Westland Aircraft

since 1915

The Wyvern was Westland's last fixed-wing aircraft. These Wyvern S.4s of No.813 Squadron based at RNAS Ford are seen near Beachy Head during 1953.

Westland Aircraft

since 1915

Derek N James

PUTNAM

BY THE SAME AUTHOR
Gloster Aircraft since 1917
Schneider Trophy Aircraft 1913–1931

For my wife, Brenda
and the James boys—
William, Benjamin, Harry, Edward and Oliver

© Derek N James 1991

First published in Great Britain 1991 by
Putnam Aeronautical Books, an imprint of
Conway Maritime Press Ltd
101 Fleet Street
London EC4Y 1DE

Revised and updated 1995

British Library Cataloguing in Publication Data
James, Derek, N.
Westland aircraft since 1915.
1. Great Britain. Aircraft, history
I. Title
629.133
ISBN 0 85177 847 X

Typeset by The Word Shop, Bury, Lancashire
Printed in Great Britain at the Alden Press, Oxford

CONTENTS

Preface

In England it is said that salt water runs in the veins of most West Countrymen. If this be so, then the rush of wings is in the ears of the others, for whom the roar of aero-engines is music to their souls.

Between the Severn and the Solent could once be found some of the great companies which, for more than half a century, were at the heart of Britain's aircraft industry. Their names have long since vanished; Supermarine Aviation and Bristol Aeroplane into the maws of British Aerospace and Rolls-Royce; Parnall long ago turned to domestic appliances for its fortunes, while Gloster Aircraft just slipped quietly into the history books.

Only Westland, a sturdy 76-year-old survivor, remains intact, but not untouched, in spite of industry rationalisation and take-over battles, still retaining the proud name first voiced in 1913 by the wife of Percy Petter, one of the twin brothers who founded the business.

Westland is unique. Despite many vicissitudes, not least the traumas of its financial restructuring during 1985–86, the company stands alone, having been the core around which other British helicopter manufacturers, under Government edict, coalesced in 1959–60. No other British aircraft manufacturer has so dramatically and successfully changed from producing one type of aircraft to another of totally different concept, or has occupied the same factory site since its inception.

The Westland story begins in an ironmonger's shop in Yeovil High Street during the late 1860s, moves into the manufacture of agricultural equipment and progresses into the sub-contract production of aircraft for other manufacturers during and after the 1914–18 War. The creation of military fighters and bombers, autogyros, civil transports and light aircraft, among which were the unusual tailless Pterodactyl family, spanned not only the 21 inter-war years but also those of the 1939–45 War. Then, in the following year, Westland struck out on a new course. This led it into the still relatively new field of rotary-winged flight through the licenced-production of Sikorsky helicopters. Thus, for the greater part of its life, Westland's design, engineering and marketing efforts have been dedicated to this class of aircraft, with great success.

The burden of responsibility for chronicling the history of this great company has been greatly eased by the willing assistance of many people, chief among them being Harald Penrose, Fred Ballam and Peter Batten. For several years this triumvirate carried the author along with their buoyant enthusiasm for Westland and all its works. Harald Penrose, the doyen of British test pilots, not only provided a mass of source material on the company's general history, but gave personal comment and reminiscences about its aircraft and access to his extensive collection of photographs. Fred Ballam cheerfully undertook the daunting task of reading and correcting the raw manuscript covering all the helicopter chapters, discovered long-forgotten project drawings and answered hundreds of questions, drawing on his lifetime service with Westland. Any errors and omissions must, however, be laid at the author's door. Peter Batten undid the Gordian Knot of differing company photographic reference systems used over countless years by his predecessors, and produced a wealth of prints depicting Westland aeroplanes, people and events. Without their never-failing and always cheerful help, advice and constructive criticism, this book could not have been completed. Many people have asked whether this book includes the story of a turbulent period in the company's history known as the 'Westland Affair'. Clearly, this vital financial restructuring operation could not be omitted; however, as at least one complete book devoted to those convoluted negotiations has already been published, readers will have to be content with a succinct summary of what then took place. I am extremely grateful to Sir John Cuckney who, as Westland's chairman, steered the company through the problem period and who kindly added important refinements to my own brief summary.

It was very gratifying to receive support and assistance from other present and past members of the Westland team, particularly Sue Eagles, David Gibbings, Peter Miles and Helen Goddard (EHI), R K Page and Ken Reed, and from A Hirst, T Jaques and W Woodford, one-time employees at Westland's Doncaster factory, and from such aviation experts as Chris Ellis, William Green, Bill Gunston, Mike Hooks, Eric Myall, Elfan ap Rees, Mike Stroud and Ray Sturtivant. Others who put their specialised knowledge and facilities at my disposal were the staff of the Public Record Office, Brian Kervell (RAE Farnborough), Gordon Day and Richard King (Air Historical Branch, MoD), the Director of Contracts/Air 4 and P A McKenna (MoD Procurement Executive), Arnold Nayler and Brian Riddle (Royal Aeronautical Society), Air Commodore Dan Honley (SBAC), Stuart Witts (Bristow Helicopters) and Marian Barnes (Museum of South Somerset). I also acknowledge with thanks the valued contributions of Carl G Ahremark, whose many fine new three-view drawings are among those in this book, and of Julian Mannering of Conway Maritime Press who applied a gentle spur to my pen, whenever it was required.

Photographs and information from overseas were of much value and I am greatly indebted to Arthur L Whittaker of Boort, Victoria, Australia, K M Molson (founder curator of the National Aviation Museum of Canada), Line Séguin (National Archives of Canada), A J Shortt (National Aviation Museum of Canada), Antoni Rudnicki (Australian War Memorial) and Pamela Garfield (Civil Aviation Authority, Australia).

Finally, I must record the immense debts of gratitude I owe to John Stroud and his late wife, Patricia, for their quiet guidance, encouragement and help with five Putnam books over many years, and to my wife, Brenda, who not only decoded my execrable fist to produce the final typescript and shared the proof-reading, but who also kept two other aviation enthusiasts, our young sons, Ben and Harry, fully occupied while I jousted with Westland.

DNJ
Barnwood, Gloucester. January 1991

Origin and History of the Company

The root stocks from which grew Great Britain's aircraft industry were legion but, sadly, it was the needs of war which provided the forcing house environment in which many of its aviation scion's early growth first flourished. It was in the peaceful creation of weirs and locks, electric tramcars, lawn mowers, motor omnibuses, architectural decoration—even wire netting—that many of the founding fathers of the companies which formed that Industry received their engineering training. It was to stand them in good stead when they became attracted to the still nascent business of aviation and used their skills and experience to set up as manufacturers of airships, aeroplanes and engines.

The foregoing horticultural analogy is particularly apt when describing the history of the Westland company for its roots are deep in the fertile soil of Somerset.

James Bazeley Petter's ironmongers shop in Yeovil's High Street during the 1890s.
(*Courtesy Museum of South Somerset*)

During 1868 a young Somerset man named James Bazeley Petter was married and, as a wedding gift, his father gave him the well-established Yeovil ironmongery business of Haman and Gillett. While young James Petter was busy with this prosperous undertaking, his wife was equally busy caring for their fifteen children among whom, the third and fourth, were twin boys born on 26 May, 1873. They were named Percival Waddams and Ernest Willoughby and were destined to play a major role in the future development of industry in Yeovil. Meanwhile, their father had decided to expand and diversify his business's interests, if only to provide the money to support his large and

1

growing family. To this end he took in a partner and by the mid-1870s the company name had been changed to Petter and Edgar and its interests now included the production of agricultural equipment; moreover, Petter was able to buy The Yeovil Foundry and Engineering Works and produce the castings for the Nautilus patented fire grate, the success of which was secured when Queen Victoria chose it for use both at Osborne House on the Isle of Wight and Balmoral Castle.

Hill and Boll's four-wheel 'horseless carriage' with a 3 hp Petter engine. The two central passengers are Percy (left) and Ernest Petter. (*Courtesy Fred Ballam*)

Their father's inventive nature was soon apparent in his children and Percy Petter has recorded how, while still attending Yeovil Grammar School, he and his eldest brother built rudimentary hand-cranked velocipedes and rode 'penny-farthing' bicycles on weekend jaunts into the surrounding countryside. After leaving school he first joined his father's foundry to learn how to make iron castings and repair agricultural machinery, then moved to the Nautilus grate section of the factory where he gained more experience before being appointed manager of the foundry in 1893 aged 20. Percy Petter admitted that he was too inexperienced but, fortunately, soon afterwards, the company engaged a new foundry foreman named Benjamin Jacobs. He proved to be an accomplished draughtsman, pattern maker, machinist and fitter who was able to teach others in all these arts. When Petter wanted an engine for one of the new 'horseless carriages' of the type which were being developed in France, Jacobs was the 'design leader' in this project. Petter records that in 1894 he had shown to Mr Jacobs a *Boy's Own Paper* article on 'How to make a model oil engine'. After looking at the drawings, Jacobs said he thought he could make a better engine for this carriage. And he did. Although Percy Petter modified and simplified this single-cylinder oil engine after initial running, which much improved it, he always insisted that the principal credit belonged to Benjamin

Jacobs. The efficiency and simplicity of this engine in comparison with others was to have a great effect on the future development of the business.

Towards the end of 1895 the 'horseless carriage' was completed when the 3 hp engine was installed in the chassis of an old four-wheel horse-drawn phaeton produced by Messrs Hill and Boll who were local coachmakers in Yeovil. On trials it reached a speed of 12 mph, was shown at the Crystal Palace in South London and appeared in the Lord Mayor's Show during 1896. In the belief that the future prosperity of the business lay in the production of 'horseless carriages', James Bazeley Petter formed a Limited Company with £1,000 capital, named it The Yeovil Motor Car and Cycle Company Limited and built a new factory on his land at Reckleford. With Ernest Petter charged with the administration of the foundry, Nautilus stove, and motor car activities, business prospects appeared bright. Again, Percy Petter records in his privately published book *The Story of Petters Ltd*, 'I remember a day when Colonel Harbin of Newton House asked my brother Hugh how the cars were getting on. "We're still pushing them", he replied. "You usually are when I see you", said the Colonel.'

But the Motor Car Company's effort to satisfy its customers' widely differing requirements, whether for a commercial traveller's car or a country bus, was financially disastrous. There were, too, the attendant problems of obtaining the correct grade of fuel and the law requiring a man with a red flag to proceed all mechanical vehicles moving on public roads. However, following a closer examination of their products and potential markets, the engine side of the business gave promise of better prospects and after moving their account from Stuckey's Bank to the Wilts and Dorset Bank (later acquired by Lloyds) to obtain a £7,000 loan, the Petter brothers were able to finance production of 1 and 1½ hp oil engines for agricultural and dairying applications. Then, in 1901, came a second financial crisis when all three businesses lost some £3,000 of which half was attributable to the engine business. Again, there was the pressing need to raise capital and, with the help of friends, £4,000 was acquired and by the following year the business had been turned around, a profit of £2,000 being made. By now the company was registered as James B Petter and Sons, Benjamin Jacobs had been appointed chief engineer and a range of engines up to 22 hp was available.

During the latter half of the nineteenth century, Somerset was to see many aeronautical events as the result of pioneering work undertaken by John Stringfellow and William Henson, both of whom lived in Chard, Henson and his family having moved to there from Nottingham in the early 1830s; moreover, many balloon and aeroplane flights were made in the county. These all served to stimulate Percy Petter's interest in human flight; indeed, in 1898 he delivered a lecture on the subject, illustrated with lantern slides and models, to the Yeovil YMCA in the Town Hall. He often discussed with Benjamin Jacobs the possibility of designing an aeroplane with a light internal combustion engine, but this never came to fruition; however, Petter did build what was intended to be a flying bicycle, which failed to fly, and later, in his garden, he constructed a powered revolving vertical shaft with four long arms carrying box kites to experiment with vertical lift. Further experimental work was made impossible due to pressure of work with the company's engine business, but it foreshadowed the advent of rotary-winged flight at Yeovil some half-a-century later.

Percy Petter's early interest in flying continued and undoubtedly influenced later decisions, first, to undertake aircraft construction during the 1914–18 War and, second, to support a proposal to build autogyros in 1933.

In 1910 Petters Limited was registered as a public company to carry on the business of making oil engines of all sizes, and two years later had about 500 employees annually producing some 1,500 engines. In order to sustain such output the foundry was working to its limits and, in spite of working day and night shifts, it was apparent that to achieve future growth it would need to be enlarged. This was not possible at Reckleford where all the available space was built on; thus it was decided to look for a new site and Mr Hardiman, the foundry manager, urged the Petter brothers to consider the possibility of finding one which could have railway sidings. As Percy Petter related in his book, 'One day he asked me to accompany him to a field at West Hendford which seemed ideal. We went . . . along a narrow lane which terminated in high wood doors. Beyond them we saw a fine piece of meadowland sloping up gradually from the Yeovil and Taunton branch railway. It seemed perfect'. The outcome of this visit was the formation of a separate small private company to purchase 75 acres to the north of the proposed foundry site. Percy Petter's brother John, who was an architect, and his partner were asked to produce a plan for a garden village with houses for Petter's employees, all linked to the foundry and works by a new main road. One Saturday afternoon in 1913 Percy Petter, his wife and two small daughters, Norah and Kathleen, were present when the first turf was cut. As this site was on the west side of Yeovil Mrs Petter chose the name 'Westland' for the proposed garden village and works.

Early in 1914 the new foundry was ready for occupation and the first castings were soon being poured. Work had also begun on the engineering department and the first bay of an intended row of buildings for machinery and erecting shops was completed during June of that year. That building was still in use in 1991.

With the start of the 1914–18 War on 4 August, most of Petter's overseas business declined, but by the end of the year the demand for engines for military use was beginning to outstrip the prewar business. The effects of the war on the people of South East England were very different, for they became the target of direct attacks by the German Air Arm which the Royal Flying Corps and the ground defences appeared powerless to prevent. Then, during early April 1915 Mr Lloyd George, Prime Minister of the National Government, made a speech in the House of Commons which shattered many popular illusions that the war would be over by Christmas. In it he revealed the shortage of suitable armament and equipment with which to continue to fight the war and called for immediate action. Shocked by the gravity of the situation the two Petter brothers responded rapidly. Ernest convened a Board meeting at which the Directors, with one exception, approved his resolution to offer the company's entire manufacturing resources to the Government for the production of whatever was required. Only the Chairman, W R Moore, was opposed to this resolution for it was against his conscience to undertake the manufacture of any kind of armament. He resigned from Petter's Board and was succeeded as Chairman by Ernest Petter.

Percival Waddams Petter (left) and Sir Ernest Willoughby Petter, the founders of the Westland company.

The subsequent immediate course of events was described by Sir Ernest in the 15 September, 1936, issue of *Petter's Monthly News*. 'A copy of this resolution was, the same day, sent to the War Office and the Admiralty. From the former nothing was heard, but almost the next day a telegram came from the Admiralty asking that two representatives might go up for a conference.' Accordingly, Ernest and Percy went to London for a meeting which was attended by five gentlemen, at least three of whom were Lords of the Admiralty, who told them that their great need was for seaplanes. They asked the brothers whether they were willing to make them. 'We explained that our experience and factory were not exactly in line with their requirements but we were willing to attempt anything which would help the Country. "Good", said they, "You are the fellows we want; we will send you the drawings and give you all the help we can. Get on with it". So we got on with it'. Shortly afterwards, Petters received a confirmatory letter from the Admiralty saying that the company might build

Naval aircraft because it was considered that the wood pattern-makers would be very suitable craftsmen for this work. The company was also asked to send representatives to Short Brothers to see the type of work required, and Percy Petter, his brother John and Mr Warren, who was foreman of the Pattern Shop, went to Rochester where Shorts had built a new factory on the right bank of the Medway during 1913. Without doubt, it was Oswald Short, who was in charge of floatplane production there, who first introduced the Petter representatives to the intricacies of aircraft manufacture. Percy Petter later confessed that, on seeing the nature of the work ' . . . my heart nearly failed me but John and Mr Warren were very sure of their ability to supervise construction of such machines'. Here Percy Petter takes up the story. 'In the first instance they were put in charge of the Works. However, I was not satisfied that their experience was really adequate for this difficult undertaking'. It was clear that in order to become a Shorts' sub-contractor an experienced aircraft engineer was required to guide Petter's staff. A year or so earlier when the company was seeking a new works manager for the engine business, one of those interviewed was Robert Arthur Bruce who was, at that time, the manager of the British & Colonial Aircraft Company at Filton, Bristol. 'Though I had not thought that management of the engine business was suitable for him, I now kept thinking that if only we could get hold of him he was the man for this aircraft business', recalled Percy Petter. 'Unfortunately, I could not get in touch until one day it occurred to me to see if he was a member of the Institution of Mechanical Engineers and, finding his name in the Directory, I wrote to him'.

The outcome of this letter was that Petter discovered Robert Bruce, by now a Lieutenant RNVR, serving as an Admiralty inspector with Sopwith Aviation Company, whose works were in a building previously a skating rink at Kingston-on-Thames. Petter wrote to the Admiralty requesting his release so that he could take up a more important role at Yeovil and in June 1915 the 46-year old Bruce became manager of Petter's new aircraft business. He brought a wealth of skills and experience to his new job, having worked in civil engineering and aircraft manufacturing and had been the hydraulics expert for Louis Brennan's gyroscopically-stabilised monowheel train and car projects. On his arrival he was faced with a contract to build twelve Short 184 floatplanes, powered by 225 hp Sunbeam engines, in a single workshop only 100 ft long and 60 ft wide. As their span was 63 ft 6 in and their length was 40 ft 7 in, this alone must have posed problems.

It is at this point in history that the paths of progress of the parent Petters Limited Company and its aircraft offspring begin to diverge. First, there was the decision by the Petters Board that this new business, though fully owned by Petters, would operate as a separate entity with Bruce as manager in control of all the business, technical and production aspects. Second, as such, it needed a name other than the Aircraft Department of Petters Ltd. The first paragraph of Sir Ernest Petter's short article in *Petter's Monthly News* of 15 September, 1936, referred to on page 5, recorded his recollection of how the name was given. 'Twenty-one years ago last April', he wrote, 'three men walked down to the corner of a field just outside Yeovil where there was a small farm hut. One of the three, the only survivor and the author of this little story, opened the door of the hut and solemnly said "This is the Westland Aircraft Works"'. Presumably

6

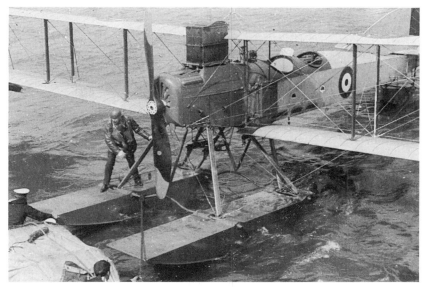

A Short 184 floatplane of the type built by Petter's Westland Aircraft Works during 1915–16.

Sir Ernest had remembered the name which Percy Petter's wife had chosen for the proposed garden village and works. Other reasons have been mooted but this author is happy to accept Sir Ernest's story for, even though it was written 21 years after that April morning, he would have recalled with great clarity such an important event in his company's history. The story of Petters Limited after 1915 encompasses massive production of diesel engines throughout the war years and after when, in association with Vickers, engines of up to 400 hp were built. Between-the-wars activity included an ever-widening overseas market for these products with civil engineering, power generation, agricultural, mining and marine applications, and the joint production with the Douglas Seaton organisation of Seaton-Petter motor cars in the 10–18 hp range between 1926 and 1933. During early 1939 the Yeovil Foundry and Nautilus Works closed when Petters was acquired by the Brush Group which moved all that production to Loughborough in Leicestershire, where the needs of the 1939–45 War were met. In 1947 Petters moved to Staines in Middlesex and ten years later became part of the Hawker Siddeley Group when it acquired the Brush Group. Then, in 1986 came a change of name when the company was merged with Listers, the long-established Gloucestershire engineering firm which also produced diesel engines. With the closure of the Staines factory in 1988 Lister-Petter engine production was centred on Dursley in Gloucestershire with a rationalised range of engines with powers from 1½ hp up to 150 hp.

To return to 1915 and Westland Aircraft Works at Yeovil, among Robert Bruce's early tasks was the employment of a team of draughtsmen and craftsmen. It has been recorded that he enlisted his wife's help in preparing drawings for assembly jigs, thus certainly making her the British aircraft

7

industry's first female jig and tool draughtsman—if that is not a contradiction in terms. The first to be recruited from Petters was 24-year-old engine designer Arthur Davenport who was appointed chief draughtsman. A number of craftsmen transferred from the Nautilus Works and they were joined by carpenters, joiners and mechanics from other local companies. In addition to human resources Bruce was aware of the need to provide them with modern 'tools'; thus he soon began installing a straight-through wind tunnel—or 'wind channel' as it was named at that time. This tunnel was modified and more powerful motors were gradually installed until, in 1938, it became a closed-circuit tunnel with an open working section. In 1942 it finally became a fully closed working section tunnel.

In response to an Admiralty telegram of 24 June, Davenport was sent to Sheerness on the Isle of Sheppey to where the third production Short 184, serialled 843, had been delivered for examination and measurement by representatives of the five companies sub-contracted to built this type of floatplane. The other four were Mann, Egerton & Co, Norwich; Phoenix Dynamo Co at Bradford; Frederick Sage & Co, Peterborough; and S E Saunders Ltd, East Cowes. At Sheerness, Davenport and the other representatives were shown over the aircraft and then they had to produce drawings to enable them to be built at their respective factories. During this visit Davenport became friendly with Victor Gaunt from Phoenix Dynamo; this friendship was to be of great value to Westland in the years ahead when Gaunt became superintendent of the company's experimental department.

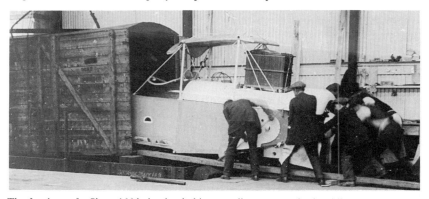

The fuselage of a Short 166 being loaded into a railway wagon in the siding of Westland's despatch department in 1916.

By early August, production of Westland's first Short 184, serialled 8356, had started and was completed by the end of December. On 1 January, 1916, having been dismantled, it left the factory on three horse-drawn carts and was taken to Yeovil Junction on the Great Western Railway. Later in the year, sidings were built in the factory so that the crated aircraft could travel all the way by rail. From there it went by rail to Hamble where the Admiralty had provided Richard Fairey with a site on the Spit at the confluence of the Hamble river and Southampton Water, at which Short 827 floatplanes, also built under sub-

8

contract, were test flown by Sydney Pickles, a freelance test pilot. Here, Westland's first aeroplane was assembled, test flown and, it is believed, was delivered to the RNAS coastal air station on Calshot Spit across Southampton Water. The story of the part which the fourth floatplane built by Westland, serialled 8359, played in the Battle of Jutland during May–June 1916 and its preservation by the Fleet Air Arm Museum at Yeovilton is referred to on page 480.

A horse-drawn cart takes Short 166 wings and centre-sections from the factory to Yeovil's Great Western Railway junction.

When production of these twelve floatplanes was nearing completion, Westland received a second sub-contract order. This was for a batch of twenty Short Type 166 floatplanes powered by 200 hp Salmson liquid-cooled radial engines which embodied the patented Swiss Canton-Unne design feature in which all the connecting rods drove a cage revolving on the crankpin on epicyclic gears. These floatplanes were of an earlier design than the Type 184 and only six had been produced by Shorts at Eastchurch on the Isle of Sheppey. Whether it was the small size of this batch or the Type 166's similarity to the even earlier Type 136, enabling them to be built 'by hand and eye', it is imposible to establish, but Shorts was unable to supply Westland with a complete set of production drawings. There was an additional problem in that the twenty Westland aircraft were to be built without torpedo carrying equipment, necessitating some redesign by Bruce and Davenport and the production of the missing drawings. In spite of these difficulties, which underlined the need to expand Westland's design office, the first Short 166, 9751, was delivered to Hamble for flight testing on 1 July, 1916.

While production of the remaining twenty-four floatplanes proceeded at Yeovil, the company was making plans against the day when orders for wheeled aircraft, rather than floatplanes, would be received. These led to the purchase of Northover Fields, part of the present aerodrome, from the Yeovil and District Hospital Board. As this was farmland, a considerable amount of work was required to grub out ancient hedges, fill ditches and generally level the site. All this work was justified when a contract for fifty Sopwith 1½ Strutter fighter-reconnaissance aircraft for the RFC was received. This 1½ Strutter

9

The first Westland-built Short 166 floatplane, 9751, in the Yeovil factory, with the Salmson radial engine of another aircraft visible at the left of the photograph.

contract was followed by orders for two more batches of 1½ Strutters for the RNAS; the first consisted of fifty single-seat bombers and the second of five single-seaters and twenty two-seater bombers designated Types 9700 and 9400 respectively by the Admiralty. Apart from the fact that these were all land aircraft, a major difference between these orders and the earlier ones was that the Sopwith Aviation Co provided excellent production drawings and instructions.

Sopwith 1½ Strutters being built in Westland's factory in 1916.

At about this time Robert Bruce and Arthur Davenport were working on the design of a biplane floatplane fighter to meet the Air Department of the Admiralty's N.1B requirement. In competiton with the Blackburn and Supermarine companies, which each received contracts for three prototypes of their pusher biplane flying-boat fighters, Westland's submission won a contract for two prototypes. Powered by a 150 hp Bentley AR1 rotary engine, the first of these compact little biplanes was flown in August 1917, the second following soon afterwards. Although they performed well while on test at the RNAS Experimental Construction Depot on the Isle of Grain, changes in naval policy

10

This N.1B floatplane fighter, N16, was the first aircraft designed and built by Petter's Westland Aircraft Works. Changes in naval policy relating to this type of fighter brought its development to an early end.

and procedures relating to ship-borne fighters ruled out further development and all contracts were cancelled later in 1917.

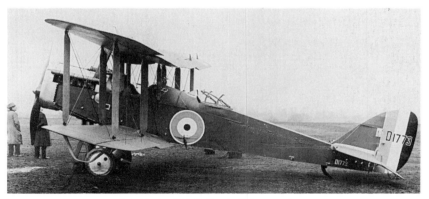

D1773, the 57th D.H.4 built by Westland.

Before the last two batches of Sopwith $\overline{1}\frac{1}{2}$ Strutters had been completed a fourth sub-contract was received, this from George Holt Thomas's Aircraft Manufacturing Company Ltd (Airco) at the Hyde, Hendon. It was for the D.H.4 two-seat day bomber designed by Capt Geoffrey de Havilland. Comprehensive production drawings were supplied to Westland and enabled construction of the D.H.4 to begin early in 1917 alongside the last batch of Sopwith 1½ Strutters. The total number of D.H.4s ordered was 175 but only about 80 of the last 100 aircraft were completed, their places in the contract being taken by the succeeding D.H.9. As with all the Short floatplanes and the early production Sopwith aircraft, a number of the first batch of twenty-five D.H.4s was crated and delivered by rail and road to The Hyde. It was not until April that BC Hucks, another freelance pilot, delivered the first Westland-built aircraft by air.

The D.H.4 order was followed by even larger ones for its successor, the D.H.9, a total of 300 eventually being ordered although, as noted earlier, some replaced D.H.4s and a small number was cancelled. Nevertheless, Westland's work on these two de Havilland-designed aircraft for the Aircraft Manufacturing Co was to be of major significance to the Yeovil company's future. Because of problems with its Siddeley Puma engine, which delivered only 230 hp instead of the expected 300 hp, the D.H.9's performance was inferior to that of the D.H.4; thus, it was not a success in its intended military role as a fast day bomber in RFC (later RAF) squadrons. A development with a more powerful engine appeared to be the solution. When the demand for the excellent Rolls-Royce Eagle VIII engines exceeded the supply rate, it was decided to re-engine the D.H.9 with the US-built Liberty engine. Designed by Jesse Vincent of Packard and E J Hall of Hall-Scott, a renowned water-cooled engine manufacturer, this engine was the subject of a massive US War Department project to provide very large numbers of aero engines quickly. Through mass-production in established motorcar factories, nearly 20,500 were delivered, the majority between October 1917 and November 1918.

This Westland-built D.H.9, B7664, with a four-bladed propeller later became a D.H.9A.

The extensive re-design of the D.H.9 to accept the Liberty engine was too much for Airco to undertake as it was heavily committed to the design of the D.H.10 Amiens twin-engined bomber. It was decided that this D.H.9 re-design task should be entrusted to Westland, with its experience of building the D.H.4 and D.H.9, rather than any of the other eleven sub-contractors which had been involved with their production.

With the assistance of John Johnson, an Airco designer who was seconded to Westland, Bruce and Davenport took full advantage of the Liberty engine's 400 hp and combined the best features of the two earlier de Havilland aircraft. The fuselage was made stronger to take the heavier engine, and wings of increased chord and span were fitted to improve the climb performance and the ceiling.

The first Westland-built D.H.9A was first flown in March 1918, powered by a Rolls-Royce Eagle engine as a Liberty engine was not available. By the end of December 1918 a total of 885 D.H.9As had been produced, about 390 by Westland and the remainder by Airco and ten other companies. Without doubt the 'Ninack', as this aircraft became known in RAF squadrons, was the best strategic bomber of the 1914–18 War. It was also to establish Westland as a major British aircraft design and manufacturing company.

A burnt out Bessoneaux hangar and a badly damaged Wagtail was the result of an employee's experiment with a cigarette and a tin of petrol.

During the latter part of 1917, Westland's small design team had prepared some preliminary designs for a small single-seat fighter, the Wagtail, powered by an ABC Wasp radial engine, to meet the RAF Type I Specification. These resulted in two Air Board contracts for a total of eight Wagtails, five aircraft ultimately being built. As part of the evaluation trials, RAF pilots flew the Wagtail, and other contenders for the Type I contract, in mock combat with a captured Fokker D VII, Germany's finest fighter in the 1914–18 War. However, a combination of engine problems and the Armistice terminated development trials of all Wasp-powered prototypes; nevertheless, the Wagtails were flown on various engine trials at the RAE, Farnborough, and the AEE, Martlesham Heath, until about 1922.

The quality of Westland's work on D.H.4 and D.H.9A production did not go unnoticed or unrecorded. A letter from the Air Council addressed to 'Messrs the Westland Aircraft Works, YEOVIL' dated 20 August, 1918, drew attention to a report written 'In the Field' on 13 August by Lieut-Col J Baldwin, commanding the 41st Wing, Independent Force, RAF. The letter reads:

'Gentlemen,
I am to inform you that a report upon D.H.4—B.3957, built by your firm, has been received from France, which it is considered should be brought to the notice of those concerned in the construction of this Machine.
On the 1st July 1917, the Machine was received in a Squadron (No. 55 at Boisdinghem) overseas after it had done 3 hours and 40 minutes flying. On the 13th August 1918 it was handed back by the Squadron to an Aircraft Depot, having been badly shot about during a raid on the previous day. The Machine had completed a total of 322 hours 5 minutes

flying time, the majority of which was over the lines.

Amongst other raids it had taken part in those on Cologne and Frankfurt and amongst various reconnaissances it had done one of 5 hours and 15 minutes. In the course of its service 4 enemy aircraft have been accounted for by its various pilots and several have been credited to the observers'.

The letter goes on to record that, apart from small repairs and replacements such as tailskids, shock absorber cord and periodic renewal of controls, the only other work on the aircraft involved internal inspection of the 'bottom planes', a new rudder and left hand elevator fitted and repairs to the wings and tailplane which had been 'shot through'. The letter continues:

'In addition, two of the longerons have had plates put on them owing to their being grazed by bullets, otherwise the Machine is exactly as received, which must approach a record for any machine on service in France.

It was considered that much of the credit of the long life of this Machine was due to the excellent material and workmanship used in doping the fabric surfaces. Its record is one which it is considered does credit to your Firm'.

The names of the eight pilots who flew B3957 were listed in the report.

Westland's covering shop where the deft fingers of girl fabric workers were halted for this photograph of Vimy control surfaces being covered.

The growing demands for aircraft for the RFC, RNAS and RAF during 1917–18 had strained Westland's design and production resources to their limits and it was becoming increasingly apparent that they would have to be expanded. This was particularly underlined when the company recieved what was to be its last wartime sub-contract order during August 1918. It was for seventy-five Vickers Vimy twin-engined bombers whose 68 ft wing span and 7,100 lb empty weight were great increases on those of earlier Westland-built aircraft. To provide production floor space for this big aeroplane a new erecting shop, with an unsupported span of 140 ft, was built, which was the largest of its kind in Britain at that time. Although it may have seemed an extravagance when the

14

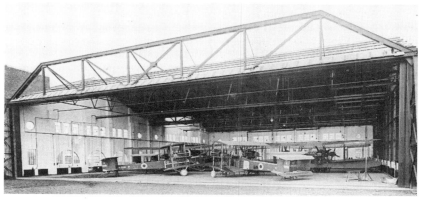

Six Vickers Vimys, with H5080 and H5081 nearest the door of the 140 ft span new 'Vimy hangar' at Yeovil.

Armistice brought cancellation of all but twenty-five Vimys, and the Air Ministry refused to pay for its construction, it has remained in use ever since, a valuable part of the Yeovil factory.

Vimy H5080 taking off from the Yeovil aerodrome.

Specification RAF Type I was just one of a number issued by the recently formed Air Ministry during the latter months of the 1914–18 War, a period when postwar aircraft requirements were being carefully studied. The Type III specification for a two-seat fighter-reconnaissance aircraft also attracted a submission from Westland. Named the Weasel it was an enlarged version of the Wagtail and in April 1918 three prototypes were ordered. However, the Weasel's allegedly 340 hp ABC Dragonfly engine, an enlarged version of the Wasp, was a disaster. It was 15 per cent down on manufacturer's claimed power output and 10 per cent heavier, was mechanically unreliable, overheated and vibrated so badly that a complete redesign would have been necessary to cure this. The most alarming aspect of the Dragonfly was that Sir William Weir, when Director General of Aircraft Production in the Ministry of Munitions, had taken the rash decision to standardise on the Dragonfly engine in almost all the specifications for new fighters and bombers planned for 1918. Hundreds of these

15

engines were produced before its many shortcomings were fully apparent. Had the War continued into 1919 a vast programme of re-engining several thousand aircraft would have been necessary, only the Armistice obviated such a drastic step. In the meantime, the Weasel prototype's flying with the Dragonfly was intermittent and by August 1919 all development of this airframe/engine combination was halted: but, yet again, these Westland prototypes were used by the RAE and AES for test-flying several other more successful aero-engines, including the Armstrong Siddeley Jaguar II and Bristol Jupiter II. This use of failed prototypes as flying test beds for engine manufacturers set a between-the-wars pattern in Great Britain; often there would be up to five contenders for a contract, for which there could be only one winner leaving several airworthy prototype aircraft surplus to requirements.

With the end of the War came massive cancellations of military contracts of all kinds, with aircraft manufacturers in particular feeling the chill draught of this dividend of peace following the Armistice. Fortunately, prospects at Yeovil were rather better than most other areas for the D.H.9A was an important general purpose aircraft in the RAF which placed Westland, as its parent company, in a position of some strength. However, its wartime success notwithstanding, the Westland Works were still regarded by the Petter brothers as merely an adjunct of their main business and looked to the oil engine to provide their future security. While the producton of the twenty-five Vimys and spares for the D.H.9A ensured an adequate cash flow, they were not averse to some diversification. It was here that Bruce's skill as a pianist, led to an attempt to produce pianos, a rare case of heart leading the head. Because of the foundry facility, which no other British piano manufacturer possessed, at which the frames could be cast, plus the company's experience of woodwork, a small number of pianos was built; however, a refusal by the woodworker's Trade Union to allow piece-work in the factory soon caused this ill-conceived venture to be abandoned. Instead, like many other aircraft companies, Westland turned to light engineering and the manufacture of milk churns.

Postwar Enterprise

During the winter of 1916–17, although the War was being waged with increasing ferocity, there were those whose thoughts were turned toward the postwar years and world of civil air transport. One of these was George Holt Thomas. An almost forgotten and largely unsung pioneer aviation industrialist, his contributions to Britain's aircraft industry included the founding, in 1912, of the Aircraft Manufacturing Co Ltd—which became the world's largest aircraft producing enterprise—and the recruitment to it, from the Royal Aircraft Factory at Farnborough, of Geoffrey de Havilland and Hugh Burroughes. It was Holt Thomas who, with the aid of some influential friends in the newspaper world (Holt Thomas was then owner of the *Daily Graphic*) persuaded Lloyd George to establish a Civil Aerial Transport Committee. Under the chairmanship of another newspaper magnate, Lord Northcliffe, the committee was formed during the summer of 1917. Its task was to consider the method of regulating civil aviation activities and to examine how the trained personnel and aircraft, which the war's end 'may leave surplus to requirements of the naval and military air services of the United Kingdom and its Overseas Dominions' could be used in establishing an air transport system.

When the War ended, it found the fledgling Royal Air Force with some 22,500 aircraft, the world's largest military air fleet, 700 airfields and 290,000 personnel.

The story of the formation and development of postwar British civil aviation is not for these pages; suffice it to say that, without exceptions, its formative years saw airlines being formed and operated exclusively with military aircraft. Some were adapted for civil passengers by merely applying civil registration markings and the fitment of seats; others were more extensively internally-modified to provide a little more passenger comfort. It was to meet the need for a purpose-built passenger aircraft that, in late 1918, Arthur Davenport began preliminary design of the Limousine.

This was one of several designs for commercial aircraft which the Westland design office was working on when a group of aviation journalists visited the factory during the first week of August 1919. Stanley Spooner, founder and editor of *Flight* magazine, reported that Westland's 'large factory, built during

G-EAJL, the Limousine II was exhibited at the 1921 Paris Aero Show in the Grand Palais.

17

the War, has the most up-to-date machinery running at full pressure producing the Vimy, for which a large order is being completed, and the Airco (DH)9'. Of more significance was his comment on the company's new designs 'one of which is already in production and ready to fly on the day of our visit'. The Limousine 'combines the qualities of a luxurious motor and a yacht'.

Although only a handful of Limousines were built—the Limousine III winning the small commerical aeroplane section of the 1920 Air Ministry Commercial Aeroplane Competition— they were a most valuable source of experience for the entire Westland team and saw service in Britain and Newfoundland.

Meanwhile, such was Great Britain's parlous postwar economic situation that, like the RAF, the Royal Navy, in its attempts to acquire new aeroplanes to replace its war-weary types, was being offered only modified and up-dated variants of existing aircraft. It was to meet a 1919 need for a three-seat carrier-borne fleet-reconnaissance aircraft that Westland's experience of D.H.9A production brought to Yeovil possibly the ugliest aircraft ever to serve with Britain's armed services. This was the Walrus, originally conceived and built in prototype form by the Sir W.G. Armstrong Whitworth Aircraft Co Ltd as a modified D.H.9A, which was handed over to Westland for further design changes and production. A total of thirty-six was built and, despite the ungainly appearance, provided good service to the Royal Navy for four years.

While milk churns and pianos may have seemed prosaic, but not unusual, products for an aircraft manufacturer in 1921, Westland's twenty-strong design team had kept pace with aerodynamic research and developments both elsewhere in Britain and overseas. It was not alone, for the Air Ministry had taken great interest in the all-metal cantilever monoplane wings being produced by the German Dornier and Rohrbach companies. Thus, despite some misgivings about the aerodynamic qualities of an internally braced cantilever monoplane designed by a Russian emigrant, the Air Ministry was keen to have a British aircraft of similar configuration and invited tenders to Specification 6/21 from George Parnall & Co at Yate and from Westland. In the manner of the era, the Specification called for a 'Postal' aircraft although, like others similarly described, it was highly unlikely that it would have carried His Majesty's mails, and this appellation was a 'title-of-convenience'. When Westland's single Napier Lion engined design, named Dreadnought, was chosen, such were the complexities of the stressing of this unusual metal multi-spar wing that a mathematician had to be employed to handle the 'sums' involved.

The design of the Dreadnought got underway in the shadow of heavy across-the-board cuts in Government departmental Estimates recommended in a Report produced by the Committee on National Expenditure with Sir Eric Geddes as its chairman. Of the three armed Services the RAF suffered the worst with a 35 per cent reduction from its estimated £15½ million expenditure; however, the Report emphasised the importance and value of the RAF and underlined the savings which could be effected in the Middle East by transferring to the RAF the Army's policing and peace-keeping roles. This latter measure had long been advocated by Marshal of the Royal Air Force Hugh Trenchard while Chief of the Air Staff and was to become known as 'air control of overseas territories'. The backbone of the RAF's light bomber and general

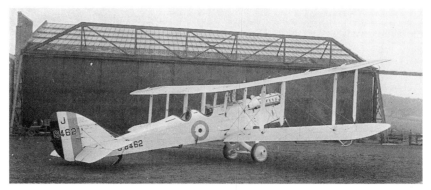

A late production Liberty-engined D.H.9A converted as a two-seat trainer by Westland in 1928.

purpose force was 663 D.H.9As of which some 270 were listed in the Report as being on active service in the Middle and Far East. Although the demands for spares and refurbishing of these aircraft was somewhat intermittent, it helped to provide work for the Westland factory with its 100 employees.

Although since 1946, which is more than half of its life, Westland has been regarded as a manufacturer of rotary-wing aircraft, the first opportunity to enter this field was presented to the Petter's Board in September or October 1923. At some time during that period, Juan de la Cierva y Cordoniu, the Spanish pioneer designer of the 'Autogiro', wrote to Westland enquiring if the company was interested in this rotary-winged concept. He was, then, working on the design and construction of his sixth aircraft, the Cierva C.6 with a 110 hp Le Rhône 9Ja engine. All of his previous aircraft had been built as private ventures with money provided by his father; but this source of finance was not bottomless and young Cierva was looking for cash and a collaborator to help him continue his work. The Petter answer, while polite, was firmly negative. It was to be 10 years before Westland began to build its first rotary-winged aircraft, the C.29 Autogiro, and a further 15 years before the company's first helicopter, the WS-51, entered production.

The first months of 1924 saw the Dreadnought nearing completion but its first flight, on 9 May ended in disaster when it crashed on take-off, seriously injuring Stuart Keep, the company's pilot who lost both legs. Happily, Keep refused to be defeated; fitted with artificial legs and aided by two sticks, he returned to work some months later to become factory superintendent. In 1934 he was appointed business manager and, soon afterwards, general manager but finally retired from the company at the end of 1935. While the crash halted further research on cantilever wings at that time, due largely to the lack of knowledge of the aerodynamics involved with the Dreadnought's wing rather than its structure, the work on this big aeroplane served to underline the need for more skilled aerodynamicists and a more powerful wind tunnel—or wind channel as it was still referred to at that time by Westland—at Yeovil.

Thus it was that, although the company had had a small 'wind channel' in 1918, in May 1924, larger electric motors were installed. Before that, Westland

Westland's open-circuit wind tunnel which was installed in the wing shop.

had relied on the use of the RAE and National Physical Laboratory tunnels, which Establishments had given the company ' . . . good service, but it was not the same as having our own wind channel' said Robert Bruce. Before going into service the tunnel was checked on a standard aerofoil supplied by the NPL from which the results obtained confirmed the accuracy of Westland's new equipment.

Without doubt, the 1914–18 War had alerted the world to the potentialities of the aeroplane, not only as a weapon but as a means of rapid travel and of 'slipping the surly bonds of earth'. That this awareness and interest in aviation came at a time when Government spending was at a minimum only served to direct attention to private flying and the creation of small economical aircraft.

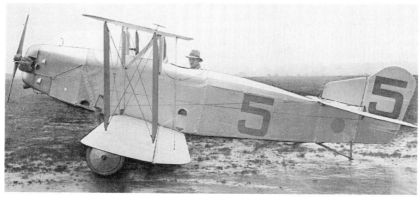

Robert Bruce kept to the proven biplane configuration for the Woodpigeon, Westland's diminutive entrant for the 1924 Light Aeroplane Competition at Lympne.

To this end, first the *Daily Mail*, which had always encouraged the growth of gliding and private flying and supported its development with very generous money prizes, then the Air Ministry, sponsored a short series of competitions or Trials during October 1922, 1923, 1924 and September 1926. For the 1924 Air Ministry Light Aeroplane Competition at Lympne, there was a dichotomy of design opinion at Yeovil regarding the best configuration for a small aircraft. Bruce favoured the traditional biplane while Arthur Davenport proposed a more advanced parasol monoplane. Unable to make a decision between the two, the Westland Board decided that both should be built. The results of this Solomon-like judgment were the diminutive Woodpigeon biplane with an empty weight of 439 lb and the Widgeon monoplane only 26 lb heavier.

Arthur Davenport's belief in the superiority of the monoplane for the Lympne Competition was more successful. This Widgeon, which ironically, was registered in Robert Bruce's name, was one of twenty to be built.

Although the Woodpigeon won none of the prize monies offered and only two were built, the superiority of the monoplane was all too evident and the Widgeon went into small-scale production in three variants. Of the twenty-six examples built, a number were exported, of which one was still airworthy in Australia in 1991, the oldest serviceable Westland aeroplane. It is interesting to speculate how much this success of the Widgeon's parasol-wing configuration influenced Davenport and even E W Petter in their design of four other Westland aircraft during the ensuing 15 years, all of which, ending with the Lysander of the 1939–45 War era, embodied this feature.

Westland's Winged-fingers

While the Westland factory was busy with production of the little Widgeons, the design office was working on a day bomber, named the Yeovil, to meet Specification 26/33 aimed at producing a successor to the cumbersome Avro Aldershot in service with No.99 Squadron RAF. It resulted in a four-cornered fight between Westland and the Bristol, Hawker and Handley Page companies. Perhaps the most noteworthy thing about the four designs produced was their marked similarity in appearance and performance. The Yeovil, of which three prototypes were built during 1924–26, was a good-looking conventional two-bay biplane with no outstanding design features or performance characteristics to set it apart from the three other contenders. In the event, Hawker's Horsley, named after Tom Sopwith's stately home Horsley Towers, won the day with the three losers going on to become useful tools in various R & D programmes. During the immediate post 1914–18 War era there had been understandable public and political reaction against anything which smacked of war-like activities. With Germany no longer a potential aggressor in Europe the swingeing cuts in the 1921 Defence Estimates, which reduced the RAF to a mere shadow of its former omnipotence, were not considered to be a dangerously weakening blow to Britain's defences. France was the only nation considered to be capable of mounting a war against Britain; not that that country showed any signs of adopting a hostile posture, but if British air defences were to be increased then there had to be a threat, real or imagined, against which to defend. Out of this Government and Air Ministry thinking came Specification 4/24. Issued in December 1924, it called for a multi-seat twin-engined fighter able to carry two automatic shell-firing guns to meet and defeat enemy aircraft which could be armed with heavy calibre cannon. The choice of this class of armament stemmed from several considerations, chief among them being the trend of bomber and bomber-escort design by French companies such as Amiot, Farman and Potez and their research into heavy armament of up to seven 7.5 mm machine-guns and even 20 mm cannon. Once again, the two West Country rivals, Westland and Bristol, responded with submissions. Although Arthur Davenport had produced schemes for a twin-engined monoplane, Westland's proposal was a conventional three-bay biplane, named the Westbury, carrying the required armament of two 37 mm cannon produced by the Coventry Ordnance Works. Two prototypes were built and the cannon were fired in air tests, but by 1927 Air Ministry interests were directed elsewhere and the development programme was abandoned. Nevertheless, Westland was impressed by the potential destructive power of the Westbury's heavy cannon armament and placed this in a mental pigeonhole marked 'For future consideration'. It was to be taken out again a decade later when considering the design of a heavily armed single-seat fighter which became the Whirlwind.

Meanwile, on 31 December, 1924, in Devil's Rest Bottom, a remote spot on the Sussex Downs, a tailless glider had made its first flight, covering 150 yards. Its designer, builder and pilot was Capt Geoffrey T R Hill who had joined Handley Page as chief test pilot in November 1918 but whose later work on the aerodynamics of wing slots with Handley Page had led him to further studies on measures to overcome an aircraft's loss of control when stalled. The powered aircraft of similar design which followed the glider were to be built by Westland, as will be revealed later in this book. Geoffrey Hill had been awarded a three-year studentship by the Royal Commission for the 1851 Exhibition and this had allowed him the freedom and time to work on the solution to the complex aerodynamic problems of stalling and spinning. During May 1923 he had submitted his proposals in Report T.1823, entitled *A Tailless Aeroplane* to the Aeronautical Research Council. In it he had concluded that safe controlled flight near and beyond the angle of stall could be achieved if a wing and aerofoil section could be designed in which the centre of pressure would remain stationary under all flight conditions instead of possessing the range of movement to which it was subject in conventionally-configured aircraft. Hill had

the Hawker Horsley. Of the four contenders—Gloster's Goral, the Handley Page Hare, Hawker's Harrier and the Witch—the Westland monoplane was the most advanced, but a combination of engine and handling problems ruled it out of the reckoning—in company with the other three prototypes, none of which was ordered.

It was realised at a very early stage of Wapiti design and production that methods which had been used to build wood, or wood and metal, aeroplanes would need some revision if satisfactory production of all-metal aircraft was to be achieved. Thus, each component was the subject of careful planning and time study so that the change from 'wood-butchering' to 'tin-bashing' could be effected without major change in personnel. With few exceptions all the employees who had worked on D.H.9A and other aircraft manufacture were successfully transferred to the production of the all-metal structured Wapiti. During the latter part of 1928 this was taken a stage further with the decision to lay down fixed track assembly lines based on the pattern of those in use at that time in the Morris Cowley Works near Oxford. To keep the assembly lines working one week's supply of all parts was constantly held in store; these included oil and petrol tanks, engine and flying controls, bulkheads and tailskids. Workbenches, vices, compressed-air lines and components were positioned by the 100 ft long track so that there was no need for the men to move away from their place of work.

Westland aircraft on parade. The first Westland IV G-EBXK, two Widgeons and two RAAF Wapiti IAs at Yeovil on 21 February, 1929, for the official acceptance of the Wapitis.

The fuselage structure was mounted on a wheeled platform running on a raised track along which it was moved by hand for all the fittings and equipment to be installed. At the end of the track the fuelage nose was supported on a wheeled tripod so that it could be removed from the track and have the main undercarriage fitted. This front tripod was removed and a small steerable 'dolly' on wheels was attached to the tail so that the complete fuselage could be moved to the erecting shop where the tail unit and wings were fitted. These methods of production resulted in some 75 per cent reduction in time for some processes. Adjoining the final assembly area was the despatch section with an enclosed railway siding and loading bay.

Thus began an era of prosperity for Westland with an extension to the design office and a new 16,700 sq ft fitting shop also being built. A Westland advertisement in the 24 July, 1929, issue of *The Aeroplane* offered jobs to 'fitters, erectors and tool-makers with press work experience. Capable men can be assured of at least 12 months' continuous work at the District Rate plus production bonus'.

Personages on parade at Yeovil. From the left, an unidentified lady, Percival Petter, Robert Bruce, Roy Fedden, Sir Ernest Petter, Lady Ryrie, Sir Sefton Brancker and another unidentified figure.

Apart from equipping some twenty RAF and AAF squadrons, Wapiti variants were exported to Australia, Canada, China and South Africa. The roll-out of the first Wapiti for the RAAF on 21 February, 1929, was the occasion for much pomp and circumstance. Westland was host to about 200 guests, many of whom travelled by train from London to Yeovil where cars carried them to the Works. The principal guests were Maj-Gen Sir Grenville de L Ryrie, the Australian High Commissioner, and Lady Ryrie who performed the acceptance ceremony; however, there were many other leading figures from Britain's

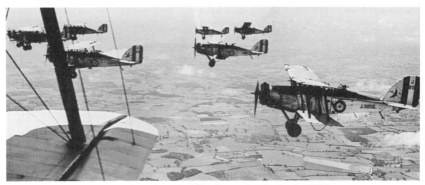

Wapiti IIAs of No.601 Squadron AAF in formation during its 1932 summer camp.

aircraft industry, including Sir Stanley White, Frank Barnwell and Roy Fedden from the Bristol company, Hugh Burroughes and David Longden from Gloster Aircraft, Sir Sefton Brancker, the Director of Civil Aviation, 17 foreign air attachés and Maj G F Davies, MP for Yeovil.

The hosts at a luncheon in Yeovil Town Hall and the subsequent visit to the Westland Works were Sir Ernest and Percy Petter, Robert Bruce, R J Norton and W Gibson, Westland commercial and works managers respectively. Afterwards, Louis Paget and Flg Off Brunton demonstrated the RAAF and RAF Wapitis and the new three-engined four-seat Westland Limousine IV, or Westland IV as it became known, made its public debut in the hands of Paget.

Production of the Wapiti was to provide more than five years of work in the West Country, not only for Westland but also for the Bristol Engine Department which supplied the Jupiter engines and Gloster Aircraft which during 1929–32, built 525 sets of all-metal Wapiti wings.

The Monoplane Era

By 1928 the sum total of Westland's experience of designing and building civil aircraft was very limited; but with it Robert Bruce and Arthur Davenport began the design of a new civil transport. This was an era when civil air services were demonstrating their ability to operate safely and reliably and their growing need for modern and cost effective aircraft. The Westland IV was to meet the need for a small 'feeder liner' and materialised as a three-engined high-wing monoplane. Although only two were built before a developed version, the Wessex, was produced, the type saw service in Britain, Belgium, Rhodesia and Egypt. It was also used by the Prince of Wales on at least two occasions and was

Official handover of Wessex OO-AGF to SABENA, the Belgian airline, on 2 September, 1930. From the left are Louis Paget with monocle, Messrs Byrom, Brunton (Westland pilot), O'Neill (SABENA's United Kingdom agent), Capt Cocquyt (SABENA chief pilot), Percival Petter and Capt Stuart Keep (Westland factory superintendent).

instrumental in the development of Railway Air Services and of an inland air mail service.

The Prince's interest in aviation was nourished when, on 31 May, 1930, he made an unexpected visit to Westland while en route from Torquay to London in his Puss Moth flown by Sqn Ldr Francis Don. As it was late in the afternoon, the factory was closed but he was met by Robert Bruce and Louis Paget and while he sat in the pilot's seat of a Wessex and drank tea his Moth was refuelled ready for his departure about an hour later.

During the early months of 1929 the Yeovil factory was beginning to bulge at the seams with work on the Wapiti, Westland IV, Widgeon and some prototypes; thus the Board, in a change of company policy, decided that it would be prepared to sell the manufacturing rights of the Widgeon to a suitable company which was 'devoted to production with the advantage of lower overhead costs. The deal would include all drawings and a sample aircraft'. It is not known whether this plan was pursued with any vigour but no such deal materialised, despite the Widgeon's high reputation as a reliable aeroplane. This was demonstrated some 18 months later when Bert Hinkler visited Westland to investigate the possibility of using a Widgeon for a flight across the South Atlantic. The Westland management proved 'unco-operative' so Hinkler turned to de Havilland, sank all his savings plus money from Lord Wakefield in a Puss Moth and made the 22 hour crossing during November 1931. Shortly afterwards Westland delivered the 500th Wapiti.

While the production of the ten Westland IV/Wessex aircraft stretched over some five years from 1929, during that period a dozen prototypes were flown. They were of a bewildering variety and most were built as 'one-offs'. First was the little single-seat Interceptor to meet the RAF's need for a fast-climbing day fighter able to engage, at 20,000 ft, enemy bomber formations attacking the British Isles. In complete contrast was the variable-geometry Pterodactyl IV three-seater which was a major advance in tailless aircraft design.

Designed almost simultaneously with the Interceptor was the C.O.W Gun

A unique photograph of the Interceptor flying at Yeovil. Below it are Armstrong Whitworth Siskin IIIAs of No.25 Squadron RAF encamped on the aerodrome in 1930.

Fighter. A single-seat aircraft armed with an enormous upward-firing 37 mm Coventry Ordnance Works piece, its development was abandoned when Air Ministry ideas on aircraft armament changed course.

The neat installation of the 37 mm cannon, which gave the C.O.W. Gun Fighter its name, is apparent in this view.

The PV.3 of 1931, while it failed to win orders as a two-seat torpedo-bomber, went on to achieve fame as one of the two Westland aircraft, used by the 1933 Houston Mount Everest Expedition, which were the first to fly over the world's highest mountain.

It was during June 1931 that another Petter, Sir Ernest's son Edward, who was a Cambridge graduate, began working in the drawing office at Westland following a period in the factory. He was to have a profound effect on the design of future Westland aeroplanes.

While production of the Wapiti was in full swing at Yeovil during 1930–31, a new building for the experimental department was being erected and other factory changes were made; however, exports of Petter oil engines had fallen disastrously and it was aircraft work which was cushioning the effect of these lost sales. Meanwhile, Arthur Davenport was wisely preparing the design of a successor to the Wapiti. This was the Wallace, the prototype of which was later chosen to accompany the PV.3 to India with the Mount Everest Expedition. A total of 174 production Wallaces were built for RAF and AAF squadrons between 1931–36.

In view of the increasing market for light aeroplanes, Petters began designing a small four-cylinder two-stroke radial engine with the view to air-testing it in a Widgeon. It ran successfully on the bench but the forecast development costs frightened the Board and the engine was scrapped.

The next four designs, built as prototypes only, could not have differed more widely. First was a large high-wing general purpose monoplane to meet Specification G.4/31. Designated the PV.7 its wing suffered from torsional weakness and twisted in flight, as Harald Penrose clearly demonstarted to a sceptical, then frightened, Davenport. Penrose later made a miraculous escape through a small side window of the PV.7's enclosed cockpit, after a wing broke off in a dive, and parachuted to safety, luckily with only some severe bruising

The triumverate which helped to put Westland on top of the world. From the left are Arthur Davenport, Harald Penrose and Robert Bruce in front of the specially converted PV.3 Wallace, later to be flown by the 1933 Houston Mount Everest Expedition, after its successful climb to more than 35,000 ft in January 1933.

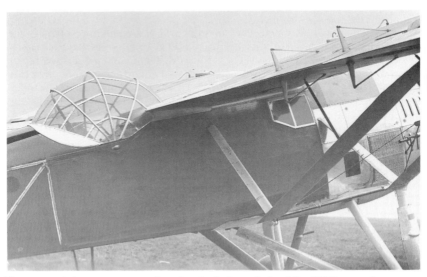

The segmented rear canopy and enclosed pilot's cockpit of the PV.7 general purpose monoplane of 1934 ensured an element of comfort for the crew.

and the loss of all his trouser-buttons to show for it. The next into the air was a single-seat biplane fighter, built to Specification F.7/30 in competition with six other types; however, the Westland aeroplane featured an engine buried in the fuselage behind the pilot and driving the propeller through a long shaft. It was the evaporatively-cooled engine which contributed to the failure of all of the submitted aircraft, the Westland F.7/30 among them, to secure a production contract. The Pterodactyl V, the last of its kind to be built by Westland, was a two-seat fighter which demanded all of Harald Penrose's skill and knowledge during its year-long test flying before being broken up at the RAE Farnborough.

First Rotary Wings

In marked contrast to the three foregoing prototypes was the C.29 Autogiro of 1934. It was in the previous year that Westland first became involved, as a company, with rotary-winged aircraft, some 10 years after Juan de la Cierva had sought some financial help from Petters, in return for collaboration in his future Autogiro projects. This had been firmly refused by Sir Ernest. For many years both Robert Bruce and Harald Penrose had been interested in rotary wings. Bruce had, earlier, done some work for Louis Brennan the inventor who, in 1919, began developing a large helicopter at the RAE Farnborough; Penrose, ever eager to add to his flying experience, had learned to fly an Autogiro in 1933 at Cierva's Hanworth Air Park and obtained his licence. In addition to these two, the RTO at Westland since 1929 was Robert Graham who had been Brennan's assistant and had done almost all of the flight testing of his helicopter.

As Westland's first foray into rotary-winged aircraft, the C.29 was a disaster, exhibiting heavy fuselage rocking when the rotor was started; this resulted from lag plane movement of the autogiro's blades and synchronous undercarriage response, or ground resonance. When Cierva came to test the C.29, he recommended that it was unwise to try and fly it as neither he nor Robert Bruce could see a solution to this problem. Thus, work on this handsome air-taxi was abandoned which set back the development of British rotary-winged aircraft by many years. During the latter part of 1933 and into 1934 an unusual aeroplane was built by Westland under sub-contract to Parnall Aircraft. This was the Hendy Heck, a two-seat cabin monoplane which had been specially designed by

Sub-contract work helped to keep the Westland factory busy in 1934. This sole example of the Parnall Hendy Heck was built at Yeovil.

Basil Henderson, the owner of Hendy Aircraft, for Whitney Straight who was a wealthy private aircraft owner. It first flew in July 1934.

The five year period from 1934 was to see major changes, re-organisation and expansion at Westland. In June 1934 came the first of these when Sir Ernest Petter decided that his son, Edward (Teddy) should be co-opted to the Westland Board, having been Robert Bruce's assistant since January 1932, and insisted that he should rank equal with Stuart Keep, the general manager. Bruce, who was then 65, would not agree to this ranking and resigned from the Board rather than accept Sir Ernest's ruling. Bruce then retired from the company, much to everyone else's regret. Bruce's natural successor was Keep, another director, who was his son-in-law, but Sir Ernest became chairman and managing director. When Geoffrey Hill learned that Sir Ernest intended to appoint Edward technical director in the near future, he, too, resigned but agreed to supervise work on the Pterodactyl V until October when he took up the Kennedy Chair of Engineering at London University. Hill's departure not only simplified Edward Petter's promotion to technical director but, because he was not interested in continuing Pterodactyl development, it meant abandoning a design contract for a tailless four-engined flying-boat with Saunders-Roe's collaboration on hull design. Keep gained something from this Board room shuffle as he was appointed general manager. The other directors were Peter Acland and John Fearn.

In spite of Robert Bruce's departure and the failure of the earlier C.29 Autogiro, there were, at Yeovil, people who still believed that rotary-winged aircraft had a great future in which Westland could play a prominent part. Among them were Harald Penrose, who had always made known his belief in them, and Edward Petter who was attracted not only by their novelty and challenge, but also because it was a new concept for Westland; thus, as the recently-appointed technical director, this placed him on an equal footing with others in the company in the matter of experience. It was through his French connection—he had married a Franco-Swiss girl—that Petter, with Arthur Davenport, produced the design of the CL.20 Autogiro which first flew in February 1935 but which, having completed over eighty test flights, was abandoned six months later with insuperable lift and control problems. Westland's lack of experience was showing.

The year 1935 also saw another major change at Yeovil when, at the 25th Annual General Meeting Sir Ernest announced that with effect from 4 July Westland Aircraft Works had ceased to be a branch of Petters Ltd and would function as a separate company with a capital of £250,000 and under the name Westland Aircraft Limited. The new Board was himself as chairman and joint managing director with Peter Acland, Edward Petter as technical director, John Fearn as works superintendent plus Air Vice Marshal N D K MacEwen. Soon afterwards Stuart Keep decided to retire and return to his native Australia, having lost his seat on the new Board, even though he had remained a Petters director. Under this management team the new company seemed to change up a gear as the pace of work quickened. With the support of powerful Roy Fedden at Bristol, who had been promoting young Edward Petter's interests, he and Davenport designed an eight-gun fighter to meet Specification F.5/34 but Petter had still to prove himself in the eyes of the Air Ministry and contracts for prototypes were given only to the Gloster and Bristol Aeroplane companies. Westland was then given the opportunity to submit a design to Specification A.39/34 calling for an army co-operation aircraft to replace the Hawker Audax in RAF service. This was to result in an order for two prototypes, designated the Westland P.8, in June 1935 with work beginning almost immediately. At that time, Westland was busy with the sub-contract production of 43 Audaxes for Hawker Aircraft using all-metal wings produced by Gloster Aircraft. During July 1935 a Wallace, possibly from the A & AEE at Martlesham Heath, played a highly significant role in the discovery of the potentialities of radar. At that time, Robert Watson-Watt, the British radar pioneer, with A F Wilkins, an early recruit to his team and A P Rowe from the Air Ministry, were conducting early trials and checks of his RDF equipment at Orfordness. On 24 July, having tracked a Vickers Valentia target at a range of 38 miles on his oscilloscope, he followed a Wallace, which was a much smaller target, on the regular Orfordness—Bircham Newton route until, at a distance of some 35 miles, the echo faded. While waiting for the echo from the returning Wallace to appear, he saw another and different type of blip which divided into two. On returning to his base the Wallace pilot reported that he had seen a formation of three Harts which divided into two. This was the first time that Watson-Watt had had confirmation of the possibility of being able to assess the size of formations in this way, something which he had always believed would be possible.

In the spring of 1936 Westland received two sub-contract orders for a total of 178 Hawker Hectors which were to have been given to A V Roe. This work was welcomed at Yeovil as it was to fill the factory throughout the latter part of the year and through to the end of 1937, a period when the possibility of producing the Hendy Heck had failed to materialise and only some work on refurbishing Wapitis and Wallaces was in hand. One of Acland's early achievements as a director was gaining the Board's approval to extend the factory. This included

The Vimy hangar on 1 March, 1937, with no less than thirty-eight Hawker Hector fuselages and aircraft visible in the original photograph.

35

A Napier Dagger engined Hawker Hector complete with armament and underwing supplies containers before delivery from Yeovil.

the re-arrangement of shops taken over from Petters, the erecton of a new boiler house and a 16,000 sq ft air-conditioned wing shop, modernisation of the dope shop and enlargement of the rib department to cope with an order from Gloster for 100 sets of Gauntlet wings, on which Westland lost £728. However, the balance was restored with a later order for 353 sets of Gladiator ailerons which made a £1,059 profit.

Meanwhile, work on the two P.8 prototypes progressed so rapidly that only

Harald Penrose sits high in the cockpit of the first Lysander in June 1936.

eleven months after receipt of the order the first one was ready for engine runs. This aeroplane, the first to be built to Edward Petter's design, was to be named Lysander and, not surprisingly, it had the high-wing configuration used in four earlier Westland types. However, this was no slavish adherence to an established design for the high wing provided the excellent all-round vision essential in an army co-operation aircraft. While the name Lysander, who was a Spartan general, followed the line of classical warriors' names given to aeroplanes with this role, General Lysander's greatest achievement was raising a Spartan fleet to beat the Athenians who were the great naval power in Greece!

When Harald Penrose first flew this prototype on 15 June, 1936, neither he nor anyone else realised that a total of some 1,650 would be produced, at Yeovil and in Canada—the great majority for use in a war only three years away. Its unique high-wing monoplane configuration (to be a wartime recognition boon to members of the Royal Observer Corps who mentally divided aeroplanes into two groups; the Lysander and all the others!) and short take-off were publicly shown in the RAF Display and SBAC Show at Hendon only twelve days later. At about the same time, Westland, in company with four other manufacturers, was submitting to the Air Ministry its proposal for a four cannon-armed fighter to meet Specification F.37/35 and later to be named Whirlwind. These two unusually-configured aeroplanes designed by Petter, were to be among Westland's contributions to the Second World War.

A Lysander II, with its palindromic serial, L6886, and camouflage, ready for delivery.

Early in 1937, possibly for the first time, the older members of the Petter family's grip on Westland was publicly contested when Edward Petter, with Peter Acland, contested Sir Ernest's proposal to merge with British Marine Aircraft Ltd in order to gain additional production facilities. After a Board room battle Sir Ernest lost the day and plans were put in hand for a vast new assembly shop, larger than the entire Petter oil engine factory, to be built at Yeovil for production of Lysanders and, hopefully, Whirlwinds, two prototypes of which had just been ordered. Through a complex chain of events, the choice of Markham & Co Ltd at Sheffield to build this new shop was to have far-reaching effects on Westland's future. Lord Aberconway, chairman of the shipbuilders John Brown & Co. was planning to acquire an aircraft manufacturer and expand it to diversify his company's interests. One of Markham's directors, Eric Mensforth, was the son of Sir Holberry Mensforth, a John Brown director. The message from him that Westland, with its Lysander work, might be a sound acquisition thus reached Lord Aberconway and the John Brown Board, which agreed with young Eric Mensforth. In July 1938 John Brown & Co acquired a controlling interest in Westland Aircraft Ltd. Sir Ernest, who retired, was replaced as chairman by Aberconway. Eric Mensforth and Acland were apointed joint managing directors, Edward Petter remained technical director with Sir Holberry Mensforth and Stanley Rawson as additional directors. Arthur Davenport and John Fearn retained their individual responsibilities as chief engineer and works manager. Soon afterwards, the Petter's oil engine business was sold to Brush Electrical Co and moved to Loughborough, leaving Westland with all of its Yeovil factory. There were questions in the House of Commons about this move which left many unemployed foundry workers in Yeovil, but Acland agreed to retrain them and all were re-employed. In September of that same year a young man named Edward Wheeldon joined Westland as a planning engineer, thus beginning a career which would eventually see him take control of the Westland empire.

With yet another Board room battle ended, a second battle to develop the Whirlwind was being fought in the experimental department and in the air. From the beginning this aircraft was so full of novel design features that it was

Only twelve more Whirlwinds were built after P7110 (seen here). Harald Penrose precisely positions his aircraft to show all its external features.

clear there would be problems. These included a one-piece Fowler flap between the ailerons which was interconnected with the leading-edge radiator-flaps and carried the rear ends of the engine nacelles; exhaust pipes running through the petrol tanks; offset rudder hinges and a concave rudder surface; a high-set tailplane and hydraulic throttle controls. Dennis Edkins, Edward Petter's personal assistant who produced most of the original drawings for his boss, said that, although the Whirlwind had great potential, its Rolls-Royce Peregrine engines and the plethora of these technical innovations plus the works management's inability to understand the amount of development work needed to get a prototype to the production stage, all militated against it.

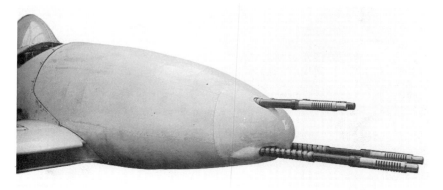

Concentrated firepower in the nose of the Whirlwind. The removable one-piece nose cowling gave unrestricted access to the armament installation.

One of Edkins' tasks was compiling data on tooling and material costs. An interesting note about Westland's labour force and wage rates at that time was discovered, literally, in a 'little black book' in the company's archives. It reveals that in September 1938, there were 10,596 people employed by Westland, 9,358 males, 187 females and 1,013 boys whose weekly wages were £3.13.10d (£3.69p), £1.17.9d (£1.87p) and 17/3d (82p) respectively, with 38 students receiving £1.16.5d (£1.62p). (The boys' wages were of particular interest to the author as they were about 50 per cent more than his own wages for a longer working week at Gloster Aircraft at about the same period!). During the following year they occupied at Yeovil a total factory floor area of 418,190 sq ft with a proposal to extend this to more than half a million square feet.

The 1939–45 War Effort

During the spring of 1939, as war in Europe became increasingly inevitable, dual managing directorship at Westland was proving difficult. Acland resigned and Eric Mensforth took full control with his accustomed vigour. When war came on 3 September these, then, were Westland Aircraft's management team, labour force and production facilities.

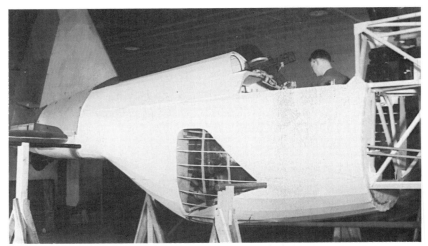

Mock-up of the 'Pregnant Perch', a proposed Lysander with ventral and dorsal gun positions for beach-straffing duties. The course of the war removed the need for it.

Throughout the 1939–45 War, the Westland factory at Yeovil and its several dispersal sites were almost wholly concerned with aircraft production, with much smaller numbers of staff being applied to development of the Lysander and Whirlwind and to basic new design work. One of the first tasks was camouflaging the main factory buildings and the aerodrome, this latter area being marked with a paint and sawdust mix to represent fields bounded by hedges and trees. Chris Barnes records in his Putnam series book *Shorts Aircraft since 1900* that this was so effective that, on a dull November afternoon in 1939, a Short Scylla four-engined transport aircraft of the recently formed National Air Communications and flown by the redoubtable Capt O P Jones, managed to land across the aerodrome in about 50 yards, coming to rest within one of the 'fields', much to the delight of some Westland employees. Next morning, Harald Penrose, delivering a Lysander to the A & AEE, made his usual '3-point take-off' and continued to climb at 45 degrees. He was followed by the Scylla which unstuck in about twice its own 84 ft length and climbed steeply out of Yeovil in a level attitude. This seriously misled another visitor, in a Miles Whitney Straight cabin monoplane, into thinking there was a strong westerly wind shear when, in fact, it was very light. His determined leap off the ground, followed by a stall from which he was able to recover, again delighted those watching on the ground.

The great majority of the production was sub-contract on various Spitfire and Seafire variants. This began in August 1940 with a contract for 300 Spitfire Mk.IAs which was changed to include 140 Mk.VBs and 110 Mk.VCs within that total. These were followed by contracts in September and October 1941 for 200 and 185 Mk.Vs, this programme ending on 5 November, 1943, with delivery of the last one. But before this even, in March 1942, Westland had begun the conversion of 213 Spitfire VBs to Seafire IIC standard; soon afterwards the company became prime contractor with design authority for all Merlin-engined

In 1941 HM King George VI visited the Westland factory at Yeovil. Accompanied by Eric Mensforth, managing director (right) and Edward Petter, technical director, he is seen inspecting Lysander production.

Lysanders and Spitfire VIIIs at Ilchester; some ex-SAR Lysanders are awaiting conversion to SOE aircraft and tropical equipment will be fitted in the Spitfires.

Seafires, a total of 913 Mk.IIIs being built at Yeovil—the last in July 1945—and 350 by Cunliffe-Owen under direct sub-contract from Westland. In conjunction with Supermarine the 'Seafire Office' at Yeovil was also responsible for the design of a manual wing-folding mechanism. Concurrently, 250 Griffon-engined

Seafire XVs and 213 XVIIs were produced by Westland during February 1944 to October 1946. Two Westland-built Spitfires were still airworthy and were being flown at displays during 1990; AR213, a Mk.IA owned by Victor Gauntlet and AR501, a Mk.VC which is in the care of the Shuttleworth Trust. This latter aircraft returned to Yeovil in October/November 1990 for refurbishment. In addition to this main production task, Westland made modifications to Curtiss Mohawk, Tomahawk and Kittyhawk single-seat fighters, this work being mainly the fitment of British radio and instrumentation in place of those fitted to suit the French Air Force which was to have been the original user of many of these aircraft. Other sub-contract production included eighteen Barracuda Mk.Is and IIs plus a large number of fuselage/wing centre-sections for the Albemarle transport and glider tug being built by A W Hawksley at Brockworth. In this latter work Westland was one of more than 1,000 sub-contractors to the Albemarle programme.

While Spitfires and Seafires were being built, the project office was busy with the P.14 which became a submission to Specification F.4/40 and which, in January 1941, was accepted for prototype production as the Welkin twin-engined high-altitude fighter. This aircraft's pressure cabin produced the need for specialised equipment and the R & D programme, on cabin pressure control valves, led by Petter and Bill Widgery, foreshadowed the postwar formation of a separate company now known as Normalair-Garrett. Westland was not alone with its Welkin pressure cabin problems; the Gloster F.9/40 twin-jet fighter prototype was similarly afflicted. There were a number of interesting parallels in these two designs, apart from the fact that, from 1941, when the F.9/40 and F.7/41 requirements became more definitive, (this latter Specification being the one to which the Welkin ultimately was developed), the P.14 was regarded as an insurance against failure of the Gloster jet fighter which was to become the Meteor. An initial requirement for six 20 mm cannon and a pressure cabin were but two of the features which they had in common. During a conversation with the author in 1968, George Carter, previously Gloster Aircraft's technical director, recalled several meetings with Petter to discuss their common difficulties and was very impressed with the advances made by Westland which put it ahead of Gloster in this field. 'He was using a lot of black Bostik and was blowing up pieces of rubber tube, like bicycle inner tubes, to seal the canopy. It

A Welkin in the welkin – or upper air. The non-appearance of very high altitude Luftwaffe attacks on Britain was, in part, the cause of the cancellation of this elegant fighter.

42

A few Lysanders remained airworthy in 1991. V9281/G-BCWL was operated by Brian Woodford and Wessex Aviation and Transport at Henstridge.

looked like Heath Robinson,* but it was working.'

Meanwhile, production of Lysanders had ceased in December 1941 when 1,652 had been built. This was Westland's largest production of an aircraft of its own design. The unit cost of these aeroplanes is worthy of note. The first twelve Lysanders were built at a fixed price of £15,189 1s 1d (£15,189.5½ p), but by the time 150 had been produced, this had dropped to £3,063 8s 5d (£3,063.42p).

If Westland's efficiency as a production unit had been recognised with the massive Spitfire and Seafire programme, then recognition of the company's management came on 1 January, 1943, when the secondment of Eric Mensforth to the Ministry of Aircraft Production, on a part-time basis, as chief production adviser to Air Marshal Sir Wilfred Freeman, its chief executive, took effect. John Fearn took over much of the responsibilities of managing director and Edward Wheeldon was appointed works manager.

As the war entered its last year, the Westland Board was looking to the future, particularly the immediate postwar years when the vast military contracts, which had kept the factory busy, would cease. Diversification into non-aviation products appeared to hold most promise; accordingly, Petter and his colleagues on the Board undertook some surveys of potential peace-time markets. However, it was the issue of Admiralty Specification N.11/44 for a single-seat carrier-borne strike fighter which most appealed to Petter, who gave his imagination free-reign in proposing a design embodying a buried mid-fuselage engine to provide good forward vision for deck-landing, and repeating this feature in a twin-jet RAF fighter-bomber to meet Specification B.1/44. This engine location while suitable for a jet aircraft, promised problems with the Rolls-Royce Eagle piston engine called for in Specification N.11/44; thus, during a fairly lengthy absence by Petter, Harald Penrose arranged for the mock-up

*The artist Heath Robinson, who died in 1944, was renowned for cartoon illustrations of vast contrivances which were absurdly ingenious and totally impractical in construction.

temporarily to be altered to a more conventional configuration which, ultimately, was accepted. This aircraft was to become the Wyvern.

At about the same time, Edward Petter was repeatedly claiming that he should be appointed chief engineer with overall responsibility for both design and production, but Eric Mensforth, who had returned to full-time work at the company soon after the war's end, would not agree. At this point, Petter decided to resign from Westland and in July 1944 he joined English Electric Aircraft Division in the coveted chief engineer appointment, taking with him, with Mensforth's agreement, his design and proposals for the twin-jet fighter bomber. This was to be developed to become the Canberra. In yet another change in management, Arthur Davenport became technical director, and John Digby took over his role as chief designer. A few months later Wheeldon was appointed works director and deputy to John Fearn.

The first fruits of the Westland Board's diversification policy came in the summer of 1945 with the formation of Westland Engineers to produce overhead and sliding doors for garages and other buildings. Further diversification came in April 1946 with the formation of Normalair Ltd, a wholly-owned subsidiary of Westland Aircraft, responsible for the R & D and production of air control equipment. While this work was to be carried on at Yeovil the registered offices were at 8 The Sanctuary, Westminster, in London. The Board, under John Fearn's chairmanship, comprised E J Boulger as general manager, chief engineer was S T A Richards, W B Hickman was secretary plus Eric Mensforth and Colonel Sorel from France. As reported in *The Aeroplane*, 'The formation of this new company is a sign of the times in that it foreshadows the need for specialised experience to meet the problems to be solved in flying commercially at high levels'. Its products were soon to find application in many British and overseas civil and military aircraft.

While the tail-end of Seafire production continued into late 1946, the repair and overhaul of Spitfires helped to keep the Yeovil factory busy: there was, too, a modest 'de-navalisation' programme in which a number of Seafire IIIs for the Irish Air Corps had their arrester hooks and other naval equipment removed, non-folding Spitfire wings were fitted and modifications were made to enable IAC radio equipment to be carried. Of prime importance was the building of the first Eagle-engined W.34 prototype of the Wyvern. This made its first flight at A & AEE Boscombe Down on 12 December, 1946, to launch a seven-year development programme before the type would enter RN squadron service. With this flight, Westland became the first company to respond to the A & AEE's invitation to contractors to use Boscombe Down, with its new runway and taxiway system, for flights of this nature.

Rotary-Wing Revolution

But for Westland 1946 was a year of major importance. At the very moment when this new prototype made its first flight at Boscombe Down, Westland's management was securing the high ground on which the company's future was to be built. It had examined many options, including the production of commercial jet aircraft after John Digby had produced some preliminary schemes, the development of high-altitude jet fighters using skills and experience gained with the Welkin, and the manufacture of light aircraft. This last option would have been exercised through licenced production of a US-built four-seat monoplane already used in Canada; however, Harald Penrose considered that, with its fabric-covered welded steel structure, it was already outdated. In the event, all the possibilities were discarded as the Board made the bold decision to move into the completely new field of rotary-wing aircraft. Having in mind the company's minimal experience with this type of aircraft, that the development of the helicopter was still in its infancy and its future uncertain, this decision was only the first of many, all equally demanding and adventurous. The major one was choosing the better method of implementing it; to take the lengthy path of building a helicopter of its own design or the quicker route, suggested by Harald Penrose, by licence-building another company's established design. Nearly 50 years later, Westland's decision to choose the latter course and to seek such a licence from the Sikorsky Division of United Aircraft Corporation at Bridgeport, Connecticut, can now be seen as being correct.

Though certainly bold, the fundamental decision to enter this new field was not taken lightly. Mensforth, Davenport, Penrose and Fearn were all keenly interested in rotary-wing development and saw a good future for it. Penrose had studied the potential helicopter market and examined the types then in production by the Sikorsky and Bell companies in the United States. Although Mensforth had no experience in the aircraft industry before joining Westland, his several war-time years at the MAP had quickly educated him. In 1944 he had contact with US helicopter development and he went to Bell, which considered he was making this approach several years too soon, and to Bridgeport to meet Igor Sikorsky who piloted him in the two-seat R-4. To enhance their understanding of helicopters in the widest sense, Penrose and Arthur Davenport spent some time at the Rotary Wing Aircraft Section of the Airborne Forces Experimental Establishment at Beaulieu, where O L L Fitzwilliams was in charge. There they examined a German Focke Achgelis Fa 223 helicopter and also flew in a Sikorsky R-4. 'Fitz' moved to Westland as helicopter engineer in March 1947 where he became responsible for all design and development work of Dragonfly, Whirlwind and Wessex helicopters until retiring in 1983.

In 1946 John Fearn led a Westland team to the United States to negotiate a licence from the Sikorsky company.

The upshot of all this 'pro-rotary wing' activity resulted in Sikorsky granting to Westland, in January 1947, a licence to build its S-51 helicopter. Ironically, Fairey Aviation had been offered a similar deal but had turned it down. This set in train a great transfer of drawings to Westland from the USA and their anglicisation before they could be issued to the shop floor.

In his book *A History of British Rotorcraft 1865–1965*, Fitzwilliams said 'Due to a prohibition on dollar content and the then wide differences between English and American materials and accessories, particularly bearings, the anglicising of the S-51 design was very extensive, every part of the helicopter being in some respects (and many parts in very major respects) different from the American original. The magnitude of this task was greatly underrated'. He went on to record that when the first Westland-built WS-51 first flew on 5 October, 1948, in the hands of Alan Bristow, there were 'only fourteen people, including the secretary and the office boy, in the department'. Small wonder that this work had taken nearly twice as long as had been anticipated when the drawings had arrived from Sikorsky.

The deal with Sikorsky included the provision of six S-51s, the first of them, G-AJHW, soon demonstrating the helicopter's unique capabilities when it was flown by Alan Bristow, then a Westland test pilot, to relieve the crew of Wolf Rock lighthouse marooned there because storms had prevented surface craft reaching them.

G-ALIK, the third WS-51, being refuelled on the roof of Olympia in London. It operated a service to and from the South Bank site for a short period in 1951.

Named Dragonfly, 139 of these helicopters were produced, the first batch as a private venture; they gave the RN and the RAF their first taste of operations in British-built rotary-winged aircraft, No.705 Squadron RN being the first helicopter squadron in the world outside of the USA. They were later used by British European Airways (BEA) for the world's first 'scheduled and sustained' helicopter passenger service between Cardiff, Wrexham and Liverpool, and by other operators.

Although rotary-winged aircraft now represented Westland's future, there was still the company's last fixed wing aircraft, the Wyvern, to progress through its lengthy development. This was beset with technical problems resulting from the use of a new gas-turbine engine, the Armstrong Siddeley Python propeller-turbine, and its complex Rotol eight-blade contra-rotating propeller.

On 9 January, 1948, a link with the company's founding was broken by the death of Robert Bruce aged 78.

Of the 124 Wyverns built, only 69 went to operational squadrons where they had a comparatively brief but exciting life. Asked for his comments on the Wyvern, an ex-Wyvern squadron pilot said, 'What I shall remember most about this aircraft was its reliability and its excellent baggage-carrying space, so useful to Naval aviators in their travels'. This was, no doubt, a tongue-in-cheek response for he had earlier described this 'heavier-than-air machine' as 'enjoyable to fly and a magnificent weapons platform as proved during the Suez operation'. In 1948 consideration was given to building a jet-powered variant but lack of both RN and RAF interest ended it. A plan to fit the unusual Napier Nomad compound engine in the Wyvern was also abandoned when mechanical problems were beyond Napier's financial and engineering resources to resolve.

While the main drawing office had been working on the development of the Wyvern, the project office initiated a number of design studies. Westland was ahead of official thinking on the matter of all-through jet training for military pilots. The W.37 was a low-wing monoplane side-by-side two-seat basic jet trainer for the type of training plan which was not to be adopted by the RAF for several years. The W.37 progressed no further than the drawing board. Thought was also given to a number of civil projects, all fixed-wing, which included a four-jet airliner similar to the de Havilland Comet, a short-haul high-wing feeder-liner like the DHC Dash 8 with two Dart propeller-turbines, and a tailless swept-wing jet aircraft echoing the earlier pterodactyl configuration. None came to fruition in the light of Westland's decision to build helicopters.

When the Westland design office's engineering load was light during 1950 it turned its attention to railway coaches under sub-contract to Cravens Railway Carriage and Wagon Co, which was a John Brown company, in Sheffield. Cravens had an order for carriages for the Canton—Kowloon railway in Hong Kong and Westland designed and strain-gauged them. Work of a still secret nature was also undertaken for the Admiralty Underwater Weapons Establishment. Meanwhile, in the factory, Gloster Meteors appeared for repair and reconditioning.

The desire to build a larger and more advanced helicopter than the Dragonfly and the decision in 1950 to do so under licence from Sikorsky were logical steps along Westland's progressive rotary-wing path. However, the first flight of the British-built 'anglicised' WS-55 did not take place until the summer of 1953. Produced in fourteen variants and named Whirlwind, this being made public in

Before its first flight, the cabin of WS-55 Series 1 G-ANFH, British European Airways *Sir Ector*, was exhibited on Westland's stand at the 1954 SBAC Exhibition.

the chairman's statement at the company's November 1953 Annual General Meeting, it was fitted with a turboshaft engine, ahead of Sikorsky.

Undoubtedly, it was the Whirlwind which helped to establish Westland as a first-rate helicopter manufacturer. Some 400 were built for the RN, RAF, many civil operators and for export. The RAF's all-yellow search-and-rescue Whirlwinds were a familiar sight around Britain's shores and over moorland and mountains until 30 November, 1981, when they were replaced by the Wessex.

During August 1953 Harald Penrose made his last flight as Westland's chief test pilot in the first pre-production Wyvern TF.2 VW872. It had been fitted with a new dihedral tailplane.

Two Whirlwind HCC.8s of The Queen's Flight had special fixed steps for easy access to the cabin.

August 1953 was to see a major change in the test pilot hierarchy at Westland when Harald Penrose made his last test flight in a Wyvern Mk.TF.2 to end 25 years as a Westland pilot, all but three of them as chief test pilot. Changing roles, he was then appointed sales manager, then a special director until retiring in 1968 with more than 400 types and variants in his log book. He was succeeded by Lieut W H 'Slim' Sear. Other senior management changes were the appointment of Eric Mensforth as chairman of Westland's Board, following the death of Lord Aberconway, and the retirement of John Fearn. Although Wyvern production was to continue until 1956, a Board decision to make it the last fixed-wing aeroplane it would design caused John Digby to resign, his place as chief designer being taken by P E Q Shunker who had been chief technician. With Dennis Hollis-Williams now as technical director in succession to Arthur Davenport, who remained a Board member, Westland's design team was readied for its next rotary-winged venture.

This Gloster Meteor Mk.F.4, RA490, was extensively modified by Westland during 1953–54 for vectored-thrust research by the RAE Farnborough.

A pioneering role in the development of another form of vertical take-off and landing aircraft was undertaken by Westland when it was charged with modifying a Meteor for RAE investigations into inflight vectored thrust characteristics, particularly reduced landing speed. This involved completely redesigning and producing a complete new centre section and nacelle structures to accept Rolls-Royce Nene engines and the development of a hydraulic operating system for the outlet nozzles. This aircraft was first flown in May 1954 by Leo de Vigne, a Westland test pilot. With 60 per cent thrust deflected on the approach, the safe landing speed was reduced by 20 per cent.

Although the Westland philosophy of licence-building helicopters from the USA was now firmly established practice, there had been initial opposition to it within some quarters of the Government and the industry; however, in the Westland Annual Report of November 1954, Mensforth underlined the value of that experience and revealed the company's intention to begin building helicopters of its own design. 'Our association with Sikorsky . . . has enabled us to make proposals to potential users to develop and produce, at an earlier date than otherwise possible, a large twin-engined helicopter. It would have a range of uses, both for passengers, where it would accomodate thirty-five people, and for Service use, particularly that of the Army where it would carry a load of five tons. We have in mind to call this helicopter the Westminster.' This showed, clearly, Westland's growing confidence and an earnest of intent to launch the design of very large helicopters for which Fitzwilliams was already producing proposals for 100- and 400-seaters. Its very name was aimed at the point from whence Westland hoped to enlist support.

Using the WS-51 Dragonfly airframe, Westland had also been working on a five-seat variant with a redesigned front fuselage. This was the Widgeon, of which only a handful were built but which provided good experience for Westland's design team.

A trio of Gnome-powered Whirlwind HAR.10s for the Royal Air Force's SAR squadrons.

This Wessex HAS.1, XS119 of No.700H Squadron, was one of 128 of these helicopters produced for the Royal Navy.

With the undoubted success of the later Whirlwind variants with turboshaft engines in mind, Westland was studying schemes to instal these engines in Sikorsky-designed airframes. The new S-58 helicopter with turboshaft engines appeared to meet the RN need for a larger helicopter which could be developed to operate in the ASW hunter-killer role. Thus was created the Wessex of which more than 230 were to be produced in ten variants for the RN and RAF, for export to overseas air forces and for civil use, this last variant principally by Bristow Helicopters, the company formed by Westland's ebullient ex-test pilot Alan Bristow.

Two Wessex HCC.4s were specially completed as replacements for long-serving Whirlwinds in The Queen's Flight.

Some three years before Wessex production and development was getting under way in 1957–58, Westland had examined the possibility of licence-building a civil variant of the Sikorsky S-56, a twin-engined 14-ton 20-seat helicopter in service with the US Marine Corps as the HR2S-1. When government support for this venture was denied, Sikorsky agreed to supply just the S-56's main and tail rotors, transmission and control systems for embodiment in a Westland-designed airframe with turboshaft engines. This unusual mixture produced the Westminster, in effect, a giant flying test rig, which first got airborne in June 1958. Sadly, its development was halted in 1961 by pressure from the Royal Navy, which believed such work would slow Wessex development, and also by the fact that the Fairey Rotodyne, which had first flown on 6 November, 1957, was a more advanced concept and well into its flight test programme.

While the armed Services were Westland's major customers, the company was always keen to promote the civil applications of helicopters and their ability to operate in and out of city centres. In August 1958, after many months of close scrutiny the Ministry of Housing and Local Government agreed Westland's plans to develop a Battersea site, bought from the John Brown company, as a temporary helicopter station to serve central London. In competition with

Westland family on show at Farnborough 1958. From the left are the Westminster G-APLE, the prototype Wessex HAS.1 XL727, Whirlwind HAS.7 XL880 and the second Widgeon G-AKTW.

The al fresco nature of the Bristol Siddeley Nimbus engine installation in the Scout and Wasp is apparent in this view of a Scout on its special handling trolley as it arrived at the 1962 SBAC Farnborough Show. (*Bristol Siddeley*)

Rotorports Ltd, which had proposed a floating platform moored in the River Thames opposite the Tate Gallery, Westland's T-shaped concrete platform built out over the water on piles with a two-level terminal building was preferred. Completed in December at an estimated cost of only £62,000 this heliport, which was opened on 23 April, 1959, was approved for scheduled services only by Westland, other operators being allowed to fly only on charter.

Rationalisation

It was in April 1957 that the not totally unexpected contents of the Government's Defence White Paper were revealed by Duncan Sandys, the Defence Minister. Apart from ruling out further development of fighter aircraft, other than the English Electric P.1 Lightning, a design with which Edward Petter initially had been involved, it pointed the way toward rationalisation of Britain's aircraft industry. This was compounded two years later when Sandys, as Minister of Aviation, was the chief architect of a plan which, ultimately, was to reduce the number of main aircraft manufacturers from sixteen to four and the engine companies from seven to one.

Within this plan the Government wanted one helicopter manufacturing organisation centred on Yeovil. In August 1959, Westland began the piecemeal acquisition of Britain's helicopter manufacturing interests. First was Saunders-Roe with its sites at Cowes and Eastleigh, gaining the promising P.531 helicopter, which it later developed into the Wasp and Scout, the Black Knight research rocket and hovercraft. During March 1960, following amicable negotiations, the helicopter division of Bristol Aircraft with its valuable Old

Rationalisation of Britain's helicopter industry in 1959 brought production of the Bristol Belvedere under Westland's control. This work was done at Old Mixon, Weston-super-Mare, previously a Bristol company factory.

Mixon factory at Weston-super-Mare and the Belvedere helicopter, was purchased for a 10 per cent interest in Westland. Finally, in May, against a hostile background, Westland bought the United Kingdom aviation interests of Fairey Aviation at Hayes, with its Rotodyne programme and the AEW Gannet. An additional dowry was the promise of some £4 million from the Government for Rotodyne development if orders justified its production. These three new elements initially operated as the Saunders-Roe, Bristol Helicopter and Fairey Aviation Divisions with the fourth being the Yeovil Division.

Apart from the acquisition of facilities, personnel and hardware, Westland also obtained the services of a number of outstanding management, commercial and technical personalities from these three other companies.

While development of the P.531 was progressed vigorously, the production and delivery of Belvederes and Gannet AEW Mk.3s went ahead, as did investigations of the Bristol 194, a 48-seat civil helicopter; however, design work on the Bristol 192C, a civil variant of the Belvedere and a larger military variant, the 192D, was to cease, while the fifteen-year-old programme which had brought the Rotodyne close to production orders was finally cancelled in February 1962.

During the foregoing period, in 1961 Westland and Boeing-Vertol signed a licence-agreement for the Vertol 107, the forerunner of the CH-47 Chinook, giving Westland non-exclusive rights to build and sell it in Europe. BEA had expressed an interest in this helicopter following the withdrawal of British Government support for the Rotodyne, and a joint BEA/Sabena agreement was a possibility. No doubt these contacts with Boeing-Vertol influenced the design of the WG.1, a project to meet Naval/Air Staff Requirement 358 for a medium lift helicopter, which bore a marked external resemblance to the Chinook, but little else resulted from this agreement.

Initially, the P.531 development soon produced the first production Scout AH

A row of Westland-Agusta-Bell 47G Sioux helicopters nearing completion at Westland's Yeovil factory.

Mk.1 five-seat general purpose helicopter, which flew on 6 March, 1961, a total of 148 being built, almost all for the British Army, only a handful being exported. The Wasp also was derived from the Saunders-Roe P.531 and was developed for RN use with a four-wheeled undercarriage, instead of the Scout's skids, and folding main rotor and tailboom. The first production Wasp HAS Mk.1 flew in January 1963, a total of ninety-eight being built for the RN and some forty more for export.

At about this time, Westland's project office was examining a series of proposals for future military helicopters to replace those currently in service. These crystallised as the WG.5, a single-engined three-seat light reconnaissance aircraft: the WG.3, a twin-engined light tactical aircraft of 8,000—11,000 lb which was to become the WG.13 Lynx; and WG.4, a twin-engined medium-sized transport and ASW aircraft of about 17,000 lb. A similar excerise was being undertaken by Sud Aviation in France, and a number of meetings between the two companies ensued to establish the level of commonality between the two nations' requirements and the helicopters envisaged. On 17 May, 1965, their respective Governments signed a Memorandum of Understanding on collaborative development and production of military helicopters.

The third small helicopter to be built by Westland during the 1960s was the Westland-Agusta-Bell 47G-3B-4, its lengthy designation stemming from the fact that Westland produced them under licence from Construzioni Aeronautiche Giovanni Agusta S.p.A in Italy to abide by a clause in its licence from Sikorsky not to build a US competitor's aircraft. Starting in 1964, Westland built 250 of these small three-seat general purpose helicopters at Yeovil under contract to the MoD, most of them going to the British Army with a few for the RAF, plus a small number more for Bristow Helicopters which was training Army pilots.

In addition to the P.531 helicopter, Westland's acquisition of Saunders-Roe had brought control not only of the Western world's largest hovercraft business, but also the Black Knight ballistic test vehicle. While Black Knight made a number of successful launches at the Woomera range in Australia with its re-entry head going up some 500 miles, the programme was terminated with the last of twenty-two firings in November 1965. Development of a smaller satellite launch vehicle, Black Arrow, was continued until 1971 when it, too, was cancelled, having failed to attain orbital velocity. Meanwhile, development of the SR-N1, -N2, -N3 and -N5 hovercraft was progressing at Cowes with a number of craft being sold to United Kingdom operators and exported. Ultimately, on 1 October, 1966, British Hovercraft Corporation was formed with Westland having a 65 per cent share, Vickers 25 per cent and the National Research Development Council (NRDC) the remainder. Its task was to control and continue the development of this new class of vehicle.

Although acquisition added to Westland's product range and R & D capabilities, it also produced a superfluity of production and flight-development capacity; thus, in the spring of 1964, the lease on the ex-Fairey Aviation White Waltham site was sold and all activities there were transferred to Yeovil and Hayes.

A major change in Westland's company structure also took place on 1 October, 1966, when a new wholly-owned company named Westland Helicopters Ltd was formed, taking responsibility for all the helicopter business of the

Westland Group. Another significant change was the appointment as chief test pilot of Ron Gellatly, who had held a similar appointment with Fairey Aviation, to succeed Slim Sear.

Meanwhile, under the stimulus of the Anglo-French MoU on military helicopter development, there had been many meetings between Westland and Sud-Aviation representatives and those of their Government departments concerned. On 22 February, 1967, a more detailed MoU confirmed collaborative production of the Sud SA 341 Gazelle to meet the need for a light five-seat communications and training helicopter, the Sud SA 330 Puma medium-sized transport helicopter and the Westland WG.13, a medium-sized multi-role helicopter capable of operating in the utility, reconnaissance, anti-tank and ASW roles. Responsibility for the development of the Gazelle and Puma was allocated to Sud while Westland had design leadership for the WG.13 which was later to be named Lynx.

Model of a 1967 tilt-rotor 80-seat transport project, a class of aircraft under active study by Westland at that time.

As far as Westland was concerned, the first fruit of this agreement was the SA 330 Puma for which about 30 per cent of the airframe, initially, was built at Hayes and shipped to Sud-Aviation. The remainder was produced by Sud at Marignane near Marseilles and La Corneuve near Paris, and supplied for the Westland production line which was moved to the Old Mixon factory at Weston-super-Mare. In addition to supplying Sud-Aviation, which, on 1 January, 1970, was merged with Nord-Aviation and SEREB to form Aérospatiale SNI, Westland was responsible for building forty-eight Puma HC Mk.1s for the RAF, the first squadron, No.33, forming in June 1971. Westland continued to produce Puma components until about 1988.

During the early 1960s, the Royal Navy had produced a requirement for a large long-range twin-engined helicopter able to operate autonomously in the ASW hunter-killer role. Westland had discussed a further extension of the licence agreement which it had with Sikorsky to include the new S-61. This was to lead to production of an anglicised variant, named Sea King, with Rolls-Royce Gnome turboshaft engines.

Four pre-production Sikorsky S-61s, designated SH3-Ds by the US Navy, had been shipped to Britain, the first one being prepared for flight on the dockside at

The Gazelle, one of the three Anglo-French collaborative helicopter projects, was flown in large numbers by the British army, with small batches being built for the other armed services.

An armed Westland-built Gazelle flies a nap-of-the-earth sortie in a ground support role.

The last of forty-eight Westland-built Pumas.

XV642, the first Westland-built Sea King HAS.1, was used in 1982 for development flying with the new composite main-rotor blades seen fitted.

Avonmouth, Avon, and flown to Yeovil on 8 September, 1967. These aircraft helped to launch the Sea King programme, for which the main erection shop was enlarged and a new air traffic control tower was built with extensive new radar and communications equipment, the first Westland-built aircraft flying on 7 May, 1969. Three months later the type entered RN service with No.700S Squadron, the IFTU, at RNAS Culdrose, such was the urgent need for this type of ASW helicopter to meet the threat from the growing fleet of large long-range Soviet submarines operating world wide. The Sea King was continually developed and has been produced in several variants for a variety of roles for RN and RAF use, principally as an ASW aircraft but also for SAR duties and as a troop carrier. It has also been widely exported and was still in production in 1991 with some 330 having been built.

Just two months after the first flight of Westland's Sea King, the British and French Governments confirmed joint production of the Gazelle. As with the Puma, one pre-production SA 341 Gazelle was supplied by Sud-Aviation for use as a trials aircraft, and joint production was undertaken by Westland and Aérospatiale.

With the manufacture of the Whirlwind and Wessex beginning to run down, the production of what would eventually be 252 Gazelles for the British Army,

A Royal Navy Sea King AEW.2 with its large Searchwater scanner radome deployed down to the operational position. This Sea King variant, seen in July 1982, resulted from an urgent need, made apparent in the Falklands' Campaign, for a carrier-borne AEW aircraft.

Two Royal Australian Navy Sea King 50s. Although the nearer aircraft's code indicates it is the fourth of the batch of ten built, its serial is the fifth in sequence.

RN and RAF was begun at Yeovil during 1971; however, later batches were built at Old Mixon leaving room for the growing Sea King production programme. The joint Westland/Aérospatiale production of Gazelles totalled 262.

The third helicopter which was the subject of the Anglo-French MoU was the Westland WG.13 which was to become the Lynx. It stemmed from a vast project programme, first by Westland and then in collaboration with France to meet the requirements of the Armies and Navies of the two countries. The Lynx differed from all other Westland-built helicopter programmes in that it was a Westland design and was the first British aircraft to be designed on metric mensuration. Design leadership gave Westland additional new responsibilities on an international scale; yet less than four years were to pass between the formation of Westland's new Project Group, in 1963, to study the future helicopter needs of Britain's armed forces, and the receipt, in July 1967, of an official Ministry ITP (instruction to proceed) with Lynx development. Initially, only six prototype, or development batch, aircraft were authorised, the first flying in March 1971, but the manifest impossibility of undertaking full development of such a complex helicopter with this comparatively small fleet resulted in a decision to build a further ten; in the event, only seven more were constructed. By this time, the widely separated elements of Westland Helicopters posed logistic and administrative problems and during the early spring of 1972 the Hayes factory was sold with all activities and many personnel being transferred to Yeovil.

Even before the first flight of the first production Lynx in February 1976, it was apparent that, apart from very large production to meet British and French requirements, the export prospects were very good. These have been realised and by the end of 1990 orders from ten countries totalled some 23 per cent of the production programme.

Six months after first flying, the seventh development Lynx, XX469, was written off with irreparable damage in November 1972 following a crash.

60

Lynx for the Brazilian, French, Netherlands and Royal Navies plus RAF and RN Sea Kings fill Westland's final assembly line.

The British Army was the first to put the Lynx into active service with units based in what was then the Federal Republic of Germany, and it was the sixth development aircraft in an Army utility configuration, XX153, which set a new world speed record over a 15—25 km course in the E.1 class for helicopters on 20 June, 1972. Flown by Ron Gellatly, this aircraft averaged 199.92 mph. Two days later, Roy Moxam, a Westland pilot, flew the same aircraft over a 100 km closed-circuit course and averaged 197.91 mph. Some 14 years later on 11 August, 1986, G-LYNX, a developed Lynx demonstrator with BERP III main rotor blades and many other modifications, and flown by Westland's chief test pilot Trevor Egginton, set a new world speed record, in the same E.1 class, of 249.09 mph to become the first helicopter to establish an over-400 kph record. The principal user of the Lynx is the Royal Navy, which flew this helicopter during the Falklands campaign of 1982 before the final stages of the acceptance trials had been completed. The Lynx again saw active service in the Gulf War. The type is scheduled to remain in service with British armed services until the latter half of the 1990s.

During the early 1970s while the preliminary flight development of the Lynx was still in hand, Westland examined the possibility of producing a civil version and began by looking again at the WG.13W project of 1966—67. The company was keen to break into the civil helicopter market, which it not only perceived as having great potential but also saw as a means of reducing its dependence on

61

Four Lynx overfly the Westland factory en route to the 1976 Farnborough Show. From the left are first prototype G-BEAD with Pratt & Whitney PT6A engines; an HAS.2, XZ166, with four Sea Skua missiles; eleventh development aircraft HAS.2 XX910 and tenth development aircraft AH.1 with Aérospatiale HOT missile pods. (*Courtesy Mike Hooks*)

Only a 1974 mock-up with a lengthened wood and metal cabin, the Westland 606 was a proposed 12-passenger civil helicopter.

military contracts from the British Government.

From these studies emerged the Westland 606, a 12-passenger aircraft employing the Lynx main rotor and transmission system, but with a lengthened fuselage and offered with the choice of either the Gem 2 or Pratt & Whitney PT6B turboshaft engines. Using Lynx XW836, the third DB aircraft, as a basis, the cockpit area was removed, a two-feet long wood and metal 'plug' was inserted to increase the main cabin length and the cockpit was replaced. The cabin was furnished to high standards of comfort but this modification precluded the aircraft from flying. Launched in January 1975 at the 27th Helicopter

Association of America Seminar and Exhibition at Disneyland where its sleek shape and promised performance were appealing, the high cost of ownership—particularly the engine element—deterred customers; thus, there was insufficient interest from potential markets for it to be put into production.

With the failure of the Westland 606 to come to fruition, in 1976 Westland again began studies of a new helicopter, larger than the Lynx, for the commercial market. Designed around the well-proven Lynx dynamic system modified slightly to suit the different role, the WG.30, as this new helicopter was designated, featured a capacious rectangular-section fuselage seating 17 passengers in airline standard accomodation plus a cabin steward. Powered by two Rolls-Royce 1,135 shp Gem engines and renamed Westland 30, this helicopter's future looked bright when first, British Airways Helicopters bought three in February 1981 then Airspur, a Californian operator with a number of short routes radiating out of Los Angeles, took delivery of four aircraft and began passenger operations with them in May 1983. Several other customers in the United Kingdom, India and the USA bought a total of 36 Westland 30 variants, but slowly the majority were either withdrawn from service or were grounded following several unexplained crashes and engine unserviceability.

Three of the four Westland 30s delivered to Airspur in the United States. From the left they are N5840T, N5830T and N5820T.

Although the Westland 30 was aimed at the civil market, Westland did not ignore its potential military application as a medium-sized tactical transport. In successful British Army trials during 1980, the Westland 30-100 prototype proved its ability not only to carry 14 fully-equipped troops but also to embark and disembark them very quickly, an important feature of a tactical transport aircraft. Unfortunately neither the civil nor the military variants of the Westland 30 were to win fu;ther o· Jers.

Meanwhile in 1978 Westland had entered into contracts with the Arab Organisation for Industrialisation (AOI) (the partners in which were Egypt, Qatar, Saudi Arabia and the United Arab Emirates) and with the Arab British Helicopter Co (ABH) of which Westland owned 30 per cent. The initial contracts had provided for orders for 250 Lynx helicopters, of which 20 were to be built by Westland and the remainder assembled in Egypt by the ABH, but in

May 1979 the AOI was terminated on instructions from the last three named partners. Westland was promised compensation for any losses suffered; however, another organisation in Egypt, also named AOI and claiming to be the same as the original four-nation AOI, alleged that Westland was in breach of contract by failing to produce the first twenty Lynx and components for the remainder. A lengthy legal battle in the Swiss Courts ensued and in 1984 an Arbitral Tribunal issued an interim award to Westland where losses were assessed to be in excess of £150 million. This unfortunate episode was to have far reaching results for Westland.

Meanwhile, in September 1978, the Westland WG.34 project, submitted to meet a Naval Staff Requirement for a new ASW helicopter to succeed the Sea King, was selected for development by the MoD. Concurrently, the Italian Navy was seeking to replace its ASH-3D helicopters in the same role. Following inter-Government discussions with Westland and Agusta, a Memorandum of Understanding was signed in the following year by the British and Italian Governments which laid the foundations for the formation by these two helicopter manufacturers of a joint company in 1980. Named European Helicopter Industries, its aim was to create and market a new multi-role helicopter, designated EH 101, not only for use by both Navies in the ASW role but also by civil operators. Project definition, the start of the integrated programme and the development phase occupied the ensuing three years.

With the prospect of diminishing helicopter production lines at Yeovil, surprisingly, Westland turned its attention to fixed-wing aircraft. In June 1983 the Ministry of Defence issued Air Staff Target (AST) 412; it called for a

An artist's impression, dated September 1984, of the AAC-Westland A-20 two-seat basic trainer to meet AST 412. It failed to meet Ministry of Defence cost and performance criteria and was rejected.

propeller-turbine basic trainer, as a Jet Provost replacement, with a performance higher than any existing aircraft of this type. By November the promise of an order for 130 aircraft with options on 15 more had attracted submissions from 15 manufacturers, but a statement in the House of Commons on 17 March, 1984, confirmed rumours that a short list of four types had been made; these were the Australian Aircraft Consortium's (AAC) A-20, the EMBRAER Tucano, Britain's Norman Aircraft Firecracker and the Swiss Pilatus PC-9.

In order to meet the requirements of an offset programme the four companies each formed partnerships with other United Kingdom manufacturers and by June 1984, when invitations to tender to Specification T301 D&P had been sent out, AAC had joined forces with Westland. The main design and development work was to be done at Yeovil with 50 per cent of the production being undertaken at Westland's Weston factory where 300 jobs would be secured. A new short list issued on 18 November revealed that, following a change in maximum speed requirements, the Westland-AAC and the Hunting-Norman Firecracker had been eliminated. Their high cost also contributed to their removal from the list. This brought two more, presumably improved, submissions from these two consortia, which appeared to motivate the MoD to invite 'Best and Final offers' from each of the four partnerships for submission by 31 January, 1985. Again, these were examined and, again, the A-20 and Firecracker were eliminated, both on performance plus the fact that the A-20 was not an 'off-the-shelf' aircraft. Yet another Westland project had failed to come to fruition.

The years 1984–86 were to be traumatic ones for Westland and, ultimately for the British Government. Westland was experiencing mounting financial and commercial difficulties on several fronts. There was the ongoing legal battle with Egypt's AOI over the losses on the Lynx contracts cancellations and there was the poor market response to the Westland 30. There was also the near £5 million acquisition of Airspur Helicopters Inc, made to protect the company's investment in the US market, and its renaming W30 Hel Inc. Westland's weakened financial position posed a very serious problem. In June 1985, following rumours that British Aerospace was planning a bid for Westland were denied, and Bristow Rotorcraft's bid to acquire a 51 per cent holding in Westland had lapsed, Sir Basil Blackwell, the outgoing Westland Chairman, had told shareholders that in the Board's view the company required an association with a substantial international business. An independent review, previously set in motion, confirmed to his successor, Sir John Cuckney, both this view and the need for an injection of new capital as part of a financial reconstruction which would be essential if Westland was to continue trading. Both the MoD and the DTI were adamant that no public funds would be made available to help a financial reconstruction and that a private sector answer to the problem would have to be found; nevertheless, they believed that Westland was a strategically important company.

A number of British and foreign companies were approached; where there was interest they were briefed on Westland's financial position and the need to consider the commercial as well as the financial problems which faced the company. Of these, in the opinion of the Board, only United Technologies made a structured response, but it was sufficient to produce additional interest by some European companies worried by the prospect of US interest in Westland.

There followed a series of meetings with United Technologies, which was subsequently joined by Fiat, and with European companies which formed what became known as 'The Consortium'. Both groups made proposals which included capital injection, licenced production of their helicopters and guarantees of sub-contract work. In mid-December the Westland Board unanimously recommended that the proposals based on an association with United Technologies and Fiat provided better prospects for the medium and long-term future of the company; indeed, the Board believed they provided the only practical solution available before Westland's annual results for the 1984–85 trading year were to be announced. However, under the active persuasion of Michael Heseltine, then Secretary of State for Defence, who supported the European companies' proposals, the Consortium persisted with its efforts to obtain a substantial interest in Westland. This led to what was, in effect, a publicly-contested financial reconstruction—and not a take-over, a development which was widely misinterpreted by many and which continued until February 1986.

The United Technologies and Fiat proposal, which was aimed at injecting some £72 million into Westland, included a licence from United Technologies' Sikorsky Aircraft Division for Westland to manufacture and sell the Black Hawk helicopter in more than fifty territories across the world, plus a guaranteed two million hours of work over a five year period beginning early in 1987. This was the form of the financial reconstruction as it was finally approved at an Extraordinary General Meeting on 12 February, 1986, and the Annual General Meeting on 25 April, 1986. A positive note was struck between these two dates when, in March, a long awaited contract was received from the Helicopter Corporation of India for twenty-one Westland 30s. These measures overcame the financial crisis. There were, however, victims. Michael Heseltine's vigorous support of the Consortium and his procurement proposals, which were at variance with British Government policy, had isolated him from his Cabinet colleagues and the Prime Minister, Margaret Thatcher. On 9 January, 1986, he had walked out of a Cabinet meeting and resigned his appointment. (It was not until five years later that, having failed in his attempt to succeed her as Leader of the Conservative Party and Prime Minister, he rejoined the Cabinet when he was invited by John Major, the new Prime Minister, to become Secretary of State for the Environment). On 24 January Leon Brittan, Secretary of State for Industry, also resigned following the allegation that one of the DTI staff had given to the press confidential information on the negotiations.

While Westland's financial structure had been stabilised and its foreseeable future had been secured by the tortuous events of the previous 12 months, some reduction of the work force to achieve cost competitiveness, particularly in the export markets, was inevitable. Thus, during the year ending September 1987, more than 1,700 employees of Westland Helicopters Ltd were declared redundant or transferred to other Westland Group companies. However, deliveries averaged almost three aircraft per month with nine Sea Kings, eleven Lynx and twelve Westland 30 helicopters being delivered during this period.

Following the agreement with United Technologies, Westland received US

State Department approval to produce a version of the Sikorsky Black Hawk helicopter, designated the WS-70. The Westland Board set aside £3 million for a demonstrator aircraft which was assembled from Sikorsky-built components to US Army S-70A battlefield transport standards. Serialled ZG468 it first flew at Yeovil on 1 April, 1987, and was allocated for training and marketing support activities. At that time, Sir John Treacher, deputy chairman of Westland Group, stated that the company still expected to export some 200 Black Hawks over a 10–15 year period despite the apparent lack of MoD interest in acquiring the type for the British armed Services. The first order for eighty aircraft for Saudi Arabia was to have been placed in July 1988 but this did not materialise.

During April, 1987, too, the first pre-production EH 101, PP1, was rolled out at a special ceremony with the first flight in the hands of Trevor Egginton, chief test pilot, taking place on 9 October after six months searching ground testing. Seven weeks later the Agusta-built PP2 flew at Cascina Costa to make a sound start to a programme aimed at getting all the nine pre-production aircraft into the air within two-to-three years of the first flight.

At Yeovil, production of the Sea King and Lynx moved at a slower pace than had been hoped but productivity was reported to have risen by 15 per cent during the previous five years, no mean achievement. The financial re-structuring of Westland Group with its now decentralised company structure in which it operated through three main subsidiaries—Helicopters, Aerospace and Technologies—was working well.

All of these changes augured well for the company's future, although Sir John Cuckney repeated his advice that it would take five years for Westland to achieve full recovery from the traumas of 1986–87. Then, in the summer of 1988, Fiat decided that its shareholding in Westland no longer accorded with its own strategic objectives; thus, in October, it was revealed that GKN had acquired Fiat's shareholding plus some others and so owned 22.02 per cent of Westland. This change underlined the British identity of the company following fears of too much foreign intervention.

In addition to its main task of building helicopters, Westland Helicopters had expanded its interests into sub-contract component production for other manufacturers, winning orders for BAe 146 and Jetstream 41 door assemblies, and engine nacelle assemblies for the Saab 340. This work was done both at the company's Yeovil and Weston-super-Mare factories.

During 1989–90 Westland Helicopters was busy developing the Lynx Mk.8 for the Royal Navy and, in parallel, the Mk.9 for the Army, this latter wheeled-variant being temporarily designated the Battlefield Lynx. Development of the Royal Navy EH 101, now named Merlin, the civil Heliliner and the utility version was being progressed. Eight of the nine pre-production aircraft had flown by the end of 1990 with the flying programme rapidly approaching 1,000 hours, the quarter-way milestone in the 4,000 hours scheduled. At that time, too, the start up of the EH 101 Merlin production programme was awaiting the outcome of a prime contractorship competition. For this Westland teamed with IBM and was opposed by British Aerospace with GEC-Marconi. A decision, expected in February 1991, was still not known in July.

Westland is, once again, moving with strength and purpose into a new era of aviation endeavour and achievement. This book is a tribute to the foresight and enterprise of Ernest and Percival Petter who founded the company and to all those who have followed in their footsteps, in whatever capacity, as employees of the Westland company.

N16, the first N.1B, with a tail float and a humped cowl over the Vickers machine-gun.

N.1B

In 1916, with a growing number of Royal Navy ships capable of carrying and launching aircraft with wheeled undercarriages or floats, the Air Department of the Admiralty was examining the potentialities of single-seat fighters. It was also considering the means whereby such an aircraft could be designed and produced to meet naval requirements. Thus the Air Department N.1B requirement was for a single-seat shipboard floatplane or flying-boat fighter having a speed of 95 knots (110 mph) at 10,000 ft and a ceiling of at least 20,000 ft. This latter requirement was particularly exacting, bearing in mind the comparatively low power/weight ratios and levels of reliability of the engines available at that time.

Three aircraft manufacturers prepared designs to meet this requirement; they were the Blackburn Aeroplane and Motor Co, the Supermarine Aviation Works and Westland Aircraft Works. Both the Supermarine and Blackburn designs were pusher biplane flying-boats but the other design, the first to emanate from the Westland Aircraft Works, was a more conventional tractor biplane floatplane. Contracts for the construction of a total of eight prototypes, all designated N.1B, were placed with the three companies; three each by Blackburn and Supermarine and two by Westland.

The design of the two Westland N.1Bs was the work of Robert Bruce and Arthur Davenport, the company's manager and chief draughtsman respectively. The construction, understandably, followed the standard pattern of that era. The fuselage was a conventional rectangular-section structure with four longerons and internal wire-braced frames of spruce with steel end fittings, the front ends of the longerons carrying the mounting for the 150 hp Bentley AR.1 (for Admiralty Rotary) rotary engine. Wooden formers on the upper longerons provided a rounded top surface to the fuselage. The cockpit surround was of leather-edged ply and had a small head fairing. The entire tail unit was an externally wire-braced wooden structure. The constant chord two-bay biplane

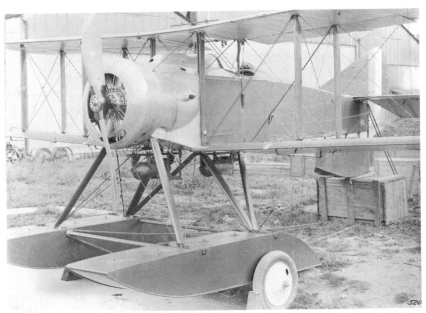

This close up of N16 shows the engine cowling's fine finish, the gun port in its cowl and two 65 lb bombs under the fuselage.

wings were built up around two ash main spars with wire-braced spruce struts and ribs, and spruce interplane struts. Ailerons and trailing-edge flaps, described as a 'wing camber-changing device patented by Robert Bruce', were fitted on all four wings. The wings were designed to fold back against the fuselage sides for shipboard stowage without requiring a jury strut to be fitted at the front spar root-end fittings. Wire-braced spruce alighting gear struts carried two rectangular-section floats, each with a number of watertight compartments. Control wires to the elevators and rudder were run externally from the cockpit but those to the ailerons and flaps were routed inside the wings. The airframe was fabric-covered with a metal engine cowling and top and side panels at the forward end of the fuselage. Armament was a fixed forward-firing Vickers .303 in machine-gun, synchronised to fire through the propeller disc and mounted in a metal 'hump' fairing on top of the fuselage in front of the cockpit, plus a Lewis .303 in gun on a swivel mounting on the upper centre-section above the cockpit. A cross-bar on the centre-section leading-edge appeared to serve the dual purpose of preventing the gun from being fired through the propeller arc and serving as a front mounting for the gun fixed to fire either slightly to port or starboard. In addition two 65 lb bombs could be carried in tandem on tubular carriers attached on the aircraft's centre-line under the fuselage.

Two N.1Bs were built by Westland with some minor differences between them. The first, N16, was fitted with 11 ft long Sopwith main floats and a 5 ft long tail float carrying a water rudder which was moved by a vertical shaft extending down from the aircraft's rudder. In N17, the second aircraft, these

N16 with wings folded and carrying a 65 lb bomb under the fuselage. Note the slotted engine cowling and absense of jury struts.

were replaced by Westland-designed floats 17 ft 6 in in length with swept-up aft ends which made the tail float unnecessary. Some reports indicate that these floats could be fitted with a through axle carrying two wheels to enable the N.1B to take-off and land on suitably equipped vessels at sea, but no evidence of this design feature can be traced. The wheels which are shown in photographs are almost certainly those of a ground-handling trolley.

Completed during the summer of 1917, in August the renowned Harry Hawker flew N16 on its first flight from Yeovil. In October at least one Westland N.1B, N16—and possibly both aircraft—went to the Royal Naval Air Service Experimental Construction Depot at Port Victoria on the Isle of Grain for evaluation where it was flown by Sqn Cmdr J W Seddon who, in 1913, as a young Lieutenant RN flying instructor, had had as a pupil the fledgling aviator and the First Lord of the Admiralty, Mr Winston Churchill. The reports of its evaluation against the PV.2, built by the Royal Naval Air Service Depot at Port Victoria, showed that the Westland N.1B performed well and exhibited good handling characteristics; however, before the type could be developed, a change of policy ensued. Landplane single-seat fighters, such as the Sopwith Pup and Camel, had demonstrated their ability to take-off and land on vessels underway at sea, thus removing the need for the carriers to heave to and either drop or pick-up seaplanes. Because of this change of emphasis, further production and development of the Blackburn, Westland and Supermarine N.1Bs was abandoned after cancellation of the contracts in 1917.

N17, the second N.1B, had a modified engine cowling and an uncowled Vickers gun.

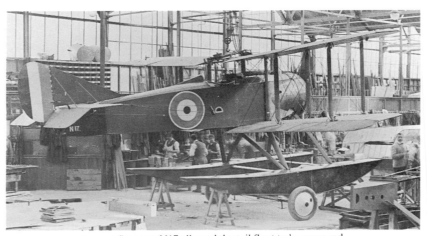

Longer floats on N17 allowed the tail float to be removed.

Description: Single-seat floatplane fighter. All-wood construction with metal and fabric covering.

Accommodation: Pilot in open cockpit.

Powerplant: One 150 hp Bentley AR.1 nine-cylinder air-cooled normally-aspirated rotary engine driving a 9 ft diameter wooden propeller.

Armament: One Vickers .303 in machine-gun firing forward and one Lewis .303 in machine-gun on a swivel mounting on the upper centre-section. Two 65 lb bombs carried in tandem under the fuselage.

Dimensions: Span 31 ft 3½ in; length 26 ft 5½ in; height 11 ft 2 in; wing area 278 sq ft.

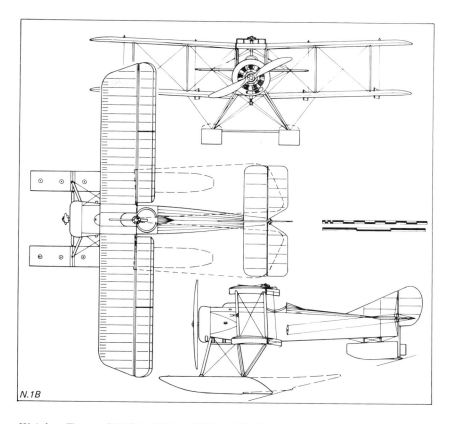

N.1B

Weights: Empty (N16) 1,504 lb, (N17) 1,513 lb. Loaded (N16) 1,978 lb, (N17) 1,987 lb.

Performance: Maximum speed (N16) 108.5 mph, (N17) 107 mph at sea level; alighting speed 50 mph; climb to 5,000 ft in 10 min.

Production: Two prototypes built by Westland Aircraft Works, Yeovil, Somerset, during 1916–17.

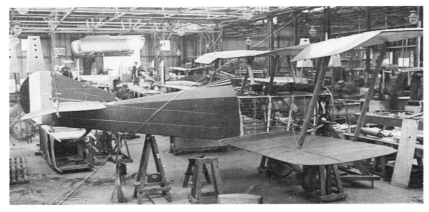

Wagtail C4291 under construction, with broad-chord fin extending forward of the tailplane, equal dihedral wings and reverse taper on inboard sections of the upper wings.

Wagtail

Although the Royal Air Force had not been founded until 1 April, 1918, during the last few months of the 1914–18 War a number of new single-seat fighters designed to meet the RAF Type I Specification were nearing completion. Among those companies producing prototypes was Westland whose small design team, led by Robert Bruce and Arthur Davenport, had been considering the design of a small fighter during the latter half of 1917. One of the requirements of the outline Type I Specification for a light fighter was that it should have an engine delivering 50 hp more than the 130 hp Clerget rotary engine in the Sopwith Camel. This increase in power, plus the smaller size implicit in the 'light fighter' description, was aimed at producing a performance which would exceed that of the Camel, both in terms of maximum speed and rate of climb, with improved handling characteristics.

At about the time when this specification was issued the Air Board was examining a recently-introduced experimental seven-cylinder air-cooled radial engine. Designed by Granville Bradshaw who had founded ABC Motors, the successor to ABEC (All British Engine Company), it weighed 290 lb, was of 657 cu in capacity and produced 170 hp. Named Wasp, it was engineered throughout for easy production; however, one of its design features, which was the use of copper-plated steel cooling fins on the cylinders, was to contribute to its future unreliability. It was this engine which the Westland design team had in mind for possible use in its private venture light fighter, provisionally known as the Hornet, and which was to power it when built as the Wagtail.

Of conventional external appearance and construction, the Wagtail had a wooden girder type fuselage, rectangular in section for most of its length, with light wood fairings to provide shape. Spruce longerons of square-section were employed with staggered vertical and horizontal spacer struts tapering to fit into

In its modified form with a reduced area fin, this Wagtail has constant-chord equal dihedral wings but with a small curved centre-section cutout.

square cups in light steel fittings bolted to the longerons. These fittings also carried attachment lugs for the swaged rods which braced each bay of the fuselage structure. The braced tailplane and fin were of similar wooden construction while the elevators and rudder were of metal. The rear fuselage aft of the cockpit, which was located under the upper wing trailing-edge, was fabric covered and removable fabric covered panels enclosed the cockpit and the forward fuselage. A wire-braced engine mounting ring with four attachment plates was carried on inwardly curved extensions of the longerons with the entire nose and engine having removable metal top and side panels and a metal cowling through which the Wasp's seven cylinders protruded. V-shaped main undercarriage legs of spruce carried a cross-axle with bungee rubber shock

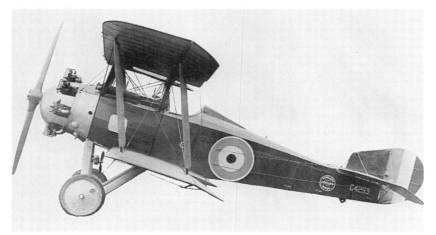

The third Wagtail, C4293, with the flat lower wing and increased dihedral on the upper wing. Retouching has removed the tailskid.

absorbers and a curved tailskid was mounted below the tailplane leading-edge. The main spars of the constant-chord single-bay wings were of ash with cross-braced drag struts and the spruce ribs of RAF 15 aerofoil section were built up from three-ply webs with spruce capping strips.

The Type I Specification stressed the need for a good all-round view for the pilot; thus the flat wide-span upper centre-section—a feature to minimise the spar bending moment—had a large trailing-edge semi-circular cut-out above the cockpit, and was supported on two pairs of outwardly-canted struts. Constant-chord wide-span ailerons were carried on both the upper and lower wings which, in the prototype Wagtail, C4291, had the same 2½ deg dihedral and were wire-braced. The wings and tail unit were fabric-covered. In this aircraft too, the fin had a long dorsal extension well in front of the tailplane leading-edge. Control wires to the ailerons and rudder ran inside the wings and fuselage but were carried externally to the elevators. Fuel was carried in a 26 gal fuselage-mounted tank in front of the cockpit, two synchronised Vickers .303 in guns were mounted on top of the fuselage and oxygen equipment was located in the cockpit.

Wagtail showing the twin Vickers guns, ring-and-bead sight, windscreen aperture for Aldis sight and centre-section configuration.

Originally six Wagtails were ordered by the Air Board and allocated the serials C4290–96 but the contract was later reduced to three aircraft, C4291–93. Construction of the first Wagtail airframe was completed by the end of February 1918 with production of two more, C4292 and 4293, well in hand; however, C4291's Wasp engine was still awaited from the manufacturer. During this period Capt F Alexander, Royal Flying Corps, was attached to Westland Aircraft Works to fly the Wagtail. With operational experience he believed that the cut-out in the prototype's centre-section should be larger. Because a

A Wagtail under construction. The elevator control system, wing aerofoil section and fuel tank locations are notable features.

modification at that stage would have delayed the first flight, a re-designed centre-section was first fitted, as a trial installation, to the incompleted third aircraft. The three central ribs aft of the front spar and the centre-section trailing-edge were removed leaving a wide aperture spanned only by the nosing and the rear spar. This new centre-section was mounted six inches lower than on the prototype and in order to use the same length faired tubular steel interplane struts and bracing wires, the lower wings were re-rigged flat and the upper wings given 5 deg dihedral. While the modified centre-section improved the pilot's view, what was not quantifiable or immediately recognisable was the effect the loss of wing area had upon wing lift and air flow disturbance.

The first flight date of C4291 has not been established; however, it is known that it took place early one morning in April 1918, and that the Wagtail's handling characteristics were such that they inspired Capt Alexander to execute a loop. This test flight also suggested that there was insufficient rudder area to counteract the nose-down effect of the fin in a side-slip; in order to minimise the time and cost involved in building a larger rudder, it was decided to cut back the fin to about half of its length. Meanwhile, work on fitting the modified centre-section and fin to the second and third aircraft was in progress.

Within a week or so the first of many engine snags, which were to plague the Wasp, were encountered and it was removed from C4291 for return to the manufacturer. Much of the trouble stemmed from valve and cylinder design and cooling. When C4291's engine was returned to Yeovil it was fitted to the second Wagtail, C4292, which had the modified centre-section and wings and was nearer completion than the third airframe. With this engine test flying was resumed on 29 April; but soon afterwards this Wagtail was badly damaged while in a canvas Bessoneaux hangar at Yeovil which had caught fire when an employee had been endeavouring to prove that he could extinguish a lighted cigarette in a can of petrol!

With the arrival of two more Wasp engines the third Wagtail was quickly completed, enabling it to fly in March 1919, and work on modifying the prototype's centre-section and fin was pressed forward. On 8 May C4293 was flown to the Aircraft Experimental Establishment at Martlesham Heath for 'fighter trials' with a number of different propellers. Unfortunately, after a badly executed landing on 18 May, the Wagtail nosed over on rough ground damaging the engine and undercarriage. After repairs this aircraft was transferred to the Royal Aircraft Factory at Farnborough on 27 May, only a few days before it was renamed Royal Aircraft Establishment, a name it was to retain for the ensuing 70 years. There it was used by the RAE and ABC to investigate the source of the Wasp's problems; but the programme was short-lived for two weeks later all trials of Wasp-powered aircraft—which included the Sopwith Snail and the BAT Bantam—were halted. However, it is recorded that, in July 1918, C4293 was at Martlesham Heath for 'motor trials' but for how long is not known.

Wagtail C4293 after its heavy landing on 18 May, 1919, during 'fighter trials' at Martlesham Heath.

The prototype Wagtail, meanwhile, had been re-engined and the airframe modifications had been embodied. It flew again at about the same time that Wasp investigations ceased; nevertheless it went to the RAE thereafter and is recorded as having been at Martlesham Heath during August for evaluation against other fighters, presumably the Camel, Snail and Bantam. Then, on 6 November it went to the Aircraft Armament and Gunnery Experimental Establishment at Orfordness for gun firing trials. By this time not only was the War finished but all flying trials with Wasp-powered light fighters had been

One of the two short fuselage Wagtails ordered in 1929. It has an Armstrong Siddeley Lynx engine, curved fin and much enlarged centre-section cutout.

terminated and production of this engine been cancelled. Nevertheless, like Charles II, the Wagtail/Wasp combination was 'an unconscionable time dying' and on 29 January, 1919, the rebuilt airframe of the second aircraft, C4292, arrived by road at Martlesham Heath where it was to remain at least until 1920.

In spite of numerous problems with the Wasp, ABC continued to develop this engine and one of the Wagtails is reported to have flown with a 200 hp Wasp II. But this was not the end of Wagtail production for in 1920 two more Wagtails were ordered, powered by the new 150 hp Armstrong Siddeley Lynx seven-cylinder air-cooled radial engine. Serialled J6581 and J6582, airframe modifications included shortening the fuselage by removing the metal-panelled bay aft of the engine to maintain the centre of gravity with the heavier Lynx, changing the shape of fin and rudder to a 'comma' shape and fitting a stronger main undercarriage to suit the increased all-up weight. These two aircraft were flown at the RAE and at Martlesham Heath until about 1922, some records indicating that at least one, J6582, having also been powered by a Wasp II.

Description: Single-seat light biplane fighter. Wood/metal construction with fabric and metal covering.
Accommodation: Pilot in open cockpit.
Powerplant: One 170 hp ABC Wasp seven-cylinder air-cooled normally-aspirated radial engine driving a two-blade 7 ft 4 in diameter wooden propeller.
Armament: Two fixed synchronised Vickers .303 in machine-guns mounted on top of the fuselage, with 1,000 rounds of ammunition.
Dimensions: Span 23 ft 2 in; length 18 ft 11 in; height 8 ft 0 in; wing area 190 sq ft.
Weights: Empty 746 lb; loaded 1,330 lb.

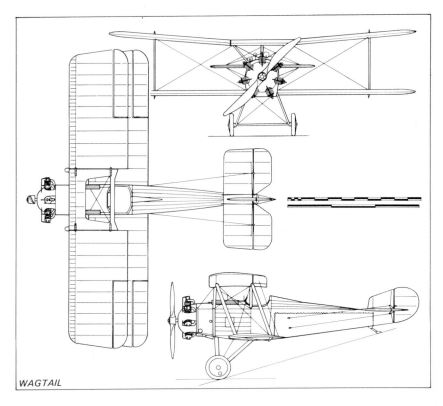

WAGTAIL

Performance: Maximum speed at 10,000 ft 125 mph; landing speed 50 mph; climb to 5,000 ft in 3.5 min, to 17,000 ft in 17 min; service ceiling 20,000 ft.

Production: Five Wagtails built by Westland Aircraft Works, Yeovil, Somerset, during 1917–20.

The second Weasel, F2913, shows off its neatly cowled Jupiter engine and wide-span wings, the apparent splaying of which is an optical illusion.

Weasel

During the final months of the 1914–18 War the Air Ministry was already giving thought to its postwar aircraft requirements and preparing some detailed specifications. Among these was RAF Type IIIA for a two-seat fighter-reconnaissance aircraft. It was intended as a replacement for the highly effective Bristol F.2B Fighter—the 'Brisfit'—which was still a comparatively new design having entered service with the Royal Flying Corps in April 1917. The Type IIIA specification called for a much improved performance, particularly in the time-to-height and service ceiling; however, the armament remained the same as the F.2B, being two fixed forward-firing guns and one gun on a Scarff ring mounting in the rear cockpit. The most unfortunate aspect was the preferred use of the ABC Dragonfly engine, a nine-cylinder radial engine designed, like the earlier Wasp which powered the Wagtail, by Granville Bradshaw. The Dragonfly proved to be a disaster in almost every way. It was claimed to produce 340 hp and weigh 600 lb but never, at any stage, delivered more than 295 hp and weighed 656 lb; moreover, it rapidly overheated having what was described as 'probably the worst example of air cooling in a production aircraft engine'. Of most importance was its designed running speed which happened to be the critical torsional vibration frequency of the crankshaft which regularly broke after a few hours running.

It was around the Dragonfly that three manufacturers designed and built prototypes, in various quantities, to meet the Type IIIA requirement. They were the Austin Motor Co which produced the Greyhound, Bristol Aeroplane Co with the Badger and Westland which scaled up its earlier single-seat Wagtail to create the two-seat Weasel.

Designed by Robert Bruce and Arthur Davenport, the Weasel was of similar construction to the Wagtail having a wooden girder type fuselage of rectangular cross-section with spruce longerons and spacer struts, the latter being tapered to fit into square steel cups bolted to the longerons. This structure was internally wire braced. Forward of the front cockpit the fuselage was plywood covered with fabric covering on the remainder; however, a small rectangular area on each side of the observer's cockpit was left uncovered to provide a 'window'. The strut-braced tail unit, which had the Westland-patented variable-incidence tailplane gear, was of similar wire-braced wooden construction and also was fabric covered. The engine mounting ring was carried on an extension of the longerons which was internally wire braced, while the complete nose section of the fuselage had removable metal panels to provide access to the engine and to the fuel and oil tanks. The engine's cylinder heads protruded through holes in the nose cowl and the Dragonfly turned a 9 ft 9 in diameter two-blade fixed-pitch wooden propeller. The fabric-covered two-bay biplane wings were built up around two ash spars with cross-braced drag struts and three-ply cut-out ribs with spruce flanges. The eight interplane struts were of streamline section spruce and, like the four centre-section support struts, were all wire cross-braced. Constant-chord ailerons were fitted to each of the four wings. As in the Wagtail, although the centre-section was smaller in span, there was an angular cut-out in its trailing edge and in that of the lower wings' trailing edge; in addition five ribs were omitted in the centre-section aft of the main spar leaving an uncovered opening above the pilot's cockpit. The two fixed forward-firing synchronised Vickers .303 in machine-guns were carried in troughs in the top of the front fuselage, with provision for one, or two, Lewis guns of similar calibre to be carried on a Scarff ring mounting in the observer's cockpit. Spruce V main undercarriage legs with a cross-axle having enclosed bungee rubber shock absorbers were used with a tailskid. A wind-driven generator was mounted on the port rear main leg. An unusual visual feature of the Weasel was the manner in which the upper and lower wings appeared to be splayed away from each other; in fact, the upper wing had 5 deg dihedral from the flat centre-section while the lower wing had no dihedral. Oxygen bottles with some 3 hours supply for the two crew and electrical heating equipment were carried in the fuselage.

An order for three Weasel prototypes was placed in April 1918 with construction starting almost immediately, but forthcoming events cast their shadows over the work with the first of a number of delays in delivery of the engine. In the event the war was ended when the first Weasel, serialled F2912,

This view of F2913 shows the large aperture in the upper centre-section, the cut-away wing roots and the generous size of the rudder and elevators.

was flown for the first time by Capt Stuart Keep during late November 1918.

Preliminary flight trials were punctuated by continuous problems with the engine, both on the ground and in the air. One incident, which could have had serious results for Westland, occurred when Stuart Keep was flying the Weasel with Robert Bruce in the observer's cockpit and the engine failed a long way from the aerodrome. Bruce immediately leaned out of the cockpit and cranked the starter magneto which was fitted on the starboard side of the fuselage, but the Dragonfly refused to start. Fortunately, the Weasel had sufficient altitude to glide back to the aerodrome, brushing through the top of the boundary hedge en route to a dead-stick landing. While company trials with this first prototype continued into the early months of 1919, construction of the second and third aircraft proceeded at a steady pace. During May F2912 went to the AEE at Martlesham Heath for 'airframe and Dragonfly motor' tests. These included some handling checks during which the lateral control was criticised. Meanwhile, as a result of the failures of the Dragonfly, it was decided to replace it with a 350 hp Armstrong Siddeley Jaguar II engine, the first airframe to be modified being the third prototype F2914 which went to Martlesham Heath during June 1922. Among airframe modifications was the fitting of horn-balanced ailerons and rudder.

While construction of the second and third Weasels had been proceeding, in August 1919, Westland received an order for a fourth aircraft to be powered by a Jaguar II. By this time all development testing of the disastrous Dragonfly had been abandoned and the production of military aircraft cut to a trickle; thus, Westland was aware that a production order for Weasels was unlikely to be placed. Nevertheless, flying with the four prototypes continued at Yeovil and at Martlesham Heath, at which latter location the Weasels made appearances until November 1924, when F2914, the third prototype was there. During November 1919 F2912, the first prototype, caught fire in the air while allegedly powered by an Armstrong Siddeley Lynx; however, its pilot, Flt Lt A H Orlebar, managed to sideslip to the ground and crash land where the fire was extinguished, the aircraft being written off charge in the following March.

By mid-summer of that year, all the Weasels had been handed over to the Royal Aircraft Establishment at Farnborough where they were being used for flight testing engines and various equipment. Although this work may have appeared mundane compared with operational flying, there was the interest of fitting and flying, in J6577, the exciting new Bristol Jupiter II radial engine which, in September 1921 was the first engine to pass the Air Ministry's type-test by delivering 400 hp at 1,625 rpm. However, there were installation problems, particularly with the Jupiter's valve gear which not only had some teething problems with its push rods which had automatic compensation for cylinder expansion, but also proved vulnerable to icing which stopped the engine when tested in climbs to altitude during the winter months. To overcome this latter snag the RAE made some wind-tunnel investigations with a number of different shaped 'helmets' to fit over the Jupiter's exposed cylinder heads, and later test flew the Weasel with this modified cowling. There were moments of glory too, the first on 24 June, 1922, when the Jupiter-powered Weasel appeared in the New Types Park at the third Royal Air Force Pageant at Hendon. However, on 11 July J6577 caught fire in the air while at AEE, crashed and burnt out. F2914

This retouched photograph of the Weasel's structure reveals a full-chord wing root without a cutout. The pilot's basket-work seat is noteworthy, as are the neat decking around the cockpit and the Scarff ring.

was a 'New Type' at Hendon on 30 June, 1923, but, with F2913, flew at the RAE until written off charge in 1925 and 1924 respectively.

Description: Two-seat biplane fighter. Wood/metal construction with fabric, wood and metal covering.

Accommodation: Pilot and observer/gunner in open cockpits.

Powerplant: One 340 hp ABC Dragonfly nine-cylinder air-cooled normally-aspirated radial engine driving a 9 ft 9 in diameter two-blade wooden propeller (F2912). One 350 hp Armstrong Siddeley Jaguar II fourteen-cylinder two-row normally-aspirated air-cooled radial engine (F2912 and F2914). One 400 hp Bristol Jupiter II nine-cylinder normally-aspirated air-cooled radial engine (F2913 and J6577).

Armament: Two fixed synchronised Vickers .303 in forward-firing machine-guns in troughs in the top of the front fuselage with Aldis and ring-and-bead sights, and one, or two, Lewis .303 in machine-guns on a Scarff mounting in the rear cockpit.

Dimensions: Span 35 ft 6 in; length 24 ft 10 in; height 10 ft 1 in; wing area 368 sq ft.

Weights: Empty 1,626 lb; loaded 3,046 lb.

Performance: Maximum speed 120 mph at sea level; landing speed 56 mph; service ceiling 22,100 ft.

Production: Four Weasels built by Westland Aircraft Works, Yeovil, Somerset, during 1918–19.

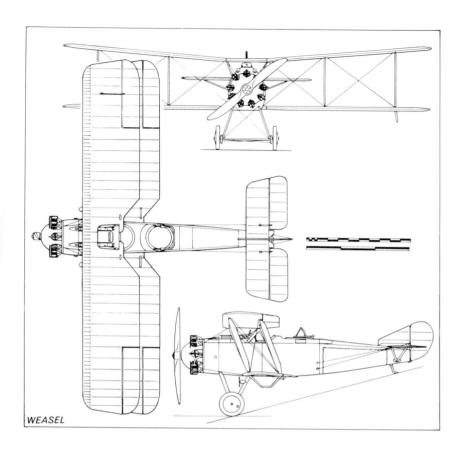

WEASEL

Limousine

With the cessation of hostilities in November 1918, Arthur Davenport was already looking to the needs of postwar civil air services. Rather than attempt to produce Westland's first commercial aeroplane by modifying a proven military type, he struck out boldly with a completely new design with the declared intention of combining in a modern aeroplane all the best points of a high-class motor car with the principal advantage of an aeroplane: speed.

The outcome was the Limousine I, a single-engined two-bay biplane of wooden construction with fabric and wood covering. Although there were few, if any, new designs of engine available, Davenport chose the 275 hp Rolls-Royce Falcon III. This was a twelve-cylinder water-cooled vee engine—only the second of its configuration to be produced by Rolls-Royce—which had given high reliability service in several of the Bristol F.2B Fighter variants. Its installation in the Limousine I and II was reminiscent of that in the Fighter in that it also used the oval-fronted radiator employed in Bristol's renowned wartime two-seater.

The fuselage was built up in separate modules: a steel tube overhung-type engine mounting, the cabin section and the rear fuselage. The engine had metal cowling panels and was fitted with very long exhaust pipes which terminated more than half way along the fuselage to minimise exhaust noise in the cabin. The engine mounting structure was bolted directly to the cabin front bulkhead which had an asbestos layer between two multi-ply panels. This 'power egg' could be easily removed if an engine change was required or if an alternative type of engine was to be fitted.

The Limousine I, K-126, seen at Yeovil in July 1919, has an oval nose radiator for its Falcon III engine. Visible are the windscreen of the offset cockpit, the very long exhaust pipe and the small fin and rudder.

To provide an unobstructed cabin the spruce and ash structure was covered with a three-ply skin which was reinforced around the door, the window and pilot's cockpit cut-out. In addition, the door, which was secured by an internal bar, had longitudinal reinforcing for additional rigidity. It was mounted on the starboard side, which had two windows, a single window being provided on the port side. A 50 gal fuel tank was carried immediately aft of the cabin front bulkhead. The rear fuselage was built up from a wood girder structure and was fabric-covered. It carried a fabric-covered tail unit, with small area vertical surfaces, of wood construction. To compensate for differing numbers and weights of passengers and their luggage, a tailplane trimming device was embodied in the design. The tailplane front spar was hinged to the top longerons and carried a hanging triangular frame inside the rear fuselage. The upper corners of the frame were attached to the two tailplane spars while the third lower corner was moved fore and aft in a rack and pinion type gear operated by a hand-wheel and Bowden cables from the pilot's position. The wings were of the traditional ash spars with spruce ribs and struts, the entire structure being internally wire-braced and fabric-covered. Ailerons of similar construction were carried on upper and lower wings and bumper bars were fitted below the two outboard pairs of interplane struts. A pair of spruce V undercarriage members carried a bungee-sprung through-axle and a tailskid was fitted.

Luxury was the keynote of the passenger cabin, which was button-back lined, carpetted and fitted with thick upholstered seats. The more austere pilot's cockpit is on the left.

The seating arrangement for the passengers and pilot certainly broke new ground. The pilot sat at the rear of cabin on the port side, his seat being raised 30 in above those of the passengers so that his head protruded through a hole in the cabin roof, a small windscreen being mounted in front of it. One wonders why Davenport placed the pilot behind the passengers. Was he influenced by a similar feature of the BAT FK.26, in which Fritz Koolhoven is reputed to have located the pilot as far aft in the fuselage as possible in order to give him the best chance of surviving a crash and thus being able to render an accurate and intelligent report on it? One passenger was seated on his lower right facing forward, a second immediately in front of him also facing forward, while the third passenger sat on the starboard side, facing aft, with a small folding table between him and the passenger behind. The reason for this seating configuration was that Davenport and Bruce saw the Limousine as an executive type aircraft in which meetings could take place and letters be dictated and typed ready for instant despatch when it landed. Thus, a secretary could fly, with her back to the engine, and a typewriter fixed to the table. It was later recorded that when the Limousine I prototype had become engaged in demonstration and sales flights, Westland's commercial manager, R J Norton, was 'ever ready to take up a secretary to demonstrate dictation in the air'.

The prototype, K-126 was completed and ready for its first flight by the end of July 1919, for which Stuart Keep was the pilot. During August, by which time the permanent civil registration G-EAFO had been allocated to this prototype, it went to the Aeroplane Experimental Establishment at Martlesham Heath for what were described as 'C of A performance trials' for the issue of its Certificate of Airworthiness on 21 August. Keep's initial reports indicated that there was some small amount of manageable longitudinal instability but that engine noise was low. This latter point was emphasised when passengers were carried, for a great deal of attention was paid to noise reduction in the cabin. The walls and roof were lined, the floor was carpeted and the luxurious grey, upholstered seats were thick and soft. All these and other measures helped to produce both a draught-free environment and noise level in flight no greater than that in a railway carriage. *Flight* reported 'Lady passengers may travel in this machine in the most delicate frocks without fear of getting them spoiled by oil'!

G-EAJL, the first Limousine II, appeared in October 1919 with an enlarged rectangular radiator and increased area fin and rudder.

Production of a second airframe, the Limousine II, was completed in October 1919. Registered G-EAJL, it also had a 275 hp Falcon III but with a larger rectangular radiator and a redesigned fin and rudder of increased area. Demonstration and test flying continued during the ensuing six months and included a period at Martlesham Heath for evaluation of handling characteristics with the revised tail unit. Following a demonstration of the Limousine I at an air meeting organised by the Bournemouth Aviation Co at Winton racecourse on 1 May, 1920, this aircraft went to Croydon where G-EAJL was on loan to Air Post of Banks Ltd. From there both aircraft were used for experimental services to Paris, the fastest being recorded in September with a time of 1 hr 52 min. The chief pilot of this company was Frank T Courtney, but like so many small aviation enterprises of its era, Air Post soon closed and both Limousines were returned to Westland.

The Limousine I K-126 (left) and Limousine II G-EAJL being prepared for demonstration flights. Note the different radiators and four-blade propellers.

Meanwhile a second Limousine II, G-EAMV, was built and was first flown in April 1920. It was intended as a test bed for the new 400 hp Cosmos Jupiter nine-cylinder radial engine designed by Roy Fedden and L F G 'Bunny' Butler. However, the Cosmos Engineering Co, based at Fishponds, Bristol, went into liquidation early in February 1920 and was not taken over by the Bristol Aeroplane Co until August. Thus it is surprising to find that the Limousine, rather than a Bristol aeroplane, was used for this work and, in the event, G-EAMV reverted to standard. A further three Limousine IIs were built, G-EARE, 'RF and 'RG, the first two, which had flown in October 1920, being leased to the new Instone Air Line, a company formed by the steamship-owning Einstein brothers, Samuel and Alfred, who had changed their name by deed poll. These two aircraft, fitted with 300 hp Hispano-Suiza 42 engines, flew regular Instone services on the routes to Brussels and Paris. In addition to a change of engine, the standard fuselage-mounted fuel tank, which was removed from its position aft of the engine where it was screened from the cabin by an asbestos-filled double-skinned wood bulkhead, was replaced by a streamlined external tank, under the port top wing, carrying 58 gal. The removal of the fuselage tank provided additional cabin volume making it even more spacious and luxurious. During 1922 Limousine IIs G-AEJL, 'MV and 'RG were overhauled for their Certificate of Airworthiness renewal and were shipped to Newfoundland, the first two in July and the third in November. (*see* Limousine III)

When the rules for the Commercial Aeroplane Competition, sponsored by the Air Ministry, were announced, they were such as to inspire Robert Bruce and Davenport to build a much larger six-passenger version, the Limousine III, powered by a 450 hp Napier Lion II engine. This was almost a new aircraft type having a 5 ft 6 in longer fuselage, three-bay wings increased in span by more than 16 ft, and a redesigned tail unit without a central fin, this being replaced by two small finlets on the tailplane. To meet the short-field landing reqirements of the Competition's rules, wheel brakes were fitted and twin nosewheels were mounted on struts attached to the bottom longerons and the undercarriage. These were to prevent the aircraft from going onto its nose if heavy braking was required during the short-landing trials. These involved landing over a 50 ft obstacle and coming to a stop within a circle marked on the ground. Sideslip landings were not permitted. As with the Hispano-Suiza-engined Limousine IIs, the fuel tanks were carried externally under the lower wings which reduced the fire-risk and permitted smoking in the cabin, where all seats faced forward.

The prototype Limousine III at Yeovil in June 1920. The two small finlets on the tailplane, the large rudder and absence of a central fin were unusual features.

The Lion-powered Limousine III with underwing fuel tanks, twin-nosewheel undercarriage and three-bay wings.

The prototype Limousine III, G-EARV, construction of which was accelerated by using the rear fuselage of Limousine II G-EARH, work on which was abandoned, was first flown by Stuart Keep during June 1920 and made ready for the flight to Martlesham Heath for the Competition. Here, in August, with silver painted wings and an eau-de-Nil fuselage, the Limousine III won the £7,500 first prize in the small commercial aircraft section, narrowly beating the Sopwith Antelope into second place on a technicality. When Harry Hawker, the Sopwith pilot, landed the Antelope in the trials, he did so with the brakes on, which burst both tyres of the main undercarriage, and one of the forward pair. The Antelope thus produced an unmatched short-distance landing, which was not officially recognised as the aircraft was not intact! However, it received second prize of £3,000. Westland's victory in this section of the Competition,

G-EAWF was the second of two Limousine IIIs to be built. It flew with the Instone Air Line at Croydon as reserve aircraft.

sadly, did not bring a rush of orders even though the Limousine III showed remarkable economy and stability—enabling Keep to leave his seat and join his passengers in flight—and was, undoubtedly, ahead of its time. Such was the state of the commercial aircraft market that only one more Limousine III was built, which was acquired by the Air Council in April 1921 having been allocated the serial J6851, but this was not taken up. Subsequently, it was loaned to Instone Air Line, registered G-EAWF, as part of a Government scheme for approved operators, where it became a reserve aircraft in company with the Limousine IIs G-EARE and 'RF, until all three were withdrawn from service in 1923.

Sidney Cotton's Limousine III G-EARV being prepared for a seal-spotting flight at Botwood, Newfoundland, in 1921. It has overwing fuel tanks. (*Ernest Maunder/Public Archives of Canada PA74266*)

91

Having taken first place, G-EARV was used by Westland for some development flying until January 1921 when it was sold to FS Cotton's Aerial Survey Company and moved to Newfoundland in a pioneering role in fishery and seal spotting operations. Flown by T K Breakell it was fitted with both ski and wheel undercarriage and was later used in the Stag Bay gold rush. By the end of 1923 'RV had logged a substantial number of flying hours carrying passengers, cargo and mail to remote communities. It was then acquired by Laurentide Air Service Ltd, with whom it was to have been registered G-CAET. However, upon arriving at Lac á la Tortue, Laurentide's maintainance base, for an overhaul and inspection, part of the Limousine's wooden structure was found to be rotted and it was scrapped in 1924.

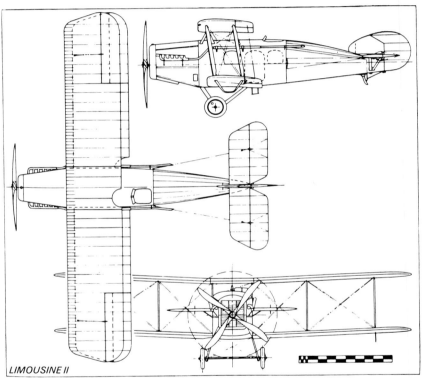

LIMOUSINE II

Description: Three/five-seat commercial biplane. Wood construction with fabric and wood covering.

Accommodation: Pilot and three or five passengers.

Powerplant: One 275 hp Rolls-Royce Falcon III twelve-cylinder water-cooled normally-aspirated vee engine driving a two-blade wooden propeller. (Limousine I and II). One 300 hp Hispano-Suiza 42 eight-cylinder water-cooled normally-aspirated vee engine driving a two-blade wooden propeller (Limousine II). One 410 hp Cosmos Jupiter III nine-cylinder air-cooled normally-aspirated radial engine driving a two-blade wooden propeller (Limousine II). One 450 hp Napier Lion 1A twelve-cylinder water-cooled normally-aspirated geared broad-arrow engine driving a 7 ft 10 in four-blade wooden propeller (Limousine III).

Dimensions: Span 38 ft 2 in (Limousine I), 37 ft 9 in (Limousine II); length 27 ft 9 in; height 10 ft 9 in; wing area 440 sq ft (Limousine I and II). Span 54 ft 0 in; length 33 ft 6 in; height 12 ft 6 in; wing area 726 sq ft (Limousine III).

Weights:	(Limousine I)	(Limousine II)	(Limousine III)
Empty	2,183 lb	2,010 lb	3,823 lb
Loaded	3,383 lb	3,800 lb	5,850 lb
Performance:			
Maximum speed	100 mph	100 mph	118 mph
Cruising speed	85mph	90 mph	90 mph
Sea level			
climb	600 ft/min	650 ft/min	600 ft/min
Service ceiling	17,000 ft	17,000 ft	12,300 ft
Range	290 miles	400 miles	520 miles

Production: A total of eight Limousines was built by Westland Aircraft Works, Yeovil, Somerset, during 1919–21 as follows: One prototype Limousine I. Five Limousine II production aircraft. Two Limousine III production aircraft.

(The Limousine I's initial registration K-126 was carried in accordance with the provisions of the United Kingdom Air Navigation Regulations, which came into force on 20 April, 1919, requiring all British civil aircraft to carry registration markings. The International Air Navigation Convention did not come into force until 22 July, 1919, and, during the interim period, the Air Ministry introduced a system of temporary markings. It required all aircraft newly constructed or built from spares to be registered in a sequence beginning at K-100. A total of 175 such registrations were allocated during the system's short life, although K-169 was the highest K-number known to have been used. Thereafter British aircraft carried a four-letter registration group prefixed by the letter G).

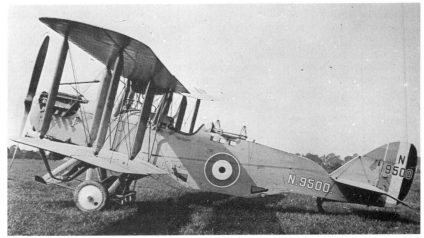

The D.H.9A ancestry of the Walrus is clearly visible in this side view of the first aircraft, N9500; so, too, are the hydrovane, arrester wire jaws and the ventral observation pannier.

Walrus

Westland could be blamed only in part for producing what was, without doubt, the company's ugliest aeroplane. In horse-breeding parlance it was 'by Tadpole out of Ninack' and bore the name Walrus, a singularly unlovely beast both in visage and gait.

During the era following the end of the 1914–18 War many RAF and Royal Navy demands for new equipment to replace their out-dated war-time aircraft were met by attempts to modify and update existing RAF types. The value of reconnaissance aircraft to hunt down an enemy fleet and exercise fire control for the guns of its own warships had been proven; however, with the development of new wireless equipment and more sophisticated fire control techniques, in 1919 it had become apparent that the existing spotter aircraft with a crew of two were inadequate. The sole observer carried could not spot, identify, code, transmit and receive signals and operate his equipment; thus, a wireless operator had to be carried. For economy reasons, and in accordance with Royal Navy policy, it was decided to adapt an existing type, the choice falling—almost inevitably—on the D.H.9A two-seater of which very large stocks of major assemblies were held. Several of these aircraft were modified by the Fleet Aircraft Repair Depot at RAF Donibristle in 1919–20 to carry a third crew member in an enlarged open rear cockpit; they then proved their effectiveness as spotters during the 1920 Fleet Gunnery Exercises. However they had earlier proved unsuitable for carrier operation due to their comparatively high landing speed and insensitive controls and the fact that their wings could not be folded.

As the direct result of these modifications a newly constituted company, The Sir W.G. Armstrong Whitworth Aircraft Co Ltd—to give it its full and imposing

With its flotation bags fully inflated, the Walrus exhibits most of its drag-producing excrescences, including the Lion engine's external 'plumbing'.

title—was busily at work on a more definitive conversion of the D.H.9A to meet the Royal Navy's need for a carrier-borne fleet-reconnaissance aircraft. This materialised during early 1920 as the one-off Tadpole, J6585. While it retained the D.H.9A's 400 hp Liberty 12 engine and basic airframe structure, modifications included unstaggered wings, a third rectangular open cockpit accomodated in a raised section of the fuselage aft of the gunner's cockpit and a ventral pannier for a prone-positioned observer. Built at the Parkside, Coventry, factory it was flown from the company's newly-acquired aerodrome at Whitley Abbey. But the Tadpole was to be only the first step toward the definitive fleet-reconnaissance aircraft, further modifications and production becoming Westland's responsibility at Yeovil where, in addition to the modifications introduced in the Tadpole by Blackburn, a number of new and important design features were instigated by Arthur Davenport. These included

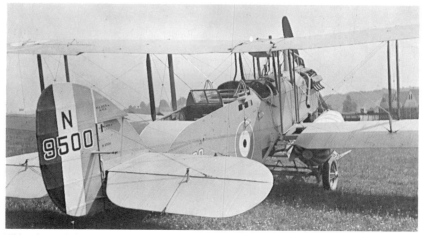

This view of the Walrus shows the large aft cockpit and its windscreen in the raised position.

replacing the Liberty engine with a 450 hp Napier Lion II, removing the radiator from the nose to a position below the front fuselage and fitting a neat nose cowling in its place; the provision of windscreens for all three cockpits and the fitting of two large flotation bags along the front fuselage sides and extending back under the wings. The main landing wheels could be jettisoned by the pilot in an emergency, such as a ditching, when the hydrovane, mounted under the nose and attached to the undercarriage legs, was relied upon to prevent the aircraft from nosing over. The cross-axle carried jaws for gripping the longitudinally-arranged arrester wires which were the standard configuration on aircraft carriers until 1930 when transverse wires were adopted. Other detail design features were the use of internally mounted compressed air bottles to inflate the flotation bags, and a Westland patented fuel jettison valve which could empty the main tank very quickly then re-seal it to act as an additional bouyancy aid. In the prototype Walrus, N9500, initially the wings were fixed, bungee rubber shock absorber cord was used in the main undercarriage and standard D.H.9A ailerons were fitted. Ultimately, N9500 and all Walrus aircraft had oleo-pneumatic undercarriage struts, and detachable wings with external horn-balanced ailerons. Fuel pumps and the generator for the wireless transmitter were driven by two small wind-driven vanes mounted on top of the fuselage in front of the pilot's cockpit. All of these added excrescences and equipment apparently added only about 200 lb to the D.H.9A's loaded weight.

The prototype Walrus was first flown at Yeovil during February or March 1921 by Stuart Keep, who found the aircraft difficult to control. This was immediately apparent at the end of this flight when he essayed a landing. As he throttled back the nose dropped and could only be picked up by opening the throttle again. Fortunately Harry Dalwood, Westland's Erecting Shop foreman had accompanied Keep on this first flight as 'living ballast': bravely Dalwood

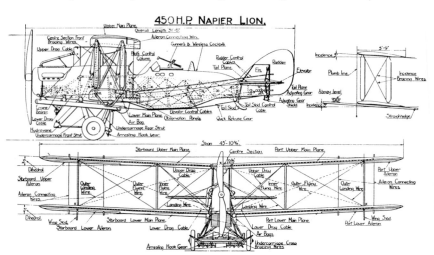

The Walrus's rigging diagram shows the multiplicity of flying, drag and bracing wires and other external features.

climbed out of the centre cockpit into the rear one and then out onto the rear fuselage where he clung until Keep, now able to close the throttle without the nose dropping, could land the Walrus. Keep's reported comment that the Walrus 'is a vicious beast' was later to be borne out by a number of crashes during test flying. These did not prevent a contract for thirty-six Walrus aircraft being awarded to Westland, some of the later-built aircraft having a high-lift wing section and enlarged rudder.

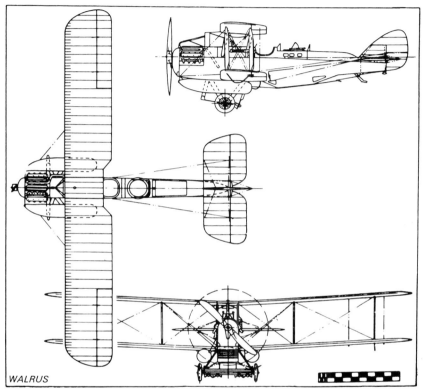

WALRUS

Deliveries began in 1921 with the Walrus initially going to No.3 Squadron RAF at Leuchars where it joined the unit's D.H.9As for coastal reconnaissance and Fleet co-operation duties. Delivery flights could also present a hazard and Harald Penrose recalls that one Walrus experienced engine failure on take-off at Yeovil and stalled, while two others could not overcome downdraughts near some low surrounding hills and were forced down, and completely written off. The Walrus served with No.3 Squadron at Leuchars until October 1922 and at Gosport until 1 April, 1923, when it was divided into Nos.421 and 422 Fleet Spotter Flights which, still at Gosport, became independent units, each with six aircraft. Some Walruses also equipped No.423 Flight from November 1923 until the end of 1924. The Walruses continued to provide unspectacular service until late 1925 when they were replaced by Blackburn Blackburns in No.421 Flight and Avro Bisons in No.422 Flight. None saw service in aircraft carriers. Perhaps the high point of the Walrus's career was its appearance in the RAF Pageant at Hendon in June 1923. With twelve other aircraft, including the Westland Weasel, it took part in a ceremonial taxi- and fly-past of new types before their Majesties King George V and Queen Mary, Queen Alexandra, and members of other European Royal Families.

Description: Three-seat carrier-borne spotter-reconnaissance biplane. Wood/metal construction with fabric and metal covering.

Accommodation: Crew of three in separate open cockpits.

Powerplant: One 450 hp Napier Lion II twelve-cylinder broad-arrow water-cooled, geared, normally-aspirated engine driving a 10 ft diameter two-blade wooden propeller.

Armament: One fixed, synchronised Vickers .303 in forward-firing machine-gun on the fuselage port side and one Lewis .303 in gun on a Scarff ring over the second cockpit.

Dimensions: Span 46 ft 2 in (production aircraft); length 29 ft 9 in; height 11 ft 7 in; wing area 496 sq ft.

Weights: Empty 3,180 lb; loaded 4,998 lb.

Performance: Maximum speed 124 mph at sea level; initial rate of climb 950 ft/min; ceiling 19,000 ft.

Production: A total of 36 Walruses built by Westland Aircraft Works, Yeovil, Somerset, during 1920–23.

Dreadnought

Although wood had been used for complete airframes, or sections of airframes of military aircraft right up to 1955 when the last Vampire, whose nose and cockpit section was of plywood and balsa construction, was phased out of RAF service, metal construction had been pioneered in 1910 in Germany by Professor Hugo Junkers. To this use of metal was coupled advanced aerofoils and structural techniques and, on 1 February, 1910, Junkers patented a twin-engined metal-skinned transport aircraft having a thick-section cantilever wing which was deep enough at its root to house the crew in order to reduce drag. This was his Nur Flügel-Flugzeug or flying-wing tailless aeroplane.

Through the war-years both the Rohrbach and Dornier companies in Germany experimented with cantilever monoplane wings and produced a number of aircraft with this feature. This work had not gone unnoticed by Air Ministry scientists and engineers in Britain who began to question their deep conviction that the biplane configuration was the only satisfactory one for military aircraft. In 1917 an opportunity for them to put theory into practice presented itself. George Holt Thomas, chairman of the Aircraft Manufacturing Company (Airco) at The Hyde, Hendon, had sent one of his staff, William Wilkins, to Russia to examine the possibility of a factory there to produce de Havilland D.H.4 and D.H.6 aircraft. Mr Wilkins returned to the United Kingdom with a Russian emigrant named Voevodskii who had earlier sent to

The merging of the Dreadnought's thick wing and fuselage is very apparent in this view.
Note the large door and position of the circular 'skylights' in the fuselage.

Airco his plans for an aerodynamically-clean internally-braced cantilever
monoplane in which the thickened wing root blended smoothly into the fuselage
in the form of a continuous aerofoil. Any Anglo-Russian plans for co-operative
production of D.H. aircraft ended with the October Revolution, but Voevodskii's plans had been passed to the Aeronautical Research Committee which saw
in them a design sufficiently advanced to equal those of the German
monoplanes. As a result, during 1920–21, models incorporating this new wing
were tested in the low-speed wind tunnel at the Royal Aircraft Establishment
(RAE), Farnborough, which proved that it produced high maximum lift but
coupled with unexpectedly high drag. An ARC Report of 1919 had revealed
that work was in progress in Britain on the aerodynamic properties of thick
aerofoils with internal bracing. 'In particular, it has been found that these
monoplanes are very liable to spin but it is hoped that model experiments will
show that this tendency can be counteracted'. In spite of this report the Air
Ministry decided that an aircraft with the Voevodskii-type wing should be built
and invited tenders to Specification 6/21 from George Parnall & Co and
Westland. Harold Bolas, Parnall's chief designer, produced designs for a
twin-engined aircraft but Robert Bruce's single-engined aircraft was chosen,
largely as the result of continuing experiments with models in the RAE wind
tunnel.

The design of this unusual aeroplane, described as a 'Postal' aircraft and
named Dreadnought, presented some considerable stressing problems. These
stemmed from the use of an 18 ft chord six-spar wing, a marked departure from
the more traditional two-spar design, and a mathematician, J D Williams, joined
Westland specially to handle this aspect of the design work. He was assisted by
John Digby who, some 25 years later, was to become chief designer. Robert
Bruce had had the opportunity to examine the Junkers multi-spar wing soon
after the war and this had, undoubtedly, influenced his approach to the
Dreadnought's 69 ft 6 in wing span, in which the top and bottom tubular steel
booms were joined by vertical tube struts and were cross-braced with swaged
rods, vertically in the plane of the spar and diagonally and transversely to the

The Dreadnought's 18 ft chord wing section and four-point attachment structure are discernible in this view. A cylindrical fuel tank was carried in each wing.

adjoining spars. The centre fuselage frames were of rectangular-section steel tube with deep triangulated structures each side carrying the wing attachment fittings. These frames formed the central cabin, which was braced longitudinally and laterally by open portal frames, the sloping sides of which provided space for the eight seats. The wing section was very similar to the RAE's T.64 section which was increased in depth to 6 ft 6 in at the inboard end of the centre fuselage frames, and 3 ft 6 in at the wing/fuselage joint. At the inboard end of the ailerons the depth was 2 ft 6 in. The top surface of the multi-ribbed front portion of the aerofoil was heavily radiused from the top of the front spar boom down to join the bottom surface in a lateral 'chine'. Therein lay a danger, for at that time aerodynamicists were unaware of early airflow separation. This danger was enhanced by the sloping sides of the centre fuselage which constituted a fillet extending along the entire length of the flat-bottomed fuselage. Harald Penrose, later to become chief test pilot, said of this feature 'Although it looked right it was empirically shaped in the absence of any known mathematical approach'.

If some of the Dreadnought's design had been based on guesstimates other more familiar problems had been carefully investigated; these included the

The Lion engine is dwarfed by the large fuselage and deep wing root section which is braced to it. External control cables to the rocking lever just aft of the cockpit and thence to the tail unit can be seen.

control surface hinge moments and both the elevators and rudder had back-set hinged balances. The ailerons were of a new design by Leslie Frise of the Bristol Aeroplane Company. When the leading edge projected below the wing it formed an air passage helping to make the aileron more effective at the stall, but principally adding drag to the down-going wing. Westland was claimed to be the first company, other than Bristol, to use this form of aileron.

The front section of the fuselage containing the two-seat open cockpit was of steel-tube construction and the 450 hp Napier Lion II engine was carried on steel mountings attached to it. Metal and wood panels enclosed the engine and cockpit section. The centre fuselage and integral inner wing were clad with finely corrugated skinning with four windows each side, two circular 'skylights' in the upper surface and a door on the port side. The rear fuselage and tail unit were of fabric-covered wire-braced wooden construction. The main undercarriage legs, with rubber-in-compression shock absorbers, were attached to the inboard end of the wing with the divided axle and radius rods fixed to the underside of the centre fuselage.

Ready for its first flight, the Dreadnought's Frise ailerons and use of corrugated metal and fabric covering for the centre and rear fuselage are clearly visible.

Manufacture of Dreadnought components and sub-assemblies began in early 1922 and continued steadily through the following year. By the end of February 1924 the aircraft was virtually structurally complete and stood in the main erecting hangar, always referred to as the Vimy Shop, ready for fabric covering. This work was completed during the end of April when the aircraft was sprayed all-over silver. Because the Dreadnought was built under an Air Ministry contract it carried RAF red, white and blue stripes and the serial J6986 on its rudder.

During the first week of May J6986's Lion underwent engine running checks and on Thursday 8th, Stuart Keep, Westland's test pilot, made some preliminary taxi-ing trials. On some of these the second pilot's seat was occupied by Robert Bruce, who was Keep's father-in-law and, of course, Westland's managing director. The following day, which was sunny with only a light breeze, Bruce, Arthur Davenport the chief designer, and a small crowd of design office and works employees gathered to watch the Dreadnought's first flight. After three practice take-offs, during one of which it became airborne after a run of only about 200 yards, the Dreadnought turned and began a fourth, this time flying clear of the grass surface as Keep held it down to build up speed before

It is surprising that Stuart Keep escaped with his life from the Dreadnought's crushed cockpit. The sharp leading edge of the wing can be seen bottom right.

allowing the nose to come up into a climbing attitude. However, it rose too steeply and as the aircraft appeared to be struggling to remain airborne the starboard wing went down and the Dreadnought suddenly lost height and hit the ground with the wingtip and the nose. The undercarriage was ripped off and the engine was forced back into the cockpit as the aircraft slid along the ground. When the first of the rescuers arrived at the scene having run across the aerodrome, they found Keep was still alive, though unconscious and with both legs broken. Sister Thomas, who was the factory nurse, was among the first group to reach the aircraft; she quickly applied tourniquets to Keep's legs, which undoubtedly saved his life, and tended him until the ambulance arrived to take him to Yeovil hospital where both legs were amputated. Although the Dreadnought wreckage was recovered—structural tests being made on the

The only flying photograph of the Dreadnought, taken seconds before it crashed on its first flight.

central cabin and the undamaged port wing—the cause of the accident remained a mystery, even though Westland and the Air Ministry made a thorough investigation. Because no exact cause could be established, the Air Ministry abandoned all interest in this project. One positive result was the recognition by Bruce that the use of empirical design methods was dangerous; thus he decided that Westland must have a more powerful wind tunnel to aid future design work.

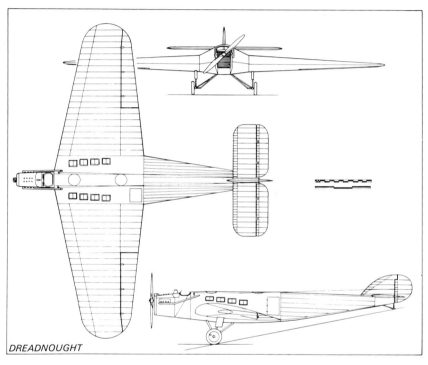

DREADNOUGHT

Description: Two-seat research/postal monoplane. Metal construction with fabric covering.

Accommodation: Two pilots in open cockpit and eight passengers in a central cabin.

Powerplant: One 450 hp Napier Lion II twelve-cylinder broad-arrow water-cooled engine driving a 9 ft diameter two-blade wooden propeller.

Dimensions: Span 69 ft 6 in; length 56 ft 0 in; height 16 ft 4 in; wing area 840 sq ft.

Weights: Empty 5,623 lb; loaded 6,900 lb (estimated).

Performance: Maximum speed 102 mph (estimated).

Production: One Dreadnought built by Westland Aircraft Works, Yeovil, Somerset, during 1922–24.

The unmarked first Woodpigeon, G-EBIY, after completion in September 1924. Clearly visible are the long front inboard interplane struts, the oleo-pneumatic undercarriage legs and the neatly cowled Bristol Cherub.

Woodpigeon

During the years following the 1914–18 War the glut of ex-military aircraft which became available for sale to private owners effectively stopped the creation of new types designed for their use and for flying clubs. The Air Ministry, while aware of this situation, had little or no money to fund such projects; however, following the qualified success of a competition for motor-gliders held at Lympne Airport, Kent, in 1923 and sponsored by the *Daily Mail* and the Duke of Sutherland, the Ministry decided to arrange another series of competitive trials the following year. This was for two-seat aircraft of the type which it believed would be needed for the flying clubs it planned to establish in many parts of the United Kingdom. Financial support in the form of £3,000 prize money was provided by the Air Council. The rules specified that only British Empire-built aircraft and their engines, of no more than 1,100 cc capacity, could enter the trials, with the emphasis on reliability and efficiency, an ability to make short take-offs and landings and carry at least a 340 lb load, excluding fuel. An airspeed indicator was mandatory and had to be visible from both cockpits! Although the Westland design team had no experience of the design of such an aeroplane, the announcement of the competition was greeted with some enthusiasm at Yeovil where the design office and factory were far from busy. Almost at once the design team was faced with a managerial dichotomy on the fundamental decision of whether Westland's entrant should be a biplane or a monoplane. Robert Bruce, a fierce protagonist of the biplane, which he believed would provide the rugged durable airframe required of a club two-seater, was at odds with Arthur Davenport who could think only in terms of a monoplane. One of the early tasks for W M 'Bill' Widgery, who was in charge of Westland's recently installed wind tunnel, was to run some comparative tests on models of the two configurations. Presumably these proved inconclusive for, in a typically British compromise, Petter's Board decided that Westland would build two aeroplanes, the Woodpigeon biplane and the Widgeon parasol monoplane, with virtually identical wing areas and power loadings.

Although externally the Woodpigeon appeared to be a conventional single-bay equal-span biplane it embodied a number of novel design features. The fuselage had four different types of structure; the first bay was of a wire-braced triangulated welded steel-tube construction attached to a fire-proof bulkhead by four bolts and carrying the engine; behind it were three bays of spruce Warren girder structure containing the two cockpits. Aft of them came four rectangular bays of spruce longerons and struts, all braced with swaged rods, then a fifth and final plywood-clad bay. On the top longerons was mounted a curved plywood coaming around the cockpits which continued aft to form the fuselage top. The wing spars were of box section built up around spruce flanges recessed to fit the plywood webs. Spruce was also used in the ribs which were of lattice girder construction. Drag bracing was provided by wire-braced spruce struts. On the first Woodpigeon there was no centre-section, the wings meeting on the aircraft's centreline; in this arrangement the front spars continued to the centreline joint but the rear spars were shorter, being hinged to inverted-V struts mounted on the top longeron and wire-braced across the fuselage. Support for the front spars was provided by two long struts, mounted outside the fuselage and attached to the top spars, and fuselage fittings to which the bottom spars were attached. They were located and acted like jury struts. This system of wing folding about the rear spar, the use of an external strut and the aileron/camber-changing flaps were developed on the earlier N1B floatplane. Outboard the interplane struts were of spruce. Full-span ailerons were fitted on top and bottom wings and could act as flaps or wing camber-changing devices to enable the Woodpigeon to meet the Air Ministry's landing and take-off performance requirements. At some stage the lower ailerons/flaps were fitted with springs to keep them lowered at low airspeed to provide greater lift. As airspeed increased they were blown back into a closed position. The spring could be adjusted in flight by the pilot or over-ridden and the surfaces locked in any of several positions. They were hinged to the rear spar of each wing, the top ailerons having spruce box spars and ribs and the bottom ailerons steel-tube spars. External control rods ran from the aileron root end rib down into the fuselage to the control column. Wing folding was achieved by raising a section of the inboard end of the top wings and removing the pin which locked the top front spars together and a plunger from the bottom end of the long front struts.

The wing aerofoil section was Airscrew 64. The tailplane had a spruce front spar and steel-tube rear spar with wooden ribs all wire-braced both internally and externally; the fin and rudder were of ash construction. With the exception of the engine and fuel tank bay, which had a metal cowling, the entire airframe was fabric covered. Rudder control cables were inside the fuselage but the elevator cables and bell cranks were carried outside. The main undercarriage was a conventional cross-axle type with V-struts, the front ones embodying a Westland oleo-pneumatic shock absorber, and the radius rods being cross-braced; the tailskid was an inverted tripod structure. For the contest streamlined fairings were fitted around the shock absorbers.

Initially, the first Woodpigeon, G-EBIY, was powered by a 61 cu in Bristol Cherub I air-cooled twin-cylinder engine, which delivered 32 hp and drove a 4 ft 5 in two-blade propeller. Designed by Roy Fedden and L F G Butler it featured connecting rods having big ends with roller bearings working on a one-piece crankshaft running in four ball bearings; it also embodied an unusual valve-actuating system which, while complex but effective, was never used on any other engine.

This view of the first Woodpigeon, G-EBIY, shows the shape of the inboard end of the upper wing, which hinged about the rear struts, and the tiny propeller.

Production of two Woodpigeons and a Widgeon were begun simultaneously, one of the former being completed first on 14 September, 1924. Westland's design team was well aware of the low power of the Cherub and of the 5 lb per sq ft wing loading; thus, before Laurence Openshaw made the first flight of G-EBIY on 17 September a runway was cut through the long grass at Yeovil with a handmower to ensure that the Woodpigeon would get airborne after failing to unstick from the rough grassy surface. When it did, Openshaw had great difficulty in keeping it in the air and under control and it was decided to modify the second Woodpigeon, G-EBJV, and to increase the span by 4 ft 9 in which increased the wing area by 45 sq ft. The design details of the modifications necessary to achieve the additional span have not been found; however, a study of photographs and general arrangement drawings show that a 2 ft 6 in span centre-section was fitted and was supported on four forward inclined and wire-braced struts on the top longerons. In addition, each half wing had an extra rib and a 13½ in extension at the tip overhang. Although this added 33 lb to the loaded weight, bringing it up to 812 lb, the wing loading was reduced to a little over 4 lb per sq ft. Lateral control remained difficult due to the complications of the combined ailerons and flaps system.

For the trials at Lympne the first Woodpigeon, G-EBIY, carried the number 5 and was flown by an RAF pilot, Flg Off S H Gaskell. The folding and unfolding tests were completed satisfactorily but in the strong wind conditions the lack of power in flight was immediately apparent. When the Widgeon,

Woodpigeon G-EBIY carrying its entry number – previously used on the Widgeon – for the 1924 Lympne Trials and showing how it could be easily ground handled by one man.

labouring under the same difficulty, was forced down by a downdraught near the Postling turning point and wrecked on Saturday 27 September, the second Woodpigeon, G-EBJV, was hurriedly completed and taken to Lympne on 2 October where it was flown the following day by Capt Winstanley who had been unhurt in the accident with the Widgeon. Strangely, when Gaskell flew G-EBJV, numbered 6, he, too, suffered a similar experience of encountering a downdraught faster than the Woodpigeon's climb rate, and was blown to the ground near to where the Widgeon had come down. Worse still, the Cherub simply was not powerful enough to get the aircraft airborne again from the field in which it had landed and it had to be returned to the aerodrome by road. This apart, G-EBJV was one of only seven qualifiers out of the sixteen aircraft which had taken part in the preliminary eliminating tests. Of these the Woodpigeon was placed seventh; however, in the Grosvenor Challenge Cup race it was second out of a field of fourteen entrants of which only nine completed the

The hurriedly-completed unmarked second Woodpigeon, G-EBJV. Note the modified centre section and struts and the slender dark jury strut fitted for wing folding.

107

course, the Woodpigeon receiving the longest handicap allowance of nearly 33 minutes.

Although the aim of the Trials was to pinpoint the best type or types of dual control aircraft for use by flying clubs, at their completion the Air Ministry announced that 'the results so far achieved warrant the formation of a small number of light aeroplane clubs', adding that it 'does not feel justified in recommending the adoption of any existing types of dual control aeroplane for the use of such clubs until the engine question (of reliability at full power) has been further explored'. The Air Ministry's assessment of the Woodpigeon underlined a fundamental error in calculating the all-up weight which proved to be much greater than expected. Thus the wing and power loadings were similarly affected which had led to loss of performance. There was criticism of the detail finish of the airframe in which control wires were carried externally, fittings were left unfaired and large gaps between the fuselage, fin and tailplane were too wide. The wing folding mechanism and the overall robust construction of the Woodpigeon were praised. Recommendations for improvements included a more powerful engine and increased wing area.

Woodpigeon G-EBJV readied for flight at Yeovil.

With the Trials completed, the Woodpigeons were returned to Yeovil where modifications were made. They were occasionally flown and in 1926, after it had been fitted with an ABC Scorpion II engine, G-EBJV was sold to the Seven Aero Club whose members were officers of No.7 Squadron RAF, then based at Bircham Newton, who entered it in the 1926 Light Aeroplane Meeting at Lympne, which was again sponsored by the *Daily Mail*. On 10 September, flown by Flt Lt Ritchie, the Woodpigeon, carrying the number 16, was unsuccessful in two attempts to clear a 25 ft high barrier after a run of not more than 300 yards. The following morning, however, now fitted with a metal propeller instead of the original wooden unit, it cleared the barrier with ease and successfully completed the landing test. Unfortunately, while taking part in the 396 miles speed and fuel consumption trial, Ritchie had to make a forced landing near Canterbury when one of the Scorpion's rocker arms seized. It was freed, which was permitted by the rules, and it returned to Lympne where another pilot, Flt

G-EBIY with a British Anzani radial engine, increased wing span and fin area, (the latter by filling the gap between it and the fuselage) to become a Woodpigeon II.

Lt Park, took over in an effort to complete the required mileage by the 8 p.m. deadline. Unfortunately he failed by 48 seconds, arriving when it was almost dark, and was disqualified. This aircraft was later fitted with a 60 hp British Anzani radial engine and, redesignated Woodpigeon II, subsequently passed through several ownerships until its last C of A ran out in May 1933. Its ultimate fate cannot be established.

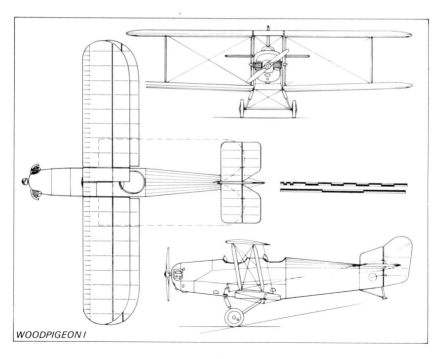

WOODPIGEON I

Meanwhile, during 1926–27, G-EBIY was also powered by a British Anzani radial and its wings were increased in span to become a Woodpigeon II. It too passed into private ownership and was last recorded as being seen during 1949 in Bower's scrap yard in Ferrybridge in Yorkshire.

Description: Single-seat light aircraft. Fabric-covered wooden construction.
Accommodation: Pilot in open cockpit.
Powerplant: One 32 hp Bristol Cherub III two-cylinder horizontally-opposed air-cooled direct-drive normally-aspirated engine driving a 4 ft 10 in diameter two-blade wooden propeller (I). One 34 hp ABC Scorpion two-cylinder horizontally-opposed air-cooled direct-drive normally-aspirated engine (I). One 60 hp British Anzani six-cylinder radial air-cooled direct-drive normally-aspirated engine (II).
Dimensions: Span 22 ft 9 in (I), 27 ft 0 in (II); length 19 ft 6 in (I), 20 ft 9 in (II); height 7 ft 0 in (I), 7 ft 1 in (II); wing area 155 sq ft (I), 200 sq ft (II).
Weights: Empty 439 lb (I Cherub), 464 lb (II Anzani); loaded 779 lb (I Cherub), 812 lb (II Anzani).
Performance: Maximum speed 72 mph at sea level (I), 70 mph (II); landing speed 32 mph (I), 35 mph (II).
Production: Two Woodpigeons built by Westland Aircraft Works, Yeovil, Somerset, during 1924.

Widgeon

The Widgeon parasol-wing monoplane was the running mate of the biplane Woodpigeon in the 1924 Air Ministry Light Aeroplane Competition and trials at Lympne, and was Arthur Davenport's conception of a two-seat aircraft for use by flying clubs. As recorded in the foregoing Woodpigeon chapter, the Widgeon was built to weigh the relative merits of the biplane and monoplane configurations.

Widgeon I and II

The construction of the Widgeon's fuselage was very similar to that of the Woodpigeon except that the front engine bay was slightly different to accomodate the triangulated steel-tube mounting for the 1,090 cc 35 hp Blackburne Thrush three-cylinder air-cooled radial engine, and the Warren girder bays containing the two cockpits were modified to accept the redesigned main undercarriage and the wing support struts. This similarity was more marked in the initial design as the Bristol Cherub engine, the same as that in the Woodpigeon, was to have been used. A small faired headrest also was fitted behind the rear cockpit in the prototype Widgeon. The major unorthodox feature of the Widgeon was its distinctive thick lozenge-shaped parasol wing, a configuration and shape which were to appear in five more Westland aeroplanes. The points of maximum thickness and chord coincided on the fifth

110

rib, at about one-third the half span, where the V support struts were attached to the underside of the wing spars. At their lower end these struts were attached to a fitting on the bottom longeron at a point directly below the rear spar. A long strut from the front spar in the centre section was also attached to this fitting, while the rear spar was supported by inverted-V struts angled sharply backwards and mounted on the top longeron.

In plan the wing root chord was small but increased markedly to the point noted previously then reduced again toward the tip. In the head-on view the undersurface of the wing was flat with all the variation in thickness being apparent only on the upper surface. The wooden spars were of I-section with three-ply webs and spruce flanges screwed and glued to each side of the webs. To reduce weight the front spar web had a series of X-shaped cutouts which, like the rear spar web, had diagonal reinforcing strips screwed and glued to it. The ribs were of the conventional spruce N-girder construction being particularly robust where the wing thickness and chord were at their maximum. As in the Woodpigeon, full-span ailerons, which doubled as flaps, were fitted and were of unusual plan form to continue the aerofoil section of the wing. This was a propeller section and was developed from R & M 322. Because of the wing thickness the duralumin-tube spar in the ailerons had a wooden 'superstructure' built up on it. Although the geometry was different from the Woodpigeon the parasol wing also folded back around the rear spar joint and the support struts' lower attachment fitting. Construction of the tail surfaces was almost identical to those in the Woodpigeon. The main undercarriage was of the cross-axle type with V struts, the front ones incorporating a coil spring shock absorber with Ferodo friction dampers, while the tailskid was an inverted tripod structure. Control cables for the ailerons were external, running through a fair-lead in the fuselage sides up to the root end rib; the tail control cables were the same as in the Woodpigeon, running internally to the rudder and externally to the elevators.

Laurence Openshaw first flew the Widgeon at Yeovil on Monday 22 September, 1924, and found it to be generally satisfactory, if underpowered. Bearing in mind that its loaded weight was slightly more than the Woodpigeon's and the wing area some 8 per cent less, the wing loading was too high at 5.5 lb per sq ft. Nevertheless, carrying the Competition number 6 on its rudder and fuselage sides and in an all-silver finish, the otherwise unmarked Widgeon I was flown to Lympne on 25 September by Capt Winstanley, an ex-RFC pilot.

The Competition began on 27 September with full-load trials, each aircraft carrying ballast weight to represent that of a passenger. Unfortunately, the day had dawned bright but very windy with gusts of more than 35 mph reported. When Winstanley set out on a circuit of the Competition course, at the first turning point he encountered a very strong downdraught from a nearby ridge and the Widgeon's Thrush engine was unable to provide enough power to counteract it. The aircraft, trying to turn quite close to the ground to avoid the high winds, was actually blown sideways into the ground where one wingtip hit the grass and the Widgeon cartwheeled and collapsed around Winstanley who was uninjured apart from some bruising.

Although the Thrush-powered Widgeon's flying hours had been few, its superiority in many ways over the biplane Woodpigeon had been perceived both

Widgeon I G-EBJT powered with a Blackburne Thrush photographed during September 1924. The unusual wing section is visible in this view.

by Westlands and the Air Ministry whose report had praised the design and engineering features even though its performance and handling characteristics had been unexplored. Thus, Robert Bruce decided that the damaged prototype should be rebuilt with a much more powerful engine and a few other airframe modifications; these included re-routed elevator control cables, the use of a smaller rudder, the removal of the pilot's faired headrest from the rear cockpit and the fitting of a larger fuel tank which created a bulge in the side of the lower front fuselage section. The engine chosen was the new 60 hp Armstrong Siddeley Genet I, a five-cylinder air-cooled radial engine. In this form it became the Widgeon II, its wings with their struts and fuselage top decking were painted green with the remainder of the fuselage and tail unit in silver. Registered G-EBJT it carried the letter G on its rudder. With an all-up weight of 1,150 lb the Widgeon II was about 330 lb heavier than in its original form, but its maximum speed of 110 mph was nearly 40 mph faster, although the handling characteristics had changed at the stall proving particularly difficult for the unwary pilot. On 18 September, 1926, G-EBJT was flown by Laurence Openshaw in the Grosvenor Trophy Race at Lympne, where it achieved the fastest time over the course averaging 105 mph. This feat was repeated in 1929 when a Widgeon III G-EBRQ won this Trophy. G-EBJT was again in action at the Easter Bournemouth Air Meeting held on a strip of land which was part of Ensbury Park race-course, during 15, 16 and 18 April, 1927. Flown by Laurence Openshaw it was 'in the frame' in several events, including second place in the quaintly named Bournemouth and District Hotels and Restaurants Handicap, known to pilots as the 'Pub-crawl Race'.

Through the remainder of 1927 G-EBJT was flown from Yeovil as a 'hack' and in connection with Widgeon III development until, in January 1928, it was sold to Dr E D Whitehead Reid who flew it from Bekesbourne, near Canterbury. He was killed in this Widgeon when he flew into some trees while making a forced landing at dusk at East Sutton Park, near Detling in Kent on 19 October, 1930.

112

Widgeon III

During the autumn of 1926, with the experience gained from building and flying G-EBJT and from the exciting performance from the parasol-winged Wizard at Yeovil, Robert Bruce believed that the time was right for the type to be developed for the private-owner market. Thus, with quantity production in mind he decided to abandon the complex design of the Widgeon II's wing, substituting a constant chord design which, with standardisation of the ribs, would be easier and cheaper to produce. He also redesigned the fuselage, tail unit and undercarriage.

Simplicity of construction was the design aim in the new Widgeon III. The fuselage was in two sections; the welded steel-tube engine mounting and the wooden centre and rear fuselage. Two types of engine mounting were available, to suit either the Cirrus inline engine or a shorter type for the Genet radial which had a duralumin face plate to which the engine was secured by four bolts. Four spruce longerons, measuring only 1 in x ½ in, with fabricated rectangular spruce frames formed the basic jig-built fuselage structure. There was no internal bracing to true up, and 1 mm thick ply skinning on the rear portion, which was increased to ¹⁄₁₆ in further forward, provided all the necessary stiffness and strength. This skin was covered with fabric which was glued on to it and then finally doped, thus eliminating the possibility of draughts through joints. In section the fuselage had a flat bottom and sides with a curved top decking, having apertures for the two cockpits. The fin, rudder and elevators were all metal but the adjustable tailplane was of wood. During construction the wing centre section had to be mounted on its four inverted V support struts which were attached to the top longeron. Only then could the starboard longeron be sawn through to make a triangular opening for a door to the front cockpit. Two types of centre section also were provided to suit the engine installation; owing to their different weights and lengths the c.g. could vary substantially. The neat solution of matching centre-sections to engines provided a slightly greater sweep back on one than on the other. The centre-section housed the 20 gal

G-EBRL, a Widgeon III with a 75 hp ABC Hornet. This aircraft later had a 95 hp Cirrus III and was converted for trials as a floatplane in 1929.

aerofoil-section gravity feed fuel tank which had an On/Off control handle on its rear face. The wings of RAF 34 section, which produced very small centre of pressure movement for widely varying conditions, were built up around two spruce box spars with spruce ribs internally braced and were fabric covered. Full-span narrow chord ailerons were hinged to an auxiliary spar and were operated by short cables running out of the fuselage side and up to their inboard end ribs. The ailerons, which had a metal structure including a tubular spar, had aluminium ribs and duralumin leading edges. Dual controls were fitted, those in the front cockpit were removable if normal passenger-carrying rather than flying instruction was to be performed. The seats were made to have separate backs so a lower seat could be fitted when parachutes were being worn. Baggage could be carried in lockers in the fuselage top decking between the cockpits and forward of the front cockpit. The cross-axle undercarriage on the Widgeon was of special Westland design having telescopic main legs of oval-section steel-tube inside which were the load-carrying steel coil springs with Ferodo friction dampers between the inner and outer tubes of the leg. These were described by Westland as being 'Durable and simple, with no rubber to perish, no glands to leak oil and no air pressure to be lost'.

Construction of the first Widgeon III powered by an 80 hp ADC Cirrus engine, advanced quite quickly under the supervision of Harald Penrose and the first flight was made by Laurence Openshaw during late March 1927 with the aircraft still in its doped undercoat. It was then painted green with a silver rudder, with these colours being reversed for the registration letters, G-EBPW, on the wings and fuselage and the G on the rudder. The front fuselage bore the aircraft's type name in silver and the silhouette of a flying duck applied with a stencil cut by Penrose.

First public mention of the Widgeon III was an advertisement which appeared in *The Aeroplane* of 13 April, 1927. It was claimed to be 'The fastest two-seat light aircraft in the world' and able to fly 20 miles per gallon of fuel. G-EBPW made its public debut in the Easter Bournemouth Air Meeting, two days after this advertisement appeared. Before it was handed over to Sqn Ldr Tom-Harry England, who was to fly the Widgeon III in some of the air races, Capt Geoffrey Hill, who was in charge of Pterodactyl design and development at Westland, took his wife for a short flight around the Bournemouth area. The Widgeon III enjoyed mixed fortunes at this meeting, coming third in the 1st heat of the Branksome Cirrus Handicap for two-seaters—and nowhere in the final. In the Bournemouth and District Hotels and Restaurants Handicap, for which England took Robert Bruce's 15-year old daughter Rachel, as his passenger, the Cirrus engine failed and in the subsequent forced-landing on boggy ground, the wheels sank into it and the Widgeon overturned. Fortunately, neither of the occupants was injured.

During 1927 production of what may be regarded as the first batch of Widgeons, which were of wooden construction, gathered momentum. There was, too, more air racing success at the Whitsun Bournemouth Meeting, when, on Saturday 4 June, Mrs Elliott-Lynn won the Ladies Race flying from scratch in G-EBPW. However, two days later Laurence Openshaw was killed in the same aircraft when it collided with Sqn Ldr Walter Longton's Blackburn Bluebird, killing him too. In the King's Cup Race, Robert Bruce's G-EBRL, which was

Previously fitted with a coupé top on the front cockpit, in 1928 a fully enclosed cabin was temporarily installed in this Widgeon III, G-EBRO.

used as the Widgeon demonstrator, was flown into second place by Capt W J McDonough, an instructor at the Midland Aero Club, averaging 102.8 mph. As an experiment in 1928 this Widgeon was fitted with a 75 hp ABC Hornet, the world's first flat-four-cylinder air-cooled engine, but there is no evidence that it ever flew with this engine. During 1929 it went to East Cowes where, powered by a 95 hp Cirrus III four-cylinder inline engine, it was converted by S.E. Saunders to a floatplane and fitted with floats made with Consuta laminated wood. The word 'Consuta' is Latin for 'stitched together' and this material was produced by stitching together the laminations with 16 SWG copper wire. However, it was found that the Cirrus engine was not sufficiently powerful to overcome the additional weight and drag of the floats and G-EBRL was refitted with its wheeled undercarriage. It ended its days in spectacular fashion by crashing at Yeovil when Louis Paget failed to recover from his usual low level spins while demonstrating the Widgeon to some visiting schoolboys. Paget broke both legs in this accident and retired from test flying.

Despite their small size and modest power, Widgeon IIIs were flown over

This Widgeon III, G-EBRQ, built in 1927, was fitted with an Armstrong Siddeley Genet five-cylinder radial.

long distances, both in Great Britian and overseas. Sqn Ldr the Hon R A Cochrane and Flt Lt Drew flew G-EBRO round a number of European cities during September 1927, covering some 4,000 miles in 52 hours flying. G-EBRN, configured as a single-seater and powered with an 85 hp Cirrus II, was fitted with an additional 60 gal fuel tank in the front cockpit space. Flown by Wg Cdr E R Manning who was to take 15th place with this Widgeon in the King's Cup Race, it took-off from Lympne on 23 April, 1928, on an attempt to fly to Australia. Manning got as far as Baghdad, an achievement in itself, but mounting problems caused the flight to be abandoned there. The aircraft was shipped home and was bought by H R Law, son of Bonar Law, who set out on a similar route to Australia in the Widgeon. Damaged, yet again, at Athens on 18 January, 1930, it returned to England where it was bought by Flt Lt Allan H Wheeler who based it first at RAF Northolt and then Andover. He flew it privately from November 1933 until the beginning of the 1939–45 War; then, after its C of A was renewed in February 1948 it was flown by N C Alderson of Stranraer but three years later it was burned because the owner had nowhere to house it. Another 'long-distance' Widgeon was G-EBRQ, which won the 1928 Grosvenor Trophy Race and was the only Widgeon III to take advantage of the choice of wing centre-sections. Because of the lower installed weight of the 75 hp Genet II radial engine the centre-section gave 11 in of sweep back instead of the standard 4 in, measured at the tip leading-edge. During the winter of 1928–29 its owner, Sqn Ldr H M 'Daddy' Probyn, and his wife made a 4,200 mile tour in this aircraft. In a flying time of 60 hours 50 minutes they visited Paris, Nice, Pisa, Naples, Catania, Tunis, Biskra, Algiers, Oran, Almeria, Seville, Madrid and Biarritz—in that order. To prove its versatility Probyn then flew it into 12th place in the 1929 King's Cup Race, maintaining 90 mph, he claimed, despite the fact that the Genet was firing on only four of its five cylinders because a rocker-arm had broken at Bristol on the first day of the race.

These long-distance flights and the growth of private ownership prompted the desire for more comfort and protection from the elements in light aircraft.

Powered by a de Havilland Gipsy I engine, G-AADE, the last Widgeon III is seen landing with its slats fully open.

Westland responded to this, ahead of almost all of its competitors, and produced a design for a cabin Widgeon with three seats in tandem, the pilot in front. A mock-up was built but no further development was undertaken; instead G-EBRO was fitted, first, with a hinged coupé top over the front cockpit and then later the fuselage was modified to have a fully-enclosed cabin. Neither of these modifications was introduced as standard fit, but G-AALE, which was taken to Canada by W J McDonough and re-registered CF-AIQ, had a coupé top fitted to its front seat by AS Carston during 1939. The last Widgeon III, G-AADE, registered to Carill S Napier in September 1927, had automatic wingtip slats and was powered by a D.H. Gipsy I engine. It was written off in a crash at Beaulieu, Hants, on 10 July, 1932.

By the early 1920s the limitations of wooden structures for military aircraft were becoming increasingly apparent, but their use in light aircraft continued as much on grounds of economy as anything else. However, in 1927 Arthur Davenport designed a metal fuselage for the Widgeon. The structure was of square-section duralumin tube with flitch plate joints and a welded steel-tube engine mounting to take the 90 hp ADC Cirrus III, the 100 hp D.H. Gipsy I, the 105 hp Cirrus Hermes I or 120 hp Hermes II engines. The engine bay had quickly detachable aluminium cowling panels. The curved top decking on the fuselage structure was wood from the engine bay to aft of the rear cockpit, behind which was a removable duralumin decking. The bottom of the fuselage was similarly metal clad for rigidity while the fuselage sides were fabric covered. A divided-axle undercarriage was also used on this variant which was designated Widgeon IIIA. This type of undercarriage was also fitted retrospectively to some of the earlier Widgeon IIIs. The first IIIA, G-EBRM, was owned by R G Cazalet of Wexford, Eire, who had it converted from a wooden Widgeon III and powered by a Hermes I. The last Widgeon to be built, G-AAGH, powered with a Cirrus Hermes I was Westland's communications aircraft from September 1930, through the war years until 27 July, 1948; then, at Merryfield, while standing with the engine ticking over and no one in the cockpit, the throttle opened slightly and the Widgeon careered into a hangar door and burst into flames.

Built in 1930, G-AAGH, with a Cirrus Hermes I engine, was the last Widgeon IIIA. It was Westland's 'hack' aircraft for many years before being destroyed in a ground accident at Merryfield on 27 July, 1948.

Widgeon III, VH-UHU, the oldest airworthy Westland aircraft. Built in 1928 it was still being flown by Arthur L. Whittaker at Boort, Victoria, Australia, in 1990.

Originally G-AALB, this Widgeon IIIA became CF-AIQ in Canada in May 1930. A coupé top was fitted on the front cockpit in 1939.

A number of Widgeons were exported, including at least five to Australia of which one, VH-UHU, owned by A L Whittaker, was still on the Australian Civil Register in 1990 and being flown from Boort, Victoria. Others went to India, New Guinea and South Africa and, it is believed, to a South American country. Although twenty-six Widgeons were built and sold there was stiff competition from other manufacturers and the Widgeon's £750 price tag made it rather more expensive than some other light aircraft. In addition, there was mounting pressure on Westland's resources at Yeovil resulting from large contracts for the Wapiti and the introduction of the Wessex. Thus, further production of the Widgeon ceased in 1930.

The major structural features of the all-metal Widgeon IIIA airframe can be seen in this Cirrus-engined example.

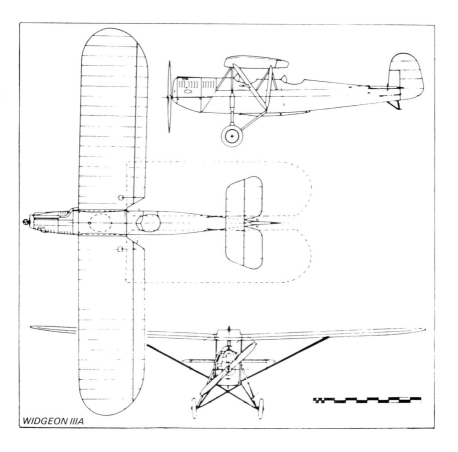

WIDGEON IIIA

Description: Two-seat parasol monoplane light aircraft. Wood/metal construction with metal and fabric covering.

Accommodation: Pilot and passenger in open cockpits.

Powerplant: One 35 hp Blackburne Thrush three-cylinder air-cooled radial engine driving a 4 ft 6 in diameter two-blade wooden propeller. (Widgeon I). One 60 hp Armstrong Siddeley Genet I five-cylinder air-cooled radial engine driving a 5 ft diameter two-blade propeller. (Widgeon II). One 85 hp ADC Cirrus four-cylinder air-cooled inline engine, or one 90 hp ADC Cirrus III four-cylinder air-cooled inline engine or one 75 hp Armstrong Siddeley Genet II five-cylinder air-cooled radial engine or one 85 hp ABC Hornet four-cylinder air-cooled horizontally-opposed engine or one 100 hp de Havilland Gipsy I four-cylinder air-cooled inline engine. (Widgeon III). One 90 hp ADC Cirrus III or one 100 hp de Havilland Gipsy I or one 105 hp Cirrus Hermes I or one 120 hp Cirrus Hermes II four-cylinder air-cooled inline engine. (Widgeon IIIA).

Dimensions: Span 30 ft 8 in (Widgeon I and II), 36 ft 4½ in (Widgeon III and IIIA); length 21 ft 0 in (Widgeon I and II), 23 ft 5¼ in (Widgeon III and IIIA); height 7 ft 3 in (Widgeon I and II), 8 ft 5 in (Widgeon III and IIIA); wing area 145 sq ft (Widgeon I and II), 200 sq ft (Widgeon III and IIIA).

Weights: Empty 475 lb (Widgeon I), 680 lb (Widgeon II), 852 lb (Widgeon III), 935 lb (Widgeon IIIA); loaded 815 lb (Widgeon I), 1,150 lb (Widgeon II), 1,400 lb (Widgeon III), 1,650 lb (Widgeon IIIA).

Performance: Maximum speed 72 mph (Widgeon I), 110 mph (Widgeon II), 100 mph (Widgeon III), 104 mph (Widgeon IIIA); landing speed 32 mph (Widgeon I), 38 mph (Widgeon II), 42 mph (Widgeon III), 48 mph (Widgeon IIIA); sea level rate of climb 300 ft/min (Widgeon I), 560 ft/min (Widgeon III), 640 ft/min (Widgeon IIIA).

Production: A total of 26 Widgeons produced by Westland Aircraft Works, Yeovil, Somerset, during 1926–30 as follows.

1 Widgeon I/II prototype
1 Widgeon III prototype
17 Widgeon III production aircraft
7 Widgeon IIIA production aircraft.

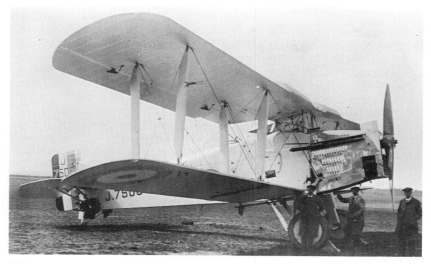

With sandbags on the tailplane struts to hold down its tail, J7508, the first Yeovil, awaits engine running in June 1925.

Yeovil

The Yeovil two-seat single-engined day bomber, built to Specification 26/23 was Westland's first military design to have been conceived, designed and built after the 1914–18 War. Although some three years earlier the Air Ministry had espoused the concept of a heavy single-engined day bomber—which material-ised in the form of just fifteen Avro Aldershots for No.99 Squadron RAF—it rapidly became disenchanted with these big cumbersome 68 ft span biplanes. Thus, Specification 26/23, received by Westland in August 1923, required an aeroplane 3,000 lb lighter and with a wing span some 10 ft less than the Aldershot, yet able to carry a 520 lb bomb load at 120 mph and with a range of 1,200 miles. As the preferred power unit was the 650 hp Rolls-Royce Condor III twelve-cylinder vee engine which had been used in the Aldershot, the Air Ministry reasoned that a much better performance would be achieved with this smaller and lighter aircraft.

Design of the new bomber began at Yeovil during late 1923, in parallel with that at Filton, Kingston-on-Thames, and Cricklewood where the Bristol, Hawker and Handley Page design teams had also taken up the challenge of Specification 26/23. Following the design submission, to its delight, Westland received an Air Ministry order for three prototypes—but so had the three other manufacturers. Construction of the first of the three Yeovils, serialled J7508, began in March 1924. Its design followed well accepted practices employing a fabric-covered wood and metal structure. The fuselage was built in three units; the forward one, being the engine mounting, was a tubular-steel structure attached to the front bulkhead of the central portion. This latter unit, like the

121

rear fuselage was all wood and built up from four spruce longerons with Warren girder spruce bracing struts which were internally wire-braced and which formed the bottom half of the fuselage. The top half was made of curved plywood skinning attached to bulkheads and with reinforced cut-outs for the close-coupled pilot's and observer's open cockpits. This central fuselage portion was bolted to the rear fuselage whose wood structure consisted of the four spruce longerons with spruce struts which were also internally wire-braced. Its top was given shape by half-round formers and stringers. The fin and braced tailplane were of wood with metal framed horn-blanced rudder and inset hinge elevators. Surprisingly, with such a large fuselage the elevator control cables were run externally. Apart from the engine bay which had metal cowling panels and wood coaming on the centre fuselage, the entire structure was fabric-covered. The radiator was mounted in front of the engine and occupied a space in the nose below the propeller shaft with its coolant header tank carried externally on top of the nose cowling. Oil tanks were fitted behind the engine in the top of the centre fuselage. The main undercarriage of the first prototype, J7508, consisted of two rubber-in-compression shock absorbing legs attached to the upper longerons and braced to the fuselage, with a pair of N-struts attached at their upper ends to the bottom longerons and at their lower ends to the articulated cross-axle and a cross-beam which was connected to the axle by two hinged links. This was an interesting configuration for the wind-tunnel model had a divided undercarriage and the two later prototypes were fitted with a more conventional cross-axle main undercarriage. A V-strut braced the tailplane. The fabric-covered two-bay wooden wing structure consisted of ash box spars with Warren girder ribs, all internally braced with spruce struts and wire rods. The four pairs of wire-braced interplane struts and short centre-section support struts were of wood and streamlined in section. Two wide but shallow 'lifting' fuel tanks were built on to the inboard section of the two top wings.

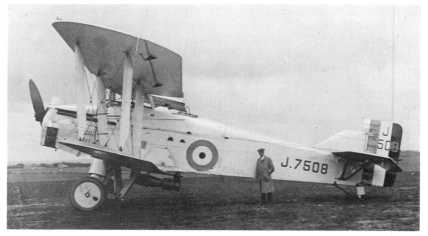

Yeovil J7508 at Andover carrying an under-fuselage 520 lb bomb. Note its small fin.

Metal-framed ailerons were carried on the top wing only and were of very wide span, occupying the entire trailing edge outboard of the tanks.

Armament was one synchronised fixed forward-firing Vickers .303 machine-gun mounted externally on top of the centre fuselage and synchronised to fire through the propeller disc, with a single Lewis gun of similar calibre carried on a Scarff ring mounting in the rear cockpit. Provision was made for ring-and-bead Aldis gun sights, the latter being fitted to the centre-section. Provision was also made for a rearward- and downward-firing Lewis gun through a hatch in the lower fuselage. One 520 lb bomb could be carried under the fuselage, or two 230 lb or four 112 lb bombs on racks under the wings and in line with the inboard bracing struts. The bomb sight was mounted in a special 'cell' beneath the pilot's cockpit, where two small windows in the fuselage sides provided light. The observer stepped down into it from his cockpit and lay prone when sighting and dropping bombs.

Production of the Yeovils continued through 1924 with the first one being completed in May 1925. After preliminary taxi-ing and engine running checks, during which some problems were experienced with the undercarriage and with the Condor engine which was started by a Bristol light-weight gas starter mounted in the fuselage and which was still in an experimental stage, the aircraft was prepared for its first flight. Because the Air Ministry believed that Laurence Openshaw, now Westland's new pilot, was short of test-flying experience, Frank Courtney, the free-lance test pilot, made the first flight at Yeovil one morning during early June. His fee was £100, and judging the Yeovil's handling characteristics to be 'satisfactory', in the afternoon he flew it to RAF Andover's aerodrome at Weyhill with Openshaw in the rear cockpit. Because Westland's aerodrome provided a maximum of only 500 yards of grass, further testing of the Yeovil was done from Andover before the aircraft's departure to A & AEE at Martlesham Heath in July.

Meanwhile, the second and third prototypes, J7509 and J7510, were being built at a slower pace to embody modifications resulting from the first aircraft's test programme. These were to include a taller fin and a simplified main undercarriage retaining the front shock absorber leg but with a rigid cross-axle and two radius rods. It is believed that J7510 had a metal fuselage and was

J7509 with a taller rudder. Noteworthy are the complex strutting of the main undercarriage and conformal overwing fuel tanks.

The third Yeovil had an increased area fin, modified and cleaned up main undercarriage and reshaped ribbed fuel tanks.

referred to as the Yeovil Mk. II. At Martlesham Heath J7508 joined No. 22 Squadron which, while nominally a bomber unit, was responsible for evaluation of new types of aircraft. The Bristol Berkeley, Hawker Horsley and the Handley Page Handcross, the three other Specification 26/23 contenders, were already with the Squadron for the evaluation trials held during August 1925. Although all four types were remarkably similar in appearance and performance, the Horsley's ability to carry the much greater bomb load, or a torpedo, required by the new Specification 24/25 tipped the scales in its favour.

Yeovil J7510 with what appears to be an adjustable-pitch two-blade propeller.

With the completion of the two remaining Yeovil prototypes, flight testing was done by Laurence Openshaw. Because of their good handling and performance characteristics all three aircraft were widely used during a number of years for research and test flying of a range of equipment; this included the fitting of non-lifting fuel tanks on the top wings of J7510 which first flew in June 1926, and extensive trials of the Gloster Hele-Shaw Beacham adjustable-pitch propellers and Leitner-Watts hollow-blade metal propellers.

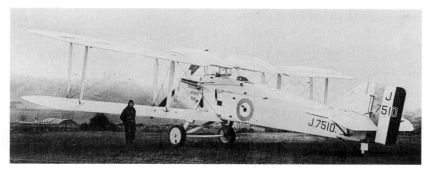

Yeovil J7510 with conformal overwing fuel tanks.

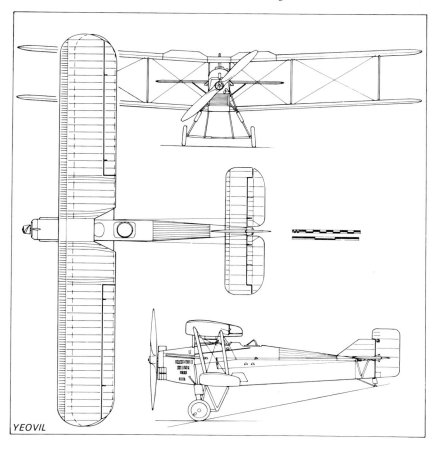

YEOVIL

Description: Two-seat biplane day bomber. Wood and metal construction with
fabric, wood and metal covering.

125

Accommodation: Pilot and gunner/bomb aimer in two open cockpits.

Powerplant: One 650 hp Rolls-Royce Condor twelve-cylinder vee inline liquid-cooled geared and normally aspirated engine driving a 15 ft 7 in diameter two-blade wooden propeller.

Armament: One fixed synchronised Vickers .303 in forward-firing machine-gun and a Scarff ring in the rear cockpit with provision for a rearward and downward firing Lewis .303 in machine-gun. One 520 lb under the fuselage and two 230 lb or four 112 lb bombs on racks under the wings.

Dimensions: Span 59 ft 6 in; length 36 ft 10 in; height 14 ft 3 in; wing area 798 sq ft.

Weights: Empty 4,660 lb; loaded 7,550 lb.

Performance: Maximum speed 120 mph; landing speed 58 mph; cruising speed 98 mph; endurance 9 hr; service ceiling 17,450 ft.

Production: Three Yeovils built by Westland Aircraft Works, Yeovil, Somerset, during 1924–26.

Wizard

If it had been difficult to acknowledge the big and bulky Westbury biplane as a fighter or, indeed, the Bristol Bagshot monoplane also built to meet the same Specification 4/24, then there was no problem in recognising the Wizard for what it was.

Strangely, the design of this aeroplane, begun in 1925, was the result of much spare-time effort by a small group of enthusiasts in Westland's design office who devoted out-of-office hours to the task of creating a 'racer'. Among them was Tony Fletcher, who had worked at Martinsyde, and Herbert A Mettam the company's experienced and skilful stressman, with advice coming from Laurence Openshaw. Perhaps the largest plus factor was that Arthur Davenport, that protagonist of monoplanes, gave this unique project his unofficial blessing. One can conjecture that this team needed something very different from the Westbury to get the design adrenalin flowing again.

Although metal construction was beginning to make its mark in new designs, in the hope that Robert Bruce would agree to build it, the design of the 'racer' was deliberately kept simple, using wood for cheapness. Of parasol monoplane configuration, employed, no doubt, because of the wealth of experience acquired with the Widgeon, the fuselage consisted of a plywood monocoque central portion of circular cross-section which embodied the cockpit. To this was attached the rear fuselage portion built up around four spruce longerons and struts all wire-braced. The untapered strut-braced wing had conventional wood box-spars with Warren girder ribs and a false aileron spar.

When the design had advanced sufficiently far to allow it to be shown to Bruce he was at once alerted to its potentialities. After he had made some modifications, which included the use of two centreline struts in place of the originally-designed cabane structure, which permitted the use of Aldis and ring-and-bead gun sights on the centreline and to port, Bruce instructed Bill Widgery, who was in charge of the company's wind tunnel, to run some tests on a model. Some 60 tests were made during the ensuing months to assess the slipstream effect with a propeller running and resulting in a change of wing section from W4 to the RAF 34 used later in the Westland IV and Wessex. Meanwhile, construction began and to keep costs down and to generally speed the programme, Openshaw proposed the use of the 275 hp Rolls-Royce Falcon III engine recovered from the wreckage of the prototype Limousine I after the Fairey Fawn had flown into it while parked at RAF Netheravon in September 1925. This engine and the absence of a propeller spinner produced a more blunt nose than originally envisaged, requiring more wind-tunnel tests, but construction continued and was well advanced by autumn 1925.

The sleek lines of the unpainted Wizard proclaim its 'racer' origins. Note area-increasing plywood glove on the rudder and the lowered retractable radiator.

About that time, Laurence Openshaw was at Martlesham Heath where the sole example of the little Hawker Heron single-seat fighter was undergoing trials. He had seen its ingenious system of metal construction, devised by Sydney Camm and Fred Sigrist, which consisted of duralumin or steel tubes swaged to a rectangular cross-section at their ends, which were bolted together with flitch plates to form the primary structure of the fuselage. Bruce at once saw the inherent benefits of this type of construction and gave instructions for the wooden front end of the 'racer' to be removed forward of the cockpit front bulkhead. In the Hawker system the ends of the tubes butted against each other; however, although it had not yet been patented (this did not take place until March 1927) Bruce decided that in the 'Westland system' there should be a one-eighth inch gap between the longerons and the struts, which would be of square section tube, and that all loads would be taken through the flitch plates with the joints being made with tubular rivets. To this structure, which included the engine mounting, was attached the two metal centre-line wing support struts. When assembled the engine and the fuselage portion in front of the cockpit had metal cowling panels while the rear portion was fabric covered; only the two banks of uncowled cylinder heads, the pilot's windscreen and faired headrest broke the overall clean lines of the fuselage. The wings, of rectangular planform, were of thick section, had a pair of struts each side bracing them to

127

the metal section of the lower longerons, and had ailerons of about quarter-span with small horn balances. The tail unit consisted of a sharply swept fin with a broad-chord horn-balanced rudder and a rectangular strut-braced tailplane with very broad-chord elevators. The undercarriage had twin Westland medium-pressure air chamber and oil dashpot shock absorbers contained inside a broad-chord fairing each side with forward-angled radius rods and a cross-axle. A pair of crossed wires braced the undercarriage and two pairs braced the wing struts.

The long gun trough in the fuselage nose, Aldis sight, horn-balanced rudder and constant-chord ailerons are visible in this view of the Wizard.

Construction of this aeroplane, now named Wizard, was completed during the early part of 1926 and engine running then began. Appropriately, for an aeroplane designed in out-of-office hours, the first flight was made on a Sunday before a small crowd of Westland employees who had been involved in its creation. After a steady take-off Openshaw delighted them with a fast run and steep climb and some steeply banked turns. On landing he reported that aileron control was heavy and unresponsive, the elevators were too sensitive and the rudder ineffective; it also tended to 'float' during the landing. Before the second flight the ailerons were increased in length with larger horn balances and the wingtips were rounded off at their trailing edges. To improve rudder effectiveness a square plywood 'glove' was fitted over the top to increase its area while the area of the elevators was initially reduced by removing their fabric covering near the trailing edges. Narrower chord elevators were later fitted.

With these modifications flight trials progressed quite well until cut short by a forced landing caused by an air-lock in the fuel system. Openshaw had just taken off from Yeovil when the engine stopped; fortunately he was able to bring the Wizard down in a narrow gap between some houses near to the aerodrome boundary, but it hit a hedge and turned over. Although Openshaw suffered only some minor cuts and bruises, the aircraft was quite severely damaged, requiring a thorough rebuild if it was to fly again. Bruce not only decided that Westland should continue to finance the Wizard but that during the rebuild some fundamental changes and improvements should be embodied. The most

Modifications embodied after the first flight of the Wizard I included increased span ailerons and removal of fabric from the elevators to reduce the effective area. The rudder's plywood glove has not yet been fitted.

important of these were a new fuselage of all-metal construction with provision for two machine-gun armament and four 20 lb bombs, and the fitting of one of the early pre-production 490 hp Rolls-Royce F.XI engines. The fuselage was built in two sections, the front one as described earlier; the new rear section employed square-section duralumin tube longerons with round-section struts. The strut ends fitted into cup sockets attached to the longerons by a single bolt. This section was internally braced by round tie rods and was given shape by conventional metal formers and stringers, all fabric covered.

The Wizard I with smaller elevators, larger rudder and rounded wingtips to accommodate the longer span aileron horn-balances.

In November 1927, the Wizard I was flown by Louis Paget, still carrying the plywood extension on its rudder but having skewed ailerons with gradually increasing chord toward the tip and shielded horn balances. During trials the Wizard I exhibited some of the qualities which its 'racer' concept had foreshadowed; it was fast, reaching nearly 190 mph, and had a spectacular rate of climb. That said, there was much which needed to be done to improve lateral control and by a process of trial and error the ailerons slowly became light and effective. While performance testing proceeded for several months, Bruce and Louis Paget kept in close contact with the Air Ministry and the RAF, extolling the virtues of the Wizard, particularly the aerodynamic benefits of the slim engine installation—enhanced by a pointed propeller spinner—and the climb, this latter feature being important in an interceptor fighter. By early 1928 the Wizard I, serialled J9252, was being prepared to go to Martlesham Heath, Paget flying it there on 29 January. The A & AEE pilots approved the aircraft's performance but were critical both of the continuing heaviness of the horn-balanced ailerons and of the pilot's forward view which was obstructed both by the wing and the two centreline support struts.

A pointed spinner and cowled engine improved the sleek lines of the Wizard, still with its two broad-chord centre-line wing supports before going to the A & AEE at Martlesham Heath. Note the machine-gun, Light Series bomb carrier and the radiator.

When the Wizard returned to Yeovil further work was put in hand to improve aileron control before the aircraft made its first public appearance in the ninth RAF Display at Hendon on 30 June, 1928. It immediately attracted attention (as did Westland's Pterodactyl IA which also appeared), its parasol wing—a configuration absent from the RAF since the Morane-Saulnier types of the First World War—making it a rare bird among British military aircraft. Its climb performance was also well displayed before Their Majesties King George V and Queen Mary and the Duke of York plus a crowd of some 200,000.

The Air Ministry was sufficiently interested to give Westland a small development contract and modest financial assistance for further development of the Wizard embodying an all-metal wing. To overcome the earlier criticism that the thick centre-section impaired the pilot's view, the new increased span duralumin wing of reduced chord, was built with a very thin centre-section and the centreline support struts were replaced by two pairs of cabane struts. In addition a supercharged 500 hp Rolls-Royce F.XIS engine was fitted. As the design of the original all-metal front fuselage had made provision for the

The Wizard II with a thinner centre-section and three of the four new struts in position, although the structure of the centreline supports has not yet been removed. It has an all-metal rear fuselage structure.

possible later installation of a supercharged engine, this was easily effected. The retractable radiator beneath the fuselage was slightly increased in area.

Flight trials of the aeroplane, now designated Wizard II, were resumed but in spite of the more powerful engine and other refinements the performance was slightly inferior to the earlier variant. This factor combined with the official preference for biplane fighters led to the abandonment of the Wizard programme.

Description: Single-seat parasol monoplane fighter. Wood/metal and all-metal construction with metal and fabric covering.

Accommodation: Pilot in open heated cockpit.

Powerplant: One 275 hp Rolls-Royce Falcon III twelve-cylinder liquid-cooled normally-aspirated vee engine driving a 9 ft 10 in diameter two-blade wooden propeller ('Racer'). One 490 hp Rolls-Royce F.XI twelve-cylinder liquid-cooled normally-aspirated vee engine driving a 10 ft 4 in diameter two-blade wooden propeller (Wizard I). One 500 hp Rolls-Royce F.XIS twelve-cylinder liquid-cooled supercharged vee engine driving a 10 ft 4 in diameter two-blade wooden propeller (Wizard II).

Armament: Two fixed synchronised Vickers .303 in forward-firing machine-guns mounted in troughs in the fuselage sides. Four 20 lb bombs carried on racks under the fuselage.

Dimensions: Span 39 ft 6 in (Wizard I), 40 ft (Wizard II); length 26 ft 10 in; height 9 ft 4 in; wing area 238 sq ft (Wizard I), 234 sq ft (Wizard II).

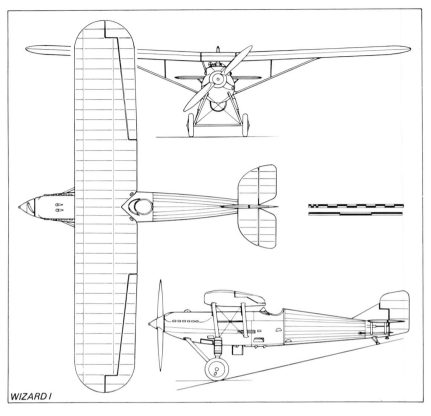

WIZARD I

Weights: Empty 2,352 lb; loaded 3,320 lb.

Performance: Maximum speed at 10,000 ft 188 mph; landing speed 56 mph; sea level rate of climb 2,600 ft/min; service ceiling 17,500 ft.

Production: One Wizard built by Westland Aircraft Works, Yeovil, Somerset, during 1926–27.

The short engine nacelles and the decked-over rear section of the aft gunner's position are well shown in this view of the first Westbury.

Westbury

During the years immediately after the 1914–1918 War, there was an understandable reaction by the general public and the politicians against anything that smacked of war-like activities. The infamous 'Geddes axe' economy move of 1920–22, which cut the operational squadrons of the RAF from 188 to 25, its aerodromes from 700 to 100 and its manpower from 291,000 to rather less than 30,000, was not considered to be a dangerously weakening blow to Britain's defences. With Germany no longer a potential aggressor it was the ex-ally France which was the only nation capable of mounting a war against Britain; not that France showed any signs of adopting a hostile posture, but if British defences were to be re-established then they had to defend against some form of threat.

The 1922 Government under Bonar Law favoured the abolition of the RAF as a separate entity, but a committee led by Lord Salisbury in June 1923 recommended an increase in Home Defence Forces from 18 to 52 squadrons as quickly as possible.

Out of this Government and Air Ministry thinking came Specification 4/24 calling for a multi-seat twin-engined fighter having a maximum top speed of 125 mph, a 50 mph landing speed and able to carry two automatic shell-firing guns to meet and defeat enemy aircraft which could be armed with heavy calibre cannon. The choice of this class of armament stemmed from several sources, chief among them being the trend of bomber and bomber-escort design by French companies such as Amiot, Farman and Potez and their research into heavy armament of up to seven 7.5 mm machine-guns and even 20 mm cannon. There had been early recognition of the potential of heavy guns by Britain before and during the 1914–18 War and attempts had been made to adapt several types, including the Coventry Ordnance Works (C.O.W.) 37 mm gun, to aircraft. It was a pair of these C.O.W. guns which were, ultimately, required to be used in fighters designed to meet Specification 4/24, although this was not initially disclosed in the Specification details.

The pilot of Westbury J7765 signals 'thumbs up' during an engine run. Note the human tail ballast's legs and front C.O.W. gun mounting.

Both the Westland and Bristol companies responded to the issue, in December of 1924, of this Specification; however, their designs could not have been more fundamentally different in concept. Bristol's design team led by Frank Barnwell favoured a monoplane configuration for its Type 95 Bagshot, having an all-metal cantilever shoulder-wing and steel-tube fuselage, all fabric-covered. Armament was carried in a nose position and in a second open position immediately behind the pilot's cockpit. Two 450 hp Bristol Jupiter VI radial engines powered the Bagshot.

Westbury J7765 under construction. The aft C.O.W. gun has been mounted temporarily and the rear section of the gunner's position is still covered.

Arthur Davenport adopted a most conservative configuration for the Westbury, the design of which began early in 1925. The original design featured a two-bay biplane configuration with diverging gap but, following work in the Westland wind-tunnel, the design was changed to incorporate high aspect ratio three-bay wings. In June 1925 Westland received an order for two prototype Westburys: the first, serialled J7765, had all-wood wings and the second, J7766, embodied wings with duralumin spars and wooden ribs. The fuselage was built in three separate units bolted together at the longerons. The forward unit, which was all-wood with spruce longerons and was covered with ply, contained the front gun turret in which the 6 ft long 37 mm gun was carried on a special Westland (later Vickers-Westland) rotatable mounting which permitted the gun to be trained through 360 degrees in azimuth.

Rex King, in his book *Armament of British Aircraft 1909–1939* describes the mounting thus, 'The gun was mounted at the apex of a pyramidal structure formed of tubes comprising a tetrahedron, the base tubes of which were connected at their apices to a central pivot by radial members, the apices being constructed to rotate about the pivot by shoes guided on a fixed base-ring. The mounting could be fixed in any position of training by a brake pad which was urged into engagement with the ring by a spring operating to rotate an eccentric shaft carrying the brake pad. The pad was released to free the mounting by depressing a pedal. The sight was carried on a crank mounted on a shaft passing through a tube and geared by a chain with a fixed central sprocket which kept the direction of the crank fixed, notwithstanding the rotation of the mounting. Training was effected by a hand-gear operating on a pinion engaging internal teeth on a base-ring. The mounting was provided with a rotary platform for the gunner and a fixed cylindrical shield carried on the ring'. The whole of this

Ballast weights in place of 37 mm C.O.W. guns and the long-chord engine nacelles are seen in this view of Westbury J7765.

135

forward unit could be unbolted for easy replacement, as a unit, in the event of being damaged in combat or nosing over on the ground for example.

The second unit was the central portion of the fuselage extending from in front of the pilot's cockpit, positioned just in front of the upper wing leading-edge, to aft of the widely separated rear gunner's position roughly amidships. The basic structure of this unit was steel-tube longerons and frames ply-covered. The gunner's cockpit aft of the wings was a multi-purpose position in which the main armament, installed at its forward end, was a second 37 mm C.O.W. gun carried on a simple trunion mounting. Although it could be moved through a very limited arc in azimuth and elevation, the gun was regarded as a fixed forward—and slightly upward—firing weapon. It was sighted by the pilot with a special sight mounted in front of his windscreen, and the gunner fired his gun at the target from a pre-determined lower level. At the rear of his position was a wind-balanced Scarff ring-mounting for a single Lewis .303 machine-gun; there was also provision for a second Lewis gun firing downward under the tail through a hatch in the floor. Wireless equipment was carried in this portion of the fuselage. It was mounted on a removable panel on the starboard side, aft of the pilot, with a small tip-up seat for an operator. Oxygen was also provided for all crew members.

The third fuselage unit was the rear section which was of mixed construction with four steel-tube longerons with spruce girder frames, the entire structure being wire-braced. The top fairing on this part of the fuselage was a ply-covered wooden unit which was attached to the longerons by clips for ease of removal and attachment. Two fairings were provided, one when the Scarff ring was fitted and the other when it was absent. The wood and fabric tail unit embodied a Westland patented tailplane incidence gear. The three crew positions were connected by an access passage through the deep-section fuselage to enable one gunner to operate both guns. The pilot could enter his cockpit by using hand and foot holds, in the fuselage side, aft of the wing, and clamber over a cat-walk on the centre-section, or could use the rear gunner's position and the inter-connecting passage.

The wooden wings of the first prototype were built up around spruce box spars and ribs internally braced by swaged steel rods, and were fabric covered, while the six pairs of interplane struts were of ash. The upper wings were joined by a small centre-section on the aircraft centreline where they were supported on a pair of inward canted N-struts attached at their lower ends to the upper

The nose ballast weight and semi-circular nose are features of J7765 in this head on view outside Westland's Vimy hangar.

longerons. Wooden fabric-covered horn-balanced ailerons were carried on all four wings. For the second prototype the wing structure was basically the same except that duralumin box spars were used with wooden ribs. Similarly, the main undercarriage, which was a pair of large triangulated wide-track units was common to both prototypes.

Power for the first Westbury was provided by two 450 hp Bristol Jupiter VI radial engines. They were carried on steel-tube mountings on the inboard section of the lower wings in corrugated metal-panelled nacelles which terminated in a vertical knife-edge at the wing trailing-edge. The fuel and oil tanks, starting magnetoes and priming pumps were all contained in the nacelle. This 'power egg' was a complete unit and, like the wing and fuselage sections, could fit into standard railway trucks of the period for ease of transport! This first aircraft was completed in 1926 and was then broken down for removal to the RAF aerodrome at Andover where Capt Frank Courtney was again engaged by Westland to make the first flight in September. With this achieved, the Westbury was flown back to Yeovil by Laurence Openshaw next day.

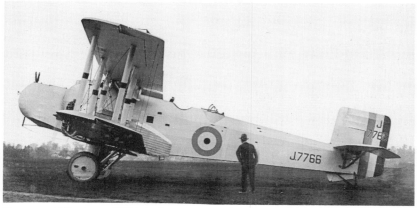

The second Westbury, J7766, had a more rounded nose, long-chord engine nacelles, a Scarff ring and a small ventral fin.

After early flight trials and further wind-tunnel work a number of modifications were made in the second prototype, J7766; these included a more rounded nose when compared with the aggressive squared-off nose of the first Westbury, the addition of a small ventral fin between the V struts of the tailplane, lengthened engine nacelles which protruded some two feet aft of the lower wing trailing-edge and the use of Jupiter VIII engines. These were first test run by Bristol in April 1927 and produced about a year later. As the first of a new family of Bristol engines they featured a 0.5:1 ratio bevel epicyclic reduction gear which enabled them to run at 2,000 or more rpm yet drive large and efficient propellers at just half that speed. The first flight of the second prototype took place at Yeovil, this time with Openshaw as the pilot. The flight test programme with this aircraft at A & AEE Martlesham Heath included firing of both C.O.W. guns, and it was the result of some damage to ribs and fabric in the upper wing caused by the powerful blast of the rear gun that a rubber-sprung steel protective shield was fitted over the central portion around the cut-out. It is recorded that the nose gun was also fired broadside in flight even though its recoil force was some 2,000 lb. When it was being 'run-up' the wheel chocks slid forward on the concrete apron and J7766 over-ran the Hucks starter, causing considerable damage to both.

Both Westbury prototypes performed well, handling easily with one engine stopped and even turning against the running engine, but official interest in such heavily-armed multi-seat fighters eventually waned; however, Westland's experience of C.O.W. gun installation and operation proved very useful when work on the Westland F.29/27 C.O.W. Gun Fighter began in 1930 even though the Specification 4/24 programme was abandoned.

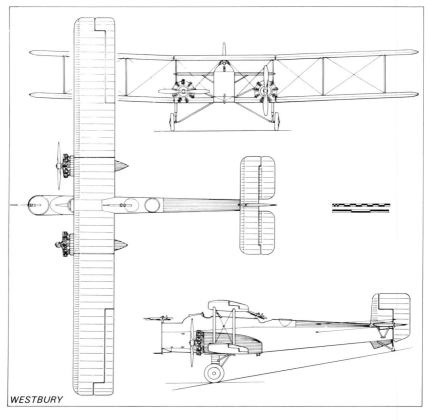

WESTBURY

Description: Three-seat biplane fighter. Wood/metal construction with wood/fabric covering.

Accommodation: Pilot in open cockpit, gunners in open front and rear positions.

Powerplant: Two 450 hp Bristol Jupiter VI nine-cylinder air-cooled normally-aspirated radial engines driving two-blade wooden propellers (J7765). Two 480 hp Bristol Jupiter VIII nine-cylinder air-cooled normally-aspirated geared radial engines driving two-blade wooden propellers (J7766).

Armament: One movable C.O.W. 37 mm gun firing 1½ lb shells at 100 rounds per min in front position, one limited movement forward-firing 37 mm C.O.W. gun and one Lewis .303 in machine-gun on Scarff ring in rear position with provision for a ventral Lewis .303 in gun firing through floor hatch.

Dimensions: Span 68 ft 0 in; length 43 ft 4¾ in; height 13 ft 9 in; wing area 875 sq ft.

Weights: Empty 4,854 lb; loaded 7,877 lb.

Performance: Maximum speed 125 mph at 5,000 ft, 113 mph at 15,000 ft; landing speed 50 mph; climb to 5,000 ft in 4½ min, 15,000 ft in 19 min; service ceiling 21,000 ft.

Production: Two Westburys, J7765 and J7766, were built by Westland Aircraft Works, Yeovil, Somerset, during 1925–27.

Wapiti

Although in the course of the last year of the 1914–1918 War British manufacturers were building a number of promising new prototype aircraft, very few entered production. Government spending on Defence during most of the postwar decade was minimal and the Royal Air Force was largely equipped with types of war-time vintage.

In that era of parsimony the concept of the General Purpose aeroplane was particularly attractive from a financial standpoint even though war-time experience had showed the greater effectiveness of aeroplanes specialising in a particular operational role. By early 1926 it was very apparent that the ageing D.H.9A, which had its origins in the D.H.4 of 1916, was in need of replacement. This need was particularly apparent in the Middle East and India where the RAF continued to be engaged in hostilities either supporting or replacing ground forces.

It was in this economic, political and operational climate that Specification 26/27 was issued, calling for a two-seat general purpose aircraft with the ability to perform bombing, reconnaissance and Army co-operation duties with equal facility. Because of the very large number of D.H.9A components and spares which still existed in Air Ministry Stores, the successor to this aeroplane was to incorporate as many of them as possible. The specification also indicated a preference for an all-metal airframe and, because of its satisfactory performance in D.H.9A variants, the use of a Napier Lion engine, of which there were large stocks, but these were not compulsory features. What was required was a performance and load-carrying capability superior to that of the D.H.9A.

With very few orders being placed for military aircraft at that time it was to be expected that the response to the issue of Specification 26/27 would be substantial. In the event seven companies—Armstrong Whitworth, Bristol, de

Havilland, Fairey, Gloster, Vickers and Westland—submitted eight aircraft types, of which only two were powered with Lion engines. As the company responsible for the development of the D.H.9A and the manufacture of some 550 of them, Westland was in a very strong position to win the order for a successor. In accordance with specified requirements Arthur Davenport embodied a number of major D.H.9A components in his design of Westland's 26/27 contender; they included the wing cellule complete with ailerons and interplane struts and the tail unit. In earlier years when Westland had been producing the D.H.9A, Davenport had designed an alternative main undercarriage with rubber-in-compression shock absorbers in place of the rubber chord then used; however, he later produced designs of an oleo-pneumatic unit and it was this which he used in his design of the new General Purpose aeroplane which featured a fuselage 5½ in wider and 12 in deeper than that of the D.H.9A.

The all-white mock-up showed Westland's 26/27 contender to be of a handsome design in which the deeper fuselage and increased wing stagger positioned the pilot much higher and further aft of the upper centre-section to give him and his gunner an excellent all-round view. Structurally, the fuselage was built in three sections; from the engine plate back to the first bay of the main section, which contained the two cockpits, and from aft of these back to the sternpost. The engine plate was carried on six diagonally-braced square-section steel-tubes canted upwards from the main section to raise the thrust line to the level of the top longerons. The main section was of square-section duralumin or steel-tube joined by steel tubular-rivetted flitch-plates to build up a very strong box girder structure. This was similar to the scheme used in the nose section of the Wizard; cleverly, it differed from the Hawker system in that, instead of butting the spacer struts onto the longerons, a one-eighth inch gap was left between them, the load being taken on the flitch plates. In the early production aircraft the rear section, aft of the cockpits, was a built-up wooden structure internally wire-braced but later this was changed to match the all-metal construction of the main section.

Shape and the additional depth was given to the basic D.H.9A-style fuselage structure by metal or wood formers and stringers attached to the top longerons of the front and main and the rear sections respectively. The fin was of wood and

The deep fuselage of the Wapiti prototype could accommodate a wealth of equipment but the pilot's Vickers Mk.II gun was carried externally.

140

was secured to a horizontal multi-ply base fixed to the top longerons on which sat the tailplane. In the prototype, serialled J8495, initially the double wire-braced tail unit was the D.H.9A type but this was later changed in shape and area. Three types of covering were used on the fuselage; immediately aft of the engine mounting the top section was occupied by a 15 gal oil tank, with a cooler mounted below and just aft of it on the port side in early aircraft, while the remainder of the main section to a point between the two cockpits was enclosed with removable aluminium panels fluted at 6 in pitch for rigidity. The top sector of the main section over the two cockpits had a curved plywood covering, attached to the top longerons and of D.H.4/D.H.9A lineage, with a leather-edged cut-out for the pilot's cockpit and a built-up circular platform for a Scarff ring gun mounting around the cut-out for the rear cockpit. The rest of the rear section and the tail unit were fabric covered. The legs of the cross-axle undercarriage were attached to the fuselage main structure close to the bottom wing front spar attachment point and the two forward inclined radius rods were pivoted to the front frame. A curved ash tailskid, which was later replaced by a straight steel unit with a steel shoe, was attached to the underside of the rear section.

Wapiti prototype, J8495, with tall rudder, horn-balanced ailerons, slatless wings and carrying two 230 lb bombs.

The major D.H.9A components, which were the two-bay fabric-covered wooden wings, were used virtually unaltered, except that the trailing-edge cut-outs in the upper centre-section and at the bottom wing root ends were reduced in size to provide more effective wing area. At a latter stage, when all-metal structure wings came into use, Handley Page automatic slats were fitted to the outer sections of the top wing. Power for the prototype, J8495, was provided not by the Napier Lion, which was beginning to reach the latter part of its development life, but by an uncowled 420 hp Bristol Jupiter VI air-cooled radial engine turning a 12 ft 6 in diameter two-blade wooden propeller. Provision was made for the carriage of a range of armament and equipment which included a fixed forward-firing synchronised Vickers .303 in machine-gun on the port side of the pilot's cockpit, a Lewis .303 in in the rear cockpit and up to 580 lb of bombs on underwing and fuselage racks. The capacious fuselage

141

provided volume for the internal installation of a 40 gal gravity fuel tank shaped to fit into the fuselage top immediately behind the oil tank, a 68 gal cylindrical auxiliary tank carried horizontally across the bottom longerons in front of the pilot's cockpit, plus oxygen, radio and photographic equipment, spares, tools, food, water and personal gear. A spare wheel, complete with tyre, was carried in the bottom of the fuselage nose covered by two hinged and slightly bulged doors. A prone bomb-aiming position in the bottom of the fuselage was fitted with a hinged ventral windscreen.

Construction of the prototype was pressed ahead quickly and, because of Westland's earlier experience with the D.H.9A and the use of its components, it was ready for its first flight during the first week of March 1927, being flown by Laurence Openshaw on Monday 7th at Yeovil. Neither Davenport, Bruce nor Openshaw had anticipated any major problems with the aeroplane having in mind the orthodox configuration and use of proven major flight control surfaces. However, Openshaw reported that the rudder had been almost completely ineffective, attributing this to the deep fuselage. Westland's Experimental Department, under its new manager, Victor Gaunt, who had joined Westland when the English Electric Company at Preston had closed its Aircraft department in March, immediately began to modify the rudder, increasing its area with plywood extensions; but as flight followed flight with only minimal improvement in control, a tall rectangular rudder, rather like that on the earlier Westbury but with the large horn-balance faired into the unmodified D.H.9A fin, was built and fitted. As the early flight trials continued and speed was progressively built up so that it exceeded that of the D.H.9A by some 22 per cent, it was found that the ailerons became unduly heavy. The remedy was a large inset horn-balance on the top ailerons.

J9078, the first production Wapiti I, with slats, the definitive fin and rudder and more neatly cowled Jupiter VI.

By the time Westland's 26/27 aspirant, complete with its unlovely tail unit, went to the A & AEE for comparative trials during March and June, it had been named Wapiti. There it was flown in competition with the Gloster Goral, Fairey Ferret III, de Havilland Hound, Vickers Valiant and the Bristol Beaver. Apart from performance and handling trials at normal flying weight and in the overload condition with simulated desert equipment, ease of maintenance and re-arming was evaluated and airframe structures were examined. Initially both the RAF engineers and the pilots at Martlesham Heath favoured the Valiant with the Ferret close behind it, but neither embodied D.H.9A components and the Valiant was very much more expensive than the Gloster and Westland products. The Hound was eliminated largely because internal stowage in its slender fuselage was minimal and its aerodrome performance did not meet the requirements, even though its Lion engine gave it the highest top speed of all the contestants. Ultimately, some five months later, the Wapiti was named the winner and Westland received an initial order for twenty-five aircraft with a modified fin and rudder. While J8495 was at Martlesham the draughtsman at Yeovil, who had drawn the fuselage structure, decided to measure it to check the tail volume against the wind-tunnel model. To his alarm he discovered that an entire 2 ft long bay had been missed out; however, as the Wapiti was performing well and receiving some favourable comments from the RAF pilots, it was decided not to rebuild the fuselage.

While production of the first twenty-five Wapiti Is of composite wood and metal construction was in progress, for which a track assembly line was installed in Westland's erection shop at Yeovil, the development programme continued, first with the prototype J8495 and then, after extensive wind-tunnel testing, with a D.H.9A (J8492) built by George Parnall & Co, this latter aircraft being used for flight trials of Handley Page automatic slats. Initially sliding on cantilever supports the slats' parallel motion produced an inefficient airflow; however, when modified to have a swinging link motion and fitted to J8495, now fitted with the definitive large D-shaped fin and rudder which characterised the Wapiti throughout its life, they proved highly effective. Fortunately, this was in time to allow them to be fitted to the first batch of Wapiti Is which had Frise ailerons. In June 1928 the prototype, powered by a Bristol Jupiter VIIIF uprated to 480 hp, went to A & AEE for further trials of what was, in effect, the Wapiti IA. It continued as a test bed for various trial installations of airframe equipment and engines for a number of years. During 1928, 1930 and 1934 it was used by Bristol Aeroplane Company's Engine Division to test fly the Pegasus radial engine.

An interesting airframe feature was that the Wapiti wing stagger could be altered to suit the engine; for example, with the 780 hp Jupiter VI it was 16 in but for the 986 lb Jupiter VIIIF it was increased to 20 in. A special engine cowling with 'helmets' for each cylinder was also tested in an effort to increase cooling and reduce drag with the Jupiter VIIIF. All of the foregoing activities with Wapiti design, construction and initial testing took place during the period when the Royal Air Force had the task of effecting British Government policy of air control of territories in the Middle East which were its mandated responsibilities until such time that they could be independently self-governing. Among them were Mesopotamia, (later to become Iraq), Palestine and Transjordan. The RAF also had a similar 'policing' role over the North West Frontier region in India and Afghanistan. To this end eleven RAF squadrons in Iraq and India were equipped with Wapitis, most squadrons retaining them until about 1935–36, although No.5 Squadron had Wapitis on charge until June 1940 when they were replaced by the Hart (India). In the United Kingdom nine squadrons of the Auxiliary Air Force flew Wapitis in the day bomber role from 1929 until 1934, with Nos.607 and 608 Squadrons not relinquishing them until 1936 and 1937 respectively. During this long service Wapitis were flown in some hazardous operations, including the evacuation by Vickers Victorias, D.H.9As and a Handley Page Hinaidi transport of 132 people and baggage from the British Legation in Kabul which was beseiged by warring tribesmen, and the subsequent airlift which raised the total number evacuated to 586 men, women and children, of which only 23 were of British nationality. The flights from Sherpur near Kabul to Peshawar in India were made via the Khyber Pass which added to the dangers, particularly for the single-engined Wapiti escorts. This operation lasted from 23 December, 1928, until 25 February, 1929, a period which was the coldest for more than a decade. Less dangerous was a 6,200 miles round trip from Ambala in India to Singapore and return by four Wapitis in January 1933.

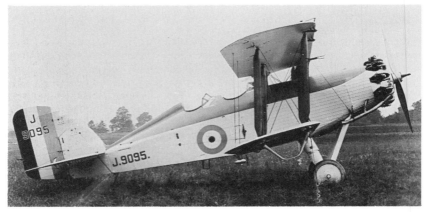

A Wapiti I specially prepared for HRH Edward, Prince of Wales, with VIP rear cockpit, Fairey-Reed metal propeller, and metal clad rear fuselage.

Wapiti I

The first Wapiti production variant was virtually identical to the prototype with its definitive fin and rudder, Handley Page slats and the direct-drive normally-aspirated 420 hp Jupiter VI engine. A total of twenty-five were built, many serving with Nos.8 RAF and 4 AAF Squadrons. Of these a number built for service in India with No.84 Squadron, were to Specification 12/30 while Specification 1/29 covered those for Home Service. J9084, the seventh Wapiti I, was fitted with metal floats made by Short Brothers and joined the Seaplane Flight at the MAEE at Felixstowe in June 1928 and March 1929. There it underwent trials to Specification 26/27 on Contract 802348/27, powered by a Jupiter VIFT engine in which forged and screwed/shrunk cylinder heads replaced the old 'poultice' heads with their tendency to leak. This modification was indicated by the suffix letter F in engine designations. The MAEE Report

F/23A of May 1929 recorded a maximum speed of 112 mph, a sea-level climb rate of 725 ft per minute after a 300 yards take-off run and a service ceiling of 13,100 ft. The Wapiti floatplane's handling characteristics were assessed as 'outstanding', with elevator and aileron controls light and responsive but with heavier rudder control. There were some criticisms of the beach handling equipment and some aspects of the maintenance. During July–August 1930, J9102, the last of the twenty-five Wapiti Is built for the RAF, was at Martlesham for trials of a new engine oil system and load carrying checks. The training role was not overlooked and J9082 and J9083 were completed as trainers with the rear armament removed and dual controls fitted.

Used for engine development, J9102, the last Wapiti I, with a 'helmeted' engine cowling to reduce drag and improve cooling and plain ailerons without horn-balances.

In 1933, as part of joint Westland/Bristol Aeroplane Company development programmes, J9102 was used as a flying test-bed for the Bristol Phoenix I, an air-cooled diesel engine which was designed to be installationally interchangeable with the Pegasus and which had first run in February 1932. Although there was a superficial similarity with the Pegasus the greater stresses and operating conditions of a diesel engine meant that there were very few common components. With the Phoenix cleared for flight in February, flight trials began in May and such was the success that in June the Wapiti appeared in the 1933 RAF Display at Hendon. By this time, bench-running of the 485 hp Phoenix II 'moderately supercharged' engine had begun with encouraging absence of 'diesel-thump' and with excellent specific fuel consumption figures. This engine was installed in the Wapiti late in the year and following early 1934 flight trials, during which a 15 per cent improvement in the time to climb to 15,000 ft was recorded, it was decided to make a ceiling climb. On 11 May, Harald Penrose flew the aircraft to a height of 27,453 ft, a record which remains unbeaten as the diesel engine altitude record. 'This was much better than expected,' he said after the climb. To prevent thickening of the fuel and lubricating oil the tanks were covered with felt and Penrose's oxygen system was electrically heated to prevent moisture in the oxygen from freezing at the reducing valve. Ballast was carried in the rear cockpit to represent the weight of a gunner and his armament.

A Royal Australian Air Force Wapiti IA. Despite the snow, the skis were fitted for ground photography only and were never flown on this aircraft.

Following recommendations by Air Chief Marshal Sir John Salmond, then Chief of the Air Staff, to the Royal Australian Air Force, Westland received an order for no less than twenty-eight Wapiti IAs, a number of which were trainers. This batch were serialled A5–1 to A5–28. This change in designation signified the embodiment of a number of modifications; including a new divided axle main undercarriage in which each wheel was carried on a stub-axle on a triangulated structure, increased wing stagger and the use of a geared 480 hp Jupiter VIII engine. Acceptance and delivery of the first of these took place in February 1929 and Sqn Ldr Smart, the RAAF Director of Training, went on record saying 'The Wapiti is ideal for desert-flying in Australia. These twenty-eight aircraft will put the training section of the Australian Air Force on a par with any in the world'. He later went on to demonstrate in Australia the

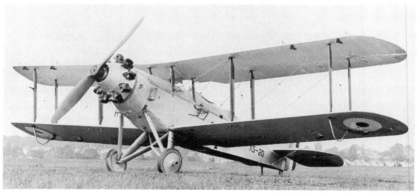

The divided-axle undercarriage was a feature of the twenty-eight Jupiter VIII-powered Wapiti IAs built for the RAAF.

146

Wapiti's capabilities with some record flights, one from Melbourne to Sydney covered the 545 miles in 225 minutes to average 145.3 mph, while at one point in another between Adelaide and Melbourne he claimed to have reached 200 mph IAS. An RAAF Wapiti was carried aboard the Royal Research Ship *Discovery II* which was looking for Lincoln Ellsworth, the US explorer and his companion who were forced down during a flight across Antarctica in a Northrop Gamma monoplane in December 1935.

Wapiti IA, J9095, delivered during April 1929, was extensively modified as a VIP version for use by the Prince of Wales (later to become King Edward VIII, then Duke of Windsor). It had all of its armament removed, the rear cockpit was given a special interior with additional instrumentation and a long faired headrest, and a long mounting step fitted below the rear cockpit. Structural changes included the use of metal rear fuselage panels while the direct-drive Jupiter VI engine drove a two-blade all-metal Fairey-Reed propeller. It is believed that a second aircraft for use by the Duke of York or possibly an Equerry was similarly modified.

On 10 October, 1929, the Duke of York (later to be crowned King George VI) used a VIP Wapiti when he flew to Brough near to Hull where he opened the Municipal Airport, his pilot being Sqn Ldr D S Don. He was attended by Maj Alexander in a second Wapiti flown by Flg Off Stemp. When the Prince of Wales returned from a visit to Egypt in 1930 he travelled as far as Marseilles in the P and O liner *Rawalpindi*, arriving on 24 April. Two days earlier the two Wapitis, flown by Sqn Ldr Don and Flg Off H W Pearson-Rogers and escorted by a Fairey IIIF, left RAF Northolt to fly to Marignane, the Marseilles airport. They arrived on 24 April. The following morning the IIIF and the Wapitis carrying the Prince and another VIP took off from Marignane at 0730 arriving at Bron, the Lyons airport, having covered the 175 miles in 90 minutes. After refuelling they departed again at 09.30 en route for Paris-Le Bourget which they reached at about 11.15. After lunch they took off again at 13.45 accompanied by a squadron of nine aircraft of the French Air Force which escorted them to the

Wapiti J9102 fitted with a Jupiter VIII.

147

coast which was crossed at Cap Griz Nez at 15.00. There an RAF flying-boat took over as escort for the Channel crossing, handing over 15 minutes later as they crossed the coast to nine Siskins of No.25 Squadron from Hawkinge led by Sqn Ldr R S Aitken. The Wapitis landed at Windsor Great Park at 1600 having flown the 650 miles from Marseilles in 6 hr 10 min to average 105 mph. Yet another Royal flight for an airport opening was that by the Duke of York on 31 May, 1930, when he flew in a Wapiti to Whitchurch, the Bristol Municipal Airport. He had the formidable escort of the second Wapiti, three Siskins and a Fairey IIIF.

Four Wapiti Is powered with 550 hp Armstrong Siddeley Panther II engines were ordered by the Chinese Central Government in 1932. Three received their C of A on 22 and 25 February and on 4 March, 1932, respectively, and were exported while the fourth aircraft was retained by Westland and registered G-ABUY in May 1932. It was subsequently delivered to the RAF as part of a production batch; its serial is not known.

It is recorded that four Wapitis built in 1932 and supplied to the South African Air Force were designated Wapiti IBs. Initially they were basically similar to the IA with a divided main undercarriage. During their Service career, their 480 hp Jupiter VIIIF engines were replaced by the 525 hp Armstrong Siddeley Panther fourteen-cylinder twin-row air-cooled radial. It is believed that in these aircraft a 75 gal fuel tank replaced the standard 25 gal auxiliary tank.

Wapiti II

A requirement for a General Purpose and Army Co-operation aircraft produced the Wapiti II, of which ten were built. As the forerunner of the Wapiti IIA, these aircraft could be regarded as its pre-production variants. They featured an all-metal rear fuselage and metal wings, matching in construction the earlier wooden structures, and were powered by the geared Jupiter VIII. Wapiti IIs were issued principally to No.84 Squadron. The all-metal wings were designed and built by the Steel Wing Company, a subsidiary of Gloster Aircraft Company, the contracts ultimately being worth £330,000 for the 525 sets of wings built during 1929–32 for Wapiti variants.

In 1929 production of 430 Wapiti IIAs, the largest number of any Wapiti variant, began at Yeovil; its major new feature heralded by the ten IIs, was the all-metal structure. Another modification was the fitment of a control column—but no rudder bar—in the rear cockpit. The prototype, J9247, was the last of the batch of eleven IIs and was built to IIA standard and with a divided main undercarriage. Records indicate that J9382, a 'metal structured version of Wapiti II', was at A & AEE as early as January 1929 for initial comparative trials powered with a Jupiter VIIIS engine. This aircraft, modified to production standard, was back at Martlesham in the autumn of 1930 for performance trials where it was joined by the prototype for similar trials, and K1129 which was flown on extended range checks with an external fuel tank under the fuselage between the undercarriage legs. A wind-driven pump on the fuselage side pumped the fuel up into the main tank. This extra fuel increased the endurance by up to two and a half hours. These latter trials were prompted by the issue of Specification 12/30 covering the aircraft intended for use with the eight RAF

A fine study of J9237, the first metal-winged Wapiti II. Later it went to Canada for cold weather trials.

squadrons based in India. The following year Wapiti IIA K1380, with modified elevators and a Jupiter VI, underwent performance trials and in 1932 J9084, the Wapiti I floatplane from Felixstowe but now with a wheeled main undercarriage plus two IIAs, K1129—with a main undercarriage having aft-mounted radius rods joining on the fuselage centreline—and K2262, were flown both at Yeovil and A & AEE with trial installations of modified windscreens, different combinations of engines, propellers and external loads. Trials of a liquid oxygen system designed by Westland were also made. Provision was also made for different types of undercarriage legs to accept a variety of wheels, floats or skis. A wide range of Jupiter engines were used to power production Wapiti IIAs and this variant was test flown at Yeovil and Filton with the geared Jupiter VIII and VIIIF, the 525 hp IXF and the geared and supercharged 530 hp X. Two Wapiti IIAs, J9497 and J9498, were completed as floatplanes and were used by Shorts on trials. Yet another IIA, K1142, was used as a receiver aircraft in 1934 flight refuelling trials with Vickers Victoria and Valentia tankers.

While the development and production testing programme of the Wapiti IIA gathered momentum, so did the production and delivery programme. The early squadrons to receive IIAs were No.60, based at Kohat in India which took delivery on 8 March, 1930, completing full conversion by mid-May, and No.27 Squadron, also at Kohat, which began re-equipping during April. On 17 May a No.11 Squadron Wapiti IIA's aircrew proved the efficacy of the control column in the rear cockpit when the pilot, Flg Off R Stroud, was hit by a tribesman's bullet during a low-level bombing attack near the Khyber Pass. When he collapsed, the gunner, AC1 C S Wiltshire, quickly fitted his control column and decided to try and return to base at Risalpur, even though he had little or no experience as a pilot. Sadly, he crashed on landing and died from his injuries.

149

J9403, one of the first production batch of Wapiti IIAs.

His courageous decision not to use his parachute but to try to get his pilot (who, unbeknown to Wiltshire, was already dead) and aircraft back to base received unique recognition. Wiltshire received posthumous promotion to the rank of Corporal.

As was to be expected, throughout the operational life of a General Purpose aeroplane like the Wapiti IIA it was called upon to perform a variety of roles, from display flying in the RAF Displays at Hendon during 1931–33 to operations in India and Iraq and patrols over the Canadian snows, the South African bush country and the Australian outback. The IIA was used for bombing, supply dropping and army co-operation, as a trainer and for target-towing. In April 1937 the Royal Canadian Air Force received twenty-five Wapiti IIAs, originally in RAF or AAF service, to equip No.3 Squadron at Trenton. To fit them for cold weather operations a special canopy was produced to enclose both cockpits. The squadron later moved to Rockcliffe in Ontario and during August 1938 was transferred to Calgary, Alberta. The squadron's Wapitis flew the 2,300 miles along a route established by Trans-Canada Airlines. This was the first time the

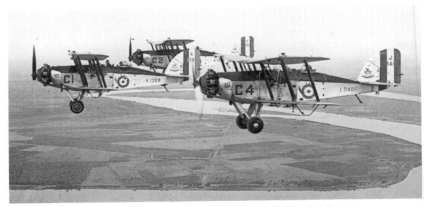

Wapiti IIAs of No.55 Squadron RAF from Hinaidi, Iraq.
Note the low-pressure tyres on the nearest aircraft.

J9498 was one of several Wapiti IIAs fitted with Shorts floats for trials. This photograph is dated July 1929.

Wapiti IIA K1132 with a Jupiter IXF for trials of underwing fuel tanks with wind-driven pumps.

RCAF had completed a move by air over such a long distance, a similar earlier move of Siskins having been accomplished by rail.

Re-designated No.10 (Bomber Reconnaissance) Squadron in 1939, it became an Air Striking Unit. Its Wapitis, replaced by Douglas Digbys in April 1940, ultimately were transferred to the RCAF School of Technical Training at St Thomas near Lake Erie.

A unique Wapiti IIA two-seat trainer was J9592 which had an all-white finish with the serial number on the rudder stripes only and which was the personal aircraft of Air Vice Marshal E Ludlow-Hewitt when Air Officer Commanding RAF Iraq during 1931–32.

A Wapiti IIA of No.27 Squadron RAF in India during 1933. Note the underwing streamlined bombs.

This engine-running Wapiti IIA, one of the last batch, is seen at Brooklands. The bulged spare-wheel stowage is visible between the undercarriage legs.

Wapiti IIA, 509, of No.3 Squadron Royal Canadian Air Force, at Camp Borden, Ontario, in 1938. (*A.D. Pearce/Public Archives of Canada PA-092489*).

Wapiti III

During 1929 four Wapiti IIIs, built to Wapiti IIA standard and with 480 hp Armstrong Siddeley Jaguar VI geared normally-aspirated air-cooled radial engines, were exported for use by the South African Air Force, the first arriving on 13 November and entering service on 25 November. In addition, twenty-seven more were built under licence by the SAAF Workshops at Roberts Heights, Pretoria. These had divided-axle undercarriages and were powered either by Jaguar VIs or 550 hp Armstrong Siddeley Panther IIA geared and supercharged radial engines. One of the licence-built Wapitis was modified to have an enclosed two-seat cabin. Bearing the civil registration 615, which was a contraction of PFA-J615, it is believed to have carried Service roundels and rudder stripes although it was allocated to the South African Civil Air Board for use by senior staff members. Knowing of the success of Wapiti 'policing operations' in Iraq, India and Afghanistan by RAF squadrons, contemporary reports record that, in 1933, the South African Government sent two SAAF Wapitis 'to deal with the disturbances in the native territory of Ovamboland'. This punitive expedition was led by Sir Pierre van Ryneveld, Director of Aviation, and although bombs were carried they were not dropped and the rebellious chief's activities were soon quelled.

Wapiti IV

During 1929–30 Westland's Project Office produced designs for a Wapiti, the fuselage of which embodied the long-missing extra 2 ft bay. It was intended for a submission by Westland to the Spanish Air Ministry and to meet its requirements was schemed with a 650 hp Hispano-Suiza 12Nbis driving a Fairey-Reed two-blade metal propeller of the type used on the Prince of Wales's aircraft. There is no evidence that a Wapiti, thus powered was built. According to contemporary reports, however, a Wapiti with the Mk.IV designation and embodying the long fuselage, divided-axle main undercarriage and a tailwheel was delivered to Marshal Chiang Hsui Liang in Mukden (now Shenyang), China.

The first Wapiti V with a cowled Armstrong Siddeley Panther II, levered-suspension undercarriage, tailwheel and message pick-up hook.

Wapiti V

The main structural differences between the Wapiti V and those variants which preceded it were the 2 ft extension to the fuselage, previously proposed for the IV, and a stronger redesigned undercarriage. The Wapiti V was powered by a 600 hp Jupiter VIIIFA engine and was designed as an army co-operation aircraft, for which role it carried a message pick-up hook hinged to the undercarriage cross-axle and operated by the gunner. These aircraft served with five RAF squadrons in India, those of No.5 Squadron still being flown until 1940.

Two Wapiti Vs received civil registrations; the prototype G-AAWA and VR-HAC, both receiving their C of A on 30 October, 1930. The first aircraft had a much modified and strengthened undercarriage; the main rubber-in-compression shock absorber legs were sharply raked forward with aft-mounted V-struts joined by a transverse strut and connected, via two pivoted trailing links, to the cross-axle, and a tailwheel replaced the skid. Power was provided by an uncowled 550 hp Armstrong Siddeley Panther IIA geared and supercharged radial.

Early in 1931 a trial installation of floats was made before G-AAWA was dismantled and crated for shipping to Buenos Aires to participate in a British Exhibition there. Harald Penrose, who was to fly the Wapiti in the Argentine and Uruguay both on wheels and floats, went to Hamble aerodrome where A V Roe & Company had a wooden slipway onto Southampton Water. There he had 20 minutes dual instruction with Louis Paget in an Avro 504N floatplane— possibly the company's well known G-EBKQ— before being sent off for an 80 minutes solo to learn all about taking-off and alighting. With this very limited floatplane experience backed up by a good deal of earlier yachting experience of wind and tide and general boat handling, he sailed in the P & O liner *Arlanza* for Buenos Aires. He was accompanied by a Westland fitter/mechanic and an assistant while the crated G-AAWA followed four days behind in a cargo ship. With the assistance of the manager of Motores Petter, the local Petters Ltd subsidiary, and a young interpreter permission was obtained from the Argentine Army Air Force for the air base at Lomas del Palomar, some 15 miles outside Buenos Aires, to be used to re-erect the Wapiti. It took approximately one

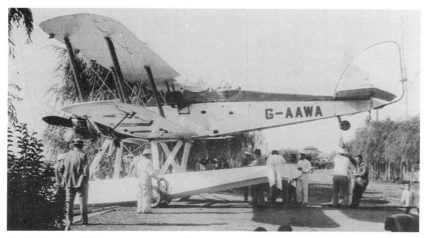
Wapiti V, G-AAWA, on floats at San Fernando air base in Argentina in connection with the 1931 British Exhibition in Buenos Aires.

month to move the crates from the ship's hold to Palomar, where there were no cranes or other engineering equipment, and to build and rig the aircraft ready for flight. In addition, there was the Westland part of the Petter stand in the Main Hall of the Exhibition in Palermo, a Buenos Aires suburb, to be prepared and manned.

A few days later the Prince of Wales was flown in to Palomar where he met General Medina, Minister of War and General Zuloaga, Commander-in-Chief of the Army Air Force. After reviewing a number of Argentine squadrons the Prince met British representatives and while talking to Penrose he turned to General Zuloaga and told him what a wonderful machine the Wapiti was and that he had one in the Royal Flight for his personal use. But the following day while returning from a flight over Buenos Aires Penrose had to make a forced landing in a field when the Panther engine failed. The cause was later found to be fuel vent pipes which had been fitted facing the wrong way. A number of Argentine pilots subsequently flew G-AAWA. During the following week Penrose flew the Wapiti across the 40-mile wide River Plate estuary to Montevideo in Uruguay for several presentations of the aircraft. Once back in the Argentine and after many vicissitudes the Wapiti was mounted on floats and taken to San Fernando naval base where several Argentine Navy pilots flew it. Although the Wapiti had been excluded from a special display of British deck-landing aircraft aboard HMS *Eagle*, which had arrived at Mar del Plata about 300 miles along the Plate estuary, Penrose was determined not to miss the chance to display the Wapiti floatplane to a great gathering of South American aviation personalities. Choosing his moment, during a brief pause in the display programme he roared low over the aircraft carrier's bows and along the flight deck, pulling up the Wapiti into a rocket loop over the bows before orbiting the ship in a vertical bank and departing. Following a final visit to Montevideo to allow Uruguayan Navy pilots to fly G-AAWA on floats, a number of Chilean and Peruvian pilots also flew the aircraft from the San Fernando base before the Westland party was summoned home at the end of the Exhibition. Unfortunately, this South American expedition did not result in orders as most countries in that region were already committed to French or US-built aircraft. The further history of Wapiti V G-AAWA is continued in the chapter dealing with the Westland Wallace. The second civil registered Wapiti V, VR-HAC, went to the Far East Aviation Co Ltd in Hong Kong for sale to China. By 1932 Westland and Bristol had jointly logged several hundreds of hours flight-testing engines in Wapitis; thus, when the Draco, a new direct fuel injection variant of the Pegasus, was ready for flight trials it was installed in J9728 and fitted with a four-blade metal propeller. However, development of this engine was abandoned.

A long-fuselage Wapiti V with modified undercarriage and used for trials of Bristol Draco direct-injection engine with a magnesium four-blade propeller. It has a message pick-up hook and light bomb carrier.

Wapiti VI

The Wapiti VI was an unarmed two-seat trainer built during 1932 to meet Specification 17/31 and powered by the Jupiter IXF. A total of sixteen are recorded as being built for service with a number of RAF and AAF squadrons.

Wapiti VII

The designation Wapiti VII was orginally given to a modified version of the Wapiti V G-AAWA, but as this differed so much from the other members of the Wapiti family it was given a new identity, first as the PV.6 prototype, P.6, then the Houston-Wallace G-ACBR and finally K3488, the Wallace I prototype.

156

A Wapiti VIII with a Panther IIA twin-row radial engine as fitted to four of these aircraft sold to China.

Wapiti VIII

Following the earlier sale of Wapitis to China, company reports indicated that a further four Wapitis with Panther IIA engines, with the modified cross-axle main undercarriage in which the oleo-pneumatic legs were in front with aft-mounted radius rods, were sold to China designated Wapiti VIII.

Description: Two-seat general purpose biplane. Mixed wood/metal and all-metal construction with metal and fabric covering.

Accommodation: Pilot and observer/gunner in open cockpit.

Powerplant: One 420 hp Bristol Jupiter VI nine-cylinder radial air-cooled direct-drive normally aspirated engine driving a 12 ft 6 in diameter two-blade wooden propeller (Prototype and I). One 480 hp Bristol Jupiter VIII or VIIIF nine-cylinder radial air-cooled geared and normally aspirated engine (IA, II and IIA). One 565 hp Bristol Jupiter XFA nine-cylinder radial air-cooled geared and supercharged engine. One 480 hp Armstrong Siddeley Jaguar VI fourteen-cylinder radial air-cooled geared and normally aspirated engine (III). One 600 hp Bristol Jupiter XFA nine-cylinder radial air-cooled geared and supercharged engine (V).One 550 hp Armstrong Siddeley Panther II fourteen-cylinder radial air-cooled geared and supercharged engine (V and VIII). One 525 hp Bristol Jupiter IXF nine-cylinder radial air-cooled geared normally aspirated engine (VI).

Armament: One fixed Vickers Mk.II .303 in forward-firing machine-gun mounted on the port fuselage side and one Lewis Mk.III .303 in machine-gun on a Scarff ring mounting in the rear cockpit. Combinations of 112 lb, 230/250 lb or 20 lb bombs to total of up to 580 lb on universal carriers under wings and fuselage.

Dimensions: Span 46 ft 5 in; length 31 ft 8 in (I, IA, II, IIA, V and VI), 34 ft 2 in (V and VIII); height 13 ft 0 in; wing area 488 sq ft.

Weights: Empty 3,330 lb; loaded 5,200 lb (I)
Empty 3,810 lb; loaded 5,410 lb (IIA)
Empty 3,260 lb; loaded 5,390 lb (III)
Empty 3,320 lb; loaded 5,410 lb (V)

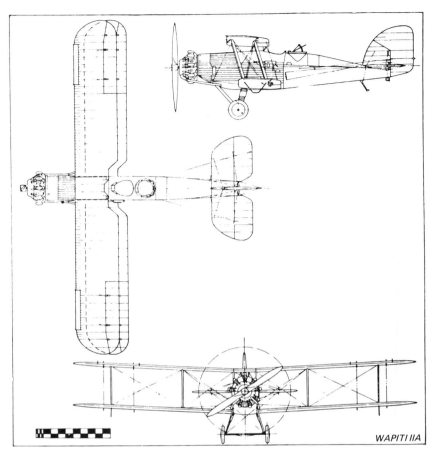

WAPITI IIA

Empty 3,400 lb; loaded 5,400 lb (VIII)
Empty 3,830 lb; loaded 5,650 lb (IIA floatplane)
Performance: Maximum speed at 5,000 ft 135 mph; cruising speed 110 mph;
    initial climb 1,150 ft/min; service ceiling 20,600 ft (IIA).
Production: A total of 558 Wapitis produced by Westland Aircraft Works,
    Yeovil, Somerset, during 1927–32 as follows:
1 prototype (1927)
28 Wapiti I production aircraft (1927–28)
28 Wapiti IA production aircraft (1929)
10 Wapiti II production aircraft (1931)
430 Wapiti IIA production aircraft (1929–32)
4 Wapiti III production aircraft (1931–32)
37 Wapiti V production aircraft (1930–31)
16 Wapiti VI production aircraft (1932)
4 Wapiti VIII production aircraft (1932)

The Witch, J8596. Its internal bomb bay position made necessary the outrigged main undercarriage units and their complex strut geometry.

Witch

The Air Ministry Specification 23/25 for a two-seat single-engined high-altitude day bomber to replace the Hawker Horsley, was also intended to establish standard bomb load requirements for the RAF. It was formulated with the earlier inadequacies of Specification 26/23 for a similar bomber in mind. The preferred—or proposed—engine was the Bristol Orion air-cooled radial which, basically, was a Jupiter VI designed against an Air Ministry contract to embody a turbo-charger developed by J Ellor at the Royal Aircraft Establishment. This exhaust-driven supercharger had been flight-tested during 1923–24 on a Jupiter III engine, driving a Leitner-Watts two-blade metal propeller, in the Bristol Seely transport which was used as a laboratory aircraft for Jupiter development. Although this power unit enabled the Seely to make climbs to some 23,000 ft from Farnborough when owned by the RAE, a number of problems were experienced with the turbo-charger. The exhaust gasses were collected in a small front ring and ducted to the turbo-charger on the rear engine cover. Unfortunately, when the turbo-charger was fitted to the Orion very many problems manifested themselves; the major difficulty was the maintenance of gas-tight exhaust joints, a close second being the difficulty of manufacturing turbine wheels and casings with rotor speeds of up to 30,000 rpm in exhaust temperatures at 650–700 deg C. Thus, development work on this engine was abandoned.

This failure by the Bristol company to provide the new engine did not come as too much of a surprise to Westland or to the three other manufacturers—Gloster, Handley Page and Hawker—who were building prototypes to meet Specification 23/25; thus Arthur Davenport decided to use the 420 hp Jupiter VI normally aspirated engine in the Witch prototype.

Without a doubt, of the contenders, Arthur Davenport's Witch was the most advanced concept. His enthusiasm for the parasol monoplane configuration, already evinced in the earlier design of light aircraft and a fighter—namely, the Widgeons and the Wizard—was continued into this exceedingly handsome bomber. But apart from its good external appearance the Witch embodied a number of advanced design features, including a metal fuselage. The fuselage was built up with square-section duralumin tube, with steel tube being used at all

The close coupled cockpits and the recessed Scarff ring mounting were features of the Witch.

load-carrying points, joined by tubular-rivetted flitch plates. An internal bomb bay was located in the front fuselage with four mechanically-operated doors. These could be opened by the weight of the released bombs in the event of mechanical failure. The tail unit was all metal with an adjustable tailplane operated through Westland patented trimming gear. Wood and metal formers gave shape to the fuselage top. The wide-track divided main undercarriage was carried on complex triangulated outriggers which provided ample space for the bomb bay in the fuselage. These consisted of the Westland oleo-pneumatic shock absorber strut with the axle, radius rod and a transverse member which were heavily braced to the top and bottom longerons. A 16 gal welded aluminium oil tank was mounted in the top of the front fuselage immediately behind the engine. The two close-coupled cockpits were located just aft of the wing trailing-edge. The wood and metal wings were sweptback 5 deg from the roots, the top wing being built in two sectons joined at the aircraft's centreline on two pairs of inverted-V struts.

The wing was built around two spruce box spars with spruce ribs and steel-tube struts in pairs superimposed and interbraced to support the deep spars against torsional loads. The leading edge was ply-covered back to the front spar, and inset horn-balanced tapering-chord ailerons were fitted. Two 95 gal welded aluminium fuel tanks were carried in the inboard section of the wings. Each

In spite of the multiplicity of wing and undercarriage bracing-struts, the Witch was a handsome aeroplane with a high top speed.

160

wing had two steel-tube struts bracing it from a mid-half-span point down to the outriggers; these struts had wooden streamlined fairings and were stiffened by vertical and horizontal fore and aft struts.

Apart from the front fuselage which had detachable metal panels, the top segment of the cockpits which had a curved plywood covering and the wing leading-edge, the entire airframe was fabric-covered. Fixed armament was a forward-firing Vickers .303 in machine-gun in the port upper side of the fuselage and a Lewis gun of the same calibre on a Scarff ring mounting in the rear cockpit. A 520 lb bomb, or combination of smaller bombs, could be carried on racks in the bomb bay. The observer could adopt a prone position for bomb aiming and had a sliding hatch in the cockpit floor.

Construction of the prototype Witch, J8596, was completed at Yeovil during late December 1927, the aircraft being taken to RAF Andover for final assembly during the following month. The first flight was made on 30 January, the pilot being Louis Paget who flew the Witch back to Yeovil. Quite early in the flight trials it was found that the aircraft was unstable in the aft c.g. condition; nevertheless, J8596 went to No.22 Squadron at A & AEE during April for performance evaluation trials more or less concurrently with the Hawker Harrier and Gloster Goring. In the event, none of the aircraft competing for an order to Specification 23/25 was selected by the Air Staff for production; this was largely because they either failed to meet its requirements

The Witch's uncovered airframe shows the oil tank, tailplane incidence control wheel, rear cockpit floor mounting and wing sweep angle.

or showed no evidence of a performance significantly above the aircraft already in service. However, the Witch had a useful life as an experimental aircraft, being fitted with a 480 hp Jupiter VIIIF geared normally aspirated engine to become the Witch Mk.II in August 1929. It ended its flying at the Home Aircraft Depot at RAF Henlow where it served with the Parachute Testing Section from October 1929 until sometime in 1931 when it was broken up.

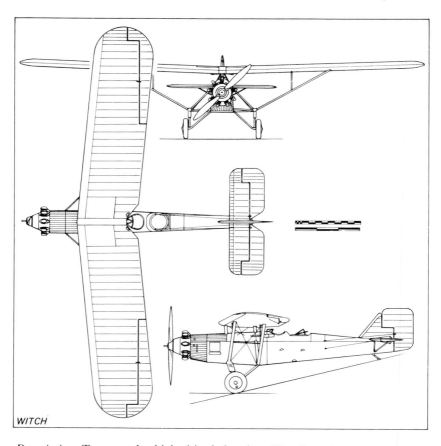

WITCH

Description: Two-seat day high-altitude bomber. Wood/metal construction with metal and fabric covering.

Accommodation: Pilot and observer in open cockpits.

Powerplant: One 420 hp Bristol Jupiter VI nine-cylinder, direct-drive normally aspirated air-cooled radial engine. One 480 hp Bristol Jupiter VIIIF nine-cylinder radial air-cooled geared and normally aspirated engine driving a 12 ft 3 in diameter two-blade wooden propeller. (Witch Mk.II).

Armament: One fixed synchronised Vickers .303 in forward-firing machine-gun in front cockpit coaming and one Lewis .303 in gun on a Scarff ring over the rear cockpit. One 520 lb bomb, or an equivalent weight of two or four smaller bombs in internal fuselage bay.

Dimensions: Span 61 ft 0 in; length 37 ft 8 in; height 11 ft 6 in; wing area 534 sq ft.

Weights: Empty 3,380 lb; loaded 6,050 lb.

Performance: Maximum speed at 10,000 ft 140 mph; landing speed 62 mph; sea level rate of climb 2,100 ft/min; service ceiling 19,000 ft.

Production: One Witch built by Westland Aircraft Works, Yeovil, Somerset, during 1926–27.

Pterodactyl IA and IB

During 1926 the Westland company became involved with a unique flying machine concept, the Pterodactyl. The early development story of this family of tailless aeroplanes and of their creator, Capt G T R Hill, is included in the Origin and History of the Company chapter of this book, to which reference should be made.

Following some confidence-building flights with his tailless glider in December 1924 and then with a powered version of it a year later, during early February 1926 Geoffrey Hill had written to Air Vice Marshal Sir Geoffrey Salmond, then Director General of Supply Research at the Air Ministry, with proposals for a high-performance single-seat fighter variant. This was to have been a pusher biplane, designated Pterodactyl Mk.II, and was followed by the Mk.III which was a two-seat tractor project with RAF 34 section wings. Although the Air Marshal's response received on 26 February was only marginally encouraging, several weeks later the Air Ministry showed that it was impressed by the performance and potential value of the home-built Pterodactyl Mk.I by giving Westland responsibility for further development work. Thus it was that, during the spring of 1926, Geoffrey Hill joined Westland to become the company's tailless aircraft designer. Seconded to him were Stanley T A Richards—known as 'Star' for very apparent reasons—who had been Handley Page's chief designer during 1921–24 and who became Hill's chief design draughtsman, and Herbert A Mettam who moved from Westland's technical office to add strength to this small but highly competent team which had access to all of Westland's resources, including the use of the company's 4 ft wind tunnel which was to prove invaluable.

Initially, all efforts were concentrated on improving the Mk.I's longitudinal control and to investigate the effects of increased wing loadings which would result from the higher performance of future Pterodactyl variants. In addition, some modifications were embodied in the airframe by Westland, but both Geoffrey Hill and the aeroplane spent some weeks at the RAE. Then, on Saturday, 3 July, 1926, the British public had the opportunity to see the Pterodactyl, for the first time. This was while leading the fly past of new types in the RAF Display at Hendon where it was flown by an RAE pilot Flt Lt J S Chick. In an all-over silver finish it carried the serial J8067. On its return to

The Pterodactyl I showing the main design features of the wing and its tip controllers, the underwing rudders and the outrigged balancing skids. It carries its 1926 RAF Display New Types Park number.

Yeovil two sets of reduced span 'controllers'—the name given to the rotating wingtip elevon control surfaces—were built for flight testing. Unfortunately, when Laurence Openshaw took off, the aircraft hit a small bump in the aerodrome surface and became prematurely airborne, the port wing dropped in spite of Openshaw's use of opposite control and spun round to hit the ground from some 10 ft. Both the wing and the undercarriage collapsed but Openshaw was uninjured due to the slow rate of descent. Another problem which arose

Suspended from the roof in an RAE hangar the Pterodactyl I's Cherub engine, tricycle undercarriage and overwing fins can be seen.

stemmed from the use of single-acting rudders on the underside of the wings. A single control wire from the rudder bar pulled the rudder to it's required control position but it relied upon airflow to return it to a neutral position. These foregoing, and other, design problems convinced the Air Ministry that to build either Hill's Pterodactyl Mk.II pusher or Mk.III tractor fighters would be too great an advance in a single stage; thus it required an interim design on which to investigate higher wing loadings and the use of the wingtip controllers at higher speeds. The stressing of the wing and the controllers, the responsibility of

Mettam and, at a later date, of Harald Penrose who joined the 'tailless team', was a highly complex task and this stage-by-stage advance was, wisely, adopted for the Pterodactyl's flight development.

The Pterodactyl IA's uncovered M-shaped wing shows the operating torque tubes for the tip control surfaces, and the tricycle undercarriage.

The interim aircraft, which was designated the Westland-Hill Pterodactyl Mk.IA, around which Specification 23/26 was written, was markedly different in external appearance from its predecessor and was a much more refined design. The elongated egg-shaped semi-monocoque fuselage with two side-by-side seats in its open cockpit, was built up from double-skinned carvel-style diagonal spruce planking with a balsa core on ash former rings. Behind the cockpit the cylindrical fuel and oil tanks sat on a wooden platform in the top of the fuselage and the fuselage terminated in two duralumin and two steel tubular struts carrying a duralumin mounting ring for the 34 hp Bristol Cherub pusher engine and its tiny 6 ft diameter propeller. The main undercarriage was a single telescopic leg and wheel strutted and wire-braced to the fuselage and strut-braced to the wings. Built mainly of spruce, the wings, which had no dihedral and R & M's No.4 aerofoil section, were of M-planform in which the leading edge was cut back at the roots to join the fuselage instead of continuing as a straight line. The entire leading edge of the fixed inboard section of the wing, spanning 30 ft, was ply-covered and, with the I-section rear spar which was located at about the three-quarters chord position, formed the two main load-carrying members. The wing root was comparatively thin with the section thickening to a maximum some four feet from the root then tapering to the tips of the controllers. Fourteen slender girder-type ribs were used in each fixed wing portion with the fifth from the root, which was the point of maximum thickness, having a solid web with lightening holes for extra rigidity. The 7 ft span TP3 aerofoil section outboard ends of the wings were the rotating 'controllers' which had a tubular spar and, like modern elevons, could be moved differentially to act as ailerons or in unison as elevators. They were moved through a long duralumin torque-tube carried inside the wing and operated by a system of push rods and bell cranks attached to the control column. A small fence was fitted to the outboard rib of each fixed wing section. An unusual feature was the use of horizontal 'electroscopic' rudders so called because they were split flaps occupying the outboard half of the fixed wing trailing edge. They also served as airbrakes when opened above and below the trailing edge. A novel spring loading device gave variable trimming in pitch. Two small spatted balancing wheels were carried on trailing outriggers attached to the underside of the wing at mid-span and in line with the trailing edge.

Rope-restrained, as if for engine running, the Pterodactyl IA's wooden monocoque fuselage showing the cylindrical fuel tank and the pusher Cherub engine.

The Pterodactyl's tricycle undercarriage, although apparently fairly basic in design, had required a good deal of testing. A special mobile test rig was built using the frame and front wheel of a bicycle. Designed—and probably built—by Stanley Seager, one of Hill's small staff, this device had two pieces of wood bolted to the frame and carrying a seat in front of the handlebars, which were reversed. A substantial 2 in by 4 in transverse wooden beam was mounted on three struts attached to the rear frame from which the back wheel had been removed. Two curved skids were fixed to the ends of the beam and balanced this do-it-yourself device which was towed behind a car to check the general handling characteristics and loads on the steering gear.

During the first week of June 1928, the Pterodactyl Mk.IA was dismantled and taken by road to RAF Andover where it was re-assembled in readiness for its first flight. In an all-over silver finish, bearing RAF wing roundels and the serial J9251 plus the black silhouette of a pterodactyl in flight on each side of the nose, it was flown by Louis Paget on 13 or 14 June. A day or so later it was flown

167

to Yeovil for some extensive test flying by Paget, Flt Lt F J Brunton and Harald Penrose. As experience on type grew the need for more power became apparent and it was decided to replace the 34 hp Cherub with a 70 hp Armstrong Siddeley Genet five-cylinder radial engine driving a Watts two-blade wooden propeller. With this heavier engine and the 200 sq ft M-plan wing the loading was 7 lb/sq ft which met the programme's design object. With this engine change the designation became Pterodactyl Mk.IB.

A bicycle, some timber and much ingenuity produced this mobile test rig for the Pterodactyl's tricycle undercarriage.

With all three pilots taking part in the test flying of the Pterodactyl, the Mk.IA had often been bumped into the air at a steep angle and insufficient flying speed by the Yeovil aerodrome's undulating surface. Because of the poor pitch damping of tailless aircraft it had flown on in a series of long-period oscillations in pitch, continually hunting above and below the level attitude. This was made worse by independent oscillations of the controllers. During September 1928 J9251 went to the RAE for trials where it was considered that the 'electroscopic' flaps required a lot of effort to operate; thus, a new balanced design was incorporated which resembled the split flap but with the leading edge moving backward along guides with pivoted arms holding the surface at about mid-chord. These required a much smaller operating force. In order to assist the pilots in controlling the Pterodactyl a variable-ratio gear system was embodied in the control system. Several months into the test programme Louis Paget was flying the aircraft with Penrose in the second seat beside him. Without warning the gear selection lever in the cockpit slipped from the low to the high position,

The Pterodactyl IA had a remarkably small frontal area. Louis Paget is in the starboard pilot's seat.

causing the aircraft to lurch forward into an unexpected dive. Paget managed to regain control and made a perfect landing, but the undercarriage collapsed, sending the Pterodactyl sliding along on its fuselage. When J9251 was rebuilt it retained its single mainwheel; however, fairly soon afterwards, a much stronger unit with two wheels in tandem was embodied which provided a much smoother ride. The front wheel was steerable and the wheel beam was pivoted on the oleo-pneumatic leg to cope with uneven landing surfaces. With the fitting of this new main undercarriage the two outrigger balancing wheels were replaced by skids and the aircraft's designation was changed again to become the Mk.IC. It was then scheduled to appear in the 11th RAF Display at Hendon on 28 June, 1930, but due to problems with the Genet engine the Cherub-powered Hill Pterodactyl flew in its place. With the Avro-built C.19 Autogiro and the Handley Page Gugnunc they formed a most bizarre trio. Another modification test-flown was a pair of thin section controllers reduced in span to 5 ft 10 in which increased the rate of roll. It is not known whether these were fitted when J9251 paid a brief visit to the RAE for a display on 14 June, 1930. Without doubt this aeroplane, which was last flown at Farnborough on 31 July, 1930, provided a great amount of information and engineering and flying experience to Geoffrey Hill's small team which was invaluable to Westland's overall tailless aircraft development programme. It is now in the Science Museum, South Kensington.

Powered by a Genet radial, the Pterodactyl IB, serialled J9251, had a strengthened main undercarriage with spatted balancing wheels, and carried RAF markings.

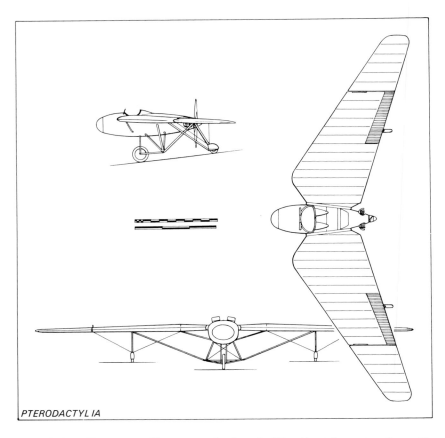

PTERODACTYL IA

Description: Two-seat tailless research aircraft. Wood/metal construction with fabric, wood and metal covering.

Accommodation: Pilot and passenger in open cockpit.

Powerplant: One 34 hp Bristol Cherub III two-cylinder horizontally-opposed air-cooled direct-drive normally-aspirated engine driving a 6 ft diameter two-blade wooden propeller. (IA). One 70 hp Armstrong Siddeley Genet five-cylinder radial air-cooled direct-drive normally-aspirated engine. (IB and IC)

Dimensions: Span 45 ft 6 in; length 17 ft 0 in; height 6 ft 8 in; wing area 200 sq ft.

Weights: Empty 900 lb; loaded 1,080 lb (Cherub III); 1,280 lb (Genet).

Performance: Maximum speed 70 mph.

Production: One prototype Pterodactyl Mk.IA built by Westland Aircraft Works, Yeovil, Somerset, during 1926–28.

170

The Mercury-engined Interceptor with small fin and rudder on Westland's compass base. Note ring-and-bead and Aldis sights, flush oil cooler and undercarriage design.

Interceptor

During the decade which followed the end of the 1914–18 War the Air Ministry's operational requirements experts and strategists were of the opinion that, in any future war, RAF Fighter Command's principal task would be to intercept and destroy enemy bomber formations attacking the British Isles. It was their deliberations and conclusions which led to the issue of Specification F.20/27 covering the requirement for a single-seat day interceptor fighter, able to engage in the shortest possible time an enemy formation passing overhead at 20,000 ft at 150 mph—this being the estimated average speed to be attained by the next generation of bombers. Manoevrability at altitude, a high rate of climb and a good all-round view were emphasised; however, the armament remained at a pair of enclosed Vickers .303 in machine-guns. The choice of engine fell on the 440 hp Bristol Mercury IIA, a geared, supercharged and reduced-stroke variant of the earlier Jupiter. Designed by Roy Fedden, Bristol's chief engineer, it featured a much reduced frontal area compared with the Jupiter, which stemmed from the shorter stroke and sloping heads of the cylinder's housing inclined overhead valves, a shape which gave them the name 'penthouse' heads. Air Vice Marshal Hugh Dowding, Director of Training at the Air Ministry, had shown great interest in the engine after it had first run in the spring of 1925 and, largely at his instigation, a short-life uprated version delivering 950 hp had been fitted in the ill-fated Short-Bristow Crusader racing floatplane which had crashed during practice flying for the 1927 Schneider Trophy Contest in Venice. In addition to this interest from 'on high', Fedden had done some very thorough lobbying, emphasising that a supercharged radial should be included among the requirements as it took less time to warm up than a liquid-cooled engine and so reduced take-off time. While, initially, the Mercury engine was written into the

Specification and a number of manufacturers had already built or submitted prototypes with this power unit, the Air Ministry later realised that only a liquid-cooled inline engine could provide the high performance required of a successful F.20/27 contender.

Nose and tail modifications to Interceptor J9124 included redesigned engine installation, extra gun blast louvres, wing-root slats and larger fin and rudder.

The issue of this specification attracted submissions from most of industry's fighter manufacturers; the Westland response to F.20/27 was a braced low-wing all-metal monoplane with a rather rotund fuselage having a basic rectangular structure built up with square-section duralumin tube with the joints formed by the company's flitch plate and tubular rivet method. Shape was provided by conventional formers and stringers. A small centre-section was built integrally with the fuselage. The tail unit, with a horn-balanced rudder, was all-metal with a strut-braced tailplane. While initially both fixed and movable tail surfaces were fabric covered, it is believed that a metal-skinned tailplane, which was ground-adjustable for incidence, was fitted at one stage of the Interceptor's test programme. Aft of the cockpit, which had a long faired headrest, the fuselage was also fabric-covered with removable metal panels being fitted to the forward section. The engine was carried on a metal mounting ring, had beaded-metal removable cowling panels with apertures through which the cylinder heads protruded, and drove a 10 ft 7 in diameter two-blade wooden propeller. Blast from the guns was released through six louvres in the metal panels on the fuselage side. A 41 gal main fuel tank and a 23 gal gravity tank were mounted in the front fuselage section. The main undercarriage which was attached to the centre-section, was of the levered-suspension type; the rear element was a pair of rigid V-struts joined by a cross-bar at the bottom, and the forward element was two oleo-pneumatic shock-absorbing legs of Westland patented design with a cross-axle linked by two levers to the V-struts. An unusual feature was the fitting of 12 in Bendix-Perrot wheel brakes, operating differentially through the rudder bar and controlled by a hand lever on the control column. The constant-chord wings were of all-metal construction with fabric covering, had long-span inset Frise ailerons and large cut-outs in the root trailing-edges to provide the pilot with a view vertically downward. The wing spars were pin-jointed horizontally at the root end to the centre-section so that the dihedral angle could be easily adjusted, and were wire-braced, having two duplicated landing wires, with tie-rods, attached to the spars and the top longeron and flying wires to the V-struts of the undercarriage. While Davenport's choice of a monoplane configuration was applauded, this method of wire-bracing was criticised by the pilots who believed that if the undercarriage was damaged the wing structure would collapse; there were others who pointed at the robust undercarriage units and discounted this theory. Certainly Davenport had embodied a number of advanced and unusual features in the Interceptor which included a gun-heating system using exhaust gas, adjustable seat and rudder pedals, plus an oxygen system, W/T equipment and a door in the cockpit metal decking to provide easier entry and exit for the pilot when wearing a parachute. There was, too, the total enclosure of the two Vickers guns within the fuselage from where they fired through spaces between the cylinders and two ports in the tapered cowling over the engine's reduction gear. Both an Aldis and a ring-and-bead sight were fitted.

The first flight, for which Louis Paget was the pilot, was made during August 1928 at Yeovil and at once the Interceptor, serialled J9124, proved to be easy to fly with precise longitudinal control during landing. However, problems quickly

The Interceptor's undercarriage and wing bracing which caused concern to some pilots. Note slat levers, gun port, 'nicked' ring cowl and case and link chutes.

became apparent with Paget reporting that it 'behaved most curiously' in loops and tight turns and discovering that at high incidences the tail vibrated with loss of longitudinal control. The 'curious' behaviour consisted of a series of inadvertent rolls off the top each time Paget essayed a loop and he described the aircraft as a 'flying corkscrew'. During the following weeks while flight testing went on, first the tailskid struts were enclosed with metal panels to create a small ventral fin, then a larger tailplane was fitted. A series of tests in Westland's own wind-tunnel with model wings and tail units showed that there was turbulence at the wing root which was to blame. While the work in the wind-tunnel was in hand it was decided to remove the Mercury IIA,which was lacking in power, and substitute an uncowled 480 hp Mercury IIIA with a small ring covering the crankcase. In addition small slats were embodied in the inboard leading-edge of the wing, but these proved ineffective and disconcerting because of the jerk which was felt in the airframe when they opened. Ultimately, the wind-tunnel tests showed that a simple wing root trailing-edge fillet would straighten out the turbulent airflow, and an air test showed this to be the answer to the inadvertent rolls during a loop. When spinning trials began the Interceptor was found to be slow to recover, and so a taller fin and rudder with increased area were fitted. Because the performance of the Interceptor was still comparatively low, even with the Jupiter engine, advice was sought from Bristol Aeroplane's engine company on the use of the US Townend cowling. With one of these recently devised engine cowling rings, J9124 was finally cleared for evaluation at the A & AEE and was flown to there during late May 1929.

The Jupiter-engined Interceptor with a Townend ring, seen at Yeovil on 22 June, 1931.

By this time several other F.20/27 contenders had been flight tested and it was clear that their performance was superior to that of the Westland Interceptor; moreover, the F.20/27 Specification had been re-written to include a requirement for an inline engine, so further development of the Interceptor was abandoned. Some further exploratory flying with a 420 hp Jupiter VII engine fitted with the Townend ring was done when the Interceptor returned to Yeovil. It was during a dive from high altitude that the forward bracing struts of the tailplane failed and Louis Paget was fortunate to escape with his life, being able

174

to recover and land without more structural damage. The Interceptor went to the RAE at Farnborough on 21 August, 1931, where it was flown on engine and other development trials until 14 March, 1933.

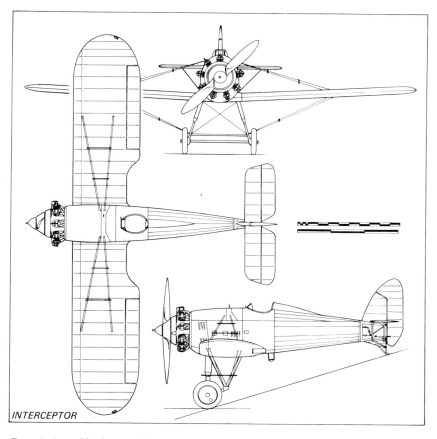

INTERCEPTOR

Description: Single-seat high-altitude monoplane fighter. Metal construction with fabric and metal covering.

Accommodation: Pilot in open cockpit.

Powerplant: One 440 hp Bristol Mercury IIA nine-cylinder radial air-cooled geared and normally-aspirated engine driving a 10 ft 7 in diameter two-blade wooden propeller. One 480 hp Bristol Mercury III nine-cylinder radial air-cooled geared and normally-aspirated engine. One 420 hp Bristol Jupiter VII nine-cylinder geared, normally-aspirated air-cooled radial engine.

Armament: Two fixed synchronised Vickers .303 in forward-firing machine-guns carried inside the fuselage sides.

Dimensions: Span 38 ft 0 in; length 25 ft 4½ in; height 9 ft 8 in; wing area 214 sq ft.

Weights: Empty 2,350 lb; loaded 3,325 lb.

Performance: Maximum speed at 10,000 ft 192 mph; landing speed 59 mph.

Production: One Interceptor built by Westland Aircraft Works, Yeovil, Somerset, during 1928–29.

The first Westland IV with ADC Cirrus III engines in February 1929.

Westland IV and Wessex

By 1928 the sum total of Westland's experience in the business of designing and producing civil aircraft amounted to eight Limousines, no more than nine Widgeons and a brace of diminutive Woodpigeons: but this was no barrier to Robert Bruce and Arthur Davenport when they began the design of a new civil transport.

It was to meet the need for a low-powered 'feeder-liner' type of aircraft that, in 1928, Westland re-launched itself into the commercial aircraft field. The name of the aircraft which was the vehicle for this move was the Westland IV, which may have seemed a bit puzzling for it was not the fourth Westland type; the answer lies in the fact that, initially, the design was officially talked of as 'the Limousine IV', but as soon as it took shape on the drawing board and in the minds of the designers it quickly acquired its own identity.

The basic design concept combined Davenport's philosophy of 'a monoplane is always better than a biplane', with that of many other aircraft engineers who believed that the ideal number of engines for a transport aircraft was 'more than two and less than four'. This configuration particularly suited the Westland IV and the Wessex which was a type intended for domestic routes where the volume of traffic was not sufficient to justify the use of a larger aircraft but where the safety and reliability of a three-engined aircraft was required. The result of his deliberations took shape as a three-engined six-seat high-wing monoplane, and powered by three 95 hp Aircraft Disposal Company Cirrus III inline engines, one in the fuselage nose and the other two mounted one on top of each of the out-rigged main undercarriage units. Three engines were chosen to provide greater in-service reliability and the ability to maintain height with a full

176

load in a one-engine-out condition; their exact position in the airframe ensured that their propeller discs did not overlap to cause turbulence and loss of propulsive efficiency. Davenport also believed that by placing the two outboard engines on the main undercarriage outriggers, braced to the top and bottom longerons, rather than on the wing, the whole of the wing surface provided uninterrupted lift; it also placed them at a more convenient height for installation, removal and servicing.

Three 105 hp Cirrus Hermes I engines initially powered the second Westland IV. Fuel gauge tubes, rear view mirror, wind-driven generator and navigation lights are visible.

Construction of the prototype Westland IV, G-EBXK, began during the autumn of 1928 with the work moving ahead very rapidly. The square-section fuselage was built up around spruce longerons and ash frames which were internally wire-braced and fabric covered. The wings employed wooden box spars with spruce flanges and three-ply webs, and spruce ribs in a Warren girder configuration. They were of RAF 34 section which was chosen because of its small centre of pressure movement which helped to make the Westland IV a very stable aircraft. The high wing was braced to the main undercarriage outriggers and the fuselage by a pair of spruce struts of streamlined section. The wooden tailplane was mounted on the top surface of the rear fuselage and was braced to it by a pair of struts each side. For expediency, Davenport decided to use a standard Wapiti rudder, purely as an experiment, but as it proved successful in flight testing, it was retained. The wide 15 ft track non-retractable undercarriage had Palmer wheels and tyres with small mudguards but, surprisingly, in an era when hydraulic shock absorbers were coming into use, this new aeroplane was fitted with bungee-type shock absorbers and was, possibly, the last multi-engined civil transport to have this design feature. As far as can be established brakes were not fitted, a tailskid being used to effect an element of braking. The flight control system was by conventional cables, bell-cranks and push rods. The rudder and elevator control cables ran outside and below the crew and passenger cabins before entering the rear baggage compartment. They emerged again from the rear fuselage in front of the tailplane leading edge, the elevator cables from the fuselage sides near the top and the rudder cables from a shrouded aperture in the fuselage top surface. Two 50 gal fuel tanks were carried in the wing roots with a gravity feed system made possible by the 'head' provided by the high positioning of the tanks.

Construction of the prototype Westland IV, was completed early in 1929, the first flight being made by Louis Paget on 21 February. It was soon discovered that, although wind-tunnel work had indicated that the Westland IV had adequate stability in all axes, longitudinal stability was lacking. The remedy was to increase the tailplane area with plywood, and this was quickly done.

Ordered by Wilson Airways of Nairobi with Cirrus Hermes engines, VP-KAD was to be fitted with Genet Major Is when the order was cancelled.

While work on G-EBXK was in hand, a second Westland IV, G-AAGW, was begun and was built almost in parallel being completed in time for exhibition in the July 1929 Olympia Aero Show. G-AAGW differed from its predecessor by having a Warren girder rear fuselage structure built from square-section duralumin tubing joined by tubular-rivetted flitch plates, internally wire-braced and fabric-covered. It was also fitted with more powerful 105 hp Cirrus Hermes I engines produced by the Hermes Engine Co which had taken over the Cirrus engines from the Aircraft Disposal Company. This change of engine produced a much more neatly cowled installation. In spite of a 600 lb increase in all-up weight to 5,500 lb the performance of this second Westland IV remained the same as that of the prototype. A minor change was to the fuel guages which, operating on the U-tube principle, were mounted externally on the wing leading-edge each side of the crew's cabin. When the Olympia Aero Show closed, G-AAGW was moved to Croydon where it was put into service with Imperial Airways' private hire section on charter flights.

In April 1929 G-EBXK was delivered to the A & AEE Martlesham Heath for performance and general handling trials. While there and being flown on fuel consumption trials by Flt Lt S N Webster, who had achieved fame by winning the 1927 Schneider Trophy Contest in a Supermarine S.5 in Venice, this prototype was involved in an 'incident'. With two passengers plus lead weights and shot bags to represent an additional two passengers, the Westland IV was fully laden. On take-off the aircraft's wheels hit one of Martlesham's many undulations with a resounding bang and sheared through a pin securing the oleo-strut of the port main undercarriage leg to its engine mounting. The strut swung down and under the fuselage where it remained suspended by its radius

Westland IV G-EBXK was brought up to Wessex standard and re-engined with Genet Major Is. (*Courtesy Mike Hooks*)

rod. Ground staff held up wheels in an effort to advise 'Webby' what had happened, but he had already noticed the absence of the wheel. As a one wheeled landing with a full load was out of the question, the passengers dumped all the ballast when the aircraft flew over a suitable part of the Heath. After debating whether to put down in the sea or attempt a landing back at Martlesham, Webster opted for the latter and flew around to burn up fuel. He then made a normal approach, sideslipping just before making gentle contact between the sound wheel and the grass. This caused the damaged wheel to move up again into the engine mounting and the aircraft heeled over, the wingtip scraping the ground with very little damage being caused.

Meanwhile, Westland had received an order from Wilson Airways Ltd in Nairobi for a Westland IV and had begun to build this aircraft, provisionally registered G-AAJI, which had had the Kenyan registration VP-KAD, allocated to it. It was intended to power this aircraft with the Cirrus Hermes I engines but, when Wilson Airways cancelled its order, Westland prepared to make some fundamental changes to the design. Drawing on the experience of some intensive flight testing and in-service flying with the Westland IV, it was decided to abandon the use of inline engines, to use Armstrong Siddeley Genet Major

Provisionally G-AAJI, then VP-KAD, this Westland IV airframe temporarily carried P-1 when re-engined with Genet Major Is to become Wessex G-ABAJ.

179

radials instead, to modify and refine some of the systems and structure and to offer this improved variant with the name Wessex. Accordingly, G-AAJI was completed to this new standard as the prototype Wessex, and re-registered G-ABAJ. The use of these uncowled radial engines enabled nacelles of an improved aerodynamic shape to be used. These were strut-braced to the wing's main spar to produce a much more rigid installation.

A modified flight control system was fitted in which push rods replaced the earlier cables, the rudder and elevator control rods passing externally under the four-passenger cabin, then upwards through the rear fuselage to a pair of rocking levers in its top surface where they continued externally to the rudder and elevators. The rudder was connected by two cables to a castoring and steerable tailwheel, while the main undercarriage was fitted with Bendix-Perrot wheels and brakes. Control surfaces were of metal construction using duralumin tube spars with pressed aluminium ribs, all fabric covered. Handley Page slots were offered as an optional extra. The crew's cabin was weatherproofed and modified to provide an improved field of view, particularly upwards, and had a two-piece vee-windscreen with a direct-vision panel, larger sliding side panels and a hinged roof for emergency exit. The throttles, tailplane trimmer and brake lever were on the pilot's left with the rudder bias handle on his right. Night flying equipment, which included navigation lights, Holt flares and a downward identification lamp, was offered as an optional extra. The passenger cabin windows and portside door plus the separate door to the luggage compartment were similar to those of the Westland IV, but the interior finish was better with a Rexine lining. A clock, air speed indicator and altimeter were also mounted on the cabin's forward bulkhead.

OO-AGE, the third of four Wessex supplied to SABENA, on a test flight over Somerset in 1931.

In this form the Wessex was offered to air service operators as a well-tried, practical aircraft suitable for feeder-liner work with passengers or freight, as a night mail carrier or an air taxi, and also to private owners who wanted something 'more ambitious then a single or two-seat aircraft'. To promote sales G-EBXK was brought up to this standard and used as a demonstrator aircraft until 1935.

The first flight with G-ABAJ came in May 1930 and after some proving flights it was re-registerd OO-AGC to become the first of four Wessex used by

SABENA, the Belgian national airline, on its European services; the others were OO-AGD, 'AGE and 'AGF.

During 1930 G-ABEG, a company demonstrator, was used for a ten-weeks tour of 22 civil aerodromes in the United Kingdom serving, it was claimed, 60 cities. A total of 6,200 miles was flown and only twice did the aircraft arrive late—on both occasions due to fog. Aerodromes visited included Norwich, Hull, Leeds, Newcastle, Belfast, Manchester, Nottingham, Northampton, Doncaster, Halifax, Huddersfield, South Shields, Dewsbury, Birkenhead, Salford and Ipswich. Over a hundred leading businessmen and representatives of the civic authorities were flown. The tour was managed by Capt H M Talbot Lehmann who also shared the flying with Louis Paget and F J Brunton, the two Westland test pilots.

With the general redesign of the Wessex well established, Arthur Davenport sought improved performance, particularly at take-off. At Armstrong Siddeley Motors in 1931, Harry Cantrill, the chief designer, had produced a new variant of the Genet Major engine with seven, instead of five, cylinders. Designated the Genet Major IA it delivered 140 hp and soon replaced the earlier variants in G-ABEG, which became known as the high performance Wessex. Although the all-up weight of the aircraft had increased by 550 lb to reach 6,300 lb the wing and span loading were still low with an improved take-off and an increase of 80 ft per minute in the initial climb rate.

On 1 June, 1931, G-ABEG was chartered by the Sheffield and South Yorks Navigation Co to undertake an aerial survey of work on one of its canal routes. A more newsworthy role for G-ABEG came on 15 July when it was used by His Royal Highness the Prince of Wales to fly to Roborough, near Plymouth, for the opening of the aerodrome there. On 18 August this same Wessex, piloted by Flt Lt E H Fielden, flew from Windsor Great Park to Le Bourget, Paris, again with the Prince of Wales as principal passenger. It was escorted by two RAF flying-boats from Lympne to the French coast. Arriving at Le Bourget at about 1 p.m., the aircraft was refuelled and took-off an hour later for Bayonne. It landed at Tours, en route, and arrived at Parmes aerodrome, near Bayonne, at 8.30 p.m. G-ABEG was subsequently bought by Imperial Airways, joining G-AAGW which had had Genet Major IA engines fitted, and G-ACHI, another 'high performance' Wessex. During November–December 1931 wind-tunnel tests were run on models of the Westland IV with Wragg flaps and with wings having a reduced chord at the roots, and with several windscreens and

G-AAGW, the second Westland IV re-engined with Genet Major IAs to become a Wessex and to fly with Imperial Airways.

181

cabin tops of different profiles.

As early as 1922 railway companies had shown an interest in the use of air transport to further their business, but their progress towards becoming transport companies in a wider sense was not achieved until 1929 when a Bill, presented in Parliament, was passed which granted them powers to operate air services. Thus, on 11 April, 1933, the Great Western Railway, which had chartered G-AAGW from Imperial Airways, began a twice-daily service on the Plymouth–Teignmouth–Cardiff route. Gordon Olley was the chief pilot and the Wessex was finished in the GWR chocolate and cream colours with the cabin upholstered in the style of a first class railway carriage. The flight was more than three hours faster than the train journey because of the direct route across the Bristol Channel. However, load factors were not up to expectations and in mid-May the fares were reduced by some 30 per cent. The Postmaster General then approved a scheme by which the aircraft could carry mail handed in at any GWR air booking office where a threepence (1p) surcharge stamp would be put on each item. On 21 May the route was extended from Cardiff to Castle Bromwich, Birmingham, until the service ceased on 30 September, 1933.

During the following year G-ABEG went on charter to the Iraq Petroleum Transport Co at Baghdad, ending its days in a disastrous forced landing in 1936 at Chirindu, Northern Rhodesia while serving with Rhodesia and Nyasaland Airways. G-AAGW and 'CHI went to Air Pilots Training Ltd at Hamble where they were used in the radio and navigation training role until they were withdrawn from use

This Wessex, G-ACIJ, has fully cowled Genet Major IA seven-cylinder radials.

and scrapped on 16 August and 23 May, 1940, respectively. On 6 May, 1935, Cobham Air Routes began flying three Wessex between Portsmouth, Christchurch and Guernsey. These were ex-SABENA aircraft OO-AGC, 'AGE and 'AGF, the first reverting to its original British registration G-ABAJ and the others becoming G-ADEW and G-ADFZ respectively. The first of this pair suffered a starboard engine failure some 30 minutes after taking off from Guernsey, limping back to make a forced alighting in the sea off The Needles, Isle of Wight, then sinking. Conversely, on 28 September, 1932, a Wessex had taken-off from Romford when, at 150 ft above a small wood on the aerodrome boundary, the starboard engine seized. The Wessex flew on to Heston on two engines and made a safe landing. 'If we had been in a single-engined or twin-engined job they would still be picking the bits of us from out of the branches' one passenger is reported as saying. This accident to G-ADEW caused Cobham to abandon this service and to sell the remaining two Wessex, G-ABAJ becoming a Portsmouth–Ryde ferry, and 'DFZ moving to National Aviation Day Displays for pleasure flying. In 1936 Trafalgar Advertising Co bought these two Wessex, fitted them with battery-powered neon tube advertisements beneath the wings and flew them at night over London.

His Royal Highness, Edward Prince of Wales inspects the Wessex destined for service with Portsmouth, Southsea and Isle of Wight Aviation. The fuselage was pale blue with buff panels, dark blue trim and silver wings. It had an enlarged fin and a tailwheel.

Only two other Wessex were built; G-ABVB was a special aircraft with strengthened wings employing square duralumin tubes in place of the normal wooden structure, and with accommodation for eight passengers being provided by reducing the baggage space; in addition, a larger rudder and stronger main undercarriage were fitted and the crew's cabin was raised to give an improved all-round view. It was put into service by Portsmouth, Southsea and Isle of Wight Aviation on the Shoreham–Portsmouth–Ryde ferry route. The last Wessex to be built, G-ACIJ, was a standard aircraft but with a metal skinned forward fuselage. It was fitted out for VIP flying and was delivered by air to the Egyptian Air Force, to be serialled W202, leaving Heston during March 1934.

Description: Four-passenger commercial high-wing monoplane. Wood or wood and metal construction with fabric and wood covering.

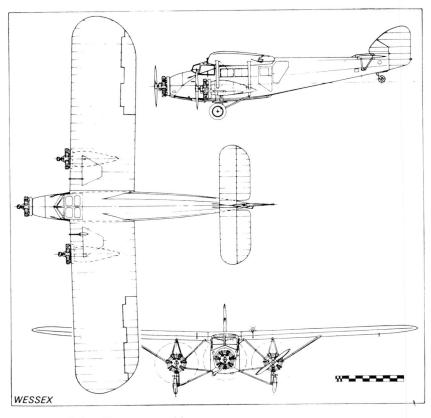

WESSEX

Accommodation: Two crew and four passengers.

Powerplant: Three 95 hp ADC Cirrus III four-cylinder inline air-cooled direct-drive normally-aspirated engines driving 6 ft 4 in diameter two-blade wooden propellers (Westland IV). Three 105 hp ADC Cirrus Hermes I four-cylinder inline air-cooled direct-drive normally-aspirated engines driving 6 ft 4 in diameter two-blade wooden propellers. (Westland IV). Three 105 hp Armstrong Siddeley Genet Major five-cylinder radial air-cooled direct-drive normally-aspirated engines driving 6 ft 4 in diameter two-blade wooden propellers (Wessex). Three 140 hp Armstrong Siddeley Genet Major IA seven-cylinder radial air-cooled direct-drive normally aspirated engines driving 6 ft 6 in diameter two-blade wooden propellers (Wessex).

Dimensions: Span 57 ft 6 in; length 38 ft 0 in; height 9 ft 6 in; wing area 490 sq ft.

Weights:	Westland IV	Wessex		
		Genet Major	Genet Major IA	G-ABVB
Empty	3,150 lb	3,810 lb	3,981 lb	3,930 lb
Loaded	5,500 lb*	5,750 lb	6,300 lb	6,300 lb

*G-EBXK 4,900 lb

Performance:

Maximum speed	108 mph	118 mph	122 mph	122 mph
Cruising speed	100 mph	100 mph	100 mph	108 mph
Sea level climb	520 ft/min	600 ft/min	680 ft/min	610 ft/min
Ceiling	12,000 ft	12,300 ft	14,900 ft	13,700 ft
Range	525 miles	520 miles	420 miles	340 miles

Production: A total of ten Westland IV and Wessex built by Westland Aircraft Works, Yeovil, during 1928–33 as follows:
Two Westland IV
Eight Wessex production aircraft.

C.O.W. Gun Fighter

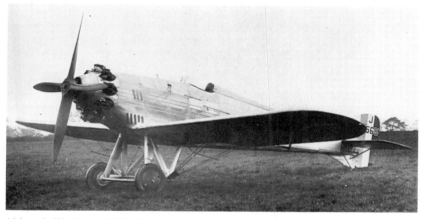

Although Westland's F.29/27 C.O.W. Gun Fighter shows a marked similarity to the earlier F.20/27 Interceptor, its longer fuselage and Mercury IIIA installation identify this unarmed aircraft.

During the middle of the 1920s the Air Ministry had recognised that, as bomber development and performance had suddenly accelerated with the introduction into RAF squadron service of the Fairey Fox, much heavier firepower would be required from future fighter designs. No longer should fighters go into battle with virtually the same one or two machine-guns which had been standard since about 1915. The issue of Specification 4/24 for a multi-seat twin-engined fighter armed with two shell-firing guns had resulted in the Bristol Bagshot and Westland's big Westbury, neither of which was ordered. But the Air Ministry's interest in increasing the armament of fighters in no way waned; moreover, it was focussing again on the big 37 mm Coventry Ordnance Works piece—the C.O.W. gun—and underlined this by releasing Specification F.29/27, this time calling for a single-seat fighter using a single C.O.W. gun as its armament.

185

Not surprisingly, tenders were issued to seven manufacturers of which three showed an initial interest in this requirement. At Yeovil Arthur Davenport had decided to use the earlier F.20/27 Interceptor as the basis for a design to meet the new Specification. An almost identical structure was used with a 4 ft 6 in longer fuselage and a wingspan increased by 2 ft 10 in which produced an extra 8 sq ft of wing area at the tips. In the F.29/27 fighter the wings were slightly swept but were of the same RAF 34 aerofoil section. External covering was a copy of that on the Interceptor with fabric on the wings and rear fuselage aft of the cockpit with metal panels, beaded for stiffness, on the front fuselage and nose. In spite of earlier expressed misgivings by some pilots at the design of the Interceptor's main undercarriage it was faithfully copied in the new fighter. Strangely, too, the F.29/27 C.O.W. Gun Fighter began life with the same small fin and rudder, Davenport perhaps believing that it would be adequate on the longer fuselage; however, a taller unit of higher aspect ratio was later fitted. These modifications added 995 lb to the empty weight of the fighter. Power was provided by a 485 hp Bristol Mercury IIIA radial engine, initially driving a four-blade propeller. Without doubt, the marked similarity between these two aeroplanes stemmed from the facts that both were being worked on at the same time and economically it was cheaper to design them alike.

If Westland's F.29/27 fighter design appeared to lack novelty, then certainly its raison d'être did not. The Specification, while calling for a high peformance to meet the potential threat of hostile bombers flying at 150 mph at 20,000 ft, also placed major emphasis on the armament and its installation. The 37 mm C.O.W. gun was to be fixed and installed so that it could fire upwards at an angle of at least 45 deg from the horizontal. It was envisaged that fighters, thus armed, would fly under formations of bombers and from this fairly secure position fire upwards at close range. Thus, general stability, accuracy of control and steadiness at altitude were other qualities required of the aircraft as a gun platform. In addition, the pilot was to be provided with easy access to the gun's breech mechanism for loading and a supply of 50 shells was to be carried. A means of sighting the gun was also required.

The front fuselage's beaded metal panels contrast strongly with the undoped fabric covering of the C.O.W. Gun Fighter's rear fuselage with its small fin and rudder.

It was in the design and engineering aspects of the armament installation that most ingenuity was exhibited by Davenport. The main and secondary structures of the 200 lb gun were attached to the bottom longeron and at two strut-braced points below and above the starboard top longeron so that it could fire upwards and forwards at an angle of 55 deg. The lower half of its length, including the breech mechanism, was enclosed by the aircraft's external metal panels and was accessible from inside the cockpit. The upper half of the gun, which emerged from the fuselage through an aperture about on the level with the upper longeron, was enclosed for most of its length by a streamlined fairing leaving about 15 in of the barrel protruding from it. In the cockpit, immediately ahead of the instrument panel and extending across almost the entire width of the fuselage, was a special rotary storage and dispensing device for the 1½ lb 37 mm shells. Designed and built by Westland, it carried 39 rounds and dispensed them, one at a time, when the pilot turned a small four-spoked handwheel. He then recharged the gun with the dispensed rounds. To show the pilot how many rounds remained an indicator rotated in step with the handwheel. The means of disposing of the empty shell cases has not been established; however, a Westland drawing shows that the bottom of the gun protruded through the cockpit floor and this may indicate their ejection point. The gun was sighted through a special periscopic sight, mounted in a fairing in front of the windscreen, the front end of which looked upwards at the same 55 deg angle as the gun.

Second development stage of the C.O.W. Gun Fighter was the installation of the 37 mm gun and sight, a two-blade propeller, larger fin, rudder and tailplane, with two bracing-struts and horn-balanced elevators.

The first flight of the C.O.W. Gun Fighter, serialled J9565, took place during December 1930 with Louis Paget as pilot. After some preliminary test flying, the four-blade propeller was removed and a two-blade unit fitted, the original small fin and rudder were replaced by ones of increased area and horn-balanced elevators were fitted; J9565 then went to No.15 Squadron at A & AEE, during April 1931 for performance and armament trials. The aircraft performed quite well but its rate of climb was criticised, as was its quite high wing loading of 17

187

lb/sq ft; however, although the fire-power was undeniable the rate of fire was considered to be too slow for effective combat. There was, too, criticism that the specified 50 rounds were not carried and that the dispenser, while a clever device, was too heavy.

But the results of the trials and the criticism soon became academic as the Air Ministry shifted the focus of its armament interest toward multiple small-bore machine-guns and further development of the F.29/27 programme was abandoned. However, fitted with a 485 hp Mercury IVA engine it remained at A & AEE from April 1932 until July 1934 before going to the Home Aircraft Depot at Henlow, where it was struck off charge on 3 December, 1935, to become instructional airframe 738M.

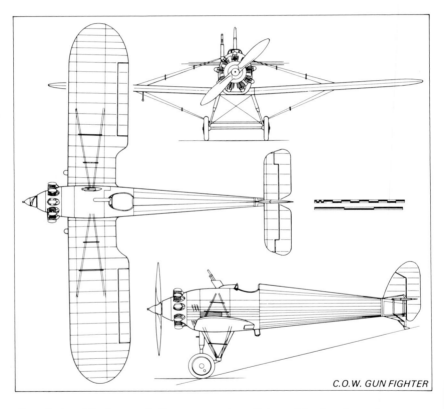

C.O.W. GUN FIGHTER

Description: Single-seat shell gun monoplane fighter. Metal and wood construction. Metal and fabric covering.

Accommodaton: Pilot in open cockpit.

Powerplant: One 485 hp Bristol Mercury IIIA nine-cylinder radial air-cooled geared and supercharged engine driving a 10 ft 7 in diameter two blade wooden propeller. (A four-blade propeller was fitted for early flight tests).

Armament: One 37 mm Coventry Ordnance Works shell firing gun mounted on the starboard side of the cockpit firing forward and upward at an angle of 55 deg. 39 rounds of ammunition were carried in a special dispenser in the cockpit.

Dimensions: Span 40 ft 10 in; length 29 ft 10 in; height 10 ft 7 in; wing area 223 sq ft.

Weights: Empty 2,615 lb; loaded 3,885 lb.

Performance: Maximum speed at 13,000 ft 185 mph; landing speed 66 mph; climb 10,000 ft in 7 min, 20,000 ft in 14.9 min; absolute ceiling 29,400 ft.

Production: One F.29/27 C.O.W. Gun Fighter, J9565, built by Westland Aircraft Works, Yeovil, Somerset, during 1929–30.

Pterodactyl IV

K1947, the three-seat cabin Pterodactyl IV in RAF markings. It has single acting wingtip rudders and fabric-covered balancing skids.

With the experience gained from the design, construction and flight testing of his earler tailless glider and the Pterodactyl I variants, in late 1929 Geoffrey Hill and his small team at Yeovil began the design of a three-seat cabin aircraft, of similar configuration, to Specification 16/29. This was the Westland Pterodactyl IV, the apparent gap between it and the Mk.I being bridged by the gull-winged Mks.II and III two-seat pusher and tractor fighter projects respectively which, in 1926, had been judged 'too much, too soon' by the Air Ministry to be built. Like the Mk.I it was of pusher configuration, the engine being a 120 hp de Havilland Gipsy III; however, having in mind the problems experienced with longitudinal control of the Mk.I Pterodactyl, Hill completely changed the design of the control system of the Mk.IV.

The short stumpy fuselage, which was only 13 ft 3 in in length, had an ash structure with the forward part, which embodied the wing centre-section, having a ply-wood skin and the rear portion being the metal-cowled engine bay. The pilot sat in the nose of the totally enclosed cabin with two side-by-side passenger seats behind him. Aft of the cabin was the luggage compartment. Access to the

189

cabin was through a large door in the port side. The engine was carried on four longitudinal steel-tube bearers and was separated from the forward cabin by a fireproof bulkhead. Air cooling of the inverted Gipsy engine was via ducts from the top and starboard side of the cowling which exhausted through a circular 'jet-pipe'-like aperture at the rear of the fuselage. The main undercarriage consisted of a tubular steel frame pivoted to a single oleo-pneumatic leg and carrying two wheels in tandem, the front one being steerable and with brakes on the rear wheel. A deep box-shaped fairing enclosed the undercarriage and extended back to a point below the cooling air outlet. This undercarriage, already proven in the Pterodactyl IC, provided smoother and more stable taxi-ing conditions. The wings, which were of RAF 34 aerofoil section, were of wooden construction having 20 closely-spaced girder ribs and riblets, a main I-section spar at the two-thirds chord position which was attached to the fuselage centre-section through a hinged joint, and a ply-covered leading-edge box. Inboard of the main V-strut attachment points, where a reinforced rib with a ply web was fitted, the wing was fabric covered, with 1 mm ply covering the outboard section which carried fabric-covered elevons in place of the Mk.I's wingtip controllers. Two balancing skids were carried on a triangular frame which was fabric-covered to provide fin area, and braced with a single strut to the underside of the wing.

The Pterodactyl IV's wing shape gave it a menacing appearance in the air.

Two major design features of the Pterodactyl IV were its control system and its variable-geometry wing. As noted above elevons were used for control in roll and pitch but, initially, the Mk.IA's 'electroscopic' type flaps mounted inboard of the elevons provided yaw control. The more notable feature was the variable wing-sweep system, covered by Patent No.352,961, which enabled the angle of wing sweep to be altered through a 4.75 degree arc. A worm-and-wheel gear turned by a hand-operated crank in the roof of the cabin, positioned so that the pilot or the port side passenger could operate it, rotated a geared double-ended turnbuckle, the threaded ends of which engaged in two nut-runners in the wing roots to swing the wings about the rear spar hinge. Although the degree of wing movement in the Pterodactyl was small when compared with that of modern variable-geometry aircraft, it produced sufficient change in the centre of pressure to compensate for the centre of gravity shift when the cabin had one, two or three occupants with additional loads.

Construction of the Pterodactyl IV proceeded at Yeovil through much of 1930 and into the early months of 1931 until completed in March. It was then dismantled and taken by lorry to RAF Andover where it was re-assembled. In an all-over silver finish with a broad green bank around its midriff and serialled K1947, it was first flown by Louis Paget who returned it to Yeovil two days later. During the early flights Paget was quick to appreciate the improvement in control; the inertia experienced with the wingtip controllers in the Mk.IC was not apparent in the Pterodactyl IV with elevons. On 2 June Paget crashed in a Widgeon and although he was fortunate enough to sustain only broken legs and other minor injuries he was unable to fly again and left Westland some months later. To add to this upset to the Pterodactyl IV's flying programme, Freddy Brunton, another Westland test pilot since 1928, had only recently left the company following some difference of opionion on flying the Mk.IC, and Harald Penrose was on leave after some four months displaying the Wapiti V in South America. He was recalled on 9 June to keep things moving generally and to fly the Pterodactyl IV.

Broad chord elevons and a variable-geometry wing were major features of the Pterodactyl IV seen here with fully-swept wings.

His first flight in K1947 almost ended in disaster before it had begun for, during the take-off run, a hump in the ground bounced the aircraft into the air in an almost stalled condition. It bounced again and Penrose's instictive corrective control only served to produce longitudinal oscillations which, coupled with rolling and yawing resulted in a generous helping of 'Dutch Roll'. As the speed built up he gained control and began a gentle climb to a safe altitude where he was able to check the effects of control inputs. He found that the aircraft was very sensitive in pitch but very heavy in roll and that the response from the 'electroscopic' rudders was slow; however, he was able to land without difficulty. After two more flights Penrose considered that he could fly the

191

The bicycle undercarriage, engine bay with its cooling air outlet, open wing root 'glove' and rear view mirror on the Pterodactyl IV.

Pterodactyl IV to good purpose. Within a few days it was flown to the RAE in readiness to take part in the RAF Display at Hendon on 27 June, where it was included among a dozen aircraft in the New Types Park.

With this first public display behind it, K1947 was returned to Westland where Harald Penrose again took up its development programme, only to discover that it was much overweight with a wing loading of 8 lb/sq ft. This prevented it from flying with two passengers, but Herbert Mettam often flew as test observer in the port seat from where he could turn the wing-sweep crank, set in the cabin roof, when Penrose was otherwise engaged. An alternative to the 'electroscopic' flap-type rudders was, meanwhile, being sought and triangular vertical rudders inboard of the elevons were tested in model form in the wind tunnel. Ultimately, single-acting oval shaped fins and rudders were mounted on the wingtips. Some spinning trials were made for which adjustable weights were carried on two rods to enable the centre of gravity to be moved.

During September 1931 the Pterodactyl IV briefly visited the A & AEE before moving to the RAE in December where it was flown by Flt Lt G H Stainforth, new holder of a 407.5 mph world speed record in the Supermarine S.6B. The RAE Report BA1026 shows that overall stability and handling characteristics were acceptable with the aircraft capable of being flown hands-off and through steep turns on either the elevons or rudders alone. Spinning was good with a slow rate of spin and quick recovery. The take-off run of 750 ft into a varying 3–6 mph wind was not good, particularly at a take-off weight of 1,900 lb which was some 150 lb below its stated all-up weight. The maximum speed was 109 mph, but as it was achieved with a propeller of too fine pitch, this figure was calculated to be 4 mph faster. Much of the Pterodactyl's performance was based on calculation and extrapolation using well-proven formulae; this was because of the incorrect propeller and overheating by the engine: thus the estimated initial rate of climb was 750 ft/min with a service ceiling of 15,000 ft. This modest performance was the major reason for Westland's decision not to develop the Pterodactyl IV design into a production civil aircraft. Nevertheless, it continued to be flown at Yeovil as a tailless research vehicle and appeared in the RAF Display on 25 June, 1932. Painted to represent a sharp-toothed monster it was exhibited again in the New Types Park before being flown by Flt Lt Stainforth in partnership with an equally ferociously painted Hart, the pair making attacks on hippopotamus-shaped balloons. These flying hours were to prove a valuable source of experience and data for Geoffrey Hill and his still small, but growing, design team at Yeovil.

Painted to represent its prehistoric ancestor, the Pterodactyl IV flies at the 1932 RAF Display at Hendon.

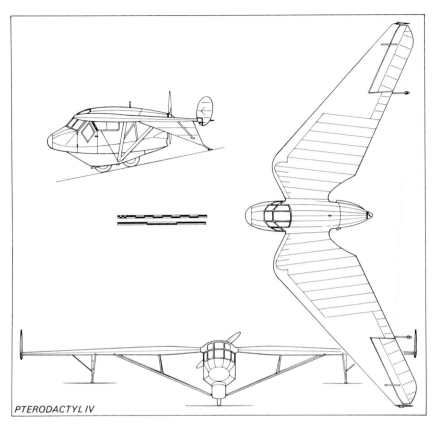

PTERODACTYL IV

Description: Three-seat tailless cabin research aircraft. Wood/metal construction with fabric, wood and metal covering.

Accommodation: Pilot and two passengers in an enclosed cabin.

Powerplant: One 120 hp de Havilland Gipsy III four-cylinder inverted inline air-cooled direct-drive normally-aspirated engine driving a 6 ft diameter Watts two-blade wooden propeller.

Dimensions: Span 44 ft 4 in; length 19 ft 6 ins; height 7 ft 6 in; wing area 259 sq ft.

Weights: Empty 1,320 lb; loaded 2,100 lb.

Performance: Maximum speed 113 mph; landing speed 54 mph; initial rate of climb 750 ft/min; service ceiling 15,000 ft; absolute ceiling 17,000 ft.

Production: One Pterodactyl IV built by Westland Aircraft Works, Yeovil, Somerset, during 1930–31.

PV.3

One of the very early concepts of naval aviation was the delivery of a torpedo to sink enemy ships. During 1930 the Admiralty was directing the development of a lightweight 1,000 lb torpedo and it was with this weapon in mind that Arthur Davenport conceived the design of a two-seat, torpedo-bomber aircraft to operate from Royal Navy Fleet carriers. He also had in mind to propose it as an RAF general purpose aircraft or to meet the requirements of an army co-operation aircraft.

Designated PV.3 it was a private venture project which, in its initial configuration, bore a marked visual, dimensional and, although metal and not wood was used throughout, structural similarity to the long-fuselage Wapiti variants which, clearly, had inspired many of its basic design features. The fuselage structure was built up from square-section duralumin tube joined by bolted and tubular-riveted flitch plates, with light alloy formers and stringers providing a rounded top surface. At the front a duralumin face plate was attached to the four longerons and formed the engine mounting. From this plate to a point immediately aft of the pilot's cockpit the fuselage was covered with quickly detachable aluminium cowling panels, the remainder of the fuselage being fabric-covered. The complete tail unit was virtually identical to that of the Wapiti but was of all metal construction and fabric-covered. Davenport again chose an air-cooled Bristol engine to power the PV.3: this time the 575 hp Jupiter XFA. Like the Wapiti installation the PV.3's Jupiter had a forward exhaust collector from which two pipes led back only two feet aft of the engine mounting plate. An oil cooler was mounted low down on the fuselage close to

Clearly a Wapiti descendant, the PV.3's clean lines were enhanced by close-fitting metal panels and neat Jupiter XFA installation. Note the prone bombing position side windows below the front cockpit.

the wing leading-edge. Fuel was carried in main and auxiliary tanks in the fuselage in front of the pilot's cockpit. A small window in each side of the fuselage low down between the two cockpits provided light for the prone bomb aimer's position. The all-metal two-bay wing structure was built up around two I-section spars with fabricated ribs. The lower wing, which was fabric-covered, was built in four sections; two inboard stub wings of 13 ft span, at the outer ends of which were attachment fittings for the two outer wings, the main undercarriage legs and the inboard interplane struts which were of streamlined steel N-form. The upper wings, which were also fabric covered, were attached to a centre-section of the same 13 ft span which was supported by four plain duralumin struts on the fuselage and by the N-form interplane struts. Inset Frise-type ailerons were carried on the lower and on the upper outer wings where leading-edge slats also were fitted. These ailerons were interchangeable between port and starboard and lower and upper wings, which were joined by plain duralumin struts. Because the PV.3 was conceived as a carrier-borne aircraft, there were dimensional limits which had to be met to allow the aircraft to fit on the carrier's lifts and enable it to be stowed in below-decks hangars with an economical use of space. For this reason the PV.3's wings could fold, hinging around the rear spars at the outer ends of the centre-section and stub wings. This reduced the wing span, when folded, to 20 ft 4 in. The main undercarriage, which had a 13 ft 6 in track, had a divided-axle hinged at the stub-wing roots and attached at its lower end to the hydro-pneumatic shock-absorber legs. A hinged radius rod was mounted between the lower point of the axle and the rear spar joint and the wheels were enclosed in large duralumin spats. The armament consisted of a single synchronised fixed forward-firing .303 in Vickers machine-gun for the pilot and a single Mk.III Lewis gun, of the same calibre, mounted on a Scarff ring over the rear cockpit. The forward-firing gun was mounted high in the port side of the fuselage and fired through a short trough in the upper cowling panels. Unusually, the Scarff ring in the rear cockpit was mounted below the top line of the fuselage which provided shelter for the

For trials at the A & AEE Martlesham Heath, the spatless PV.3 had a Scarff ring, message pick-up hook and underwing Universal bomb carriers.

196

observer/gunner. The disposable war load could be either the 1,000 lb torpedo carried in crutches under the fuselage and between the main undercarriage units, or a pair of 550 lb bombs, four 250 lb or 112 lb bombs or sixteen 20 lb bombs on four universal carriers beneath the lower wings just outboard of the undercarriage. A combination of these bombs, not exceeding 1,100 lb in weight, could also be carried. Provision was also made for three 250 litre oxygen cylinders and associated system, radio equipment and an F24 camera.

The PV.3 in December 1932 being modified for its pioneering flights over Everest. Rear cabin windows are in place and the Pegasus IS3 engine is being installed.

The PV.3 was first flown by Louis Paget during February 1931, going to the A & AEE in March, with the Class B marking P3, for preliminary evaluation where its general performance and handling proved satisfactory. Its outstanding attributes, apart from a high top speed, were its rate of climb and, more importantly, its high altitude capability, climbing to a corrected service ceiling of over 26,000 ft. But this was not enough to prompt a production contract and when the development of the 1,000 lb torpedo was abandoned it seemed that there was no further use for the lone PV.3 prototype. For many months it was to languish in a hangar at Yeovil being flown only occasionally as a 'hack'. Its fortune was to change, however, when, in November 1932, it was chosen with the Westland PV.6 which had become the Wallace prototype, for modification and use by the 1933 Houston Mount Everest Flying Expedition team. Following a recommendation by Flt Lt Cyril Uwins, a test pilot at the A & AEE, Sqn Ldr the Marquis of Douglas and Clydesdale, MP, visited Yeovil to discuss the possibility of these aircraft being made available to the Expedition of which he was the chief pilot. He also went to Filton from where Uwins, on 16 September, 1942, had flown a Vickers Vespa biplane powered by a Bristol Pegasus S3 radial engine to a height of 43,876 ft to capture the world's altitude record held by a United States Navy aircraft. With Clydesdale's report that these three aircraft types were the only ones capable of flying over Mount Everest, it was decided

Harald Penrose in the Houston-Westland PV.3 at Yeovil. Note narrow-chord engine cowling and outside air temperature gauge on inboard rear interplane strut.

that, if only for ease of maintenance, it would be preferable to have two aircraft made by the same company. Other advantages of the Westland aeroplanes included a deep fuselage with room for cameras and other equipment, the ability to accept the Bristol Pegasus engine with a minimum of airframe modifications and a tall undercarriage to provide ground clearance for a large diameter propeller. Accordingly, the PV.3, with the prototype Wallace which is described in a following chapter, was extensively modified to meet the challenge of flying two people and a range of specialised equipment over the 29,000 ft high peak of the world's highest mountain. Aircraft weight was a vital factor, for the aircraft would have to carry sufficient fuel not only to climb to over 30,000 ft but also for the 330 mile return flight between Lalbalu aerodrome at Purnea, the Expedition's base, and Everest. To this end all military equipment such as attachment fittings for the underwing bomb carriers and the torpedo crutches, their control and release mechanisms and for the Scarff ring were removed, as were the front Vickers gun and its associated equipment, the main undercarriage wheel spats and even the brakes. The two major changes were the installation of a 630 hp Bristol Pegasus IS3 supercharged engine and the replacement of the open rear cockpit with an enclosed cabin. The fuel system was simplified by removing the auxiliary fuel tank and hand pump and relying solely on the main and gravity tanks and the engine pump. Drawing on Uwin's experience with the Vespa all grease and oil was to be cleared off control surface hinges and pulleys and from the tailplane incidence-changing gear. The wooden propeller, made by the Airscrew Co of Weybridge, was given a special coach finish 'to withstand the heat while the aircraft was on the ground'. Because the airframe was built of aluminium and duralumin and the control cables were of steel, their different coefficients of contraction and expansion posed problems at very low temperatures. To overcome these spring boxes were fitted in the control cable runs. To minimise draughts the pilot's open cockpit was provided with a floor and was enclosed fore and aft with sealed three-ply wooden bulkheads and fitted with a large three-section wrap-around Triplex glass windscreen. The observer/photographer's cabin was totally enclosed, access being provided by two longitudinally hinged panels in the top of the fuselage, each with two oval windows. These were folded inwards and secured inside to enable the observer to stand up to take still photographs or cine film with a hand-held camera. An additional pair of hinged outwardly-opening rectangular windows was provided high in the fuselage side immediately below the hinge line of the folding panels, and the cabin floor had sliding panels so that a camera could take vertical or oblique photographs of the mountain. The seat was designed to be vertically adjustable. Provision was made for the use of electrically-heated flying suits, gloves, boots, helmet and goggles plus a complete oxygen system, also electrically-heated, supplied from three 750 litre cylinders carried inside the rear fuselage. A reserve cylinder was also carried. Electrically-heated blankets were provided to wrap around the cameras, there were heaters inside the camera bodies and each film magazine had its own heater. A Williamson Automatic Eagle III survey camera was carried to make exposures at regular intervals during the flight and obtain overlapping photographs for a mosaic from which it was hoped that an accurate and detailed map could be produced.

G-ACAZ airborne at Yeovil during January 1933.

Work on both the PV.3, now named the Houston-Westland to honour Lady Houston who was financing the venture, and on the Wallace had been pressed ahead as rapidly as possible and by the middle of January 1933 the PV.3 was the first to be ready for initial engine running. On 21 January Harald Penrose, wearing one of the sets of electrically-heated flying clothing, made a 35-minute first flight of this aircraft, registered G-ACAZ, at Yeovil, and two days later he did a check climb to 24,000 ft to try out the oxygen system. On the 24th Col Stewart Blacker who originated the idea to overfly Everest, Air Commodore P

F M Fellowes who had been appointed to lead the Expedition, and the Marquis of Douglas and Clydesdale, each similarly clad, had a short familiarisation flight in the rear cabin. Finally, on the following day, Harald Penrose took Fellowes on a 1 hr 40 min flight to a corrected height of 35,000 ft, where the outside temperature recorded was minus 60 deg centigrade, to prove that the PV.3 could achieve, and improve upon, their required performances at extreme height. G-ACAZ was then officially handed over to Lord Clydesdale who made a number of familiarisation and check flights in it. Thereafter, it was dismantled and crated for shipment in the ss *Dalgoma* from Tilbury.

The Houston-Westland PV.3 G-ACAZ approaching Everest on 3 April, 1933.

After the successful flights over Everest G-ACAZ, with the Wallace G-ACBR, was returned to England by sea where, after a period at Yeovil and an appearance in the Royal Air Force Display at Hendon on 30 June, 1934, this pioneering Westland aeroplane, now serialled K4048, enjoyed long service at the RAE and with No.501 Squadron before use as a flying test bed for the development of Bristol aero-engines. Its ultimate fate has not been recorded.

Description: Two-seat biplane torpedo bomber. All-metal construction. Metal and fabric covering. Converted to high-altitude photographic and research aircraft.

Accommodation: Pilot and observer in open cockpits. Rear position converted to enclosed cabin.

Powerplant: One 575 hp Bristol Jupiter XFA nine-cylinder radial air-cooled geared and supercharged engine driving an 11 ft diameter two-blade wooden propeller (PV.3). One 630 hp Bristol Pegasus IS3 nine-cylinder radial air-cooled geared and supercharged engine driving a 12 ft 6 in diameter two-blade wooden propeller (G-ACAZ).

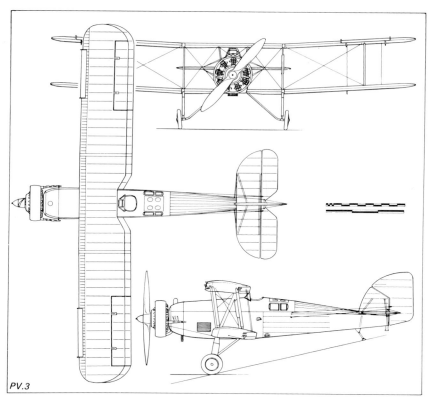

PV.3

Armament: One .303 in fixed synchronised forward-firing Vickers machine-gun and one .303 in Lewis Mk.III machine-gun on a No.7 Scarff ring mounted over the rear cockpit. One 1,000 lb torpedo in crutches below the fuselage or two 550 lb or four 112 lb or sixteen 20 lb bombs in underwing carriers (PV.3).

Dimensions: Span 46 ft 6 in (20 ft 4 in folded PV.3); length 34 ft 2 ins; height 11 ft 8 in; wing area 500 sq ft.

Weights: Empty 3,580 lb; loaded 5,600 lb (PV.3).
Empty 3,420 lb; loaded 5,100 lb (G-ACAZ).

Performance: Maximum speed 163 mph; landing speed 59 mph (PV.3), 51 mph (G-ACAZ); climb 5,000 ft in 4.7 min, 10,000 ft in 8.9 min, 20,000 ft in 20 min; ceiling 26,000 ft (PV.3), 35,000 (G-ACAZ).

Production: One prototype PV.3 built by Westland Aircraft Works, Yeovil, during 1930–31. Converted during 1931–32.

Once Wapiti V G-AAWA, the Wapiti VII, or PV.6, in November 1931. Note the bulged Townend ring through which the pilot's gun fired, and modified undercarriage.

Wallace

Some two years before the last Wapiti was delivered in August 1932 Arthur Davenport's fertile brain was at work scheming a successor. It was only to be expected that, when it emerged, his design for a new two-seat general purpose biplane should be similar in configuration and construction to that of the Wapiti. However, there was one other important input; this was a sketch of an improved Wapiti sent to Davenport by Harald Penrose when he was in South America flying the Wapiti demonstrator G-AAWA. It included a divided main undercarriage and a Rolls-Royce inline engine. Penrose had discovered while in the Argentine, that the Wapiti's cross-axle undercarriage posed a danger when landing on aerodromes with long grass; thus, Davenport took note of this when draughting the proposed new design—but omitted the inline engine, preferring a radial engine, as in the Wapiti, on grounds of economy.

Evolution rather than revolution was his guiding principle with this aeroplane. As originally envisaged, it was intended to have five hours duration and be used principally for army co-operation and light bombing duties but later other roles such as long-range escort fighter, two-seat trainer and as a fighter/reconnaissance floatplane were proposed. At one stage consideration was also given to providing a range of engine mountings which could enable either a Pegasus, Jaguar, Panther or Gnome-Rhône Mistral engine to be fitted, but this scheme was abandoned.

In order to speed the construction of the prototype as a private venture it was decided to use the airframe of the Wapiti V G-AAWA as its basis, this initially giving the aircraft the designation Wapiti VII. While the basic structure remained virtually unchanged, there were some major changes to secondary structures, undercarriage units, engine and equipment. In the first stage of its metamorphosis, the fuselage cross-section with flat sides and bottom was retained; later, re-designed metal and wood formers and stringers were fitted to

202

produce a more rounded shape to the sides of the front fuselage, increasing its overall width at the mid-point by some 10 inches. As in the Wapiti, from a point between the cockpits the forward part of the fuselage was covered with easily removable curved metal panels; aft of this the fabric covering was provided with large zip-fastened panels for ease of internal inspection. At first the main undercarriage units of the Wapiti V were also retained, but soon a new design was incorporated with raked back shock-absorbing main legs, inverted V cross-axle rods and two radius rods, in the form of a V, attached to the outer ends of the axle rods and to a common attachment point on the centreline of the fuselage underside. The wheels were enclosed in spats and had Dunlop differential brakes operated by toe-pedals on the rudder bar. An un-spatted castoring tailwheel replaced the standard skid. The change of engine involved the installation of a 550 hp Bristol Pegasus IIM3 radial in a narrow-chord drag-reducing Townend ring. This was considered to be a more simple but effective modification than the fitment of the more advanced NACA cowling. It had the additional benefit of being cheaper. The Townend ring had a noticeable bulge on the port side to provide a clear path for the bullets from a fixed synchronised Vickers machine-gun, now totally enclosed in the rounded fuselage side and firing between the engine cylinders and through the propeller disc. Later a small 'dent' was embodied near the ring's top to give an uninterrupted line of sight for the repositioned pilot's gun sight.

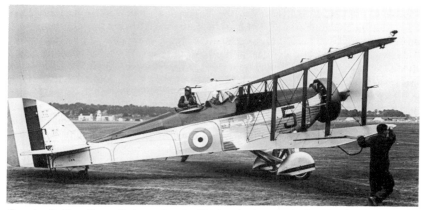

Carrying its New Types Park number the PV.6 taxies in on arrival at Hendon for the RAF Display in June 1932.

Conversion work on G-AAWA went on through the summer of 1931 until in late October it was completed. By then, the aircraft was so different from the Wapiti that it was given a new Westland designation, the PV.6; however, it was still referred to as the Wapiti VII in some quarters. On 31 October Harald Penrose made the first flight at Yeovil with this prototype which carried the Class B marking P6. Early flight trials with a 655 hp Pegasus IV installed, revealed that it was faster and had a better rate of climb than the Wapiti, while the re-designed Frise ailerons, rudder and elevator made the PV.6 much more

K3562, the first production Wallace I, converted from Wapiti IIA K1346, flies low at Yeovil.

tractable in the air. Oxygen, radio and photographic equipment was carried. Westland was keen to have the aircraft accepted for trials at Martlesham Heath and after an initial reluctance on the part of the Air Ministry, P6, carrying RAF roundels, was eventually flown by RAF test pilots—but at Westland's risk—during November 1931. On its return to Yeovil further development work and test flying continued; later, on 25 June, the PV.6 made its public debut in the New Types Park and Fly Past in the RAF Display at Hendon, two days later flying in the first SBAC Display held there, too. However, the PV.6 had clearly impressed the A & AEE pilots and in September 1932 Westland received a contract for twelve aircraft, which had received the name Wallace in August, and which were to be created by converting this number of Wapiti IIAs, to meet Air Ministry Specification 19/32. These Wallace Mk.Is were delivered to No.501 (City of Bristol) Squadron RAF at Filton during January–March 1933. During

Originally Wapiti IIA K2313, this Wallace I, K4344, was the receiver in an inflight refuelling demonstration in the 1935 RAF Display before conversion for target towing.

the conversion work a number of modifications were embodied; they included the fitting of a tip-up seat in the rear cockpit and 'firing steps' to enable the gun to be fired almost vertically downward, floor mountings for a remotely-operated camera, rudder bias gear and provision for trim weights in the rear fuselage when the aircraft was flying without the observer. During 1933–34 Westland received five more similar contracts which resulted in a total of fifty-eight conversions of Wapitis to Wallace Is to Specifications 7/33 and 9/33 plus eight aircraft built as new. They served with Nos.501, 502, 503 and 504 Squadron all of which were formed as Special Reserve Squadrons.

During 1932–33 the PV.6 was modified for use by the Houston Everest Expedition and registered G-ACBR. Here it flies high over the Himalayas.

Meanwhile, the Westland PV.6/Wallace had been selected to equip the 1933 Houston Mount Everest Flying Expedition and was being extensively modified and rebuilt to the same standard as the Westland PV.3 already described. During the first days of February 1933 the Wallace was ready for engine runs and on the 4th Harald Penrose flew it for its acceptance climb and altitude test. He had with him, as a passenger in the rear enclosed cabin, Col Stewart Blacker. As the aircraft climbed through the 20,000 ft mark, Penrose began to suffer oxygen starvation and immediately throttled back and lost height; however, he found that a coupling in the oxygen supply pipe to his mask was undone. With the coupling secured again he continued the climb reaching an indicated height of 37,500 ft somewhere over Beachy Head. As he turned back towards Yeovil the engine spluttered and stopped, and there began a long power-off glide down through cloud with the ignition, fuel and heated flying suits all turned off. Breaking cloud at about 8,000 ft Penrose found himself—as he had hoped—near the Solent and was able to make an emergency landing at Hamble where it was found that the quill shaft turning the single fuel pump had sheared. With a Certificate of Airworthiness granted on 10 February and the aircraft registered G-ACBR, it was dismantled and crated for shipping to Karachi in the ss *Dalgoma* sailing from Tilbury.

205

West country aircraft, West country squadron. No.501 (City of Bristol) Special Reserve Squadron's Wallace Is are shown in this cleverly faked picture, in which two studies of the same four-aircraft formation have been combined.

Following the success of the Expedition's flights over Everest, G-ACBR was shipped back to England and Yeovil where it was reconverted to Wallace I standard and, serialled K3488, was delivered to No.501 Squadron at Filton during December 1933. It later went to A & AEE Martlesham Heath.

As the result of RAF Squadron experience with the Wallace Is and their open cockpits, plus Davenport's and Penrose's long-held conviction that, with the ever mounting speed and ceiling of aircraft, such cockpits were outdated,

The PV.6/Wallace II prototype in October 1934 with closed cockpit canopies, stowed rear gun and underwing bomb carriers.

Davenport produced a scheme for totally enclosing the Wallace's pilot and gunner. For the pilot, he designed a jettisonable tunnel-shaped canopy which could be opened by sliding it forward, over the windscreen, on two round rods fixed to the cockpit edges, while the gunner had a hinged three-piece segmented hood, with slipstream deflectors on its rear edge, which folded up and forward, where it was housed in a fixed tunnel-shaped section of the enclosure when the gun was to be used. The gun was to be stowed in a shaped trough in the curved top section of the fuselage on the starboard side, from where it could be swung when required for use. To enable Westland to make a trial installation of this cockpit enclosure, the old Wallace prototype and ex-Everest aircraft, now K3488, was returned to Yeovil during early January 1934. During February or March it went to Martlesham Heath for a two month period of evaluation after which, it is believed, it went back to Westland for further engineering development and flight trials during that year. There was no doubt, however, that the RAF pilots at Martlesham Heath liked it, or that the Wallace I airframe, despite its similarity to the Wapiti, had development potential; thus, in 1935 the Air Ministry issued Specification G.31/35 written around the Wallace with enclosed cockpits and powered by a 665 hp Bristol Pegasus IV radial engine. In April K3488 went to Martlesham Heath for handling trials and on 29 June, 1935, the first order for seventy-five of the new Wallace Mk.IIs was received by Westland. Deliveries began on 31 December with these aircraft going to the four Special Reserve Squadrons which, thus, became the first in the RAF to fly aircraft with enclosed cockpits. An ITP with a follow-on order for twenty-nine Wallace IIs was placed on 21 February, 1936, the first aircraft being delivered on 22 July and the last on 13 October. In addition to service with the four Special Reserve Squadrons noted earlier, Wallaces also were used by the Anti-Aircraft Co-operation Flight at RAF Biggin Hill and a number were equipped with target-towing gear. One of these, Wallace I K4344, had been used experimentally as a tanker aircraft and, flown by Flt Lt Ryder in the 1935

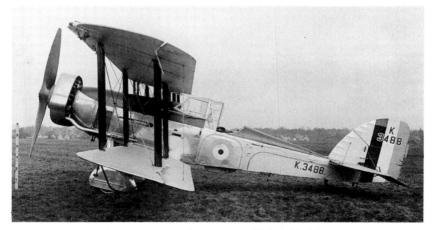

The PV.6's last development stage as the prototype Wallace II with full cockpit canopies, the rear one stowed, and ventral camera blister.

207

RAF Display at Hendon, had demonstrated inflight refuelling with a Hawker Hart, flown by Flt Lt Swayne, acting as the receiver aircraft.

An unusual role for the Wallace was undertaken on 2 February, 1938, when Flg Off D E Gillam flew a Station Flight aircraft from Aldergrove to the island of Rathlin, some seven miles off the County Antrim coast. Fierce storms had isolated the island and its inhabitants for three weeks and the Wallace's 350 lb load of food and candles relieved their plight. After a 30 minutes flight Gillam managed to land in a field with a 200 yards run which was bounded by stone walls, and to take-off from it for the return flight.

At the outbreak of the 1939–45 War, eighty-three Wallaces remained on RAF strength and served in various roles until finally being withdrawn during 1943, the last one, Wallace II K6019, in December.

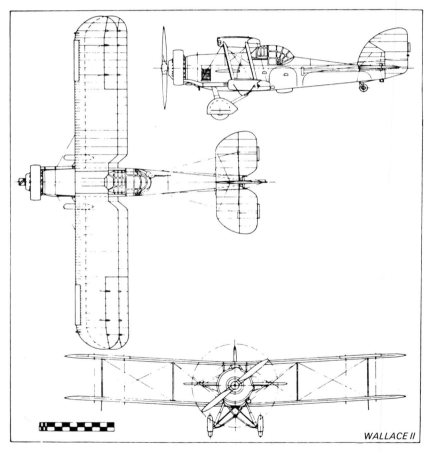

WALLACE II

Description: Two-seat general purpose biplane. Mixed metal/wood construction with metal and fabric covering.

208

Accommodation: Pilot and observer/gunner in open cockpits (Mk.I) or enclosed cockpits (Mk.II).

Powerplant: One 550 hp Bristol Pegasus II nine-cylinder radial air-cooled geared normally aspirated engine driving an 11 ft 10 in diameter two-blade wooden propeller (Prototype and Mk.I).
One 665 hp Bristol Pegasus IV geared and supercharged nine-cylinder radial air-cooled engine driving a 12 ft 6 in diameter two-blade wooden propeller (Mk.II).

Armament: One fixed Vickers .303 in forward-firing machine-gun mounted in the front fuselage and one Lewis .303 in machine-gun on a Scarff ring mounting in the rear cockpit (Prototype and Mk.I) or on a special mounting in the rear cockpit (Mk.II). Combinations of 112 lb, 230/250 lb or 20 lb bombs to a total of 580 lb on universal carriers under the wings and fuselage.

Dimensions: Span 46 ft 5 in; length 34 ft 2 in; height 11 ft 6 in; wing area 488 sq ft.

Weights: Empty 3,340 lb; loaded 5,300 lb (Prototype).
Empty 3,450 lb; loaded 5,450 lb (Mk.I)
Empty 3,680 lb; loaded 5,750 lb (Mk.II)

Performance: Maximum speed at 15,000 ft 158 mph; cruising speed 135 mph; initial climb 1,350 ft/min; climb to 10,000 ft in 6.2 min; service ceiling 24,100 ft.

Production: A total of 174 Wallaces produced by Westland Aircraft Works Ltd. Yeovil, Somerset, during 1931–36 as follows:
1 prototype (Wapiti G-AAWA conversion)
8 Wallace I
58 Wallace I (conversions from Wapiti IIA and VI).
1 Wallace I (conversion from civil Wallace G-ACJU).
107 Wallace II

PV.7

A major challenge to British aircraft manufacturers was the first issue of Air Ministry Specification G.4/31 during July 1931 calling for a general purpose aircraft which the Air Ministry was seeking to serve as a successor to the Wapiti and the Fairey Gordon, both still comparatively new in RAF squadron service. That this requirement should be notified so early showed a good deal of courage and forethought on the part of the Air Ministry. The challenge stemmed from the fact that this aircraft had to be capable of operating in no less than seven disparate roles: these were army co-operation, day and night light bombing, casualty evacuation, dive-bombing, photography and overland reconnaissance. As if these were not enough for one design, in October 1931, the specification was amended, in order to further widen its scope, with the addition of coastal reconnaissance and torpedo bombing. This multiplicity of roles did not dissuade a record number of nine manufacturers from submitting designs to meet the many requirements of this specification. They were Armstrong Whitworth, Blackburn, Bristol, Fairey, Handley Page, Hawker, Parnall, Vickers and Westland, of whom all but Handley Page and Westland stuck rigidly to the biplane configuration.

Standing 12 ft tall and with a 60 ft wingspan, the big PV.7 echoed earlier Westland aircraft and foreshadowed the Lysander. The open cockpit and horn-balanced rudder of the original configuration are noteworthy.

Clearly drawing on his experience with three earlier Westland high-wing monoplanes, Arthur Davenport chose this configuration for the company's two-seat private venture multi-role aircraft, designated the Westland P.7. Design work is believed to have begun late in 1931 or early 1932 with component production beginning in the autumn of that year. By April the following year the basic structure of this prototype was beginning to take shape in the Westland experimental department at Yeovil. The fuselage was of the standard Westland type of construction, being built up with square-section duralumin tubing—steel being used at major load-carrying stations—which were joined with flitch plates and tubular rivets. Light alloy formers and stringers gave shape to the rear fuselage top surface. The deep-section forward fuselage structure housed the prone bomb-aiming position which had a sliding panel in the floor, and the pilot's cockpit, positioned well forward in front of the wing leading-edge to give an excellent all-round view. A single synchronised Vickers machine-gun was to be carried in the port side of the front fuselage to fire through the propeller disc. The second crew member occupied a large cockpit positioned just aft of the wing

The PV.7, with open cockpit but modified fin and rudder, in one of the many roles for which it was designed, carries a 1,000 lb torpedo with apparent ease.

210

trailing-edge. Initially, at the request of the Air Ministry, the pilot's cockpit, unlike that of the second crew member, was open but its position, only six feet behind the very large propeller, made it extremely draughty, buffeting the pilot's head and, on one occasion, almost removed his goggles. Thus, after early flight trials, it was modified to become enclosed by the windscreen, a hinged roof, with three transparent curved panels aft of it which sloped downward to the fuselage top surface to make a clear view tunnel for the pilot, and by two semi-circular segmented side windows. A small window was fitted in each side of the fuselage beneath the wing to give light to the prone bomb-aiming position. The rear cockpit was fitted with a Westland patented segmented hood which could be folded forward to allow the full use of a machine-gun. The tail unit, which embodied a braced tailplane was of metal construction. The fuselage and tail unit were fabric-covered with the exception of plywood decking around the rear cockpit and metal panels which clad the forward fuselage. A large oil cooler was fitted on the starboard side of the nose just aft of the engine. The P.7 was powered by a 722 hp Bristol Pegasus III M3 radial engine, in a Townend ring, turning a two-blade wooden propeller having a small metal spinner. At the opposite end of the fuselage was a fixed castoring tailwheel unit.

The segmented side window through which Harald Penrose made a successful exit from the PV.7 after structural failure of a wing strut.

The 60 ft 3 in span wings, of RAF 34 section, which visually dominated this large aeroplane, were of two-spar all-metal construction with the ribbed structure internally braced by inter-spar swaged rods. Wide-span ailerons, also of metal construction, occupied half of the trailing edge, with patented Westland 'electroscopic' trailing-edge split flaps, about 4 ft 9 in in span, mounted immediately inboard of the ailerons. These flaps acted as dive-brakes to limit the aircraft's speed when dive-bombing. Handley Page leading-edge slats were carried on the outboard wing section. In order to provide the pilot with an improved rear view, the inboard sections of the wings were reduced in thickness by sloping the upper surface downwards, and their leading edges were swept back to give an unobstructed upwards view. A 120 gal fuel tank was carried at the inboard end of the constant thickness section of each wing. The wings joined the fuselage at its top surface, its line curving downwards, following that of the clear view transparency tunnel and virtually matching that of the wing section, to the rear cockpit. They were braced to the fuselage bottom longeron by two cranked broad-chord struts of aerofoil section, which contributed additional lifting area. The wide-track divided main undercarriage units consisted of two V struts with their tops attached to the fuselage and their lower ends to the wheel axle on an oleo-pneumatic main leg. The top of this leg was attached to the forward wing strut at the point where it was cranked. At this point, too, a diagonal bracing strut was attached to transfer landing loads to the fuselage. The forward wing strut was braced to a similar point on the rear strut and also had a diagonal strut to the fuselage. The whole of this complex wing strut system was stiffened by cross-bracing wires.

Construction of the P.7 continued through the summer of 1933 until it was pushed out for preliminary engine running and adjustments during the last week of October. The original design had included a large rudder having a curved trailing-edge and an enormous horn-balance, and it was a rudder of this shape which was fitted for the initial 30 minute flight. This came on 30 October after Harald Penrose had made some preliminary 'straights' to check the general feel of the aircraft and engine response. At once he was aware that the ailerons were too heavy, that some harmonisation of the controls was needed and that the

PV.7's design features included Westland 'electroscopic' flaps, wind deflectors on the open aft cockpit canopy and fuselage side window for prone bombing position.

pilot's open cockpit was much too draughty. While modifications were put in hand to improve the handling, development flying of the aircraft, now designated PV.7, continued with the open pilot's cockpit throughout the winter of 1933–34. This must have been particularly irksome for Penrose as the flying programme included flight tests and modification checks on the rear cockpit canopy. As the flight envelope was expanded another, more serious, snag was encountered. This was torsional weakness of the wing which twisted when the ailerons were applied, reaching dangerous proportons with increases in speed. Both Robert Bruce and Davenport found it hard to accept the reported extent of the wing twist, so Davenport offered to accompany Penrose on a test flight. Unable to convince his passenger that the wing twisted when the ailerons were moved in level cruising flight, Penrose put the aircraft into a gentle dive and, when speed had built up, he applied full aileron. The desperate shouts from the rear cockpit as Davenport instructed the pilot 'Stop— or you'll have the wings off!' proved not only the efficacy of the demonstration but also the truth of the flight test reports in the most convincing manner. As a result the wings were removed and the swaged rods in the wing structure were replaced by triangulated tubular members between the spars. At the same time the pilot's open cockpit was enclosed as described earlier.

In its final form the PV.7 was a pugnacious looking aircraft.

With these modifications embodied, development flying was resumed, but with increased speeds rudder 'tramping', caused by overbalancing, became apparent. To cure this a large constant-chord rudder without the large horn-balance was fitted. It was during this period that the PV.7 lost its port wheel on take-off. Penrose flew round for three hours to use up as much fuel as he could with safety, before landing, the axle digging into the ground and swinging the aircraft to an abrupt halt. Fortunately, the robust undercarriage did not appear to be damaged; but what lay in store for the aircraft tends to indicate some hidden cracks in an end fitting—or fittings—on the wing struts. With confidence in the PV.7 building steadily, on Saturday 30 June it was flown in the 1934 RAF Display at Hendon, carrying the marking P7 on the fuselage, where its advanced monoplane design compared very favourably with the several biplanes present which were produced to Specification G.4/31 by rival manufacturers. As was then customary the aircraft in the New Types Park and the attendant facilities were retained at Hendon until the following Monday when the member companies of the SBAC invited guests to see their latest products, which included the PV.7. Soon afterwards it went to the A & AEE for official evaluation by the RAF where, during July and August, it received some encouraging reports by the pilots involved. The flight tests included the customary number of flights with the aircraft loaded to move the c.g. aft of its normal position. Then the Air Ministry called for a further test involving dives to check the stability of the aircraft with the c.g. moved even further aft, these to be made by the manufacturer's pilot. This requirement was telephoned to Penrose who was at Martlesham Heath. Accordingly, on 25 August, the aircraft was loaded to the new condition, Penrose borrowed an A & AEE parachute, took off and, in gusty conditions, climbed the PV.7 to 14,000 ft from where he made some preliminary dives. Just after he had taken off, a telegram from Yeovil had arrived at the A & AEE reading 'Postpone flight. Strength requirements not met at proposed loading'. Unfortunately, the aircraft was not fitted with radio and Penrose could not be warned. Thus, unaware of the telegram, he began another dive at a higher speed than before when, at about 220 mph, the port wing broke off and carried away the tail unit. Penrose tried to open the cockpit roof but it was jammed, so he pulled down the segments of the small port side window and managed to get out through this restricted aperture, making a safe descent by his borrowed parachute. This was the first such jump from an enclosed cockpit of a British military aircraft. Following this accident, the wreckage, which was scattered along a seven miles path, was recovered—the fuselage and starboard wing from a small river—and returned to Martlesham Heath for a lengthy Air Ministry and Westland investigation into the cause of the mid-air break up of the aeroplane. This revealed that the port rear wing strut had failed in compression under severe down load caused by turbulence.

Unfortunately, the PV.7 prototype was not covered by insurance, Westland having cancelled this when the aeroplane was taken on charge by the A & AEE.

The Pegasus III M3 engine is dwarfed by the PV.7's fuselage. Note the front cockpit's segmented side window and rear cockpit hood and the broad-chord aerofoil section wing struts.

However, the Air Ministry would not accept liability because it was being flown by a civilian pilot. Westland could not afford to build another G.4/31 prototype as a private venture and its high hopes of a substantial contract were dashed.

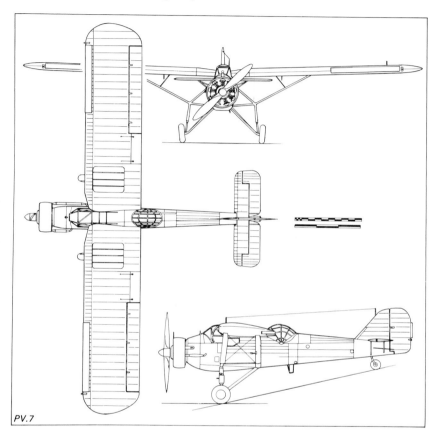

PV.7

Description: Two-seat general purpose aircraft. All-metal construction with fabric, metal and wood covering.

Accommodation: Pilot and observer in enclosed cockpits.

Powerplant: One 722 hp Bristol Pegasus III M3 nine-cylinder radial air-cooled geared and normally-aspirated engine in a Townend ring cowling, driving a 12 ft 4 in diameter two-blade wooden propeller.

Armament: Provision for a fixed synchronised forward-firing .303 in Vickers machine-gun mounted in the side of the front fuselage. A .303 in Lewis gun could be carried on a Scarff ring over the rear cockpit. The design maximum bomb load was two 500 lb bombs carried externally on racks under the centre fuselage. Alternatively provision was to be made for carrying a 1,000 lb torpedo in crutches.

Dimensions: Span 60 ft 3 in; length 38 ft 8 in; height 12 ft 0 in; wing area (including bracing struts) 537 sq ft.
Weights: Empty 4,515 lb; loaded 7,172 lb.
Performance: Maximum speed 173 mph at 5,000 ft; landing speed 48 mph; climb to 10,000 ft in 8 min; absolute ceiling 22,700 ft.
Production: One PV.7 built by Westland Aircraft Works, Yeovil, Somerset, during 1932–33.

Pterodactyl V

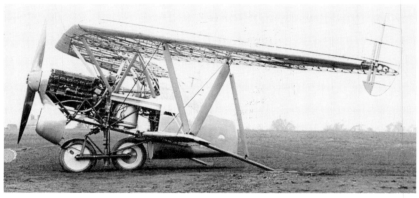

In its initial uncovered state, the condenser, stub-exhausts, fuel tank, rear gunner's position and balancing skids of the Pterodactyl V are visible features.

Although the earlier development programme with the Pterodactyl IV had produced an aeroplane with good handling characteristics and with a three-seat cabin having space for luggage, its performance with the Gipsy III engine was inferior to that of some other club and private-owner types on the market. With this fact in mind plus the limited civil market in the prevailing depressed economic climate in Great Britain, Westland had decided not to put the Pterodactyl IV into production.

This decision left Geoffrey Hill and his team free to concentrate their attention on a high-performance military application for the next Pterodactyl, something which Hill had always cherished since his 1926 submissions to the Air Ministry of two fighter projects. Clearly, the field of fire provided for flexibly-mounted rear guns in the Pterodactyl configuration made it most suitable for development as a two-seat fighter; thus, this was the basis of proposals submitted to the Air Ministry by Westland during 1931. It was around them that Specification F.3/32 was written, covering a two-seat tractor fighter armed with two fixed forward-firing Vickers machine-guns and a single flexibly-mounted Lewis gun in the rear cockpit. The engine specified was the Rolls-Royce PV.G evaporatively-cooled variant of the Kestrel which became

216

known as the Goshawk and which delivered 600 hp. With this encouragement detail design of the Pterodactyl Mk.V was launched with Herbert Mettam, who was responsible for the stress work, finding that this was a very long and complex task exacerbated by the lack of data on the safe limits for load distribution on swept wings with combined bending and torsion loads. Wind-tunnel tests with models also showed up areas of potential aerodynamic problems with the different stalling characteristics of the straight centre-section and the 47 deg swept outer wings.

While Hill retained the same basic configuration of its predecessor, the Pterodactyl V was a much more advanced and ambitious design to meet the requirements of a military aircraft. The increased strength and rigidity required for fighter manoeuvrability, including inverted flight, was obtained by adopting a sesquiplane configuration, which also had a number of other advantages. Because of the small fuselage with little internal stowage space the small unswept lower wing could contain ammunition, be fitted with a Light Series bomb carrier and serve as the mounting for the outrigger undercarriage balancer struts. Of most importance was their ability to provide extra lift without an increase in wingspan.

Early modifications to the Pterodactyl V were the larger condenser with hexagonal intake, balancers with small wheels and wingtip slats moved inboard.

The fuselage structure was of square-section duralumin tubing joined by tubular-riveted flitch plates, the engine mounting being of square-section steel-tubes similarly joined. Because the fuselage was only 17 ft 4 in in length very few formers, or panel support members, were required, these being mainly the reduction gear cowl, engine bay rear bulkhead, instrument panel support structure, cockpit front frame and seat bulkhead. They carried detachable metal panels, as did the main undercarriage; only the condenser—or radiator, the fuselage underside, and the pilot's and gunner's cockpit surrounds being skinned. Initially the exhaust gasses from both cylinder banks exited through stub pipes. Aft of the engine bay were mountings for the oil tank and the cooler, which protruded from the starboard side of the fuselage, and the vertical thimble-shaped fuel tank. The pilot's cockpit was situated well aft of the upper wing trailing edge from where it provided an excellent all round view. Two Vickers machine-guns were to be mounted with their breeches mid-way down the sides of the pilot's cockpit under slightly bulged fairings and be fired through long troughs in the fuselage sides. Empty links and cases were to be ejected through a chute in the fuselage side. The rounded rearmost section of the fuselage was stepped down from the pilot's cockpit and was designed to carry a Hill-designed electro-hydraulic gun-turret, for which Patent No.436071 was granted in June 1935 in the names of Capt G T R Hill and Petters Ltd. A fixed mounting ring, which was part of the fuselage structure, had an inner ring which revolved on ball bearings and carried the gun mounting, adjustable seat, the gun sight, all the control and actuating mechanism, spare ammunition drums and the cupola. A single Lewis gun was mounted on its side, with the ammunition drum inboard to save space and give easy access for drum-changing. It is believed that while this turret may have been 'offered up' to the airframe, no documentary or photographic evidence has been found to show that a fully-equipped working turret was installed or flown. However, Harald Penrose clearly recalls flying the Pterodactyl V fitted with a mock-up 'aerodynamic shape turret to check the effects of air flow around it'. The two-wheel tandem main undercarriage unit was arranged in a rocking frame carried on a single oleo-leg. A shock absorber was carried on a stirrup over the front wheel, which was steerable through a small angle, and the rear wheel only was braked. Oxygen and radio equipment was fitted in both cockpits. The fabric covered RAF 34 section wings were separate units, port and starboard. They had two I-section spars built up from duralumin booms and webs with rolled section stiffeners and fabricated duralumin girder ribs. At their 'root' ends the heavy ribs were pin-jointed but, surprisingly, the joint did not have any supporting struts. The entire leading edge was also of duralumin and extended back to the front spar to make a strong rigid box structure. To add strength, at major load bearing stations the ribs were duplicated; where the straight centre-section terminated the second rib at its outer end had a plate web, and these additional ribs were also located where the two pairs of centre-section support struts from the upper longerons were

The Pterodactyl V's lower wing was a robust structure to which various struts were attached. The pilot's gun trough in the fuselage can be seen.

218

attached to the wings and where the V interplane struts were attached. Tubular compression struts were fitted at an angle between the front and rear spars linking the reinforcing ribs. Elevons of similar tubular spar and rib construction were carried at the outer ends of the upper wing, as were Handley Page automatic slats initially linked to leading-edge spoilers. Oval fins and rudders were mounted at the wings' tips, the rudders being able to be used as air-brakes. The smaller lower wing was of similar construction but had no control surfaces; however, it provided a strong mounting point for the outrigger undercarriage balancer units which, initially, consisted of a long straight skid, braced to the top of the V interplane struts and the lower wing, and fitted with a protective shoe.

Construction of the Pterodactyl V moved ahead rapidly during 1932 and by the autumn it was completed; the aircraft was then prepared for ground engine running and taxi-ing trials at Yeovil. Harald Penrose took over the aircraft and successfully taxied it for the first time, but, as the second run began, the port wing collapsed when the small strut between the rear spar and the undercarriage balancer strut failed. It was subsequently discovered that a minute error had been made in calculating that strut's eccentric loading. Back in the factory the top wings were removed and some structural tests and general redesign work began. These led to a rebuilt main wing with strengthened undercarriage balancer struts plus other small modifications. During the engine running and the single taxi run it was discovered that the evaporative cooling system was allowing the Goshawk I to overheat; thus a larger condenser was planned with some system modifications. This work occupied about sixteen months before the Pterodactyl V was again ready for further taxi trials at Yeovil, and with these completed during May 1934, the upper and lower wings were removed and the aircraft, as yet unmarked, was taken by road to RAF Andover for its first flight.

Before this flight Harald Penrose made the customary five or six straight runs, almost to the point of becoming airborne, to check the aircraft's characteristics in this ground-borne phase, then he taxied it back to the hangar for some final engine adjustments and checks on control movement. With the take-off successfully accomplished, Penrose put the aircraft into a gentle climb to about 4,000 ft during which he found that while lateral control was heavy the response

With the more powerful Goshawk II, modifications included a longer front fuselage, pear-shaped air intake and suppressed outlets, recessed exhaust system, underwing fins and larger rudders.

in pitch was light and quick. At this altitude with 'hands off' it flew straight and level and showed no dangerous tendencies. Although the early wind-tunnel tests had indicated stall problems these were not apparent; however, although the elevons proved to be overbalanced they could be easily controlled. After a 20 minute flight Penrose landed; later in the day he flew the aircraft back to Yeovil where the test flying programme was continued.

Almost immediately, engine problems appeared; the Goshawk's evaporative cooling system required an even larger condenser with a redesigned hexagonal air intake replacing the circular style of the original unit, while the engine's torque reaction on take-off tilted the aircraft on to its port undercarriage balancer skid. This latter problem was eased by off-setting the two mainwheels about two inches to that side of the fuselage, adding a cranked bracing strut to the skids and replacing the shoes with small wheels. Other modifications included moving the Handley Page slats inboard from the wingtips, wire-locking the spoilers in the closed position as they were found to be unnecessary, bracing to the wing the strut which had failed during the second taxi trial, and adding a trim tab to the starboard elevon. In this configuration the Pterodactyl V carried the Westland designation P8 in black on the sides of the rear cockpit, and on 29 August, 1934, it was flown at a presentation to the aeronautical Press at Yeovil. Later its Service serial K2770 was applied with RAF roundels.

In the head-on view it is easy to forget that the Pterodactyl V was designed as a turret fighter.

As flight testing proceeded it was found that, in a dive, the wings were twisting due to lack of torsional stiffness; thus, the outer wing section was redesigned and strengthened. When Geoffrey Hill left Westland in October and design became the responsibility of the inexperienced Edward Petter, it was Herbert Mettam's task to supervise the on-going development of the Pterodactyl V. Directional instability caused by an interaction between lateral and directional yawing produced a marked 'Dutch roll' which was partially cured by fitting larger toed-in fins and rudders. In preparation for the planned testing of the aircraft with the extra weight of the installed turret, during the winter 1934–35 a second modification programme was undertaken. This involved the installation of the more powerful 615 hp Goshawk II engine which, to counterbalance the weight of the turret, was moved 2 ft forward by adding an extra bay to the front fuselage. An exhaust collector was fitted to each cylinder bank with a large discharge pipe angled downwards and recessed into the nose cowling, while the air intake to the condenser was changed to pear shape, with recessed outlets positioned below the lower wing roots. These modifications produced a more sleek appearance to the fuselage. Others introduced two bars carrying weights which protruded from the rear fuselage to enable the c.g. to be altered, an anti-spin parachute in the fuselage underside and further changes in the engine cooling system. In this form flight tests revealed that the increased side area of the longer fuselage upset the longitudinal stability and two large strut-braced fins were attached under the upper wing inboard of the elevons. As further corners of the flight envelope were explored, Penrose found that in certain manoeuvres the controls were heavy while in the loop they became very sensitive to control surface position. In the dive at around 170 mph the elevons twisted along their length seriously affecting control. However, development flight testing continued and when the 'turret' was fitted—although this probably consisted only of the cupola secured to the mounting ring—Harald Penrose recalls carrying out a series of dives from altitude to check its effect on the control and handling of the aircraft.

During the summer of 1935 it was planned to send K2770 to the RAE for trials, but a few moments after take-off from Yeovil on the delivery flight to Farnborough the engine seized at about 200 ft, from which height Penrose made a skillful 'deadstick' landing. It was discovered that, during taxi-ing on the rutted airfield, the undercarriage front wheel had ridden up and knocked a coolant cock to the 'off' position. As Rolls-Royce's total production of Goshawks numbered only twenty-four, of which twelve were allocated for use in eight different prototypes, there was no spare engine available as a replacement for the Pterodactyl V; thus development was abandoned. However, on 11

Harald Penrose airborne in the Pterodactyl V.

December, 1935, the Aeronautical Research Committee wrote to the Air Ministry to say that the ARC's Stability and Control Sub-Committee recommended that the Pterodactyl V should go to the A & AEE ' . . . for ordinary performance and handling tests and should be kept in case further research was needed on it at a later date'. The Director of Scientific Research at the Air Ministry replied on 20 February, 1936, stating that because of the control difficulties at take-off and the unsuitability of the Martlesham Heath aerodrome plus the time required for RAF pilots to gain sufficient experience on type to fly K2770 without undue risk, 'it has been decided that no further flight testing or development should be undertaken, but that Mr Penrose's report should be accepted as the best authoritative flying experience of the type'. The letter confirmed that the aircraft would be stored at the RAE and be available for any further research required in the future.

Subsequently Westland dismantled this last of the Pterodactyl family and took it by road to Farnborough for storage. It never flew again and was finally struck off charge on 15 July, 1937, and broken up.

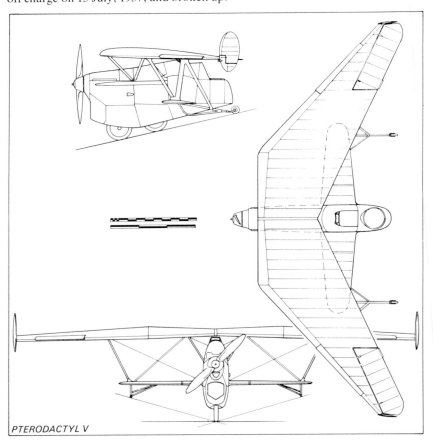

PTERODACTYL V

Description: Two-seat tailless fighter.

Accommodation: Pilot in open cockpit, gunner in proposed turret.

Powerplant: One 600 hp Rolls-Royce Goshawk I twelve-cylinder vee inline evaporatively-cooled geared and supercharged engine driving a 9 ft 6 in diameter two-blade wooden propeller. One 615 hp Rolls-Royce Goshawk II twelve-cylinder vee inline evaporatively cooled geared and supercharged engine driving a 9 ft 6 in diameter two-blade wooden propeller.

Armament: Two fixed synchronised Vickers .303 in forward-firing machine-guns and one Lewis .303 in machine-gun either on a No.19 ring mounting in the rear cockpit or in a turret. Four 20 lb bombs on a Light Series carrier under the port wing.

Dimensions: Span 46 ft 8 in; length 20 ft 6 in; height 11 ft 8 in; wing area 396 sq ft.

Weights: Empty 3,534 lb ; loaded 5,100 lb.

Performance: Maximum speed 165 mph at 15,000 ft; landing speed 66 mph; climb 12 ¾ min to 15,000 ft; service ceiling 30,000 ft.

Production: One Pterodactyl V built by Westland Aircraft Works, Yeovil, Somerset, during 1932.

C.29

Although the C.29 was the last Westland aeroplane for which Robert Bruce had a design input, it was appropriate that it should be the company's first rotary-winged aircraft.

Design thought began in 1933 and centred around a five-seat cabin configuration, much larger and heavier than any other autogyro previously envisaged in Great Britain. The basic fuselage structure was of typical Westland warren girder layout consisting of square-section steel and duralumin tubing with duralumin and wood stringers and formers to produce an oval cross section. The engine mounting ring for the 600 hp Armstrong Siddeley Panther II radial engine was angled downward in relation to the aircraft's longitudinal axis to provide an initial airflow through the rotor blades, and was carried on a triangulated structure forward of the cabin. Duralumin tubing and pressings were used to construct the tail unit which consisted of a two-piece strut-braced tailplane, in which the aerofoil section of the port segment was inverted to offset propeller torque effect, and four fins. A small ventral fin was built integrally with the fuselage and a large dorsal fin and rudder of broad chord were attached to the basic structure and two fins were tip-mounted on the tailplane with the upper sections canted outward to provide clearance for the rotor; these carried small elevators. The 50 ft diameter three-blade rotor was mounted on an inverted V structure on top of the cabin which was wire-braced to the main undercarriage outriggers. An enclosed clutched shaft, driven off the back of the engine, passed vertically upwards in front of the windscreen to provide start-up for the rotor. The entire structure was fabric-covered for lightness, apart from a small area of the cabin sides and the hinged door which were clad with duralumin. The main undercarriage consisted of two long-stroke shock absorber legs attached at their tops to pyramidal outriggers on the fuselage sides, and at their bottoms to a pair of V radius rods hinged on the fuselage centreline. A castoring tailwheel was attached to the extreme end of the fuselage structure. The cabin was well glazed with a large windscreen and deep side screens and with additional sliding windows in the cabin door and side. Seating was arranged two forward and three aft. Fuel and oil tanks were carried under the cabin floor.

The Cierva Autogiro Co was responsible for the design and construction of the rotor and rotor mechanism which employed the direct-control system; thus the 'hanging stick' control column passed down from the rotor head into the cabin via a universal joint in the cabin roof.

The portly fuselage of the C.29 provided ample space in the cabin for five people. The angle at which the engine and its one-piece twisted metal propeller are inclined downward is very apparent.

Construction of the C.29 began late in 1933 and was completed early in the following year. During this period the Spanish airline LAPE was reported to have an interest in the C.29's commercial possibilities and with this in mind the take-off weight was increased from 4,150 lb to a notional 5,000 lb. Tethered ground running tests were scheduled to begin in April and Cierva came to

The uncovered C.29 airframe shows its Warren girder main structure, wood and metal formers and stringers, and the inverted aerofoil section of the port tailplane.

Yeovil to undertake these. However, when the engine was started there were serious ground resonance problems with the fuselage rocking from side to side and vibration from the rotor. The control column was secured with rope to prevent it lashing about the cabin but each test produced similar results, with the C.29 showing no ambition to get airborne.

Neither Bruce, Davenport nor Cierva could come up with answers. These problems had not been encountered with any of Cierva's earlier Autogiros and there was, at that time, no experience or knowledge of the ground resonance phenomenon. Cierva was of the opinion that the C.29 was too dangerous to fly and all work on it was suspended until more experience had been gained from other autogyro programmes. However, later in 1934, the Air Ministry decided that the C.29 should go to the RAE for experimental ground running and it arrived at Farnborough on 11 December serialled K3663. The vibration and resonance problems were not solved and after a long period of storage it was finally struck off charge on 26 June, 1939, and broken up.

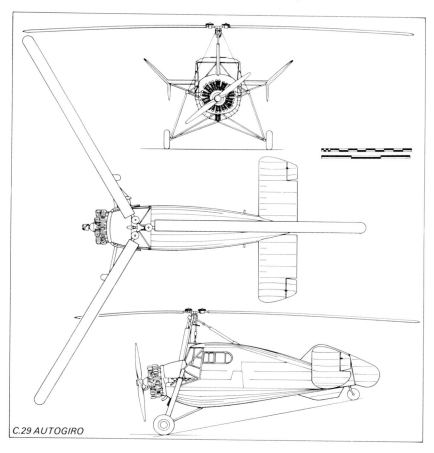

C.29 AUTOGIRO

Description: Single-rotor five-seat cabin Autogiro. Metal and wood construction with fabric and metal covering.

Accommodation: Pilot and four passengers.

Powerplant: One 600 hp Armstrong Siddeley Panther II fourteen-cylinder two-row, air-cooled, geared and supercharged radial engine driving a two-blade fixed-pitch metal propeller.

Dimensions: Rotor diameter 50 ft; rotor blade chord 1 ft 3 in; fuselage length 38 ft 0 in; height 12 ft 9 in.

Weights: Empty 3,221 lb; loaded 5,000 ft.

Performance: (Design estimate) Maximum speed 160 mph; landing speed 21 mph; climb 1,500 ft/min.

Production: One C.29 built by Westland Aircraft Works, Yeovil, Somerset, during 1933–34.

F.7/30

The Westland F.7/30, K2891, in its original configuration with open cockpit, which gave Harald Penrose problems, and small fin and rudder.

The Air Ministry's Specification F.7/30, issued to the aircraft industry late in 1931, was probably the most important and far seeing requirement formulated up to that time; indeed, when viewed in retrospect in the light of the, then, evolving pattern of air defence, its importance cannot be too highly rated.

The principal aim of F.7/30 was to produce an aeroplane for Royal Air Force fighter squadrons which could meet on equal—or better—terms any hostile airborne threat to the British Isles. Thus, the Specification, calling for a single-seat day and night interceptor, contained many stringent requirements; they included a maximum speed in excess of 250 mph coupled with a 50 mph landing speed and a very rapid rate of climb. The range, manoeuvring envelope and service ceiling were pitched at levels far superior to those of any Hawker Fury fighters, the armament was effectively doubled with four synchronised .303 in Vickers machine-guns and ammunition, and an oxygen system and two-way radio were to be carried. For night flying a good all-round view, free from visual interference by exhaust glare, and a low wing loading were specified. Because of the earlier success of the Rolls-Royce F, or Kestrel, liquid-cooled engine in many British aircraft, the Air Ministry specified the Kestrel IV, its evaporatively-cooled variant, for the new fighter. This engine resulted from a Rolls-Royce survey of competitive weaknesses which served to underline the massive weight and other shortcomings of the water cooling system. In 1928 a special F engine was designed to use steam cooling. As the heat dissipator, or radiator, in this type of cooling system is filled mainly with steam and not water, it weighs much less, and condensing the steam releases some 30 times more heat as cooling the same flow of water. During ground running this engine, known within Rolls-Royce as the PV.G—Private Venture Type G—and which became the Goshawk, performed well producing about 600 hp, but flight development revealed a number of problems; these included the virtual impossibility of pumping the nearly boiling condensate from a condenser carried lower in the aircraft than the header tank. Nevertheless, with the Goshawk nearing production—if an eventual total of only twenty-four engines can be accorded that status—it was the preferred power unit for F.7/30 aspirants. It was to be a contributory factor in the downfall of several of them.

Open exhausts show the F.7/30's engine location in the fuselage. Ailerons are only on the upper wing. The F.7/30 carries its 1931 Hendon New Types Park number.

The projected completion date for prototypes was 1933; this took into consideration not only the anticipated increase in design time for an aircraft meeting such a demanding specification but also to give Rolls-Royce sufficient time to complete Goshawk development and production planning. This time allowance was to prove insufficient, however.

One of the more interesting facets of Specification F.7/30 was its reception by the aircraft industry which greeted it with much enthusiasm for there was the promise of large production orders for the successful contender. Although the specification presented challenges to industry's design and engineering skills, it would also sharpen and advance them. The first result was that seven manufacturers submitted twelve design proposals. Of Westland's two design submissions one, the PV.4, was an unusual gull-wing biplane of very clean appearance having the engine mounted within the fuselage behind the pilot and driving the propeller through a long shaft. The pilot's open cockpit was above it in front of the top wing's leading-edge. This layout, which was conceived by Penrose and Davenport to provide an excellent all-round view, was not immediately acceptable to Robert Bruce but he was finally persuaded to adopt it. The second design, a strut-braced high-wing monoplane, was Davenport's favoured submission; however, in order to achieve a low wing loading, the span had grown to 40 ft and the landing speed was still 8 mph above the required figure. As a result the Air Ministry rejected the more advanced-looking monoplane in favour of the biplane PV.4. The structure of the PV.4 followed earlier Westland design, with the rectangular fuselage frame being of square-section duralumin tubing joined by flitch plates and tubular rivets and strut-braced internally. Because of the unusual position of the engine additional heavier frame members carried the engine mountings and extended upwards to provide attachment points for the centre-section spars. The main frame extended well forward to support the cockpit, armament and undercarriage. The oval-section nose was formed by shaped rails clad with detachable metal panels extending from the propeller to a point just aft of the engine bay, and the radiator was mounted in a streamlined cowl under the fuselage between the undercarriage radius rods. The rear fuselage was given shape by metal formers and stringers and was fabric-covered. The all-metal tail unit, which embodied a variable-incidence tailplane, had sheet metal leading-edges with fabric covering. The divided-axle undercarriage had oleo-pneumatic main legs and both the main and tail wheels were spatted. The four Vickers machine-guns and their ammunition boxes were mounted in the fuselage nose and synchronised to fire through the propeller arc. The guns were in two staggered pairs, the uppermost pair being mounted so far forward that the flash eliminators were in line with the clearance space between the fuselage nose and the spinner. Almost all of the cooling jackets of the upper guns were exposed in their troughs while the back-set lower pair of guns protruded only a short way out of the fuselage. Because the top line of the nose sloped downward very sharply in front of the windscreen the ring-and-bead sight was carried on a forward-raked inverted-V support. The two-spar single-bay wings were of duralumin and were fabric covered, as were the ailerons which, with automatic slats, were fitted only to the upper wings, and a rack for four small bombs was attached under the port lower wing. The centre-section, to which the upper wings were attached, had marked

The gull upper wing, the Goshawk's radiator and the spatted divided undercarriage are noteworthy in this view of the F.7/30.

dihedral from the centreline of the fuselage to which it was attached and was supported by two struts at its outboard ends. This created the gull-wing appearance of the upper wings. Outward canted N interplane struts were fitted and the wing cellule was wire-braced. All control runs were carried internally; and provision was made for internal fitment of two-way radio, night flying and oxygen equipment.

K2891 with modified exhausts, an enlarged fin and rudder and enclosed cockpit. The clearance between the upper gun muzzles and the propeller is minimal.

Of the seven manufacturers competing for the ultimate F.7/30 contract, tenders were accepted from Blackburn, Supermarine and Westland. At Yeovil construction of a prototype, K2891, began soon after Westland received an Instruction to Proceed with this work during July 1932. The appointed date in 1933 for completion of the prototypes and their evaluation came all too soon but none of the contenders was ready. It was not until the first week of March 1934 that final preparations were made for a first flight. On 15 March, after some ground running with the Goshawk, Harald Penrose did some taxi-ing and several straight runs to check the ground handling, but the braking system was faulty and there were problems with the cooling system. Next day Penrose made some more straights before the wings were removed and the complete aircraft was taken by lorry to RAF Andover. After re-assembly some more straights were made and the first flight took place on 23 March. Penrose found that the F.7/30 flew quite well and that everything was working well enough for him to fly it back to Yeovil, and this he did having previously made landings at Andover and being pleasantly surprised at the short run required. The view from the open cockpit high above the nose was superb but Penrose found that, at the higher speeds, unless he held his head on the cockpit's centre line it was buffetted about from one side to the other by the slipstream. This, understandably, caused him to throttle back to cruising speed at which the aircraft could be flown comfortably. However, in spite of experimenting with different throttle settings the engine coolant temperature was permanently near the upper limit. Subsequent test flights from Yeovil revealed that the steam condensers were

229

unable to perform effectively through the varying range of flight and atmospheric conditions. When coolant temperatures rose above the red line and the system blew plumes of steam, the engine had to be throttled right back and cooled down with the aircraft in a gliding descent before continuing with the test flight. At Westland it quickly beame clear that the theory of evaporative cooling did not meet the demands of fighter performance. It was too complex and vulnerable in combat for Service use. Nevertheless, flying continued in spite of these difficulties of cockpit buffeting and engine overheating, and during the following ten days speed checks were made over the measured course, only to find that the maximum speed was about 30 mph below the estimated figure. This revelation added urgency to the task of enclosing the cockpit not only for pilot comfort but also to improve the top speed.

Although there were some differences of opinion among squadron pilots and within the Air Ministry about the need for fighter aircraft to have open cockpits, Davenport designed a deep-sided canopy, which could be jettisoned in an emergency, faired into the 'valley' of the centre-section with a fixed clear view section. Subsequent flights proved that it did not affect control or stability and that, in fact, after some aileron adjustments, the controls were well harmonised. In addition, the mounting of the engine, cooling system and fuel and oil tanks around the aircraft's centre of gravity contributed to a high degree of manoeuvrability. This midships position of the engine and its exhaust caused an unforeseen problem when Penrose first slow-rolled the F.7/30, and found that the fabric covering of the rear fuselage and one side of the tailplane was on fire.

The F.7/30's Goshawk installation showing the long drive-shaft and reduction gear, the upper wing attachment structure and undercarriage and lower spar attachment fittings.

Following modifications to the fuel system, on the next flight Penrose repeated the slow roll with the same result. Fortunately, a redesigned exhaust system in which a single exhaust manifold replaced the original open stub exhausts, prevented a recurrence of in-flight fires.

During May 1934 K2891 went to the A & AEE for evaluation against the other F.7/30 aspirants, before returning to Yeovil and being prepared for participation in the New Types fly-past in the RAF Display at Hendon on Saturday 30 June. Two days later it was on show again as part of the third SBAC Exhibition and Display at Hendon, being flown—albeit with some aileron problems—by Flt Lt. J F X McKenna as Penrose was busy displaying the new Westland PV.7 general purpose monoplane. After this flurry of activity there was disappointment for Westland when its fighter failed to win the F.7/30 competition. This was not totally unexpected for the A & AEE Report M676 stated that from early in the trials the Westland P.4's performance proved to be far below that of the other aircraft built to specification F.7/30. Following instructions from the Air Ministry's Directorate of Technical Developments the evaluation trials of this aircraft were therefore abandoned. But Westland was not alone in its disappointment for none of the other manufacturers fared any better in the competition and no contract was awarded. Thus K2891 was used for experimental flying at Yeovil and the RAE Farnborough, during one period

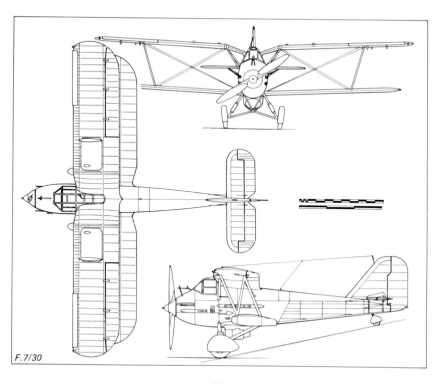

F.7/30

231

being fitted with a new rudder for which the hinge line was sharply raked forward. Its ultimate fate cannot be established only that on 3 July, 1935, it went to RAF Halton in component form.

Description: Single-seat biplane interceptor fighter. Metal construction. Metal and fabric covering.

Accommodation: Pilot in enclosed cockpit.

Powerplant: One 600 hp Rolls-Royce Goshawk IIS twelve-cyclinder vee inline evaporatively-cooled normally aspirated engine driving a 10 ft 4 in diameter Watts two-blade wooden propeller.

Armament: Four fixed synchronised Vickers .303 in forward-firing machine-guns each with 140 rounds of ammunition mounted in the fuselage nose. Four 20 lb bombs on a carrier under the port wing.

Dimensions: Span 38 ft 6 in; length 29 ft 6 in; height 10 ft 9 in; wing area 370 sq ft.

Weights: Empty 3,624 lb; loaded 5,170 lb.

Performance: Maximum speed 185 mph at 15,000 ft; landing speed 55 mph; climb 17 ½ min to 20,000 ft.

Production: One P.4 F.7/30 built by Westland Aircraft Works, Yeovil, Somerset, during 1932–34.

Lysander

During the 1939–45 War there were many stories about the Lysander, some probably apochryphal, which served to highlight its remarkable low-speed capabilities and its unique appearance in the air, both of which set it apart from all other aircraft.

The Lysander was born out of the need for a replacement for the Hawker Hector army co-operation aircraft, which the Air Ministry had hastened into production by Westland during 1936 to meet the urgent demands of the RAF Expansion programme. But the Hector could be regarded only as an interim type and by early 1935 a new requirement had been formulated with the result that, in April, Specification A.39/34 was issued calling for a two-seat army co-operation aircraft. At this time a good deal of lobbying was in progress at the Air Ministry where the technical abilities of W E W Petter, the recently appointed technical director of Westland Aircraft were being actively promoted. It was this factor, plus the company's experience with this type of aircraft which led to the addition of Westland to the list of companies which had been invited to tender to this Specification. There was a response from Bristol with its Type 148 low-wing monoplane while Hawker submitted a biplane contender and A V Roe produced some preliminary designs of the Avro 670 during October, neither of the last two reaching prototype stage.

The design of Westland's contender to Specification A.39/34, designated the P.8, was principally that of Arthur Davenport under Petter's technical direction. Still smarting under the criticism, implied if not expressed, that his earlier design for a single-engined interceptor had been turned down because of his lack of experience and knowledge of the end user's requirement, Petter sought the

K6127, the first prototype Lysander, in red oxide finish and with a two-blade wooden propeller ready for its first flight. The main undercarriage fairings and cowling gills have not been fitted.

views not only of Westland's pilots but also those of the aircrews and engineers from the RAF's army co-operation squadrons—principally No.59 based at Old Sarum—at that time flying the Hawker Audax. While their responses were disparate a number of fundamental design features predominated. Davenport and Petter had already decided that their new design would be a monoplane, while the results of their survey showed that a good all-round view for the pilot and observer, a short take-off and landing, good low-speed control and general handling characteristics were essential. Davenport, with all the experience of half a dozen high-wing Westland designs behind him, emphasised the value of this configuration to provide the view. He produced some preliminary designs embodying this feature and with the undercarriage retracting into a stub-wing. Petter dismissed this latter proposal by his chief designer, opting instead for a streamlined non-retractable undercarriage, with heavily spatted wheels. The fuselage and wings were an intriguing mixture of well-established forms of construction with unique engineering features. The fuselage was a conventional metal girder structure, the front section employing the Westland system of square-section duralumin tubes with bolted flitch plate joints while the rear section was of seamless steel tubes welded together. These two sections were joined at a point just aft of the observer's cockpit by bolted flitch plate joints. The engine mounting plate was attached to the front of the four longerons while the front of the fin was attached to the two upper longerons and the rear end was bolted to a bridge fitting between them. The tailplane was cantilevered out from the rear fuselage structure. This rectangular girder structure was given its rounded shape by light alloy and wood fairings with metal or fabric covering. The main undercarriage was a one-piece cantilever hairpin-shaped duralumin hollow extrusion, machined to a tapered square-section, which was carried in two massive forged stirrups bolted to the front fuselage structure. Stub-axles attached to its lower extremities were fitted with Dowty internally-sprung wheels, which avoided all the problems of oleo legs, and which were fully spatted. The spats carried machine-gun mountings on a welded steel-tube frame and a landing light and stub winglets could be attached to the main leg to carry light bombs or other stores. Fairings were attached to the main leg and had a hinged door on the top surface for access to ammunition chutes and electrical equipment. The tailwheel unit was fully castoring and self-centring with an oleo-pneumatic shock absorber. Initially, the prototype's Bristol Mercury radial engine turned a two-blade wooden propeller and its long-chord cowling lacked gills; later a three-blade metal propeller and a gilled cowling were fitted to all Lysanders.

The completed first prototype Lysander with fixed tailplane and RAF Display New Types Park number.

The front part of the fuselage around the pilot's cockpit was clad in removable metal panels, the rest of the fuselage being fabric covered. To provide access to equipment and permit easy inspection almost all of the starboard side below the cockpit canopy sill had removable fabric-covered panels. A unique feature was the location of a window on each side of the fuselage in front of the fin so that ballast weights could be checked before flight. The all-metal tail unit had light alloy skinning on the two-spar fin and two-spar variable-incidence tailplane with fabric-covered rudder and elevators. Both units had removable aluminium alloy tips and their rear spar webs were curved to match the metal nosings of the rudder and elevators which housed internal mass balance weights. Push rod control systems were used for both surfaces. The pilot's cockpit was set high in the fuselage in front of the wing leading-edge and had an abnormally low 'waistline' which helped to provide excellent all-round visibility. A sliding roof and vertical sliding side windows provided access for the pilot. The long unbroken cockpit canopy extended well aft of the high wing and enclosed the observer's position, which also had a sliding roof section. Both crew seats were adjustable for height, the observer's also being laterally adjustable. Hinged floor panels in the rear cockpit gave access to the bomb and supplies dropping sight. Both cockpits were heated and had individual controls. A Fairey mounting for a machine-gun was fitted in the rear cockpit. Full radio, W/T and oxygen systems were carried with a chart board positioned over the main 95 gal fuel tank located between the two cockpits. A message pick-up hook attached to the fuselage underside was operated by the observer, as was the camera and flare gun which were carried.

The wings were a triumph of engineering and aerodynamic design, being unusual from whatever standpoint they were viewed. Visually, in plan the inboard sections had reversed taper leading-edges and straight trailing-edges while the outboard sections had straight leading-edges and tapered trailing-edges; thus the root chord was only 3 ft 6 in while the maximum chord outboard was 6 ft 6 in. Similarly, the wing thickness at the roots was less than half that at the maximum chord position, echoing the shape and section of the Widgeon's wing from some twelve years earlier. There was no centre-section, the wing root ribs being attached to fuselage frames and were separated by the long cockpit canopy. Structurally and aerodynamically the single-spar wing also was unusual and was the first fully-flapped and slatted wing to be used on a Service aircraft. Petter had been impressed by the ply and spruce D-section torsion box nose and single spar of Harald Penrose's little sailplane Pegasus, which he had designed and built, and this may have been one of the factors which caused him to use this feature in the P.8's wing design. The main spar had machined Hiduminium extruded sections forming the booms which were rivetted to a plate web with top-hat stiffeners. The pressed nose ribs attached to it were clad with light alloy skinning to produce a torsion box leading-edge, while the main rib sections were of light alloy tubular construction and were fabric covered. Triangulated drag bracing of square section light alloy and steel tubing aft of the main spar was attached to a false spar carrying the flap and aileron hinges and control system bearings. Although the sailplane had only a single bracing strut on the Lysander Petter decided to relieve the torsion by using an additional strut to support his novel wing structure.

Harald Penrose in the cockpit of the prototype Lysander. Note the open leading-edge slats and the internal wing attachment structure.

The Y-shaped wing bracing struts were attached at their lower ends to the main undercarriage leg and at their upper ends to a specially strengthened plate rib at the maximum chord and thickness point of the wing. They were I-section light alloy extrusions to which duralumin front and rear fairings were screwed. The all-metal ailerons were fabric-covered and were controlled through a push-rod and chain and sprocket system. The entire wing had leading-edge slats, each divided into two sections and operating on ball-bearing rollers in three I-section runners in the main spar. The slats were on adjustable fittings, so that the vent between the slat's trailing-edge and the nose of the wing could be set as required, and had pneumatic dampers to eliminate oscillations. Slotted Handley Page flaps were fitted on the inboard sections of the wings and were moved by the inboard slats to which they were coupled by chain and sprocket systems.

K6127 with production standard radio and rear armament fitted. The window beside the fin was for checking whether ballast weights were in position before flight.

During June 1935 Westland received a contract to produce two prototypes and work began at once, to such good effect that at the end of May 1936, still in its red oxide undercoat, the first was ready for initial engine runs. Harald Penrose began the first taxi-ing trials on 10 June after which the aircraft, now painted silver, serialled K6127 and named Lysander, had its wings removed and it was taken by road to Boscombe Down, then a disused grass aerodrome, for its first flight on 15 June and a cross-country return to Yeovil. Penrose recalls that on the first take-off ' . . . heading into a gentle west wind, the throttle was steadily opened; already the tip slats were fully out and within the first few yards the root slats pulled forward and partly lowered the interconnecting flaps. In less than 150 yards the machine was climbing away'. During the flight it was discovered that the controls were a little heavy and that the aircraft was unstable; then, on landing ' . . . I ran out of elevator when ten feet up because the tailplane was not adjustable, so the engine had to be used to help flatten out', said Penrose. An immediate remedy was the addition of a wide strip to the elevator trailing-edge to increase the chord, but this made little difference, and it became increasingly evident that, with the slats and flaps fully deployed there was a much greater nose-down trim change than the wind-tunnel tests had predicted. However, on 27 June the P.8 prototype made its public debut in the RAF Display at Hendon and two days later flew to Hatfield for the SBAC

236

Show. On 8 July K6127 was among some ten of the newer types of RAF aircraft drawn up at the A & AEE for inspection by HM The King. It returned there on 27 July for a week's preliminary handling trials during which the pilots encountered the same landing and instability problems which Harald Penrose had been experiencing. The instability was largely overcome by increasing the tailplane area, but this made flattening out during landing virtually impossible. The answer was a variable-incidence tailplane, but this introduced another real danger; if full throttle was applied during an overshoot, the aircraft pitched upwards sharply, even though the control column—with some effort—was held fully forward. Only by using minimum power to maintain flying speed and resetting the tailplane to neutral could an overshoot be accomplished without fear of stalling. Penrose saw, only too clearly, the dangerous possibilities and refused to accept it, but Petter and Westland's production staff argued vehemently against any further modifications to the tail on the grounds that it would delay production by six months; further, they claimed that a warning notice in the cockpit would be sufficient. At some stage an automatic trimming device was proposed but this was rejected as being too complex.

Meanwhile, in September, the Air Ministry had ruled out the Bristol Type 148 as an A.39/34 contender and had issued to Westland the first production contract for 169 Lysander Mk.Is to Specification A.36/36. This set the scene for what was to become the largest and longest running production programme for

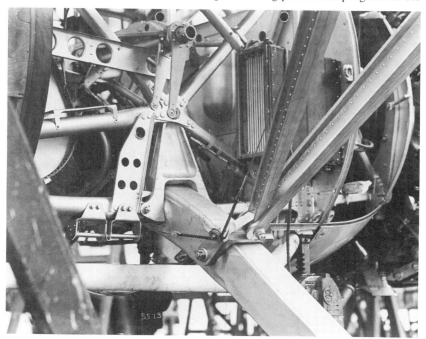

Construction of the Lysander undercarriage showing the square-section 'hairpin' extrusion, its attachment stirrups and the wing struts attachment.

any fixed-wing Westland-designed aircraft. Shortly afterwards, on 11 December, 1936, the second prototype, K6128, made its first flight and, during the month at the company's Annual General Meeting, the chairman, Sir Ernest Petter, told shareholders that orders for Lysanders would keep the works fully employed for two years.

Almost all of the development flying was done by the two prototypes whose tail units remained un-modified following the A & AEE pilots' acceptance of the aircraft with its landing problems. 'Inevitably in later service there were scores of crashes . . . because the pilot was unable to prevent stalling with full engine', said Harald Penrose. There was a near disaster of a different kind while K6128 was at Martlesham Heath during March 1937. To save weight and as an experiment a lightweight fabric, instead of the Irish linen used on the first prototype, had been used on this aircraft. On the wings the fabric was attached to the main spar boom by a metal strip secured with Simmonds stop nuts. When K6128, flown by Sqn Ldr R W Collings, pulled out after a high-speed dive at the A & AEE all the fabric on the top surface began to rip and come off. The pilot sensed that something serious had occurred but bravely elected to stay with the

The Dowty internally sprung wheel which enabled a single cantilever undercarriage leg to be used. A landing light is housed in the wheel spat. (*Dowty Group*)

aircraft and landed safely, earning an Air Force Cross for his courage and tenacity.

As production of Lysanders got under way, development flying continued at Yeovil, the A & AEE and RAE and during early 1938 K6128 was shipped out to No.5 Squadron, a Wapiti-equipped unit based at Miramshah in Waziristan, for some successful tropical and general field trials. Then, on 25 March, L4673, the first production Lysander, was flown by Harald Penrose, the second following it a few days later. On 15 May L4673 went to the A & AEE for performance trials, while L4674 was retained by Westland for trials to a new Mk.II standard with a Bristol Perseus engine. The third aircraft, L4675, had dual controls and was meant for the CFS at Upavon but, in the event, a standard production Lysander was required to enable the pilot's handling notes to be written up, so L4676 went to the CFS instead.

K6127, the first Lysander prototype, with an experimental installation of two 20 mm Oerlikon cannon for a ground attack role.

Deliveries to RAF squadrons also began on 15 May, No.16 Squadron at Old Sarum, where the School of Army Co-operation was located, being the first to replace its Audaxes with Lysanders when it received L4675. The Air Staff had originally planned to re-equip Nos.4,16,2,208,13 and 26 Squadrons in that order, but due to the recent re-equipment of No.2 Squadron with Hectors and a delay in sending Lysanders to No.208 Squadron due to the Munich Crisis, the squadrons received their new aircraft between September 1938 and April 1939 but not in that order.

As anticipated by Harald Penrose, there were a number of accidents on the squadrons. During a demonstration on 28 April, 1939, by a No.2 Squadron Lysander at Hawkinge, the pilot essayed a steep climb out of a low and slow fly-by but stalled and crashed. About the same time a No.13 Squadron pilot making a steep climb on take-off, stalled in a turn with insufficient height to recover. Then, during an Empire Air Day display, a Lysander stalled off a low, slow turn and crashed while a fourth stalled during a night take-off with the same result.

Mock-up of a proposed Boulton Paul Type A Mk.III four-gun turret installation in a Lysander.

At this time considerable interest in the Lysander was being shown by several overseas air forces whose pilots came to Yeovil to fly the aircraft. Harald Penrose recalls a moment of tension when a very large and heavy Turkish pilot set out to emulate his 150 yard take-off and apparent climb out over an abandoned cottage on the aerodrome boundary; in fact, Penrose took-off slightly to one side of the cottage. The Turk, however, positioned the aircraft immediately in front of it, but managed to just clear the obstruction. A French pilot was not so lucky; his heavy landing broke off part of the undercarriage leg but he succeeded in climbing away again. When he essayed a second landing he held the aircraft level on the remaining wheel before dropping on to the

Mock-up of a proposed ventral gun position in a Lysander.

opposite wingtip and ending up on its nose.

Because of its speed-range and comparatively docile handling characteristics—other than during overshoots or outside prescribed limits—the Lysander was used not only in a number of different operational roles, which included army co-operation, air-sea rescue, target towing, Special Duties and radar calibration, but also as the vehicle for testing a number of interesting and bizarre experimental configurations and equipment. The fuselage, wings, tail unit and undercarriage were all the subject of experimentation, only the radial engine installation remaining virtually unchanged. During late 1939 a scheme was devised to arm the Lysander with a 20 mm cannon for use as a ground or

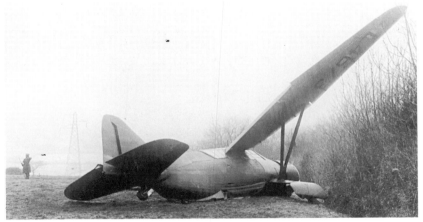

'The Pregnant Perch', the first production Lysander L4673, with a ventral gun position, ended its days with its nose in a ditch in June 1940.

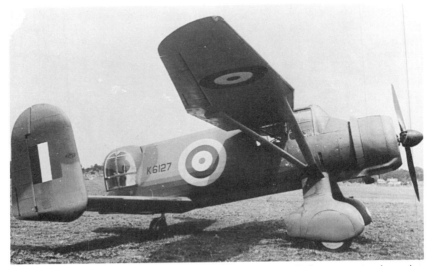

The first prototype Lysander rebuilt during 1940–41 with a Delanne-type tandem wing configuration and a mock-up tail turret.

Twin end-plate fins and rudders and the very realistic mock-up tail turret on the tandem wing Lysander.

surface-vessel attack aircraft in the event of an attempted German invasion of the British Isles. A drum-fed Oerlikon gun was fitted to each of K6127's main undercarriage legs, their front barrel mountings picking up on the stub-winglet attachment points and the breeches being supported on V-struts attached to the fuselage sides. In this position the guns were able to fire outside the propeller disc, as did the standard .303 in Browning guns in the wheel spats. After some preliminary firing trials the project was abandoned during the summer of 1940. It is believed that a similar two-cannon armament was also fitted to L4673, the first production Lysander Mk. I. Three other armament-oriented projects were the installation of a Boulton Paul Type A Mk.III four-gun turret immediately aft of the wings, a ventral gun position and the installation of a Boulton Paul tail turret. The dorsal turret project did not progress beyond the mock-up stage but the other two were built and flown, again with their use against invading enemy troops in mind. After a mock-up had been built and a trial installation of a mock-up turret in P1723, a Lysander Mk.II, a modification of L4673 to accommodate a ventral gun position earned this Lysander the nickname 'Pregnant Perch'. This project was suddenly terminated in June 1940 when engine failure caused George Snarey, who had joined Westland some 18 months earlier as assistant test pilot, to force land 'somewhere in Devon'. The port

Harald Penrose flies the tandem wing Lysander, K6127, at Yeovil in July 1941.

243

undercarriage leg carried away and luckily this stopped the aircraft sliding into a deep ditch.

During work on the dorsal turret project it was recognized that the additional weight would move the c.g. too far aft; thus the idea of fitting a very large tailplane to restore the longitudinal stability was mooted. In France Maurice Delanne had built just such a tandem wing light aircraft, the Delanne 20T, and was also constructing a fighter prototype of similar configuration. After Petter and Penrose had visited him during the spring of 1940, and Penrose had flown this light aircraft, Petter quickly redesigned a Lysander with a shortened fuselage, to be fitted with a tail turret of either Frazer-Nash or Boulton Paul design, and an aft cantilever wing with tip-mounted fins and rudders. Following a series of wind-tunnel tests with different models, the detailed drawings were issued to Harringtons, a Hove coach builder, who produced the rear wing under sub-contract while Westland modified and shortened K6127's rear fuselage. Although the intention was to fit an operational turret at a later stage the modification work was completed without any electrical or hydraulic power supply lines to the rear fuselage; instead, a Perspex and plywood mock-up was fitted and lead ballast was added to simulate the weight of a real turret and its associated systems. This work occupied a year and it was not until 27 July, 1941, that Harald Penrose first flew this strange looking aeroplane, now designated P.12. He found that its take-off and handling characteristics were markedly similar to the standard production Lysander, except that the twin rudders were less effective. This did not prevent him from looping the aircraft on this first flight. After completing Westland's flight test programme K6127 went to the A & AEE for handling trials which were aimed principally at proving the concept; thus, the P.12's very wide c.g. range was fully explored, the aircraft proving very stable. By then the need for a beach-strafing aircraft had passed and, although K6127 proved very tractable, further development was abandoned. It was struck off charge on 13 June, 1944.

Hydraulically-operated dive-brakes were fitted to one Lysander as an experiment.

A Lysander Mk.II, P9105, was used for test flying a special high-lift wing designed by H Steiger and built by Blackburn Aircraft. As the inventor of the monospar wing structure, Steiger had employed this feature in a 38 ft span parallel-chord wing with full-span flaps and slots and the use of wingtip spoilers for lateral control. Yet another trial installation was under-wing air-brakes fitted to one aircraft only. While photographs have been widely published purporting to show a Lysander with a castoring main undercarriage 'to enable it to land, pointing into wind on an out-of-wind strip', this was erroneous. Special Duties squadrons had found that the shock absorbing elements of the Dowty internally sprung wheels on their Lysanders were bottoming when landing in rough fields in Occupied France. In an effort to overcome this problem, Westland bolted two high energy absorbing Dowty Liquid Spring shock absorbers, with internally sprung wheels, to the main undercarriage extrusion: however, this undercarriage was fitted as an experiment on only one aircraft. In service with RAF and RCAF squadrons during the 1939–45 War, Lysanders initially saw service in Europe, the Middle East and South East Asia in their primary role of army co-operation aircraft. After 1940, when Allied forces withdrew from mainland Europe after the Battle of France, there was little or no requirement in the European theatre for aircraft in this role. Thus, these Lysanders and their crews were a ready-made force immediately available to equip many air-sea rescue, coastal patrol and Special Duties squadrons in which they provided an outstanding service.

Lysander Mk.I

A total of 169 aircraft were built, from which seven RAF squadrons were equipped beginning in June 1938. During the ensuing fifteen months these

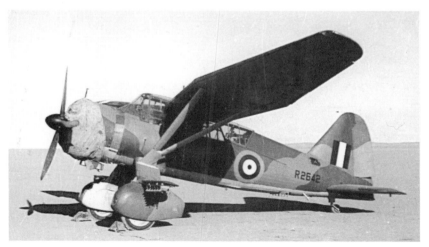

This Lysander I, R2642, with its engine cover and the stub-wings fitted is seen in the Western Desert in 1942.

squadrons continued their peacetime conversion to the Lysander and training to bring themselves up to operational standards of efficiency. By September 1939 many of these Lysanders, which were powered by 890 hp Bristol Mercury XIIs, had been replaced by Mk.II aircraft, the Mk.Is being shipped to the Middle East. There they saw action in the Western Desert, East Africa, Greece, Crete, Palestine and Egypt alongside the later Mk.IIs. Some twenty Lysander Is were converted to TT.Is and TT.IIIs being fitted with electrically-powered winches for target-towing duties.

Egyptian Lysander Mk.I

The last of eighteen Mercury XII powered Lysander Is for the Royal Egyptian Air Force, with carburettor intake filters and short sliding rear canopies.

During the autumn of 1938 the Egyptian Government signed Contract 555425 for nineteen Lysander Mk.Is for the Royal Egyptian Air Force. Serialled Y500–Y518 the unit price of these aircraft was £5,600 each. The first one, Y500, first flew on 6 October, 1938, and deliveries began one week later, being completed on 15 December.

Finnish Lysander Mk.I

Contrary to some reports that nine Lysander Mk.Is were flown to Finland during the summer of 1939, a 'little black book' discovered by a member of Westland's technical staff shows that an order for these nine aircraft was not signed by the Finnish authorities until 8 February, 1940, and that it was met by diverting them from a cancelled Estonian contract for ten aircraft. In addition the book indicates that a further eight ex-RAF Lysander Mk.Is were also sold to Finland, the whole deal initially being worth £149,311, which was later reduced to £147,897.8s.8d (£147,897.40p). A further element of mystery is that no

Lysanders were ever included in official inventories of Ilmavoimat aircraft. As the order was signed only a month before Finland capitulated to overwhelming invading Soviet forces to end the 14-week Russo-Finnish War, the maintenance of such records could have been an impossibility.

French Lysander Mk.I

Serialled 01, this was the sole Lysander I sold to France.

France ordered one Lysander Mk.I at a cost of £11,985. As a French pilot had earlier damaged a Lysander demonstrator aircraft at Yeovil, perhaps the repairs are reflected in the high unit price! Serialled 01, this lone Lysander was delivered on 6 July, 1939, to the Armée de l'Air.

Lysander Mk.II

This Lysander variant was powered by the 905 hp Bristol Perseus XII sleeve-valve radial engine, which was the major difference between the two Marks. Four Lysander squadrons, Nos.2,4,13 and 26 went to France in 1939 with the BEF Air Component, leaving No.16 Squadron at Old Sarum. In France they were used for artillery spotting, reconnaissance and bombing, but were no match for the large formations of Messerschmitt Bf 109s and 110s which were encountered daily, even though a number of these Luftwaffe fighters were destroyed by Lysander crews. Nevertheless, despite crippling losses, Lysanders played a vital role in the Battle of France in the supply dropping and bombing roles. During the Battle some 70 per cent of the 175 Lysanders which went to France were lost. Like the earlier Lysander Mk.Is, the Mk.IIs served in the Middle East and were also operational in South East Asia against Japanese forces. A total of twenty-one were later converted to TT Mk.Is and IIs.

The twelfth of thirty-six Lysander IIs supplied to the Turkish Air Force in 1939. Note bead sight on the engine cowling and the rear gun installation.

Canadian Lysander Mk.II

Before the start of the 1939–45 War the Royal Canadian Air Force had shown an interest in acquiring the Lysander and National Steel Car Corporation Ltd obtained a licence to build the aircraft at Hamilton, Ontario, where a new factory was built during April–June 1938. Tooling began immediately, the first metal was cut in September with the first Lysander Mk.II, 416, making its first flight on 16 August, 1939, at Malton, piloted by E L Capreol. A total of seventy-five aircraft were produced, some as target tugs. After the war ex-RCAF Lysanders 433 and 451 were converted as crop sprayers and registered CF-DRL and CF-DGI-X respectively.

N1256, a Lysander II of No.225 Squadron RAF 'somewhere over England' in 1940.

Turkish Lysander Mk.II

On 29 June, 1939, Westland received an Instruction to Proceed with production of thirty-six Lysander Mk.IIs, for the Türk Hava Kuvvetleri, the contract, No.981730/39 being worth £365,940. Records indicate that, initially, the serial numbers 711–746 were allocated but those finally applied were 3101–3136. The first of these flew on 8 January, 1940, and deliveries began on 1 February, 1940, being completed on 12 April.

Irish Lysander Mk.II

Six Lysander Mk.IIs, serialled 61–66, the first of which flew on 8 June, 1939, were delivered to the Irish Air Corps between 15 June and 11 July, 1940, each costing £6,250. The long gap between the date of the contract No.611814/37 and these deliveries is inexplicable. Of these six aircraft 61 and 66 were converted to TT Mk.IIs during September 1944 and were struck off charge during November 1946, 63 remained serviceable until April 1947 and the other three were written off in accidents during 1941–42.

Lysander II, R1999, of No.225 Squadron being serviced at Old Sarum in 1940. The variable-incidence tailplane is fully nose down and control surfaces are centralised indicating that control locks are on.

French Lysander Mk.II

At least twenty-two ex-RAF Lysander Mk.IIs were transferred to the Free French Forces during 1940.

Lysander Mk.III

Strangely this was the lowest-powered Lysander variant, being fitted with an 870 hp Bristol Mercury XX or 30 radial engine, yet it was the heaviest. In its main and sub-variants, the Mks.III and III (SD), IIIA and IIIA (SD) it equipped twenty-four squadrons in the United Kingdom, Middle East and South East Asia operating in the army co-operation, reconnaissance, air-sea rescue and radar calibration roles. It was, however, in service with Nos.138, 161 and 357 Special Duties squadrons that it earned undying fame. Based first of all at Newmarket, Suffolk, but later moving to Tempsford, Bedfordshire, Nos.138 and 161 Squadrons played a 'cloak-and-dagger' role under the auspices of the Special Operations Executive, a secret organisation established in June 1940 to put into effect Winston Churchill's directive to 'Set Europe ablaze'. From August 1941 the squadrons' task was to maintain contact with Resistance forces in France, to drop supplies of arms, ammunition, explosives, radios and other equipment and to deliver and pick up agents and Resistance leaders or rescue downed Allied airmen. All this to be done under cover of darkness. For the hazardous tasks of carrying agents—or 'Joes' as they were referred to, their real names remaining a close secret—these Lysanders, usually painted matt black, were fitted with an external ladder alongside the rear cockpit for ease and speed of exit and entry by the 'Joes', who were sometimes 'Josephines'. Each sortie was highly dangerous with accurate navigation by the pilot being the first essential to the success or failure of the operation. That said, the highest standards of airmanship and courage were required when the small field had been located, the three torches in the form of an L to show wind direction, and hopefully held in friendly hands, had been snapped on and the landing had to be made. Most of these early flights were accomplished with Lysander Mk.III (SD) aircraft but in 1942 the Mk.IIIA (SD) was introduced to enable these flights to penetrate deeper into France than before. This variant had the Mk.IIIs twin rear guns removed and a large 150 gal fuel tank was carried under the fuselage between the undercarriage legs to extend the endurance to eight hours. The loaded weight was increased by some 58 per cent and cruising speed was reduced

V9287, a Lysander IIIA (SD) of No.161 Special Duty Squadron, with long-range fuel tank
and ladder for clandestine SOE operations into Occupied Europe.

by about 25 mph but the range was almost doubled at 1,100 miles.

Late in 1944 six Lysander Mk.IIIA (SD) aircraft were shipped to Karachi for use by 'C' flight, No.357 Squadron, which was engaged on Special Duties, mainly for picking up agents and supplying Force 136 operating behind the Japanese lines. Although the Squadron base was Jessore the Lysanders were detached to Meiktila and Mingaladon.

Canadian Lysander Mk.III

In Canada during 1942 the National Steel Car Corporation built 150 Lysander Mk.IIIs with Bristol Mercury XX engines but completed them as Lysander IIIA TTs. Like most Lysanders in Canada they had a cockpit heater. The first to fly, 2305, got airborne during mid-December 1941 flown by E H Taylor. Later twelve were converted for target towing and twelve more as glider tugs by Central Aircraft Ltd at London, Ontario. A plan for Westland to assemble Lysander Mk.IIIs built in Canada, for which a batch of fifty serial numbers V8920–V8969 had been reserved, was cancelled. Postwar, two Lysander IIIs were used for crop spraying and were registered CF-FOA and CF-GFJ.

Portuguese Lysander IIIA

Westland's only overseas deliveries of Lysander IIIAs was to Portugal during September 1943 when eight aircraft went by sea in ss *Fort Cumberland* to Lisbon. As this was 21 months after production had ceased they were all ex-RAF aircraft.

United States Lysander TT IIIA

Substantial numbers of Lysanders were transferred to other air forces, twenty-five TT Mk.IIIAs being supplied to Gunnery Flights and Schools of the US 8th Air Force in 1942 and remaining in service in the United Kingdom for about two years. They retained their RAF serials and fin stripes but carried USAAF insignia. Apart from two which crashed they were all returned to the RAF in 1945. Lysanders were also transferred to the South African and the Free French Air Forces.

During January 1946 all RAF Lysanders were withdrawn from service and were ferried to Maintenance Units for scrapping. They were last used operationally by the Royal Egyptian Air Force against Israeli forces during 1948. A total of sixty-four Lysanders of all Marks were converted for use as instructional airframes.

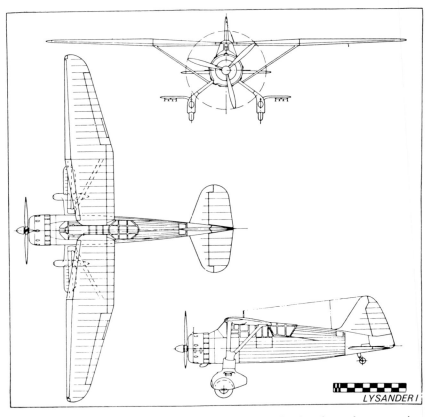

LYSANDER I

Description: Two-seat army co-operation aircraft. Metal and wood construction with metal and fabric covering.

Accommodation: Two crew in enclosed cabin.

Powerplant: One 890 hp Bristol Mercury XII nine-cylinder radial air-cooled geared and supercharged engine driving an 11 ft diameter variable-pitch three-blade metal propeller (Mk.I). One 905 hp Bristol Perseus XII nine-cylinder radial air-cooled, sleeve-valve, geared and supercharged engine driving an 11 ft diameter variable-pitch three-blade metal propeller (Mk.II). One 870 hp Bristol Mercury XX or 30 nine-cylinder radial air-cooled, geared and supercharged engine driving an 11 ft diameter variable-pitch three-blade metal propeller (Mk.III).

Armament: One fixed forward-firing .303 in Browning machine-gun in each wheel spat and one .303 in Lewis or Vickers gas-operated machine-gun on a Fairey mounting in the rear cockpit (Mk.I) or two Lewis guns (Mk.II). A removable stub-winglet on each main undercarriage leg could carry six 20 lb HE bombs, Mk.II practice smoke bombs or Mk.I reconnaissance flares. Alternatively the load could be four Mk.VII 112 lb or 120 lb general purpose bombs, two 250 lb HE bombs, incendiary bomb canisters, smoke canisters or

Mk.VB supply droppers. A Light Series carrier under the fuselage could carry four 20 lb HE Mk.I bombs.

Dimensions: Span 50 ft 0 in; length 30 ft 6 in; height 14 ft 6 in; wing area 260 sq ft.

Weights: Empty 4,044 lb (Mk.I), 4,160 lb (Mk.II), 4,365 lb (Mk.III); loaded 5,920 lb (Mk.I), 6,030 lb (Mk.II), 6,330 lb (Mk.III), 10,000 lb (Mk.IIIA (SD)).

Performance: Maximum speed 211 mph at sea level, 219 mph at 10,000 ft (Mk.I); 206 mph at sea level, 230 mph at 10,000 ft (Mk.II); 209 mph at sea level, 212 mph at 5,000 ft (Mk.III); minimum speed 54 mph (Mk.1 and II), 56 mph (Mk.III); climb to 10,000 ft in 6.9 min (Mk.1 and II), 8.0 min (Mk.III); service ceiling 26,000 ft (Mk.1 and II), 21,500 ft (Mk.III); take-off run to clear 50 ft 250 yards (Mk.I and II), 305 yards (Mk.III).

Production: A total of 1,427 Lysanders built by Westland Aircraft Ltd. Yeovil, Somerset, and Westland (Doncaster) Ltd during 1935–1942 as follows:

2 P.8 prototypes (1935–36)
169 Lysander Mk.I production aircraft.
442 Lysander Mk.II production aircraft.
367 Lysander Mk.III production aircraft.
347 Lysander Mk.IIIA production aircraft.
100 Lysander TT Mk.IIIA production aircraft.

A total of 225 Lysanders built under licence by the National Steel Car Corporation Ltd, Malton, Ontario, Canada, during 1938–1942 as follows:

75 Lysander Mk.II producton aircraft.
150 Lysander TT Mk.IIIA production aircraft.

CL.20

Even before the earlier C.29 Autogiro had failed to get off the ground and began gathering dust in a hangar at Yeovil, Edward Petter was investigating the possibilities for Westland to collaborate with another autogyro designer in the creation of a second rotary-winged aircraft. Through his contacts at Cierva Autogiro Co and with the help of Westland's agent in France, Petter met Georges Lepère, an experienced design engineer who had, with ex-Schneider Trophy pilot Charles Weymann, formed Avions Weymann–Lepère in 1929 and had designed and built several Cierva Autogiros. One of these was the CL.10, a small two-seat side-by-side aircraft with a 75 hp Pobjoy R Cataract engine.

Edward Petter and Lepère soon established a great rapport and with Sir Ernest Petter's agreement to finance the manufacture of a new Autogiro, Lepère began design work. To help with this project he arranged for the CL.10B, a modified direct-control cabin variant of the CL.10 to be sent to Yeovil from the Cierva Autogiro Co at Hanworth where it was being test-flown by Juan Cierva and Allan Marsh. Understandably, the design of the new aircraft, designated Westland CL.20, was similar to the CL.10B.

Construction of the CL.20 began in August 1934 with both Edward Petter and Arthur Davenport supervising detail redesign and manufacture. The rear fuselage was a departure from established Westland practice, having a welded seamless steel-tube structure in a flat-based triangular configuration with circular frames which was given shape by light alloy formers and stringers to produce a multi-faceted fabric-covered exterior. The cabin had a sturdy light-alloy rear arched member, a wooden floor and a large door with a window on each side. It was enclosed by a deep three-section windscreen, a large transparent panel in front of the door which extended downward to the floor, and a two-section curved roof. Aft of the cabin there were more transparent panels on each side and over the fuselage top. The mounting plate for the 95 hp Pobjoy S Niagara engine was carried on a braced steel-tube structure attached to the forward triangular fuselage structural member. The engine bay, forward of the windscreen was clad with metal panels. The tail unit, which was of fabric-covered metal construction, consisted of three fins mounted on a tailplane, without elevators, but which had ground-adjustable incidence. One half of the tailplane was set at negative incidence and had an inverted aerofoil section to counter the propeller torque. The main undercarriage units were outrigged, the vertical shock absorbers being carried on a braced triangulated system of struts attached to the two forward frames in the fuselage. Wheel brakes were fitted and were cable operated by a lever in the cabin floor. All three undercarriage wheels were spatted, the tailwheel being steerable. The three-blade folding rotor was mounted on a longitudinal streamlined inverted V structure attached to the front and rear frames of the cabin and braced by a lateral inverted V of two steel-tubes. The tilting rotor head was moved by a

The CL.20's polished fuselage panels, spatted wheels and enclosed rotor start-up mechanism were essential if the planned performance was to be achieved.

hanging control column which passed vertically through the cabin roof, where a universal joint was located, to a position in front of the pilot. The Niagara engine was specially modified with a rear power take-off bevel gearbox driving through a friction clutch, the long transmission shaft which, at its upper end, drove a crown wheel integral with the rotor hub. This was for power starting the rotor rather than having to resort to the earlier manual starting procedures. As a safety measure the release mechanism for the clutch and wheel brakes could not be operated until the control column was freed from its locked position and the rotor became auto-rotating as the propeller slipstream took effect.

Building work on the CL.20 was completed in December 1934, and on 21 January, 1935, bearing the civil registration G-ACYI, flight trials began at Yeovil. These were in the hands of Harald Penrose who, in 1932, had taken a conversion course to rotary-winged aircraft in the direct-control C.30 with Cierva at Hanworth. With these completed G-ACYI was dismantled and transported to Hanworth for Juan Cierva to continue these trials. He made the first short flight followed by a second on 5 February, but a number of small

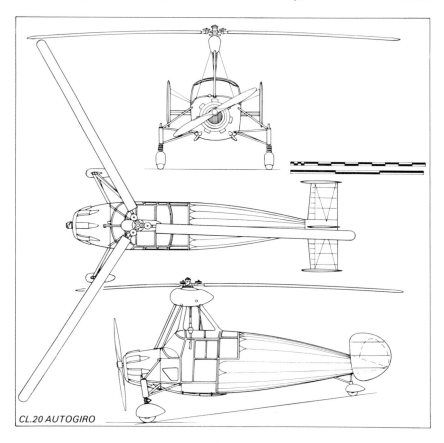

CL.20 AUTOGIRO

control problems were encountered. The tailplane incidence was changed and the outboard fins exchanged. Further test flights ensued and, with attention focussing on the lack of lift, the rotor was removed for incidence checks on the blades. On 15 March Allen Marsh, the Cierva test pilot, made his first flight in the CL.20 during which he experienced the aircraft's inability to exceed a height of about 300 ft; however, he found that it was pleasant to fly even though its lateral control was over sensitive. A more powerful Niagara engine was fitted, flying with it for the first time on 18 July; but even this made little difference to the generated lift. Thus, after a further eight test flights during that month, Marsh made what was to be the last one on 21 July when he carried a passenger for just a 2 min flight. This brought to an end the CL.20's 61 test flights during which only 8 hr 31 min flying time had been logged. The CL.20 was dismantled and returned to Yeovil where Edward Petter was still convinced that there would soon be a market among private owners for such an aircraft. He had managed to persuade his father to allow Westland to build six CL.20 airframes while the lack of lift and control problems were being solved, but although work was begun during March 1935, the programme was abandoned to enable Westland's design office to concentrate on work of more immediate importance.

Description: Single-rotor two-seat Autogiro. All-metal construction with fabric and metal covering.
Accommodation: Pilot and passenger in side-by-side seats in an enclosed cabin.
Powerplant: One 95 hp Pobjoy S Niagara seven-cylinder radial air-cooled, geared and normally-aspirated engine driving a 7 ft 3 in diameter two-blade wooden propeller.
Dimensions: Rotor diameter 32 ft 0 in; length 31 ft 9 in (rotor turning), 18 ft 6 in (folded); height 10 ft 3 in.
Weights: Empty 840 lb; loaded 1,400 lb.
Performance: Maximum speed 106 mph; landing speed 25 mph.
Production: One CL.20, built by Westland Aircraft Works, Yeovil, Somerset, during 1934–35.

Whirlwind

In parallel with the Air Council's launching, in November 1934, of a series of schemes for the expansion of the Royal Air Force, there was the issue of a number of Specifications aimed at providing new fast and heavily armed monoplane fighters as replacements for the ageing biplanes. Among them were F.9/35 and F.10/35 for a two-seat and single-seat day and night fighter respectively. Two companies, Boulton Paul and Hawker received orders to build prototypes of their submissions to Specification F.9/35; with the former company's Defiant turret-fighter being chosen for quantity production rather than Hawker's Hotspur.

In the meantime, Specification F.10/35 had been the subject of a good deal of re-thinking by the Operational Requirements staff who believed that it had been

The camouflaged first prototype Whirlwind in 1940 with production standard canopy, radio mast, pitot head, interim exhaust system and black/white wing undersurfaces.

largely met by the Hawker and Supermarine prototypes being built to F.36/34 and F.37/34, which became the Hurricane and Spitfire. One of the major features of F.9/35 and F.10/35 was the heavy armament called for; six or, preferably, eight 20 mm cannon. This number of guns had been decided by a careful analysis of the weight of projectiles which needed to be fired during a two-second burst to ensure the destruction of an enemy aircraft. In May 1935 the Air Staff considered two alternatives to proceeding with F.10/35; these were to suspend it for a time or to re-write it and call for an even more advanced design. In the event, F.10/35 was withdrawn and was superceded by F.37/35 calling for a single-seat, single-engined day and night fighter. Among the detailed performance requirements were a maximum speed of at least 40 mph more than the contemporary bombers at 15,000 ft and not less than 330 mph at this altitude, a 30,000 ft service ceiling and with take-off and landing runs over a 50 ft barrier to be not more than 600 yds. Other requirements included retractable undercarriage, an enclosed cockpit with heating, night flying equipment, and a variable-pitch propeller. The armament specified was 20 mm or 23 mm cannon in sufficient numbers to meet the 'two second burst destructive effect' referred to earlier. Initially there was also a recommendation that they should be able to be traversed, but this was later removed from the Specification. So, too, were the words 'single-engined' type to allow submissions of twin-engined designs.

Clearly this Specification was a milestone in fighter development history for not only was it the first formal British requirement for a four-cannon fighter but was among the front runners in the world to specify such a heavy armament.

Rather surprisingly, in view of the limited experience of some manufacturers in the field of high-speed fighters, eight companies were invited to tender to F.37/35, of which five were able to respond. They were Boulton Paul, Hawker, Bristol, Supermarine and Westland, which submitted the twin-engined P.9.

The P.9 project drawings produced by Arthur Davenport's team of designers, all under the guidance of Edward Petter who had been appointed technical director in July 1935, centred around the concept of a fighter with the most heavy concentration of firepower possible with four 20 mm cannon, a good all-round view for the pilot and absolute minimum frontal area. Grouping the cannon in the nose demanded a twin-engined configuration, while a slender fuselage and carefully streamlined engine nacelles helped to ensure minimum drag. The engines chosen were 885 hp Rolls-Royce Peregrine vee inline liquid-cooled units, but to avoid the use of high-drag frontal radiators these were carried in the centre section. The oil cooler was mounted on the front spar and the coolant radiators received cooling air from a spanwise intake in the leading edge. Similarly, to avoid protruding external air intakes for the down-draught carburettors, internal intakes projected into the radiator air duct.

L6844, the dark grey Whirlwind first prototype. Note the through-wing exhaust outlets above the nacelle, early cockpit canopy, pitot head, mudguards and lack of tail unit acorn fairing.

At the submission stage the P.9 featured a tailplane mounted in the mid-position on the finely-tapered rear fuselage, with twin endplate fins and rudders. Advanced design features included Fowler area-increasing flaps on the centre-section, Handley Page automatic slats on the leading edges of the outer wings and hydraulically-actuated slats on the upper leading edge of the centre-section radiator intake which were interconnected with the flaps. The rear portion of the engine nacelles moved with movement of the flaps. Structurally, the design of the P.9 was innovative, particularly in the use of magnesium alloy skinning and of electron castings. The fuselage was to be built in three sections; the front section from the nose to just aft of the cockpit, which embodied the centre-section, and rear section and the tail cone which, it is believed, originally would have included the integrally built fin and tailplane. The front section from the nose to just aft of the cockpit was of stressed skin construction with aluminium alloy extruded main members, vertical and horizontal formers and frames. Most of this front section forward of the cockpit was used to house the armament pack which extended forward from an armoured bulkhead. The four cannon were carried on a tubular structure and a duralumin base plate to which armour plates could be clipped to protect the four amunition drums and the cockpit. The cockpit was enclosed by a sliding canopy which, although it could not be jettisoned, could be opened by winding a handle.

The rear fuselage section was of magnesium alloy stressed skin, flush-rivetted and carried on aluminium frames and stringers. The mainplane was built in three parts; a centre-section built integrally with the front fuselage section, and port and starboard outer panels. The main spar ran the full width of the centre section and had booms of aluminium alloy extrusions machined to a U section to accept the aluminium webs, with integral fork ends at the outboard ends to which the outer panels were attached. Two lighter spars between the engine nacelles carried the inboard leading-edge slats and the Fowler flaps. The steel-tube engine mountings were attached to the front spar. A 67 gal fuel tank and a 10 gal oil tank were carried each side in the centre section between the engine and the outboard rib. The outer wing panels were built up around the main spar, a false aileron spar and 10 duralumin plate ribs. Handley Page slats occupied the whole of the leading edge outboard of the profiled 24 gal oil tank. All the control surfaces were of metal construction and were metal covered. Operation of the leading-edge inboard slats was through a linkage to the Fowler flaps and combined with the radiator shutter operation. The first flap movement opened the shutters to permit maximum airflow through the radiators for ground engine running, taxi-ing and climbing. Further movement of the flaps opened the leading-edge slats, for take-off and initial climb, which then remained open until the flaps were retracted through the same position. All the flying controls were operated by systems of push-pull rods, bell cranks and rocking levers. Trim tabs, operable through Bowden cables, were fitted on the elevators and rudder and a ground-adjustable tab on the ailerons. All three tabs had a servo action. Exactor hydraulic control systems were used for the throttles and mixture controls and for the propeller pitch control. A Dowty hydraulically-actuated undercarriage with a retractable castoring tailwheel was fitted, all three units being enclosed by doors when retracted.

The pitch of the de Havilland propellers shows that the Peregrine engines are handed on Whirlwind L6844. The centre-section radiators and small fuselage frontal area are seen to advantage.

In his efforts to avoid external excrescences, Petter adopted a unique but highly dangerous engine exhaust system. Two long exhaust pipes, suitably insulated, were led through ducts in the fuel tanks and exited aft of the wing trailing-edge. It was a complex installaton, too, requiring more than 60 bolts and nuts.

This, then, was Westland's submission to meet Specification F.37/35, a proposed design which, like every one of Petter's aircraft, embodied many unusual and unique features. It was submitted during the summer of 1936.

Although originally F.37/35 had called for a single-engined aircraft, the results of the Tender Design Conference were heavily in favour of the three twin-engined proposals by Bristol, Supermarine and Westland, even though their estimated delivery dates were, understandably, later than those for the single-engined designs. It appears, too, that neither Westland's long estimated lead time of up to 24 months for the P.9 prototype—which was more than any of the other submissions except the Supermarine Type 313—nor the £27,500 price, which was the highest, counted against Westland in the final deliberations of the September 1936 Design Conference.

L6845, the second prototype Whirlwind in August 1939, with Rotol propellers on same-rotation Peregrines, small fin/tailplane acorn and experimental nose mounted pitot head.

Thus it was that, early in 1937, the Air Staff chose the P.9 as the sole F.37/35 design to proceed to the prototype construction stage, the company receiving Contract No.556965/36 for two aircraft, serialled L6844 and L6845 on 11 February, 1937. There was some surprise and alarm in the aircraft industry that Westland, which had had little involvement with high-speed fighter design since

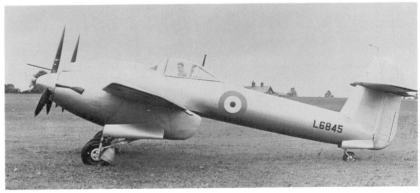

This side view of Whirlwind L6845 shows the modified, horn-balanced rudder and interim exhaust.

the biplane F.7/30, should have been preferred to other companies with more experience. There was, however, no doubt that the entire concept of the P.9 was in advance of that of the other submissions and that the Westland design office had the capacity to undertake the work involved; these two vital factors clearly weighed heavily in the Air Staff's final choice. However, there were still a few lingering doubts in the minds of some Air Ministry staff, as witness an important clause in the Contract. At the time of its award nearly all new aircraft were ordered into quantity production 'off the drawing board'; in the case of the Whirlwind no production order was to be placed until the prototype had completed handling trials. This was to delay the entire programme with serious consequences.

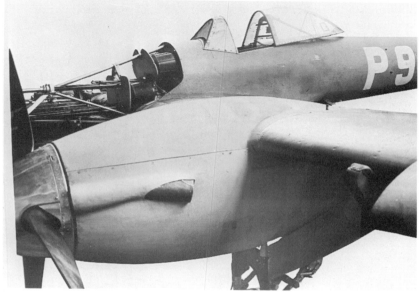

This view of Whirlwind L6845 shows the closely cowled port engine and the manner in which the nose panels could be removed for access to the armament installation.

With detail design work in hand, wind-tunnel testing of the originally projected configuration with twin fins and rudders showed that, while a high top speed of around 370 mph was possibly attainable, the position of the tailplane could cause instability and the elevators could become almost ineffective due to 'blanketing' when the large Fowler flaps were fully lowered. A major redesign of the tail unit resulted in the substitution of a single fin and rudder with a high set tailplane. This was embodied in the mock-up which was finally approved in June 1937 after Air Ministry and Air Staff inspection.

Although construction of the prototype L6844 at Yeovil was hindered by late delivery of many major components, including the engines and undercarriage, this aircraft was completed by late September 1938 and Harald Penrose began initial ground handling and taxi-ing trials on 4 October. These revealed that the engines tended to overheat and 'steam' during prolonged high-power running, and that the Exactor controls, which had replaced the earlier Simmonds-Corsey system, were not entirely satisfactory. With these trials completed, the aircraft, with its outer wings and engines removed, was prepared for transporting by road to RAF Boscombe Down, the home of Nos.88 and 218 Squadrons flying Fairey Battles, which offered a very much bigger aerodrome with better approaches than did Westland's own. After re-assembly, there were further taxi-ing and high-speed runs on 11 •October, to enable Penrose to obain the 'feel' of the controls, during which he experienced engine overheating yet again. When the Peregrines had cooled he essayed another fast run, but 'overcooked' it and when, on throttling back, it appeared that the aircraft would run out of aerodrome, Penrose opened the throttles fully and managed to get airborne with only a few yards to spare.

The bulged nose cone of Whirlwind L6844, previously used for a four-abreast cannon installation was retained for trials with a single 20 mm cannon.

After a short period at Boscombe Down, L6844 was flown back to Yeovil for preliminary contractor's trials which began on 10 November. Inevitably, with this combination of so many advanced engineering and design concepts, combined in a new airframe with untried engines, there were many snags which arose. The two Peregrines were the fourth and seventh engines to be built, and although their performance and power output were satisfactory they continued to run hot, so much so that the starboard engine seized and was removed. There were, too, directional control problems which were partially overcome by increasing the rudder area above the tailplane. The rudder was in upper and lower sections and, because of the control run geometry, was carried on offset hinges. In its original form it proved ineffective at small angular movements and

A 12-gun 'weapon egg' built by Martin-Baker for trials on a Whirlwind prototype.

too heavy thereafter. Various cures were tried before the problem was solved by giving the rudder concave surfaces on both sides of the lower section and on the starboard side of the upper section. Other control problems included tail buffeting at the stall and in tight turns, marked nose down pitching in the higher speed range, the ailerons were too heavy and the outboard slats tended to slam open. Later, in Service use, these slats invariably were locked shut. By the year's end many other problems had been encountered and some had been overcome. It was with a number of them still unsolved that L6844 went to the RAE at Farnborough on 31 December, 1938, for brief handling trials, Westland having been informed that upon the outcome hung a production order for two hundred Whirlwinds! After only two-and-a-half hours flying during the month that the Whirlwind was at RAE, which entirely confirmed Penrose's findings, L6844 returned to Yeovil to continue the flight-test programme but by April only 25 hours flying had been logged. Some 250 modifications were made, including changes to the slats, aileron leading-edge, servo tab gear ratio and cockpit layout. More major changes were a fin-shielded horn-balance to the upper rudder section and a small wooden torpedo fairing at the fin and tailplane joint, this last addition to cure buffeting in tight turns. Meanwhile, construction of the second prototype Whirlwind, L6845, was proceeding at a steady rate until completion was delayed so that modifications could be embodied and, while waiting for its engines, the 11th and 12th Peregrines, to be built. It finally flew on 29 March, 1939.

While L6844 was at Farnborough, Westland received a production contract for two hundred Whirlwinds and responded by promising delivery of the first aircraft in nine months' time. Unfortunately, there was no parallel order placed with Rolls-Royce for Peregrine engines, largely because the Air Ministry was awaiting the outcome of flight trials of L6844 fitted with handed engines and L6845 with engines that both rotated the same way. Clearly, the hope was that the handed engines would not show any major benefits so that only one type of Peregrine could be ordered. During June L6845 was flown with both types of engine by two A & AEE pilots. Their reports showed that the handling characteristics were the same with both engine combinations.

P6966, the first production Whirlwind I, still in its primer finish, at Yeovil during June 1940.

One design aspect which had always worried Harald Penrose, and, indeed, many other people, was the somewhat frightening routing of the exhaust pipes through ducts in the fuel tanks. Penrose believed that failure or damage to the duct could result in a catastrophic explosion. Proof of the dangers inherent in this system became evident on 10 June, 1939, when the starboard aileron push rod on L6844 failed, and the aileron went up, causing it to roll. However, Penrose immediately applied up-aileron on the opposite side to produce 'washed out' wingtips which got the aircraft flying straight and level and then, by skilful piloting, he landed the aircraft back at Boscombe Down.

It was later found that part of the exhaust system duct had failed, happily in the nacelle and not in the fuel tank, which allowed hot exhaust gas to burn the aileron push rod causing it to fracture under load. A more worrying aspect was that this failure was close to the main spar, failure of which would have meant the loss of the aircraft and possibly of Penrose too. Although Petter had been loth to change the design before this incident, the Air Ministry insisted that a more conventional external system be used.

Development flying continued in an intermittent way with the two prototypes during the spring and summer of 1939. While a number of the many problems which had beset the prototypes were being cleared, particularly their handling which was much improved in spite of the still somewhat heavy ailerons, there

A Whirlwind I 'fully furnished' cockpit, complete with gunsight, in January 1941. Missing from the right hand panel is the IFF recognition device switch.

remained the recalcitrant Peregrines which still overheated, failed in flight and which did not produce their specified power at altitude. These engines were still being 'hand-built' almost in the manner of prototype units and production standard engines would not become available for many months. Two other criticised shortcomings in the Whirlwind were the tail buffet in tight turns, and the long landing run resulting from the need of a landing speed to provide sufficient elevator control for hold off. This limited the choice of usable aerodromes for Whirlwinds.

One of the major problems with the slow delivery of engines was the small number of staff and limited engineering facilities which Rolls-Royce was able to allocate to the Peregrine programme, in view of the company's heavy work load on the Merlin variants, the Vulture and the beginning of the Griffon design.

As development and production test flying proceeded through the summer months, Whirlwind manufacture slowly got under way in the shadow of the continuing Lysander programme. A good deal of project work was being done to improve the Whirlwind's armament, not only by adding Browning .303 in machine-guns to four Hispano Mk.I 20mm cannon but also by using belt-fed ammunition in two belts with 150 rounds and two with 200 rounds each in place of the 60 round drums. Thought was also given to the use of twelve .303 in machine-guns with up to 5,000 rounds. A mock-up of this installation was first produced by Martin-Baker before this twelve-gun installation was built as a 'weapon egg' for rapid attachment to the aircraft. It had a cadmium-plated steel-tube structure complete with the guns, their mountings and twelve ammunition boxes. Another armament installation was the mounting of a single 40 mm cannon in a slightly modified nose. The first prototype aircraft, L6844, with an extended nose, was used at the RAE for trial installations of a four-cannon belt-feed mechanism with the cannon mounted four-abreast instead of being paired one above the other, and for the single 40 mm cannon, although there is some doubt whether this weapon was ever flown. Armament experts argue over the photographs which purport to show it in the nose of L6844, some believe that it is, in fact, a single 20 mm cannon doing duty for the larger weapon.

This work on alternative nose armament was part of Petter's plans for the Whirlwind II, which included the installation of two extra 35 gal fuel tanks, one in the nose and a second one in the rear fuselage. This arrangement would have resulted in the pilot sitting in the middle of 194 gal of high octane fuel. One of the failures of the Whirlwind was its fuel system which was, in effect, two entirely separate systems with no provision for crossfeeding fuel from one main tank to the other to supply the engine on the opposite side. One wonders what form the system would have taken in the Whirlwind II to ensure that fuel was drawn equally from these two additional and widely spaced tanks to avoid trim problems.

During August 1939, only a few weeks before the War began, Rolls-Royce, having earlier abandoned work on the Exe, a twenty-four cylinder X-configuration engine being test flown in a Fairey Battle, decided to further rationalise its engine programme and announced the early termination of the Peregrine and Vulture to enable a greater concentration of effort on the many Merlin variants being designed and built. Then, a letter to Westland from the Air Ministry Contracts Branch, dated 26 October, 1939, gave instructions that the contract for two hundred Whirlwinds was 'not to be proceeded with'. It was not until 6 December that the go-ahead for 114 aircraft was given in a second letter. These came as major shocks to Westland even though Petter, Eric Mensforth and Peter Acland were aware of the undercurrent of dissatisfaction with the Whirlwind in certain sections of the Air Ministry.

Whirlwind I, P6984, was the 19th production aircraft and was typical of the 114 built. Note the large fin acorn and the rear-view mirror on the windscreen arch.

Throughout the 1939–40 winter, flying with the two prototypes continued with L6844 going to the RAE at Farnborough in February 1940 where it was installed in the 24 ft wind-tunnel for drag analysis. By taping over the gaps around the control surfaces and undercarriage doors and by adding fairings to the exhaust outlets it was calculated that the reduction in drag could provide a 15 mph increase in maximum speed.

Harald Penrose banks Whirlwind I, P7110, for the camera revealing the empty case collector and the smaller camera gun blister.

When the original production order for the two hundred Whirlwinds had been placed with Westland, the company's nine-month first delivery date was to prove wildly optimistic. It was not until 22 May, 1940, 17 months after receipt of the order, that P6966, the first production aircraft, first flew. Thus five years had elapsed between the initial issue of Specification F.37/35 in June 1935 and the delivery of the first production Whirlwind to No.25 Squadron RAF in June 1940. This lengthy period was exceeded by only one of the eight other fighter types put into production for the RAF during the Second World War. It seemed that the surprise and alarm expressed earlier by the aircraft industry in Britain when Westland won the F.37/35 competition was justified.

The first production aircraft trials at the A & AEE were made with P6980, the 15th production Whirlwind which went to Boscombe Down on 16 November, 1940. It remained there just three weeks during which a series of dives from up to 14,000 ft were made at speeds up to the design diving speed of 410 mph. These were to check on tail vibration which had become apparent in some of the earlier production aircraft and which had been overcome with the fitting of a large acorn fairing at the fin and tailplane junction.

During April and May 1941 P6997, the 32nd production Whirlwind, was test flown at Boscombe Down to check the handling characteristics with the outboard slats locked in. This followed a number of incidents in which the slats of other Whirlwinds had opened so violently that they broke away from their mountings. On at least one occasion this was followed by structural failure of the wing and the tail unit and the death of the RAF pilot. As these trials proved that there was little or no difference to the handling or performance, it was recommended that these slats should be permanently closed and locked in. After a period with the Air Fighting Development Unit, P6997 went back to Westland for modifications before returning to Boscombe Down for trials of the aircraft carrying an external bomb-load. These were to check the Whirlwind's suitability for operations as a fighter-bomber. With two 500 lb bombs, carried one under each wing, the aircraft was cleared for speeds up to 350 mph above which the handling and control characteristics deteriorated. Assymetric loading with a single bomb was considered operationally unsatisfactory and unsafe in certain flight modes, particularly during low-level evasive manoeuvres.

Meanwhile, the Whirlwind production programme was gathering momentum despite delays due to non-delivery of Peregrine engines from Rolls-Royce which was unable to obtain delivery of the special down-draught carburettors from Hobson.

This Dark Sea Grey civil-registered Whirlwind, G-AGOI, originally P7048, was used by Westland as a 'hack' during 1945–47. The change of colour aft of the cockpit resulted from the use of paint from two competing manufacturers. The supplier of that on the rear fuselage won!

May and June 1940 was a very busy period for No.25 Squadron, a night interception unit which was heavily involved with operational RDF (radar) trials with Blenheim IFs carrying experimental airborne radar equipment, the AI Mk.III. Temporarily based at North Weald, but having been detached to Hawkinge for a short period, it returned to North Weald in time for its pilots' first viewing of the Whirlwind on 30 May when L6845, the second prototype, arrived from Boscombe Down. On 1 June Sqn Ldr K A K McEwan, No.25's Commanding Officer, demonstrated the aircraft. During the next two weeks

P6966 and P6967 were flown to North Weald for the squadron to fly; however, very shortly afterwards the Air Ministry decided not to lose the expertise and experience gained by the squadron with its radar-equipment and to re-equip it with the new Beaufighter. During July the two Whirlwinds left North Weald, both going to No.263 Squadron at Grangemouth. This squadron, which had been decimated when, after flying Gladiators in Norway and re-embarking in HMS *Glorious*, only to be sunk on 8 June, 1940, with the loss of all the aircraft and most of the air-crew, was intended to become the first operational Whirlwind unit in place of No.25. However, due to production delays it was equipped with Hurricane Is during later June and flew them operationally until November. A good deal of the squadron's efforts went into some intensive flying of Whirlwinds to overcome a number of snags, chief among them being armament and engine problems. Production aircraft were being delivered straight from Yeovil to Drem, the squadron's base.

No.263's score-book with Whirlwinds was opened on 12 January 1941, when, operating from Exeter, and with a detachment at St Eval, a section intercepted a Junkers Ju 88 off the Scilly Isles, Pilot Officer Stein being credited with its 'probable' destruction. The squadron also was undertaking 'Chameleon' patrols against E-boats cruising in the English Channel searching for survivors from returning night raiding Luftwaffe bombers which had come down in the sea. The first confirmed victory came on 8 February when an Arado Ar 196 reconnaissance floatplane was shot down by Pilot Officer Traham who also crashed into the sea, presumably having died in the successful attack on the enemy aircraft.

In order to exploit to the full the Whirlwind's heavy firepower No.263 took the offensive and prepared to make low-level point attacks on enemy-held aerodromes in France. The first of these was on 14 June, 1941, when a

One of eleven presentation Whirlwinds, P7056, *The Pride of Yeovil*, was paid for with donations from the people of the town.

six-Whirlwind force attacked Messerschmitt Bf 109 coastal aerodromes at Querqueville and Maupertus, west and east of Cherbourg respectively. Unfortunately poor weather conditions with limited visibility hampered the operation. Further Whirlwind attacks during July and August, with the code-name Warheads, were more successful. On 12 August No.263's Whirlwinds escorted as far as Antwerp six Blenheim squadrons attacking the Fortuna, Knapsack and Quadrath power stations near Cologne. In parallel with these the squadron was also involved in development flying to prepare the Whirlwind for ground attack operations against armoured vehicles.

A second Whirlwind squadron, No.137, was formed at Charmy Down on 20 September, 1941, and worked-up to operational status, one flight flying its first operation on 24 October. This was a Ramrod with the Whirlwinds escorting bombers in an attack on railway sidings at Landernau some 10 miles from Brest. During the winter months No.137 undertook sweeps and coastal patrols from Coltishall and then Matlaske from where it had detachments at Snailwell and Drem. On 12 February, 1942, the squadron was detailed to escort some destroyers; however, it became involved with part of the gigantic 'umbrella' of Luftwaffe fighters escorting the German warships—*Scharnhorst, Gneisenau* and *Prinz Eugen*, forcing their way up the English Channel after breaking out from Brest. In the ensuing engagement four Whirlwinds and their pilots were lost.

From September 1942 both squadrons' aircraft were fitted with a Mk.III universal bomb carrier under each wing following the trials with P6997 referred to earlier. Thus equipped, the aircraft became known unofficially as the 'Whirlibomber', taking part in many Rhubarbs which were low-level cross-Channel fighter attacks on targets of opportunity. These included shipping, locomotives, harbours, bridges and aerodromes with attacks being made by day and by night.

In June 1943 No.137 Squadron gave up its Whirlwinds and converted to Hurricane IVs, while No.263 continued to fly its Whirlwinds until December, two years after production ceased at Yeovil. The lack of replacement aircraft and pilots had reduced the operational state during the last few months of the year, even though some of No.137 Squadron's aircraft had been transferred to No.263.

In total, only 116 Whirlwinds, of the 200 ordered, were built, but of these, 114 were production aircraft which all saw squadron service. That only two prototypes were built is a unique record of achievement, particularly in view of the Whirlwind's many advanced structural, aerodynamic and system design features.

Description: Single-seat day and night fighter or fighter/bomber. All metal construction.

Accommodation: Pilot in enclosed cockpit.

Powerplant: Two 885 hp Rolls-Royce Peregrine I twelve-cylinder vee inline liquid-cooled geared and supercharged engines driving 10 ft diameter de Havilland 4/4 three-blade variable-pitch metal propellers.

Armament: Four British Hispano Mk.I 20 mm forward-firing cannon in the fuselage nose with 60 rounds per gun. Provision for one Mk.III universal bomb carrier beneath each outer wing.

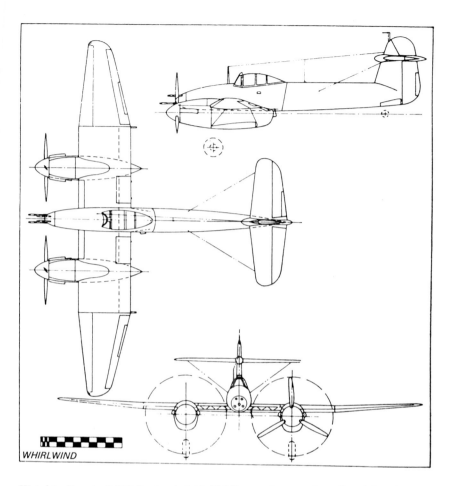

WHIRLWIND

Weights: Empty 8,310 lb; loaded 10,356 lb; maximum take-off weight with two 500 lb bombs 11,388 lb.

Performance: Maximum speed 355 mph at 15,800 ft; landing speed 110 mph; climb to 30,000 ft in 24.6 min; service ceiling 30,300 ft; range 800 miles.

Production: A total of 116 Whirlwinds built by Westland Aircraft Ltd, Yeovil, Somerset, during 1937–41 as follows:

2 Whirlwind prototypes
114 Whirlwind Mk.I production aircraft.

Welkin

In its primer undercoat the first prototype Welkin, DG558/G, is towed out for engine running on a wet October day in 1942.

Although the Welkin twin-engined fighter, designed for operating at very high altitude, did not fly until November 1942, the concept of providing pilots with a pressurised cabin for extended stratospheric flight had been studied and become the subject of much experimental work in Great Britain for a number of years during the 1930s. From 1938 this work culminated in several prototype aircraft with pressure cabins including the experimental General Aircraft ST.25 which was redesignated the GAL.41, the Vickers Type 432 which never, in fact, flew with such an installation, and the Vickers Wellington V and VI. Without doubt General Aircraft's submission to the Air Ministry in October 1939 of the GAL.46, a private-venture project for a twin-engined two-seat high altitude fighter-bomber, was never regarded seriously as a viable proposition; however, it proved to be the catalyst which helped to change the official mind on the matter of pressure cabins for operational aircraft. However, it was quick to assert that the receipt of the submission by General Aircraft was not the prime reason for this change. By April 1940 the Air Ministry's interest had hardened to the point where it had decided to encourage the development of a high-altitude fighter to combat expected air attacks on the British Isles by very high flying Luftwaffe bombers, Germany's work on pressurisation of aircraft being no secret. This it did by issuing, early in July, Specification F.4/40 to five manufacturers—Fairey Aviation, General Aircraft, Hawker Aircraft, Vickers-Armstrongs and Westland Aircraft. In the initial flush of enthusiasm, the broad requirements of this Specification called for a two-seat high-speed aircraft, able to operate, ultimately, at 45,000 ft but with a pressure cabin able to maintain a 10,000 ft cabin altitude equivalent. Armament was to be six fixed forward-firing 20 mm cannon, airborne interception radar equipment was to be carried and a top speed of 450 mph at 25,000 ft was required. The preferred power units were the Rolls-Royce RM.65M engines, which were the forerunners of the Merlin 60 series with two-speed two-stage superchargers. These were the initial core of

F.4/40 requirements; others included a fuel capacity sufficient for two hours maximum economic cruise at 25,000 ft in addition to 30 minutes level flight at maximum power settings (all of this fuel to be carried in self-sealing tanks), the provision of armoured protection for the crew and a service ceiling of 34,000 ft.

Little time was given to those five companies who were invited by the Air Ministry to submit tenders, the submission date being set for 20 July, 1940. Of these five, Vickers-Armstrongs, which was busy with the design of its Type 414, a twin-engined fighter to meet Specifications F.22/39 and later F.16/40, and Fairey Aviation, then fully occupied with design and development work on the Fulmar and Barracuda, did not make submissions. Thus the choice lay between the Hawker P.1004, which was a larger development of the Typhoon incorporating six-cannon wings, a set of which were built, the re-vamped version of General Aircraft's GAL.46, which had become a pure fighter, and two design proposals by Westland.

It was, perhaps, to be expected that at least one of these Westland proposals should be of unorthodox design and Edward Petter did not disappoint, with a brochure showing an engine layout featuring twin tandem-mounted Merlins turning counter-rotating propellers through a single reduction gearbox. The six-cannon armament was mounted in a 58 ft span wing, the crew sat back-to-back in a pressure cabin and the estimated maximum speed was 428 mph at 35,000 ft. Although the Specification had listed the use of a nosewheel undercarriage as optional, Petter clung to the conventional tailwheel; this was, almost certainly, because it would have provided better braking characteristics on the grass aerodromes lacking hard runways and enable the aircraft to meet the 700 yards landing run requirement with fuel remaining for 500 miles flight. With two Merlins in the nose it would have posed a problem finding space for a retracted nose undercarriage leg! The other design submitted by Westland was the P.14, clearly a development of the Whirlwind being of markedly similar configuration and considered to be the principal proposal. It was a low-wing monoplane with two Rolls-Royce Merlin Mk.XX engines in the 60 ft span wing and with the tailplane mounted on the fin but lower than in the Whirlwind, with a large acorn fairing where these two surfaces joined. Two 20 mm cannon were to be mounted in the centre-section and four more in the fuselage nose. The two crew members were seated back-to-back in an armoured pressure cabin having bullet-proof windscreens and a jettisonable top cover, while the maximum speed at 35,000 ft was calculated to be 395 mph, some 30 mph slower than the other Westland proposal.

Air Ministry assessment of these four proposals began on 17 October, the criteria not only being their technical merit and ability to meet the Specification for a fighter which could out-climb and out-gun whatever the Luftwaffe might fly against Britain in the foreseeable future, but also the perceived capability of the individual companies to turn their designs into effective prototype hardware and to have the manufacturing ability and capacity for quantity production. Applying these latter criteria General Aircraft was ruled out on its lack of experience and facilities allied to the under-developed nature of its proposal. Initially the Hawker P.1004, being structurally close to the Typhoon/Tornado twins, was considered to be the most suitable from the production point of view; however, Hawker's design office was already overloaded with ongoing

Hurricane development as well as work on the Typhoon and the first stirring of its thin-wing successor the Tempest. Thus, all Ministry of Aircraft Production attention appeared to be focusing on the submissions by Westland—whose design office was ready to take on new work. During the following month Westland suggested a reduction in the armament to four cannon but each with more rounds, and in mid-December, proposed the fitting of two .303 in machine-guns in each wing; moreover, it was suggested that provision should be made only for a pilot. Almost inevitably it was the P.14 which was of major interest, the two fuselage-mounted Merlin installation of the second proposal, which was complex, badly obstructed the pilot's forward view and needed a lot of development work, resulted in its rejection. The use of a pressure cabin was an essential element in the design of all four proposed high-altitude fighters and Westland was well ahead in the basic research associated with pressurisation systems. Bill Widgery, the company's chief experimental engineer, had devised and laboratory-tested a pressure cabin control valve, in the form of a 'leaking altimeter', and it had been flight tested in a pressurised Spitfire Mk.II by Harald Penrose. In addition, this work was now to be supplemented by the RAE and by Vickers-Armstrongs which was working on the pressure cabins in the Wellington V and VI.

While all this work was in hand, progress was being made with wind-tunnel testing to establish the definitive configuration, initial detail design and the construction of a mock-up. The wind-tunnel results showed that a mid-wing position would be more efficient than the proposed low wing and that the tailplane position, low on the fin, placed it satisfactorily clear of any turbulent airflow from the wings or flaps, particularly when the latter were lowered. Various tail unit shapes and sizes were also model-tested in Westland's wind tunnel to ensure effective control throughout the speed and height ranges. In a letter to Petter, dated 23 December, 1940, W S Farren, the director of technical development at the Ministry of Aircraft Production, indicated a strong possibility that Westland's high-altitude fighter would soon get the go-ahead. Finally, on 9 January, 1941, Eric Mensforth received instructions from the Minister of Aircraft Production himself, the fiery little Lord Beaverbrook, to proceed with the design and production of two P.14 prototypes, the value of this contract being some £175,000.

At the design conference on 13 February while production of the two P.14s was progressing, a number of fundamental changes were made to the F.4/40 requirements; these included the reduction of the crew to just the pilot and the armament to four cannon 'with provision for two more' while the performance of the cabin pressurisation system was also less exacting so that at 45,000 ft the cabin altitude equivalent was raised to 25,000 ft. This was to be achieved with a pressure differential of only 3.5 psi. In addition, the maximum speed required was reduced from 450 mph to a minimum of 400 mph. These changes were notified in a re-issue of requirements dated 3 June, 1941. Meanwhile, at Yeovil, design changes were in hand with an increase in span of 5 ft to reach 65 ft which, happily, left the all-up weight still some 600 lb short of the specified 16,000 lb. The removal of the second crew member and his equipment enabled an additional 77 gal of fuel to be carried internally; but inevitably the weight crept ever upward and when the span was increased yet again to 70 ft, providing 460 sq ft of wing area, it rose to 18,300 lb. By March 1941 the basic mock-up was ready for assessment by the various Air Ministry operational requirements, engineering and aviation medicine experts who found a number of features to criticise. These included the heavy framing of the windscreen and canopy—necessarily large to cope with the needs of the pressure cabin—and the position of the nacelles on the mid-wing, all of which restricted the pilot's view to each side and downward below an angle of about 8 deg. It was also considered that the position of the pilot's head was too far from the windscreen. There were, too, some rumblings about the wide span causing ground handling and hangarage problems, but these clearly lacked evidence and future events were not to provide it. On the engineering side there was the design and provision of an effective system for airframe de-icing, while the aviation medicine physiologists considered the requirement for a separate portable oxygen system for the pilot for use if he baled out at very high altitude. Then on 26 April, Specification F.7/41 was issued with the definitive requirements and it was to these that the P.14 was developed. Structurally, the P.14, which was to be officially named Welkin—the poetic name for the sky or upper air—had an all-metal stressed skin airframe of conventional design, the configuration having been used previously in the Whirlwind. The fuselage was built in three main sections; the front fuselage containing the pressure cabin, the four cannon and their individual ammunition boxes; the rear fuselage built up around oval frames with stringers; and the tail unit. The pressure cabin was built as a separate unit, using ½ in thick bullet proof light alloy material, with armoured steel front and rear bulkheads, and a heavy gauge light alloy floor. Covering the top of the cabin was a thick armoured double windscreen, with an airspace between the two layers through which hot air was passed to demist it on the inside and prevent ice accretion on the outer surface, and a sliding canopy of similar construction in which the thick inner shell withstood the air pressure. A thick bullet proof glass bulkhead was carried on top of the rear armoured bulkhead and was shaped to match the canopy contour. Aft of this glass bulkhead was a clear-view Perspex fairing extending over what was intended to be the second crew member's cockpit but which was now the ammunition bay. Sealing of the pressure cabin was effected by a Bostik rubberised liquid sealant at all the joints, by specially designed bellows and gland seals at points where hydraulic pipes, electric cables and control rods passed through the cabin bulkheads or walls, and by inflatable rubber seals around the sliding canopy frame. Air for the pressurisation system came from a small intake in the leading edge of the starboard outer wing panel which was ducted to a blower on the starboard engine and thence through a filter and silencer to a non-return valve on the aft face of the cabin's rear bulkhead and into the cabin. Westland's patented automatic control valve maintained the required cabin altitude to suit the operating altitude. This complete pressure cabin unit was attached to the centre-section front spar by bolts passing through its strengthened web. The four cannon and their associated systems were mounted beneath the cabin floor and a camera gun and air intake were on the forward face of the front bulkhead under the nose cone. The rear fuselage section carried a vertically cylindrical 79 gal fuel tank (shades of the Wapiti main tank installation) plus radio, oxygen and emergency equipment. It terminated in a strengthened frame to which the tail unit was attached, this unit comprising the fin and tailplane, their respective control surfaces each having a trim tab, and the retractable tailwheel.

The 70 ft span wing was also built in three sections; a centre-section extending to a point 5 ft 4 in beyond the engine nacelles and two outer wing panels. The centre-section spars inboard of the nacelles had T-section booms with Warren girder webs instead of the plate webs with vertical stiffeners which were used outboard of that point. This centre-section carried the two Rolls-Royce Merlin engines in very close-cowled nacelles. which extended aft of the trailing-edge and contained the main undercarriage, the coolant tanks and radiators, oil tanks and coolers, the supercharger intercoolers, with intakes in the wing leading-edge. The flaps which occupied all of its trailing-edge both inboard and outboard of the nacelles, also acted as radiator flaps, a device first used in the Whirlwind. Two fuel tanks were also carried in the centre-section outboard of the engines; in the leading edge was a 60 gal tank with a 140 gal tank positioned between the two spars. With the fuselage tank they provided a total fuel capacity of 479 gal. The outer wing panels carried the long-span ailerons each with a trim tab.

When first flown, DG558/G had a rounded top fin and rudder and short engine nacelles. The G suffix indicated the secret nature of the prototype which required an armed guard while on the ground, particularly after an emergency landing away from its base.

Production of the two Welkin prototypes, DG558/G and DG562/G progressed to such good effect that by the early part of October 1942 the first of these was being prepared for preliminary ground engine running and taxi-ing. During the last week final checks and adjustments culminated in the first flight on 1 November, Harald Penrose first making several long runs to check the effect of the rudder and elevators before getting airborne after a 500 yards ground run. During this flight Penrose experienced directional instability with the rudder bar free in level flight; he also found that, while the pressurisation system was most effective it was intolerably hot in the cabin. This historic flight of a pressurised aircraft was notified to N E Rowe, the new director of technical developments at the MAP who, in return, congratulated Westland on its great achievement.

With this flight completed there began the customary long programme of turning a prototype into an acceptable operational aircraft. On the ground wind-tunnel tests on the rudder and nacelles resulted in the removal of the horn-balance to improve directional control and stability, and lengthening of the nacelles aft of the wing to reduce the drag figures; in addition, the pressurisation

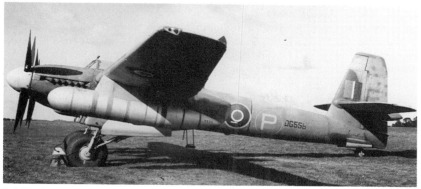

DG558/G, after modifications to the fin and rudder and with longer engine nacelles, carrying two 200 gal underwing fuel tanks. Respraying has obliterated the G suffix.

system was modified to provide cooler air and friction in the aileron control rod run was reduced. Meanwhile, in the air, the second flight was made the following day with two more on 3 November. Unfortunately the fourth flight ended in a forced landing at RAF Zeals, about 18 miles northeast of Yeovil, after failure of the constant-speed unit controlling the port variable-pitch propeller, which 'ran away' to overspeed the engine. This was the first of no less than five forced landings made with this prototype in the following thirteen months, all resulting from propeller or engine snags. That it survived is a great tribute to Penrose and to the other pilots involved in these and other forced landings during the Welkin flight-test and development programme. However, by the end of 1942, 19 test flying hours had been logged by DG558, during 23

Welkin front fuselage mock-up and cut-out engine nacelle to check pilot's view from the cockpit. The mock-up of the tail unit is on the left.

flights. The top speed at 29,000 ft was close to the predicted 385 mph, with the pressure cabin functioning well at this altitude; during February 1943 the Welkin was flown at 41,000 ft where, again, the pressure cabin could not be faulted. On one of these very high altitude flights engine failure forced a landing at RAF Swinderby in Lincolnshire, this time some 180 miles from Yeovil.

The first flight of the second prototype, DG562/G, took place in March 1943, and after some preliminary flying during which it had been dived at 370 mph and climbed to its service ceiling of 44,000 ft, it went to the A & AEE at Boscombe Down on 21 April.

To boost high-altitude performance liquid oxygen, carried in a fuselage tank, was injected into the engines. Here engine running with the second prototype DG562, is under way.

While the early test flying of the two Welkin prototypes gathered momentum, production of the first batch of one hundred Welkin F.Mk.Is had begun at Yeovil. Although the engine and propeller-associated problems had not been overcome it was believed that they could be alleviated by the use of propellers with fully-feathering blades; thus a 12 ft 6 in four-blade Rotol Aircrews propeller was chosen as the standard unit. However, as these were not immediately available, the first fifty production aircraft were planned to be fitted with de Havilland three-blade feathering propellers of the same diameter currently equipping the Mosquito F.Mk.VI. The first production Welkin, DX278, appeared during August 1943, and in the middle of September was allocated to the A & AEE. It had logged 30 hours before catching fire and forced landing at Chilbolton on 24 October following loss of oil pressure on one engine. This began a series of problems and accidents which dogged the assessment of the Welkin. Fortunately, the second and third production aircraft, DX279 and DX280, arrived at Boscombe Down during the following week but this latter aircraft suffered an inflight engine fire and was written off in the forced landing. Its replacement, DX282, survived until 21 January, 1944, when,

Although early production Welkin Is had standard day fighter camouflage and markings as on DX281, later aircraft had blue undersurfaces.

being flown by Flg Off G B Willerton, it too was written off in a collision with the prototype Supermarine Seafire Mk.III, MA970, on the ground at Boscombe Down, after the starboard engine lost power on take-off and the Welkin developed an uncontrollable swing. This left only DX279, with infrequent assistance by the two prototype Welkins, to shoulder the burden of testing at A & AEE until the first production aircraft DX278 could be rebuilt and returned to the programme. Nevertheless, between October 1943 and January 1944, DX279, was used to investigate performance and handling in dives up to a limiting 315 mph and in level flight, explore control effect and response while rolling and in stalls and single-engined handling. In none of these was the Welkin trouble-free, a major problem being in the dive from high altitude. During one dive from 35,000 ft with the aim of accelerating to the limit of 315 mph indicated air speed at 30,000 ft, the control column began to move backwards and forwards, the pilot being unable to stop it. He could, however, pull the column back slightly but found that the up elevator, thus applied, was

DX281 strapped down for engine running in October 1943. Note the dihedral on the outer wing panels and the air intake on the nose.

completely ineffective and he could not pull out of the dive until, at 20,000 ft, the pitching stopped and control was regained. A & AEE investigations revealed that with increasing Mach number there was a marked decrease in the maximum lift coefficient which limited the speed and the amount of g which could be applied in the dive if these loss of control characteristics were to be avoided. Thus, when the maximum g was reached in an attempted pull-out at any given height and speed, a high speed stall occurred which made the elevator totally useless. If the pilot persisted in his attempts to pull out severe buffetting was experienced. This unfortunate characteristic was to plague the Welkin throughout its admittedly short flying life.

The overall assessment, recorded in A & AEE Report 808 dated 2 March, 1944, was that the Welkin, as flown, was easy to fly and had adequate stability, the elevators were effective except at high Mach numbers as described above, but the ailerons were heavy and produced a very poor rate of roll. In the landing configuration the stalling speed was 86 mph and in the clean configuration 105 mph. Single-engined handling characteristics were unacceptable because of very severe rudder oscillations. The assessment also included mock combat trials against a Mosquito Mk.IX at 35,000 ft which revealed that, while the Welkin could cope with a hostile bomber or reconnaissance aircraft, if it engaged a

This tail-on view of Welkin I DX281 shows the concave skinning of the 'hollow ground' rudder.

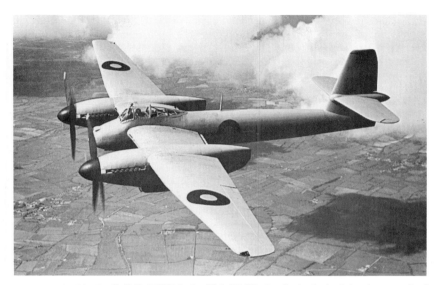

Photographed in April 1943, DX318, the 29th Welkin I to be built, had the then standard P.R. blue undersurfaces.

single-engined fighter it would certainly be outmanoeuvred and its low limiting diving speed would make pursuit in a dive impossible. The A & AEE engineers liked the ease of access to internal equipment for line maintainance; however, they believed it was 'too complex for its own good' and were concerned that the Welkin had inherited the Whirlwind's susceptibility to fire on its structure and the effect. The A & AEE reports allied to the non-appearance of the long-expected high-altitude attacks on Britain by the Luftwaffe, the raison d'être of Specification F.4/40 and the Welkin, resulted in a growing lack of interest in, and requirement for, the Welkin as a high-altitude fighter. This had been signalled earlier when two hundred Welkins ordered in the spring of 1943,

PF370, the sole two-seat Welkin II prototype, was converted from DX386, Welkin I airframe. It had increased dihedral on outer wings and lowered windscreen arch. There was a rear cockpit window in the fuselage side and a long cannon-firing trough resulting from the 31 in extension of the front fuselage.

were cancelled. Nevertheless, production of Welkin F.Mk.Is continued, as did development flying; these were supplemented by a number of new variants being proposed by Petter and Davenport. The Air Ministry played its part with a suggestion in July 1943 that there could be a need for the Welkin as an unarmed photographic reconnaissance aircraft; Westland was also asked to produce a brochure for a fighter-bomber Welkin, but nothing was to come from these studies. Two months later, Petter proposed a two-seat radar-equipped night fighter variant and another with a laminar-flow wing and powered by Rolls-Royce Griffon engines which could give a 50,000 ft ceiling and a 425 mph top speed at 40,000 ft. These seemed viable, but yet another proposal for a high-altitude high-speed mail-carrying variant was too fanciful. Other proposals included the use of a V tail unit, which could have improved the handling characteristics and reduced the weight, and the use of a wing with increased chord. Petter's contacts with George Carter at Gloster Aircraft had alerted him to the potentialities of the jet engine and he examined the possibility of a jet Welkin.

In spite of a substantial investment of time and effort in these proposed developments only a single example of the radar-equipped night fighter Welkin was built. This work was done with the blessing of the MAP which had approved it on 4 February.

The Welkin NF.Mk.II was developed to Specification F.9/43 which was issued in April 1943 and written around this prototype. The major design changes were to the front fuselage. This was extended forward by 31 in to provide space for an additional cockpit to house the second crew member in an aft facing seat, and for the AI Mk.VIII radar scanner and other equipment under a thimble-shaped radome. The front windscreen arch was lowered and raked forward and a one-piece sliding canopy was proposed. A mock-up of this new fuselage was quickly built in time for an Air Ministry meeting on 13 May. Two prototypes were ordered and were to be created by modifying a pair of Mk.I Welkins from the production line; DX386 and, it is believed, DX408. The first flight of this prototype, now serialled PF370, took place at Yeovil on 23 October, 1944, with Harald Penrose as pilot. During initial handling trials conducted at Yeovil and Merryfield, he experienced problems with rudder control and some modifications were made to the balance. The performance of the Mk.II Welkin was rather disappointing with the maximum speed of 333 mph at 40,000 ft being more than 50 mph slower than the Mk.I at this altitude, and the service ceiling some 3,000 ft below that of the single-seater, the additional 2,100 lb increase in weight undoubtedly contributing to this latter performance reduction. These figures were confirmed when PF370 was briefly evaluated at A & AEE. Two Welkin Mk.Is had been delivered to the Fighter Interception Unit at RAF Wittering during May, where they remained for two months on trials before these were prematurely terminated. Thus, by the autumn of 1944 it was clear that the Welkin would never enter operational squadrons. With the second two hundred production batch of Mk.Is having been cancelled following interim plans to build sixty of them as Mk.II night fighters, the first batch of one hundred Mk.Is was cut to seventy-five aircraft. Nevertheless, Westland's production of sub-assemblies plus the production programmes of its many sub-contractors were in top gear and it seemed that the manufacturing process could not—or would not—stop. Neither, it seemed, could development flying with the prototypes and selected production aircraft. The second prototype DG562 was being used for engine trials in which liquid oxygen, carried in a stainless steel tank in place of the fuselage fuel tank, was injected into specially-modified Merlin engines to produce more power and, thereby, an increase in speed at altitude. The hazards and technical problems of handling and pumping LOX on the ground and in the aircraft prompted the abandoning of this development.

The Welkin II taking part in the 1946 SBAC Display at Radlett.

Yet another trial which began in June 1945 with DX340 was the installation of two Merlin RM.16SM engines with chin radiators plus the wing-mounted units. These raised the maximum speed by 11 mph to reach 398 mph at 30,000 ft, but no further development was undertaken. Ultimately, seventy-seven complete Welkins were built plus twenty-six airframes, possibly in the serial block HS680-HT521, without engines. The great majority of these were flown away for storage at No.5 MU at RAF Kemble, and No.18 MU at RAF Dumfries. Once there, a few were test flown but all were either broken up at these units or moved to other locations for final destruction. The Welkin Mk.II survived for a number of years after the War, first being flown by Westland in a lengthy pressure cabin development programme and then by the Ministry of Supply, which re-acquired it for radar trials. During these two periods of flying it bore the identification markings P.17 and then WE997. It made its public debut in 1946 at the first postwar SBAC Exhibition and Display at Radlett aerodrome, then owned by Handley Page, where it was flown by Penrose. With the completion of these various tasks WE997 was put into storage, minus its outerwing panels, at Merryfield, where it remained until sold to Coley, the scrap dealers. There is also the story, probably apochryphal, that it was dismantled by gypsies and taken away by them as scrap metal.

Thus ended the Welkin programme, one which had failed to produce an operational aeroplane but which had pioneered high-altitude flying and so laid the foundations both for future developments by the British aircraft industry and for a new Westland subsidiary company, Normalair Ltd, now Normalair-Garrett Ltd, a part of Westland Technologies Division.

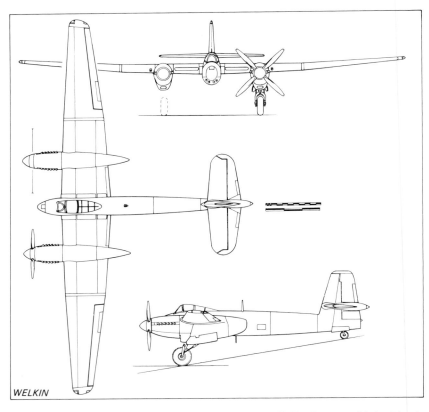

WELKIN

Description: Single-seat high-altitude day fighter (Mk.I). Two-seat high-altitude night fighter (Mk.II). All-metal construction.

Accommodation: Pilot and crew in enclosed cockpits.

Powerplant: Two 1,560 hp Rolls-Royce Merlin 61 twelve-cylinder vee inline liquid-cooled supercharged engines driving 13 ft diameter de Havilland four-bladed variable-pitch non-feathering metal propellers (P.14 prototypes). Two 1,630 hp Rolls-Royce Merlin 72 (port) and 73 (starboard) or Merlin 76 (port) and 77 (starboard) twelve-cyliner vee inline liquid-cooled geared and supercharged engines driving 12 ft 6 in diameter Rotol Airscrews four-blade fully-feathering metal propellers.

Armament: Four British Hispano Mk.II 20 mm forward-firing cannon under the fuselage nose with 566 rounds of ammunition arranged 145 rounds each outer gun and 138 rounds for each inner gun.

Dimensions: Span 70 ft 0 in; length 41 ft 6 in; (44 ft 1 in Mk.II); height 15 ft 3 in; wing area 460 sq ft.

Weights: Empty 11,974 lb (13,580 lb Mk.II); maximum take-off weight 19,775 lb (21,892 lb Mk.II).

Performance: Maximum speed 387 mph at 26,000 ft. (346 mph at 20,000 ft Mk.II); landing speed 88 mph; climb to 40,000 ft in 20 min (to 35,000 ft in 20 min Mk.II); service ceiling 44,000 ft (41,000 ft Mk.II); range 1,480 miles (1,200 miles Mk.II).

Production: A total of 77 Welkins built by Westland Aircraft Ltd, Yeovil, Somerset, during 1940–45, as follows:
2 prototypes
75 Welkin F.Mk.Is (one converted to the Mk.II)
26 Welkin F.Mk.I airframes.

Wyvern

The initial conception of the Wyvern, the last fixed-wing aeroplane to be produced by Westland, was that of Edward Petter who had received considerable encouragement and support from Commodore (later, Rear-Admiral Sir Matthew) Slattery, when he was Director General of Naval Aircraft Development and Production at the MAP. During March–August 1943 Petter and Dennis Edkins, his personal assistant, had produced a number of project drawings for naval torpedo-carrying aircraft, at least two of which, to meet the Specifications S.6/43 and S.11/43, had piston engines driving contra-rotating propellers. Later Edkins had drawn a low-wing monoplane, with a Rolls-Royce Eagle twenty-four cylinder horizontally-opposed flat-H engine buried in the centre fuselage and driving contra-rotating propellers through a long shaft. The cockpit was located in the nose, much in the manner of the Westland F.7/30, affording the pilot a superb forward view. A mock-up was built but weight calculations showed that this configuration would be very heavy and it certainly found little favour with pilots, including Harald Penrose. A second mock-up with a more conventional nose-mounted engine was built. It was this project which formed the basis of the Westland W.34, of which the predominant features were a large 'humped' fuselage with the cockpit high on top to provide the pilot with an excellent forward view, a near-elliptical planform low wing and a large fin and rudder of similar shape.

Without the customary formalities of a preliminary competitive Design Study stage, Westland representatives attended a meeting with, the Controller Supplies (Air) on 14 April, 1944, at which the company was nominated to design an aircraft based on the W.34 to meet a new requirement, N.11/44, being drafted around it. A follow-up meeting took place one week later and on 1 May Westland submitted proposals for the use of propeller-turbine engines instead of the agreed Rolls-Royce Eagle. On 2 August the Ministry of Supply decided that the W.34 should begin life with the Eagle and that twenty pre-production aircraft should be built with this engine. By the end of September 1944 the broad design had been settled and the main requirements established, and both the Advisory Design Conference and the Mock-up Conference had been held; thought also had been given to the ordering of six flying prototypes, a complete airframe for structural testing plus three sets of wings for aerodynamic development and what was described as 'development with turbine engines'. In addition, the Air Ministry had shown some interest in the new Westland N.11/44 aeroplane in the long-range escort fighter role for possible use by the RAF in the Far East theatre of operations and two of the six prototypes proposed had been reserved as variants for RAF use. Later, Specification F.13/44 was drafted to cover this; however, with the advent of the Gloster Meteor jet fighter and gas-turbine engine development generally, this interest was to wane during the following year and ultimately, all prototypes were allocated for Naval development flying.

The first Eagle-engined Wyvern prototype, TS371, being flown by Westland test pilot Peter Garner during October 1947. It lacked folding wings, arrester gear and cannon.

By this time Petter had left Westland and had been succeeded by Arthur Davenport who, in turn, had appointed F J W W Digby to succeed him as chief designer. Thus it was John Digby who was charged with the task of establishing the detailed design of the W.34. Specification N.11/44 called for a long-range day fighter, able to operate from aircraft carriers and shore stations. As a fighter, air-to-air combat was envisaged as the aircraft's principal operational role, but it was also required to be able to carry weapons suitable for attacking ships or land targets without prejudicing the primary fighter role. The type of engine was not specified, only a preference for a British product being expressed. (In fact, of course, the Rolls-Royce Eagle had already been selected for the initial design, it being the most powerful aero-engine then available; however, Petter had been well aware of the potentialities of the gas-turbine, as recorded in the General History pages of this book, and he had examined and discussed the possibilities of installing a propeller-turbine in a developed W.34 airframe). The maximum speed was expected to be 500 mph with a cruising speed of at least 340 mph and a duration of 2½ hours at this speed plus 15 minutes combat at 10,000 ft and 45 minutes at the maximum speed attainable at 20,000 ft. A minimum radius of action of 275 miles plus a 15 minutes loiter at 10,000 ft were also required. Power wing-folding and spreading, an undercarriage designed for a rate of sink of 12 ft per second but with attachment points capable of accepting 14 ft per second, and the possibile use of the undercarriage as a dive-brake were part of this exacting Specification. A comprehensive array of communications and navigation equipment was required, as was a heavy fixed armament of four 20 mm British Hispano Mk.V cannon with sufficient ammunition for 25 seconds firing. The disposable weapon load, carried externally, was eight 60 lb rocket projectiles, one 2,000 lb bomb or three 1,000 lb bombs, or an 18 in Mk.XVIII torpedo or a 1,820 lb Mk.VI mine as required. Once again, it was stressed that provision for the carriage of these weapons was not to prejudice the aircraft's primary air combat function. Surprisingly perhaps, while there was no limit placed on the maximum all-up weight, the landing-on weight was not to exceed 17,500 lb, but this was to include all the ammunition and sufficient fuel for one hour's flying. Major constraints on the design were the maximum external dimensions which were specified as 18 ft width and 15 ft 9 in height with the wings folded and an overall length of 40 ft. These were to allow the aircraft to fit onto existing aircraft carrier lifts and occupy minimum space in the below-deck hangars where the deck-head height was a major limiting factor.

That the N.11/44 aircraft was marking the end of an era, not only at Westland, was underlined by the choice of the Eagle engine, however enforced it may have been, for this was to be the last big piston engine to be built by Rolls-Royce. Sadly, N.11/44 had been initiated at a time when a fundamental change was occurring in aircraft power units under the stress of war conditions; thus, Westland's new fighter was to be developed during a period when development of reciprocating engines was declining and major effort was being put into gas-turbine development by the engine manufacturers.

Design of the Eagle had begun in 1942 with the aim of producing an engine more powerful than any other then running. In its essentials it echoed, on an enlarged scale, the Napier Sabre but avoided that engine's many shortcomings, benefitting from Rolls-Royce's massive experience with the thousands of engines it had produced since the first engine to carry the name Eagle had run at Derby in February 1915. This 2,808 cubic inch capacity engine, equivalent to 46 litres, had two crankshafts, each driven by twelve sleeve-valved cylinders, turning a two-stage two-speed supercharger with inter-coolers at the rear of the engine and, initially, a single propeller shaft at the front. Later, when adopted for the Westland W.34, a new reduction gearbox to turn the 13 ft diameter eight-bladed contra-rotating propeller was embodied in the Eagle 22. It was the high power of the Eagle which not only made this type of propeller essential if the diameter was to be kept within reasonable bounds, but also brought a train of other design problems in its wake. The size of the propeller made necessary a main undercarriage leg long enough to provide adequate tip clearance with the deck, or runway, during take-off and landing. When retracted the wheels had to leave space for the carriage of a torpedo or other external load but the track was prescribed by the folded width of the aircraft. The solution, provided by Dowty Equipment, was a device on the main oleo legs which shortened them as they retracted, a technique first employed on the Gloster Meteor.

During November 1944 Westland received a contract for the six prototypes, while instructions to proceed with the manufacture of jigs and tools for the construction work came on 7 February, 1945. Production of the first of the six prototypes, which had been allocated the serial number TS371, had already begun at Yeovil with the manufacture of details and small components.

TS371, the first Wyvern prototype, under construction at Yeovil on 1 October, 1948. One end of Westland's erecting shop was curtained off for this work. It has the original rudder and small fin.

The Wyvern's Dowty undercarriage shortened as it retracted to fit the available space in the centre-section.

Meanwhile, design work relating to the re-engining of the W.34 with a propeller-turbine was receiving top priority after the work on TS371 and the second prototype TS375, both of which were powered by the Eagle. That the engine was causing concern both at Westland and the Ministry of Supply was evidenced by a meeting on 2 October, 1944, to discuss the future development of the N.11/44 aircraft with the Eagle and with a propeller-turbine. Among those who attended were Ernest Hives, director and general manager of Rolls-Royce, John Fearn and John Digby, Westland's joint managing director and chief designer respectively, and senior Ministry of Supply representatives. Their discussion centred on the Eagle-engined Mk.1 aircraft and a Mk.2 variant powered by the new RB.39 Clyde propeller-turbine which was still on the drawing board at Rolls-Royce's Barnoldswick site. Some forecasts were made for deliveries of both types of engine, none of which, in the event, were to be met. Deliveries of four Eagle powerplants were expected to begin in July 1945; three bare engines, which Westland would equip as powerplants, would follow from November 1945, with all seven Eagles for the six N.11/44 prototypes to be at Yeovil by August 1946. Forecasts for Clyde deliveries were wildly optimistic. The first was expected to be ready in December 1945 with two more in July and September 1946; in fact, the first Clyde did not run until 5 August, 1945, with the first engine not being delivered until the summer of 1948.

Throughout 1945 and 1946 the failure of engines to be delivered on time continued to plague the N.11/44 programme; moreover, in October 1945, under

The Rotol eight-bladed contra-rotating propeller, shallow radiators and the Dowty levered-suspension undercarriage of this Eagle-engined prototype Wyvern are noteworthy.

pressure from the MoS, Rolls-Royce agreed to abandon further development of the Eagle engine and concentrate maximum effort on gas-turbine work. Production of a small batch of about thirty Eagles was approved to power the six prototypes and the twenty pre-production aircraft to be built to Specification 17/46P. Meanwhile, at an MoS meeting on 7 December, 1945, the decision was taken to change from development of the Mk.1 Eagle-powered aircraft and, instead, concentrate on the Mk.2 with the Clyde, contract details for three prototypes to Specification N.12/45 being sent to Westland immediately after Christmas. It was not long before this plan was upset, for in March 1946, Rolls-Royce signalled a substantial delay in work on the Clyde. This was not altogether surprising for this engine was the company's first propeller-turbine designed as such from scratch and was also the world's first two-spool engine. At yet another MoS meeting on 1 May Westland was instructed to investigate use of the Armstrong Siddeley Python propeller-turbine in place of the Clyde. Although the Python was reckoned to be inferior to the Clyde, at least it had the benefit of being created, as the ASP, by adding a propeller gearbox to the front end of the ASX axial-flow turbojet which had been flown in a Lancaster test bed during 1943. However, like the Clyde, the Python was still in a very early stage of its development.

In the factory at Yeovil, production of the prototypes proceeded. Structurally they were typical of their era, being of light alloy stressed skin construction. The fuselage was in three sections; the engine mounting structure and air intake forward of a firewall, the centre fuselage with the integral wing centre-section, and the rear fuselage with the integral fin. The engine mounting, in the thirteen aircraft built with Eagle engines, differed from that of the subsequent aircraft with propeller-turbines in which it consisted of a ring carried on a fuselage frame in which the Python power plant was mounted, complete with all its accessories, and fully cowled. It was surrounded by the annular air intake formed by a two-piece cowling which had built-in walkways to simplify maintenance. The two four-blade contra-rotating propellers were mounted on their drive shafts well forward of the intake. The centre fuselage contained the cockpit with its one-piece sliding canopy, a 95 gal forward fuel tank contoured to the fuselage top decking immediately in front of the pilot and a 173 gal aft fuel tank including the transfer tank, behind the cockpit and between the bifurcated jet pipes. Beneath the cockpit floor was a massive cruciform-braced centre-section structure. Outside the fuselage side walls the integral centre-section was built up around a deep main spar and the wide-chord leading edge box with fabricated ribs and heavy gauge skinning which contained the well for the wide-track hydraulically-retractable main undercarriage units. The inboard 20 mm cannon of the pair mounted in each wing was carried in the outer end of the centre-section leading-edge. In the aft position of the centre-section on each side was a 30 gal fuel tank with Youngman-type three-position trailing-edge flaps, the outboard links of which were housed in a prominent fairing on the upper surface of the wing. The rear fuselage, which was a monocoque structure, housed a range of ancillary equipment, the tailwheel, which retracted into an enclosed box in the underside of the fuselage, and the arrester hook. Its last four frames extended upwards to form the basic fin structure, the penultimate frame acting as a main spar to which preformed ribs were attached. A heavy gauge skin was spot-welded to this fin structure. The inset horn-balanced rudder had a trim tab. The fixed tailplane was of a similar construction and carried horn-balanced elevators with trim tabs. Initially mounted without dihedral the tailplane was later modified to have a 10 deg dihedral angle and two auxiliary fins. The outer wing panels were built up around the main spar and a sealed leading-edge box which, with pressed ribs, formed an integral 100 gal fuel tank. Inboard of the fuel tank in the leading edge was mounted the second of the pair of cannon. Aft of the main spar, rib structure carried an auxiliary spar to which the ailerons were hinged, each aileron having a spring tab and the port aileron also being fitted with a trim tab. A plain split-flap was fitted inboard of the ailerons. Although not included initially, when it was discovered that the reversible-pitch propellers could not be used as a speed- or dive-brake, a small dive-brake was fitted in the upper surface of the wing to open and close in unison with the split-flap. The entire outer wing panel could be folded by hydraulic jacks, the hinge line being between the two cannon; in addition the wingtip could be folded in a similar manner. External loads could be carried at five points; a mounting beam for a torpedo or ventral fuel tank was located under the cruciform centre-section structure, two wing tanks could be carried under the centre-section outboard of the main undercarriage units and six rocket launching rails were fitted under each outer wing panel.

The mighty 3,500 hp Rolls-Royce Eagle engine which powered the Wyvern prototypes, was 9 ft long without the co-axial propeller shafts.

Westland W.34 and Wyvern TF.Mk.1

Construction of the first prototype, TS371, was completed during October 1946, and after some preliminary ground running of the Eagle and other system checks at Yeovil, the aircraft was taken by road to the A & AEE aerodrome at Boscombe Down, with its long runway, for the first flight. This took place on 16 December, the pilot being Harald Penrose who found that, in flight, the Eagle engine ran smoothly and the propellers worked satisfactorily; in addition, the stability and handling were good enough for him to decide to fly the aircraft back to Yeovil where he made a satisfactory landing on the grass aerodrome. This was a remarkably historic flight for not only was it the first to be made by Westland's last fixed-wing aeroplane, which was named Wyvern TF.1 early in

1947, but it was also the first flight of the Eagle, the most powerful and the last piston-engine to be produced by Rolls-Royce and of the first eight-blade contra-rotating propeller to be developed in Britain. The task of proving so much combined novelty was to be long and arduous.

TS378 with wings folded aboard HMS *Illustrious* in 1949. It has a six-bladed de Havilland propeller.

To speed the manufacture of TS371, it had been built without folding wings and arrester gear and the cannon and ejection seat were omitted. During 1947, while the second prototype, TS375, was being made to the same standard, TS371 was being test flown principally on handling trials. A number of problems mainly associated with the engine and propeller, soon became apparent. The Eagle's long overhanging shaft carrying the front propeller was found to flex badly and it was difficult to obtain satisfactory lubrication of the pitch change bearings between the two propellers. TS375 was completed in August and first flew from Yeovil on 10 September, 1947, joining the first prototype Wyvern on handling trials. However, on 15 October, while flying as the subject of air-to-air photography, the propeller bearing failed and being unable to overcome the enormous drag from the stationary propeller blades, TS371 crashed in a field killing Peter Garner, its Westland test pilot. Only two days earlier, the Ministry of Supply had informed Westland that it now favoured the Python propeller-turbine rather than the Clyde for use in the Wyvern. This was yet another upset to the Wyvern programme and was to lead to further delays. Following this unfortunate loss, the second prototype was fitted with an experimental ML ejection seat and the 10 deg dihedral tailplane.

Manufacture of the four subsequent prototypes continued through 1948, all being completed to naval standard with armament, wing folding gear and arrestor hook. TS378, the third prototype, was unique in being fitted with a six-bladed de Havilland Propellers contra-propeller, and elevators with smaller horn-balances for its early flights. The standard eight-blade Rotol propeller and elevators were fitted later. The fourth Wyvern 1, TS380, came into the programme to clear the carriage of external stores and when this was accomplished it became the back-up aircraft to the third prototype on initial deck-landing trials, replacing TS384, the fifth Wyvern which undertook the range of armament firing and dropping trials. On 4 June, 1948, it was flown to Hucknall from where Rolls-Royce began engine trials with it. TS384 was eventually written-off in a forced landing at Lichfield on 14 April, 1949, while being flown by Herbert C Rogers, a Rolls-Royce test pilot.

In pristine condition Wyvern TS380 stands prepared for the flight-test programme.

This Wyvern prototype, probably TS375, carries an 18 in torpedo with an air tail.

Following a series of Airfield Dummy Deck Landings (ADDLS) at Boscombe Down in May 1948, the first round of deck landing trials began on 9 June with TS378 in HMS *Implacable*. These were halted for a time when, as a result of a propeller failure on TS380, all the prototypes were grounded; however, the trials were resumed on 13 July when TS378 made fifteen take-offs and landings and TS380 followed these with seven more the next day. A further series of deck landing trials were made with TS378 during May and June 1949 in HMS *Illustrious*.

Wyvern TF.Mk.2

With flaps lowered and air-brakes out, Harald Penrose 'lands on' at Merryfield in VP109, the first of three prototype Python-engined Wyvern 2s. It had a flat tailplane and a small dorsal fin.

While flight trials with the six Eagle-engined Wyvern Mk.1 prototypes proceeded at Yeovil and Merryfield and at A & AEE Boscombe Down, RAE Farnborough, and Rolls-Royce, Hucknall, construction of the first two Westland W.35 Wyvern TF.Mk.2s, VP109 which was fitted with a Python and VP120 with the Clyde engine and of the early pre-production Mk.1s was progressing at Yeovil. The Clyde was a more compact engine than the Python and the Wyvern's airframe required only a modest amount of alteration to enable this engine to be installed; thus it was the first to be completed. The first flight by VP120 took place at Boscombe Down on 18 January, 1949. 'It was the shortest first flight I ever made' Harald Penrose told the author, 'Almost immediately after getting airborne a thick cloud of smoke filled the cockpit. I couldn't see out or even the instrument panel and opening the hood made it worse'. Fortunately with great skill he managed a short circuit and made a successful landing. Back in the hangar it was found that there was a leak in the fuel system which had allowed fuel to drop onto the Clyde's hot exhaust duct. Once again it had fallen to Penrose to make the first test flight of a new engine in an airframe which was still under development. With this snag cleared, he flew the aeroplane to Yeovil to begin its test programme. During the early flights Penrose found that the engine's response to throttle movement was too sensitive and he experienced the effects of power surging. Development of the Clyde was soon to be abandoned by Rolls-Royce which was becoming heavily involved with work on the RB.53 Dart propeller-turbine and the AJ.65 which became the Avon turbojet. Thus, after a few months at Yeovil VP120 was flown to Rolls-Royce at Hucknall on 4 July, 1949, but after only 50 hours flying it went to D Napier & Son at Luton on 20 April, 1950. There, as part of a project to create a Wyvern Mk.IA variant, it was planned to fit a Nomad compound engine, but work on this engine, too, was abandoned due to the complexity of the design and the solutions to its problems. Later, a Wyvern Mk.5E was proposed, powered by a Napier Double Eland propeller-turbine, but there was no interest expressed in this variant.

The elegant Rolls-Royce Clyde engined prototype Wyvern 2, VP120, on thrust measuring trials at Yeovil. The 40 ton 'anchor' was part of a fuselage structural test rig. Arthur Davenport is the figure in the hat.

The second Wyvern Mk.2, VP109, which was fitted with the Python, had posed some installation problems. There was a 21 inch increase in fuselage length and the fuselage depth was also increased partly to provide space for the bifurcated exhaust ducts under the cockpit. The AS.P.3 Python I in the Wyvern Mk.2 had a type-test power rating of 3,560 shp with about 1,000 lb of residual jet thrust during take-off. It was with this engine that the first flight of VP109 was made at Boscombe Down on 22 March, 1949, the pilot being Sqn Ldr Mike Graves who had previously flown the Eagle-engined Wyvern Mk.1 and the Mk.2 with the Clyde. On this first flight of yet another new engine and airframe combination at least the Python had been previously air-tested by Armstrong Siddeley in a Lancaster flying test-bed. Even so, Graves discovered that this engine's throttle response and tendency to surge were worse than those of the Clyde. The second Wyvern TF.Mk.2 with a Python, VP113, first flew on 20 August, 1949, and there was sufficient confidence in the aircraft for Mike Graves to fly it in the SBAC Display at Farnborough during the week 5–11 September and demonstrated that it could be 'looped, rolled and thrown all over the sky, as could the new Python engine as well', as one contemporary report

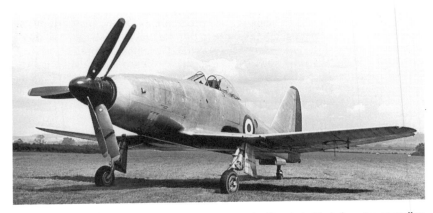

Wyvern VP120's neatly cowled Clyde engine turned a Rotol six-bladed contra-propeller, seen strapped to prevent risk of windmilling.

described it. A few days later VP113 was at RAE again for some discussions on spinning and returned there again in October. Graves had made full spinning trials following earlier tests with a free-spinning model in the RAE's vertical wind-tunnel. Sadly he was to lose his life on 31 October, 1949, at Yeovil when, after demonstrating this aircraft to Air Ministry and RAF representatives the Python appeared to flame-out and stop. Instead of attempting a belly landing he elected to lower the undercarriage and try for a normal landing, but he touched down too far across the small aerodrome and overshot into a housing estate killing himself and the occupants of the house which the aircraft demolished.

Wyvern T.Mk.3

Before the initial test flying of the Clyde and Python powered prototypes had begun a pre-production batch of twenty Wyvern TF.Mk.2s, VW867–VW886, had been ordered to Specification 21/48P. In addition, a single Wyvern T.Mk.3 was ordered to Specification T.12/48 for a two-seat trainer variant. Originally known as the Westland W.38, this aircraft was powered by a Python 1 and had a deepened rear fuselage to accommodate a second seat for an instructor behind the standard Wyvern TF.Mk.1 cockpit. A periscope was fitted between the two cockpits to provide a better forward view for the instructor. This aircraft, VZ739, first flew on 11 February, 1950, and remained with Westland for trials; however, as this variant did not go into production it was used as a company 'hack'. Then, on 3 November, 1950, Sqn Ldr Derek Colvin successfully force-landed it in the saltings of the Axe estuary at Seaton, Devon, after turbine-blade failure stopped the engine. It was later written-off after an unsuccessful attempt to recover it complete from the marshy surface where it had come down. Ironically, it was not until 22 December, 1950, that the Admiralty finally advised Westland that there was no case for development of a two-seat Wyvern.

February 1950 also saw the first flight of the first of twenty pre-production Wyvern TF.Mk.2s, VW867, which took place on the 16th of that month. During its five-year life it was used to replace VP113 in the test programme, taking part in deck landing trials on HMS *Illustrious* in May and June 1950. It was flown with great elan by Harald Penrose while carrying a torpedo and rocket projectiles in the SBAC Display during September before going on to Armstrong Siddeley Motors at Bitteswell in January 1951 for three years of engine development flying. This was the first of five Wyvern TF.Mk.2s used by this engine manufacturer for development of the Python.

An Armstrong Siddeley Python powered pre-production Wyvern 2, VW880, had the cut-back nose cowling, production standard fin, a rudder with an inset horn-balance and ejection seat.

The flight-test programme of the Wyvern and Python was destined to be even longer than that of the Wyvern 1 as Westland, Armstrong Siddeley and Rotol Airscrews sought to provide answers to the aerodynamic problems coupled with precise control of the engine/propeller combination. In order to improve the handling characteristics the airframe was progressively modified. The introduction of small air-brakes necessitated the fitting of small boundary layer fences on the wing trailing-edge to prevent aileron twitch when the air-brakes were operated; a taller fin with an experimental dorsal fin and a horn-balanced rudder were embodied, the aileron trim tabs were modified, and the leading-edge of the annular air intake was cut back to facilitate the loading of engine starter cartridges. Following the in-flight collapse of several cockpit canopies, which caused head injuries to two pilots and may have caused a crash in which an A & AEE pilot lost his life, the canopy was strengthened. Equally taxing were the problems associated with engine and propeller control; these included the lag in power response to movements of the throttle and the surges of power when stored energy in the rotating core of the engine or the propeller was transmitted from one to the other in either direction. A series of different types of control units and systems were devised by the engine and propeller manufacturers over a period of more than two years during 1950–52. The need to solve this surge problem overshadowed all other development work so that progress towards MoS approval for the aircraft to be released to the squadrons was slow. During August 1951 Westland and Rotol decided to blank off a device called the 'anticipator' in the constant-speed control system developed by Armstrong Siddeley. Some promising flight trials were made by Westland test pilots, but the engine manufacturer believed that the system was inherently unstable and recommended that the Wyvern should be restricted to speeds less than 400 mph until a new inertia control system could be perfected by Rotol. This became available during the winter of 1951 and was so successfully tested by Armstrong Siddeley pilots that an aircraft fitted with it was sent to A & AEE for assessment. Unfortunately, after a few hours flight-testing at Boscombe Down the control system failed, as did others flown by Westland and Rotol pilots. Subsequently, it was found that the failure was due to a mechanical fault in the Rotol unit, but at the time the effect of this failure was disastrous for the Wyvern programme.

Air Marshal Sir John Bootham, CS(A) at the MoS, called a conference in February 1952 to resolve this impasse; as a result Westland was asked to demonstrate the safety of the blanked-off 'anticipator' system by undertaking five hours of high speed and aerobatic flying to include five dives on each of six Wyverns. In the event, Westland pilots performed a total of 237 dives to maximum speeds in excess of 350 mph on seven aircraft during these trials. However, on the first flight an unexplained surge had developed and this single occurrence was seized upon as proving that the system was unsafe. As a result, all flying of Wyverns other than by Westland, was stopped. In April 1952 the RAE and the NGTE joined the investigation and a report by Dr Arnold Hall, Director of the RAE, dated 21 April stated that this system was safe and stable, with the reservation that instability might increase with altitude, and that near the Wyvern's ceiling violent throttle movements should be avoided. Wyvern flying then started again at the RAE and A & AEE.

Wyvern S.Mk.4

But the Wyvern had one more snag which it reserved until the final stages of evaluation during August 1952. When only 15 hours flying was required to complete all the test work necessary for a preliminary CS(A) release of the aircraft to the Service, an A & AEE pilot reported that it was possible to cause the Wyvern rudder to lock-on under sustained sideslip at medium and low speeds. It took four months for Westland to find and apply the solution; this was the fitting of finlets to the tailplane. With this modification embodied, a limited release for the Wyvern S.Mk.4 was granted on or about 19 December, 1952; the limitation was that, until the new engine control unit was fully developed by Rotol, the Wyvern would be operated only from shore stations. This was a sad start to the Service career of the Royal Navy's latest carrier-based strike aircraft. This release galvanised Westland and the other suppliers into rapid action preparing the eighteen aircraft modified up to the full interim standard for use by No.813 Squadron, which gave up its Blackburn Firebrands to become the first unit to be equipped with the Wyvern. By the end of December Westland had produced forty-eight aircraft of various marks and delivered all but a few to Merryfield for flight testing, and production was continuing at the rate of four Wyverns a month.

VZ748, the third production Wyvern 4, was used for a variety of trials. Here it carries two 100 gal underwing tanks.

Originally, the Admiralty had planned to form the first shore-based Wyvern squadron at RNAS Ford on 1 February, 1953; in the event the first aircraft to reach the squadron, VZ755, arrived on 20 May having been delivered to RNAS Stretton for the fitment of certain items of Service equipment on 8 May. By the end of July No.813 Squadron had received twelve Wyverns and continued to receive new aircraft until October 1954 by which time twenty-nine aircraft had been taken on charge by the squadron. Following the establishment of this first squadron, No.703W Flight was formed at Ford in October 1954 to provide pilot training for No.827, the second Wyvern squadron which was commissioned in the following month. Meanwhile, with fully-modified Python 3s incorporating the definitive Rotol engine control unit being fitted in the Wyvern S.4s, No.813 Squadron, which had been shore-based, embarked in HMS *Albion* in September but following problems with fuel-starvation and flame-outs during high g loading catapult launchings, it disembarked at Hal Far, Malta, remaining there until

A Wyvern 4 all set to engage the first arrester gear wire as it lands on a carrier.

VZ782, a No.813 Squadron Wyvern 4 on HMS *Eagle* during 1955. The folding wingtips was a feature abandoned in that year.

March 1955 when it returned to Ford in *Albion*. It was following engine failure on a catapult launch that Lieut B O Macfarlane's Wyvern VZ783, fell into the sea and he survived by making the first underwater ejection using the Martin-Baker 1B seat unit when the aircraft was cut in two by the ship. Both Nos.813 and 827 Squadrons then embarked in HMS *Eagle*; they remained aboard until returning to Ford to disband in November 1955 when Nos.830 and 831 Squadrons commissioned, initially equipping with Wyverns from the earlier

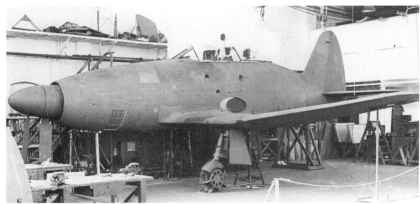

Mock-up of the Wyvern 3 two-seat trainer with a flat tailplane and full-length nose cowling.

VZ789, a Wyvern 4 of No.827 Squadron, 'bolting' with 420 ft of HMS *Eagle*'s deck remaining.

squadrons before receiving new aircraft from Stretton in January 1956. In April No.831 embarked in HMS *Ark Royal* serving until returning to Ford to be disbanded on 10 February, 1957. Meanwhile, also in April, No.830 embarked in HMS *Eagle* to become the sole Wyvern squadron to operate in the Anglo-French campaign in Suez in October 1956. Placed on standby on the last day of the month, it painted black and yellow stripes on its nine Wyverns for easy

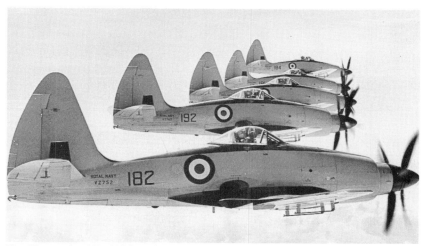

Five Wyvern 4s of No.813 Squadron in stepped-down echelon while based at RNAS Ford during 1953. All have the full Perspex canopies.

301

identification and on 1 November the squadron flew 18 sorties strafing and bombing Dekheila aerodrome and photographing other targets. By 6 November the squadron had flown 79 sorties and lost two aircraft, both pilots ejecting in the sea and being rescued. The squadron returned to the United Kingdom early in 1957 and disbanded at Lee-on-Solent on 5 January. No.813 Squadron had reformed in October 1956, and when No.831 disbanded in February 1957, it became the last active Wyvern squadron. When it finally disbanded at Ford on 29 March, 1958, this ended the Wyvern's career in operational squadrons. Small numbers of Wyvern 4s were also operated by Nos.700, 703 and 764 Squadrons at Ford for type conversion and development flying before the Wyvern Conversion Unit took over the former role. No.787 Squadron, Naval Air Fighting Development Unit at RAF West Raynham used four Wyverns until its task was taken over by No.700 Squadron.

Seen in January 1950, VZ739, the sole Wyvern 3 two-seat trainer, showing the deep rear fuselage and twin canopies. The instructor's periscope between the cockpits has not yet been fitted.

As the result of squadron experience a number of modifications were introduced in the Wyvern after it had entered service. These included a change to a Martin-Baker Mk.2B ejector seat, the use of a composite canopy with a metal rear end to replace the stiffened one-piece type, the introduction of perforated air-brakes under the centre-section and a flat bullet-proof windscreen in place of the earlier curved type, and elimination of the folding wingtips. Trials with 200 gal underwing fuel tanks and 100 gal Venom-type wingtip tanks did not result in modifications to production Wyverns. Of the 127 Wyverns built, about forty were lost or were scrapped having served as instructional airframes. Almost all of the survivors went to the Naval Aircraft Holding Unit at RNAS Lossiemouth during late 1957 and early 1958 from where they were sold as scrap to British Aluminium at Warrington. Only one Wyvern survived; this is VR137, the last Eagle-engined Mk.1 to be built which is in the care of the Fleet Air Arm Museum at RNAS Yeovilton.

The Wyvern, which was the first Westland-designed aircraft to serve with the Royal Navy since the Walrus of 1921, will be remembered as the first propeller-turbine powered aircraft to serve in aircraft carriers and, of course, the last fixed-wing type of Westland design to be built. Its epitaph could very well be a comment by Harald Penrose. 'The Wyvern was very nearly a very good aircraft'.

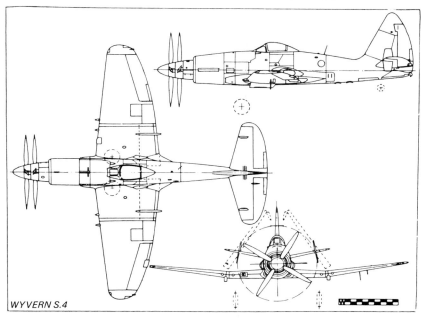

WYVERN S.4

Description: Single-seat carrier-borne strike aircraft. All-metal construction.
Accommodation: Pilot in enclosed cockpit.
Powerplant: One 2,690 hp Rolls-Royce Eagle 22 twenty-four cylinder horizontal-H liquid-cooled geared and supercharged engine. (TF.Mk.1). One 4,000 shp Rolls-Royce Clyde twin-spool reverse axial-flow propeller-turbine with 1,550 lb residual thrust driving a 13 ft diameter Rotol Airscrews eight-blade contra-rotating propeller (TF.Mk.2). One 3,560 shp Armstrong Siddeley AS.P.3 Python 1 axial-flow propeller-turbine with 1,100 lb residual thrust driving a 13 ft diameter Rotol Airscrews eight-blade contra-rotating propeller (TF.Mk.2). One 3,670 shp Armstrong Siddeley Python 3 axial-flow propeller-turbine with 1,180 lb residual thrust driving a 13 ft diameter Rotol Airscrews eight-blade contra-rotating propeller (T.Mk.3 and S.Mk.4).
Armament: Four fixed forward-firing 20 mm British Hispano Mk.V cannon in the wings with 200 rounds per gun. Provision for one 2,500 lb torpedo in crutches under the fuselage or one 1,000 lb bomb under the fuselage and one under each wing or sixteen 25 lb or 90 lb rocket projectiles under the wings.
Dimensions: Span 44 ft 0 in; width folded 20 ft 0 in; length 42 ft 3 in; height 15 ft 9 in, folded 18 ft 2 in; wing area 355 sq ft.
Weights: Empty 15,443 lb (TF.Mk.1), 15,600 lb (S.Mk.4); loaded clean 19,194 lb (TF.Mk.1), 21,200 lb (S.Mk.4); loaded with torpedo 21,879 lb (TF.Mk.1), 24,550 lb (S.Mk.4).

303

Performance: Maximum speed 365 mph at sea level, 456 mph at 23,000 ft; initial rate of climb 2,900 ft/min; service ceiling 32,100 ft; maximum range 1,186 miles (TF.Mk.1). Maximum speed, 383 mph at sea level, 380 mph at 10,000 ft; initial rate of climb 2,350 ft/min; service ceiling 28,000 ft; maximum range 910 miles (S.Mk.4).

Production: A total of 124 Wyverns built by Westland Aircraft Ltd, Yeovil, Somerset, during 1945–56 as follows:
6 Westland W.34 prototypes.
7 Wyvern TF.Mk.1 pre-production aircraft.
3 Wyvern TF.Mk.2 prototypes.
20 Wyvern TF.Mk.2 pre-production aircraft (nine completed as S.Mk.4 aircraft).
1 Wyvern T.Mk.3 prototype.
87 Wyvern S.Mk.4 production aircraft.

Dragonfly

The first fruit of Westland's decisions to enter the rotary-wing field and to do so by licence-building another company's design as a private venture, was the granting of a licence to Westland by the United Aircraft Corporation, the agreement being signed on 10 January, 1947. This saved Westland a great amount of time and money; moreover, it covered the construction of the Sikorsky S-51 powered by a British engine and using British materials, components and equipment. It also included the supply of six US-built S-51s to enable Westland to steepen its own 'learning curve' and to demonstrate to potential customers such as British European Airways and the Ministry of Supply. The use of British engines and other equipment, while desirable, was largely due to Britain's shortage of United States currency which would have hampered the purchase of US engines and Sikorsky components. In addition, the agreement allowed Westland to improve the Sikorsky design and, of most importance, to sell the aircraft, initially designated the WS-51, throughout the world with the exception of North America. This was a clause which was to have far-reaching benefits for Westland. Because work on the Bristol 171, Fairey Gyrodyne and Cierva's Skeeter and Air Horse was already underway, there was no time to be lost by either Westland or Sikorsky in preparing for this programme of work. During January 1947 J M Barr, United Aircraft Corporation's export manager and B L Whelan, general manager of the Sikorsky Division, came to Yeovil to discuss and help plan production in Westland's factory. One of the problems was the 'anglicisation' of Sikorsky drawings which began to arrive at Yeovil in May. There was also the preparation of production plans. This was the task of the new Westland Helicopter Division led by Oliver Logie Lloyd Fitzwilliams who had joined the company as helicopter engineer. He had gained a good deal of rotary-wing experience prewar with G and J Weir Ltd and had had charge of the Rotary Wing Aircraft Section of the Airborne Forces' Experimental Establishment at Beaulieu during 1944–46.

Westland's first helicopter, G-AKTW, the anglicised Sikorsky S-51. It was to lead the way to the company's production of some 2,500 helicopters by 1991.

It was hoped to have the first WS-51 completed within a year but, in the event, its manufacture took much longer. This was due, in part, to the need to replace the 450 hp Pratt & Whitney Wasp Junior engine with a 520 hp Alvis Leonides 50 but, in fact, almost every part of the aircraft differed from the US-built model. To avoid having to re-draw all the Sikorsky drawings, of which there were some 2,700, each was carefully examined and details of design alterations to suit British equipment or materials were incorporated in design sheets attached to each existing drawing before issue to the production shop. This was done by a team of draughtsmen led by A R (Tony) Yates. Thus, it was not until September 1948 that the first prototype, registered G-AKTW, was being prepared for its first flight at Yeovil.

The WS-51's fuselage was of mixed construction, the forward cabin and tail cone were light alloy semi-monocoque structures with a steel-tube centre-section and rotor pylon which housed the engine and gearbox respectively. A monocoque 'bath' structure formed the floor and the major structural support member of the cabin which was extensively glazed with heavy framing and with a large sliding door on each side. The pilot's seat and instrument panel were located on the aircraft's centreline with a bench seat for three passengers side-by-side behind it. A dual control cabin configuration was possible with the pilot and co-pilot or pupil seated in tandem when the bench seat was removed and a second-pilot's seat installed. A tricycle undercarriage with a castoring nosewheel was fitted; the main units each consisted of a tubular V-frame with a light alloy fairing, hinged to the bottom 'longeron' of the centre-section structure and carrying a stub-axle for the wheel. This was braced to the centre-section structure by a single oleo-pneumatic shock absorber strut. The engine was mounted horizontally on a welded steel-tube ring above the bottom truss of the centre-section structure and drove the rotor head through a vertical shaft and a two-stage epicyclic gearbox. Fireproof bulkheads fore and aft of the engine bay separated it from the two 42 gal fore and aft fuel tanks; two more fireproof screens were situated above and below the engine with its accessories

305

carried below the lower screen. Cooling air entered through an intake in the front face of the pylon which, like the centre-section, was clad with light alloy panels, and the exhaust pipe projected through the starboard side of the fuselage. Each of the three blades of the main rotor was built up around a tubular metal spar with wood leading and trailing edges, all fabric covered. The three-blade tail rotor had wood spars and was ply covered. There was no fin or tailplane fitted. Control cables from the cabin to the engine and main rotorhead ran along the floor and up the rear bulkhead to actuate torsion shafts driving screw jacks whose rods connected to the rotor swash plate assembly. In this form G-AKTW was first flown on 5 October, 1948, at Yeovil by Alan Bristow. While this was later than had been anticipated it was, nevertheless, a great achievement by Westland as only 16 months had elapsed since work had begun on building this prototype.

VZ961, the eighth production Dragonfly HR.1, in standard Royal Navy all-over silver finish. Note the squared-off fuselage rear-end carrying mountings for two F24 cameras.

Although Westland foresaw production of civil and military variants of the WS-51, now designated Dragonfly, it was to the Services that it looked for major orders. Both RAF and Royal Navy interest in helicopters had been stimulated in 1945 when the Sikorsky R-4 Hoverfly I had entered service with No.529 Squadron and No.771 Fleet Requirements Unit respectively. Thus, it was in anticipation of demands from both Services for Dragonflies that speculative production of thirty aircraft was begun. Because of the very high cost of creating full production tooling, they were to be built by hand. For that reason, when these orderes arrived, an 18-month delivery time was quoted to allow the production shops to be tooled up.

Meanwhile, on 14 January, 1949, G-AJHW, the first of the six Sikorsky-built S-51s which were part of the licence agreement, had been delivered on charter to the Royal Navy's No.705 Helicopter Squadron at HMS *Siskin* at RNAS Gosport for a two months trials period. During this, serialled WB220, it operated from the aircraft carrier HMS *Vengeance*, undertaking pilot conversion, day and night ASR trials, training of winchmen and cold weather trials. It returned to Yeovil on 22 March. This led to official confirmation of initial orders for thirteen Dragonfly HR.Mk.1s for the Royal Navy and for three HC.Mk.2s for the RAF.

A Dragonfly 1, VZ962, of No.765 Squadron used for trials with a pylon-mounted winch. It is now in the International Helicopter Museum at Weston-super-Mare.

While the Services prepared to receive their first Dragonflies, civil operators were already showing a practical interest in its use. Having seen Los Angeles Airways begin the world's first scheduled helicopter mail service on 1 October, 1947, in Britain during early 1948, BEA's Helicopter Unit, under Capt J Cameron, began flying three of Westland's Sikorsky S-51s, G-AJOV, G-AJOR and G-AKCU. This last aircraft was written off in an accident in North Wales during May 1949 and was replaced by S-51 G-AJHW which had been returned to Yeovil after RN trials as WB220. An experimental dummy postal service was operated during April over a 120 mile circuit of Devon and Somerset, landing on the outskirts of villages, with 96 per cent regularity in poor weather conditions. In spite of the high operating cost of £28 per hour, which dashed hopes that the Post Master General would agree to a permanent helicopter mail service, BEA continued to operate an experimental service by day in East Anglia. On 21 February, 1949, a night mail run was begun between Norwich and Peterborough with which a great deal of experience was accumulated by BEA. This was followed in May 1950 by what has been claimed as 'the world's first scheduled helicopter passenger service'. It ran for 10 days, 9–19 May, between Barnes Park, London, and Castle Bromwich, Birmingham, the site of the British Industries Fair, and was operated by a Westland WS-51 G-ALIL flown by Ken Reed. Flying two return trips each day, 120 passengers were carried between these two points. Then, on 1 June, 1950, BEA inaugurated what was to become the world's first 'scheduled and sustained' helicopter passenger service between Liverpool, Wrexham and Cardiff. It was officially opened by Lord Pakenham, then Minister of Civil Aviation, who flew on the first service out of Speke accompanied by Lord Douglas of Kirtleside, BEA's chairman, and Lady Douglas. This service continued until 31 March, 1951, when BEA withdrew it while plans were made for a similar service between London and Birmingham.

Dragonfly HR.Mk.1

A total of thirteen Dragonfly HR.Mk.1s powered by Alvis Leonides 521/1 engines of 500 hp, were built for the Royal Navy, the first production aircraft,

VX595, being first flown on 18 June, 1949, by Ken Reed. This aircraft and the last HR.Mk.1, VZ966, were each flown experimentally with a four-blade rotor. VX595 was also used for development of metal rotor blades. VZ966 was flown in collaboration with an RAE programme to investigate high advance ratio main-rotor blade behaviour, this being the ratio of the forward speed of the aircraft to the blade tip speed. As flight at reduced rotor speed was to be undertaken an additional rotor blade was required to maintain adequate lift. A camera was mounted on the rotor head to obtain photographs of a tufted blade. These showed that in certain flight regimes some of the tufts rose vertically from the blade surface and rotated violently.

It was not until 13 January 1950, however, that the first Dragonfly was delivered to No.705 Squadron at Gosport and which was to train pilots for air-sea rescue and general utility and photographic duties. These were almost exclusively day operations because the Dragonfly Mk.1 had only rudimentary instruments not suited to all-weather or night flying. Dragonflies in aircraft carriers replaced destroyers as 'plane guards'. When operating in this role, for which they were fitted with a pilot-operated winch on the port side of the rotor pylon, the Dragonflies flew on the port quarter or beam of the carrier when deck-flying was in progress to provide an instant air-sea rescue service. Initially, however, this Dragonfly variant could lift only one survivor at a time, but a modification to enable fuel to be dumped rapidly was embodied to enable two to be rescued. A number of Dragonfly Mk.1s were converted to HR.Mk.3 standard by Westland.

Dragonfly HC.Mk.2

The Royal Air Force's Dragonfly HC.Mk.2, which was powered by an up-rated 540 hp Alvis Leonides 524/1 engine, was basically the same as the Royal Navy's HR.Mk.1, but could be fitted with an enclosed pannier on each side of the fuselage to carry two stretcher cases when used in its primary role as a casualty evacuation aircraft. Only three Dragonfly Mk.2s went into RAF service, the first to fly—on 11 February, 1950—and to be delivered by Ken Reed during March was WF308; this was originally a civil Westland S-51 Mk.1A, G-ALMC. Two more, serialled WF315 and WF311 and first flown on 24 February and 2 March by Reed, were delivered during the same month and in April went to RAF Seletar, Singapore, for operational trials before becoming the nucleus of the Far East Casualty Evacuation flight, formed on 1 May, for jungle rescue in Malaya. This Flight eventually formed the basis of No.194 SAR Squadron.

One of the problems encountered was that of loading the aircraft due to centre of gravity movement. Flown solo, the Dragonfly was supposed to carry six lead weights in the front of the cabin; for each additional person carried, two weights were to be moved aft. Because of the difficulties of doing this, which involved stopping the engine, it became normal practice to fly with only two weights in the nose. This reduction in forward ballast brought a train of control and handling problems in its wake which were never wholly solved. By this time no less than twenty-seven civil and military helicopters had been built by Westland.

G-ALEI, a WS-51 1A, belonging to Pest Control Ltd. It carries two pesticide tanks under the fuselage and a rear-mounted spreader array. A large amount of ballast can be seen on the front mounting while crop spraying in Normandy on 28 May, 1949. (*Courtesy Fred Ballam*)

Westland S-51

Two variants of the WS-51 were built, the Mk.1A powered with the 500 hp Alvis Leonides 521/1 and the Mk.1B with imported 450 hp Pratt & Whitney R-985-B4 Wasp Juniors. Very similar to the Dragonfly HR.Mk.1, the internal cabin furnishing was upgraded to suit its civil passenger role. A total of fifty-one was built by Westland of which twenty-seven appeared on the British civil register.

That there was a mounting interest in helicopters in Great Britain for civil and military use was exemplified by the range of customers. G-AKTW, the Westland-built prototype, was evaluated by the RAF serialled XD649, before being converted to become the prototype Widgeon in 1955 and going to Bristow Helicopters as G-APPR in 1958. In 1949, G-ALEI, the fourth WS-51, was bought by Pest Control Ltd which used it for crop-spraying development work. When it crashed at Sion in Switzerland on 4 May, 1950, it was returned to Westland and, with components from a crashed S-51, G-AJOO, had a useful life as a rotor test rig. Then in 1953 Evening Standard Newspapers Ltd bought G-ANAL for use as a photographic aircraft and general communications duties, but encountered so many difficulties in operating it in and around Greater London that it was sold to Fairey Aviation Ltd as G-ANZL but crashed in October 1959. The newspaper's operating problems were instrumental in launching Westland into a series of protracted negotiations and planning which resulted in the establishment of its Heliport at Battersea in 1959. Following BEA's earlier experience with helicopters, Silver City Airways bought G-ANLV in 1954 and operated it from Lydd in Kent on some cross-Channel services; however, it crashed at Montfort-l'Amaury some 20 miles southwest of Paris on 14 June, 1957. G-ALIL became an MoS aircraft serialled WB810 and was flown extensively by Westland for development work on the Leonides 524/1 engine with +8 lb boost rating. It also flew with a Leonides 531/8 long-stroke

A Westland demonstrator WS-51 1A, the orange and ivory G-AMRE, was used for trials before going to Norway as LN-ORG in 1952. It returned to Westland in 1954.

The nose of G-AMRE showing the heavy black rubber seals around the glazing panels. In the Sikorsky S-51s, the panels were mounted directly into the frames. Outside air temperature equipment is fitted by the footstep for trials.

Originally G-ALMB, this WS-51 1A was exported to Italy in March 1951. The vertical exhaust at the front of the tail cone is, in fact, a distant factory chimney.

engine but it was not a success due to very high levels of torsional vibration induced in the transmission.

A substantial number of the Mk.1As which appeared on the British civil register were exported, the Air Forces of Italy and Thailand buying two and three respectively, four more going to Japan's Air Self Defence Force, while single aircraft were bought by civil operators in Italy and Norway. In addition overseas sales of WS-51 Mk.1As were made in Ceylon (2), France (9) and Iraq (2), and of Mk.1Bs in Yugoslavia (10). All of the five Mk.1Bs on the British civil register were exported, two to the Egyptian Air Force and three to the Belgian Congo, two of which were sold to Mexico. It is of interest to note that three of the original Sikorsky-built S-51s were also exported to Canada.

This Westland WS-51 1B with a Pratt & Whitney Wasp Junior engine was originally G-ALKL but went to the Egyptian Air Force, serialled 9, in November 1949. It does not have the rear-end camera bay.

Dragonfly HR.Mk.3

This Dragonfly variant was built in greater numbers than any of the others, a total of seventy-one being produced for the Royal Navy. The first of these, serialled WG661, first flew on 1 February, 1952. It differed from the HR.Mk.1 in having three all-metal rotor blades, rather than the earlier metal and wood blades from which the fabric covering sometimes parted company in flight, and a hydraulic powered control system. With the HR.Mk.1s, these Dragonflies were

311

Still carrying its Service serial number, Dragonfly 3, WG670, was one of a number converted to Mk.5 standard, and later sold to civil operators. Ultimately this one went to Southend Historic Aircraft Museum in 1972.

widely used in aircraft carriers for general communications work and in the 'plane-guard' role. The RN Dragonflies flown in the Korean War with their metal bladed main rotors and powered controls were in advance of otherwise comparable helicopter types being used by US forces. Most coastal air stations were also equipped with two Dragonflies for air-sea rescue duties, replacing the veteran Sea Otter amphibians; in addition they took part in many civil rescue operations. A number of this variant was converted to HAR.Mk.5 standard.

WN497, a Dragonfly 3, in a rather dilapidated condition, with its main-rotor blades folded. The starboard sliding door is held on, but not in position, by rope. (*Courtesy Mike Hooks*)

312

WG661, the first production Dragonfly HR.3, undergoing winch trials in 1951. This aircraft was used for development flying by Westland. Rear fuselage-mounted 17½ lb ballast weights are visible above the port wheel.

Dragonfly HC.Mk.4

Twelve of this Dragonfly variant were supplied to the RAF between 1952 and April 1954 with all-metal rotor blades and a hydraulic servo-control system. Like the earlier HC.Mk.2, it was intended for casualty evacuation, equipped to carry two stretcher cases in enclosed panniers on the fuselage sides. In this form the HC.Mk.4s played an important role with the Far East Air Force in the Malayan jungle campaign and proved their ability in hundreds of rescue and supply operations.

Dragonflies were finally withdrawn from FEAF on 29 June, 1956, by which time substantial numbers of Whirlwind helicopters had entered service.

313

Dragonfly HR.Mk.5

To extend the capabilities and operational life of its earlier Dragonfly variants, in 1953 the Royal Navy began a programme of modification and modernisation of about twenty-five HR.Mk.1s and Mk.3s at RNAS Donibristle in Scotland. The more powerful 540 hp Alvis Leonides 523/1 engine was fitted, and the instrumentation and communications equipment was updated. In this form these aircraft were re-designated HR.Mk.5s.

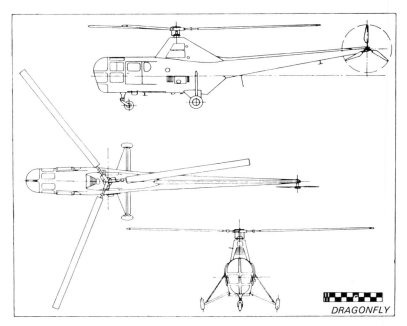

DRAGONFLY

Description: Single-engined single main-rotor multi-role helicopter. All metal structure with metal covering.

Accommodation: Pilot plus three passengers or one crew member in enclosed cabin, or two stretcher cases in external enclosed panniers to suit roles.

Powerplant: One 500 hp Alvis Leonides 521/1 nine-cylinder, air-cooled, geared and supercharged radial engine (HR.Mks.1 and 3, HC2, and 4, WS-51A). One 540 hp Alvis Leonides 523/1 nine-cylinder air-cooled, geared and supercharged radial engine (HR.Mk.5). One 450 hp Pratt & Whitney Wasp Junior nine-cylinder air-cooled geared and supercharged radial engine (WS-51B).

Dimensions: Rotor diameter 48 ft; length 57 ft 6½ in; height 12 ft 11 in; main rotor disc area 1,808 sq ft.

Weights: Empty 4,367 lb, loaded 5,700 lb (WS-51 Mk.1B)
Empty 4,380 lb, loaded 5,870 lb (Mks.1,2,4)
Empty 4,397 lb, loaded 5,880 lb (Mk.3, WS-51 Mk.1A)

314

Empty 4,420 lb, loaded 5,900 lb (Mk.5)

Performance: Maximum speed at sea level 100 mph (all variants); cruising speed 85 mph (all variants); rate of climb at sea level 800 ft/min (Mks.1,2,4, WS-51 Mks.1A, 1B), 950 ft/min (Mks.3,5); service ceiling 12,400 ft (Mks.1,2,4 and 5), 13,200 ft (Mk.3); range 300 miles (all variants).

Production: A total of 149 Dragonflies produced by Westland Helicopters Ltd, Yeovil, Somerset, during 1949–54 as follows:

13 Dragonfly Mk.1 production aircraft
2 Dragonfly Mk.2 production aircraft
71 Dragonfly Mk.3 production aircraft
12 Dragonfly Mk.4 production aircraft
22 WS-51 Mk.1A production aircraft
5 WS-51 Mk.1B production aircraft
2 WS-51 Mk.1A production aircraft (Ceylon)
9 WS-51 Mk.1A production aircraft (France)
2 WS-51 Mk.1A production aircraft (Iraq)
1 WS-51 Mk.1A production aircraft (Japan)
10 WS-51 Mk.1B production aircraft (Yugoslavia)

Widgeon

The prototype Widgeon was converted from WS-51 1A G-ALIK. Maintenance was simplified by built-in hand and foot holds and a platform. Note the internal cowling on the Leonides on top of which was the cooling fan.

The improvement in the lifting capabilities of the Westland WS-51 Dragonflies with the more powerful Leonides engine variants prompted Westland, during 1954, to examine the possibilities of redesigning the WS-51's front fuselage to accommodate an additional passenger. This would have the added benefit of overcoming the centre of gravity difficulties. Thus, having studied several ways of doing this, the company took the bold decision to proceed with a private venture project.

Re-registered G-APPS, the prototype Widgeon was used by British United Airways for civil engineering work, including pipe laying 1961. (*British United Airways*)

The two major design changes were to the cabin, which had a new profile, and was extended by 10 inches and could seat the pilot and one passenger side-by-side with three more on the rear bench seat, and to the main rotor and gearbox. This last modification involved removing the top of the WS-51 gearbox, substituting a WS-55 gearbox top and main-rotor shaft to allow the use of the WS-55 rotor head and shortened blades. This WS-55 Whirlwind unit had more efficient offset flapping hinges which increased the centre of gravity range and overcame the earlier ballasting problems. In addition, metal main-rotor blades were fitted and a three-blade laminated wood S-51 tail rotor. The weight penalty of the new rotor head was almost exactly balanced by a weight saving in

One of British United Airways' Widgeons lifting a pallet of bricks to the top of a new Thames-side building in 1961. (*British United Airways*)

the new nose structure if the Dragonfly and the new helicopter were compared to the same standard. Named Widgeon, the second Westland type to bear this name, it was produced as a general purpose helicopter able to operate in a variety of roles.

As the empty weight of the Widgeon was almost the same as the Dragonfly, the increase of some 200 lb in loaded weight was used almost entirely for extra payload. Westland therefore envisaged the Widgeon as a passenger or cargo-carrier, as an air ambulance using a hinged nose-door to admit two stretchers or as a rescue aircraft for which role a winch could be fitted. For military use in the ASW role or other over-water operations, inflatable neoprene pontoons were available, while the side-by-side seating in the nose made the Widgeon adaptable as a trainer.

Conversion work on three WS-51 Mk.1As, G-AKTW, G-ALIK and G-ANLW began during early 1955 with the first flight of this last aircraft taking place on 23 August at Yeovil. G-ALIK first flew with the new rotor-gearbox

317

A Widgeon gearbox being prepared for installation in a new airframe on the Yeovil production line.

Executair's Widgeon G-APTW at Yeovil. The logo on the nose shows a cine-camera with wings.

arrangement but with a standard WS-51 airframe. G-AKTW followed it a few days later and both aircraft completed the mandatory 10 hours flying before appearing at the SBAC Flying Display and Exhibition at Farnborough which opened on 3 September. G-ALIK, piloted by Roy Bradley, flew a synchronised display with a Whirlwind Mk.5, XJ 396 flown by Slim Sear and Derek Colvin.

Despite the good performance of the Widgeon, only twelve were built as new aircraft and three were converted WS-51 Mk.1As. They were used by Bristow Helicopters Ltd in the Persian Gulf on oil rig communications flying, by the Hong Kong Police with 'sky shouting' loudspeaker equipment while others found their way to Nigeria. Others were sold to the Brazilian Navy and Royal Jordanian Air Force while one was used in Japan for electrical power-line inspection. The last Widgeon left the factory in September 1959. Two years before this, the Royal Navy had expressed an interest in the Widgeon as a small commando-type carrier and plans were in hand to convert twenty-four Dragonflies to Widgeon standard. But this was an era of Government stringency in matters of defence spending and this programme was abandoned. It was to have been the Dragonfly HR.Mk.7.

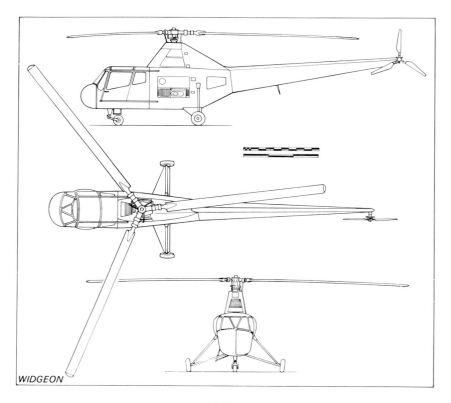

WIDGEON

Description: Single main-rotor utility helicopter.

Accommodation: Pilot and up to four passengers or crew in enclosed cabin.

Powerplant: One 520 hp Alvis Leonides 521/2 nine-cylinder air-cooled geared and supercharged radial engine.

Dimensions: Rotor diameter 49 ft 2 in; length 41 ft 10 in; height 13 ft 4 in; main rotor disc area 1,898 sq ft.

Weights: Empty 4,322 lb; loaded 5,900 lb.

Performance: Maximum speed at sea level 109 mph; cruising speed 88 mph; rate of climb at sea level 700 ft/min; service ceiling 11,800 ft.

Production: A total of 15 Widgeons produced by Westland Aircraft Ltd, Yeovil, Somerset, during 1955–59 as follows:

Three Widgeons converted from WS-51 Mk.IAs.

12 Widgeon production aircraft.

Whirlwind

G-AMHK, a Sikorsky S-55 registered to Westland in January 1951 for use as a demonstrator.

Almost before the Dragonfly had entered service with No.705 Squadron of the Royal Navy in January 1950, Westland's management had set its sights on building a larger and more advanced helicopter. The most obvious way to achieve this was to seek an extension of the licence which Westland had earlier negotiated with United Aircraft Corporation's Sikorsky Division for production of the S-51 at Yeovil. The new round of discussions began in June 1950 and on 15 November Westland announced that it had, that day, secured the rights to licence-build the Sikorsky S-55, the prototype of which had first flown at Bridgeport almost exactly a year earlier. As before, Westland was permitted to export these aircraft, other than to North America; this time, however, the British company bought a single example of the S-55, (c/n 55016) which was immediately shipped to Yeovil for use as a demonstrator Whirlwind. This was first registered to Westland in January 1951 as G-AMHK and was first flown by Ken Reed on 6 June. The following year it went to the A & AEE for evaluation

320

serialled WW339. Although the Westland design team had had experience of this 'anglicisation' of US design drawings with the S-51, the more complex S-55 posed a number of problems; in addition it was found that some of the British components specified were heavier than their US counterparts. Almost without exception all the major design features of the Sikorsky S-55 were embodied in the Westland aeroplane. One exception was the main-rotor gearbox which was redesigned by Westland to embody new castings and stiffer gears. The fuselage was a rectangular light alloy semi-monocoque structure with a rear cone-shaped extension carrying the tail rotor pylon, the sharp step up from the bottom line of the cabin to that of this extension being filled by a large triangular fin. A 600 hp Pratt & Whitney 1340-40 air-cooled radial engine was mounted on an inclined axis in the lower part of the nose and drove the main-rotor gearbox, which was in the cabin roof, through a long sloping shaft passing upward between the two pilots' seats located high above the cabin. Access to the engine was via two clamshell nose doors, these and the position of the engine making it very accessible from ground level for servicing. Fuel tanks under the cabin floor had a total capacity of 179 gal. The three-blade main-rotor embodied offset flapping hinges with hydraulic damping about the drag hinges. The two-blade tail rotor gearbox was driven by a shaft running through the upper part of the rear extension cone. There were two small fins forming an inverted V below the tail rotor pylon. The undercarriage was a non-retractable four-wheel type, the smaller front units were fully castoring and the two main units consisted of one oleo-pneumatic shock absorber strut and one radius rod. Accommodation in the cabin was for eight passengers, ten fully-armed troops or six stretchers, with

Whirlwind 1, XA863, keeps station on G-ANJT, a WS-51 Series 1 during August 1954. Both have undrooped tail cones and anhedral tailplanes. (*Courtesy Dowty Group*)

access through a large sliding door on the starboard side. Cargo capacity was 340 cubic feet.

Construction of G-AMJT, the first Westland WS-55 Series 1 helicopter, continued through 1951–52 with the first hovering test taking place on 12 November, 1952. There followed some six months of tethered and hovering trials of the transmission and other systems and components. While the aircraft was still in its yellow primer and unmarked, it first flew during the summer of 1953, but it was not until 15 August that the 'official first flight' of this helicopter, XA862, took place. It was to become the first of ten Mk.1s to be built for the Royal Navy. The second aircraft built, XA864 (G-17-1) was to fly ahead of XA863 which was the next to get airborne and was shown in the Static Aircraft Park at the 1953 SBAC Exhibition leaving a Dragonfly Mk.1, VZ966, and a Wyvern Mk.S.4, VW870, to represent Westland in the Flying Display. Before deliveries to No.848 Squadron RN began in July 1954, XA862 was flown as the Type Test aircraft and XA864 was used by Westland for strain-gauge checks of its rotor and transmission systems. Following the RN variant a batch of ten HAR Mk.2/4 were produced for the RAF, beginning with XD163. Except for some equipment differences, these two variants were very similar; however, the Mk.4 had the R-1340-57 engine, a low altitude rated variant instead of the Mk.2's R-1340-40 engine. At the Westland AGM on 16 December, 1953, the chairman's Statement to Shareholders revealed that the WS-55 had been named Whirlwind.

The fifth production Whirlwind 1, XA866 was a Westland undercarriage development aircraft. It had the straight undrooped tail cone and anhedral tailplane.

Production and development of the Whirlwind can be sub-divided into three groups. The Series 1 consisted of the Whirlwind HAR. Mks.1–4 and the WS-55 Series 1 civil helicopter, all with US-built radial piston engines; Series 2 covered the HAR.Mk.5, HAS.Mk.7, HCC.Mk.8 and the WS-55 Series 2 civil variant all having British Alvis Leonides Major radial piston engines, while the Series 3 comprised the HAR.Mks.9–10, HC.Mk.10, HCC.Mk.12 and the WS-55 Series

3 civil helicopter which were powered by Bristol Siddeley/Rolls-Royce Gnome 1000 turboshaft engines.

Whirlwind HAR.Mk.1

A batch of ten Whirlwind HAR.Mk.1 helicopters was built for the Royal Navy and was delivered to No.848 Squadron, beginning in July 1954 to replace its Sikorsky-built S-55 Whirlwind HAR.21s delivered in 1952 as part of the Mutual Defence Aid Programme. With the HAR.1 the squadron operated in the general utility and SAR role. During September and October 1954 five aircraft were sent to Malaya with the squadron but the always hot, and often high, operating conditions affected their performance, the 600 hp Pratt & Whitney engine being insufficiently powerful to lift more than a very much reduced load of men or equipment. Thus, about nine months later, they were recovered to the United Kingdom. This variant did, however, provide excellent service aboard the ice patrol ship HMS *Protector* in the Antarctic and while operating patrols from a Falkland Islands base from 1955–66. For these duties the Whirlwind was fitted with special radio equipment and flotation gear. During 1955 a Mk.1 undertook trials as a minesweeper but the lack of power again made this exercise inconclusive.

Whirlwind HAR.Mk.2 and Mk.4

Although basically similar to the HAR.Mk.1, these two Whirlwind variants had different internal equipment; in addition, while the Mk.2 had the same engine as the Mk.1, the Mk.4 had a Pratt & Whitney R-1340-57 engine having a supercharger ratio increased from 10:1 to 12:1 for improved performance, and equipment for operations in tropical climates. They were built for the RAF in six production batches, totalling seventy-one aircraft. During September 1954 the first Mk.4s entered service with No.155 Squadron, FEAF, based at Seletar but with a detachment at Kuala Lumpur where they were used for jungle rescue

XJ426, a Whirlwind 2, originally serialled XD795 and which was converted to a Mk.10, winches in a 'survivor' on a practice ASR mission.

and transport duties. About thirty were issued to the RAF, the last one, XL113, being delivered on 4 December, 1956.

The first deliveries of the Mk.2s did not begin to reach No.22 Squadron, Coastal Command, at Thorney Island until February 1955 soon after it had reformed as a postwar SAR unit. The Mk.2s served longest with this squadron, not being fully replaced by Whirlwind HAR.Mk.10s until 1963. In an all-yellow finish when serving as part of the United Kingdom's SAR Organisation, these aircraft played a vital and pioneering role in the build up of the SAR helicopter fleet. A small number of Mk.2s from the Joint Experimental Helicopter Unit at Middle Wallop took part in the Anglo-French amphibious landing at Port Said during the Suez Crisis in November 1956.

A Whirlwind 2 gunship. An experimental machine-gun installation in an aircraft, XK969, of the Joint Experimental Helicopter Unit at Old Sarum. (*Courtesy Fred Ballam*)

During February 1957 Whirlwind Mk.2s of No.217 Squadron were detached to Christmas Island in the Pacific in support of Operation Grapple 2, during which Britain's first hydrogen bomb was dropped from a Vickers Valiant on 15 May, 1957.

A number of both these Whirlwind variants were converted to HAR.Mk.10s.

Whirlwind HAR.Mk.3

Although thirty-seven Whirlwind HAR.Mk.3s were 'laid down', three were completed as Mk.5s and nine as Mk.7s. This RN variant was similar to the Mk.1 but was intended as a replacement for the Dragonfly for plane-guard duties on aircraft carriers and was powered by a 700 hp Wright 12-1300-3 air-cooled radial

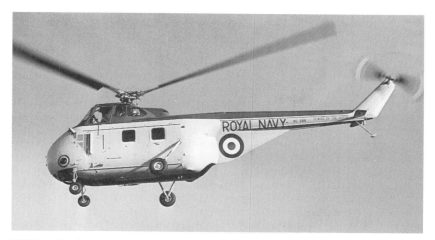

XG586, with the drooped tail cone and flat tailplane, was a hybrid Whirlwind 3 completed as a Mk.7 airframe with a Wright Cyclone R-1300–3 engine. The launching aperture under the rear fuselage was for torpedoes carried internally for warmth. (*Courtesy Fred Ballam*)

engine. The prototype, XJ393, first flew on 24 September, 1954, and the Whirlwind Mk.3 entered service in November 1955 to serve at several shore establishments and aboard HMS *Albion, Ark Royal, Bulwark, Eagle, Victorious* and *Warrior*. It was while as part of the ship's flight for plane-guard duties in this last carrier that four Mk.3s also participated in Operation Grapple. During the

XK970, a Whirlwind 2, was modified by the Joint Experimental Helicopter Unit at Old Sarum to carry four small air-to-ground missiles. (*Courtesy Fred Ballam*)

previous year, Whirlwind Mk.3s also took part in the amphibious landing at Port Said. With Bristol Sycamore HR.Mk.14s and Whirlwind HAS.Mk.22 helicopters, they airlifted 45 Royal Marine Commando ashore from two light Fleet carriers, HMS *Theseus* and *Ocean*.

Initial trials of vertical replenishment of vessels at sea were made by a Whirlwind Mk.3 during February 1962 between the RFA *Resurgent* and the Fleet carrier HMS *Victorious*. This Whirlwind variant was phased out of RN service during 1964. Among the tasks undertaken by RN and RAF Whirlwind Mks.1–4 were ASR and jungle rescue, casevac, troop and general transport, static line parachuting and plane-guard duties.

Some Whirlwind HAS.3s were equipped with US Asdic 194 (AQS-4), licence-built by R.B. Pullin and Co. From XJ402 they were fitted with a 3 deg drooped tail cone with an integral fin and flat tailplane. This gave greater clearance for the main-rotor blades.

WS-55 Series 1

A total of forty-five WS-55 Series 1 civil helicopters were built by Westland during 1951–60; in addition the company assembled one Sikorsky-built S-55 which was registered G-AMHK in January 1951 and from which the WS-55 was developed.

Structurally the Series 1 was virtually identical to the Sikorsky helicopter, and was powered by a 600 hp Pratt & Whitney Wasp R-1340-40 engine, with accomodation for two crew and for seven passengers and luggage. The cabin of G-AMHK was upholstered and soundproofed and its first public showing in the United Kingdom was at the Commonwood House Country Club at Chipperfield, Bucks, where it was flown by Ken Reed on 22 June, 1951.

The first Westland-built S-55, G-AMJT, first flew on 12 November, 1952, piloted by Derek Colvin, Westland's test pilot, who successfully completed three five-minute hovers; this aircraft then began a 50 hours ground running test programme on the engine, gearbox, transmission and rotors. G-AMYN was flown by Westland with the Class B registration G-17-3 before being delivered to France for the Aéronavale on 15 April, 1954. At the SBAC show in

BEA WS-55 Series 1 G-ANFH giving a crop-spraying demonstration on 25 May, 1959. The large barrel in the open cabin can be seen. (*British European Airways*)

September 1954, G-ANFH, the third civil Whirlwind was exhibited on the Westland stand minus its tail boom, main rotor and engine and with its cabin having three forward-facing seats and two rear-facing. It was named *Sir Ector*, but a wall plaque in the cabin warned 'The good Sir Ector should not be confused with Sir Ector de Maris, brother of the great Sir Lancelot'. One wonders if this classical reference was inspired by the good and great Harald Penrose! A Whirlwind HAR.Mk.1, XA817, was the sole Westland representative in the Static Aircraft Park.

This amphibious WS-55 Series 1, G-ANUK, of BEA flew service trials on the Waterloo–London-Heathrow route along the Thames.

By far the largest operator of WS-55 Series 1s was Bristow Helicopters at Redhill which, at one time or another during their lives, owned twenty-five, of which several were sold on to other operators, only to be bought back again later. Bristow flew these Whirlwinds in support of early off-shore industry operations and civil engineering projects and on general transport and emergency duties from 1961 until 1969 by which time the Wessex 60 had almost entirely replaced it. The second largest customer was The South Georgia Co which, during 1954–56, bought six WS-55 Series 1s for whaling operations in the South Atlantic and Southern Ocean. The first three, G-ANJS, 'T and 'U were lost in the sea while flying from two whaling factory ships. G-ANUK, South Georgia's fifth aircraft, had been used by BEA Helicopters Ltd and, named *Sir Kay*, on experimental helicopter services from Waterloo to London-Heathrow Airport, while early in 1953 BEA and Westland had undertaken noise tests with an S-51, G-AJOR, at the South Bank site. During the third week of January 1955 trials of Vokes exhaust silencers were begun on the site, with particular attention being paid to noise readings in nearby offices while the aircraft was taking-off and landing. These were found to be 'acceptable'. In May, further trials with the silencers, and with floats fitted, were undertaken along the South

Bank–Heathrow route, the aircraft finally being cleared for operation at a maximum take-off weight of 7,500 lb. This reduced the seats from seven to five. Ultimately, these trials resulted in the inauguration of the service on 25 July, 1956, when Capt 'Jock' Cameron, BEA's senior helicopter pilot, flew John Boyd-Carpenter and three other dignatories in float-equipped G-ANUK. These canoe-shaped appendages were fitted in case of engine-failure along the mandatory route over the Thames. The single fare was £1.15.0 (£1.75p) and there were eight services per day, but BEA abandoned these helicopter services during the following year.

G-APWN, a WS-55 Series 1, was converted to a Series 3 by Bristow Helicopters in 1964. (*Bristow Helicopters*)

Two more aircraft were sold to the Norwegian whaling company, Melsom and Melsom, during September 1953; the first was the US-built S-55, originally registered G-AMHK, which became LN-ORK and the second was registered LN-ORL. One of these landed at Durban on 7 November after flying off a platform on the factory ship *Norvhal*. This company found the helicopter's hovering capability of great value when counting whales in a school!

On 20 September, 1955, two WS-55 Series 1s, bought by the Royal Dutch Shell Group, to service oil rigs and platforms, left Eastleigh Airport, Southampton, on the, then, longest delivery flight ever attempted by a British helicopter. Flown by Alan Bristow and Alan Green, these aircraft were fitted with long-range fuel tanks for the more than 3,000 miles journey to Doha on the Persian Gulf via France, Italy and Greece, Cyprus and Iraq.

Of the thirty-three Whirlwind Series 1s on the British Civil Register, twenty-three eventually were sold overseas with a further thirteen being delivered to Brazil (3), Cuba (2), France (6), Norway (1) and Yugoslavia (1).

Still extant is G-ANFH in the International Helicopter Museum.

Shell Refining Co used inflatable pontoons on this WS-55 Series 1, G-AODB, in Bahrein in 1956. (*British United Airways*)

Whirlwind HAR.Mk.5

The performance-limiting power of the US-built Pratt & Whitney R-1340 piston engines in the Whirlwind Series 1 helicopter was overcome in two stages, the first being the introduction of the Series II aircraft with British 750 hp (derated) Alvis Leonides Major 755 air-cooled radial piston engines. Among a number of modifications embodied in this variant were a tail boom with 3 deg of droop to provide increased main-rotor blade clearance, a sprung tail bumper and a redesigned horizontal stabiliser. All three HAR.Mk.5s, XJ396, XJ398 and XJ445, were converted from airframes laid down as Mk.3s and taken from the production line.

The prototype, XJ396, was converted and first flew in its modified form with a Leonides Major engine on 28 August, 1955; a week later it appeared in the SBAC Flying Display at Farnborough. An Armstrong Siddeley AS.181 turboshaft was installed in XJ398 and during late 1955 XJ445, which was also taken from the Mk.3 production line for conversion to, but never completed as, a Mk.6, was fitted with a Turboméca Twin Turmo turboshaft. This was Westland's first venture into turbine-powered helicopters and was to pave the way for many hundreds more. Unfortunately, neither of these two latter installations proved a success and were abandoned, XJ445 being re-engined with a Leonides Major and going to the RAE Farnborough.

Whirlwind HAS.Mk.7

The Whirlwind HAS.Mk.7 was the first British helicopter designed for front-line service in the anti-submarine role. The prototype, XG589, first flew on 17 October, 1956, powered by the Leonides engine. As a Gannet replacement in the ASW role the 'hunter' Whirlwind HAS.7 was equipped with a dipping sonar for submarine detection, while the 'killer' HAS.7 could carry a lightweight homing torpedo, initially the Mk.30 but later the Mk.44 was introduced, or depth charges. These weapons were housed in a bay below the cabin floor, from which position the fuel tanks were moved, the 'bathtub' was made some 9 in deeper by raising the floor level to obtain the same fuel capacity.

The fourth production Whirlwind 7, XG592, ready for delivery.

This Whirlwind variant went to No.700H Squadron for intensive flying trials in June 1957 and to No.845 Squadron shortly afterwards. Unfortunately its early Service life was marred by a series of engine-associated problems and failures, a number of which resulted in fatal accidents. This variant made its public debut when Whirlwind XK941 was flown in the 1957 SBAC Display at Farnborough. During April–November 1959 all HAS.7s were grounded and Gannets were returned to service in place of the ASW helicopters which were undergoing modification of their engines and transmission systems. The first operational squadron to receive these modified helicopters was No.815. A total of eight operational and four training squadrons flew the HAS.7s; however, they began to be replaced in the ASW role by Wessex HAS.Mk.1s during 1960. Many HAS.7s were converted for use as Commando support helicopters. In October 1959 No.848 Squadron re-equipped with this variant which could accommodate eight fully-armed Royal Marine Commandos. Two other squadrons, Nos.846 and 847, were similarly equipped. The HAS.7 was flown in Sarawak, Brunei and other regions of Borneo and in Kuwait in support of RM Commando operations during 1961–64.

The RN retired its last piston-engined helicopter, Whirlwind HAS.Mk.7 XN299 on 22 July, 1976. Based at the Joint Helicopter Tactical Development Unit at Old Sarum, Wiltshire, it had been dubbed the 'Iron Chicken'.

This reduced-weight Whirlwind 7, XN358, has had the ventral fin, tail rotor drive-shaft cover, brakes and some internal equipment removed to improve its lifting capabilities in the ASR role, here being practised off Portland Harbour. (*Courtesy Fred Ballam*)

Whirlwind HCC.Mk.8

One of two Queen's Flight Whirlwind 8s, XN127, at Yeovil.

Only two Whirlwind HCC.Mk.8s were built. Serialled XN126 and XN127, they were for service with the Queen's Flight and joined that unit at RAF Benson on 5 November, 1959. Powered by 740 hp Leonides Major 160 engines, they were the only helicopters in the RAF with these engines. They were fitted with dual controls and had special soundproofing and furnishings in the four-seat cabin.

WS-55 Series 2

White and blue G-AOCZ, a WS-55 Series 2, was a Westland demonstrator for some ten years from 1955 before conversion to a Series 3. (*Courtesy Fred Ballam*)

Only eight WS-55 Series 2 aircraft, powered by the 750 hp Alvis Leonides Major 755 engine, appeared on the British Civil Register, three of which were built as such and five were conversions from Series 1s and HAS.Mk.7s. Exports were to

One of four WS-55 Series 2 for Spain. The prominent carburettor air intake filter under the nose is noteworthy.

Austria (10), Royal Jordanian Air Force (2) and Spain (4) plus two to Canada, G-AOYY and 'YZ, which became CF-KAD and 'AE in July 1957. The two ex-RN HAS.7s, XK940/G-AYXT and XM685/G-AYZJ, are still extant, 'XT still on the Register and 'ZJ in the Newark Air Museum. Ultimately, all the others were exported.

Whirlwind HAR.Mk.9

Although the rotary-wing element of the RAF had received its later turbine-powered Whirlwind HAR.Mk.10s in November 1961, it was not until the middle of 1966 that the Royal Navy equivalent, the HAR.9, entered service with No.829 Squadron in the SAR role.

A total of sixteen HAR.9s were created by re-engining a batch of Whirlwind HAR.Mk.7s with the 1,050 shp Bristol Siddeley/Rolls-Royce Gnome H 1000 turboshaft. This was an anglicised licence-built variant of the US General Electric T58 with a Lucas fuel system and a Hawker Siddeley Dynamics control computer. The Gnome, which was only 54 in long with a 2 sq ft frontal area, was only one-third of the weight but produced more than 40 cent more power than the earlier Leonides Major radial engine. These enhanced the Whirlwind's performance, reliability and flight safety. It was mounted horizontally and offset to port in the fuselage nose, which was lengthened by 30 in, thus producing a more streamlined shape. The space now provided on the other side of the nose became an electrical equipment bay for components moved from the tail boom. The main-rotor gearbox and transmission system of the radial engine installation was retained unchanged to simplify the conversion of existing Whirlwinds to turbine power. Accommodation was provided for three crew and up to five survivors.

In RN service the HAR.9s were based principally at RNAS Brawdy, Culdrose and Lee-on-Solent; two served in HMS *Endurance* and *Protector* on Antarctic ice-patrol duties.

Whirlwind HAR. and HC.Mk.10

Basically similar to the RN Whirlwind HAR.Mk.9, which it pre-dated in service by some five years, the RAF Whirlwind HAR.10 and HC.Mk.10 were short-range tactical transports, ground support or SAR helicopters with accommodation for three crew and up to eight passengers.

The prototype airframe, XJ398, had been laid down as an HAR.3 which became the second HAR.5; in 1958 it was again re-engined with a General Electric T58 turboshaft and first flew in this form on 28 February, 1959. A total of sixty-eight production Whirlwind HAR. and HC.10s were built powered by the 1,050 shp Bristol Siddeley Gnome H.1000 turboshaft. A number of others were converted from HC. and HR.Mk.2s and Mk.4s and first entered service on 4 November, 1961, with No.225 Squadron, Transport Command, at RAF

Ground forces abseiling from RAF Whirlwind 10 XP357 at Kuching, Borneo, in 1964.

Odiham. This variant was also issued to Coastal and to Flying Training Commands and to RAF Germany. In FEAF service it operated in Borneo during the Indonesian Confrontation period, being the last RAF aircraft to fly in support of Malaysian forces before being withdrawn in November 1967.

Whirlwind HCC.Mk.12

Early in 1964 two Whirlwind HCC.Mk.12s, XR486 and XR 487, joined the Queen's Flight. They were specially furnished and equipped variants of the HAR.Mk.10. In July 1967, while on its way to Yeovil for a conference about the introduction of the Wessex Mk.4 to the Flight, one of these aircraft XR487 suffered structural failure and crashed while carrying a crew of two plus Air Commodore John Blount, then Captain of the Flight, and the Flight's Engineer

Officer. All four lost their lives. Initially it was believed that this accident was due to a fatigue crack found in the spar of one of the main-rotor blades; all Whirlwinds were grounded, except for operational flights, pending the outcome of non-destructive testing of the blades. It was not until December 1967 that it was revealed that the Queen's Flight accident followed loss of the rotor head caused by fatigue failure of the drive-shaft. This was traced back to the manufacturing process of this high tensile steel shaft which was unique to the Whirlwind. As a result, all Whirlwinds were grounded and their gearboxes were returned to Westland for examination. Over 100 shafts were inspected and a number were rejected, making replacement a matter of extreme urgency. Although there was official confirmation after this accident that it had not been the practice for Her Majesty to use the helicopters, when this rotor drive-shaft defect had been remedied, HRH Prince Philip and other members of the Royal Family resumed flying in the surviving Whirlwind HCC.Mk.12 pending its replacement by the Wessex.

WS-55 Series 3

Produced both as a new-built aircraft and by the conversion of Series 1 and 2 aircraft, this Whirlwind variant ultimately was powered by a 1,050 shp Bristol Siddeley/Rolls-Royce Gnome H.1000 turboshaft. The installation of this engine was designed so that conversion from the piston-engined variants was comparatively simple, and followed closely that of the similarly-powered Whirlwind HAR.9 and 10. The piston engine, clutch and fan unit were removed but the gearboxes and transmission system were unchanged. The prototype, first flew on 28 February, 1959. About twenty-five WS-55 Series 1s and 2s and HAR.Mk.1s/3s were converted to the Series 3 standard, many by Bristow Helicopters; among the 'converts' was G-APDY, which had been Westland's Series 2 demonstrator.

An early Whirlwind 2, F12, delivered to France. It has a winch on the fuselage side.

335

French Whirlwind HAR.Mk.2

A total of thirty-seven Whirlwind HAR.Mk.2s, serialled F1–F37, were delivered to the French Navy during 1954–56.

Yugoslav Whirlwind HAR.Mk.5

In 1957 Yugoslavia bought four Whirlwind HAR.Mk.5s plus four airframes without engines and four complete aircraft sets of sub-assemblies. These aircraft were for the Yugoslav Air Force.

Yugoslav Whirlwind HAR.Mk.7

Two Whirlwind HAR.Mk.7s, plus two airframes without engines and two complete aircraft sets of sub-assemblies were supplied to Yugoslavia in 1959 for use by the Yugoslav Navy.

Assembly of both the Whirlwind Mk.5s and Mk.7s was done in a special facility; in addition, there was an interchange of Westland and Yugoslav engineers during the 1961–63 period in connection with this and other associated work.

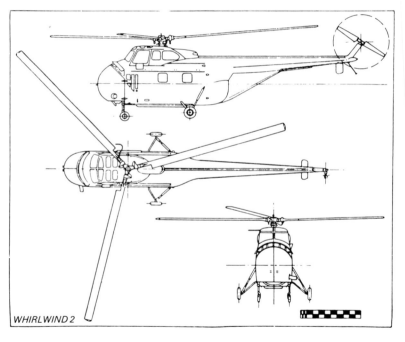

WHIRLWIND 2

Description: Single-engined single main-rotor civil or military helicopter.
Accommodation: Two crew and eight passengers or ten troops in the main cabin.

Powerplant: One 600 hp Pratt & Whitney R-1340-40 nine-cylinder radial air-cooled geared and supercharged engine (Series 1, Mks.1, 2 and 3). One 600 hp Pratt & Whitney R-1340-57 nine-cylinder radial air-cooled geared and supercharged engine (Mk.4). One 700 hp Wright R-1300-3 nine-cylinder radial air-cooled geared engine (Mk.3). One 750 hp Alvis Leonides Major 755 fourteen-cylinder two-row radial air-cooled geared and supercharged engine (Series 2, Mks. 5, 6, 7 and 8). One 1,050 shp Bristol Siddeley Gnome H.1000 turboshaft (Series 3, Mks.9, 10 and 12).
Armament: One Mk.30 or Mk.44 homing torpedo or depth charges (Mk.7). Four Nord SS.11 air-to-surface missiles (Mk.2).
Dimensions: Main-rotor diameter 53 ft 0 in; length 41 ft 8½ in (Series 1 and 2, Mks.1, 2, 3, 4 and 8)), 44 ft 2 in (Series 3, Mks.9, 10 and 12); height 15 ft 7½ in (all Mks); main-rotor disc area 2,205 sq ft.
Weights: Empty 4,990 lb (Series 1), 5,327 lb (Mk.1), 5,435 lb (Mk.2), 5,610 lb (Mk.3), 5,387 lb (Mk.4), 5,170 lb (Series 2), 5,993 lb (Mk.7), 4,644 lb (Series 3), 5,483 lb (Mk.9), 4,760 lb (Mk.10), 4,800 lb (Mk.12); normal loaded 7,200 lb (Series 1, Mks.1, 2 and 4), 7,500 lb (Mk.3), 7,800 lb (Series 2 and 3, Mks.5–12).
Performance: Maximum speed 99 mph (Series 1, Mks.1, 2 and 4), 109 mph (Series 2, Mks.5, 7 and 8), 110 mph (Series 3, Mks.9, 10 and 12); cruising

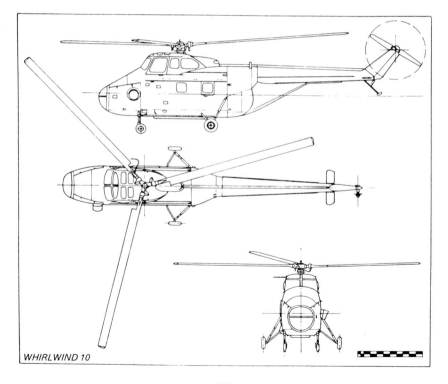

WHIRLWIND 10

speed 85 mph (Series 1 and 2, Mks.1, 2, 3 and 4 and 8), 106 mph (Series 3, Mks.9, 10 and 12); sea level rate of climb 600 ft/min (Series 1, Mks.1, 2 and 3), 800 ft/min (Mk.4), 910 ft/min (Series 2, Mks.5, 7 and 8), 1,200 ft/min (Series 3, Mks.9, 10 and 12); service ceiling 8,600 ft (Series 1, Mks.1, 2, 3 and 4), 10,000 ft (Mk.9), 13,000 ft (Series 2, Mks.5, 7 and 8), 16,600 ft (Series 3, Mks,9, 10 and 12); range 320 miles (Series 1), 335 miles (Series 2), 300 miles (Series 3).

Production: A total of 364 Whirlwinds produced by Westland Aircraft/ Helicopter Ltd, Yeovil, Somerset, during 1953–66 as follows:

10 Whirlwind HAR.Mk.1 production aircraft
33 Whirlwind HAR.Mk.2 production aircraft
25 Whirlwind HAR.Mk.3 production aircraft
24 Whirlwind HAR.Mk.4 production aircraft
3 Whirlwind Mk.5 development aircraft
129 Whirlwind HAR.Mk.7 production aircraft
2 Whirlwind HCC.Mk.8 production aircraft
68 Whirlwind HAR.Mk.10 production aircraft
2 Whirlwind HCC.Mk.12 production aircraft
44 WS-55 Series 1 production aircraft
19 WS-55 Series 2 production aircraft
5 WS-55 Series 3 production aircraft.

Westminster

During the early 1950s Westland was pursuing its long considered design of a gas-turbine-powered large heavy-lift helicopter for civil and military use. In April 1951 in response to a specification issued by British European Airways (BEA), a Westland proposal envisaged a 30-seater powered with an Armstrong Siddeley Double Mamba and in the following year an even larger 50-seater with either four Rolls-Royce Darts or three Napier Elands was submitted to meet a BEA requirement. Other projects in 1953 included the giant 400-seat W.90 troop transport, but none of these came to fruition. During January 1954 Westland actively considered licenced production of a re-engined civil version of the Sikorsky S-56, replacing its two pylon-mounted Pratt & Whitney radial engines with either Rolls-Royce Tynes, Mambas or Elands side-by-side above the main cabin roof. Westland's chairman, Sir Eric Mensforth, later wrote to the MoS to seek funding of this project and in July provided specific proposals. During subsequent negotiations the company forecast completion of twelve S-56s, five with turboshaft engines, by June 1958. Westland's proposals failed to gain Government support. On 29 June, 1955, Westland completed negotiations for an extension to the inter-company licencing agreement with Sikorsky to cover the S-56's 72 ft diameter five-blade main-rotor and gearbox, the four-blade tail rotor and the transmission and control system in a Westland-designed airframe. In spite of this sad lack of Government support Westland decided to go ahead with the private venture design and development of a heavy-lift transport helicopter.

The first Westminster, G-APLE, tied down for engine running before the first flight. It has a five-bladed main-rotor, internal fuel tanks and unguarded engine air intakes. Westland said the Westminster was 'an ordinary helicopter drawn on bigger pieces of paper'.

Because of Westland's heavy commitment to the Wessex programme only the minimum staff, finance and engineering resources could be allocated to this new aircraft. Initially two variants were planned; a 40-seat short-range civil transport intended for stage lengths of not more than 100 miles, and a flying crane able to lift a 15,000 lb load. Westland produced a wooden mock-up cabin of the civil variant with 40 seats in eight rows of five-abreast with vestibules, luggage racks and entrance doors at each end. A major design feature was the location of the power units on top of the cabin to provide the maximum internal volume for passengers or cargo and an improved rotor drive system. This feature was made possible by the comparatively low weight of 1,500 lb of the 2,920 shp Eland 229A turboshafts chosen to power this aircraft which had been named Westminster. Westland was among the early helicopter manufacturers to take advantage of the good power/weight ratio of turboshaft engines in this way.

Westland's earlier experience with the Whirlwind and Wessex had shown the need for comprehensive test facilities for all parts of the dynamic system and ground test rigs were originally envisaged. However, in March 1956, the bold step of deciding to build a flying test rig to integrate the propulsion and control system was taken. It was believed that it would be a unique opportunity to gain flying experience with all systems which needed 'live' development and to check the aircraft's handling characteristics and cockpit layout while saving time and money. With these considerations in mind, the first prototype, which was designated WG.6, was designed as the simplest possible welded steel-tube space frame which, in effect, located the fully-equipped cockpit, the engines and

Westminster G-APLE, as a flying crane with a five-blade main-rotor, lifting a section of bridge at the Military Engineering Experimental Establishment, Christchurch.

transmissions, rotor systems and undercarriage in the correct positions they would occupy in a passenger-carrying helicopter for which, at that time, there was no specific fuselage layout.

The tapering rectangular-section fuselage was built up from jig-welded steel-tube modules to produce a two-part structure with four 'longerons' and twelve rectangular 'frames' having longitudinal and transverse diagonal compression struts. The forward part which was about half the overall length comprised five bays of near constant height and width at the front of which was attached an almost completely glazed 'fish head' shaped monocoque structure which was the two-seat cockpit. The flight test observer and his instruments were housed in a rectangular 'box' at the rear of this part. The aft part of the

The Terylene covering gave the Westminster visual appeal as a passenger helicopter in June 1960. External fuel tanks, air intake guard, nose pitot boom and six-bladed rotor are noteworthy.

fuselage consisted of six bays of tapering rectangular section to which the tail rotor pylon of similar construction, but with light alloy cladding, was attached. Economy was one of the guiding factors in the Westminster's design and existing components and equipment were used wherever possible. Thus, the two 250 gal fuel tanks which were carried in the forward fuselage were Whirlwind overload

Airborne with a five-bladed rotor Westminster G-APLE had a tailplane for handling trials.

tanks with an added section. The undercarriage, which was attached to this portion of the fuselage, was originally intended to be similar to that of the Wessex but calculations revealed the risk of ground resonance and so a more simple design, using a single near-standard Dowty oleo-pneumatic shock absorber strut, was used. The mainwheels came off a Bristol Freighter, their weight being reduced by removing half the brakes, while the tailwheel was a standard S-56 unit. The two engines, which were on loan from D Napier and Son, the main gearbox and rotor head and associated control equipment were carried on a platform attached to the top of the forward fuselage. Each engine, which was on trunnion mountings, was in its own isolated bay separated from the other by longitudinal and transverse fireproof bulkheads and completely cowled. The tail rotor transmission ran in bearings mounted in transverse members on top of the rear fuselage and inside the enclosed rotor pylon. The main gearbox, which was also enclosed, turned the five all-metal bladed main-rotor hub which had offset combined drag and flapping hinges to increase the c.g. range, and hydraulic drag dampers. The Westminster's powerplant was, in essence, a constant-speed system in which variations in load caused by rotor pitch changes provided a power demand on the engines. Load changes caused a change in rpm, which was sensed by a governor on the engines which adjusted the fuel input to maintain constant-speed. Electric de-icing of both rotors was planned for the production aircraft.

Construction of this unusual flying test rig occupied some 18 months and was completed in February 1958. The next three months saw the usual static and systems testing until the first engine runs began on 3 June. During the ensuing

The second Westminster had a redesigned structure and nose. An oil cooler was added above the engine air intakes.

twelve days 20 hours of 'tied-down' engine running and dynamic system testing were successfully completed in preparation for the first flight, which took place at Yeovil on 15 June in the hands of 'Slim' Sear. Flight testing continued during the summer but a good deal of vibration was being experienced, however, and proved difficult to eradicate; thus a number of changes were made in the design of the second aircraft, WB.7. These included the use of tubes of different size and gauge in the fuselage construction plus a six-blade main-rotor from the Sikorsky S-64. With the statutory 10 flying hours being achieved, the Westminster, now registered G-APLE, appeared in the SBAC Display at Farnborough during 1–7 September. It was described as 'a flying cut-away drawing'.

While test flying continued with the first prototype, Westland began building the second Westminster. This was to have been representative of an airline configuration with a totally enclosed monocoque airframe. In the event, it remained uncovered but had a small enclosed cabin for the flight test observer and equipment in the rear fuselage to overcome some forward c.g. problems. At this time, there were rumblings within the Admiralty to the effect that work on the Westminster variants was distracting Westland's attention from the Wessex development programme. That this was unwarranted was later proven when the Wessex first flew five months ahead of schedule. Because of this pressure by its best customer, Westland saw the writing on the wall for the heavy-lift transport helicopter project, but work on both aircraft continued. G-APLE's space frame structure was given a streamlined shape by the addition of plywood frames and wooden stringers covered with Terylene fabric to which a special coating was applied to protect it from gearbox and transmission lubricating oil; G-APLE first flew with this new covering on 17 June, 1960. A new six-blade main-rotor was also fitted to investigate blade stall problems at certain speeds. These changes raised the maximum speed to 155 mph and reduced the inflight vibration.

Meanwhile, the second Westminster, G-APTX, was nearing completion and was first flown at Yeovil by Sear on 4 September, 1959. The initial stage of the flight-test programme proceeded satisfactorily but it was against a background of a major change in Britain's helicopter industry; this was Westland's piecemeal acquisition of the helicopter interests and facilities of the Saunders-Roe, Bristol and Fairey companies. In their subsequent reorganisation, which placed a great burden on the Yeovil headquarters staff, the rationalisation of their combined product range resulted in the abandonment of work on a number of prototypes and projects. Among those under scrutiny was the Westminster, which was evaluated with the Bristol Type 194 project and Fairey's Rotodyne in the large civil helicopter role. The Royal Navy's growing need for the Wessex in the ASW role was one of the major factors in the early demise of the Westminster; the other was that Westland could not continue all the current programmes of its new acquisitions and those with uncertain futures faced cancellation. Without official Government support plus the fact that the Rotodyne was a more advanced concept the Westminster was abandoned in September 1960.

Ultimately all the equipment supplied by Sikorsky, which included the rotors, drive heads and gearboxes, was stripped out of both Westminsters and returned to the United States to avoid demands from HM Customs for payment of duty.

The airframes were then cut up and sold to Coley, the scrap metal merchant, a sad end for two promising prototypes.

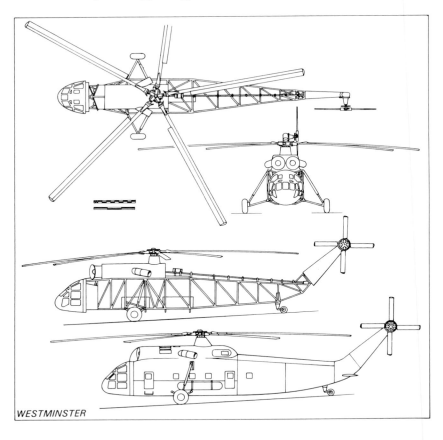

WESTMINSTER

Description: Twin-engined single main-rotor transport or heavy-lift helicopter. All-metal unclad structure (later plastic-covered).

*Accommodation:*Two crew on enclosed flight deck. (40 passengers projected) plus two observers (different provisions on G-APLE and G-APTX)

Powerplant: Two 2,920 shp Napier Eland E220 turboshafts.

Dimensions: Main-rotor diameter 72 ft 0 in; length 86 ft 9 in; height 21 ft 1 in; main rotor disc area 4,069 sq ft.

Weights: Empty 21,245 lb; loaded 33,000 lb.

Performance: Maximum speed 155 mph, cruising speed 115 mph; sea level rate of climb 1,750 ft/min. (Estimated performance for production aircraft: cruise 150 mph; sea level rate of climb 2,000 ft/min; range 120 miles).

Production: Two aircraft built by Westland Aircraft Ltd, Yeovil, during 1956–58.

Wessex

The Whirlwind family of helicopters had been a marked advance over the earlier Dragonfly and, in the gas-turbine-powered HAS.9 variant, had proved highly effective in an anti-submarine role when paired to form the two elements of a hunter/killer team. However, by 1955 the Admiralty was conscious of the fact that in anti-submarine warfare the two disparate tasks of search and strike could be performed even more efficiently and economically if they could be done by one aircraft. This dual role would require a larger and more powerful aircraft which could carry a heavier warload with an extensive avionic fit.

The Royal Navy had, even earlier, set its sights on a large twin-engined helicopter able to operate in the hunter/killer role. This was the Bristol 173 tandem-rotor design, built to Specification CAOR 2/46, which had first flown on 3 January, 1952, and had undergone a three-day series of trials in the aircraft carrier HMS *Eagle* the following year. During 1953 a Naval requirement, HR 146, was issued. It was for a general purpose ship-based helicopter for use in the anti-submarine and surface vessel role but also able to undertake search-and-rescue duties. The Bristol Helicopter Division tendered the tandem-rotor Type 191 to meet the Royal Navy's requirement and during 1954 received a contract for three prototypes each with two 850 hp Alvis Leonides Major piston engines and sixty-five production Type 191s each powered by two 1,405 shp Napier Gazelle turboshaft engines. Work was well advanced when the Admiralty

The Sikorsky-built HSS-1N Seabat, serialled XL722 in Royal Navy finish on its first Gazelle-powered flight. The engine protrudes through a hole in the nose doors. (*Courtesy Fred Ballam*)

cancelled the programme, its basic reasons being the difficulties being experienced with the transmission system, rotor interference problems and, inevitably, the rising cost of the programme. It also saw a quicker way, with Westland collaboration, to get the type of helicopter it needed.

Thus it was that, following the cancellation of the Bristol 191 and with the somewhat qualified success of its licenced-production of Sikorsky S-51 and S-55 helicopters for the Royal Navy in mind, in 1956 Westland sought and was granted a similar licence to build the comparatively new S-58 which had made its first flight on 8 March, 1954. The Westland design team had long considered a scheme to re-engine Sikorsky airframes with turboshaft engines in place of their radial piston engines, and the S-58, with its single nose-mounted 1,525 hp Wright R-1820-84 radial engine, appeared ideally suited for such a conversion. This engine was mounted behind large clam-shell doors in the nose of the fuselage to give complete accessibility from ground level. In order to speed this conversion programme and prove the efficacy of turboshaft power applied to this helicopter, during 1957 a US-built S-58 airframe—which was, in reality, a US Navy HSS-1N Seabat anti-submarine variant—was crated and shipped to Yeovil, where it was rebuilt with the Wright radial engine and test flown to obtain standard performance figures and handling characteristics. With this part of the programme completed, the Wright engine was removed and the installation of a 1,100 shp Napier Gazelle NG.11 free turbine turboshaft began.

An early modification to XL722 was a ring cowl around the Gnome engine's air intake.

Initially, with economy and speed of progress in mind, the clam-shell nose doors were retained with a large hole cut in them to allow the Gazelle to breathe. Designed as a helicopter engine the Gazelle was also a comparatively new engine having run for the first time on 3 December, 1955. It had the accommodating feature of being able to run equally well whether mounted in a

XL722's nose air intake nears its definitive early shape.

horizontal, vertical or inclined attitude. Equally convenient was its narrow radial-slot type intake at the front of the engine. Thus, in the S-58 airframe the Gazelle was mounted inclined at an angle of 39 deg from the vertical with its intake protruding a short way through the nose doors. This was the same angle at which the Wright piston engine had been installed and this simplified the Gazelle's connection to the S-58's rotor drive system. With an integral 6:1 ratio epicyclic reduction gear, the engine drove the standard S-58 main and tail rotor systems through the main-rotor gear box. Although the Gazelle was not as powerful as the Wright piston engine its weight was a little over a half; thus, at only the modest 1,100 shp delivered at that early stage of its development the Gazelle's power/weight ratio was 1.31 shp/lb compared with 1.03 hp/lb of the Wright R-1820-84 itself a dedicated helicopter engine. This produced a performance rather better than that of the S-58.

Apart from the advantages of the turboshaft engine, the S-58's fuselage was much larger than that of the Whirlwind with room for two crew in the cabin and all the dipping sonar equipment. Weapons, such as missiles, gun pods or lightweight torpedoes could be carried externally on or around the main undercarriage unit. With these potentialities in mind, conversion work was progressed rapidly and on 17 May, 1957, the re-engined S-58, now serialled XL722, made its first flight at Yeovil piloted by 'Slim' Sear, Westland's chief test pilot. The initial test flying programme was sufficiently encouraging to warrant further development and initial building of three pre-production aircraft, serialled XL727–XL729, was begun under MoD contract towards the end of 1957. In the event, eight more pre-production aircraft were built, serialled XM299–301 and XM327–XM331. The first of these was rolled out for preliminary engine running during the first week of June 1958 with a first flight taking place on 20th of the month, the pilot being 'Slim' Sear.

Wessex HAS.Mk.1

The construction of the new Westland-built helicopter followed closely that of the Sikorsky design but incorporated much anglicised detail. The fuselage was a light-alloy semi-monocoque structure with a forged steel ring mounted on a four steel-tube frame carrying the main-rotor gearbox. This frame served to stiffen the airframe and minimise vibration which had manifested itself with the change from the Wright Cyclone engine to the Gazelle. The tail pylon, which carried a small horizontal stabiliser, could be folded to help reduce the overall length by some 27 ft for hangar-stowage in aircraft carriers and other ships. The flight deck was located above and in front of the main cabin with two side-by-side seats. The 1,450 shp Napier Gazelle Mk.161 turboshaft was mounted in the fuselage nose below and in front of the flight deck. The air intake, which was of various configurations to suit the role and operating environment, was in the extreme nose with exhaust gas outlets on each side of it. The shaft-drive to the four-blade all-metal main-rotor was through a double epicyclic reduction gearbox while the shaft-drive to the four-blade all-metal tail rotor was through intermediate and tail gearboxes. The two non-retractable main undercarriage units were attached to the fuselage sides below the flight deck, each consisting of an oleo-pneumatic shock absorber strut and a single radius rod. The non-retractable tailwheel unit was fully castoring and self-centering with an anti-swivelling lock. A large rectangular sliding door with a window in it, which was fitted on the starboard side of the main cabin, and the sliding windows of the flight deck could be jettisoned in an emergency. A group of bag-type fuel tanks with 300 gal capacity was carried under the cabin floor with provision for

XL727, the first pre-production development Wessex 1 with a further modified nose. The horizontal and vertical markings on the fuselage are where rows of rivet dimples have been filled before painting. (*Courtesy Fred Ballam*)

XL728, the second pre-production development Wessex 1. A single large jet-pipe replaces the two small ones on XL722. It became a Mk.2 and was the RAE's radio trials aircraft.
(*Courtesy Fred Ballam*)

additional 100 gal auxiliary drop tanks to be carried externally on the torpedo carriers. Normally, however, only the port side tank was carried. Although intended primarily for the ASW role and capable of carrying four Nord SS.11 or AS.12 wire-guided missiles, machine-guns, 2 in rocket projectiles and the Mk.44 torpedo, the Wessex HAS.1 was also suitable for SAR duties, freight carrying, casevac, training or general communications work. The maximum disposable load, which included the crew and 270 gal of fuel, was 5,100 lb allowing 16 fully-armed troops to be carried over short distances. Of major importance was the new electronic flight control system with auto-stabilisation which permitted night and nearly all-weather operation.

This, then, was Westland's latest aircraft for which David Hollis Williams had earlier chosen the name Wessex. It was the Royal Navy's first helicopter to be designed as an anti-submarine aircraft and the world's first quantity-produced helicopter to be powered by a free gas turbine. The use of this type of power unit eliminated the need for high octane petrol to be stored in an aircraft carrier in addition to kerosene which is more easily carried in the ship's tanks, as is its own boiler fuel oil.

The flight development and evaluation trials of the pre-production batch of Wessex HAS.Mk.1s began in July 1958. During this programme initially XL727 was used for transmission type-testing; XL728 went to the RAE Farnborough after conversion to an HC.Mk.2; XL729 was extensively strain-gauged and flown on vibration checks; XM299 was employed on trials with dipping sonar equipment; XM300, XM327 and XM328 were allocated to development of the

Full power engine running at Yeovil with XM299, a development Wessex 1. There are fore and aft restraining cables at the main undercarriage and on the tail cone. (*Courtesy Fred Ballam*)

flight control system; XM301 flew on engine development and XM330 and XM331 were used for weapons trials. Later in the programme, XL728 was also used for engine and transmission development and XM299 for development of both the Type 194 and 195M sonars, the former being a Bendix AQ54 licence-built by Rank-Pullin in the UK and the latter built by Plessey Marine to an AUWE design.

The Wessex made its public debut in the SBAC Flying Display and Exhibition at Farnborough during 1–7 September, 1958, and also appeared at the Paris Air Show in the following June. Production Wessex HAS.1s began to be issued to No.700(H) Squadron Intensive Flying Trials Unit, Royal Navy, in April 1960

'Bootsie' Wessex 1 XM329, was used for trials at the Admiralty Underwater Weapons Establishment with the first and only available Plessey 195 sonar equipment. To ensure its safety over water this aircraft was fitted with special flotation gear.

with service trials beginning in June at RNAS Culdrose. This unit was charged with completing the acceptance trials, building up Service experience on type and formulating operating procedures and tactics for day and night ASW operations. The Wessex HAS.1 and its new systems were finally approved for issue to squadrons in June 1961 and entered front-line service with No.815 Squadron at Culdrose when it commissioned on 4 July, 1961. This squadron embarked in HMS *Ark Royal* in September 1961, to become the first carrier-borne Wessex unit in an operational role.

XS121, a production Wessex 1 which was converted to Mk.3 standard with the thimble radome and 'horsecollar' main-gearbox fairing.

Meanwhile at Yeovil, production and development flying with the Wessex HAS.1 continued with a number of the pre-production and early production aircraft being flown at the RAE and at A & AEE on trials at Boscombe Down, in France for high-altitude flying, in Canada on de-icing trials and in Malta and North Africa for tropical trials. Deliveries to the Royal Navy were such that the second Wessex unit, No.819 Squadron, commissioned at Eglinton, Northern Ireland, on 5 October, 1961. Ultimately, the Wessex HAS.1 operated with seven front-line ASW squadrons in Fleet carriers and with Ship's Flights in County Class destroyers, these latter ships having a hangar designed to match the Wessex dimension. In addition, this variant of the Wessex served in four training squadrons. It was not until August 1979 that the Wessex HAS.1 was finally retired from Royal Navy service.

Wessex Commando Mk.1

The overall improvement achieved by Westland in the operational capabilities of the Wessex commended this helicopter as a replacement for the earlier

Whirlwind HAS.Mk.7s in service with the Royal Navy's Commando Helicopter Squadrons. During 1961 Westland's design office produced proposals for a troop-carrying and general logistics variant of the Wessex. Basically similar to the Wessex HAS.1, all the automatic flight control system and the sonar equipment were omitted from the Commando variant. A batch of twelve of these aircraft equipped No.845 Squadron which commissioned on 1 April, 1962, enabling the Commando Forces to mount helicopter assaults from Royal Navy carriers.

Wessex 1 XS154 of No.845 Squadron being serviced at Nanga Gatt, Borneo, in 1963. It has the armament and camouflage of a Mk.5.

In 1963 the Squadron began to see active service in Borneo during the three-year confrontation with Indonesia, this Wessex being finally retired in 1965.

Wessex HC.Mk.2 and HAR.Mk.2

In order to meet a Royal Air Force requirement for a powerful general duties helicopter for troop and equipment transport and casualty evacuation, which could also be used for ground attack, Westland made a fundamental design change to the basic Wessex airframe. This was the replacement of the single Gazelle engine with two coupled 1,350 shp Bristol Siddeley Gnome H.1200 Mk.110/111 turboshafts in a nose installation. While this minimised the modification work, Westland had to strengthen the aircraft's airframe and redesign the transmission system with a more robust main gearbox, having a power limitation of 1,550 shp at the rotor head, to make use of the additional power. The twin-engine installation, in effect, doubled the operational capabilities of this Wessex variant and also provided added safety with one-engine-out, enabling it to retain cruising performance even when carrying a 4,000 lb underslung load or 16 fully armed troops.

352

XR521, one of the first batch of Wessex HC.2s for the RAF, lifting rolling road matting at Aldergrove in Northern Ireland.

During August 1961 a total of thirty Wessex was ordered for the RAF and designated Wessex HC.Mk.2. In order that development of this variant should proceed with the minimum delay, two development batch HAS.1 airframes, serialled XM299 and XL728, were converted to near Mk.2 standard for preliminary engine and control system development trials by the installation of two 1,050 shp coupled Gnome H.1000 Mk.101 turboshaft engines with appropriate transmission and other equipment modifications. The first flew on 18 January, 1962, and after manufacturer's handling and development flying it went to the A & AEE for preliminary engine handling. Two more aircraft, XR497 and XR498 were flown by Westland as development Wessex and by A & AEE on various trials during May–December 1963. Meanwhile, the manufacture of the first Wessex HC.2 got under way at Yeovil with the first prototype aircraft, XR588, making its first flight on 5 October, 1962. However, it was not until February 1964 that the Wessex HC.2 entered RAF service with No.18 Squadron at RAF Odiham, retaining them until December 1980. The Wessex HC.2 served with seven RAF squadrons in the various roles noted earlier, operating in the United Kingdom, Aden and the Persian Gulf, Cyprus, Germany, Hong Kong and Singapore, while the UK-based No.22 Squadron and No.84 in Cyprus flew this Wessex variant, designated HAR.2, in the SAR role. A total of seventy-four Wessex HC.2s was produced by Westland, the last being delivered in July 1965.

Wessex HAS.Mk.3

In parallel with the development of lightweight radar equipment and advanced flight control systems, Westland produced designs for a new Wessex variant for the ASW role. Basically a more powerful version of the Wessex HAS.1, it was to prove a much more effective and potent weapons system. Powered by a 1,600 shp flat-rated Gazelle 18 Mk.165 turboshaft engine with a compressed-air starting system replacing the AVPIN (isopropyl-nitrate) starters of the HAS.1's 1,450 shp Gazelle Mk.161, the Wessex HAS.3 carried more complex search radar equipment and was fitted with a duplex—in place of the earlier simplex—automatic flight control system designed by Louis Newmark and developed by Westland. This latter system enabled a complete anti-submarine sortie to be performed automatically, controlling the aircraft from take-off through the ASW operation, into and out of the hover mode, and on transits between sonar dipping operations. This Newmark/Westland system, operated in conjunction with the Ecko lightweight search radar and the Marconi doppler navigation system, enabled the Wessex HAS.3 to operate at night or in bad weather without the need to rely on information from a surface vessel's radar. This Wessex also could carry a formidable range of weapons, including four Nord SS.11 or AS.12 wire-guided missiles, or two Mk.44 or 46 lightweight homing torpedoes plus depth charges, machine-guns or rocket projectiles. The HAS.3 had an extended and raised fairing aft of the main gearbox and rotor head plus a thimble-shaped dorsal radome, these two protuberances causing this Wessex variant to be nicknamed 'the Camel'. This fairing, or 'horsecollar' as it was known, was fitted to smooth out the airflow around the radome which had affected the tail rotor and caused an airframe twitch. It was also used to house an additional alternator and its associated equipment.

Operated in the ASW role by a crew of four, the Wessex HAS.3 provided the Royal Navy with a helicopter which could work quite autonomously, being able

The second of three development Wessex 3s, XT256, complete with 'horsecollar' and thimble radome. The theodolite target on the gearbox cowling was used for trials in 1965 with the Newmark automatic flight control system.

to combine the search and strike role; however, its limited endurance produced a very short time on station. Thus, this Wessex variant was used to develop inflight refuelling techniques, taking on fuel from ships underway while remaining airborne.

The majority of the Wessex HAS.3s were produced by converting forty-three HAS.1 airframes to the new standard. Three HAS.3s, serialled XT255–XT257, were built as pre-production aircraft in Westland's Experimental Shop and served to develop and integrate all of the equipment developed in isolation in various Wessex Mk.1 development batch aircraft.

On 9 January, 1967, No.700 H Squadron commissioned at RNAS Culdrose as the Wessex HAS.3 Intensive Flying Trials Unit, ultimately being equipped with five aircraft. It operated in this role until 15 September, 1967, when it was disbanded. During the following month this Wessex variant entered front-line service with No.814 Squadron which was equipped with six aircraft. Four operational squadrons plus two training squadrons flew the Wessex HAS.3, and it was the Royal Navy's standard ASW helicopter until the arrival of the Sea King in February 1970. No.819 Squadron was the last front-line squadron to operate the Wessex HAS.3, disbanding on 29 January, 1971, leaving single aircraft to operate from County class guided missile destroyers.

Wessex HCC.Mk.4

Two Wessex aircraft, XV732 and XV733, were ordered from Westland during 1968 for use by the Queen's Flight. Designated Wessex HCC.Mk.4, these aircraft were built to HC.2 standard but with the main cabin having VIP interior finish and furnishing plus an external folding step below the cabin door. Additional navigation equipment was installed on the flight deck. The first flight of the HCC.4 took place at Yeovil on 17 March, 1969, and these aircraft entered service with the Queen's Flight on 25 June, 1969, their first official operation coming on 1 July in support of the Investiture of the Prince of Wales at Caernarvon.

As this book went to press, the choice of a successor helicopter to the Wessex HCC.4s in the Queen's Flight had not been made.

Wessex Commando HU.Mk.5

Although the Wessex Commando Mk.1 had given sterling service to the Royal Navy's Commando Forces, its single engine and limited load carrying ability were restrictive factors in its operation. Early in 1962 Westland began the design of a more powerful load-carrying variant of the Wessex, designated HU.Mk.5 for use by the Commando helicopter squadrons. Basically similar to the HC.2, it was powered by two coupled Bristol Siddeley Gnome Mk.110 and 111 turboshaft engines and had a strengthened airframe to withstand the rigours of continual low-level flying. At one period Westland believed that it would not be necessary to build a prototype of the HU.5 as it was so similar to the HC.2; however one, serialled XS241, was built to the new standard which showed the very many differences between these two variants which had been embodied over a period of time.

XT771, a Wessex 5, lifts a Snocat tracked vehicle during an annual Exercise Clockwork in Norway.

The first order for forty aircraft was received during August 1962, although construction of the prototype Wessex HU.5 at Yeovil had begun earlier during May, this aircraft first flying on 31 May, 1963, with the first production aircraft, XS479, getting airborne for the first time on 17 November, 1963. The first of six HU.5s for No.700V, Intensive Flying Trials Unit, was delivered to RNAS Culdrose on 5 December, 1963, and during October 1964 No.848 Squadron became the first operational unit to equip with this Wessex variant. A second order for sixty aircraft was placed during June 1964, enabling a total of four operational squadrons and two training squadrons to be equipped with the Wessex HU.5. No.845 was the last Squadron to relinquish its Wessex HU.5s, during 1987.

Australian Wessex HAS.Mk.31

During June 1961 Westland received an order for twenty-seven Wessex designated HAS.Mk.31, principally for use in the ASW role in HMAS *Melbourne*. In effect, the HAS.31 was an export version of the Wessex HAS.1 but powered with a 1,575 shp flat-rated Gazelle 13/2 Mk.162 turboshaft engine in place of the Gazelle Mk.161 of lower power. Deliveries of three aircraft a month from Yeovil began during September 1962 with the first aircraft arriving at Nowra Naval Air Station on 1 November, 1962, for No.725 Squadron. No.817 Squadron was the first unit to join an aircraft carrier when, in August 1963, it embarked in HMAS *Melbourne* to undertake its allotted task as the RAN Fleet's ASW and SAR squadron. Following some five years' RAN service, in 1968 it was decided that the Wessex 31A was still underpowered and not wholly

356

WA200, the first of twenty-seven Wessex 31s, based on the HAS.1, produced for the Royal Australian Navy during 1962–63.

effective in either of these two roles. Accordingly, a programme was begun to modify the airframe to accept 1,600 shp Gazelle 22 Mk.165 turboshafts and to fit improved and updated navigation and ASW equipment. In this modified configuration the aircraft were re-designated Wessex HAS.Mk.31B. Four squadrons ultimately were equipped with these Wessex variants.

Iraqi Air Force Wessex Mk.52

Twelve Wessex Mk.52 helicopters were ordered from Westland during 1963 for use by the Al Quwwat al-Jawwiya al-Iraqiya—the Iraqi Air Force, all twelve aircraft being delivered between April 1964 and February 1965.

They were basically similar to the Wessex HC.2 but with different communications equipment, and it is believed that four of them were in an airworthy condition before the Gulf War in 1991.

Ghana Air Force Wessex Mk.53

The Ghana Air Force took delivery of two Wessex Mk.53s during 1966 for use in the VIP transport role and for other general support duties. They were similar in appearance and equipment to the Wessex HC.2 and Mk.52. Subsequently both helicopters were sold to a civilian organisation.

357

Iraq bought twelve Wessex 52s in 1963. There is a fuel jettison pipe under the fuselage.

Brunei Wessex Mk.54

One Wessex Mk.54. similar in configuration and equipment to the Wessex HC.2, Mk.52 and Mk.53, was ordered and delivered during 1967 for service in the Sultanate.

The sole Wessex 54, similar to the HC.2, produced for the Sultanate of Brunei. The large all-purpose nose air filter is prominent.

A Royal Flight Wessex HCC.4. The red and Royal blue finish and the folding step just visible under the starboard door are distinguishing features. (*Courtesy Fred Ballam*)

Wessex 60 Series 1

During 1964, Bristow Helicopters Ltd, then a part of Airwork International, was seeking a new type of helicopter to replace the twenty-five Westland Whirlwinds and five Widgeons which were among its fleet of forty-five

The Great G-ATBY! One of Bristow's fleet of Wessex 60s. There is pop-out flotation gear stowage on the main undercarriage wheels. (*Courtesy Mike Hooks*)

rotary-wing aircraft. It was not altogether surprising that Alan Bristow, the holding company's managing director, should look to Westland to provide it for he had been a test pilot with the Yeovil company during 1947–49 and knew its products well. Bristow Helicopters operated in many parts of the world and was becoming involved with Britain's offshore oil and gas exploration operations. The twin turboshaft engines of the Wessex with their power reserves and quiet operation made this aircraft suitable for long overwater flights to service drilling rigs and production platforms, and for hot-and-high operating conditions in a number of countries around the world.

In service with the Royal Navy and Royal Air Force the Wessex had already proved itself in the Near and Far East, and its ability to carry external

Under contract to Trinity House, Bristow Helicopters used the Wessex 60s for lighthouse support duties. Here work on the base of the Royal Sovereign light tower in the English Channel is in progress. (*Bristow Helicopters*)

long-range fuel tanks enabling it to service offshore installation up to 230 miles from the coast made this helicopter very attractive to the potential operator. To meet these needs, Westland modified the RAF's Wessex HC.Mk.2 design to produce a proposal for a civil aircraft to carry either 16 passengers with the main cabin in its utility transport configuration, or 10 passengers in airline standard seating; moreover, it could accommodate up to eight stretchers, two seated casualties and a medical attendant or up to 15 survivors in a rescue operation. Power was supplied by two 1,350 shp Bristol Siddeley Gnome Mk.110 and 111 turboshaft engines. The standard of radio communications and navigational equipment fitted was of a high order and the general specification earned the Wessex 60 a public transport Certificate of Airworthiness and approval for VFR/IFR operations. Dual controls were standard. The main cabin was soundproofed and heated and had a special protective floor. Emergency equipment included individual life jackets for the passengers and crew, an 18-man liferaft and a sonar locator beacon.

Servicing the twin Gnome turboshaft installation in the Wessex was facilitated by the hinged air filter and large access doors, as illustrated by this Wessex 60. (*Bristol Siddeley Engines*)

A total of twenty Wessex 60s was built by Westland between 1965 and 1971; of these, nineteen were either operated by Bristow Helicopters as new aircraft or were acquired by Bristow from other operators. Bristow received its first

Wessex 60 in September 1966 and subsequently operated the type from eleven bases in the United Kingdom and fifty-four others in Africa, Asia, Australia, Europe, the Middle East and South America. However, after three unexplained accidents the company grounded all of its Wessex 60s on 13 August, 1981, and sold them to other operators or back to Westland.

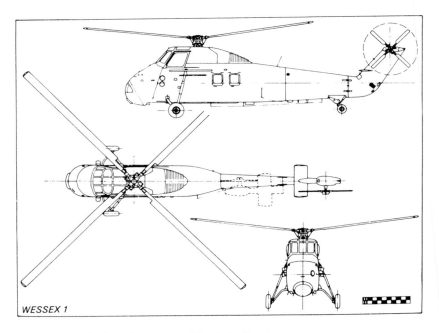

WESSEX 1

Description: Single main-rotor multi-role helicopter.

Accommodation: Pilot and co-pilot on flight deck, one or two crew in main cabin depending on role (Mks.1, 3, 31). Up to 16 troops or passengers (Mks.2, Commando 1 and 5, 60) eight stretchers, two seated survivors (Mks.1, 2, 3, 31, 60).

Powerplant: One 1,100 shp Napier Gazelle 11 turboshaft engine (prototype XL722). One 1,450 shp Napier Gazelle 13 Mk.161 turboshaft engine (Mk.1, Commando 1). One 1,600 shp Napier Gazelle 18 Mk.165 turboshaft engine (Mk.3). Two coupled 1,350 shp Bristol Siddeley Gnome H.1200 Mk.110/111 turboshaft engines (Mks.2, 4, Commando 5, 52, 53, 54, 60). One 1,575 shp Napier Gazelle 13/2 Mk.162 turboshaft engine (Mk.31A). One 1,600 shp Napier Gazelle 22 Mk.165 turboshaft engine (Mk.31B).

Armament: Two Mk.44/46 homing torpedoes, depth charges, (Mk.1, 5, 31 A and B). Two or four Nord SS.11 or AS.12 wire-guided missiles, two 2 in rocket pods, 7.62 mm and .303 in machine-guns, (Mk.2, 5, Commando 1 and 5).

Dimensions: Rotor diameter 56 ft; length 65 ft 10 in (38 ft 2 in folded); height 15 ft 10 in over tail rotor.

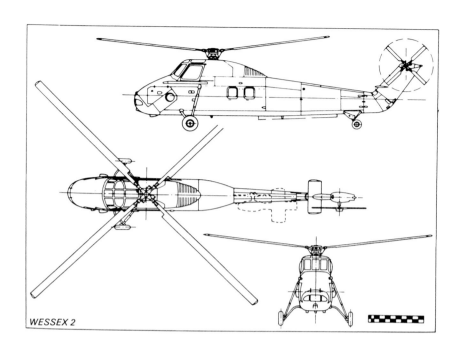

WESSEX 2

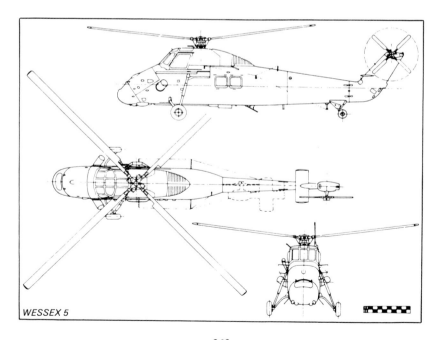

WESSEX 5

Weights: Empty 7,600 lb; loaded 12,600 lb (Mk.1)
  Empty 8,340 lb; loaded 13,500 lb (Mk.2, 4, 52, 53, 54)
  Empty 9,350 lb; loaded 12,600 lb (Mk.3)
  Empty 8,657 lb; loaded 13,500 lb (Mk.5)
  Empty 7,850 lb; loaded 13,500 lb (Mk.31)
  Empty 8,657 lb; loaded 13,600 lb (Mk.60).

Performance: Maximum speed at sea level 135 mph (Mks.1, 3, 31), 132 mph (Mks.2, 4, 5, 52, 53, 54, 60); cruising speed 122 mph; rate of climb at sea level 1,750 ft/min (Mk.1), 1,650 ft/min (Mks.2, 4, 5), 1,540 ft/min (Mks.3, 31, 60); service ceiling 14,100 ft (Mks.1, 3, 5, 31), 12,000 ft (Mks.2, 4, 52, 53, 54, 60); range with standard fuel 478 miles (Mk.5), 390 miles (Mks.1, 3, 52, 53, 54), 334 miles (Mk.60), 310 miles (Mks.2, 4), 302 miles (Mk.31).

Production: A total of 382 Wessex produced by Westland Helicopters Ltd, Yeovil, Somerset, as follows:
12 Wessex Mk.1 pre-production aircraft
128 Wessex Mk.1 production aircraft
74 Wessex Mk.2 production aircraft
3 Wessex Mk.3 pre-production aircraft
2 Wessex Mk.4 special aircraft
101 Wessex Mk.5 production aircraft
27 Wessex Mk.31 production aircraft
12 Wessex Mk.52 production aircraft
2 Wessex Mk.53 production aircraft
1 Wessex Mk.54 production aircraft
20 Wessex Mk.60 production aircraft.

Scout

The first Saunders-Roe P.531, G-APNU, with a Blackburn-Turboméca Turmo 600 engine, being flown by Ken Reed at Eastleigh in July 1958.

During the late 1950s, the British Army was quickly becoming aware of the value of its little Saunders-Roe Skeeter helicopter in a number of roles; it was also aware of the need for a rather larger turbine-powered replacement. It was not until the summer of 1957 when the 425 shp Blackburn-Turboméca Turmo free-turbine engine became available that Saro was able to project such a helicopter. This was the P.531 of which two prototypes, G-APNV and G-APNU, were built, powered by de-rated 400 shp Turmos. The second of these, G-APNU, was the first to be flown, by Ken Reed Saro's test pilot, on 20 July, 1958, with G-APNV first flying on 30 September. These two aircraft were followed by three P.531-0s, XN322, which was G-APNV developed and fitted with a 960 shp Blackburn A.129 Nimbus free-turbine engine, plus XN333 and XN334. It was soon apparent that this aircraft, which had the notional name Sprite, would not meet the Army's requirements, and major redesign work began. It resulted in the first P.531-2, which was 33 per cent heavier at 5,000 lb AUW and had a de-rated 635 shp A.129 free-turbine, an engine developed from the Turboméca Artouste and which was to be further developed to become the Bristol Siddeley Nimbus. This prototype, G-APVL, first flew at Eastleigh on 9 August, 1959, during an intense period when Westland was acquiring the Saunders-Roe Helicopter Division. With this change in the company's structure, all future development of the P.531 was driven by Westland; thus, it was decided to build a second P.531-2, G-APVM, first flown on 3 May, 1960. It was fitted with the more powerful 1,050 shp de Havilland Gnome turboshaft engine, an anglicised licence-built General Electric T58 derivative which had first run on 5 June, 1959, de-rated to 685 shp.

P.531–2, G-APVL, the first Mk.2, became XP116 for Scout development flying. It had a skid undercarriage and different tail unit. (*Courtesy Mike Hooks*)

Evaluation of these prototypes at A & AEE had impressed the Army Air Corps and RN pilots, and although the increased weight of the P.531–2 promised some ground handling challenges to the Army, a small pre-production batch of eight P.531-2 Mk.1s was ordered in May 1960 for further familiarisation

G-APVM, the second P.531–2, had a de Havilland Gnome H.1000 engine.

and evaluation flying. The first of these, XP165, flew on 4 August, 1960; a month later an order was confirmed for the production aircraft to Specification H.201D, now designated Scout AH.Mk.1, with forty being built at Hayes, where XP846, the first one, flew on 20 October, 1961. This factory belonged to Fairey Aviation which had been acquired by Westland in May 1960.

While the P.531 prototypes' construction had embodied many Skeeter components for economy and speed of manufacture, the later P.531-01 and -02 prototypes had been much modified. Further development by Westland had brought more changes, including the use of powered controls, which were first flown in XP190, the sixth pre-production aircraft, on 6 March, 1961.

The third development Scout AH.1, XP167, which was used for various rotor head trials.
(*Courtesy Mike Hooks*)

XP189, one of eight development Scout 1s, was used for rotor trials including Lynx rigid-rotor development. Note the bulged rear cabin door and the triangulated undercarriage bracing.

Scout AH.Mk.1

Structurally, the Scout fuselage was of all-metal semi-monocoque construction of the 'pod-and-boom' type. It was manufactured in two main sections: the cabin with the engine bay and the rear fuselage cone with the fin/tail-rotor pylon. The forward portion was constructed of frames and the cabin floor, which were attached to two main longitudinal members extending aft, through the tank bay behind the cabin and up to a platform carrying a tubular structure for the main-rotor mounting. Further aft was a fireproof platform on which the engine and accessories were mounted externally. From the primary gearbox at its rear end the Nimbus drove a shaft which extended forward to the secondary gearbox at the base of the vertical main-rotor shaft. Three interconnected bag-type fuel tanks were carried behind the cabin with other accessories and services. The forward cabin, with two doors on each side, could accommodate the pilot and crew member side-by-side with three others—or four when bulged rear doors were fitted–on a bench seat behind. Provision was made for carrying a stretcher or freight in the cabin and for an external sling and two stretcher panniers. The 32 ft 3 in diameter main-rotor had four folding all-metal blades carried on a fully-articulated hub with drag and flapping hinges and a torsion-bar blade suspension system. The undercarriage was of the tubular skid type with removable ground manoeuvring wheels. A semi-monocoque construction was used in the tail which was built separately. It carried the fin/tail-rotor pylon with a horizontal stabiliser having small end-plate fins. The tail-rotor drive-shaft ran externally along the top of the tail cone and was enclosed by spine covers. At the base of the pylon a gearbox drove the shaft up the pylon to the two-blade rotor with wooden blades. Provision was made for fitting two 7.62 mm general purpose machine-guns on the landing skid mounting booms plus another gun on a fixed or flexible mount on the port or starboard side of the rear cabin. For the

367

A Lynx rotor on Scout XP189 while at RAE Bedford. (*Courtesy Fred Ballam*)

AAC Scout 1 XT614 on patrol in Malaysia. (*Courtesy Rolls-Royce*)

anti-tank role, two Nord SS.11 wire-guided missiles could be carried on each side of the rear fuselage and a gyro-stabilised binocular sight was fitted in the cabin roof over the port front seat.

First deliveries of the Scout to Army units did not begin until March 1963, this long delay resulting from the transfer of the Scout production to Hayes and a lengthy period of engine unserviceability during Army development trials. Soon after delivery these aircraft went to Borneo, where they were almost immediately engaged in combat with terrorists, and to Army Air Corps units in the United Kingdom. Later, Scouts were operated in Aden, Brunei, Malaya and Zimbabwe and, most recently, in the Falklands. In this latter campaign, AAC and Royal Marine air crews flew Scouts to great effect in the ground support, reconnaissance, supply and casevac roles. The Scout's longest operational task has been in Northern Ireland where they provided vital air support to the Army and Police forces. In this role some Scouts were equipped with colour television equipment transmitting pictures to a Brigade head-quarters.

XT642, a Scout 1, armed with four Vigilant anti-tank missiles.

A total of 149 production Scout AH.Mk.1s were built at Hayes with quantity production ending in 1970; however, five replacement aircraft were built two years later. Three Scouts were sold to the Royal Jordanian Air Force, and two each to the Royal Australian Navy and the Bahrain and Uganda Police.

Description: Single-engined single-rotor general purpose helicopter.
Accommodation: Pilot, one crew member and up to four passengers in enclosed cabin.
Powerplant: One 1,050 shp Rolls-Royce (Bristol Siddeley) Nimbus 101 or 102 turboshaft engine, derated to 685 shp.

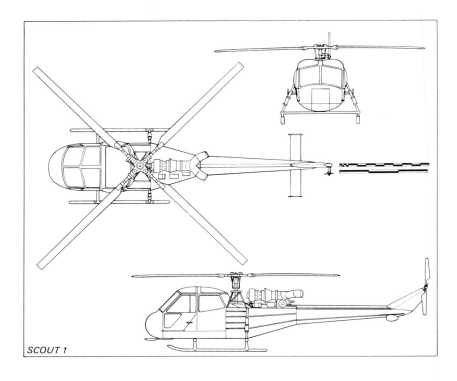

SCOUT 1

Armament: Two fixed forward-firing 7.62 mm general purpose machine-guns or a fixed or flexibly-mounted machine-gun in the rear cabin. four SS.11 wire-guided missiles on fuselage sides.

Dimensions: Main-rotor diameter 32 ft 3 in; length 30 ft 4 in (blades folded); height 8 ft 10 in; main rotor disc area 816.16 sq ft.

Weights: Empty 3,084 lb; loaded 5,350 lb.

Performance: Maximum speed 131 mph; cruising speed 122 mph; sea level rate of climb 1,670 ft/min; service ceiling 17,700 ft; range 316 miles.

Production: A total of 149 Scout AH.Mk.1 aircraft built by Westland Aircraft-Fairey Aviation Division, Hayes, Middlesex, during 1961–1972, as follows:

8 Scout AH.Mk.1 development aircraft.

141 Scout AH.Mk.1 production aircraft.

Wasp

While development and testing of the Saunders-Roe P.531-0/N and P.531–2 prototypes was under way, the Royal Navy had expressed an early interest in this aircraft. G-APNV, the first development prototype which first flew at Eastleigh on 30 September, 1958, piloted by Ken Reed, was serialled XN332 and, with the second and third prototypes, XN333 and 334, went to the RN in October–November 1959 for evaluation by No.771 Squadron at RNAS Yeovilton extending over an 18 months period. During this time several hundred take-offs and landings were made aboard frigates in order to develop not only the aircraft but also establish satisfactory techniques of deck handling. This programme involved the trials with some twenty different undercarriage arrangements and deck securing devices, which included the use of suction pads on the ends of both skids, skids with long-stroke oleo legs and a four-wheeled undercarriage. The principal requirements were that the undercarriage should enable a safe landing to be made within the prescribed ship motion limits and provide stability and immobility of the helicopter after it had landed on the platform. A 24 ft square 'rolling platform' was built at RAE Bedford to help in developing techniques and solving problems associated with helicopter operations from small ships. Trials also were made in HMS *Undaunted* from a 21 ft by 26 ft platform on the aft deck to assess the best type of undercarriage to meet these requirements. Ultimately a four-wheel fully-castoring lockable undercarriage was selected with a harpoon-type deck-securing system. While these trials were in progress, development of an autopilot/autostabiliser system was taking

Wasp HAS.1, XT431, carrying two Mk.44 torpedoes on under-fuselage crutches. Note flotation gear container, bulged rear door and splayed wheels.

371

place using a Saunders-Roe Skeeter 12 helicopter, XM563, re-engined with a Blackburn-Turboméca Turmo turboshaft engine. This system provided control in height, roll, yaw and pitch. Other development work included trials of main-rotor blade and rear fuselage folding mechanisms and of flotation gear.

Following these lengthy trials in which Westland's Yeovil and Fairey Aviation Divisions were fully involved, an order was placed in September 1961 for a pre-production batch of Sea Scout HAS.Mk.1s for the Royal Navy. The type name was subsequently changed to Wasp—probably because of the noise made by the several elements of its propulsion system!

The first of two pre-production Wasps, XS463, built at Hayes, Westland's Fairey Aviation Division, was first flown by Ron Gellatly, the Division's chief test pilot, on 28 October, 1962. A second pre-production aircraft, XS476, was followed by XS527, the first production Wasp HAS.Mk.1, which first flew in January 1963. This Wasp was taken on RN charge on 6 June, 1963, and was not withdrawn from service until November 1985 having operated with HMS *Endurance* during and after the Falklands Campaign. Further trials with these aircraft, principally in HMS *Nubian*, involved more than 200 landings and take-offs in various sea states and wind strengths during February–March 1963.

Wasp HAS.Mk.1

The structure of the Wasp HAS.Mk.1 was almost identical to that of the Scout with which it had been designed and developed almost concurrently. The major differences between these two aircraft were that the Wasp was powered by a 1,050 hp Rolls-Royce (Bristol Siddeley) Nimbus 103 or 104 shaft-turbine engine de-rated to 710 shp; it also featured a folding rear fuselage for hangar stowage in frigates, a four-wheel undercarriage in which the wheels were carried on Lockheed shock absorber struts with the rear wheels toed outwards at 45 deg to provide stability on the deck, a metal two-blade tail rotor and a single horizontal stabiliser carried on the starboard side of the fin opposite to the rotor. The avionics fit was different to suit the ASW role and included an autostabilisation/autopilot system with a radio altimeter which was not fitted in the Scout.

A variety of anti-submarine weapons totalling 540 lb could be carried on launch points under the cabin between the undercarriage legs; these included depth charges or two Mk.44 homing torpedoes but only one Mk.46 torpedo could be carried owing to its greater weight. Alternatively, for the ASV role a Nord AS.12 wire-guided air-to-surface missile could be carried on a pylon on each side of the fuselage aft of the cabin. As the Wasp was not fitted with any sophisticated detection equipment, it was vectored onto its target by a ship or sonar-equipped helicopter. Wasps with these missiles were fitted with gyro-stabilised cabin-roof-mounted sights above the left hand seat.

A total of ninety-eight Wasps, including the two pre-production aircraft, were produced at Hayes for the Royal Navy, the first batch going to No.700W Squadron, the Intensive Flying Trials Unit, at RNAS Culdrose which commissioned on 4 June, 1963. Its task was to develop handling techniques and sort out engineering problems with the new helicopter. There the first Small Ship Flight for HMS *Leander*, formed on 11 November, 1963. The ITFU operated until 4 March, 1964, when it was disbanded. On the following day

Note AS.12 launcher on the starboard side of this Wasp about to land on a frigate's aft platform.

No.829 Squadron commissioned as the Headquarters Squadron to be parent for all Small Ships Flights and provide operational flying training for Wasp pilots. It moved to RNAS Portland in December 1964.

Wasps were operated from Leander, Tribal and Rothesay class frigates and from early Type 21 Amazon class frigates before the Lynx entered service. A Wasp also was often carried in the Commando carriers *Albion* and *Bulwark*, being attached to the Wessex squadrons for forward air control and liaison duties. No.706 Squadron at Culdrose flew six Wasps in the training role during the 1960s and early 1970s and the Britannia Flight of the Royal Naval College at Dartmouth had a Wasp for air experience flights.

During the Falklands Campaign the Task Force's Wasps were used for gunnery spotting, as armed escort for troop carrying helicopters and in the casevac role. Wasps from HMS *Antrim*, *Brilliant* and *Plymouth* disabled the Argentine submarine *Sante Fé* on 24 April, 1982, and put it out of action for the remainder of the war. The Wasp was finally retired from RN service in April 1988 after 25 years.

Indonesian Navy Wasp

Four Wasps, ordered for the Indonesian Navy, were handed over to the Indonesian Defence Attaché in the United Kingdom on 7 October, 1981, at Westland's Weston-super-Mare factory. Six ex-RNNAS Wasps, refurbished by

This Indonesian Navy Wasp has a civil registration, naval serial number and the often used Class B G-17-1.

Westland, were acquired in 1981. Their serials, with RNNAS serials in brackets, were HS434(240), HS435(233), HS436(237), HS437(238), HS438(242) and HS439(245).

Royal Netherlands Naval Air Service Wasp

A Royal Netherlands Naval Air Service Wasp, designated an AH 12A, photographed on 12 December, 1968. (*Courtesy Mike Hooks*)

Some doubt remains about the numbers of Wasps delivered to the RNNAS. Records indicate that twelve, and perhaps thirteen, were acquired as their serials range from 233 to 245.

Royal New Zealand Air Force Wasp

Records indicate that, initially, six new Wasps were delivered to the RNZAF. Two refurbished ex-RN Wasps, NZ3907(XT435) and NZ3908(XT781) were delivered in 1975. These aircraft were for operations from the frigates *Canterbury, Southland, Westland* and *Waikato* and the survey ship *Monwai*.

South African Air Force Wasp

A total of seventeen Wasps were ordered for the South African Air Force in 1962, of which only sixteen were delivered. Serial numbers allocated are believed to have been 81–97. The first batch of six aircraft was delivered during 1963 and a repeat order for four Wasps was despatched in 1966. In 1972 seven more were ordered, of which the last of the six delivered, known to be serialled 96, did not leave Westland until 1974 due to an embargo on exports to South Africa. In 1988 it was reported that eight surviving Wasps were about to be withdrawn from SAAF service.

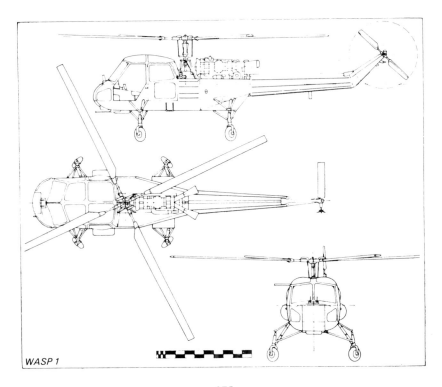

WASP 1

375

Brazilian Navy Wasp

Some doubt remains about the exact numbers of new Wasps delivered but it is believed to be four. In 1977 seven refurbished ex-RN Wasps were also acquired serialled N7036(XT419), N7037(XS564), N7038(XV633), N7039(XT433), N7040(XS530), NX7041(XT792), NX7042(XS542).

Description: Single-engined single-rotor light anti-submarine helicopter.
Accommodation: Pilot, one crew member and three, or four passengers in an enclosed cabin. Provision for one stretcher across rear of cabin.
Powerplant: One 1,050 shp Rolls-Royce (Bristol Siddeley) Nimbus 103 or 104 shaft-turbine engine de-rated to 710 shp.
Armament: Two Mk.44 or one Mk.46 homing torpedoes or two depth charges in crutches between the undercarriage legs or two Nord AS.12 air-to-surface guided missiles on fuselage sides.
Dimensions: Main-rotor diameter 32 ft 3 in; length 40 ft 4 in, (folded) 25 ft 9 in; height 8 ft 11 in; main-rotor disc area 816.86 sq ft.
Weights: Empty 3,452 lb; loaded 5,500 lb.
Performance: Maximum speed 120 mph; cruising speed 110 mph; sea level rate of climb 1,440 ft/min; service ceiling 12,200 ft; range 303 miles.
Production: A total of 98 Wasp aircraft built by Westland during 1963–68 as follows:
2 Wasp HAS.Mk.1 pre-production aircraft.
96 Wasp HAS.Mk.1 production aircraft.

Sea King

The concept and design of the Westland Sea King has its roots deeply in the US Navy's Operational Requirements section and the Design Office of Sikorsky Aircraft Division of the United Aircraft Corporation. With its experience of operating pairs of HSS-1 (S-58) Seabat helicopters in the anti-submarine hunter/killer role, in 1957 the US Navy drew up a requirement for a new helicopter in which these two roles could be combined. Among the detailed requirements was the ability to carry search equipment and an 840 lb weapon load, have a range of 530 miles, a cruising speed of about 140 mph and be able to operate in all weathers.

Clearly, this sort of specification predicated the need for a much larger helicopter than those already in US Navy service. Thus was born the Sikorsky S-61 Sea King, a large aircraft more than 72 ft long with a 62 ft five-bladed main-rotor which, ultimately, was to be powered by two 1,500 shp General Electric T58-G-100 turboshaft engines. Of conventional Sikorsky configuration with its single main-rotor and an anti-torque tail rotor, the S-61 embodied the unusual feature of a watertight boat-shaped hull with stabilising floats, while the systems equipment included automatic stabilisation for all-weather operations.

This view of XV370, the first Sikorsky-built S-61D-2 Sea King to be delivered in October 1966 to Yeovil as a 'pattern' aircraft, shows its flexible fuel tank made by FPT, now a Westland company. It also reveals the ½ in steel tie-down box on the fuselage, just aft of the sponson strut, which was used for full-power engine running trials.

The US Navy awarded a development contract to Sikorsky for the S-61 on 24 December, 1957, and the first flight was made on 11 March, 1959, with deliveries to two squadrons beginning in September 1961. Initially, in US Navy service, the S-61 was designated the HSS-2 but during July 1962, when a common three-Service system of designations was adopted by the US armed forces, it became the SH-3A Sea King.

In Britain the Royal Navy had watched the evolution of the S-61/SH-3A with great interest. Although the Wessex in no way had been a stop-gap aircraft following the demise of the Bristol 191 programme and had performed every role with which it had been tasked with great efficiency since entering Royal Navy service in July 1961, during the early 1960s the need for a larger longer-ranging hunter/killer helicopter for use in the anti-submarine warfare role was of paramount importance. Soviet Russia had earlier embarked on a major programme of building large numbers of submarines with conventional and nuclear power and these were operating in the world's oceans where they were being encountered with increasing frequency.

This need had been foreseen not only by the Royal Navy but also by Westland which, as early as 1959, had discussed further licence agreements with Sikorsky to cover the development and production of the S-61 in Great Britain. This latest agreement allowed Westland to use the basic S-61D/SH-3D airframe and rotor head but to make modifications to permit the use of an alternative British engine, which was, in fact, a licence-built General Electric T58 known as the

Gnome, rotor blades and other equipment. Although the licence agreement had been signed by the two companies soon after the first flight of the prototype S-61, it was not until September 1967 that the first of four aircraft supplied to Westland by Sikorsky made its first flight. This aeroplane, an SH-3D (61-343/G-ATYU, subsequently serialled XV370), was cocooned and shipped as deck cargo to Avonmouth where, on the dockside, it was prepared for flight by Westland and Sikorsky engineers. On completion of this work, it was flown to Yeovil, a distance of some 40 miles, on 8 September by 'Slim' Sear. For about three months XV370 was used for performance trials with its General Electric T58 engines and other US-built equipment before being stripped down for its anglicisation programme. This first aircraft was followed by three more pre-production aircraft from Sikorsky, XV371–XV373. XV372 was allocated to Rolls-Royce for flying on an engine development programme but unfortunately crashed on 15 January, 1969, during a flight between Yeovil and Filton. When an engine flamed out after ice ingestion the pilot, Jim (Binnie) Barnes, attempted to make a landing but this was unsuccessful, the aircraft rolling over on touchdown. Meanwhile, construction of the first Westland-built Sea King, HAS.Mk.1, XV642, was progressing at Yeovil. Structurally, it closely followed the Sikorsky S-61, the single-step boat-hull fuselage being of all-metal semi-monocoque construction. A cantilevered stabiliser is carried on the starboard side of the tail-rotor pylon. The main undercarriage consists of two twin-wheel units which are hydraulically retracted rearwards into stabilising sponsons braced to the fuselage sides. A non-retracting tailwheel is carried below the hull step. Pop-out flotation bags are carried on the stabilising floats. The pilot and co-pilot are seated side-by-side on the flight deck with two crew members, one of whom acts as tactical co-ordinator in the ASW role, in the main cabin. Sliding doors are fitted on the cabin side walls.

The first Westland-built production Sea King HAS.1, XV642, with a six-blade tail rotor, dorsal radome and 'barn door' foreign object damage shield which has the de-icing strips.

A major difference between the US and British Sea Kings is the powerplant which in the early Westland aeroplanes consisted of two 1,400 shp (Bristol Siddeley) Rolls-Royce Gnome H.1400 turboshaft engines, mounted side-by-side outside the fuselage on top of the main cabin. The Gnomes were fitted with the Hawker Siddeley Dynamics/Rolls-Royce full-authority electronic engine control system, which was much more advanced than the Hamilton Standard electro-mechanical system on the General Electric T58 engines. The main-rotor has five metal blades which can be power folded and spread. Both engines drive through free-wheel units to the main gearbox; the five-bladed tail rotor is driven through intermediate and tail gearboxes and shafts, the latter housed in a 'spine' which runs along the top of the rear fuselage and up the rotor pylon. Electronic equipment, the flight control system and the various hydraulic, pneumatic and electrical systems vary with the role of the individual Marks of Sea King. While the Westland Sea King is externally similar to the Sikorsky S-61/SH-3, they share only the basic airframe structure and the rotor system.

Sea King HAS.Mk.1

The first production contract for Sea Kings announced on 27 June, 1966, was for fifty-six HAS.Mk.1 anti-submarine aircraft, and the first of these production Sea Kings built by Westland, XV642, was first flown at Yeovil on 7 May, 1969. It was to fly as a trials aircraft until mid-1988 which must set a record for longevity for a research and development aircraft. To XV642, too, goes the honour of making the first deck landing when, on 2 July, 1969, in the hands of Lieut-Cdr C J Horscroft and Lieut P J G Harper from the Aircraft Handling Squadron at the A & AEE Boscombe Down, it landed on the Royal Fleet Auxiliary *Engadine* off Portland. On 11 August XV645 was flown from Yeovil to RNAS Culdrose by Lieut-Cdr V Sirett, then the Commanding Officer designate of No.700S Squadron, the Royal Navy's Sea King Intensive Flying Trials Unit. By 19 August, when the Squadron was commissioned, two more Sea Kings, XV644 and XV646, had been delivered. During the ensuing nine months the unit flew 2,700 hours with its six aircraft, which included XV647–649, to prove the type fit for operational use.

Meanwhile at Yeovil, Westland test pilots had flown some 160 hours with the Sea Kings before they were handed over to No.700S Squadron and undertaken more than 1,500 hours of the manufacturer's flight test and development programme. The first operational unit to be equipped with the Sea King was No.824 Squadron which formed on 24 February, 1970, also at Culdrose. It later embarked in HMS *Ark Royal* and remained aboard until the end of this renowned aircraft carrier's last commission. This was an historic event for it represented a major advance in the Royal Navy's anti-submarine warfare capabilities. By using the large main cabin of the Sea King as the tactical control centre of the Sea King 'weapon system', Westland provided space for a range of equipment enabling the aircraft to operate autonomously in the twin roles of a submarine hunter and killer. Thus, the HAS.1 carried a tactical display provided by the Ecko AW 391 search radar, Plessey 195 sonar, Marconi AD 580 Doppler processing and bathythermographic facilities and a Louis Newmark Mk.31 automatic flight control system; in addition the retractable undercarriage, boat

XV648, one of the six Sea King 1s allocated to No.700S Squadron, the Intensive Flying Trials Unit in 1969.

Sea King 1 XV651 was modified to accept the Ferranti Sea Spray radar as part of the Lynx development programme, and flown from Defford for the RRE. It was the only Sea King 1 to be converted directly to a Mk.5 and was returned to the Royal Navy for service with No.814 Squadron. (*Courtesy David Gibbings*)

hull and the main-rotor power-folding and spreading capability were all new features in a Royal Navy helicopter. Armament on the Sea King HAS.1 was either four Mk.44 homing torpedoes, four Mk.11 depth charges or a nuclear depth bomb.

The second operational unit to be equipped with Sea King HAS.1s was No.826 Squadron which embarked in HMS *Eagle* having formed at Culdrose on 2 June, 1970. During the 1970s three more operational squadrons—Nos.814, 819 and 820—plus Nos.707 and 737 training squadrons were equipped with Sea King HAS.1s serving ashore and afloat with the Royal Navy. From February 1978 these aircraft were either allocated to Royal Fleet Auxiliary Ships, were retrospectively modified to HAS.Mk.2/2A standard or relegated to other duties. The conversion to Mk.2 standard was done by Westland and to Mk.2A by RNAS Fleetlands. Forty-five HAS.1s were converted to HAS.Mk.5 standard.

Sea King HAS.Mk.2

XZ570, the first production Sea King 2. It was to become Westland's 'hack' aircraft for development of EH 101 avionics and radar.

With the five years experience gained by the Royal Navy with the Sea King as its principle anti-submarine helicopter, Westland decided to update the aircraft and improve its operational capabilities. This was in answer to the growing fleet of Soviet conventional and nuclear-powered submarines with enhanced performance. Designated Sea King HAS.Mk.2, this variant was powered by two more powerful 1,535 shp Gnome H.1400–1 turboshaft engines; however, as in earlier helicopters, the power was limited to that which the transmission system could accept. To handle this additional power, a new and more robust main gearbox was fitted with similarly improved intermediate and tail gearboxes and a six-bladed tail rotor to improve yaw control in the hover. Fifteen new aircraft were ordered during 1975, the first of these, XZ570, was flown at Yeovil on 18 June, 1976. In addition, as noted earlier, thirty-seven HAS.Mk.1 airframes were brought up to HAS.2 standard.

The first operational unit to re-equip with this variant was No.826 Squadron which converted to it during December 1976. Ultimately all front-line Sea King squadrons and No.706 Training Squadron converted to the HAS.Mk.2.

During the Falklands Campaign all the ASW equipment in No.824 Squadron's Sea Kings was removed and the aircraft were modified to carry up to 24 troops or 16 stretchers when used in the casevac role.

Described as a 'professional research aircraft', XZ570 was used for Sea King 5 and composite blade development before being fitted with twin box beams along the fuselage to carry Ferranti Blue Kestrel or other radars. From 1987 it was used on the EH 101 development programme. (*Courtesy David Gibbings*)

Sea King AEW.Mk.2A

One of the important Sea King developments which resulted from the 1982 Falklands Campaign was the very rapid conversion of two Mk.1 aircraft, XV649 and XV650, for an airborne early warning role. Within a few days of the loss of HMS *Sheffield* a Type 42 destroyer, on 4 May as the result of a direct hit by a sea-skimming Exocet missile launched by a Super Etendard of the Argentine Air Force, a scheme to give the Sea King an AEW capability was conceived by the Royal Navy, Westland and Thorn EMI Electronics. Under a programme known as Project LAST (low altitude surveillance task) it was developed in only eleven weeks using the two Sea Kings as testbeds.

The Thorn EMI Searchwater maritime surveillance radar employed was similar to that used in the Nimrod and was housed in an air-pressurised thimble-shaped dome of impregnated Kevlar fabric. The entire assembly was carried on a swivel mounting on the starboard side of the fuselage in line with the aircraft's dorsal radome. It was moved hydraulically, using a standard Sea King undercarriage hydraulic jack, from the horizontal position, adopted during take-off and landing, to swing forward and downward to below wheel level when deployed for operation. The scanner is pitch and roll stabilised and provides a full 360 deg scan.

Trials of the radar system were conducted during June and were followed by flying trials in HMS *Illustrious* in which the two Sea Kings were embarked during August for deployment to the South Atlantic, even though Argentine forces had surrendered on 14 June. There these Sea Kings were able to provide initial airborne early warning for British naval vessels within the 200 mile radius total exclusion zone surrounding the Falkland Islands. A VHF radio link provides voice and data communications with the Fleet, enabling warnings of a target's course, speed, coded identity, range and bearings to be transmitted very rapidly. Targets can be detected at a range of more than 100 miles from a normal service ceiling of 10,000 ft. The normal four-hour endurance can be extended by ship to air 'in-flight refuelling' with the helicopter in the hover mode.

The two original Sea King AEW.2A aircraft formed the nucleus of No.849 Squadron which reformed at RNAS Culdrose on 9 November, 1984. A further seven AEW.Mk.2As, XV656, 671, 672, 697, 704, 707 and 714, were produced by modification of these HAS.1 aircraft. No.849 Squadron's 'A' Flight was commissioned with three of these helicopters on 31 May, 1985, for service in HMS *Illustrious* in August 1985.

XV671, a Sea King 1 modified to become a Mk.2A AEW aircraft. It carries a retractable Thorn EMI Searchwater radar in an inflatable dome. The engine intake FOD shield has de-icing strips applied.

Sea King HAR.Mk.3

While the primary role of the Sea King had been as an anti-submarine strike helicopter, it also was capable of secondary support roles including underslung load carrying, troop transport, as an armed close support aircraft and as a search and rescue (SAR) aircraft. It was this last role which interested the Royal Air Force which had operated all of the earlier Westland-built helicopters in the SAR role.

The fifth production Sea King 3 in Royal Air Force SAR configuration lifts a crew member and stretchered casualty under the watchful eye of the winch operator.

Thus, on 24 September, 1975, Westland announced an initial contract to build fifteen Sea King HAR.Mk.3s for the RAF. Powered by two 1,535 shp Rolls-Royce Gnome H.1400–1 turboshaft engines, this variant's navigation system included a Decca TANS F computer accepting inputs from a Mk.19 Decca receiver, Decca Type 17 Doppler, and MEL lightweight radars, plus distance measuring equipment, automatic direction finder and a radar altimeter. Other changes included fuel tank capacity increased by 113 gal and the fitting of a cabin door winch with a cable four times longer than that of earlier helicopter winches to reduce hazards encountered in cliff and beach rescues. Up to three stretcher cases could be carried and twelve survivors plus the crew of four. Additional space was provided in the main cabin by moving the rear bulkhead aft. The first HAR.Mk.3, XZ585, was first flown at Yeovil on 6 September, 1977, with deliveries of all fifteen aircraft to No.202 Squadron being completed during 1979. Earlier, in February 1978, in preparation for the arrival of the Sea King, the RAF Sea King Training Unit was established at RNAS Culdrose and by August 1978 a sufficient number of aircrews had been trained to begin conversion of No.202 Squadron from the Whirlwind HAR.Mk.10 to the Sea King. Sea Kings from this squadron operated in the SAR role in the Falklands Campaign during 1982. Three additional HAR.3s were ordered in 1983 and were delivered during June–September 1985. During April 1986 Sea Kings joined RAF Chinook helicopters to equip No.78 Squadron based at RAF Mount Pleasant in the Falkland Islands.

Sea King HC.Mk.4

A No.846 Squadron Sea King 4 Commando, ZA292, on an exercise in Norway. It has a load-carrying low-response beam under the fuselage.

During 1972 Westland's Design Office had projected a land-based troop transport variant of the Sea King to which the type name Commando had been given. It was devoid of all equipment relating to its anti-submarine warfare role and had only a basic avionic fit. In addition, the flotation sponsons were omitted but the emergency flotation bags were retained and the undercarriage was not retractable. It had the same engines, gearboxes and six-bladed rotors as those used in the ASW.Mk.2 variant. In this form it was calculated that 28 fully-armed troops or an equivalent 7,500 lb of equipment could be air-lifted over a 300 miles range. None of the British Services showed any overt interest in this aircraft but some export orders were secured.

During 1978 the Royal Navy asked Westland to examine a development of the Commando to replace the Wessex HU.Mk.5 as the main lift helicopter for the Royal Marines' commando forces. Designated Sea King HC.Mk.4 the first of an initial order for fifteen aircraft, ZA290, first flew on 26 September, 1979, at Yeovil. A few of these aircraft were delivered during November 1979 in time for use by No.45 Royal Marine Commando during the NATO Exercise Clockwork

A Sea King 4 Commando of No.846 Squadron lifting a 3¼ ton Volvo Bandvagn over-snow vehicle in Norway during September 1985. The load is attached to a low response beam below the fuselage. The beam prevents the load oscillating and affecting the aircraft's centre of gravity.

in Norway. This was most fortuitous as the wartime role of No.846 Squadron, based at RNAS Yeovilton, was to provide helicopter transport facilities for amphibious forces deployed in defence of NATO's northern flank. Further orders for eight in 1982, four in 1984 and ten in 1985, brought total production of this variant for the Royal Navy to thirty-seven. Sea King HC.4s of No.846 (Commando) Squadron were used for general troop and cargo transport work during the 1982 Falklands Campaign. Further orders for batches of eight, fourteen and four aircraft brought the total production of this variant for the Royal Navy to forty-one. Two additional aircraft, ZB506 and 507, were designated Sea King Mk.4X and were ordered as development vehicles for use by the RAE at Bedford and Farnborough respectively. External identification features of this variant were the non-retractable undercarriage, in which the sponsons were replaced by stub-wings, and additional windows in the main cabin. The 30th Mk.4, ZF115, was the first production Sea King to fly from the start with composite main-rotor blades, on 3 June, 1986, although others had been retrofitted with this type of rotor. A folding tail pylon was an optional feature.

Sea King HAS.Mk.5

The reliability and all-round success of the Sea King airframe and engine combination prompted its further development to meet the threat posed by the ever increasing performance of Soviet submarines. Design work began at Westland during late 1978 and was aimed principally at increasing the size of the main cabin and embodying a new navigation/attack system. The additional space was obtained by moving the rear bulkhead some 6 ft further aft into the tail. Other structural modifications included strengthening the cabin floor to take the weight of the new equipment and stiffen the hull, and altering the underfloor fuel tanks to allow for the aft movement of the c.g. The nav/attack system of this new variant, designated Sea King HAS.Mk.5 used the Decca TANS G coupled to Decca Type 71 Doppler and the MEL Sea Searcher radar, this last piece of equipment having almost twice the operating range of earlier radars. Also fitted was the Racal MIR-2 ESM, passive sonobuoy dropping

ZB506, one of two Sea King 4Xs specially prepared for use by the RAE Farnborough and Bedford for research and testing new helicopter radar systems. It has a large flat-topped radome, modified main undercarriage and 'raspberry-ripple' finish.

equipment and associated GEC Avionics lightweight acoustic processing and display system. (LAPADS). The increased size of the Sea Searcher rotating antenna necessitated a larger dorsal radome, with a flat top profile, which externally, characterised the HAS.Mk.5.

This range of new equipment enabled the Sea King HAS.5 to pinpoint the position of a submerged submarine at a far greater range than before and to attack the target with Sting Ray torpedoes. A major advance was the Sea King's ability to handle information provided by sonobuoys dropped from RAF Nimrods as well as monitoring the signals from its own sonobuoys.

A total of thirty new Sea King HAS.5s were ordered in three batches of seventeen, eight and five aircraft. The prototype was a converted HAS.Mk.2, XZ916, which first flew as an HAS.5 on 1 August, 1980, and was used for development flying by Westland before going to the A & AEE on 12 November. It was followed into the air by the first production HAS.Mk.5, ZA126, on 26 August, 1980. This aircraft and the second production example, ZA127, were officially handed over to the Royal Navy on 2 October, 1980. The first front-line unit to receive this Sea King variant was No.820 Squadron which became operational with the type in June 1981 while embarked in HMS *Invincible*. Delivery of the first batch of HAS.5s was completed during October 1982 with deliveries of the next eight aircraft beginning on 13 September, 1984, the last batch of five production aircraft being delivered by July 1986. In addition to these new-built aircraft, virtually all of the surviving force of some fifty HAS.2 helicopters were converted to HAS.5 standard, this programme being undertaken principally by RNAS Fleetlands and Culdrose starting during 1981.

Some HAS.5s were fitted with a modified starboard sponson with an integral winch and stowage for MAD equipment. These sponsons were identical to those used in the US Navy's SH-3H helicopter and were bought direct from Sikorsky.

Pictured in September 1985, this Sea King 5 lifts its dunking sonar body. Two of the four torpedoes and the radome are noteworthy.

388

During the Falklands Campaign, Sea King HAS.5s of Nos.820 and 826 Squadrons were tasked with providing an anti-submarine screen for the Fleet; in addition these units also became involved in their SAR role.

West German Navy Sea King Mk.41

A German Navy Sea King 41 at Yeovil during January 1974.

On 20 June, 1969, Westland announced the first export success for Westland Sea Kings. This had been achieved in May when the West German Navy ordered twenty-two Sea King Mk.41s for SAR duties in succession to Grumman Albatross amphibians used previously. Based on the Sea King HAS.Mk.1, they were fitted with very similar radar and navigation equipment but none of the sonar equipment was carried. In addition the main cabin heating system was improved and the fuel capacity was increased to a total of 800 gal. The aircraft were serialled 89-50 to 89-71, the first one flying on 6 March, 1972. One of these aircraft, 89-61 (c/n WA765), was written off in an accident early in 1974 before delivery and was replaced in July 1975 by a second aircraft (c/n WA 830) with the same serial number. These aircraft were updated in the latter part of the 1980s by the installation of Ferranti Seaspray radar and other equipment.

Indian Navy Sea King Mk.42, 42A, B and C

The Indian Navy Sea King Mk.42s were for use in the anti-submarine role. They were built to the HAS.1 standard but fitted with communications equipment which was suitable for use in conjuction with existing Indian Navy systems. In addition, an improved cabin ventilation system was embodied plus other modifications to suit the local climatic conditions. Initially six aircraft were ordered in November 1969, the first one flying on 14 October, 1970, with deliveries starting on 15 March, 1971, and being completed on 23 August. These aircraft served with No.330 Squadron in INS *Vikrant* or were used for training at INS *Garuda*, a shore-base at Cochin. Six more Sea King Mk.42s were ordered during July 1972 with deliveries in batches of three aircraft during September–October 1973 and June–July 1974. These twelve Sea Kings were serialled IN501–IN512, and deliveries enabled the Indian Navy's second Sea King squadron, No.336, to commission at Cochin on 20 December, 1974. Three more were ordered in 1978, the aircraft in this batch approximated to the HAS.Mk.2 with 1,535 shp Gnome H.1400–1 turboshaft engines and with a haul-down capability for small ship operation. Designated Sea King Mk.42A they were delivered in March 1980, serialled IN551–IN553.

A Sea King 42B launches a British Aerospace Sea Eagle long-range anti-ship missile in July 1987. The launching beam can be seen on the fuselage side.

In July 1983 twelve Advanced Sea King 42Bs were ordered for the Indian Navy, with orders for a further nine coming later. These aircraft were powered by Gnome H.1400-IT engines, developed to meet the requirements of 'hot-and-high' operating conditions, and were fitted with uprated main gearboxes and strengthened main lift frames. Other changes included composite main-rotor blades and a reversion to five-bladed tail rotors which had cambered composite blades rather than symmetrical-section metal units. This new tail rotor produced some 10 per cent more thrust than the six-blade unit. In addition updated ASW equipment, including MEL Super Searcher radar and Marconi acoustic processing equipment, was installed. Provision was also made for the carriage of the British Aerospace Sea Eagle long-range anti-ship missile. The twenty-one Sea King Mk.42Bs were serialled IN512–531 and IN533 the first one flying on 17 May, 1985; due to political and financial problems in India,

IN555, one of six Sea King 42Cs ordered for the Indian Navy. It has a nose-mounted radome for the Bendix radar.

deliveries were delayed, the main bulk not being delivered until 1989–90.

The six Sea King 42Cs ordered for the Indian Navy were built as the SAR and utility transport variant of the Mk.42B. The navigation system was similar to that of the Sea King HAR.3 except that the MEL radar was replaced by a nose-mounted Bendix unit and some other electronic equipment was produced by the Hyderabad Division of Hindustan Aeronautics Ltd. Serialled IN555–IN560 the first flew on 25 September, 1986, deliveries beginning on 5 February, 1987, and being completed on 1 November, 1988.

Royal Norwegian Air Force Sea King Mk.43

During December 1970 an order was received for ten Sea Kings for use by the Royal Norwegian Air Force in the SAR role. These aircraft, which were serialled 060, 062, 066 and 068–074, were built to the same standard as the West German Sea King Mk.42s but with different communications equipment. The first of these aircraft first flew on 19 May, 1972, and went into service with No.330 Squadron RNAF based at Bodø, deliveries being completed with three aircraft on 15 November, 1972.

During August 1989 Westland received a £12 million order for one new Sea King Mk.43B for delivery in June 1992 and for updating the existing RNAF fleet. This work included modernisation of the navigation and communications equipment and the installation of FLIR and dual radar systems.

The first three of ten white and dayglo red Sea King 43s for Norway. 062 and 066 were delivered in December 1972.

Arab Republic of Egypt Air Force Commando Mks.1 and 2

A specially fitted VIP transport Commando 2B, one of two delivered to the Arab Republic of Egypt in 1975–76.

During 1973 Saudi Arabia ordered five Commando Mk.1 aircraft, designated Mk.70s, for use by the Egyptian Air Force as a general transport helicopter. These aircraft were similar to the Sea King HAS.Mk.1 but were equipped to carry troops or cargo or to operate in the casualty evacuation role. The first aircraft first flew at Yeovil on 12 September, 1973, and was delivered on 29 January, 1974. Serialled 261–265, deliveries were completed on 15 January, 1974. This initial order was followed by a further order for nineteen Commando

Mk.2s, powered by Gnome H.1400–1 engines fitted with air-intake sand filters and with up-rated gearboxes and six-bladed tail rotors, of which the first aircraft first flew on 16 January, 1975, carrying the B-class marking G-17-12, and was delivered on 21 February. Two of the Commando Mk.2s had specially fitted main cabins for VIP transport and were designated Mk.2Bs. All of these Commando aircraft were delivered by 14 February, 1976, ten reaching the Egyptian Air Force by the end of 1975.

This was the first Egyptian Commando 2E equipped for electronic countermeasures operations and has additional domes on the fuselage. It also carries British civil registration G-BFSE and Westland build number 866. In Egypt it became SU-BBJ.

In 1978 the Egyptian Air Force examined the possibility of acquiring four Commando aircraft specially equipped for electronic countermeasures operations and, designated Mk.2E, these were eventually ordered. The first one flew on 1 September, 1978, and, carrying the Egyptian civil registration SU-BBJ, it was delivered on 9 December, 1980. The three other aircraft, SU-ARR, 'RT and 'RP, were delivered on 3 April, 1979. Like the earlier Commando Mks. 2 and 2B they featured engine air-intake sand filters and several hemispherical radomes on the fuselage sides plus a thimble-shaped dorsal radome.

Pakistan Navy Sea King Mk.45

During December 1972 the Pakistan Navy ordered six Sea King Mk.45s, which were virtually identical to the RN HAS.Mk.1s and Indian Navy Mk.42s, for ASW operations. Five of these aircraft were subsequently modified for an alternative role as anti-surface vessel (ASV) aircraft and were equipped to carry two AM-39 Exocet missiles.

The first of these aircraft, which were serialled 4510–4515, flew on 30 August, 1974, at Yeovil. They then were delivered to RNAS Culdrose where, during the autumn of 1975, Pakistan Navy personnel began training with their aircraft. For two periods during April–June 1976 and again during June–October 1977, 4514 carried the French registration F-ZWRM for Exocet firing trials based at St Raphaël.

The penultimate Pakistan Navy Sea King 45 en route to the Larkhill ranges for dropping trials with an Exocet air-to-surface missile.

It is believed that final deliveries of this batch of six aircraft to Pakistan took place during 1977; however, a single HAS.Mk.5, ZE421, was converted and delivered on 11 January, 1989.

Arab Republic of Egypt Navy Sea King Mk.47

Six Sea King Mk.47s were ordered during 1973 by Saudi Arabia for use by the Egyptian Navy in the ASW role. These aircraft were based on the Royal Navy's Sea King HAS.Mk.2 with some variations of the communications equipment and avionics, but with provision for the same armament to be carried.

The first of these six aircraft, flew on 11 July, 1975, and was delivered to RNAS Culdrose on 29 August where it was used to train Egyptian Navy personnel, before final delivery to Egypt on 18 May, 1976. Two other Sea Kings went to Culdrose before delivery to Egypt, the last of the six being delivered on 14 January, 1976.

Belgian Air Force Sea King Mk.48

On 22 April, 1974, five Sea King Mk.48s were ordered for the Belgian Air Force for SAR operations. Similar in most aspects to the RAF Sea King HAS.Mk.3s, they were fitted with communications equipment to suit the Belgian SAR System.

The first of these aircraft, which were serialled RS01–RS05, flew on 19 December, 1975, and was delivered to RNAS Culdrose where the Belgian Air Force personnel underwent training. It was followed there by the other five Sea Kings, the last one arriving on 14 July, 1976. By October 1976 the aircraft were in Belgium where they entered service with No.40 Escadrille, a joint Air Force/Navy SAR unit based at Coxyde, replacing Sikorsky S-58s.

During 1987–88 Westland supplied thirty replacement composite main-rotor blades for these aircraft and in the following year began updating the navigation systems in all five Sea Kings. Westland and Belgian Air Force personnel jointly undertook this work at the Coxyde air base.

Royal Australian Navy Sea King Mk.50

The first Royal Australian Navy Sea King 50A, N16-239, carrying Class B markings G-17-12 in January 1983. It has a six-bladed tail rotor.

An initial order for ten Sea King Mk.50s for the Royal Australian Navy was placed during May 1973. These aircraft were to be employed in the ASW, SAR, casualty evacuation and utility roles. Powered by Gnome H.1400–1 engines, they embodied the stronger gearbox and six-bladed tail rotor which provided improved directional control when moving on an aircraft carrier deck and increased stability in the hover. These Sea Kings were also fitted with a winch-operated inflight refuelling system to enable them to refuel from a ship under way without having to alight on the ship. While this could allow long duration sorties to be made, the limiting factor was crew fatigue. Certain sections of the avionics in the Sea King 50s were updated to suit RAN requirements. The ten aircraft were serialled N16-098, -100, N16-112–114, N16-117, -119, N16-124 and -125, the first one flying on 30 June, 1974. Four months later, on 23 October, the RAN formed its first Sea King Flight at RNAS Culdrose where the air and ground crews of No.817 Squadron RAN underwent training with its new aircraft. Initially this squadron served in HMAS *Melbourne* but when this aircraft carrier was retired it became shore-based at Nowra.

In 1981 two more Sea Kings, designated Mk.50As were ordered. Serialled N16-238 and -239, the first one flew on 7 December, 1982, and was delivered on 22 February, 1983.

Qatari Emiri Air Force Commando Mks.2A, 2C and 3

QA22, a Qatari Emiri Air Force Commando 2A in March 1976 before the fitting of air-intake sand filters.

The Gulf State of Qatar, which has a treaty with Great Britain, bought four Commando Mk.2s during January 1974. This was the major production version of the Commando and was powered by the Gnome H.1400–1 engines. Three of these aircraft, designated Mk.2As and serialled QA20–22, were intended as general utility helicopters able to carry 27 fully-armed troops; the fourth, a Mk.2C, was fitted out internally as a VIP transport. Only the three Mk.2As appear to have been fitted with sand filters over their engine air intakes. The first one flew on 9 August, 1975, and was delivered on 10 October, the last aircraft being delivered on 17 May, 1976.

This initial order was followed by a second for eight Commando Mk.3s with Gnome H.1400-IT engines and equipped to carry a range of armament, including Exocet missiles or sixteen SURA or eighteen SNEB rocket projectiles or two .5 in machine-guns in pods. These Commando Mk.3s, serialled QA30–QA37, were unusual in that they used Sea King sponsons with retractable undercarriages. The first one flew for the first time on 14 June, 1982, and was delivered on 26 November. All deliveries were completed by 4 January, 1984.

Description: Twin-engined single main-rotor multi-role helicopter. All metal construction.

Accommodation: Pilot and co-pilot on flight deck, two crew in main cabin (Mks.1, 2 and 5 ASW variant); main cabin will carry up to 22 survivors (Mk.3 SAR variant) or 28 troops (Mk.4 and Commando variants).

Powerplant: Two 1,400 shp (Bristol Siddeley) Rolls-Royce Gnome H.1400 turboshaft engines driving a 62 ft diameter five-blade metal main-rotor and a 10 ft 4 in diameter five-blade metal tail rotor. (Mks.1, 41, 42, 43, 45 and

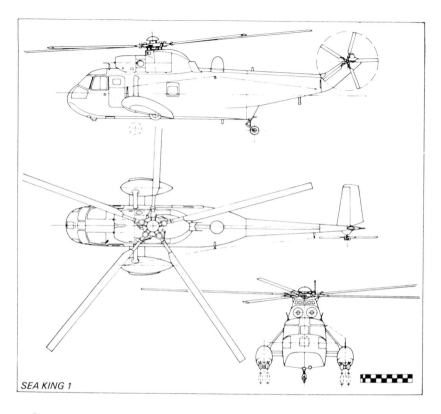

SEA KING 1

Commando Mk.1). Two 1,535 shp Rolls-Royce Gnome H.1400–1 turboshaft engines driving a 62 ft diameter five-blade metal main-rotor and a 10 ft 6 in diameter five- or six-blade metal tail rotor. (Mks.2, 3, 4, 4X, 5, 6, 43A, 45A, 48, 50 and Commando Mk.2). Two 1,465 shp Rolls-Royce Gnome H.1400-IT turboshaft engines driving a 62 ft diameter five-blade metal or composite main-rotor and a 10 ft 4 in six-blade metal or composite tail rotor (Mk.42B and Commando Mk.3).

Armament: Four Mk.44, Mk.46 or Sting Ray torpedoes, or four depth charges, or one nuclear depth bomb, or four Sea Eagle missiles. Other operational equipment includes sonobuoys, marine markers, smoke floats and a pintle-mounted 7.62 mm machine-gun in the main cabin.

Dimensions: Main rotor diameter 62 ft; length overall (rotors turning) 72 ft 8 in, (rotor and tail pylon folded) 47 ft 3 in; fuselage length 55 ft 10 in; width overall 16 ft 4 in; height (rotors turning) 16 ft 10 in; main-rotor disc area 3.019 sq ft.

Weights: Empty 12,170 lb (HAS.Mk.1), 12,194 lb (typical weight depending on variant); maximum take-of weight 21,500 lb.

Performance: Never exceed speed at sea level 140 mph; cruising speed 126 mph; maximum rate of climb 808 ft/min; service ceiling (one engine out) 4,000 ft (all these at maximum take-off weight). Never exceed speed at sea level 169 mph, cruising speed 152 mph (at typical mid-mission weight).

Production: A total of 321 Sea Kings built by Westland Helicopters Ltd, Yeovil, Somerset, during 1968–1990 as follows:

1 Sea King HAS.Mk.1 prototype
56 Sea King HAS.Mk.1 production aircraft
21 Sea King HAS.Mk.2 production aircraft
19 Sea King HAR.Mk.3 production aircraft
41 Sea King HC.Mk.4 production aircraft
2 Sea King Mk.4X aircraft
30 Sea King HAS.Mk.5 production aircraft
6 Sea King HAS.Mk.6 production aircraft
23 Sea King Mk.41 production aircraft
12 Sea King Mk.42 production aircraft
3 Sea King Mk.42A production aircraft
21 Sea King Mk.42B production aircraft
6 Sea King Mk.42C production aircraft
10 Sea King Mk.43 production aircraft
1 Sea King Mk.43A production aircraft
6 Sea King Mk.45 production aircraft
6 Sea King Mk.47 production aircraft
5 Sea King Mk.48 production aircraft
10 Sea King Mk.50 production aircraft
2 Sea King Mk.50A production aircraft
5 Commando Mk.1 production aircraft
17 Commando Mk.2 production aircraft
3 Commando Mk.2A production aircraft
2 Commando Mk.2B production aircraft
1 Commando Mk.2C production aircraft
4 Commando Mk.2E production aircraft
8 Commando Mk.3 production aircraft

Sea King continues in production in 1991.

The all-yellow first WG.13 Lynx XW835, during its first flight on 21 March, 1971, at Yeovil. It carries the build number 00-01 on its nose. Its external appearance was markedly similar to that of the later production aircraft.

Lynx

Following Westland's acquisition in 1959–60 of the other British helicopter interests at Saunders-Roe, Fairey Aviation and Bristol Aircraft, project design activity at those companies was discontinued. It was then centred at Yeovil where, in 1962, a new Project Group was formed. Its prime task was to examine the future needs of the British armed Services who were seen to be Westland's major customers in the future and who would need replacements for the helicopters in current service. Westland hoped that this military market would also pave the way into civil and export markets.

At that time Naval/Air Staff Requirement 358 was the only officially circulated call for a medium helicopter for the Royal Navy and the RAF, and Westland, which had projected a series of four helicopters to meet all the anticipated needs of the Services, submitted WG.1. This was a twin-rotor design bearing a close resemblance to the Boeing-Vertol CH-47 Chinook: it was, however, only one of four projected designs intended to cover the entire spectrum of the Services' helicopter requirements. One of these, the single-rotor WG.3, was for use by the Army as a light tactical aircraft able to carry up to ten fully-armed troops and a crew of two. It had an all-up weight of 8,000–11,000 lb and was powered by two Pratt & Whitney PT6A turboshaft engines. Because it was intended for battlefield operations as a Whirlwind and Scout replacement, it was designed to be easily maintained and quickly repaired, to be highly reliable with minimum turn-around times and to be air-portable. For economy and reliability, initially the WG.3A design incorporated proven components and engines, including the Whirlwind gearbox and the use of a Bristol Belvedere rear rotor as the main-rotor. This latter unit was to be extensively redesigned in the future. Into the design of the WG.3A went a great deal of experience gained by the Bristol element of the Project Group with the Bristol Type 203 which had been projected as a Sycamore replacement.

Inevitably, as the WG.3A design was refined and developed into the WG.3B, using a Sycamore gearbox, and the WG.3C, which could lift fifteen troops, so the size and weight went up and encroached on the WG.4 project which was intended as a Wessex replacement. Thus, although this larger helicopter was the basis for discussion and presentations to all three Services, Westland concentrated on the original smaller 8,000 lb aircraft now re-designated WG.13. This basic design was extensively modified to meet differing user requirements, a major change being the re-location of the engines, from inside to above the cabin roof in front of the main-rotor to provide the increased internal head room required by the Army. Much of the project design work was centred around overcoming the modest amount of power available, for although 800 shp engines were required, none existed; thus a stub-winged variant was studied to allow the 49 ft 4 in main rotor diameter to be reduced. Then, in October 1964, General Staff Operational Requirement 3335 was issued, detailing the Army's Specification for a helicopter required for service in 1972.

For development flying, powered by two Pratt & Whitney PT6B-34 engines, XW835 became G-BEAD.

GSOR 3335 was very far reaching; it called for a multi-role helicopter able to carry a crew of two and seven fully-armed troops or a maximum load of 3,000 lb of supplies as an underslung load. In addition it was to have defensive and offensive armament and be able to operate in the casualty evacuation, reconnaissance, or liaison roles. The performance requirements included a maximum speed of 170 mph, a radius of action of up to 170 miles depending upon the load to be carried and a 900 miles unrefuelled ferrying range. These, and a number of other specified requirements, could all be met by the WG.13 project.

Meanwhile, Westland was aware that the 750 hp PT6A engines were not sufficiently powerful for several other projected WG.13 variants and the Project Group considered the use of two 770 hp Continental T72 free-turbines mounted aft of the main-rotor. These were seen as rather more suitable for the WG.13Q utility variant, the R armed escort and the WG.13S in which both roles were combined, and which Westland submitted in July 1965 to meet GSOR 3335.

While the S variant was not proceeded with, the concept of one aircraft being developed for use in more than one role was pursued by Westland, and in 1966 WG.13 variants for Army, Navy and civil applications were studied. This work produced the WG.13T for armed reconnaissance and the U utility variant for the Army, plus the WG.13V for the Royal Navy and the civil variant designated WG.13W. These projects had many features in common including the same engines and 44 ft diameter main-rotor and, of more importance perhaps, the use of a new gearbox with conformal gears, which Westland had been researching for a long time. These gears, also known as CIRCARC (circular arc) profiles, have teeth whose mating profiles conform, both sets having instantaneous centres of curvature on the same side of contact. They are smaller and lighter for a given load than earlier gear designs, provide a greater reduction ratio per stage and, with the simplified main-rotor hub, help to create a much lower profile.

While Westland was developing the WG.13 design, a Joint Service Requirement was issued in June 1966. This replaced the Army's GSOR 3335 and detailed the specific needs of the Army and Royal Navy. The RN requirement was for a second generation helicopter able to operate from small ships such as frigates and destroyers in high sea states. France's parallel need for a range of helicopters and their joint development and production was being planned under the terms of a Memorandum of Understanding signed by the British and French Governments on 17 May, 1965. The final Anglo-French Agreement was signed on 22 February, 1967, and in general terms, while France's needs for a tactical medium transport helicopter and a light observation helicopter were to be met by its own SA.330 Puma and SA.341 Gazelle, Britain was to provide WG.13 variants to meet the French Army need for an armed reconnaissance helicopter and an ASW helicopter for the French Navy. About 70 per cent of the French W.13 production was to be Westland's, which also had design leadership, with the remainder being done by Aérospatiale. It was to be the first British aeroplane to be designed using Metric, rather than Imperial mensuration. In addition, there were requirements for an RAF trainer and an ASW helicopter for the Royal Navy. It was at the end of 1966 that, at last, a more powerful new turboshaft engine was announced. It began life at Bristol Siddeley Engines as the 900 shp BS.360 whose design and development was continued, as the RS.360, after Rolls-Royce's acquisition of Bristol Siddeley in October 1966. This was exactly what Westland required, particularly for the French WG.13 variants which could accommodate a rotor diameter no greater than 42 ft 8 in and three seats in the armed reconnaissance helicopter. In the event, this Army requirement was cancelled in October 1969. Although the use of this BSE/R-R engine would produce the classic case of a new engine and airframe combination, never a popular arrangement with airframe manufacturers, its modular construction and excellent forecast power/weight ratio and specific fuel consumption made it extremely attractive. Westland's fears were to be realised, however.

The embodiment of the BS.360 was a major step forward in the WG.13 project programme and detailed design work on the Army utility and naval variants was passed to the Hayes design office. By this time all elements of the company were operating under the new name of Westland Helicopters Ltd, a wholly owned Westland Aircraft Ltd company, formed on 1 October, 1966, and embracing the Westland Aircraft, Bristol Helicopters, Fairey Aviation and Saunders-Roe aviation interests. During July 1967 Westland was notified of the official intention to proceed with the WG.13 and work on the production and development programme was stepped up. Initially, it was planned to build sixteen aircraft to handle the complex airframe, systems, engine and rotor development flying, but this number was cut to thirteen. In addition a number of ground test rigs and airframes for structural and systems testing were required. Production planning was aimed at having the first prototype ready for flight during the middle of 1970, and in anticipation of this, the mock-up of what was placarded as the 'Westland-Sud WG.13' was exhibited on the Westland stand in the Paris Air Show during May–June 1969. But, almost inevitably, there was slippage in the programme and it was not until October 1969 that Rolls-Royce announced that the BS.360 had run successfully for the first time; even then, when the engine began running on test, it was delivering about 200 shp below its forecast 900 shp. The engine power problems stemmed from a mismatch between the gas generator spools and power turbine sections of the engine. There was, too, some public airing of problems with cost over-run on both the airframe and engine development programmes which helped neither company. However, a major element of the WG.13, now named Lynx, had flown close to the programmed date; this was the semi-rigid main-rotor of which scaled-down versions were flown on two Scout helicopters, XP189 and XP191, the first on 31 August, 1970. One of the things which came to light during the ground and flight testing of the semi-rigid rotor on the Scouts was 'air resonance', a phenomenon not previously encountered by Westland. The problem was solved by fitting hydraulic lag plane dampers in parallel with the outboard rotor head component (known universally as the 'dog bone' or 'os du chien' by Aérospatiale engineers). This solution was transferred to the Lynx design which has always embodied dampers.

These two Scouts logged some 30 development flying hours with this highly effective rotor. This was closely followed by the main-rotor ground test rig, which embodied a remote control cabin with a replica of the Lynx controls and instrument installation, and which was first 'flown' on 24 September. These two development 'tools' were invaluable to the Westland test pilots who were able to gain handling experience before flying the Lynx which was ready for initial ground running checks during the second week of March 1971. These occupied about a week, the first flight coming on 21 March, the all-yellow first Development Batch Lynx (DB) XW835, being flown by Ron Gellatly at Yeovil. This eight months slippage was not wholly surprising having in mind the very advanced nature of this new airframe/engine/propulsion system. Even then, the flight engines being delivered by Rolls-Royce's Leavesden factory were down on power which prevented Westland from exploring the corners of the full flight envelope. However, the pre-flight trials of the semi-rigid main-rotor had provided evidence of its great superiority over the earlier more complex and bulky rotor heads, and this was being experienced with the full-sized rotor on the first Development Batch aircraft. While the grey-painted second DB Lynx, XW836, was undergoing ground resonance testing—even though no problems had been experienced with the first aircraft—the scarlet third DB aircraft,

XW837, was the next Lynx to fly, on 28 September, 1971, still with the under-powered BS.360. During March 1972 both XW838, the all-blue fourth DB Lynx and XW836 made their first flights on 8th and 24th respectively, while the first Army utility development AH.Mk.1 Lynx, XX153, got airborne on 12 April. Thus, within little more than a year following the first flight of the Lynx, five aircraft were on the test and development programme.

Structurally they were basically similar to the production aircraft which followed them in the factory; however, the airframe was subjected to major detail redesign for production because the original design by the Hayes drawing office was very complex, used a frightening number of detail components, was overweight and deficient in both strength and stiffness. In the initial DB airframes, two A-frames, each with a trunnion box at the apex, carried the main gearbox, in an effort to minimise the transfer of in-plane rotor vibrations to the airframe by using the gearbox and engine masses as vibration absorbers. It didn't work; thus, at an early development stage, the gearbox casting was redesigned with integral feet which were attached to the transmission deck on the cabin roof at the same points as the discarded A-frames.

The original rotor heads were designed to be built using a steel central 'flower pot' vertical member to which four titanium arms were bolted. This enabled development flying to begin, and to continue for a lengthy period, while the problems of making satisfactory forgings for the titanium 'monobloc' heads were sorted out.

Having in mind Westland's close links with the Sikorsky design office it is understandable that the first helicopter to be wholly designed by the British company should employ the well-proven US 'pod-and-boom' configuration. That said, Westland embodied very many completely new design features in the Lynx which set it apart from the Sikorsky products. The fuselage and tail unit are of conventional semi-monocoque construction, mainly of light alloy, although fibre-glass access panels, doors and fairings were used. The well glazed cabin has a deep wrap-around windscreen with large 'eyebrow' windows in the fibreglass roof over the two crew seats. In the prototypes and early development aircraft the two sliding doors in the cabin sides each had three small windows which were replaced by a single large rectangular window in production variants. There is provision for internally mounted defensive armament and mountings on the exterior for weapons or stores. The pilot and co-pilot, or observer, are seated side-by-side and have their own doors. A hollow box-section frame behind the crew contains all control runs to the rotor head to give an unobstructed floor. In the maximum high-density general purpose configuration a pilot and ten armed troops can be carried, the latter on lightweight bench seats in the soundproofed cabin. These can be quickly removed to premit the carriage of about 2,000 lb of freight internally, for which tie-down rings are provided. A 3,000 lb load can be carried on an external attachment below the cabin floor. A fixed twin-skid type or tricycle wheeled undercarriage is attached to the main fuselage. The tailboom is a light alloy monocoque structure with a swept fin/tail-rotor pylon carrying a half tailplane to starboard. The pylon's leading- and trailing-edges and the fairing over the tail-rotor gearbox are of glassfibre. In the RN variants of the Lynx the pylon can be folded and spread manually to reduce the overall length by some 8 ft 6 in for stowage. The two engines, whose designation was changed to RS.360 in 1967 and which were named Gem in 1971, are mounted side-by-side on the cabin roof aft of the main-rotor shaft and gearbox and separated from the fuselage, transmission area, and each other by firewalls. Fuel is carried in five crashproof bag tanks within the fuselage structure one of which is located under the floor of the forward cabin area. Additional tanks can be installed in the rear of the cabin to increase the ferrying range. The two engines drive the four-blade semi-rigid main-rotor and the four-blade tail-rotor through the main gearbox. The rotor hub and inboard portions of the four flexible arms are a one-piece titanium forging. Each blade consists of a two-piece two-channel stainless steel D-shaped box spar to which is bonded a GRP rear skin stabilised by a paper honeycomb core, and with a moulded GRP tip. The blades are attached to the rotor hub by titanium root attachment plates and a flexible arm. Later production Lynx have more advanced composite blades with paddle tips developed under the British Experimental Rotor Programme (BERP). The tail-rotor blades have a light alloy spar and a rear section similar to that of the main-rotor blades.

The first utility variant development Lynx, XX153, in Army Air Corps finish. It went on to set a World Speed Record in June 1972. It is seen with redesigned skids.

With the first Army Lynx AH.Mk.1 DB Utility aircraft, XX153, beginning its flight test programme, the first Royal Navy HAS.Mk.2 DB aircraft, XX469, first flew on 25 May, 1972, and differed from the earlier airframes by having a lengthened nose to accommodate a radar scanner and a wheeled undercarriage. Then on 29 June Roy Moxam, Westland's test pilot, flying XX153 in the Army utility configuration, set a new world speed record in the E.1 Class for helicopters over a 15–25 km course of 199.92 mph; 48 hours later, flying the same aircraft over a 100 km closed-circuit course, he achieved 197.914 mph. This aircraft also was the first helicopter to be rolled, the pilot being Moxam, who publicly demonstrated this at the Farnborough Show on 4–10 September 1972.

By October the Gem engine had at last delivered its maximum rated power on the test bed and Rolls-Royce had produced sufficient engines to equip all of the development aircraft flying on the programme. The first Lynx to be lost was XX469, the first Royal Navy aircraft which crashed on 21 November, 1972, sustaining Category 5 damage and was written off. However, the second RN DB

XX510, the HAS.2 development Lynx to the definitive Royal Navy standard, over the ill-fated HMS *Sheffield*. Note the splayed main undercarriage wheels.

aircraft, XX510, made its first flight on 5 March, 1973, and joined the other development aircraft. It was this Lynx which, on 29 June, made the first at-sea landing of the type aboard the helicopter support ship RFA *Engadine*. As the flight development programme got into its stride with the rest of the DB aircraft being built, they were allocated to a variety of tasks. Initial icing trials had been completed in Norway and Denmark early in 1975 with XW837, the third prototype, reserved for development of the automatic flight control system. Initially, the sixth aircraft, XX907, was allocated to Rolls-Royce for engine development, but later it became the second Lynx AH.1 development aircraft. Seven more aircraft were used on the main military development programme; they were XX469, the first DB RN (first flight 25 May, 1972), XX510 the second DB RN aircraft (5 March, 1973), XX904 and XX911, the first and second Aéronavale Lynx dedicated to French equipment trials as part of the joint programme (6 July and 18 September, 1974). They were followed by the last RN development aircraft XX910 which was the basic RN version (23 April, 1974), XW 839, the fifth basic aircraft (19 June, 1974) and XZ166 (5 March, 1975). During June 1975 one utility Lynx and two RN Lynx went to the A & AEE for type testing and certification, and by early 1976 these thirteen development aircraft had logged some 2,800 test flying hours. During May 1974 Westland had received the first order for one hundred Lynx, comprising twenty-two AH.1s for the AAC, sixty HAS.2s for the RN and eighteen Mk.2(FN)s destined for the Aéronavale.

Lynx AH.Mk.1

The first production Lynx AH.1 for the Army Air Corps, XZ170, with 900 shp Gem 2 engines, first flew on 11 February, 1977. The AAC received its first Lynx

The first Lynx AH.1 to be delivered to the AAC, XZ172, seen in June 1977 in company with Scout XW280, a type the Lynx replaced in service.

during 1977 and the type became operational with BAOR Germany at Detmold in August 1978. A total of 113 were built, all being delivered by February 1984.

Although the Army's original intention had been to use the Lynx as a tactical troop and supplies 'mover', a casevac aircraft or an airborne command post, its agility and performance during flight trials caused these plans to be modified to include the anti-tank role. Westland's demonstrator aircraft, G-LYNX, which first flew on 11 May, 1979, demonstrated the helicopter's capabilities with a wide range of weapons which included the Hughes TOW anti-tank guided missile, rocket projectiles, machine-gun pods and Hispano 820 anti-armour cannon. It also showed its ability to airlift three-man anti-tank teams armed with Milan missiles and their associated equipment. In addition to these roles, the

FPT flotation gear on test in a development Lynx.

406

Lynx has been operated on SAR and reconnaissance duties and as armed escort to troop-carrying helicopters.

During its first four years of AAC service, the Lynx was employed in its utility role but a retrofit programme on sixty AH.1s, begun in 1981, created a force of anti-tank helicopters armed with eight TOW missiles and eight more reloads in the cabin, a roof-mounted sight plus associated equipment.

While the AAC Lynx did not take part in the Falklands Campaign, it served there soon afterwards providing an immediate response force in the event of an attempted Argentine landing, supplying remote missile and radar sites around the Islands, armed reconnaissance and general liaison duties. In Northern Ireland the Lynx continues to serve with great success on patrols by day or night, providing the Army with rapid response transport and armed reconnaissance capabilities.

An AAC Lynx in West Germany carrying eight Hughes TOW missiles. It has a cabin roof mounted Hughes sight.

A small number of Lynx AH.1s were supplied to 3 Commando Brigade Air Squadron, based at Yeovilton, in 1984 to replace its ageing Scout AH.1 aircraft, plus one or two HAS.2s for evaluation. These aircraft were repainted in a black and green camouflage finish with the words 'Royal Marines' in black replacing the white 'Royal Navy'. This followed a decision not to proceed with a hybrid Army/RN Lynx Mk.6 for beach assault duties. The last AH.1, ZD285, was completed as the first AH.5 (interim), with uprated gearbox and Gem 2 engines. First flown on 21 November, 1984, it went to the RAE Bedford for trials with new avionics and other equipment to enhance future variants.

About twelve Lynx AH.1s were used for experimental and development flying trials by Westland and various Establishments.

Lynx HAS.Mk.2

This version of the Lynx was developed principally for ASW hunter-killer duties operating from guided-missile destroyers and frigates. It is also capable of operation in the air-to-surface vessel search and strike, SAR, troop transport,

XZ234, a Lynx HAS.2, flew with the IFTU at Yeovilton in 1977. It operated off a small 40 ft by 30 ft platform of the Royal Danish Navy's fishing protection vessel *Beskytteren* off Copenhagen in April 1978.

reconnaissance, fire support, fleet liaison and communication roles. The original production order was for sixty Lynx HAS.2s but this was later increased to eighty, the additional twenty aircraft having GEM 41-1 engines and being designated HAS.Mk.3 (qv). The Lynx HAS.2 differs from the AH.1 in a number of areas; it has a fixed tricycle undercarriage in which the mainwheels can be splayed outward and locked at 27 deg to enable the aircraft to rotate on the ship's deck to the most suitable take-off heading; the main-rotor can produce some 3,000 lb of negative thrust to give the Lynx some post-landing stability and maintain its contact with a probably heaving deck until the hydraulically actuated Fairey Harpoon deck-lock system can be engaged; the Sea Spray lightweight search and tracking radar is carried in the extended nose and the weapons systems and avionics fit differ to suit the various roles. The sixty Lynx HAS.2s were built in two batches of thirty each, production of the second batch beginning in early 1979.

The first production Lynx HAS.2, XZ227, first flew on 10 February, 1976, and entered RN service with the Intensive Flight Trials Unit No.700L Squadron: which commissioned at RNAS Yeovilton in September of that year. This squadron was unique in that it was a joint RN/Royal Netherlands Navy operational evaluation unit. At full strength it had six RN and two RNethN aircraft, the latter being transferred to a shore base in the Netherlands in May 1977 following their initial evaluation. During this period, deck handling trials were completed in HMS *Birmingham*, a Type 42 destroyer, at sea off Portland in

February 1977. Trials at the IFTU continued until December when the first Lynx to go into front-line operational service joined the frigate HMS *Sirius*. The first RN Lynx squadron, No.702, commissioned at Yeovilton on 26 January, 1978, while the first Lynx deployment at sea came on 8 February, 1978, in the Leander class frigate *Phoebe*. The phased introduction of the Lynx in more than 40 ships, mainly Type 21 frigates and those of the Leander and Tribal classes and the Type 42 destroyers, soon got under way and in January 1981 No.815 Squadron commissioned at Yeovilton as the Headquarters Squadron for Lynx Ships' Flights.

About twenty-five RN Lynx from No.815 Squadron took part in the Falklands war, their first action being on 25 April, 1982, when a pair of Lynx HAS.2s from the Type 21 frigates *Antelope* and *Alacrity* attacked the Argentine Navy's submarine *Santa Fé* off Grytviken harbour with a torpedo and machine-gun fire. Later that day Lynx HAS.2s escorted Sea Kings landing Marine Commandos on South Georgia, about 700 miles southeast of the Falkland Islands. The British forces subsequently re-captured the island. On 3 May HMS *Coventry*'s Lynx launched its two Sea Skua missiles at a vessel it had detected on its radar and scored direct hits. Shortly afterwards the Lynx from another Type 42 destroyer, HMS *Glasgow*, was fired at by what was at first thought to be the same vessel. It launched its Sea Skua from nine miles range and completely destroyed the upperworks of what turned out to be a second vessel. Subsequently, two more enemy vessels were attacked by Lynx HAS.2s armed with Sea Skuas, each of the four missiles launched scoring direct hits. Apart from torpedoes and guided missiles, MAD equipment and ECM pods were carried by a number of RN Lynx operating in the South Atlantic theatre.

Lynx HAS.2, XZ236, converted to represent an interim Mk.8 and used for central tactical system development, flies alongside HMS *Gloucester*.

Among the Lynx HAS.2s used for experimental and development flying, were XZ227 (A & AEE; RAE Aberporth, Sea Skua back-up trials), XZ236 (WHL and A & AEE) and XZ698 (A & AEE TOW trials).

Lynx HAS.Mk.3

Basically similar to the Lynx HAS.2, the HAS.3 is powered by two 1,120 shp Gem 41-1 turboshaft engines with an uprated transmission to permit the all-up weight to increase to 10,500 lb. These aircraft had the 'three-pinion' main gearboxes with a torque-sharing device built in which permitted much greater single-engine power inputs from the uprated engines in an emergency; these offered an improved safety margin for flyaway following an engine failure. A total of twenty aircraft were ordered but when three Lynx HAS.2s were lost in the Falklands when HMS *Antelope* and *Coventry* and the conveyor ship *Atlantic Conveyor* were destroyed, three more HAS.3s were ordered as replacements plus one for the ETPS. Deliveries began in March 1982 and were completed by April 1985, but in July a further seven aircraft were ordered. In May it had been revealed that Westland, with Racal Avionics as a sub-contractor, was developing a Racal-designed central tactical system (CTS) for the HAS.3 to reduce the crew's workload in later Lynx variants.

ZD267, a Lynx HAS.3, was modified to become the Mk.8 aerodynamics trials aircraft with a 360 deg radome, passive identification device in the nose, Orange Crop ESM and main-rotor-head vibration absorber.

In June 1990 three Royal Navy Lynx HAS.3s, ZF557, ZF558 and ZF563 were fitted with the CTS and entered service with No.700 L Squadron, the RN Lynx Operational Flight Trials Unit (LOFTO), at RNAS Portland on 6 July for initial sea trials in HMS *Argus*. These were completed in August and more CTS-equipped Lynx were scheduled to join the squadron for further trials during early 1991 as part of the Lynx Mk.8 development programme. Three more Lynx Mk.3s were allocated to this programme at Yeovil; XZ236, originally an HAS.2 which, ultimately, was converted to Mk.8 standard and was involved in the avionics systems development, ZD266 was used for CTS development and integration with existing equipment and further enhancements for ECM, MAD and other equipment. ZD267 was extensively modified to incorporate a new passive identification device, having the nose re-configured and radar aerials and other equipment re-located. The all-up weight was increased to 11,300 lb, a reverse direction tail rotor, and the Sea Spray 180 deg radar re-positioned in a chin-mounted radome. It went to the A & AEE during mid-1990 for testing the Mk.8 airframe, and was also used for flight testing advanced composite rotor blades with anhedral tips developed from the BERP composite blades.

Lynx AH.Mk.5

Soon after the last Lynx AH.1 had been modified to produce the first of two AH.Mk.5 (Interim) aircraft, ZD285, and had flown on 21 November, 1984, a second trials aircraft, the Mk.5X, ZD559, was built to the same standard with two 1,120 shp Gem 41-1 engines, the three-pinion uprated gearbox and the same 10,000 lb all-up weight. It first flew on 11 February, 1985, and joined the first aircraft at RAE Bedford for trials of new avionics and other equipment for use in future Lynx variants. Eight AH.5s were ordered for the AAC. The first definitive AH.5, ZE375, first flew on 23 February, 1985, and was used for engine trials. Only one more of this batch, ZE376, was completed to this standard; it first flew, converted to become the first AH.7, on 23 April, 1985. With the remaining six aircraft it was integrated with a new order for four AH.Mk.7s received in June. Later, a single AH.5, ZD560, was built, first flew on 16 June, 1987, and went to the EPTS. During 1987, ZD285 completed a two-year modification programme and went to the RAE Farnborough fitted with a swivelling nose turret. After trials it was used to test-fly an airborne mission management system with a 'glass cockpit'.

Lynx AH.Mk.7

Based on the Lynx AH.5 this is an uprated aircraft to meet the GSR 3947 requirement for the AAC. Modifications include improved cockpit management systems, a reversed-direction of rotation tail rotor with composite blades and a 10,750 lb loaded weight. The more powerful tail rotor reduces noise and improves the ability to hover for extended periods at high weights, an important factor during anti-tank operations. In addition to the seven aircraft transferred from the AH.5 contract, four more were ordered in 1985. The first AH.7, ZE376, was the converted second Mk.5. Deliveries were completed with the 11th aircraft by July 1987. Conversion of AH.1 Lynx to AH.7 standards was done at the RN workshops at RNAS Wroughton, the first of these, XZ614 was returned to service on 30 March, 1988. Eight more were finished by the end of that year.

Lynx HAS.Mk.8

The first Lynx HAS.3, ZD249, was not Super Lynx but was reconfigured as an aerodynamic representation of the Mk.8. It featured BERP main-rotor blades, 360 deg radome and a PID. Here it carries four British Aerospace Sea Skua anti-ship missiles. Mountings for the Norwegian Kongsberg Penguin 3 anti-ship missile also were fitted.

This is a development of the Lynx proposed for the RN which embodies an improved composite tail rotor, BERP main-rotor blades, a central tactical system and an 11,300 lb loaded weight. One HAS.2 and two HAS.3s were converted to participate in the Mk.8 development programme, the first, XZ236, flying on 25 January, 1989, for use as the CTS test-bed aircraft. It was followed by ZD266 and by ZD267 which became the aerodynamic trials aircraft.

Lynx AH.Mk.9

This Lynx variant is the equivalent of the so-called Battlefield Lynx with a tricycle undercarriage, composite main-rotor blades with advanced BERP tips and exhaust diffusers as standard and with the maximum take-off weight increased to 11,300 lb. The first prototype, XZ170, first flew as such in 1989. It had been built as the first AH.1 and spent most of its time on trials work, including development of the AH.5, AH.7 and BERP blades and was used for high agility flying. Sixteen new aircraft were ordered in 1987 for delivery starting in 1991 plus eight conversions of Lynx AH.1 airframes. These were for the newly formed Nos.672 and 673 Squadrons for support of the rapid intervention 24th Armoured Brigade, some operating in command post or tactical transport roles.

412

It is difficult to recognise XZ170, the first Lynx AH.1, in its guise as the Lynx 9 prototype. Modifications include BERP blades, tricycle undercarriage and jet-pipe IFR diffusers. XZ170 was a trials aircraft for Lynx AH.1, 5, 7 and 9 development.

Lynx 3

The roots of the Lynx 3 can be found in a Franco-German combat helicopter requirement PAH-2 of the mid-1970s. Although the instigators' interest in it waned, it was revived again in 1981 and in June the following year, Westland revealed its intent to develop an increased-weight Lynx with heavier armament and a number of advanced features. This was to be known as the Lynx 3, which has been confused with the Lynx HAS.Mk.3.

When France and Germany began their own PAH-2 programme, Westland continued its work on the Lynx 3 as a private venture. A full-scale mock-up was built around a proposal for an Army helicopter designed and engineered to provide increased survivability in a battlefield environment and to provide greater firepower in a ground support role. Design features included an 11¾ in plug in the forward fuselage, to give a better rear view and more room for missile reloads, and a strengthened Westland 30 type tail cone. The loaded weight was 27 per cent greater than the production Lynx AH.1 and additional power came from two 1,260 shp Gem 60–3 engines. Lateral air-intakes were to have particle filters and exhaust diffusers and BERP main-rotor blades were specified. A redesigned tricycle wheeled undercarriage had a crash absorption system to accept 20 fps descent rates and the armoured crew seats had shock absorber strut mountings. The cabin could accommodate up to ten troops or eight reload missiles. Armament could be a 20 mm cannon, machine-gun or RP pods or anti-tank missiles on stub-pylons on the cabin sides. Full day and night

Instrumented BERP main-rotor blades on the long-serving first Lynx AH.1 XZ170. The rotor head carried a telemetry package and the small bracket on the tip held a reflector for optical tracking.

vision sensors could be fitted in the nose, roof or be mast mounted, and a raked forward cable-cutter was carried on the cabin roof.

For naval applications a second Lynx 3 mock-up was produced with the longer forward fuselage. The design embodied air intakes and a stronger undercarriage

Wooden mock-up of the Army Lynx 3, completed with BERP blades, sideways-facing air intakes and IFR diffusers, plus a Westland 30 tail cone with low tailplane. Note the mast-mounted sensors, two Stinger air defence weapons and eight Hellfire anti-tank missiles.

of near standard Lynx configuration, a 360 deg radome and a passive identification device in the nose. Two Sting Ray torpedoes were carried on the mock-up.

In order to get a flying example into the air as quickly as possible the 301st Lynx airframe was modified to the new Lynx 3 standard. An additional feature of this aircraft was that it embodied a Westland 30 tail unit with endplate fins on the tailplane. This aircraft, serialled ZE477, first flew on 14 June, 1984, and was displayed at Farnborough International in September.

A September 1985 mock-up of naval Lynx 3 with BERP blades, 360 deg radar and PID, Westland 30 tail cone and low tailplane. It carries two Sting Ray torpedoes.

415

ZE477, the Lynx 3, with modified main undercarriage, and sideways-facing intakes with standard exhaust outlets. It has the Westland 30 type tail cone and tail unit.

Despite extensive sales promotion and some 100 hours development flying, no orders were placed for the Lynx 3 and when the programme was abandoned in 1987, ZE477 went to the International Helicopter Museum at Weston-super-Mare.

Lynx demonstrator G-LYNX

A special demonstrator Lynx, registered G-LYNX, the 102nd airframe in the production programme was built in 1979 and was widely used by the Westland sales team. It was also used for armament trials with HOT and Hellfire missiles, during which it was serialled ZA500. For subsequent 20 mm cannon and machine-gun trials it became ZB500. This was to meet a CAA objection to civil registered aircraft flying in the United Kingdom with armament.

Westland has a long-standing prominence in rotor blade design and manufacture since it produced the first metal blades for the Dragonfly. The company also quickly recognised the great potential of composite materials for blades. During the early 1980s Westland and the MoD jointly sponsored the British Experimental Rotor Programme (BERP). This embraced the company's research work on new main-rotor blade aerofoil sections which was undertaken in collaboration with the RAE, and during it what became known as the BERP blade was evolved. The first flight of a BERP main-rotor on an Army Lynx, XZ170, was made on 9 August, 1985. By the early spring of 1986 considerable experience had been gained with the rotor and it became apparent that at weights within the usual operating range of an Army Lynx it would allow flight at very high speed if enough power was provided. On trials the aircraft was flying some 70 mph faster than a standard Lynx. This much improved performance enabled Westland to consider the possibility of attacking the

416

World Helicopter Speed Record in two categories; these were the Absolute Speed of 368.40 km/h (229.20 mph) held by a Mil A-10, and the Class E1E speed for helicopters of 3,000–4,500 kg held by a Sikorsky S-76A at 340.40 km/h (211.51 mph). With the agreement of the Westland Board, granted on 16 May, 1986, the preparation of G-LYNX for the record attempt began.

Flying fast requires high power and so two 1,200 shp Rolls-Royce Gem 60 engines were installed to take full advantage of the benefits of the BERP rotor blades. These engines were allowed to operate at maximum contingency turbine inlet temperatures for five minutes which, with water-methanol injection, produced very high power for limited periods. In order to transmit this extra power to the rotor, a main-rotor gearbox, similar to that in the Westland 30 was fitted. As the existing Lynx tail rotor was not capable of counteracting the main-rotor's increased torque at the planned forward speed, a Westland 30 tailplane with 8 deg offset fins was embodied. A small Gurney flap was added to the existing cambered central fin—or tail rotor plyon—to increase its side force. To increase the total propulsive power the tailpipes on the engines were turned directly aft and their nozzle areas were reduced. This produced an additional 800 lb of thrust.

These and other modifications included drag-reduction by the removal of windscreen wipers, weapon fittings, steps and all aerials except one communication antenna, reducing the size of cooling air intakes for the intermediate and tail rotor gearboxes and fairing the rotor head and blade joints. First installed engine runs were made on 30 July with a first flight on 1 August.

The required measured 15 km (9.33 miles) course was across the Somerset levels at Sedgemoor with 'gates' at Hartlake Bridge at the eastern end and East Huntspill at the western end. The flight crew for the attempt was Trevor Egginton, Westland's chief test pilot and Derek Clews, flight test engineer. In the ground team were official observers from the Royal Aero Club representing the FAI, aided by members of the Royal Observer Corps, ATC, Territorial Army and the company. The efforts of the entire team were rewarded in the early evening of 11 August when a new record of 400,87 km/h (249.10 mph) was established, the first to exceed the 400 km/h barrier. The experience and

G-LYNX, the World Speed Record holder, embodied a Westland 30-type tail cone and tail unit, BERP blades with fairings on the head and blade-to-'dogbone' joint and ejector exhausts producing 800 lb thrust. Windscreen wipers and steps were removed and cooling air intakes for the intermediate and tail rotor gearbox were of minimum effective size.

information gained has benefitted subsequent production aircraft.

With the record secured, G-LYNX formed the basis for a mock-up for Lynx 3 shown at Farnborough International '88, its wheeled undercarriage ultimately being developed and incorported in the Lynx AH.9.

This historic aircraft is still in use by Westland. In January 1991 it was being prepared for flight trials with 1,200 shp AVCO Lycoming/Pratt & Whitney T.800 engines.

Aéronavale Lynx Mk.2

The flight deck of a Lynx HAS.2 of No.700L Squadron, the IFTU, showing the central tactical system display.

This Lynx is very similar to the Royal Navy HAS.2 but has different equipment specified by the French Navy. The first order covered a batch of eighteen aircraft, of which the first production aircraft was retained by Westland for trials, with eight more being ordered later. Deliveries to St Raphaël naval air base began in September 1978. Serials were 260–268, 270–278 and 620–627.

Aéronavale Lynx Mk.4

In May 1980 Westland received an order for fourteen aircraft with Gem 41-1 engines and uprated transmissions to permit an increase in all-up weight to 10,500 lb. The airframe, transmission and rotors were identical to the Lynx HAS.3. Deliveries began on 28 February, 1983, and were completed during early 1984. The French Lynx is equipped with dipping sonar and a modified automatic flight control system providing automatic transition into and out of

The first Lynx (FN)2 for the French Navy. On its fin it has the British serial XZ260, the numerals of which were adopted as the French serial.

the hover. The Lynx equips four front-line Aéronavale squadrons based on the Atlantic and Mediterranean seaboards and also serves on a number of warships. Serials were 801–814.

Brazilian Navy Lynx Mk.21

Based on the RN Lynx HAS.2, this variant had some minor changes in the avionics equpment. A total of nine aircraft were delivered, serialled N3020–N3028.

Argentine Navy Lynx Mk.23

Two aircraft of this mark were built and they were similar to the RN Lynx HAS.2 but had a different avionics fit. Serialled 3-H-41 and -42, they were not delivered, the first aircraft becoming a Mk.90 for the Royal Danish Naval Air Service, serialled S035.

Royal Netherlands Naval Air Service Lynx Mk.25

The first of three Lynx variants to be supplied to the Royal Netherlands Naval Air Service, the Lynx Mk.25, was designated the UH 14A by the RNethNAS. It had all the basic features of the RN Lynx HAS.2 and was for use in the SAR and utility role. A batch of six aircraft was ordered, serialled 260–265.

The second of two Argentine Navy Lynx 23s.

Royal Netherlands Naval Air Service Lynx Mk.27

Based on the RN Lynx HAS.2 this variant, designated the SH 14B by the RNethNAS, was ordered for use in the ASW role, operating from Tromp, Kortenaer and Van Speijk class frigates. A total of ten aircraft was built. They were serialled 266–275.

State of Qatar Police Lynx Mk.28

This multi-role helicopter was based on the British Army's Lynx AH.1 but was fitted with different avionics and equipped with engine air intake sand filters. Three aircraft were supplied to this customer, bearing the serials QP1–QP3 having previously flown at Yeovil with Class B markings G-17-20–'22.

Air-intake sand filters on QP2 identify this as one of three Lynx 28s ordered by the State of Qatar Police.

The first Lynx 80 for the Royal Danish Naval Air Service, S-134, was handed over on 15 May, 1980, on board HDMS *Hvidbjørnen* moored in the Port of London.

Royal Danish Naval Air Service Lynx Mk.80

The Lynx Mk.80 was based on the RN Lynx HAS.3 but had a non-folding tail. The RDNAS took delivery of eight aircraft which were serialled S-134, S-142, S-170, S-175, S-181, S-187, S-191 and S-196, these being the build numbers. They had previously flown as G-BHHM, G-BHHL, G-17-18— -23; these last Class B markings were also used on three Lynx Mk.28s for the Qatar Police.

Royal Netherlands Naval Air Service Lynx Mk.81

This third batch of Lynx helicopters for the Netherlands was similar to the RN Lynx HAS.3 and was designated the SH 14C by the RNethNAS. These aircraft, of which eight were ordered, were for use in the ASW role and were the first with the uprated transmission system which became standard in the Lynx HAS.3. They were built while the HAS.2s for the RN were still on the production line at Yeovil, and were serialled 276–283.

Royal Norwegian Air Force Lynx Mk.86

Like the Danish Lynx Mk.80, this variant was based on the RN Lynx HAS.3 and had a non-folding tail. A total of six were ordered plus one major rebuild. They were serialled 207, 216, 228, 232, 235 and 237, which again, were the build numbers. However, when 235 underwent its major rebuild after an accident, it was given the new build number 350. These aircraft had earlier carried the markings G-BIFX, 'EW and 'ZS, G-17-11—13.

The Royal Norwegian Air Force's first Lynx 86, 207, pictured in April 1981. The British civil registration G-BIFX has been applied without the hyphen and, just aft of it, is the Leigh crash locator beacon.

Argentine Navy Lynx Mk.87

Delivery of this Argentine Navy Lynx 87, 3-H-143, was embargoed and, for a period it was demonstrator G-BKBL. It is seen operating from a 38 ft by 26 ft platform on an 800 ton corvette.

Delivery of these eight aircraft was stopped by a British Government embargo on the sale of military equipment to the Argentine. The Mk.87 was based on the RN Lynx HAS.3 and the first aircraft was built and ready for delivery in Argentine Navy markings, serialled 3-H-143 having previously carried G-17-10. It subsequently was marked G-BKBL as the Westland demonstrator, and ZE388 for missile trials before going to the Royal Danish Navy as Mk.90 S-249. The second Mk.87, G-17-11, followed it as S-256, the third was not completed and the remainder were not built. The serials allocated were 3-H-143–150.

West German Navy Lynx Mk.88

The first order for twelve Lynx Mk.88s was placed in 1980. An ASW helicopter, this variant is similar to the RN Lynx HAS.3 but with Gem 41–2 engines and a non-folding tail boom. This batch was delivered between late 1981 and early 1983. Two more aircraft were ordered during 1982 for delivery during 1986, with a further order for five aircraft being received during February 1986. Deliveries of these Lynx, to Marinefliegergeschwader 3 at Nordholz were completed in January 1989. These aircraft were serialled 83-01–19 having previously been G-BIHJ–'M, G-17-25–'32,—, —, and ZG867–871 respectively.

Nigerian Navy Lynx Mk.89

Yet another export variant of the Lynx to be developed from the RN Lynx HAS.3, Nigeria ordered three of these aircraft. Their serial numbes were 01-F-89 to 03-F-89 and previously were flown as G-17-4, -15 and -16.

Two Nigerian Navy Lynx 89s, derivatives of the Royal Navy Lynx Mk.3.

Royal Danish Naval Air Service Lynx Mk.90

This was an improved version of the Royal Danish Navy Lynx Mk.80 equipped with updated avionics and other modifications. The first of these aircraft ordered, S-249, was converted from an embargoed Argentine Navy Mk.87, 3-H-143, which had become the Westland demonstrator G-BKBL. It first flew on 15 April, 1987, and was delivered on 22 May. The second Lynx Mk.90, S-256, was the second Mk.87, 3-H-144, and was delivered towards the end of 1987, while a surviving Argentine Navy Mk.23, 3-H-41, was bought during 1987 for modification by Westland to Mk.90 standard as S-035. The Kongelinge Dansk Søvaernets Flyvetjaeneste is wholly equipped with Lynx helicopters which are maintained by Royal Danish Air Force personnel. These aircraft are mainly based at Vaerlose but five Danish warships, the frigate *Beskytteren* and four Hvidbjornen class frigates, each carry one Lynx.

Portuguese Navy Lynx Mk.95

An order for five Super Lynx, for the Portuguese Navy was confirmed in an announcement during the 1990 Farnborough International Show. Designated the Lynx Mk.95 and scheduled to enter service in 1993, these aircraft will be the first of the Lynx family to be equipped with the Racal RNS 252 Tactical Data System and Doppler 91 Navigation System and a Bendix 1500 radar. They will also carry Bendix AQS-18 dipping sonar equipment and will operate from the new Vasco da Gama class frigates.

Republic of Korea Navy Lynx Mk.99

The first Lynx 99, ZH219, for the Republic of Korea Navy, which first flew on 16 November, 1989.

During the 1988 Farnborough International Show, Westland announced an order for a then unspecified number of Lynx aircraft for the Republic of Korea Navy designated Lynx Mk.99, the first aircraft, ZH219, first flew on 16 November, 1989, and the second, ZH220, in January 1990. This was the first time Westland had sold aircraft to Korea and the order was the first for Westland's new generation of navy Lynx and the largest defence contract concluded by Great Britain with the Republic of Korea.

The first two aircraft of a then unspecified 'substantial number' subsequently ordered were officially handed over to the ROK Navy at Yeovil in July 1990, several weeks ahead of schedule, where they were used initially for pilot conversion training. The Lynx Mk.99 entered ROK Navy service late in 1990. Serial numbers allocated to these aircraft ran from 90-0701.

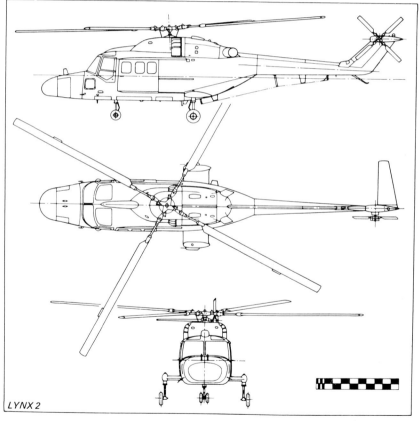

LYNX 2

Description: Twin-engined single main-rotor multi-role helicopter. All metal structure with metal and GRP covering.
Accommodation: Two crew, and with up to ten troops in the main cabin.

425

Powerplant: Two 700 shp Bristol Siddeley/Rolls-Royce BS/RS.360 turboshaft engines (early development aircraft). Two 900 shp Rolls-Royce RS.360-07/ Gem 2 turboshaft engines (AH.1, HAS,2, Mk.2). Two 1,120 shp Rolls-Royce Gem 41-1 turboshaft engines (HAS.3, AH.5, AH.7). Two 1,120 shp Rolls-Royce Gem 42-1 turboshaft engines (Mk.8, Mk.9). Two 1,200 shp Rolls-Royce Gem 60 turboshaft engines (G-LYNX, ZA500, ZB500).

Armament: One, or two, 20 mm cannon, 7.62 mm Miniguns, gun or RP pods; six AS.11 or eight HOT, Hellfire, TOW or ATOW or two Stinger or similar air-to-surface missiles (AH.1, AH.5, AH.7). Two Mk.44, Mk.46 or Sting Ray homing torpedoes; four Sea Skua semi-active homing missiles; four AS.12 or similar wire-guided missiles; 7.62 mm Miniguns (HAS.2, HAS.3).

Dimensions: Main-rotor diameter 42 ft 0 in; length 49 ft 9 in; height 12 ft 0 in; main-rotor disc area 1,385 sq ft.

Weights: Empty 5,683 lb (AH.1, 5 and 7), 6,040 lb (HAS.2 and .3); loaded 10,000 lb (AH.1 and 5), 10,500 lb (HAS.2 and .3), 10,750 lb (AH.7).

Performance: Maximum continuous cruising speed 161 mph (AH.1, 5 and 7), 144 mph (HAS.2 and 3); maximum forward rate of climb 2,480 ft/min (AH.1, 5 and 7), 2,170 ft/min (HAS.2 and 3); hovering ceiling 10,600 ft (AH.1, 5 and 7), 8,450 ft (HAS.2 and 3); maximum range 392 miles (AH.1, 5 and 7), 368 miles (HAS.2 and 3).

Production: A total of 382 Lynx produced by Westland Helicopters Ltd, Yeovil, Somerset, during 1985–90 as follows:

13 Lynx development aircraft
113 Lynx Mk.AH.1 production aircraft
86 Lynx Mk.HAS.2 production aircraft
30 Lynx Mk.HAS.3 production aircraft
14 Lynx Mk.4 production aircraft
5 Lynx Mk.AH.5 production aircraft
10 Lynx Mk.AH.7 production aircraft
16 Lynx Mk.9
9 Lynx Mk.21 production aircraft
2 Lynx Mk.23 production aircraft
6 Lynx Mk.25 production aircraft
10 Lynx Mk.27 production aircraft
3 Lynx Mk.28 production aircraft
8 Lynx Mk.80 production aircraft
8 Lynx Mk.81 production aircraft
6 Lynx Mk.86 production aircraft
2 Lynx Mk.87 production aircraft
19 Lynx Mk.88 production aircraft
3 Lynx Mk.89 production aircraft
5 Lynx Mk.95 production aircraft
12 Lynx Mk.99 production aircraft
1 Lynx demonstrator G-LYNX
1 Lynx 3

Westland 30

Although during the early 1970s Westland's Project Office had studied a 13-seat civil version of the Lynx based on the earlier WG.13W project of the mid-1960s, due to lack of interest it had not entered production. However, with the development of the highly efficient Gem 41 turboshaft engines and the uprated three-pinion Lynx gearbox, during 1976 Westland began again to examine a larger private venture helicopter as the next progressive stage from the Lynx. With this was coupled the company's continuing desire to obtain a foothold in the commercial helicopter business which it believed held great potential. This belief stemmed partly from the US Government's de-regulation of its airlines and the rapid growth of the off-shore industry in many regions of the world.

Design work on this new aircraft, then designated WG.30, began in 1977 and although it embodied an almost unchanged Lynx engine and transmission installation it featured a much larger rectangular cross-section fuselage, a new tail unit and undercarriage and an increased diameter main-rotor. Structurally it followed that of the Lynx, the large box-like fuselage was a conventional semi-monocoque structure of light alloy frames with stringers having constant spacing throughout the airframe. The well-glazed cockpit had a deep wrap-around windscreen with side windows in the two doors. A large rectangular sliding door was fitted on each side of the main cabin which had 5 ft 5 in head room. A baggage compartment with external doors was located aft of the cabin. The two engines were mounted side-by-side above the cabin aft of the gearbox, all three units being carried on a vibration-absorbing raft with elastomeric suspension units carried on two lift frames. Fireproof walls separated the engines from each other and from the main cabin. Roof panels, bulkheads and surrounds for the fuel tanks—which supported the front and rear seats in the main cabin—were of aluminium honeycomb construction while the flooring was of GRP.

G-BGHF, the first prototype WG.30 (later Westland 30), in India where it was demonstrated to the Indian Oil and Natural Gas Commission in September 1983.

The main-rotor was of the semi-rigid hingeless type with four blades, each having a stainless steel D-section spar with a bonded GRP rear skin stabilised by a plastics honeycomb core. The rotor head was a forged titanium unit. Four composite blades with a glassfibre-skinned rear section with foam filling, were used in the tail rotor which was carried on a swept fin.

The prototype, G-BGHF, was first flown on 10 April, 1979, two weeks ahead of schedule. Following early test flights, during which some problems with stability in yaw and pitch were encountered, the single tailplane on the starboard side of the fin was replaced by a conventional tailplane with endplate fins mounted on the bottom of the rear fuselage boom forward of the fin. In addition, to provide more yaw control and reduce internal noise the tail rotor diameter was increased, the speed of rotation reduced whilst the direction of rotation was reversed. The blades of this new tail rotor were Sea King Mk.42B cambered composite blades with cropped outboard ends. The results were encouraging, so much so that Westland decided to lay down an initial batch of twenty-five aircraft on a speculative basis.

Westland 30 Series 100

The first production aircraft, now re-designated Westland 30 Series 100, was G-BIWY; it first flew on 27 September, 1981, with 1,135 shp Gem 41-1 engines, although this variant's range and load carrying limitations with these engines was recognised by Westland. Flight testing with this aircraft and the prototype continued through the remainder of that year with British CAA type certification being received in December and US FAA certification in December of 1982. This latter approval was a pre-requisite to the operation of the Westland 30 by Airspur of Los Angeles.

The launch customer for the Westland 30 was British Airways Helicopters which ordered three Series 100 aircraft, the first of which G-BIWY, was

In British Airways Helicopters' livery, G-BIWY, the first production Westland 30 Series 100, off-loads survival-suited passengers on a North Sea platform.

428

A British Airways Helicopters 30-100 calls at Bromma Airport, Stockholm, during a Scandinavian demonstration tour.

delivered on 6 January, 1982, to Beccles, Suffolk, the heliport operated by BAH. From there off-shore industry workers and equipment were flown to gas and oil rigs and platforms in the southern North Sea. BAH was to operate two more Westland 30-100s, G-BKGD and G-OGAS until 1986 when the company was taken over to become British International Helicopters which continued to operate the three aircraft. Helicopter Hire was the second United Kingdom company to operate the Westland 30-100, leasing two aircraft in 1983, while overseas there were a number of 'alarums and excursions' in the USA and India. As noted earlier, Airspur leased four aircraft, beginning operations from Los Angeles International Airport on 9 May, 1983, with services linking outlying areas and provincial airports with the hub airport. However, the amount of business generated was disappointing and during the following year Evergreen Helicopters took over the aircraft to run the operation on a much reduced basis. During 1984 Omniflight Helicopters, acting on behalf of Pan American Airways, introduced scheduled services with Westland 30-100s between John F

N5830T, a Westland Westland 30-100 initially operated by Airspur Helicopter between Los Angeles International Airport and Fullerton some 20 miles away.

Kennedy International Airport and downtown New York where, in contrast with Los Angeles, there are a number of heliport facilities. However, although Omniflight believed the Westland 30 to be ideally suited to its New York shuttle service, on 1 February, 1988, it closed down this operation largely due to the downturn in PanAm's fortunes and to problems with the Gem engines. In India during September 1983, at the invitation of its Government, G-BGHF was demonstrated to officials of the Indian Oil and Natural Gas Commission; this was followed in December 1984 by a presentation by G-BLPR, which also carried the marking OIL-I on the boom, which was a Westland 30 Series 100-60 powered by 1,260 shp Gem 66-3 engines. The Indian Government had also expressed an interest in buying six Series 100-60s for the Indian Air Force and Westland expected, with all confidence, that orders would ensue, but these could not be secured. However, following a successful demonstration to the newly formed Helicopter Corporation of India, since renamed Pawan Hans, in 1987 a contract for twenty-four Series 160 aircraft was signed; these were to be supplied under a £65 million overseas aid package from the United Kingdom Government.

G-BKKI, a development Westland 30-100 demonstrates a military role as it unloads an Army three-man mortar team.

Apart from these civil applications, Westland also proposed the Westland 30 as a military tactical transport, and during 1980 the prototype, G-BGHF, was demonstrated in this role in trials with the Army School of Infantry. These showed the aircraft's ability not only to lift up to twenty-two lightly-armed troops over short ranges or fourteen fully-equipped fighting men, but also to embark and unload them very quickly, an essential attribute for aircraft in this category. In the casevac role it could accommodate up to ten walking wounded, six stretcher cases and an attendant. The succeeding variants of the Westland 30 were all projected for military as well as civil applications.

Westland 30 Series 200

Further development of the Westland 30 concept was essential if more markets were to be exploited. In 1981 Westland had sought Government aid for a comprehensive development programme and in the following year the Secretary of State for Industry announced that the Government would provide £41 million launch investment to support development of the Westland 30 Series 200 and 300. The first fruit of this programme was G-ELEC, a Series 200 (TT 30) helicopter which was first flown on 3 September, 1983. The 'TT' suffix to the designation indicated its potential military role as a tactical transport helicopter. The major improvement was the use of two 1,712 shp General Electric CT7-2B engines which drove the same conformal main gearbox as the Series 100 but through an additional reduction gearbox on each engine because of its higher output speed. Structural changes included sideways facing air intakes and a lengthened fuselage upper decking to accommodate the longer raft which carried the engines and main gearbox. Following flight testing at Yeovil, G-ELEC and G-BKKI, a Series 100-60, went to Mojave Airport, California, for high temperature and to Leadville in Colorado for high altitude trials during 1984.

The sole Westland 30-200 Series. G-ELEC, was powered by two General Electric CT7-2B engines, giving unrestricted single-engine capability at high temperatures. Note the sideways facing intakes and longer fuselage upper decking.

Westland 30 Series 300 and 400

The last Westland 30 variants were the Series 300 (TT 300) and 400–404 powered by General Electric CT7s, and the Rolls-Royce/Turboméca RTM.322 respectively. The prototype 300, G-HAUL, was first flown on 5 February, 1986. It had the standard large main cabin with a much improved cruising speed and payload/range, these stemming from an increased loaded weight and a five-blade main-rotor with Westland's BERP advanced technology composite blades. Further development of the rotor head, gear box and the engine mounting raft resulted in even lower levels of noise and vibration. Other

431

Only one Westland 30-300 Series, G-17-22, was built. Here it is camouflaged to represent a TT 300 variant powered by General Electric CT7-2Bs.

improvements included a composite tailplane, a stronger fuselage and tail boom, a crashworthy undercarriage plus updated avionics and engine management system. This variant was actively promoted by Westland in the military transport role to meet the RAF ASR 404 for a successor to the Puma and Wessex.

While Westland had some export success with the Westland 30 in the civil market further interest failed to materialise. This was due initially to the Gem engine's lack of power and reliability and the low payload and in part to the generally depressed state of the helicopter market. On the military side there was too much competition from well-established US and European helicopter manufacturers and the MoD decision to re-cast its Puma and Wessex replacement plans. And over all these factors there were the political and financial considerations which plagued Westland during the mid-1980s. Thus the Westland 30 line was closed in about January 1988, and although the company expressed a willingness to re-open it if sufficient orders warranted this, it has remained closed ever since.

Westland 30s continued to operate in the United Kingdom with BAH and BIH for a number of years; the last one, G-BKGD, was still flying as a back-up to the Sikorsky S-61Ns on the Penzance-Scilly Islands route during December 1990, having logged over 5,000 hr and was written into the 1991 schedules. Overseas, of Pawan Hans fleet of twenty-one Westland 30s, nineteen were assigned to work for the Oil and Natural Gas Commission in India, the others being used by State Governments. However, in July 1988 VT-EKO crashed at Jammu killing all seven on board; VT-EKR crashed, after tail rotor failure, at Kohima in February 1989 with the loss of three lives, and when a third crash occurred, with VT-EKQ on 11 December, 1989, the entire fleet was grounded by the Indians.

Description: Twin-engined single main-rotor general purpose civil or military helicopter. All metal construction with metal and GRP covering.

432

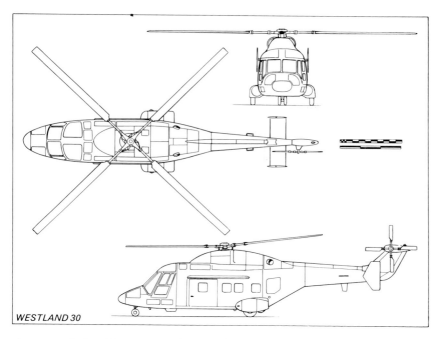

WESTLAND 30

Accommodation: Two crew and up to 20 troops in the main cabin or up to 19
   passengers.
Powerplant: Two 1,135 shp Rolls-Royce Gem 41-1 turboshaft engines (WG.30
   and Westland 30 Series 100 (TT 30)). Two 1,260 shp Rolls-Royce Gem 60-3
   turboshaft engines (Series 100-60 (TT 30)). Two 1,712 shp General Electric
   CT7-2B turboshaft engines (Series 200 (TT 30), and Series 300 (TT 300)).
   Two 2,100 shp Rolls-Royce/Turboméca RTM.322 turboshaft engines (Series
   400).
Dimensions: Main rotor diameter 43 ft 8 in; length 52 ft 2½ in; height 15 ft
   6½ in; main rotor disc area 1,497 sq ft.
Weights: Empty 6,982 lb, loaded 12,350 lb (Series 100)
   Empty 8,353 lb, loaded 12,800 lb (Series 100-60)
   Empty 7,520 lb, loaded 12,800 lb (Series 200)
   Empty 8,300 lb, loaded 16,000 lb (Series 300)
   Empty 8,850 lb, loaded 17,950 lb (W30-400-404)
Performance: Maximum continuous cruising speed 138 mph (Series 100, 100-60
   and 200), 172 mph (Series 300); hovering ceiling 3,800 ft (Series 100), 2,600 ft
   (Series 100-60); range 466 miles (Series 100), 455 miles (Series 100-60), 380
   miles (Series 200), 420 miles (Series 300).
Production: A total of 40 Westland 30s produced by Westland during 1978–86 as
   follows:
2 Westland 30 Series 100 development aircraft.
12 Westland 30 Series 100 production aircraft.
24 Westland 30 Series 100-60 production aircraft.

1 Westland 30 Series 200 development aircraft.
1 Westland 30 Series 300 development aircraft.

PP1, ZF641, the first of nine pre-production EH 101s, undergoing ground resonance checks before the first flight. The fin leading-edge and sections of the top fuselage decking have been removed and various umbilicals attached.

European Helicopter Industries EH 101

Following design and feasibility studies by the MoD (Navy) to establish the requirements for a new ASW helicopter to succeed the Sea King, in the spring of 1977 Naval Staff Requirement 6646 was issued. The Westland response was the submission of the WG.34 project which, in September 1978, was selected by the MoD for development. About that time the Marina Militari Italiana (MMI) was examining a similar need to replace its Sikorsky ASH-3D helicopters which had been licence-built by the helicopter division of Agusta SpA in Italy. After a series of inter-company discussions on this need for a new helicopter, the British and Italian Governments signed MOU1 in November 1979. This led, in June 1980, to the formation by Westland and Agusta of a joint company. Named European Helicopter Industries (EHI), it was to manage the development, production and marketing of a new multi-role helicopter designated the EH 101. This was to meet the needs of both Navies and to have other civil and military applications. There was a popular story, probably apocryphal, that this designation should have been EHI 01 but a typing error, followed by a printer's error, produced the one adopted!

In June 1981 MOU2 was signed by the two Governments and the project definition phase followed immediately. It was a careful examination of the feasibility of this joint product being built to meet both Navies' requirements. In spite of the different marine sonar environments in which the two Navies would operate—the North Atlantic and the Mediterranean—March 1982 marked the start of the integrated programme, while 1983 saw the beginning of the full development phase. MOU3 of January 1984 gave the go-ahead for the rest of this phase of the programme, with a contract for the Naval variant of the EH 101 being signed on 7 March. Following an EHI market survey the results indicated that the requirements of a medium-sized commercial helicopter and also of a military tactical transport helicopter were also compatible with the basic airframe requirements of the naval EH 101 variant. Thus it was decided that two other variants would be developed; these were the civil transport and a civil or military utility helicopter with a rear loading ramp, for which latter aircraft Agusta would have design leadership. An Integrated Development Plan was initiated to ensure that, for the first time in a major helicopter project, development of three different variants would proceed simultaneously in such a way that work on each would make a continuous contribution to the whole. This meant that civil and military customers would get the best of both worlds.

The overall design philosophy was to provide a helicopter which, when compared with other existing types, would provide substantial improvements in integrity, performance and reliability, with reduced cost of ownership and which would have a high degree of crew and passenger acceptability. Design features were to include three engines to provide high power margins, fail-safe

With a handful of collective pitch applied, Trevor Egginton gets EH 101 PP1 airborne at Yeovil. The tailplane has inverted aerofoil section.

435

damage-tolerant airframe structures and rotating components with on-board monitoring of the engines, transmission, avionics and other main systems. The RN variant was to be designed specifically for autonomous all-weather operations from a 3,500 tons frigate; thus it had to fit into a given size of hangar. It had to be capable of being launched and recovered from a frigate's platform in sea states of 5 or 6 while the ship was on any heading and with wind speeds of up to 55 knots from any direction. While the MMI variant met a number of common requirements the emphasis was placed more on shore-based operations than those at sea.

The arrowhead formation of the EH 101's General Electric CT7–6 engines can be seen in this rather shadowed view of PP3, G-EHIL, the first civil variant.

Ten pre-production aircraft were planned as being necessary to complete the comprehensive 4,000 hours development programme, one of these to be used for varous ground installations and trials. The division of the major design responsibilities was that Westland was allocated the forward fuselage incorporating the flight deck with its advanced multi-function displays, main cabin and undercarriage, the installation for the three 1,720 shp General Electric CT7-2A turboshaft engines, main-rotor blades and the flight control and fuel systems; Agusta has the rear fuselage and tail unit, the main-rotor head and transmission system—this latter system being sub-contracted to Fiat Aviazione—and the electric and hydraulic systems. The cost of this programme was to be shared equally between the two countries' Ministries and principal manufacturers involved. The aircraft were to be produced by single source manufacture of their components with the final assembly in each country of its own aircraft.

Component manufacture for the first two pre-production aircraft, PP1 and PP2, began during March 1985 at Yeovil and at Cascina Costa near Milan respectively. While these aircraft lacked the vast range of ASW systems and equipment to be carried on the operational helicopters they embodied the major features of the definitive configuration. The fuselage was designed in four sections with a tail cone, the front and centre sections being common to all three variants and of aluminium alloy stressed skin construction. The rear fuselage, while of similar construction, was modified with a slimmer after end to accommodate the rear loading ramp/door in the utility variant. The tailcone and integral tail-rotor pylon are produced in composite materials and designed to fold on the naval variants. While the naval variants are intended for single-pilot operation, the flight deck can accommodate two pilots. The ASW helicopter also has accommodation for an acoustic systems operator and an observer with the major elements of the avionics equipment being carried in the main cabin. The scanner is housed in a shallow cylindrical dome under the forward end of the cabin. In the civil transport variant the air-conditioned cabin is designed to seat 30 passengers and one cabin attendant in airline standard four-abreast seats with a centre aisle, a galley, toilet, overhead lockers and baggage stowage aft of the cabin.

The EH 101's three engines give Category A VTOL performance without payload restrictions, a 193 mph cruising speed over a 580 miles range which will enable it to operate offshore to drilling rigs and platforms, or on scheduled flights into inner city heliports at high loaded weights under the more exacting civil operations rules anticipated in future years. Up to 28 fully-equipped troops or an equivalent 6 tons load of equipment can be carried in the utility variant. The civil requirements were, in fact, in excess of those for the RN variant. The three engines are carried in an arrow-head formation above the main cabin on advanced-design anti-vibration mountings and housed in reinforced Kevlar cowlings with side-facing air intakes. Fireproof bulkheads separate the engines from each other and from the main cabin. All three engines front drive into the main gearbox. The five-blade main-rotor hub has a metal core encased in composite materials. The composite blades which can be power-folded—as can the rotor pylon—in the naval variant, have an advanced aerofoil section with special high-speed tips which embody design and aerodynamic features which stem from Westland's work on the BERP. Four composite blades are used in the tail rotor. The tricycle-type undercarriage is retractable, the twin-wheel steerable nose gear retracting into the front fuselage and the single-wheel main units into sponson-like fairings on the centre fuselage. Emergency flotation is provided by four Kevlar-reinforced polythene floats inflated from helium-charged pressure bottles. Two floats are attached to the sponson fairings and two to the aircraft's nose. Operational equipment and armament includes a 360 deg search radar, dipping sonar and sonobuoy systems, plus four Sting Ray or equivalent homing torpedoes, air-to-surface missiles, depth bombs and small calibre machine-guns. In addition to the ASW role, others envisaged for the Naval variant include over-the-horizon targeting, anti-shipping surveillance and tracking and anti-ship strikes, while troop and equipment transport, casevac and surveillance duties are foreseen for the utility variant.

Construction of the two prototypes and a cockpit simulator continued through 1985–86 with the simulator being officially commissioned by John Lee, Under Secretary of State for Defence—Procurement, on 14 May, 1986. PP1 was rolled out at a special ceremony at Yeovil, on 7 April, 1987, involving the almost mandatory light show and clouds of dry ice, at which the principal guest was

George Younger MP, then Secretary of State for Defence. Although by then the programme had slipped some six months behind schedule, EHI chairman Sir John Treacher said that it was hoped that the in-service date of 1992 would be met. There followed six months of ground testing with PP1, serialled ZF641, and of the 'iron bird' test rig at Cascina Costa before the first flight, made by Westland's chief test pilot, Trevor Egginton, and his deputy, Colin Hague, on 9 October. It was quickly followed by the second pre-production aircraft, PP2, which was flown flown by Agusta's chief test pilot Raff Longobardi, with Egginton in the left-hand seat, at Cascina Costa on 26 November. All three pilots expressed themselves delighted with their aircrafts' inflight handling characteristics, which were good in both the hover and in forward flight, the aircraft reacting smoothly to pilot inputs.

PP1 keeps station on PP3 as the first two Westland-built EH 101 development aircraft fly together for the first time in October 1988.

The first four pre-production prototypes, PP1–PP4, were used in the flight-test programme for basic development; PP5 and PP6 were to be used for development of the RN and MMI naval variants respectively; PP7, the utility variant was allocated to development of the rear ramp and its associated systems and PP8 and PP9 were allocated to development trials for the civil and utility variants respectively and for reliability and proving trials. During December 1987 ZF641 was taken off the flying programme for a lay-up after completing 50 hours running, which included eight flying hours. The aircraft was inspected, some modifications to reduce vibration in the accessory gearbox were embodied, fairings aft of the main-rotor head were re-shaped to improve the airflow over the rear fuselage and the instrumentation capability was enhanced to enable it to record some 600 parameters. ZF641 began flying again early in March 1988. While most public mention and attention appeared to be focussed on the RN and MMI variants, EHI's intention to make an early attack on the civil market was underlined when PP3, the civil variant G-EHIL, was the third EH 101 to fly, getting airborne at Yeovil on 30 September, 1988. It was piloted on its 15 min flight by Colin Hague who had succeeded Trevor Egginton as chief test pilot in April of that year. Meanwhile, Agusta was completing PP6 the MMI variant, first flying it on 26 April, 1989; then, seven weeks later on 15 June, PP4, designated the avionics development aircraft ZF644, was flown at Yeovil. It featured a full glass cockpit electronic instrument system and aircraft management computer plus a central multiplexed control unit and an RN communications system.

PP5, serialled ZF649, first flew at Yeovil on 24 October, 1989, to become the dedicated RN pre-production prototype and the first to fly with fully integrated avionics/mission systems. On this first flight with this equipment it remained airborne for one hour, then made an instrument landing in the dark, which was not on the flight plan!

In October 1988 PP1 joined PP2 at Cascina Costa where a joint Westland/ Agusta team pooled their resources in the development of the EH 101 airframe and the critical transmission and the dynamic components, the last having suffered some problems. PP1 was fitted with a modified main-rotor pylon fairing of improved aerodynamic shape and with a main-rotor having anhedral tips to the blades. This latter modification reduced by 250 hp the power required in the hover, which was much below the forecast figure. Both aircraft were flown without their low-set tailplanes, PP2's rear fuselage also being wool-tufted during this phase of the test programme. A rotor head vibration absorbing device, weighing some 200 lb, was fitted to PP1 while PP3 at Yeovil flight-tested Westland's Active Control of Structural Response (ACSR) system which senses vibration frequency and amplitude and produces an anti-phase response to counter it. It was planned to fit all production EH 101s with this ACSR which proved to be several times more powerful than any other ever flown. PP1 was scheduled to be returned to Yeovil in early 1991 ready for preliminary ship trials in the middle of the year. At Cascina Costa work on PP7, the utility variant prototype with a rear loading ramp was pressed ahead, the first flight taking place on 15 December, 1989. This aircraft was followed into the air by the

EH 101 PP5, ZF649, the Royal Navy Merlin, made its first deck landings on HMS *Norfolk* in November 1990. Notable is the large 360 deg radome under the cabin.

second civil variant, G-OIOI, which first flew on 24 April, 1990, to join G-EHIL, the first civil prototype, in the certification programme. At that time a number of civil operators had expressed interest in this EH 101 variant both for offshore and onshore operations, with the most urgent need being in the former. While Westland perceived a substantial worldwide market for the commercial aircraft, it was aware that success depended not only on early certification and in-service date but also on the long awaited production decision by the MoD.

Outside of the United Kingdom and Italy, the major source of interest in the naval variant of the EH 101 was Canada which needed a replacement for some 35 ship-borne Sikorsky CH-124 Sea King ASW/utility helicopters being flown by Canadian Armed Forces Maritime Command. That United Technologies' injection of capital in Westland had strengthened and warmed the association between the two companies was illustrated in early 1987 when Sikorsky withdrew its bid for the Canadian New Shipborne Aircraft (NSA) and endorsed the EH 101. Having eliminated the Aérospatiale Super Puma, which was seen to be near the end of its possible development life and did not measure up to the CAF specification, in August 1987 the Canadian Government confirmed its selection of the EH 101 to meet Maritime Command's NSA requirement. This was followed up in April 1988 by a contract to define an EH 101 to meet the specification of the NSA programme which, inter alia, called for a helicopter able to operate from patrol frigates and destroyers as a fully autonomous weapons system. Canada anticipated ordering forty-five EH 101s and during the contract definition phase EHI was joined by five Canadian companies; Bell Helicopter Textron Division, Canadian Marconi Co, Amtec Group, IMP Group and Paramax Electronics. To co-ordinate this international team and manage the Canadian programme, EHI formed a new company EH Industries (Canada) Inc. By early 1991 the project definition phase had been completed.

The 4,000 hours flight development programme with the eight pre-production prototypes continued through 1990 and by the end of the year they had flown

Colin Hague and the Merlin ZF649 make a precision landing on HMS *Norfolk* in November 1990.

some 850 hours in nearly 900 separate mission flights. A pitch-up problem which was identified required a redesign of the tail unit for ship-based operations of the RN Merlin and Italian naval variants. Agusta flew PP2 with a single tailplane mounted high on the starboard side of the fin, but solved the problem with a low-set high aspect ratio tailplane. Meanwhile, at Cascina Costa, a programme of rotor blade and tail fold development with PP2 confirmed that the EH 101 met its design criteria of operating from small frigates. This was followed by three days of flight trials with PP2 in the Mediterranean with Maestrale class frigates operating off the Italian Navy base at Luni. Flown by Raff Longobardi and Colin Hague with British and Italian Service pilots, PP2 was used for flying deck approaches, hovering in ship-induced turbulence and landing on the ships' platforms. During these trials the high aspect ratio assymetric tailplane, mounted on the starboard side of the rear pylon, to cure 'pitch up' during transition from or to the hover mode was also verified. Meanwhile, at Yeovil, the EH 101 'Drop Test Vehicle' which consisted of the main and nose undercarriage units and a platform carrying a 31,500 lb load of weights, was used for dropping onto steel decks.

Development and promotion of the EH 101 as a 30-seat passenger aircraft took a step forward when PP8, now named the Heliliner, made its public debut in this guise at the 1990 Farnborough International Show. Resplendent in a red, white and blue finish, it embodied a number of modifications to smooth out and direct the airflow around the main-rotor and engines. They include a 'beanie' on top of the rotor head, changes to the shape of the forward and aft cowling, which was given a 2 ft extension, and fairings over the rotor blade tension links at the root ends. These will be standard on production aircraft. The 'beanie', a circular deflector, was developed to combat 'shuffle', a low frequency lateral vibration caused by turbulence from the main-rotor head hitting the tail pylon. This quantly-named device deflects the rotor wake downwards away from the tail

The resplendent red, white and blue Heliliner, G-OIOI, alias EH 101 PP8, as it appeared in the September 1990 SBAC Display.

unit. Earlier, in April it had been decided that all production EH 101s for the Royal Navy would be powered by three 2,100 shp Rolls-Royce/Turboméca/Piaggio RTM.322-01 turboshaft engines. The fourth pre-production Westland-built aircraft PP4, which is the civil variant with a rear ramp and first flew on 16 January 1991, was scheduled as the first to be modified to accept the RTM.322 at the end of 1991.

During November 1990 PP5, the Merlin ZF649, flown by Colin Hague, made the first deck landings on HMS *Norfolk* and full ship handling trials with this vessel were scheduled to begin in June 1991.

By the end of 1990 the EH 101 programme milestones included British troop trials, which had produced two minute loading times for 30 combat-equipped troops and support weapons and 40 seconds for deplaning; rotor blade de-icing tests and single-pilot operation. EHI was awaiting the signature of MOU 4 and the move into the EH 101 production phase. This had been delayed due to an MoD desire, expressed in February 1990, to put this in the hands of a single prime contractor. Two consortia were bidding for the EH 101 Merlin prime contractorship. Westland had teamed with IBM, this latter company having had the experience of successfully integrating the ASW mission system in the US Navy's Sikorsky H-60 Sea Hawk helicopter, while British Aerospace and GEC formed a competing consortium under the name Merlin Management. With Westland still having responsibility for provision of the aircraft, the prime contractorship is principally concerned with risk taking, ensuring performance and the mission system integration. In Britain, while the Royal Navy had stated a requirement for fifty anti-submarine EH 101 Merlins and the MoD had expressed an intention to buy twenty-five tactical support variants to improve Army air mobility, these quantities were subject to variation. These latter helicopters are for operation by the Royal Air Force. The Italian Navy requirement was for forty-two EH 101s for use in the anti-submarine and anti-shipping roles while Canada had expressed a firm intention to acquire forty-five EH 101s for the ASW role. Future worldwide sales were predicted as being 800 helicopters.

In September 1991 MOU4 was signed, the MoD choosing the Westland – IBM partnership as prime contractor for an RN anti-submarine/surface vessel weapons system, the Merlin. Later, IBM Federal Systems was sold to Loral ASIC. Westland does most hands-on integration work: Loral directs activities, handles planning and contracts with Westland and Agusta. Merlin production began early in 1995. In late 1993 following a change of Government, Canada cancelled its EH101 order. When GKN – owning 22 per cent of Westland – acquired United Technologies' shares in the Group, it followed this, in February 1994, with a successful bid for the remaining shares. Westland is now a wholly-owned GKN subsidiary. Team Apache, announced at the 1994 SBAC Show, brought together Westland, McDonnell Douglas, Martin Marietta and Westinghouse to offer the Westland Apache attack helicopter (based on the US Army Longbow Apache) to meet British Army needs into the next century. A significant EH 101 milestone reached in December 1994 was civil certification of the 30-seat transport and rear-ramp variants. For the first time a helicopter was certificated simultaneously by three Authorities: the Civil Aviation Authority, Registro Aeronautico Italiano and the US Federal Aviation Administration.

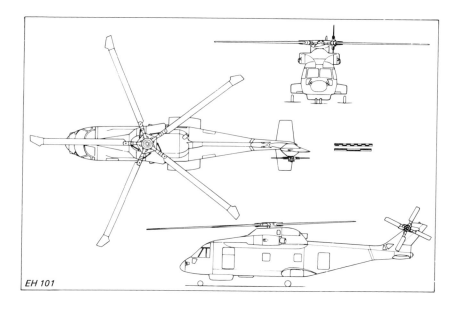

EH 101

Description: Three-engined single main-rotor civil and military multi-role helicopter. Metal and composite construction and covering.

Accommodation: One pilot plus observer and acoustic systems operator (naval variant), two pilots and 30 passengers plus one cabin staff (civil variant), two pilots and 30 fully-equipped troops or 10,000 lb cargo internally or on external sling.

Powerplant: Three 1,279 shp General Electric CT7-2A turboshaft engines (naval and utility variants) or 2,000 shp CT7-6 turboshaft engines (civil variant). Three 2,100 shp Rolls-Royce/Turboméca/Piaggio RTM.322 turboshaft engines (production variants).

Armament: Four Sting Ray or equivalent homing torpedoes, Harpoon, Sea Eagle, Exocet, or similar air-to-surface missiles, or depth bombs.

Dimensions: Main-rotor diameter 61 ft 0 in; length 75 ft 3 in (spread), 52 ft 0 in (main-rotor and tail-pylon folded); width 18 ft 0 in (main-rotor and tail-pylon folded); height 21 ft 4 in; main-rotor disc area 2,924.8 sq ft.

Weights: (N-naval, C-civil, U-utility).
Empty 15,862 lb (N), 16,126 lb (C), 16,891 lb (U)
Loaded 28,660 lb (N), 31,500 lb (C and U).

Performance: Never-exceed speed 200 mph; normal operational limit speed 193 mph; cruising speed 173 mph; design ceiling 15,000 ft; ferry range 1,150 miles; time on station for sonar dunking cycle with full weapon mission load 5 hr.

Producton: A total of nine pre-production prototypes built by Westland Helicopters and Agusta SpA as follows during 1984–1990:
PP1, PP3–5, PP8 (Westland Helicopters)
PP2, PP6–7, PP9 (Agusta SpA).

443

APPENDIX A

Individual Aircraft Notes

In this section can be found the basic data on production quantities, airframe serial and Contract numbers and service of all Westland types. Other details, not exhaustive, indicate where aircraft were allocated to the Westland company, other manufacturers or to Ministry Establishments for trials. Wherever possible the duties on which these aircraft were engaged are also included. No attempt has been made to include details of all the development flight trials conducted by Westland.

Abbreviations most frequently used in these notes and throughout the book refer to the following:

AAC	Army Air Corps
ACC Flight	Anti-Aircraft Co-operation Flight
AACU	Anti-Aircraft Co-operation Unit
A & AEE	Aeroplane and Armament Experimental Establishment
AAS	Air Armament School
ADC	Aircraft Disposal Company
AEE	Aeroplane Experimental Establishment
AFS	Advanced Flying School
A & GS	Armament and Gunnery School
AH	Army Helicopter
AOC	Air Officer Commanding
AOS	Air Observer School
ASM	Armstrong Siddeley Motors
ASR	Air-Sea Rescue
ASW	Anti-Submarine Warfare
ATC	Armament Training Camp
ATDU	Air Torpedo Development Unit
BERP	British Experimental Rotor Programme
BGS	Bombing and Gunnery School
CA	Controller of Aircraft (MoS)
CFE	Central Fighter Establishment
CFS	Central Flying School
CGS	Central Gunnery School
C.O.W.	Coventry Ordnance Works
CSA	Controller of Supplies (Air)
DTD	Directorate of Technical Development
EFTS	Elementary Flying Training School
EMC	Electro-magnetic compatibility
ETPS	Empire Test Pilots School
EWS	Electrical and Wireless School
FAA	Fleet Air Arm
FAF	French Air Force

FEAF	Far East Air Force
FFF	Free French Forces
FTS	Flying Training School
GDGS	Ground Defence Gunners School
GP	General Purpose
GRU	Gunnery Research Unit
HAD	Home Aircraft Depot
HAR	Helicopter, Air Rescue
HAS	Helicopter, Anti-Submarine
HC	Helicopter, Cargo
HT	Helicopter, Training
IAF	Indian Air Force
IFF	Identification Friend or Foe
IFTU	Intensive Flying Trials Unit
IR	Infra-red
MAEE	Marine Aircraft Experimental Establishment
MAP	Ministry of Aircraft Production
MoD	Ministry of Defence
MoS	Ministry of Supply
MoU	Memorandum of Understanding
MU	Maintenance Unit
NF	Night Fighter
ntu	not taken up
PTS	Parachute Testing Section
PV	Private Venture
RAAF	Royal Australian Air Force
RAE	Royal Aircraft Establishment (after 1988 Royal Aerospace Establishment)
RAFRS	Royal Air Force Regiment School
RCAF	Royal Canadian Air Force
RFC	Royal Flying Corps
RN	Royal Navy
RNAS	Royal Naval Air Service/Royal Naval Air Station
RNZAF	Royal New Zealand Air Force
RP	Rocket Projectile
RRE	Royal Radar Establishment
SAAF	South African Air Force
SAR	Search and Rescue
SBAC	Society of British Aircraft Constructors (after 26 February, 1964, Society of British Aerospace Companies)
S of AC	School of Army Co-operation
SOC	Struck off charge
SS	Signals School
TAF	Turkish Air Force
TI	Trial Installation of equipment
TRE	Telecommunications Research Establishment
TT	Target Tug
UHF	Ultra high frequency

VHF	Very high frequency
WAL	Westland Aircraft Ltd
WHL	Westland Helicopters Ltd

N.IB Two aircraft, N16 and N17, built to Admiralty Air Department N.IB Requirement by Westland under contract CP13699/16 during 1916–17. Development abandoned in 1917.

Wagtail. Three aircraft, C4291–4293, built to RAF Type IA Specification by Westland under Contract 41838/1/17, and two aircraft, J6581–6582, under Contract 35a/454/C448 during 1917–20. All used for ground and air trials of engines and equipment. C4291 AES (competitive evaluation August 1918); AES (gun firing trials November 1918). C4293 AES (fighter trials May 1918); RAE (engine trials May 1918). AES (engine trials July 1918). J6581 AES (December 1920 and November 1921); RAE (comparative trials with Lynx and ABC Wasp March 1921); AES (January 1922). J6582 AEE (December 1920, 23 October 1921 and April 1922); RAE (comparative trials with Lynx and ABC Wasp March 1921).

Weasel. Four aircraft, F2912–2914 and J6577, built to Specification D or R Type 2 by Westland under Contract 35a/1020/C381 during 1918–19. All used for ground and air trials of engines and equipment at Yeovil, AES and RAE. F2912 AES (Dragonfly engine and handling checks April 1919, crashed November 1919); F2913 AES (performance trials September 1920); RAE (level speed trials 1923 and Jupiter IV exhaust manifold and temperature checks 1924). F2914 AEE (Jaguar engine and handling checks November 1919 and stability tests November 1920); RAE (Jaguar supercharger trials 1923 and carburettor and steel variable-pitch propeller tests 1924). J6577 AEE (Jaguar engined performance trials July 1920, November 1921 and March 1922).

Limousine 1. One prototype, K126 (later G-EAFO) built by Westland during 1919. Written off in a ground collision with a Fairey Fawn at RAF Netheravon on 3 September, 1925.

Limousine II. Five aircraft, G-EAJL, 'MV, 'RE, 'RF and 'RG, built by Westland during 1919–22. 'RE scrapped 19 June, 1923; 'RF scrapped 16 May, 1923; 'RG scrapped 10 September, 1923. Construction of sixth aircraft, G-EARH was abandoned and the rear fuselage was used in building the Limousine III G-EARV in 1920.

Limousine III. Two aircraft, G-EARV and 'WF, built by Westland during 1920–21. 'RV scrapped during 1924. Second airframe, built under Contract 254221/20 dated 11 November, 1920, was allocated serial J6851 but it was not taken up. It was scrapped on 12 April, 1922, after service with Instone Air Line at Croydon.

Walrus. A total of 36 aircraft, N9500–9535, built by Westland during 1920–23. Operated by RAF Squadrons: No.3 (later 421 and 422 Flights), 423 Flight. Trials aircraft: N9500 AEE (evaluation trials May 1921). N9502 RAE (radiator tests 1924 and 1925, oil cooler and fuel pump tests 1925 and 1926). N9506 RAE (aerial target and glider tests 1925). N9515 AEE (handling trials with high-lift wing August 1921). N9521 RAE (vapour separation tests 16 October, 1922). N9523 AEE (performance trials April 1921). N9529 RAE (general handling tests July 1923).

Dreadnought. One aircraft, J6986, built to Specification 6/21 by Westland under Contract 382430/23 during 1922–24. Crashed during first take-off at Yeovil on 9 May, 1924, and written off.

Woodpigeon. Two aircraft, G-EBIY and G-EBJV, built by Westland during 1924 for Lympne Light Aeroplane Competition. G-EBIY sold to Flying Officer A F Scroggs, finally Miss C O'Brien, was in Bowers' scrap yard at Ferrybridge, Yorks, during 1949. G-EBJV sold to L Taylor, then to L J C Mitchell, then J E Crossland-McClure. C of A last renewed 6 May, 1932.

Widgeon I/II. One aircraft, G-EBJT, built by Westland during 1924. First flown with a Blackburne Thrush engine on 22 September, 1924. Crashed on 27 September while taking part in the Air Ministry Light Aeroplane Competition at Lympne. Rebuilt with some modifications and an Armstrong Siddeley Genet I to become the prototype Widgeon II. Written off in a crash near Detling, Kent, on 19 October, 1930.

Widgeon III. One prototype, G-EBPW, built by Westland during 1926–27. First flown with a Cirrus II during late March 1927. Crashed after colliding with a Blackburn Bluebird at Bournemouth on 6 June, 1927. Eighteen other Widgeon IIIs as follows: G-EBRL used by Robert Bruce, crashed at Yeovil 3 June, 1931; G-EBRM to R G Cazalet, converted to Widgeon IIIA in 1929; G-EBRN to Wg Cdr E R Manning, burned at Stranraer in 1951; G-EBRO to Westland, scrapped during 1939–45 war; G-EBRP to the French Motor Car Co., Delhi, India, became G-IAAW; G-EBRQ to Sqn Ldr H M Probyn, Old Sarum, withdrawn from use January 1936; G-EBUB to Australia as G-AUHU, became VH-UHU and still airworthy in February 1991; G-EBUC registration reserved for Westland but not taken up; spare airframe; G-EBUD to Brockway Motors Ltd, Sydney, Australia, as G-AUIN, became VH-UIN, crashed at Grenfell, New South Wales; G-EBUE (same as G-EBUC); G-AADE to Carill S Napier, crashed at Beaulieu, Hants, 10 July, 1932. In addition G-AIGI sold to Airgold in New Guinea, but became VH-UGI in Australia; G-AUIY, 'KA, 'KE and 'KP to Australia; G-UAAH to the Port Elizabeth Light Aero Club, South Africa, plus one other, c/n WA 1683, for which no evidence can be found to confirm its reported export to Newfoundland.

Widgeon IIIA. Five aircraft built by Westland during 1929–30 as follows: G-AAFD *Miss Ethyl* for the Anglo-American Oil Co; G-AAFN Westland demonstrator; G-AAGH Westland communications aircraft 1930–48 crashed after unmanned take-off on 27 July, 1948: G-AAJF to Miss C R Leathart; G-AALB to W J McDonough, Winnipeg, Canada; G-EBRM, a Widgeon III, owned by R G Cazalet, was converted to Widgeon IIIA standard during 1929.

Yeovil. Three aircraft, J7508–7510, built to Specification 26/23 by Westland under Contract 445077/24 during 1924–26. All used for development and trials flying. J7508 A & AEE (performance trials April–July and September–October 1926). J7509 No.11 Squadron (service trials August 1925); RAE (Condor trials September 1925, supercharger trials 1927 and Condor IIIA with Hele-Shaw Beecham propeller trials 1928). J7510 RAE (R/T transmission trials December 1926) last flown 22 March, 1928.

Wizard. One aircraft built by Westland as a private venture during 1926–27. First flown with a Rolls-Royce Falcon III. Rebuilt with a Rolls-Royce F.XI and designated Wizard I, J9252, in 1927. Rolls-Royce F.XIS fitted and aircraft designated Wizard II. A & AEE (performance trials June 1926, January–April 1928; performance and handling trials August 1929–April 1930. March and November 1931).

Westbury. Two aircraft, J7765–7766, built to Specification 4/24 by Westland under Contract 542527//24 during 1925–27. J7765 A & AEE (initial evaluation October 1926); J7766 A & AEE (handling trials February 1927, C.O.W. gun trials August 1931).

Wapiti. One prototype, J8495, built by Westland to Specifiction 26/27 under Contract 720155/26 during 1927. First flown on 7 March, 1927. A & AEE (evaluation March 1927); Westland (April 1927) No.12 Squadron (service trials) and A & AEE (June 1927); No.39 Squadron (service trials) and A & AEE (July 1927); Bristol Aeroplane Co (600 hp Pegasus IM trials 1928); Westland (February 1929); RAE (July–September 1929); A & AEE (September–November 1929); Bristol Aeroplane Co (October 1930); RAE (October 1931); Westland (October 1931) RAE (Pegasus development February–June 1934).

Wapiti Mk.I. First production batch of 25 aircraft, J9078–9102, built by Westland under Contract 790464/27 during 1927–28.
Operated by RAF: Nos.5,11,20,30,39,60,84,100,601,602,604,605 Squadrons. Trials aircraft: J9082 A & AEE (1928–30); J9084 MAEE (on floats, June 1928 and March–May 1929), A & AEE (dropping trials October 1932); J9101 RAE (July–August 1928) 39 and 101 Sqns (Jupiter tests October–November 1928); J9102 Bristol Aeroplane (Jupiter development 1929) A & AEE (oil pump tests July 1930), RAE (Phoenix I CI engine. Heated clothing trials June 1933). Bristol Aeroplane (Phoenix I trials; with Phoenix II set a height record for diesel engines at 27,453 ft in May, 1934). Special aircraft: J9095 (modified for use by Prince of Wales 1928); J9096 (modified for VIP transport, 24 Sqn June 1928–July 1930, 605 Sqn January 1931. Crashed 16 February, 1931, 605 Sqn 1934).

Wapiti Mk.IA. First production batch of 28 aircraft, A5-1–A5-28, built by Westland for Royal Australian Air Force during 1928–29.

Wapiti Mk.II. First production batch of 10 aircraft, J9237–9246, built by Westland under Contract 813644/27 during 1928–29.

Operated by RAF: Nos.55 and 84 Squadrons. Trials aircraft: J9237, Rockcliffe, Canada (cold weather trials on skis, March 1930–May 1932); J9238 A & AEE (comparison trials, December 1928, performance evaluation September 1930).

Wapiti Mk.IIA. One prototype, J9247, built by Westland under Contract 805331/27 during 1928. RAE (June 1928), Westland (November 1928), A & AEE (September 1930), Westland (Jaguar VI fitted as Mk.III prototype), A & AEE (July 1931–June 1932), Westland (Panther IIa fitted as Mk.VIII prototype), A & AEE (February–March 1934)

Wapiti Mk.IIA. First production batch of 35 aircraft, J9380–9414, built by Westland under Contract No.834731/28 during 1928–29.
Operated by RAF: Nos.5,11,20,27,28,30,31,39 and 84 Squadrons. Trials aircraft: J9382 A & AEE (comparative tests Jupiter VIIIS January 1929 and March 1931); Westland (fit bomb racks June 1931); A & AEE (October 1931); RAE (December 1931); Shoeburyness (SOC July 1936).

Wapiti Mk.III. First production batch of four aircraft, P601–604, built by Westland for South African Air Force during 1929.

Wapiti Mk.IIA. Second production batch of 34 aircraft, J9481–9514, built by Westland under Contract 880023/28 Part I during 1929.
Operated by RAF: Nos.5,11,20,27,28,30,31,39,55,60 and 84 Squadrons and other units including HQ Flights New Delhi and Lahore, Communications Flight New Delhi, FTS and IAF. Trials aircraft: J9487 MAEE (on floats May 1929); J9498 Shorts (on floats July 1929); J9501 A & AEE. Other aircraft: J9496, J9499 (IAF).

Wapiti Mk.IIA. Third production batch of 45 aircraft, J9592–9636 built by Westland under Contract 880023/28 Part 2 during 1929.
Operated by RAF: Nos.30,55,84,500,600,601,602,603,605,608 Squadrons. Trials aircraft: J9604 RAE (propeller and IR photo trials February 1932, camera gun trials June 1933). Other aircraft: J9612 and J9617 (to RCAF as 539 and 540 October 1937); J9618 (sold to Essex Flying Club January 1938); J9633 (IAF).

Wapiti Mk.IIA. Fourth production batch of 17 aircraft, J9708–9724, built by Westland under Contract 915859/29 during 1929–30.
Operated by RAF: Nos.5,11,20,27,28,31,39 and 60 Squadrons, and IAF. Other aircraft: J9711 (IAF).

Wapiti Mk.IIA. Fifth production batch of 37 aircraft: J9835–9871, built by Westland under Contract 933774/29 during 1929–30.
Operated by RAF: Nos.5,30,55,84,501,600,601,602,603,605,607 and 608 Squadrons. Other aircraft: J9854 (IAF); J9867 (sold to Essex Flying Club January 1938); J9868–71 (to RCAF as 541–4 October 1937).

Wapiti Mk.V. First production batch of 35 aircraft, J9725–9759, built by Westland under Contract 915859/29 during 1930.

449

Operated by RAF Nos.5,11,20,27,28,31 and 60 Squadrons and IAF. Trials aircraft: J9728 Westland (fitted with Bristol Draco I diesel engine), A & AEE (July and August 1930), RAE (August 1930 and November 1931, brake trials 1932, IFR with Virginia June 1934, last flown December 1936); other aircraft: J9735, '38,'40,'42,'54,'57 (IAF).

Wapiti Mk.IIA. Sixth production batch of 36 aircraft, K1112–1157, built by Westland during 1930.
Operated by RAF: as for previous batch. Trials aircraft: K1129 A & AEE (long-range trials September 1930, windscreen trials August 1932). Other aircraft: K1126 (IAF); K1139,'43,'46,'48,'49,'52 (to RCAF as 527–29, 508,530,509).

Wapiti Mk.IIA. Seventh production batch of 56 aircraft; K1254–1309, built by Westland during 1930–31.
Operated by RAF: Nos.2,5,27,28,31 and 60 Squadrons and IAF. Other aircraft: K1254,'57,'60,'63,'66,'69,'73,'76,'89,'90,'98, K1308 (IAF).

Wapiti Mk.IIA. Eighth production batch of 100 aircraft; K1316–1415, built by Westland during 1930–31.
Operated by RAF: Nos.30,55,60,84,501, 600,601,604,607 and 608 Squadrons and IAF. Trials aircraft: K1380 A & AEE (performance trials 1931). Other aircraft: K1394, K1403 (IAF); K1318,'22,'24–'26,'28–'30,'36,'42,'66,'78 (to RCAF as 510,'31,'32,'11–'13,'33–'35,'38,'37,'36).

Wapiti Mk.VI. First production batch of 16 aircraft: K2236–2251, built by Westland during 1931.
Operated by RAF: Nos.501,502,503,601,602,605,607 and 608 Squadrons. (K2248–2251 not delivered).

Wapiti Mk.IIA. Ninth production batch of 69 aircraft, K2252–2320, built by Westland during 1931–32.
Operated by RAF: Nos.5,27,31,60,503,504 Squadrons and IAF. Trials aircraft: K2262 (RAE November 1931); K2287 (RAE); Other aircraft: K2276–7,'89,'94, K2303–4 (IAF); K2257,'62,'66,'68,'86,'87 (RAAF).
(All Wapitis converted to Wallaces listed under Wallace aircraft notes).

Wapiti Mk.VI. First production batch of 16 aircraft, K2236–2551, built by Westland during 1932.
Operated by RAF: Some squadrons equipped with Wapiti Mk.IIA aircraft and other units.

Wapiti VIII. First production batch of four aircraft built by Westland for China about 1932.

Witch. One aircraft, J8596, built to Specification 23/25 by Westland under Contract 716899/26 during 1926–27. First flown at RAF Andover on 30 January, 1928. A & AEE (performance trials April 1928); became Witch II with Bristol

Jupiter VIIIF; A & AEE (August 1929); Henlow Parachute Test Section (1929–31).

Pterodactyl IA. One aircraft, J9251, built to Specification 23/26 by Westland under Contract 730449/27 during 1926–28. Used for ground and air trials at Yeovil. Re-engined to become Mk.IB. RAE (handling trials 11 September, 1928). New undercarriage fitted to become Mk.IC. Displayed at RAE Farnborough 14 June, 1930, and last flown there on 31 July, 1930.

F.20/27 Interceptor. One prototype, J9124, built to Specification F.20/27 by Westland under Contract 813869/27 during 1928–29. First flight during August 1928. A & AEE (handling trials, May 1929–March 1930); RAE (handling trials October 1931–32, last flown 14 March, 1933).

Westland IV. One prototype, G-EBXK, and one production aircraft, G-AAGW, built by Westland during 1928–29. Both were converted to Wessex standard. G-EBXK (to National Aviation Day Displays July 1935, withdrawn from use May 1936) G-AAGW (to Imperial Airways November 1929; withdrawn from use with No.11 Air Observer and Navigator School, RAF Watchfield, August 1940).

Wessex. Eight aircraft built by Westland during 1929–33. G-ABAJ (previously provisionally registered G-AAJI but with Kenyan registration VP-KAD allocated for Wilson Airways, Nairobi. Neither taken up. To SABENA as OO-AGC June 1930, restored to British Register March 1935. To Sir Alan Cobham. Scrapped 1938); OO-AGD (previously allocated G-AULF for Shell Company of Australia. To SABENA July 1930 when Shell order cancelled. Destroyed by fire at Evère, Brussels, 8 December, 1934); G-ABEG (to Imperial Airways May 1933. Damaged beyond repair N Rhodesia 1936), G-ABVB (to PSIoWA 1932. Damaged beyond repair Isle of Wight 30 May, 1936); G-ACHI (to Imperial Airways 1933. Withdrawn from use May 1940) G-AGIJ (to Egyptian Air Force as W202 May 1934); OO-AGE (to SABENA 6 August, 1930. To Sir Alan Cobham as G-ADEW March 1935. Ditched in English Channel 3 July, 1935); OO-AGF (to SABENA 30 August, 1930. To Sir Alan Cobham as G-ADFZ March 1935. Registration cancelled 1 December, 1946)

F.29/27 C.O.W. Gun Fighter. One aircraft J9565, built to Specification F.29/27 by Westland under Contract 881545/28 during 1929–30. A & AEE (performance and handling trials April 1931 and March 1932–July 1934): Henlow (26 November, 1935. Instructional airframe 738M 31 December, 1935).

Pterodactyl IV. One prototype, K1947, built to Specification 16/29 by Westland under Contract 948111/29 during 1930–31. Development and evaluation flying at Yeovil. A & AEE (handling trials September 1931); RAE (stability and control checks May 1932 and 1934, and pilot training May 1933, struck off charge 12 August, 1938).

PV.3. One prototype, P.3 (later K4048) built as a private venture by Westland to Contract 279524/33 during 1930–33. A & AEE (March 1931). Development halted. Converted to a high-altitude photographic and research aircraft, G-ACAZ, for use by the 1933 Houston Mount Everest Expedition team during 1932–33. Made first successful over-flight of Mount Everest on 3 April, 1933. Serialled K4048, it flew with No.501 Squadron before being used as a flying test-bed for engine development by Bristol Aeroplane Co. RAE (Pegasus development June 1934 and preparation for RAF Display, Hendon.)

Wallace. One prototype Wallace, P.6, a converted Wapiti V G-AAWA, built by Westland as a private venture during 1931. First flew on 31 October, 1931. Modified for use by Houston Mount Everest Expedition, registered G-ACBR, and flown over the peak on 3 and 19 April, 1933. Returned to UK in May and exhibited in RAF Display at Hendon on 24 June, 1933. Reconverted to Wallace I standard. To No.501 Squadron as K3488, then to Westland and A & AEE (gunner's cockpit evaluation February 1934). As Wallace II it was at A & AEE (handling trials April 1935).

Wallace Mk.I. Production batch of 12 aircraft, K3562–3573 (converted from Wapiti IIAs K1346, '45, '32, '33, '47, '31, '51. '48, '49, '50, '52, '53) built by Westland under Contract 200962/32 during 1932–33.
Operated by RAF: No.501 Squadron and other units including AACU, AAF, AAS, AOS, ATC, BGS, FTS, GDGS and Station Flights. Trials aircraft: K3562 A & AEE (performance trials and type test March 1933).

Wallace Mk.I. Second production batch of 14 aircraft K3664–3677 (converted from Wapiti IIAs K1354–1365, J9864, J9605) built by Westland under Contract 249751/33 during 1933–34.
Operated by miscellaneous RAF units including AAF, AACU, AAS, AOS, ATC, BGS, GDGS and Station Flights. Trials aircraft: K3573 A & AEE (performance tests December 1933), K3673 A & AEE (performance trials December 1933). This latter Wallace was presented to Tonbridge School Officers' Training Corps.

Wallace Mk.I. Third production batch of eight new aircraft, K3906–3913, built by Westland under Contract 251009/33 during 1933–34.
Operated by RAF: Nos.501, 504 Squadrons and other units including AAS, AOS, ATC, BGS, EWS, GDGS.

Wallace Mk.I. One aircraft, K4010 (converted from Wapiti VI K2245) built by Westland under Contract 49752/33 during 1933–34. Trials aircraft RAE and A & AEE (handling trials in October 1934).

Wallace Mk.I. Fourth production batch of nine aircraft, K4012–4020, (converted from Wapiti IIAs K1334, '39, '41, '44, '70, '72–'75) built by Westland under Contract 251010/33 during 1933–34. Operated by RAF: Nos.504 Squadron and other units including AAC Flight, AOS, BGS, EWS, RAFC.

Wallace Mk.I and Mk.II. Fifth production batch of 12 aircraft, K4337–4345 (Mk.I) K4346–K4348 (Mk.II) (converted from Wapiti IIAs K2306–2317) built by Westland under Contract 330688/34 during 1934–35.
Operated by RAF: Nos.24, 502 and 503 Squadrons and other units including AAS, AOS, ATC, BGS, EWS, GDGS, GRU. Trials aircraft: K4344, K4345 (RAE), K4346 A & AEE (weighing and handling trials February 1935).

Wallace Mk.I. Sixth production batch of 12 aircraft, K5071–5082, (converted from Wapiti IIAs K2318–K2320, '79, '80, K2252, '54, '60, '64, '66, K1412, '13) built by Westland under Contract 375777/34 during 1935.
Operated by RAF: Nos.502, 503, 504 Squadrons and other units including AOS, ATC, BGS, EWD, GDGS, RAFC.

Wallace Mk.I. One aircraft, K5116 (converted from civil-registered Wallace G-ACJU) built by Westland under Contract 375777/34 during 1935.
Operated by miscellaneous RAF units including AOS, ATC, BGS.

Wallace Mk.II. First production batch of 75 aircraft, K6012–6086, built by Westland under Contract 410770/35 during 1935–36.
Operated by RAF: Nos.501, 502, 503, 504 Squadrons and other units including AAC Flights, AACU, AAS, AOS, ATC, BGS, EWS, FTS, GDGS, RAFRS, SS, Station Flights. Trials aircraft: K6039 (RAE), K6055 (A & AEE).

Wallace Mk.II. Second production batch of 29 aircraft, K8674–8702, built by Westland under Contract 496398/36 during 1936.
Operated by miscellaneous RAF units including AAC Flights, AACU, AOS, ATC, BGS, FTS, GDGS, SS, Station Flights. Trials aircraft: K3571 RAE (target towing 1933), K3673 RAE (arrester system trials and IFR with Overstrand trials April 1930), K4010 Bristol Aeroplane and RAE (Pegasus IV development 1936), K4344 and K4345 RAE (stabilised bomb sight and target towing 1938), K4344 RN Lee-on-Solent (smoke generator trials 15 November, 1939), K8679 (A & AEE).

PV.7. One aircraft, P.7, built as a private venture to Specification G.4/31 by Westland during 1932–33. A & AEE (evaluation trials July-August 1934). Written off in a crash at A & AEE on 25 August, 1934.

Pterodactyl V. One aircraft, P.8/K2770, built to Specification F.2/32 by Westland during 1932. First flown at RAF Andover during May 1934. Development flying at Yeovil until summer 1935. Transported to RAE on 8 June, 1936, for storage. Struck off charge 15 July, 1937.

C.29. One prototype built by Westland during 1933–34. Ground testing begun and abandoned in April 1934 at Yeovil. RAE (ground running 11 December, 1934. Struck off charge 26 June, 1939).

PV.4 F.7/30. One aircraft, K2891, built to Specification F.7/30 by Westland under Contract 189221/32 during 1932–34. First flown at RAF Andover on 23

March, 1934. Subsequently used for experimental flying at Yeovil. A & AEE (evaluation trials May 1934 and performance trials February 1935). Development terminated in 1934. Subsequently used for experimental flying at Yeovil and RAE. To RAF Halton S of TT (sent as components 3 July, 1935).

P.39 Lysander. Two prototypes, K6127 and K6128, built to Specification A.39/34 by Westland under Contract 415936/35 during 1935–36. K6127 first flown on 15 June, 1936. Hendon (RAF Display 27 June, 1936), A & AEE (Inspection by HM the King 8 July, 1936, handling trials 27 July, 1937, and evaluation trials July 1939), RAE (handling, September 1936, 28 July, 1937; research handling 18 June, 1938, 1939 and 9 October, 1940). K6128 first flown on 11 December, 1936. A & AEE (handling and performance trials, December 1936 and handling July 1939). Miramshah (tropical and field trials with No.5 Squadron RAF 1938), instructional airframe 8 July, 1940.

Lysander Mk.I. First production batch of 66 aircraft, L4673–4738, part of mixed Mks.I and II batch, built by Westland under Contract 555425/36 during 1937–38. Operated by RAF: Nos.2,4,6,13,16,26,173,208,237,287,613,614,695 Squadrons and other units including S of AC. Trials aircraft: L4673, final conference aircraft; A & AEE (performance trials 1938), ventral gun installation, crashed June 1940. L4674 A & AEE (performance trials 1938). L4678, L4681, L4682, L4703 (Finland as LY123–LY126).

Lysander Mk.II. First production batch of 78 aircraft, L4739–4816, part of mixed Mks.I and II batch, built by Westland under Contract 555425/36 during 1937–38.
Operated by RAF: Nos.2,4,6,13,16,20,26,28,81,116,208,225,231,237,239,241, 268,285,286,287,288,400 (ex-110 RCAF), 614 and 695 Squadrons and other units including S o AC. Other aircraft: L4798 (FFF).

Lysander Mk.I. Second production batch of 35 aircraft, P1665–1699, part of a mixed Mks.I and II batch, built by Westland under Contract 611814/37.
Operated by RAF: Squadrons as first batch. Other aircraft, P1666, P1668, P1680–81, P1683 converted to TT Mk.III.

Lysander Mk.II. Second production batch of 174 aircraft, L6847–6888, N1200–1227, N1240–1276, N1289–1320, P1711–P1745, part of a mixed Mks.I and II batch, built by Westland under Contract 611814/37.
Operated by RAF: Squadrons as first batch. Other aircraft: L6869, N1208, N1245, N1300, P1713, P1735–36, P1738 (FFF), N1209, N1320 converted to TT Mk.III, 01 (FAF), 61-66 (IAC), P1723 (dorsal turret TI).

Lysander Mk.I. Third production batch of 68 aircraft, R2572, R2575–R2600, R2612–R2652, part of a mixed Mks.I and II batch, built by Westland under Contract 981730/39.
Operated by RAF: Squadrons as previous batches. Other aircraft R2650 (REAF), R2572, R2575, R2578, R2581, R2587, R2588–89, R2591, R2593–4, R2597–8, R2632, R2638 converted to TT Mk.I. R2650 (REAF).

Lysander Mk.II. Third production batch of 100 aircraft, P9051–P9080, P9095–P9140, P9176–P9199, part of a mixed Mks.I and II batch, built by Westland under Contract 981730/39.

Operated by RAF: Squadrons as previous batches. Other aircraft P9105 RAE (Stieger wing research 1940–41), P9059, P9078, P9102–3, P9134, P9181, P9184 (FFF), P9109–11, P9113–5, P9117, P9123, P9125, P9128, P9130, P9133 converted to TT Mk.III. 3101–3136 (TAF).

Lysander Mk.II Fourth production batch of 47 aircraft, R1987–R2010, R2025–R2047, built by Westland under Contract 994551/39.

Operated by RAF: Squadrons as previous batches. Other aircraft R2036, R2039–40, R2043, R2045–6 (FFF) R2047 (RCAF).

Lysander Mk.III. First production batch of 350 aircraft, R8991–R9030, R9056–R9079, R9100–R9135, T1422–T1470, T1501–T1535, T1548–T1590, T1610–T1655, T1670–T1709, T1735–T1771, built by Westland under Contract 23637/39.

Operated by RAF: Nos. 4,13,16,116,225,231,237,239,241,285,287,288,309,400 (ex-110 RCAF) 613,614 Squadrons. Other aircraft: R8991–R8999 (Finland as LY114–LY122 1940), R9000 (REAF), T1570 (RN as TT Mk.III), T1739 (BOAC), T1445, T1450, T1453, T1456, T1458, T1461, T1532, T1534, T1571, T1583, T1616, T1623, T1626, T1633, T1642, T1674–79, T1688, T1692, T1699, T1746, T1750, T1752, T1763 converted to TT Mk.III.

Lysander Mk.III. Second production batch of 500 aircraft, W6675–W6724, W6733–W6782, W6788–W6817, W6824–W6863, W6869–W6888, W6896–W6938, W6961–W6990, W6999–W7048, W7053–W7082, W7091–W7140, W7145–W7184, W7192–W7241, ordered under Contract B54504/39, part of a mixed Mks.III and IIIA batch. Only 17 aircraft, W6939–W6945, W6951–W6960, built by Westland (Doncaster), the remainder were cancelled.

Operated by RAF: Squadrons as first batch.

Lysander Mk.IIIA. First production batch of 347 aircraft, V9280–V9329, V9347–V9386, V9401–V9450, V9472–V9521, V9538–V9557, V9570–V9619, V9642–V9681, V9704–V9750, built by Westland under Contract B54504/39 part of a mixed Mks. III and IIIA batch.

Operated by RAF: Nos. 4,13,16,138,148,161,225,275,276,277,278,285,309,357, 414,598 Squadrons. Other aircraft V9317, V9506, V9583, V9741 plus some 20 other aircraft (USAAF), V9614 (FFF), V9309, V9321, V9363, V9439, V9555, V9594, V9705, V9729 (Portugal), V9372, V9579, V9679, V9726 converted to glider tugs.

Lysander TT Mk.IIIA. First production batch of 100 aircraft, V9751–V9753, V9775–V9824, V9844–V9868, V9885–V9906, built by Westland.

Operated by RAF. As previous batch.

Lysander Mk.II. First production batch of 75 aircraft, 416–490, built by National Steel Car Corporation under three contracts for 21, seven and 47 aircraft during

1938–42.
Operated by RCAF: Nos.2,110,112,118,123 Squadrons and other units including 11 RCAF BGSs. Postwar 433 became CF-DRL, 451-CF-DGI-X, 700 and ex-RAF R2047-CF-GFJ.

Lysander Mk.III. First production batch of 150 aircraft, 2305–2454, built as TT Mk.IIIs, by National Steel Car Corporation during 1942. Operated by RCAF: Eleven RCAF BGSs as part of the BCATP. Postwar 2382 became CF-FOA.

CL.20. One aircraft, G-ACYI, built by Westland during 1934–35. Development abandoned and aircraft scrapped in 1938.

P.9 Whirlwind. Two aircraft, L6844 and L6845, built to Specification F.37/35 by Westland under Contract 556965/36 during 1937–39. L6844 first flew 11 October, 1938. RAE (handling trials, January 1939); A & AEE (evaluation trials, March 1939); RAE (wind-tunnel tests February–May 1940); A & AEE (July 1940); AFDU (February 1942); 4S of TT (April 1942 became 3063M). L6845 first flew 29 March, 1939. A & AEE (propeller comparative trials June 1939); No.25 Sqn (May 1940); A & AEE (July 1940); No.263 Sqn (July 1940 and August 1941).

Whirlwind Mk.I. First production batch of 200 aircraft, P6966–P7015, P7035–P7064, P7089–P7122 to be built by Westland under Contract 980384/39 during 1940–41, (114 aircraft built). P7123–P7128, P7158–P7177, P7192–P7221, P7240–P7269 cancelled.
Operated by RAF: Nos.137 and 263 Squadrons. Trials aircraft: P6980 A & AEE (handling trials November 1940). P6997 A & AEE (handling trials April–May 1941).

Whirlwind Mk.I. Second production batch of 200 aircraft, R4243–R4283, R4296–R4325, R4345–R4384, R4400–R4445, R4460–R4479, R4499–R4521 to be built by Westland under Contract 20186/39, was cancelled.

P.14 Welkin. Two aircraft, DG558/G and DG562/G built to Specification F.4/40 by Westland under Contract Ctts/Acft/633 during 1940–42. DG558/G first flew 1 November, 1942. A & AEE (handling trials January 1943). DG562/G first flew in March 1943. A & AEE (propeller trials April 1943; armament trials August 1943, assessment of Merlin RM.165M engines 1945).

Welkin Mk.I. First production batch of 100 aircraft, DX278–DX295, DX308–DX349, DX364–DX389, DX407–420 to be built by Westland under Contract Ctts/Acft/1350/SAS/C.23(a) during 1942–44 (75 aircraft built plus 25 airframes less engines). None issued to RAF squadrons. Two aircraft, DX286 and DX289, issued to Fighter Interception Unit, RAF Wittering, May–July 1944 and later to the Air Fighting Development Unit.
Trials aircraft: DX278 A & AEE (intensive flying October–November 1943); DX279 A & AEE (handling trials September 1947); DX282 A & AEE

(intensive flying December 1943–January 1944); DX327 A & AEE (aileron checks March 1945); DX328 RAE (March 1945); DX329 Rotol Airscrews (propeller development November 1944 and March 1945). DX330 Rotol Airscrews (propeller trials 1944–47); DX340 Rolls-Royce (engine development).

Welkin NF.Mk.II. Two aircraft, PF370 and PF376 to be built as conversion of Welkin Mk.I, DX386 and possibly DX408, to Specification F.9/43 by Westland under Contract SB.26569 during 1943–44. PF370 first flew 23 October, 1944. A & AEE (evaluation trials January 1945). Westland pressure-cabin trials as P.17, and MoS Radar trials at TRE Pershore. Re-serialled WE997. Second prototype, PF376, cancelled.

W.34. Six aircraft, TS371, TS375, TS378, TS380, TS384, TS387 built to Specification N.11/44 by Westland under Contract Acft/4522/C.23(c) during 1945–48. TS371 first flew on 12 December, 1946. Crashed 15 October, 1947; TS375 first flew 10 September, 1947, A & AEE (handling trials, March 1949, and May 1950); TS378 A & AEE and HMS *Implacable* (deck handling and ADDL trials, May–June 1948); A & AEE and HMS *Illustrious* (deck landing trials, May–June 1949); A & AEE (May–June 1950); TS380 A & AEE and HMS *Illustrious* (deck landing trials, July 1948); RAE (NAD trials, July-November 1949); TS384 (armament trials, WAL); Rolls-Royce (engine development, June 1948–April 1949, written off in forced landing); TS387 A & AEE (handling trials, March 1949); RAE (crash barrier trials, July 1950). SOC 1951.

Wyvern TF.Mk.1. Ten pre-production aircraft, VR131–VR140, to be built to Specification 17/46P by Westland under Contract 6/Acft/386/CB.9(c) during 1948–49. There is no evidence that the last three aircraft were completed. VR131 de Havilland Propellers (May 1949), Rotol Airscrews (August 1949). VR132 A & AEE (handling trials February–April 1950); RNEC Manadon (instructional airframe, 1954); VR133 HMS *Eagle* (carrier trials, 1952); RAE (crash barrier trials, 1953); VR134 A & AEE (handling trials, February–April 1950); RAE (propeller development trials, November 1950, SOC November 1953); VR135 RNAS Yeovilton (instructional aircraft, May 1950); RNAS Bramcote (instructional airframe, A2227 June 1957); VR136 RNAS Gosport (instructional aircraft, May 1950); VR137 College of Aeronautics, Cranfield (vibration testing techniques demonstrator airframe, November 1950–May 1963); RNAS Yeovilton (FAA Museum, February 1966).

W.35 Wyvern TF.Mk.2 Three aircraft, VP109, VP113, VP120, built to Specification N.12/45 by Westland under Contract Acft/5982/CB.9(c) during 1948–49. VP109 first flew 22 March, 1949. A & AEE (handling trials, August 1949); RAE (arresting trials, May–June 1950); RAE (vibration investigation, December 1950, crashed 24 April 1952); VP113 first flew 30 August, 1949, SBAC Display, Farnborough, 5–11 September, 1949; RAE (various pre-spinning checks, September and October 1949); crashed at Yeovil 31 October, 1949; VP120 first flew 18 January, 1949. Rolls-Royce (July 1949); Napier (April 1959); RAE (crash barrier trials, September 1950, SOC February 1951).

Wyvern TF.Mk.2. Pre-production batch of 20 aircraft, VW867–VW886, built to Specification 21/48P by Westland under Contract 6/Acft/1536/CB.9(c) during 1947–48. All used for flight handling and engine development trials variously by A & AEE, RAE, WAL, ASM and FAA between May 1950 and 1958. VW870, VW873, VW880–VW886 converted to Wyvern S.Mk.4s.

Wyvern T.Mk.3. One aircraft, VZ739, built to Specification T.12/48 by Westland under Contract 6/Acft/2998 during 1949–50. First flew on 11 February, 1950. Manufacturers trials. Force landed on 3 November, 1950, and written off.

Wyvern S.Mk.4. First production batch of 50 aircraft, VZ745–VZ766, VZ772–VZ799 built by Westland under Contract 6/Acft/2879/CB(a).
Operated by Royal Navy Fleet Air Arm; Nos.703,787,813,827 Squadrons.
Trials aircraft: VZ745 A & AEE (emergency hydraulic system investigations, July–November 1952); A & AEE (handling trials); RAE (arrester trials, February–September 1955), Rotol Airscrews (propeller development, February–September 1953); ASM (engine development, October 1953. Crashed 18 May, 1954). VZ748 RAE (rudder overbalance trials, January–June 1953); A & AEE (handling and performance checks, December 1953–February 1954); A & AEE (cockpit canopy jettisoning trials, May 1954 and January–February 1955); HMS *Ark Royal* (deck handling, November–December 1956); VZ749 Rotol Airscrews (propeller development, November 1952–May 1954); 813 Sqn (November 1956–March 1958). VZ750 A & AEE (June–October 1953; 813 Sqn (November 1956–August 1952). VZ774 A & AEE and HMS *Eagle* (deck-landing trials, October–November 1953); HMS *Illustrious* (deck landing trials, high altitude handling trials January 1954–June1955); 700 Sqn (January–December 1957). VZ775 A & AEE (July 1953–June 1954); RAE (armament trials, June 1954); A & AEE (August 1954–February 1955). VZ776 RAE (September 1953–January 1955 and proofing trials, April 1955–February 1957). VZ777 A & AEE and HMS *Eagle* (flying limitations investigations and deck landing trials, October–November 1953); ASM (engine development, November 1954–April 1955); HMS *Eagle* (deck handling, June–July 1957); HMS *Ocean* (deck handling July–August 1957). VZ790 A & AEE (handling trials with RPs July–November 1954).

Wyvern S.Mk.4. Second production batch of 13 aircraft, WL876–WL888, built by Westland under Contract 6/Acft/5056/CB.9(c) during 1953–54.
Operated by Royal Navy Fleet Air Arm: Nos.813,827,830,831 Squadrons.
Trials aircraft: WL881 ASM (engine investigations during catapult launch, October–December 1954 and April 1955–January 1956); RAE (engine investigations during catapult launch, October–December 1954); RAE (May–August 1956 and November 1956–March 1957). WL884 WAL (tip tank trials April 1955). WL885 A & AEE (gun icing trials, performance and handling checks March 1955–November 1956). WL886 WAL (window dispenser and overload tank installations and trials, October 1954–March 1958).

Wyvern S.Mk.4. Third production batch of 13 aircraft, WN324–WN336, built by Westland under Contract 6/Acft/6269/CB.9(c) during 1955.

Operated by Royal Navy Fleet Air Arm: Nos.830,831 Squadrons.

Wyvern S.Mk.4. Fourth production batch of 11 aircraft, WP336–WP346, built by Westland under Contract 6/Acft/6345/CB.9(c) during 1955–56.
Operated by Royal Navy Fleet Air Arm: Nos.700,830,831 Squadrons.

Dragonfly HR.Mk.1. First production batch of six aircraft, VX595–600, built by Westland under Contract 6/Acft/2432/CB9(a) during 1948–49. VX595 first flew 18 June, 1949. Some conversions to HR.Mks.3 and 5.
Operated by Royal Navy Fleet Air Arm: No.705 Squadron.

Dragonfly HR.Mk.1. Second production batch of seven aircraft, VZ960–966, built by Westland under Contract 6/Acft/2798/CB9(a) during 1950–53.
Operated by Royal Navy Fleet Air Arm: No.705 Squadron.

Dragonfly HC.Mk.2. First production batch of two aircraft, WF311, WF315, built by Westland under Contract 6/Acft/4450/CB9(a) during 1949–50. Dragonfly HC.Mk.2, WF308, was also converted from WS-51 Mk.1A, G-ALMC, under this Contract.
Operated by RAF: No.194 Squadron.

WS-51 Mk.1A. One prototype, G-AKTW, built by Westland as a private venture during 1947–48. First flown on 5 October 1948. WAL (flight and general evaluation), A & AEE (evaluation trials as VD649 1952), later converted to Widgeon in 1955, became G-APPR with Bristow Helicopters Ltd in October 1958 and 5N-ABV in Nigeria in June 1962. Trials aircraft G-ALEG. WAL (development flying 1948), A & AEE (evaluation trials as WZ749 1951). G-ALEI Pest Control Ltd 1949, crashed Sion, Switzerland, (4 May, 1950). WAL (components used as rotor test rig 1951–1956). G-ALIK WAL (1949) later converted to Widgeon in 1955, became G-APPS with Bristow Helicopters in October 1958 and 5N-AGA in Nigeria in January 1963. G-ALIL RAF (evaluation as WB810, March 1949). WAL (Leonides 524/1 engine with +8 lb boost development 1950). G-ALMC RAF (trials in Malaya, November 1950).
British register: G-ALMB (Italy as I-MCOM March 1951); G-AMAK, 'AS and 'AT (Thai Air Force August 1950); G-AMJW (Thai Air Force May 1953); G-AMOW and 'OX (Italian Air Force as MM80038 and 40, 26 and 27 February, 1953); G-AMRE (Norway as LN-ORG October, 1952 restored as G-AMRE to WAL February 1954); G-ANAL, 'AM (Japan as JA-7014 June 1953); G-ANGR and 'GS (Japan February 1954); G-ANLV, 'LW (converted to Widgeon 1958); G-AOAJ, G-AOHX (Japan as JA-7025 May 1956).
Direct Exports: Ceylon (2) as CH 501–2; France (9); Iraq (2) as 332, 345; Japan (1).

WS-51 Mk.1B. British register: G-ALKL and 'MD (Egyptian Air Force November 1949); G-AMHB 'HC and 'HD (Belgian Congo as OO-CWA, 'CWB and 'CWC May 1951), January and February 1952.
Direct Exports: Yugoslavia (10) 11501–10.

Dragonfly HR.Mk.3. First production batch of 34 aircraft, WG661–672, WG705–709, WG714, WG718–726, WG748–754, built by Westland under Contract 6.Acft.3789/CB.9(a) Part 1 during 1950–51. Some conversions to HR.Mk.5s.
Operated by Royal Navy Fleet Air Arm: No.705 Squadron and some Station Flights.

Dragonfly HR.Mk.3. Second production batch of four aircraft, WH989–992, built by Westland under Contract 6/Acft/3789/CB.9(a) part 2 during 1950. Some conversions to HR.Mk.5s.
Operated by Royal Navy Fleet Air Arm: No.705 Squadron and some Station and SAR Flights.

Dragonfly HR.Mk.3. Third production batch of nine aircraft, WN492–500, built by Westland under Contract 6/Acft/6203/CB.8(a) part 1 during 1951. Some conversions to HR.Mk.5.
Operated by Royal Navy Fleet Air Arm: as previous batch.

Dragonfly HR.Mk.3. Fourth production batch of 12 aircraft, WP493–504, built by Westland under Contract 6/Acft/6203/CB.8(a) part 2 during 1952–53. WP505–510 on same Contract cancelled. Some conversions to HR.Mk.5s.
Operated by Royal Navy Fleet Air Arm: As previous batches.

Dragonfly HR.Mk.3. Fifth production batch of 12 aircraft, WV933–944, ordered under Contract 6/Acft/6203/CB.8(a)—Cancelled.

Dragonfly HC.Mk.4. First production batch of two aircraft, WT845–846, built by Westland under Contract 6/Acft/6545/CB.8(a) Part 1.
Operated by RAF: As previous batches.

Dragonfly HC.Mk.4. Second production of one aircraft, WX953, built by Westland under Contract 6/Acft/6545/CB.8(a) Part 2.
Operated by RAF: As previous batch.

Dragonfly HC.Mk.4. Third production batch of six aircraft, XB251–256, built by Westland during 1952–53.
Operated by RAF: As previous batches.

Dragonfly HC.Mk.4. Fourth production batch of three aircraft, XF259–261, built by Westland under Contract 6/Acft/9739/CB.8(a).
Operated by RAF: As previous batches.

Dragonfly HR.Mk.5. About 30 Dragonfly HR.Mks.1 and 3 were converted to HR.Mk.5 standard during 1955–58.
Operated by Royal Navy Fleet Air Arm: Nos.701,705,727,777 Squadrons and Station and SAR Flights.
In addition an HR.Mk.1, WB810, and HC.Mk.2, WZ749 and a third aircraft, XD649, were produced by conversion of three WS-51s, G-ALIL, G-ALEG and

G-AKTW for service evaluation. WB-810 was fitted with bomb shackles beneath the fuselage to carry a 1,000 lb bomb during trials with the Porton Chemical Weapons Establishment.

Widgeon. A total of 15 aircraft built by Westland during 1955–59. Prototype G-ALIK, converted from WS-51 Mk.1A, first flew on 23 August, 1955. WAL demonstrator; Bristow Helicopters (as G-APPS October 1958); Nigeria (as 5N-AGA January 1963). G-AKTW WAL (August 1958 converted to Widgeon), Bristow Helicopters (as G-APPR) (October 1958). Nigeria (as 5N-ABV June 1962). G-ANLW WAL (December 1958, converted to Widgeon). G-AOZD WAL (August 1957), Bristow Helicopters (December 1960), Nigeria (as 5N-AGL December 1966). G-AOZE WAL (August 1957), Bristow Helicopters (December 1960), Nigeria (as 5N-ABW June 1962). G-APBK WAL (December 1957), Hong Kong Police (as VR-HFL December 1957), Malaysia (as 9M-AOP 1962). G-APBL WAL (December 1957), Hong Kong Police (as VR-HFM October 1957). G-APTE WAL (April 1959), Bristow Helicopters (April 1959), Nigeria (as 5N-AGM December 1966). G-APTW WAL (June 1959) Executair Ltd, (July 1959), later WAL communications aircraft. G-APVD WAL (July 1959) Ferranti Ltd (June 1963). G-APWK WAL (September 1959 withdrawn from use 10 September, 1973).

Direct Exports: Brazilian Navy (2), Royal Jordanian Air Force (1), Japan (1).

Whirlwind HAR.Mk.1. First production batch of 10 aircraft, XA862–871, built by Westland under Contract 6/Acft/8379/CB.9(b).
Operated by Royal Navy: Nos.700,705,777,781,829 and 848 Squadrons.
Trials aircraft: XA862 Type Test aircraft; XA863 A & AEE (CA release with Pratt & Whitney Wasp engine, 27 March, 1954); XA864 WAL (main and tail rotor strain gauging, March 1953–54), A & AEE (blind flying research October 1957), RAE (radar research 12 January, 1959); XA865 A & AEE (side trials in casevac role 29 April 1954), RRE (radar trials 15 February, 1955—February 1958), RAE Bedford (February 1958), BEA Helicopter Experimental Unit, Gatwick, (drop tests and other trials 20 August, 1962—15 July 1963); XA866 WAL (undercarriage development 10 April, 1954); XA871 RAE (radar and Sea Slug missile checks 25 October, 1954).

Whirlwind HAR.Mk.4. First production batch of 10 aircraft, XD163–165 and XD182–188, ordered from Westland under Contract 6/Acft/8593/CB.9(b). XD183–188 cancelled.
Operated by RAF: Nos.22 and 155 Squadrons.
Trials aircraft: XD163 RAE (Donut flotation gear for Queen's Flight trials 21 May, 1964). XD164 A & AEE (evaluation flight trials 13 July, 1954).

Whirlwind HAR.Mk.4. Second production batch of 12 aircraft, XD777–784, XD795–797 and XD800, built by Westland under Contract 6/Acft/9409 CB.9(B) part 1. (These aircraft were re-serialled XJ401–408, XJ426–428 and XJ431 respectively).
Operated by RAF: Nos.155,225,228 and 275 Squadrons.

Whirlwind HAR.Mk.2. First production batch of eight aircraft, XD798–799 and XD801–806, built by Westland under Contract 6/Acft/9409 CB.9(B) part 2. (These aircraft were re-serialled XJ429–430 and XJ432–437 respectively). Operated by RAF: Nos.22,217,225,228 and 284 Squadrons.

Whirlwind HAR.Mk.3. First production batch of eight aircraft, XJ393–395, XJ397 and XJ399–402, (originally serialled XD763–765, XD767 and XD769–772). XD766 and XD768 were taken from production line for conversion to Mk.5s under Contract 6/Acft/11427/CB.9(b); built by Westland under Contract 6/Acft/9410/CB.9(b).
Operated by Royal Navy: Nos.700,701,705,728,737,781,815 and 845 Squadrons.
Trials aircraft: XJ393 WAL (Wright Cyclone engine type 30 September, 1954), RRE (low-altitude radar target March 1956–October 1960); XJ394 WAL (main and tail rotor blades strain gauging); A & AEE (range surveillance 10 October, 1957); XJ395 A & AEE (CA handling and performance trials February 1956); XJ397 WAL (Cyclone engine trials 24 June, 1966); XJ402 WAL (transmission system strain gauging).
Conversion: XJ401 to WS-55 Series 3 G-AYTK.

Whirlwind HAR.Mk.3. Second production batch of 16 aircraft, XG572–585 and XG587–588, built by Westland under Contract 6/Acft/10586/CB.9(b).
Operated by Royal Navy: As previous batch.
Conversions: XG576,'583,'587,'588 to WS-55 Series 3 G-AYNP, G-BAGD, G-AYYI, G-BAMH respectively.

Whirlwind. One aircraft, XJ445, was taken from the Mk.3 production line and converted to a Mk.5 by Westland under Contract 6/Acft/10586/CB.9(b).

Whirlwind HAR.Mk.3. One hybrid aircraft, XG586, built by Westland under Contract 6/Acft/10587/CB.9(b). (Completed as a Mk.7 airframe with a Wright Cyclone R-1300–3 engine).
Trials: A & AEE (Development trials 31 December, 1956); ATDU (torpedo dropping 6 February, 1957).

Whirlwind HAS.Mk.7. First production batch of nine aircraft, XG589–597, built by Westland under Contract 6/Acft/10587/CB.9(b).
Operated by Royal Navy: Nos.700H,705,737,814,815,820,824,845,846,847 and 848 Squadrons.
Trials aircraft: XG589 Alvis (Leonides Major engine trials 4 May, 1957), RRE (2 March, 1960); XG590 A & AEE (CA handling); XG591 A & AEE (UHF trials 20 May, 1959); XG592 WAL (pylon strain gauging at increased AUW); XG593 A & AEE (UHF trials 20 May, 1957), WAL (autopilot installations trials).

Whirlwind HAR.Mk.4. Third production batch of eight aircraft, XJ723–724, XJ761 and XL109–113, built by Westland under Contract 6/Acft/11387/CB.9(b) part 1.
Operated by RAF: As previous batches.

462

Whirlwind HAR.Mk.2. Second production batch of 16 aircraft, XJ725–730, XJ756–760 and XJ762–766, built by Westland under Contract 6/Acft/11387/CB.9(b) part 2.
Operated by RAF: As previous batch.
Some conversions to HAR.Mk.10s.

Whirlwind HAR.Mk.5. Two development aircraft, XJ396 and XJ398, were taken from the Mk.3 production line and converted to Mk.50 by Westland under Contract 6/Acft/11427/CB.9(a).

WS-55 Series 1. A total of 44 aircraft were built by Westland between 1953–59. G-AMJT(WAL), G-AMYN (French Navy), G-ANFH (BEA *Sir Ector*), G-ANJS–'JV (Christian Salveson), LN-ORL (Melsom and Melsom, Norway), G-ANUK (BEA *Sir Kay*) G-ANZN–'ZO (Bahamas VP-BAG, 'F), G-AOCF (BEA *Sir Lionel*), G-AODA–'DB (Shell), G-AOCZ (WAL Demonstrator— converted to Series 2). G-AODO–'DP (Fisons-Airwork), G-ATLZ (Bristow), G-AOHE (Christian Salveson), G-AORT (Saudi Arabia HZ-ABE) G-AOYB, G-AOZK, G-APKC (Fison Airwork), G-APRV–RW (Bristow VR-BBE, 'F) G-APWM (Kuwait 9K-BHD) G-APWN–'WO (Bristow), G-APXA, 'XB, 'XF (Kuwait 9K-BHA–'C), G-APXI ntu.
Exports: Brazil (3) N7008–10; Cuba (2) H10–11; France (6); Yugoslavia (1).

Whirlwind HAR.Mk.2. Third production batch of nine aircraft, XK968–970 and XK986–991, built by Westland under Contract 6/Acft/12881/CB.9(b).
Operated by RAF: As previous batches.

Whirlwind HAS.Mk.7. Second production batch of 20 aircraft, XK906–912 and XK933–945, built by Westland under Contract 6/Acft/12725/CB.9(b).
Operated by Royal Navy: Ships' Flights.

Whirlwind HAR.Mk.2. Fourth production batch of nine aircraft, XK968–970 and XK986–991, built by Westland under Contract 6/Acft/12881/CB.9(b).
Operated by RAF: As previous batches.
Some converted to HAR.Mk.10s.

Whirlwind HAS.Mk.7. Third production batch of 45 aircraft, XL833–854, XL867–884 and XL896–900, built by Westland under Contract 6/Acft/13955/CB.9(b).
Operated by Royal Navy: As previous batches.
Conversions to HAR.Mk.9s: XL839, '875, '880, '898 and '800.

Whirlwind HAS.Mk.7. Fourth production batch of 15 aircraft, XM660–669 and XM683–687, built by Westland under contract 6/Acft/15633/CB.9(b).
Operated by Royal Navy: As previous batches.
Conversion to HAR.Mk.9: XM666.

Whirlwind HAR.Mk.7. Fifth production batch of 40 aircraft, XN258–264, XN297–314, XN357–362 and XN379–387, built by Westland under Contract

KF/2N/015/CB.25(a).
Operated by Royal Navy: As previous batches.
Trials aircraft: XN285 A & AEE (preparation for tropical trials in Kano, Nigeria, 18 September, 1959).
Conversions to HAR.Mk.9s: XN298, '306, '309–311, '357.

Whirlwind HCC.Mk.8. Production batch of two aircraft, XN126–127, built by Westland under Contract CK/2N/01/CB.25(a).
Operated by: The Queen's Flight.
Converted to HAR.Mk.10.

WS-55 Series 2. A total of 19 aircraft were built by Westland.
G-APDY (WAL Demonstrator) 'PY–'PZ (Iran Heli-Taxi Co EP-BSK-CSK).
Conversions: ex-Series 1 G-AOCZ, 'YY, 'YZ, ex-HAR.Mk.7 XK940/G-AYXT.
Exports: Austria (10) 3D, AX-'DX, 3D, XL-'XQ; Jordan (2) 303–304; Spain (4) Z1–Z4.

Whirlwind HAR.Mk.10. First production batch of 12 aircraft, XP299–303, XP327–333, built by Westland under Contract KF/2N/037/CB.25(a).
Operated by RAF: Nos.22,28,32,84,103,110,202,225,228 and 230 Squadrons.
Trials aircraft: XP299 A & AEE (CA release 5 July, 1961).

Whirlwind HAR.Mk.10. Second production batch of 40 aircraft, XP338–363 and XP392–405, built by Westland under Contract KF/2N/042/CB.25(a).
Operated by RAF: As previous batch.

Whirlwind HAR.Mk.10. Third production batch of 18 XR453–458, XP477–487 and XS412, built by Westland under Contract KK/K/04/CB.25(a). (XR486–487 completed as HCC.Mk.12s).
Operated by RAF: As previous batches.

WS-55 Series 3. A total of five aircraft were built by Westland.
G-ASOU (Germany D-HODE), G-ATIU, 'KV (Bristow), 'LZ (ex-French Air Force; Bristow), G-AWWA (ex-Ghana Air Force; Bermuda VR-BDD).
Conversions: ex-HAR.3s XG576, XJ401, XG587, '583, '588/G-AYNP, 'TK, 'YI, G-BAGD, 'MH respectively.
Exports: Brunei (1) G-AXZS/AMDB-102.

Westminster. Two aircraft, G-APLE and G-APTX, built by Westland during 1956–58. G-APLE first flew 15 June, 1958; SBAC Display, Farnborough, September 1958; G-APTX first flew 4 September, 1959. Development abandoned in 1960, both aircraft retained at Yeovil and Yeovilton until broken up in 1962 and sold as scrap. The dynamic systems were returned to Sikorsky.

Wessex HAS.Mk.1. Pre-production batch of 12 aircraft, XL727–729, XM299–301 and XM326–331, built by Westland under Contract 6/Acft/13323/CB.25(a).

Operated by Royal Navy:
Trials aircraft: XL727 Rolls-Royce (engine development 6 December, 1965); XL729 A & AEE (pre-view preliminary handling 9 June, 1959); XM300 A & AEE (autopilot assessment 5 February, 1960, and 19 April, 1960), RAE Bedford (rotor performance assessment and underslung load trials 11 November, 1970), RAE Farnborough (internal noise level checks 5 July, 1970); XM301 A & AEE (handling trials 29 September, 1959, and 4 February, 1960);, RDTU Culdrose (armament trials 23 June, 1960, and 11 August, 1960), Napier Ltd (engine development 21 January, 1961, and 26 January, 1962), Rolls-Royce (engine development 2 April, 1962), Shoeburyness (vulnerability trials 26 February, 1969); XM326 A & AEE (performance and stability characteristic checks 16 February, 1960, and performance analysis 17 May, 1961); XM327 HMS *Hermes* (lift trials 23 June, 1960), A & AEE (flight control system evaluation 14 December, 1960), RAE (flight-testing hover coupled control and flight director 4 July, 1962); XM328 A & AEE (rotor governor preliminary evaluation 26 July, 1960, and EMC trials May 1968); XM329 A & AEE (radio trials 12 February, 1960), UDE Portland (Asdic trials 17 January, 1961); XM331 A & AEE (to Canada for winterisation trials 11 October, 1961), RRE (light-weight radar development 22 January, 1963).

Wessex HAS.Mk.1 First production batch of 40 aircraft, XM832–845, XM868–876, and XM915–931, built by Westland under Contract 6/Acft/15487.
Operated by Royal Navy: Nos.700H, 815 and 819 Squadrons.
Trials aircraft: XM834 A & AEE (production standard aircraft trials 23 December, 1966); XM836 Vickers-Armstrongs (cold chamber tests on complete aircraft 4 May, 1960), A & AEE (flight control system assessment 17 November, 1966); XM837 A & AEE (winterisation trials, Canada 19 September, 1960), 771 Squadron (service handling trials 5 December, 1963), 829 Squadron (pressure refuelling trials 6 April, 1965), Rolls-Royce (high-speed compressor surge investigation 30 September, 1965); XM838 A & AEE (gyro-magnetic system evaluation 7 September, 1961); XM871 A & AEE (armament trials 10 November, 1966); XM874 A & AEE (HF radio clearance 12 December, 1962); XM923 A & AEE (icing and snow trials 3 October, 1968); XM926 RRE (rotor blade aerial, mapping and terrain avoidance radars trials and evaluation 8 March, 1973), RAE Bedford (rotor aerial trials 9 September, 1975).
About 19 of this batch were converted to HAS.3 standard.

Wessex HAS.Mk.1. Second production batch of 40 aircraft, XP103–118, XP137–160, built by Westland under Contract KF/N/07/CB25(a).
Operated by Royal Navy: Nos.700H,706,737,771,772,814,815,819,820,826 and 845 Squadrons.
Trials aircraft: XP137 A & AEE (engine air intake and armament installation winterisation trials 7 January, 1970); XP153 AHU Fleetlands (engine checks 1969).
About 16 aircraft from this batch were converted to HAS.3 standard.

Wessex HC.Mk.2 First Mk.2 prototype aircraft, XR588, built by Westland under Contract KF/N/026/CB.25(a).
Operated by Royal Air Force: No.22 Squadron.

Wessex HC.Mk.2 First production batch of 30 aircraft, XR497–511 and XR515–529, built by Westland under Contract KF/N/019/CB.25(b).
Operated by Royal Air Force: Nos.18,22,28,72 and 78 Squadrons and No.2 FTS.
Trials aircraft: XR497 A & AEE (CA release 24 May, 1963, and clearance for Canada trials 21 November, 1963), RRE (IR Linescan equipment trials 4 October, 1965); XR498 A & AEE (tropical trials preparation 10 July, 1963), crashed Idris 30 August, 1963, and repaired; XR505 A & AEE (Mk.2 Wessex radio clearance 18 October, 1963).

Wessex HAS.Mk.1 Third production batch of 20 aircraft, XS115–128 and XS149–154, built by Westland under Contract KK/M/029/CB.25(a).
Operated by Royal Navy: as previous batches.
Trials aircraft:XS118 Rolls-Royce (engine control development 12 June, 1963, and flight test for engine life expectancy 10 February, 1964), crashed 26 May, 1965, SOC 17 November, 1965; XS121 A & AEE (EMC trials 30 June, 1964); XS122 A & AEE (CA release electrics/radio compatibility 18 November, 1967); XS127 A & AEE (post CA release development of Wessex Mk.3 and Gazelle 165 engine 27 February, 1969).
About eight aircraft from this batch were converted to HAS.3 standard.

Wessex HU.Mk.5. One pre-production aircraft, XS241 built by Westland under Contract KF/2N/042/CB.25(a).

Wessex Mk.10. One replacement aircraft, XS412, built by Westland under Contract KF/2N/042/CB.25(a).

Wessex HU.Mk.5. First production batch of 40 aircraft, XS479–500 and XS506–523, built by Westland under Contract KK/M/020/CB.25(a).
Operated by Royal Navy: Nos.700V,707,771,772,845 and 848 Squadrons.
Operated by Royal Air Force: No.84 Squadron.
Trials aircraft: XS484 A & AEE (radio altimeter assessment 23 April, 1968, icing trials 10 December, 1970, AUW trials in HMS*Bulwark* and CA release 24 April, 1979); XS499 A & AEE (avionics clearance 20 October, 1966); XS506 A & AEE (cold weather trials 28 October, 1964).

Wessex HAR.Mk.2 Second production batch of six aircraft, XS674–679, built by Westland under Contract KK/M/64/CB.25(a).
Operated by Royal Air Force: Nos.22 and 72 Squadrons and No.2 FTS.
Trials aircraft: XS679 A & AEE (re-assessment of radio/avionics equipment 20 June, 1966, CA release-doppler trials 13 October, 1967, and general avionics trials 24 January, 1969).

Wessex HAS Mk.1 Fourth production batch of 28 aircraft, XS862–889, built by Westland under Contract KK/M/68/CB.25(a).
Operated by Royal Navy: As previous batches.
Trials aircraft: XS863 A & AEE (general R&D flight trials 10 October, 1983).
About 10 aircraft from this batch were converted to HAS.3 standard.

Wessex HAS.Mk.3 First development batch of three aircraft, XT255–257, built by Westland under Contract KK/M/017/CB.25(a).
Trials aircraft: XT255 A & AEE (preview of DB Wessex Mk.3 31 May, 1965, and CA release 20 October, 1965); XT256 A & AEE (CA release-systems 16 May, 1966, flight director trials 13 September, 1967, and Seawolf trials 25 October, 1963).

Wessex HU.Mk.5. Third production batch of 40 aircraft, XT448–487, built by Westland under Contract KK/M/70/CB.25(a).
Operated by Royal Navy: Nos.707,772,781,845,846,847 and 848 Squadrons.
Operated by Royal Air Force: No.608 Flight and No.47 Parachute Regiment.
Trials aircraft: XT457 A & AEE (EMC trials 2 November, 1965); XT458 A & AEE (EMC trials 2 May, 1966); XT460 A & AEE (engine intake assessment in blower tunnel 5 February, 1971); XT463 A & AEE (handling trials 18 April, 1984).

Wessex HC.Mk.2 Third production batch of 22 aircraft, XT601–607 and XT667–681, built by Westland under Contract KK/M/111/CB.25(a).
Operated by Royal Air Force: Nos.22,28,72,78,84 and 103 Squadrons and No.2 FTS.
Trials aircraft: XT667 A & AEE (EMC trials 5 November, 1971).

Wessex HU.Mk.5. Fourth production batch of 20 aircraft, XT755–774, built by Westland under Contract KK/M/120/CB.25(a).
Operated by Royal Navy: Nos.707,771,772,781,845,846,847 and 848 Squadrons.
Trials aircraft: XT774 A & AEE (Mk.3 RP launcher clearance 29 September, 1967, and emergency flotation gear clearance 26 March, 1968).

Wessex HC.Mk.2. Fourth production batch of 15 aircraft, XV719–733, built by Westland under Contract KK/M/169/CB.25(a). Last two airframes completed as HCC.Mk.4 aircraft under Contract KK/M/192/CB.25(a) for The Queen's Flight.
Operated by Royal Air Force: Nos.22,72 and 84 Squadrons, No.2 FTS and The Queen's Flight (HCC.Mk.4).
Trials aircraft: XV726 A & AEE (CA release—fuel system and EMC clearance 5 March, 1981); XV727 A & AEE (winterisation trials in Norway 6 November, 1968), crashed 30 January, 1969, SOC 30 January, 1970; XV729 A & AEE (increased AUW trials 26 March, 1969); XV732 A & AEE (CA clearance 10 May, 1969), The Queen's Flight, RAF Benson (ground and flight trials 1 December, 1982).

Wessex HAS.Mk.1. Conversions to HAS.Mk.3 standard were made under Contract KK/M/019/CB.25(a).

Wessex HAS.Mk.31. A batch of 27 aircraft was built for the Royal Australian Navy by Westland during 1962–64.

Wessex Mk.52. A batch of 12 aircraft was built for the Iraqi Air Force by Westland during 1963–64.

Wessex Mk.53. Two aircraft were built for the Ghana Air Force by Westland during 1965–66.

Wessex Mk.54. Two aircraft were built for the Sultanate of Brunei by Westland during 1967.

Wessex 60 Series 1. A batch of 20 aircraft was built by Westland during 1965–71. The following were operated by Bristow Helicopters in the UK on the British register and/or overseas with non-UK registrations: G-ASWI, 'TBY-'Z, 'TCA-'B, 'TSC, 'VNE, 'VEW, 'WOX, 'WXX, 'XPJ, 'YNC, 'ZBY-'Z, 'ZCA, G-BAWJ, 'BCE, 'GER and 'GWT.

Scout AH.1. Development batch of eight aircarft, XP165–167, XP188–192, built by Saunders-Roe/Westland during 1960–62. XP165 first flew 29 August, 1960, A & AEE (performance, handling and engine assessment 7 April, 1961), Blackburn Engine Division (Turmo engine control and handling 10 October, 1961), A & AEE (CA release 6 June, 1962, and tropical trials, Idris 26 June, 1962, ETPS (20 March, 1964), SOC 26 August, 1971; XP166 (ex-Saro P.531-2 G-APVL). First flew 9 August, 1959, A & AEE (autopilot assessment 6 August, 1963), RAE (HUD development trials 9 June, 1965), SOC 21 May, 1976; XP167 First flew 4 August, 1960. Various rotor head trials, RAE (structural research 15 September, 1970), SOC 24 September, 1970; XP189. Various flight trials including Lynx semi-rigid rotor August 1970–January 1974, A & AEE (blower tunnel checks 6 February, 1975), XP190 A & AEE (radio trials 18 December, 1961), Bristol Siddeley Engines (tropical trials, Khartoum, 26 May, 1962), Rolls-Royce (7 December, 1967); XP191 Various flight trials including semi-rigid rotor, RAE Bedford (performance and handling 5 August, 1971), Army Apprentice College (instructional airframe 5 January, 1978); XP192. AAC Middle Wallop (intensive flying 15 September, 1961), A & AEE (CA release 24 January, 1962).

Scout AH.Mk.1. First production batch of 40 aircraft, XP846–857 and XP883–910, built by Westland Fairey Aviation Division under Contract KF/2Q/06/CB.25(a).
Operated by AAC.
Trials aircraft: XP846 A & AEE (c.g. limit extension 11 October, 1963), Bristol Siddeley Engines (intensive flying of Nimbus 105 31 August, 1965, and 9 September, 1966); XP847 A & AEE (radio assessment 3 March, 1964, instrument panel assessment 23 September, 1966, spray tank trials 29 June, 1967, operational reliability 23 August, 1967, jettison and firing of Swingfire missile 27 May, 1970); XP848 A & AEE (operational reliability trials 11 October, 1962); XP849 A & AEE (cold weather preparations to Canada 27

November, 1962); XP850 A & AEE (operational reliability assessment 26 June, 1962); XP851 A & AEE (operational reliability assessment 8 June, 1962); XP857 A & AEE (trials of troops entering, exiting and abseiling from aircraft 17 August, 1962); XP889 (external stretcher installation check 3 October, 1963); XP902 A & AEE (CA release-radio 29 November, 1984); XP907 Bristol Siddeley Engines (engine flight development 3 November, 1964); XP908 A & AEE (performance checks at 5,200 lb AUW 17 June, 1964, and 2 in RP assessment 21 April, 1967); XP909 Flight Refuelling Ltd (flight refuelling tests with turning rotors 8 December, 1969).

Scout AH.Mk.1. Second production batch of 24 aircraft, XR595–604 and XR627–640, built by Westland Fairey Aviation Division under Contract KF/2Q/09/CB.25(a).
Operated by AAC.
Trials aircraft: XR632 Rolls-Royce (free turbine strain-gauging 18 June, 1969).

Scout AH.Mk.1. Third production batch of 36 aircraft, XT614–649, built by Westland Fairey Aviation Division under Contract KK/N/80/CB.25(a).
Operated by AAC.
Trials aircraft: XT624 A & AEE (radio and aerial assessment 18 June, 1969); XT626 A & AEE (icing trials 17 July, 1972); XT632 (CA release 24 February, 1976, and flight test 5 April, 1977); XT637 A & AEE (autopilot assessment 11 December, 1964); XT640 A & AEE (assessment of production aircraft 27 August, 1965).

Scout AH.Mk.1. Fourth production batch of 24 aircraft, XV118–141, built by Westland under Contract KK/N/102/CB.25(a).
Operated by AAC.
Trials aircraft: XV121 A & AEE (CA release SRIM equipment 22 August, 1984).

Scout AH.Mk.1. Fifth production batch of five aircraft, XW280–284, built by Westland under Contract KK/N/155/CB.25(a).
Operated by AAC.
Trials aircraft: XW280 A & AEE (EMC clearance of SS.11 system 11 April, 1970, and EMC trials with AF120 sight 30 July, 1970).

Scout AH.Mk.1. Sixth production batch of five aircraft, XW612–616, built by Westland under Contract KK/N/182/CB.25(a).
Operated by AAC.

Scout AH.Mk.1. Seventh production batch of seven aircraft, XW795–801, ordered from Westland under Contract K25A/223/SW/CB.25(a), but XW800–801 not built.
Operated by AAC.

Wasp HAS.Mk.1. Two pre-production aircraft, XS463 and XS476 (ex-G-17-1 and G-17-2 respectively), built by Westland under Contract KN/N/O14/

CB.25(a).
Trials aircraft: XS463 A & AEE (flotation equipment flight trials 2 July, 1964, performance and handling at 6,500 lb AUW 29 September, 1964), RAE Bedford (CDRE trials 9 October, 1970); XS476 A & AEE (handling trials 11 June, 1963).

Wasp HAS.Mk.1. First production batch of 30 aircraft, XS527–545 and XS562–572, built by Westland under Contract KK/N/O11/CB.25(a).
Operated by Royal Navy: Nos.700W and 829 Squadrons.
Trials aircraft: XS527 A & AEE (radio/armament trials 15 July, 1963, and tropical trials preparation 10 July, 1964); XS528 A & AEE (tropical trials 3 December, 1963, autopilot checks 20 July, 1965, torquemeter assessment 12 May, 1966, assessment of light aircraft spray system 22 November, 1967, CA release 18 July, 1973); XS529 A & AEE (functioning flotation system in icing conditions 7 April, 1971); XS530 A & AEE (vibration investigation 12 September, 1963); XS532 A & AEE (external load trials 20 March, 1964); XS564 RRE (Sea Dart instrumentation 1965); XS569 A & AEE (clearance of AS.12 installation 5 June, 1968), HMS *Daedalus* (Zeiss Oberkochen camera trials 9 October, 1978).

Wasp HAS.Mk.1. Production batch of 30 aircraft, XS802–812 and XS834–852 cancelled.

Wasp HAS.Mk.1. Second production batch of 30 aircraft, XT414–443, built by Westland under Contract KK/N/49/CB.25(a).
Operated by Royal Navy: Nos.703,706,829,845 and 848 Squadrons and Britannia Flight, Royal Naval College, Dartmouth.
Trials aircraft: XT414 A & AEE (electric assessment 13 October, 1964, Mk.44 torpedo trials), ATDU Culdrose (Mk.44 torpedo dropping 8 February, 1965), A & AEE (electric assessment 22 February, 1965), ATDU (Mk.44 torpedo dropping clearance 26 February, 1965), A & AEE (X-band transponder trials 20 July, 1965); XT417 A & AEE (clearance of 600 lb bomb and SS.11 installations 13 January, 1967, assessment of AS.12 equipment 6 July, 1967, anti-icing trials 27 November, 1969); XT423 A & AEE (icing and snow trials 29 September, 1963); XT435 A & AEE (EMC trials 13 October, 1965).

Wasp HAS.Mk.1. Third production batch of 18 aircraft, XT778–795, built by Westland under Contract KK/N/93/CB.25(a).
Operated by Royal Navy: As previous batch.
Trials aircraft: XT778 A & AEE (EMC trials 30 June, 1966); XT793 A & AEE (CA release and flying in HMS *Sheffield* 3 May, 1975).

Wasp HAS.Mk.1. Fourth production batch of 18 aircraft, XV622–639, built by Westland under Contract KK/N/142/CB.25(a).
Operated by Royal Navy: As previous batch.
Trials aircraft: XV633 A & AEE (Mk.31 torpedo trials 21 July, 1969); XV636 (screen wiper trials in wind tunnel 5 August, 1976).

Sea King HAS.Mk.1. First production batch of 56 aircraft, XV642–677 and XV695–714, built by Westland under Contract KK/191/055 during 1969–72. Operated by Royal Navy: Nos.700S,706,824,826 Squadrons.
Trials aircraft: XV643 A & AEE (Temperate CA release 8 July, 1969); XV644 Rolls-Royce (engine failure investigations 18 December, 1969); XV647 RAE (26 September, 1969), A & AEE (equivalent CA release trials for Sea King in Iranian Navy ship *Larak* 9 April, 1975, and flying trials in HMS *Invincible* 16 October, 1980); XV651 A & AEE (datum checks in preparation for tropical trials 10 June, 1976), RRE (Blue Tit radar trials 3 November, 1979); XV654 WHL (TI manoeuvre recording equipment trials 1 November, 1979); XV656 A & AEE (CA release for Mk.46 Mod.2 torpedo 6 July, 1973); XV671 A & AEE (CA flying trials in RFA *Olmeda* 16 July, 1975), A & AEE (sonobuoy trials 9 February, 1977).
Sea King HAS.Mk.1 conversions: XV642 converted to Mk.2, 643/5, 644/A2664, 647–8/5, 649–50/2A, 651/5, 653–55/5, 656/2A, 657/6, 658/WO, 659–61/5, 663/6, 664/2, 665/6, 666/3, 669/A2659, 670/5, 671–72/2A, 673–75/5, 676–77/6, 696/5, 697/2A, 699–700/5, 701/6, 703/5, 704/2A, 705–06/5, 707/2A, 708–11/5, 712/6, 713/5 and 714/2A.

Sea King Mk.42. First production batch of six aircraft, IN501–506, built by Westland for the Indian Navy during 1971.

Sea King Mk.41. First production batch of 22 aircraft, 89-50–71, built by Westland for the West German Navy during 1972–74.

Sea King Mk.43. First production batch of 10 aircraft, 060, 062, 066, 068–074, built by Westland for the Royal Norwegian Air Force during 1972.

Sea King Mk.42. Second production batch of six aircraft, IN507–512, built by Westland for the Indian Navy during 1973–74.

Commando 1. First production batch of five aircraft, 261–265, built by Westland for the Arab Republic of Egypt Air Force during 1973.

Sea King Mk.50. First production batch of 10 aircraft, N16-098, N16-100, N16-112–114, N16-117–119, N16-124 and N16-125, built by Westland for the Royal Australian Navy during 1974–75.

Sea King Mk.45. First production batch of six aircraft, 4510–4515, built by Westland for the Pakistan Navy during 1974

Commando 2 and 2B. First production batch of 19 aircraft 721–723, and WA806–821, built by Westland for the Arab Republic of Egypt Air Force during 1975–76.

Sea King Mk.47. First production batch of six aircraft, WA822–827, built by Westland for the Arab Republic of Egypt Navy during 1975.

Commando 2A and 2C. First production batch of four aircraft, QA20–QA22 plus one unmarked VIP 2C variant, built by Westland for the Qatari Emiri Air Force during 1975–76.

Sea King Mk.41. One replacement aircraft with previously used serial 89-61, built by Westland for the West German Navy during 1974–75.

Sea King Mk.48. First production batch of five aircraft, RS01–RS05, built by Westland for the Belgian Air Force during 1975–76.

Sea King HAS.Mk.2. First production batch of 13 aircraft, XZ570–582, built by Westland under Contract K/Acft/12/821 during 1976–77.
Operated by Royal Navy: Nos.706,814,819,820,824,825,826 Squadrons.

Sea King HAS Mk.2 conversions: XZ570/EH 101 development, 571/5, 574–75/5, 576/development aircraft, 577–79/5, 580/6, 581/6, 582/5.

Sea King HC.Mk.4. Four aircraft XZ870–873, built only to Stage 2 during January–April 1977. Subsequently they were completed as ZA290–293 (q.v.) during 1979–80.

Sea King HAR.Mk.3. First production batch of 15 aircraft, XZ585–599, built by Westland under Contract K/Acft/12/846 during 1977–78.
Operated by RAF: Nos.78 and 202 Squadrons.
Trials aircraft: XZ585 A & AEE (CA release 26 January, 1978); XZ586 WHI (development flying for Mk.3 clearance 27 September, 1977).

Commando 2E. First production batch of four aircraft, SU-ARP, '-ARR, '-ART and '-BBJ, built by Westland for the Arab Republic of Egypt Air Force during 1978.

Sea King Mk.43A. One aircraft, 189, built by Westland for the Royal Norwegian Air Force during 1978.

Sea King HAS.Mk.2. Second production batch of eight aircraft, XZ915–922, built by Westland under Contract A12/1201 during 1977–79.
Operated by Royal Navy: As previous batch.
Trials aircraft: XZ916 A & AEE (CA release flying 12 November, 1980, and Sea Searcher radar tests 24 April, 1983).

Sea King HAS.Mk.2 conversions: XZ916/5, 918–22/5. The first three aircraft XZ915–917 flew with the incorrect serials XV915–917.

Sea King Mk.42A. Third production batch of three aircraft, IN551–553, built by Westland for the Indian Navy 1979–80.

Sea King HAR.Mk.3. One aircraft, ZA105, built by Westland under Contract KA12/846 during 1980.

Sea King HAS.Mk.5. First production batch of 17 aircraft, ZA126–137 and ZA166–170, built by Westland under Contract A12/1321 during 1980–82. (Records indicate that these aircraft were ordered as Mk.2s but were built as Mk.5s).
Operated by Royal Navy: Nos.706,810,814,819,820,824 and 826 Squadrons.
Trials aircraft: A & AEE (MAD trials of first installation 20 January, 1981).

Sea King HC.Mk.4. First production batch of 15 aircraft, ZA290–299 and ZA310–314, built by Westland under Contract A12/1450 during 1979–82.
Operated by Royal Navy: Nos.707,845 and 846 Squadrons.
Trials aircraft: ZA290 WHL (development trials); ZA293 WHL (development trials continuing from ZA290 28 January, 1980), A & AEE (20 June, 1980).

Commando 3. First production batch of eight aircraft, QA30–QA37, built by Westland for the Qatari Emiri Air Force during 1982–83.

Sea King Mk.4X. Two development aircraft, ZB506 and ZB507, built by Westland under Contract A12/1550 during 1982–83. Delivered to RAE Farnborough on 23 December, 1982, and 4 February, 1983, for development flying, ZB506 as test airframe for use in WG.34, Sea King replacement programme.

Sea King Mk.50A. First production batch of two aircraft, N16–238 and -239, built by Westland for the Royal Australian Navy during 1982–83.

Sea King HC.Mk.4. Second production batch of eight aircraft, ZD476–480 and ZD625–ZD627, built by Westland under Contract A23b/19 during 1983–84.
Operated by Royal Navy: as previous batch.

Sea King HAS.Mk.5. Second production batch of eight aircraft, ZD 630–637, built by Westland under Contract A23b/19 during 1984–85.
Operated by Royal Navy: as previous batch.

Sea King HAR.Mk.3. Second production batch of three aircraft, ZE368–370, built by Westland under Contract A23b/46 during 1985.
Operated by RAF: as previous batch.

Sea King HAS.Mk.5. Third production batch of five aircraft, ZE418–422, built by Westland under Contract A23b/87 during 1986.
Operated by Royal Navy: as previous batches.
(ZE421 was converted to a Mk.45 and was delivered to the Pakistan Navy in January 1989 serialled 4516).

Sea King HC.Mk.4. Third production batch of 14 aircraft, ZE425–428 and ZF115–124, built by Westland under Contracts A23b/98 and A23b/130 respectively during 1985–87.
Operated by Royal Navy: Nos.772,810,814,820,826,845,846 Squadrons.
Trials aircraft: ZF116 A & AEE.

Sea King Mk.42B. Fourth production batch of 21 aircraft, IN512–531 and IN533, built by Westland for the Indian Navy during 1985–89.

Sea King Mk.42C. Fifth production batch of six aircraft, IN555–560, built by Westland for the Indian Navy during 1986–88.

Sea King HC.Mk.4. Fourth production batch of four aircraft, ZG820–822 and ZG829, built by Westland under Contracts H11a/333 and A23b/295 respectively during 1989.

Sea King HAS.Mk.6. First production batch of six aircraft, ZG816–819, and ZG875–876, built by Westland under Contract H11a/333 during 1989–90.

WG.13 Lynx. Development batch of 13 aircraft built to Specification H.273 by Westland during 1970–74. Aircraft serials and Contract numbers were: XW835–839 (K2/A/7/CB.67(c)), XX153 (K2/A/CB.85(a)), XX469 (K2/A/13/CB.25(a)), XX510 (K2/A/13/CB.25(a)), XX904 (K/A25A/04), XX907 (K2/A/14/CB25(a)), XX910–911 (K2/A/7/CB.25(a)) and XZ166 (K2/A/7/CB.25(a)).

XW835	WHL first flew 21 March, 1971, (development programme April 1972), became G-BEAD in July 1976 and ultimately an instructional airframe at AAC Centre, Middle Wallop.
XW836	First flew 24 March, 1972. Became the mock-up for the civil Lynx 606 and was shown at the 1972 Farnborough Show.
XW837	First flew 28 September, 1971.
XW838	WHL first flew 8 March, 1972, (development programme 1972), sustained Cat 5 damage in development flight 29 August, 1974, struck off charge and transferred to Army 20 August, 1978.
XW839	First flew 19 June, 1974.
XW153	WHL first flew 12 April, 1972, (AH.Mk.1 development programme April 1972). A & AEE (CA release 6 August, 1975, and ARC 340 trials 17 June, 1976). Struck off charge 11 December, 1979, Shoeburyness.
XX469	WHL first flew 25 May, 1972, (HAS.Mk.2 development programme May 1972), sustained Cat 5 damage 21 November, 1972, scrapped.
XX510	First flew 5 March, 1973, WHL (HAS.Mk.2 development to definitive RN Standard).
XX904	First French Navy DB Mk.2. First flew 6 July, 1973, (F-ZKCU) SNIAS (Marignane 25 July, 1973). Taken on charge by French

Navy 1 December, 1978.

XX907   AH.Mk.1 first flew 20 May, 1973, Rolls-Royce (engine development, Filton 28 June, 1973, Leavesden 12 August, 1977), RAE (cabin noise research 10 March, 1980).

XX910   WHL first flew 23 April, 1974 (HAS.Mk.2 development programme 2 October, 1974), A & AEE (service assessment 8 May, 1975), Farnborough (SBAC Show 5–12 September, 1976), RAE (flight experience and assessment for future use 3 March, 1978).

XX911   Second French DB Mk.2 (F-ZKCV) first flew 18 September, 1973. SNIAS (Marignane, Development of French Navy armament and navigation equipment installation 28 September, 1973), taken on charge by French Navy 14 February, 1978.

XZ166   WHL first flew 5 March, 1975, (development programme 17 March, 1975). A & AEE (Blower tunnel trials 31 March, 1978), Rolls-Royce (engine development, Filton, 15 October, 1979), Boscombe Down (ETPS 11 February, 1980), struck off charge 18 December, 1980, RAE (Apprentice Training School 18 February, 1981).

Lynx AH.Mk.1. First production batch of 50 aircraft, XZ170–199, XZ203–222, built by Westland under Contract K/A25(a)/04 during 1976–78. VZ170 first flew 12 February, 1977, and deliveries completed in 1979.
Operated by ACC Nos. 651–657,659,662,663,665,669 and 671 Squadrons and RM 3C BAS.
Trials aircraft: XX153 A & AEE (CA release); XZ170 and XZ171 A & AEE (CA release; environmental trials in USA and Canada); XZ172 and XZ174 AAC IFTU (Middle Wallop, October 1977), A & AEE (roping and abseiling trials 1978); XZ176 WHL (TOW installation tests 21 June, 1978), A & AEE (CA release 7 August, 1980); XZ178 A & AEE (military free-fall parachute trials 24 February, 1981); XZ221 WHL (jet deflector system January 1980. Ship trials on logistic landing ship *Sir Geraint* 6–20 October, 1980); and XZ609 (A & AEE, CA release).

Lynx HAS.Mk.2. First production batch of 30 aircraft, XZ227–252, XZ254–257, built by Westland under Contract K/A25(a)/04 during 1975–78. XZ227 first flew 10 February, 1976, and deliveries completed by 5 March, 1979. Operated by RN Squadrons: Nos.700L,702,815.
Trials aircraft: XZ229–234 IFTU (Yeovilton September 1976–March 1978); XZ227 A & AEE (general development August 1976–78, and CA release-instrumentation 1 May, 1980), RAE (Aberporth, Sea Skua missile trials and firing 7 February 1980 and 4 December, 1980); XZ228 A & AEE (CA release Mk.2 8 July, 1976); XZ230 A & AEE (Lynx/Skua system trials 9 July, 1981, and CA release—HMS *Leeds Castle* 29 January, 1982); XZ234 A & AEE (ESM

development 16 May, 1978);XL235 WHL (Evaluation assessment and ship trials 9 January, 1978), A & AEE (for trials in HMS *Broadsword*); XZ237 RAE (Aberporth Sea Skua development 4 March, 1980, 9 January, 1981, 23 June, 1981–5 May, 1983).

Lynx Mk.2 (FN). First production batch of 18 aircraft, XZ260–268, XZ270–278, built by Westland for the French Navy during 1977–78 and fitted out at Marignane. XZ260 first flew 4 May, 1977. Contract K/A25(a)/04.

Lynx AH.Mk.1. Second production batch of 13 aircraft, XZ605–617, built by Westland under Contract K/A25(a)/04 during 1979–80. Originally ordered as RAF trainer aircraft but policy change caused order to be transferred to AAC. XZ605 first flew 21 November, 1979, and deliveries completed by May 1980.
Operated by AAC: Nos.654,657,659,671 Squadrons.
Trials aircraft: XZ609 A & AEE (CA release EMC tests 2 May, 1980).

Lynx Mk.2.(FN). Second production batch of eight aircraft, XZ620–627, built by Westland under Contract K.A25(a)/04 during 1979–80. XZ620 first flew 24 October, 1979. Trials aircraft: XZ263 Rolls-Royce (engine checks, Filton, 2 April, 1979).

Lynx AH.Mk.1. Third production batch of 37 aircraft, XZ640–655, XZ661–681, built by Westland under Contract K/A25(a)/29 during 1979–81. XZ640 first flew 7 May, 1980.
Operated by AAC: Nos.652–657,659,663,665,668 and 671 Squadrons and RM3C BAS.

Lynx HAS.Mk.2. Second production batch of 12 aircraft, XZ689–700, built by Westland under Contract K/A25(a)/29 during 1978–80. XZ689 first flew 15 December, 1978, and deliveries completed by April 1980.
Operated by Royal Navy. Nos.702,815 and 829 Squadrons.
Trials aircraft: XZ698 A & AEE (TOW trials 9 July, 1981).

Lynx HAS.Mk.2. Third production batch of 18 aircraft, XZ719–736, built by Westland, under Contract K/A25(a)/29 during 1980–82. XZ719 first flew 16 April, 1980, and deliveries completed by May 1982.
Operated by Royal Navy: Nos.702,815 and 829 Squadrons.
Trials aircraft: XZ734 A & AEE (CA release—Sting Ray torpedo 5 January, 1982); XZ735 A & AEE (CA release—Sting Ray torpedo 19 May, 1981).

Lynx HAS.Mk.3. First production batch of 20 aircraft, ZD249–268, built by Westland under Contract A25a/159 during 1981–83.
Operated by Royal Navy: Nos.702,815 and 829 Squadrons.
Trials aircraft: ZD256 A & AEE (armament trials and CA release 6 September, 1984); ZD264 A & AEE (EMC radio trials 26 September, 1983).

Lynx Mk.4. First production batch of 14 aircraft, 801–814, built by Westland for the Aéronavale during 1982–84.

Lynx AH.Mk.1. Fourth production batch of 13 aircraft ZD272–284, built by Westland under Contract A25a/213 during 1982–84.
Operated by AAC:

Lynx HAS.Mk.3. Second production batch of three aircraft, ZD565–567, built by Westland under Contract A25a/322 during 1984–85.
Operated by Royal Navy: Nos.702 and 815 Squadrons.

Lynx HAS.Mk.3. Third production batch of seven aircraft, ZF557–563, built by Westland under Contract A25a/322 during 1987–88.
Operated by Royal Navy: Nos.815 and 829 Squadrons.

Lynx AH.Mk.5. (Interim) Three aircraft, ZD285, ZD559 and ZD560 built by Westland under Contracts A25a/322 and A25a/339 in 1983/88.
Trials aircraft. ZD285 and 559 RAE Bedford (avionics development 1985–86); ZD560 (ETPS).

Lynx AH.Mk.5/7/ First production batch of eight aircraft, ZE375–382, ordered from Westland under Contract A25a/322 but only first two built. They were later converted and the remaining six completed to AH.Mk.7 standards as part of the second batch during 1984–86.
Operated by AAC: No.665 and 671 Squadrons and No.4 Regiment.

Lynx AH.Mk.7. Second production batch of four aircraft, ZF537–540, built by Westland under Contract A25a/402 during 1986–87.
Operated by AAC: Nos.654 and 669 Squadrons.

Lynx AH.Mk.9. First production batch of sixteen aircraft, ZG884–889 and ZG914–923, built by Westland under Contract H11b/38 during 1990–91.
Operated by AAC: Nos.672 and 673 Squadrons.

Export Lynx

Lynx Mk.21. First production batch of nine aircraft, N3020–3028, built by Westland for the Brazilian Navy during 1972–78.

Lynx Mk.23. First production batch of two aircraft, 3-H-41 and 3-H-42, built by Westland for the Argentine Navy during 1978.

Lynx Mk.25. First production batch of six aircraft, 260–265, built by Westland for the Royal Netherlands Naval Air Service during 1976–77.

Lynx Mk.27. First production batch of 10 aircraft, 266–275, built by Westland for the Royal Netherlands Naval Air Service during 1978–79.

Lynx Mk.28. First production batch of three aircraft, QP1–QP3, built by Westland for the State of Qatar Police during 1977–78.

Lynx Mk.80. First production batch of eight aircraft, S-134 S-142, S-170, S-175, S-181, S-187, S-191 and S-196, built by Westland for the Royal Danish Naval Air Service during 1974–81.

Lynx Mk.81. First production batch of eight aircraft, 276–283, built by Westland for the Royal Netherlands Naval Air Service during 1980–81.

Lynx Mk.86. First production batch of six aircraft, 207,216,228,232,235 and 237, built by Westland for the Royal Norwegian Air Force during 1980–81.

Lynx Mk.87. First production batch of eight aircraft, 3-H-143–3-H-150, ordered for the Argentine Navy. Only the first two built during 1982, but not delivered and became Danish Mk.90s S-249 and S-256.

Lynx Mk.88. First production batch of 12 aircraft, 83-01–83-12, built by Westland for the West German Navy during 1981–82.

Lynx Mk.89. First production batch of nine aircraft, 01-F-89–03-F-89, built by Westland for the Nigerian Navy during 1983–84.

Lynx Mk.90. First production batch of three aircraft, S-249, S-256 and S-035, converted from two ex-Argentine Lynx Mk.87s and one Mk.23 respectively by Westland for the Royal Danish Naval Air Service during 1986–87.

Lynx Mk.88. Second production batch of seven aircraft, 83-13–83-19, built by Westland for the West German Navy during 1986–88.

Lynx Mk.95. First production batch of five aircraft, ordered during 1990 from Westland for the Portuguese Navy for delivery during 1993.

Lynx Mk.99. First production batch of 12 aircraft, 90-0701–90-0712, built by Westland for the Republic of Korea Navy during 1988–90.

The following proposed Lynx variants were not built for a variety of financial, political and commercial reasons: Lynx Mk.6 (Royal Marines), Mk.22 (Egyptian Army), Mks.24 and 26 (Iraqi Army), Mk.82 (Egyptian Army/Air Force), Mk.83 (Saudi Arabia), Mk.84 (Qatari Army), Mk.85 (United Arab Emirates Army) and Mk.87 (Argentine Navy—embargoed).

Westland 30 Series 100. Two development aircraft, G-BGHF and G-BKKI were built by Westland. Both were converted into Series 160 aircraft.

Westland 30 Series 100. A batch of 12 aircraft was built by Westland. G-BIWY 'KGD and 'KNW went to British Airways Helicopters; G-BKFD, 'KFE, 'KFF and G-17-31 were delivered to Airspur, USA, to become N5820T, '30T, '40T and '80T; G-KATE and G-VAJC were leased to Helicopter Hire; N112WG, N113WG and N115WG were sold to Midway Airlines, USA; N113WG and N115WG were later converted to Series 160 variants by Westland.

Westland 30 Series 100-60. A batch of 24 aircraft was built by Westland. G-EFIS went to Omniflight Helicopters, USA as N114WG; N116WG and N118WG were delivered to Westland Inc, USA; G-BLKR, 'TY and 'PR became VT-EKF, 'KG and 'KE with the Helicopter Corporation of India and were followed by 18 more, VT-EKH–'EKY.

Westland 30 Series 200. One development aircraft, G-BKNV, which became G-ELEC, built by Westland.

Westland 30 Series 300. One development aircraft, G-17-22, which became G-HAUL built by Westland.

European Helicopter Industries EH 101. Pre-production batch of nine aircraft: PP1–PP9, ZF641, 02, G-EHIL, ZF644, ZF649, 06, 07, G-0101 and 09 respectively, built by Westland Helicopters Ltd and Agusta SpA under Contract during 1984–1990.

Westland-built aircraft. PP1, ZF641, first flown 9 October, 1987. Allocated to basic type development with PP2, 02, at Cascina Costa as a Single Site development operation in October 1988. PP3, G-EHIL, first flown 30 September, 1988. Allocated to the commercial programme with PP8. Supplementary role providing support to PP1 and PP2. Handling and performance assessment; AFCS development initial evaluation of ACSR; main-rotor blade envelope and stall margin. First icing trials scheduled for 1991. PP4, ZF644, first flown 15 June, 1989. Avionic development involving AMS, cockpit displays, navigation and communications systems. PP5, ZF649, first flown 24 October, 1989. Dedicated to specific integration of Royal Navy weapon systems. PP8, G-OIOI, first flew 24 April, 1990. Civil variant, as Heliliner, made passenger-carrying debut at Farnborough Show, 2–9 September, 1990. Allocated to flight trials associated with Civil Type Certification.

Agusta-built aircraft. PP2, 02, first flew 26 November, 1987. Allocated to basic type development with PP1 at Cascina Costa. PP6, 06, first flew 26 April, 1989. Dedicated to specific integration of weapons systems for the Marina Militare Italiana. PP7,07, first flew 24 April, 1990. First utility variant with rear ramp door; trials primarily concerned with military clearance including vibration evaluation. PP9, 09, first flew 16 January 1991. Allocated to civil utility variant trials and demonstrations.

Construction of Other Manufacturers' Aircraft

Like a number of other British aircraft manufacturers, Westland gained its initial experience of the business of building aeroplanes by the sub-contract production of another company's designs.

As related earlier, it was the Petter brothers' desire to contribute to the War effort in 1915 which brought their company its first order for aircraft. This was for twelve Short Type 184 floatplanes, often referred to as 'the Two-two-five' because of its 225 hp Sunbeam engine. Westland was not alone in receiving orders for this aircraft. When Shorts got some very big contracts totalling 153 Type 184s during the summer of 1915, its two factories were unable to cope with the work; thus five other companies were given orders for 78 aircraft in total to supplement the 75 being produced by Shorts. Ultimately nine sub-contract manufacturers built 829 Type 184s with Shorts adding a further 117 to the grand total.

The only surviving Type 184 is the fourth Westland-built aircraft, serialled 8359, which has a special place in naval aviation history. Flown by Flt Lieut F J Rutland ('Rutland of Jutland') with Assistant Paymaster G S Trewin as his observer, this aircraft took-off from the seaplane carrier *Engadine* during the afternoon of 31 May, 1916, which was the beginning of the Battle of Jutland. The crew soon spotted three enemy cruisers and ten destroyers and, in spite of low cloud and limited visibility, their position and course were reported. Continuing bad weather made any further aerial acitivity impossible, but this reconnaissance flight was a major milestone in naval air warfare. After the war, 8359 went to the Imperial War Museum but it was badly damaged during an air raid in 1940; however, the fuselage has been restored and is now in the care of the Fleet Air Arm Museum at Yeovilton, only a few miles from the factory where it was built.

Short Type 184. Single-engine two-seat torpedo-spotter. One 225 hp Sunbeam eight-cylinder liquid-cooled vee engine. Span 63 ft 6 in; length 40 ft 7 in; height 13 ft 6 in; empty weight 3,500–3,800 lb; loaded weight 5,100–5,560lb; maximum speed 75–88 mph; service ceiling 9,000 ft; endurance 2¾–4½ hr. Serial numbers of Westland-built aircraft: 8356–8367.

Following this order Westland received a second one for twenty Short Type 166 floatplanes which were forerunners of the Type 184. Shorts had built only six of these Type 166 torpedo-carrying aircraft, although, in fact, none were ever carried although equipped to do so. The Westland-built examples were without torpedo gear and, beginning in July 1916, were delivered to Hamble by rail for flight testing which was undertaken by Sydney Pickles, a well-known civil test pilot.

Short Type 166. Single-engine two-seat torpedo-bomber. One 200 hp Salmson nine-cylinder liquid-cooled radial engine. Span 57 ft 3 in; length 40 ft 7 in; height 13 ft 9 in; empty weight 3,500 lb; loaded weight 4,580 lb; maximum speed 65 mph; service ceiling 8,200 ft; endurance 4 hr. Serial numbers of Westland-built aircraft: 9751–9770.

That Westland could produce high-quality work in its Yeovil factory was recognised by Sopwith Aviation and the Air Board with the award of three sub-contract orders for a total of 125 Sopwith 1½ Strutter two-seat fighters and single- and two-seat bombers, all of which were built during winter 1916–17.

Sopwith 1½ Strutter. Single-engine two-seat fighter. One 110 hp Clerget 9Z nine-cylinder air-cooled rotary engine. Span 33 ft 6in; length 25 ft 3 in; height 10 ft 3 in; empty weight 1,259 lb; loaded weight 2,150 lb; maximum speed 96½ mph. Serial numbers of Westland-built aircraft: A1511–1560.

Sopwith 1½ Strutter Admiralty Type 9400. Single-engine two-seat bomber. One 130 hp Clerget 9B nine-cylinder air-cooled rotary engine. Dimensions as above. Empty weight 1,305 lb; loaded weight 2,150 lb; maximum speed 97½ mph; service ceiling 1,500 ft. Serial numbers of Westland-built aircraft: N5605–5624.

Sopwith 1½ Strutter Admiralty Type 9700. Single-engine single-seat bomber. Engine and dimensions as Type 9400. Empty weight 1,316 lb; loaded weight 2,342 lb; maximum speed 98½ mph; service ceiling 13,000 ft. Serial numbers of Westland-built aircraft: N5120–5169 and N5600–5604. (N5161 and N5168 converted to Type 9400).
Before this programme was completed the Aircraft Manufacturing Company's D.H.4 day bomber was beginning to appear in Westland's factory, and some 140 examples of this classic aeroplane were built at Yeovil.

De Havilland D.H.4. Single-engine two-seat reconnaissance bomber. One 200 hp BHP six-cylinder liquid-cooled inline engine, or one 250 hp Rolls-Royce Eagle Mk.III or Mk.IV twelve-cylinder liquid-cooled geared vee engine. Span 42 ft 4½ in; length 30 ft 2 in; height 10 ft 0 in; empty weight 2,303 lb; loaded weight 3,313 lb; maximum speed 117 mph; service ceiling 16,000 ft. Serial numbers of Westland-built aircraft: B3954–3970, B9476–9500 and D1751–1775 (BHP engines), N5960–6009 (built under Admiralty Contract CP.100786 with Rolls-Royce engines), N6380–6429 (BHP or 200 hp RAF 3a engines).
When its successor, the D.H.9, was ordered into production, Westland was again a major sub-contract manufacturer completing most of the 300 aircraft ordered from it.

De Havilland D.H.9. Single-engine two-seat day bomber or maritime patrol aircraft. One 230 or 290 hp Siddeley Puma six-cylinder liquid-cooled inline engine. Span 42 ft 4 ⅝ in; length 30 ft 6 in; height 11 ft 3½ in; empty weight 2,203 lb; loaded weight 3,669 lb; maximum speed 109½ mph; service ceiling 15,500 ft. Serial numbers of Westland-built aircraft: B7581–7680 (under Contract AS 19174), D7201–7300, F1767–1866 (not all built).
When this type's performance failed to measure up to requirements and Rolls-Royce Eagle VIII engines were in short supply, it was decided to fit the US-built Liberty engines in the D.H.9. Because the Aircraft Manufacturing Company was busy with other design work, the task of redesigning the D.H.9 to accept the US engine was given to Westland. The resulting D.H.9A became another classic aeroplane, with Westland producing 355 examples.

De Havilland D.H.9A. Single-engine two-seat general purpose aircraft. One 400 hp Liberty twelve-cylinder liquid-cooled geared vee engine. Span 45 ft 11⅜ in; length 30 ft 3 in; height 11 ft 4 in; empty weight 2,800 lb; loaded weight 4,654 lb; maximum speed 114½ mph; service ceiling 15,100 ft; endurance 5¼ hr. Serial numbers of Westland-built aircraft: F951–1100, F1603–1652, H3396–3545 (J401–450 under Contract 35a/3093/C3565 and AS 31684, cancelled), J6957–6952 (under Contract 375546/22 to Spec. 22/23), J7799–7819 (under Contract 602586/25), J7855–7866 (under Contract 640047/25), J8460–8482 (under Contract 730775/26).

In August 1918 Westland was given a sub-contract order for seventy-five Vickers Vimy twin-engined bombers but in the three months before the war ended, this was reduced to twenty-five aircraft. This was the be the largest aircraft type to be built in the Yeovil factory.

Vickers F.B.27a Vimy. Twin-engined three-seat heavy bomber. Two 360 hp Rolls-Royce Eagle VIII twelve-cylinder liquid-cooled geared vee engines. Span 68 ft 0 in; length 43 ft 6½ in; height 15 ft 7½ in; empty weight 7,101 lb; loaded weight 12,500 lb; maximum speed 103 mph; service ceiling 7,000 ft; endurance 11 hr. Serial numbers allocated to Westland-built aircraft: H5065–5139 (under Contract 35A/2388/2689. 25 built, remainder cancelled).

It was not until 1934 that Westland again undertook sub-contract aircraft production, if the building of a single prototype can be given that description. The aircraft was the Hendy Heck, a small low-wing monoplane with a manually retractable main undercarriage. It had been designed by Basil B Henderson for Whitney Straight who specified a high-speed cruise with a low landing speed.

Hendy 3308 Heck. Single-engine two-seat private aircraft. One 200 hp de Havilland Gipsy Six six-cylinder air-cooled inline engine. Span 31 ft 6 in; length 26 ft 1½ in; height 8 ft 6 in; empty weight 1,811 lb; loaded weight 2,600 lb; maximum speed 170 mph. For its early flights it bore the Westland Class B marking P but was subsequently registered G-ACTC.

The first of two types of Hawker aircraft built by Westland was the Audax which was produced in two batches of eighteen and twenty-five during 1935–36. Then, during early 1936, Westland took over an order, scheduled to go to A V Roe, for all 178 Hectors ordered, all being delivered by the end of the following year.

Hawker Audax. Single-engine two-seat army co-operation aircraft. One 575 hp Rolls-Royce Kestrel X twelve-cylinder liquid-cooled geared vee engine. Span 37 ft 3 in; length 29 ft 7 in; height 10 ft 5 in; empty weight 2,938 lb; loaded weight 4,386 lb; maximum speed 170 mph; service ceiling 21,500 ft; endurance 3½ hr.
    Serial numbers of Westland-built aircraft; K5586–5603 and K8311–8335 (under Contract 389426/35).

The first Westland-built WS-70 Black Hawk, ZG488, armed with a machine-gun pod, SNEB and MATRA rocket pods.

Hawker Hector. Single-engine two-seat army co-operation aircraft. One 805 hp Napier Dagger IIIMS twenty-four-cylinder air-cooled geared and supercharged H engine. Span 36 ft 11½ in; length 29 ft 9¾ in; height 10 ft 5 in; empty weight 3,389 lb; loaded weight 4,910 lb; maximum speed 187 mph; service ceiling 24,000 ft; endurance 2½ hr. Serial numbers of Westland-built aircraft: K8090–8167 (under Contract 497301/36), K9687–9786 (under Contract 521856/36).

The outbreak of the 1939–45 War again brought sub-contract work to Yeovil, this time for Supermarine Spitfire IAs, VBs and VCs of which 685 were built.

Supermarine Spitfire IA, VB and VC. single-engine single-seat fighter. One 1,030 hp Rolls-Royce Merlin II (IA) or 1,440 hp Merlin 45/50 (VB and VC) twelve-cylinder liquid-cooled geared and supercharged vee engine. Span 36 ft 10 in; length 29 ft 11 in; height 11 ft 2 in; empty weight 4,000 lb; loaded weight 5,800 lb (IA), 5,050 lb/6,650lb (VB), 5,110 lb/6785 lb (VC); maximum speed 353 mph (IA), 375 mph (VB and VC); service ceiling 31,500 ft (IA), 35,500 ft (VB and VC). Serial numbers of Westland-built aircraft: AR212–261 (IA), AR274–298, AR318–347, AR362–406 and AR422–461 (VB), AR462–471, AR488–532, AR546–570 and AR592–621, EE600–644, EE657–690, EE713–753, EE766–811, EE834–867, EF526–570, EF584–616, EF629–656, EF671–710 and EF715–753 (VC) (under Contract 124305/40).

In addition to this Spitfire programme, deliveries from which began on 18 July, 1941, and ended on 5 November, 1943, Westland also produced 2,115 Seafire IICs, IIIs, XVs and XVIIs, initially as a Supermarine sub-contractor but later as prime contractor for all Merlin-engined Seafire production. Westland was involved, jointly with Supermarine, in the design of the wing-folding mechanism and took sole responsibility for the modification of later Seafire variants to enable a bubble-type clear-view canopy to be fitted.

Supermarine Seafire IIC and III. Single-engine single-seat fighter. One 1,340 hp Rolls-Royce Merlin 45/46 or 1,640 hp Merlin 32 (IIC), one 1,640 hp Merlin 32 (III). Span 36 ft 10 in; length 30 ft 2½ in; height 11 ft 2 in; empty weight 6,103 lb (IIC), 6,204 lb (III); loaded weight 7,010 lb (IIC), 7104 lb (III); maximum speed 332 mph (IIC), 352 mph (III); service ceiling 28,000 ft- 31,300 ft. Serial numbers of Westland-built aircraft: LR631–667, LR680–712 and LR725–764 (IIC), LR765–820 and LR835–881 (III) (under Contract B.124305/40 as amended). NF418–445, NF480–526, NF531–570, NF575–607 and NF624–665 (III), NM984–999, NN112–157, NN169–214, NN227–270, NN283–330, PP921–957, PP969–999. PR115–156, PR170–215, PR228–271, PR285–334, RX156–194, RX210–256, RX268–313 and RX326–353 (LFIII) (under Contract Air/2605/CB.23(c)), RX354–530 cancelled.

Supermarine Seafire XV and XVII. Single-engine single-seat fighter. One 1,850 hp Rolls-Royce Griffon VI, 2,035 hp Griffon 61, 87 or 88 or 2,375 hp Griffon 85 twelve-cylinder liquid-cooled geared and supercharged vee engine. Span 36 ft 10 in; length 32 ft 3 in; height 10 ft 8 in; empty weight 6,168 lb (XV), 7,015 lb (XVII); loaded weight 7,948 lb (XV), 8,010 lb (XVII); maximum speed 384 mph (XV), 387 mph (XVII); service ceiling 32,000 ft (XV), 39,500 (XVII). Serial numbers of Westland-built aircraft: SR446–493, SR516–547, SR568–611, SR630–645, SW781–828, SW844–875, SW876–879 and SW896–921 (XV) (under Contract Air/2605/CB.23(c)). SW922–939 and SW951–985 cancelled. SW986–993, SX111–139, SX152–201, SX220–256, SX271–316, SX332–370 and SX386–389(XVII) (under Contract Air/3853). SX390–432, SX451–490 and SX503–546 cancelled.

Deliveries of Seafires began on 23 January, 1943, and continued until 12 October, 1946.

Westland had expected to take a major role in the production of Fairey Barracudas with the receipt of an initial order for 250 aircraft, but, in the event, this total was progressively reduced and only eighteen were built, the Spitfire and Seafire production taking priority.

Fairey Barracuda I and II. Single-engine three-seat torpedo/dive bomber. One 1,260 hp Rolls-Royce Merlin 30 (I), 1,640 hp Merlin 32 (II). Span 49 ft 2 in; length 39 ft 9 in; height 15 ft 2 in; empty weight 10,012 lb (I), 10,818 lb (II); loaded weight 13,068 lb (I), 14,100 lb (II); maximum speed 235 mph (I), 228 mph (II); service ceiling 18,400 ft (I), 15,000 ft (II). Serial numbers of Westland-built aircraft: DN625–629 (I), DN630–642 (II). DN643–669, DN693–730, DN756–805, DN839–874, DN897–935 and DN957–998 cancelled.

Westland also was involved with modifying US-built fighters to suit their operation by the RAF. These were Curtiss P-36 Mohawks, and P-40 Tomahawks and Kittyhawks, some of which had been ordered by France for the Armée de l'Air but were diverted to Britain when it took over the contracts following the fall of France in July 1940. On Mohawks Westland installed British instrumentation and radios in place of French-specified equipment with metric calibration. The other types were fitted with British radios, although this work was ultimately undertaken by operational units in the Middle East to where these aircraft were despatched. One Tomahawk, AX900, was retained by Westland as a radio trials aircraft.

The rationalisation of the British Aircraft Industry during the 1958–60 era resulted in Westland acquiring the aviation and helicopter interests of the Saunders-Roe, Fairey and Bristol companies. These acquisitions brought several of their fixed and rotary-wing aircraft into the Westland fold; they included the Saunders-Roe P.531 helicopter and SR-N1 Hovercraft, Fairey's Gannet and Rotodyne, and the Bristol Belvedere. All of these, except for the Gannet, were eventually referred to as Westland SR-N1, Rotodyne and Belvedere even though, in the case of the SR-N1, Gannet and Belvedere, they continued to be built or developed in their original factories under new Westland ownership; in fact, all Belvedere deliveries were made after Westland's acquisition of Bristol Helicopter Division.

When, in late 1963, the Bell Model 47 helicopter was chosen as standard British Army equipment and was designated the Sioux AH.Mk.1, Westland received orders to begin producing this aircraft under licence from the Agusta company in Italy, itself a licencee of Bell. Under the designation A-B47G-3B-4, a total of 250 was built at Westland's Yeovil factory, beginning in 1964.

A Westland-built Agusta-Bell 47G-4, one of a number used by Bristow Helicopters for initial training of British Army pilots.

Westland Agusta-Bell 47G Sioux production line at Hayes during the late 1960s.

Westland/Agusta-Bell Sioux AH.Mk.1. Single-rotor single-engined three-seat light helicopter. One 260 hp Avco Lycoming TVO-435-A1A six-cylinder supercharged flat engine. Rotor diameter 37 ft 1½ in; length 43 ft 2½ in; height 9 ft 3¾ in; empty weight 1,778 lb; loaded weight 2,950 lb; maximum speed 105 mph; service ceiling 20,000 ft. Serial numbers of Westland-built aircraft: XT126–250, XT498–516, XT540–570, XT824–849 (under Contract KK/191/033/CB.25(a)), XT798–820 (under Contract KK/2C/2/CB.25(a)), XW179–195 (under Contract KK/2C/22/CB.25(a)), XV310–324 (HT.Mk.2) (under Contract KK/2C/12/CB.25(b)).

On 17 May, 1965, the Governments of Britain and France signed a Memorandum of Understanding agreeing to a collaborative programme of development and production of military helicopters to meet their common needs. Studies of current helicopter programmes in both countries led to the signing of another MOU on 22 February, 1967, in which they agreed to collaborate on a light observation and communications helicopter based on the Sud-Aviation SA.341; a tactical medium transport helicopter which was the Sud SA.330 Puma plus an ASW and anti-tank helicopter, for which Westland had design responsibility, based on the WG.13 and which became the Lynx.

Production of the SA.341 Gazelle for British forces was centred on Westland's Old Mixon factory at Weston-super-Mare. The first prototype first flew on 28 April, 1970, with the first production Gazelles AH.1 and AH.2, flying on 31 January and 6 July, 1972, respectively. A total of 262 Gazelles were built, 197 AH.1s for the AAC and Royal Marines, 31 HT.2s for the Royal Navy and 34 HT.3s for the RAF.

Westland-Aérospatiale Gazelle. Single-rotor single-engined five-seat multi-role helicopter. One 592 shp Turboméca Astazou IIIA turboshaft engine. Rotor diameter 34 ft 5½ in; length 31 ft 2¾ in; height 9 ft 0 in; empty weight 2,002 lb; loaded weight 3,747 lb; maximum speed 164 mph; service ceiling 16,730 ft.

An Army Gazelle AH.1 exercising with RFA *Engadine* off Portland. Note the flotation gear and exposed tail-rotor drive-shaft.

Serial numbers of Westland-built aircraft: XW842–849, XW851–858, XW860–866, XW868, XW870–871, XW884–895, XW897–900, XW902–904, XW906–913, XX370–373, XX374–389, XX391–396, XX398–399, XX403, XX405–414, XX416–419, XX431–457, XX460, XX462, XZ290–292, XZ294–305, XZ307–312, XZ314–349, XZ930–XZ942, ZA726–737, ZA765–777, ZA801–804, ZB625–629, ZB646–649, ZB665–693.

A Westland-built Gazelle over London. It was used by aptly named Point-to-Point Helicopters to fly jockeys between race meetings.

Royal Navy Gazelle, XW845 at RNAS Yeovilton on 8 July, 1972. The fenestron replaces the conventional tail rotor. (*Helicopter International*)

The second helicopter in the Anglo-French collaborative production programme was the SA.330 Puma. Westland was responsible for the production of some 30 per cent of the airframe and some components and for the final assembly and flight testing of 48 aircraft for the RAF. Rolls-Royce had a similar amount of involvement in the provision of the Turboméca Turmo engines. The first Westland assembled Puma, WX198, first flew on 25 November, 1970. No.300 Squadron RAF was the first to receive these aircraft, forming in June 1971.

The first Westland-built Puma HC.1, XW198 (left) gets airborne with another of its kind.

487

ZA941, the last Westland-built Puma, in 'raspberry-ripple' finish at the RAE, with French 'polyvalent' engine intakes.

Westland-Aérospatiale Puma. Single-rotor twin-engine tactical medium transport helicopter. Two crew, accommodation for 16 troops and 5,500 lb slung load. Two 1,320 shp Turboméca Turmo III C4 turboshaft engines. Rotor diameter 49 ft 2½ in; length 48 ft 5 in; height 16 ft 10 in; empty weight 7,562 lb; loaded weight 14,110 lb; maximum speed 174 mph; service ceiling 15,750 ft.
Serial numbers of Westland-assembled aircraft: XW198–237, ZA934–941.

APPENDIX C

Fixed-wing Projects

In common with many other British manufacturers, Westland adopted several different systems for identifying its designs which, ultimately, were translated into production aircraft or remained as projects. Generally the company used the aircraft's role and type of engine or the official specification to which it was designed. Some helicopter project drawings had no identification and many were undated. Unfortunately, it is believed that no complete list of Westland projects survives; however, the company numbered and photographed its wind-tunnel models and these have helped to swell the following list which is not exhaustive.

Designation	Date
Twin Jaguar-engined bomber to 39/24	1924
Twin Jaguar-monoplane bomber to 39/24	1924

Twin Jaguar sesquiplane bomber to 39/24   1924

Twin-engined seven-seat passenger or postal aircraft.   1928

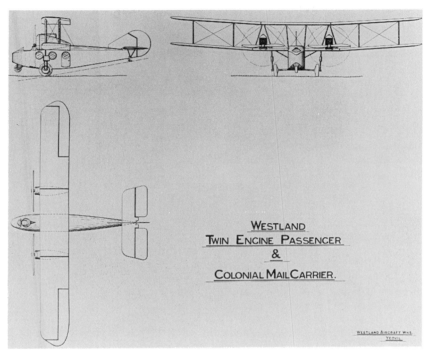

This 45 ft 9 in span seven seater of 1928 was also envisaged as a colonial mail carrier with two Napier Lions. (*Westland drawing*)

Three-engined Limousine V 10-seat monoplane to 6/29   1929

Single-seat monoplane fighter to F.7/30   1930

Single Kestrel sesquiplane day bomber to P.27/32   1933

Single Kestrel pusher Pterodactyl VI to F.5/33   1933

Four Gipsy VI Pterodactyl VII flying-boat to R.1/33   1933

Single Perseus monoplane fighter to F.5/34   1933

Twin Perseus GP TSR aircraft to G.24/35   1936

P.9 Single Hercules fighter to F.37/35. Design study   1936

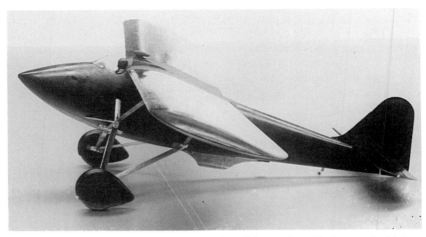

1930 wind-tunnel model of the F.7/30 monoplane fighter rejected in favour of a biplane configuration.

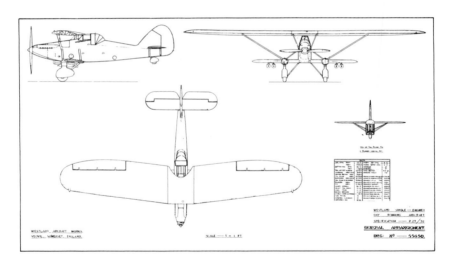

A 60 ft span sesquiplane bomber proposed to meet Specification P.27/32 which produced the Fairey Battle. (*Westland drawing*)

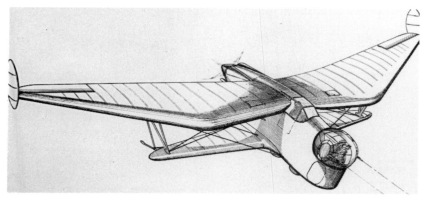

Designed to Specification F.5/33, the Pterodactyl Mk.VI two-seat fighter had a nose turret.

The 63 ft span Pterodactyl Mk.VII flying-boat with four de Havilland Gipsy Six engines was produced only in model form.

P.9 Twin turbojet fighter to F.37/35. Design study	1936
P.8 Single Perseus army co-operation aircraft to A.3/37	1937
P.10 Single Taurus torpedo/dive-bomber to S.24/37	1938
Twin tractor or pusher Griffon long-range fighter to F.6/39. Design studies	1939
Single Taurus army co-operation high/low-wing monoplanes to A.7/39. Design studies.	1939
Single Griffon/Taurus naval fighter to N.8/39. Design studies.	1939

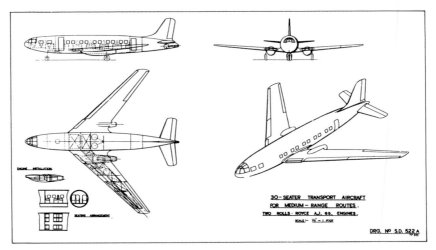

One of several Westland 30-seat twin-jet airliner projects to Brabazon IIA recommendation with Rolls-Royce AJ.65 turbojets. (*Westland drawing*)

Single Taurus naval fighter to N.9/39. Design study.	1939
P.14 Twin Merlin high-altitude fighter to F.4/40	1940
Twin tandem-mounted Merlin high-altitude-fighter to F.4/40. Design study.	1940
Twin W2B turbojet Delanne tandem wing high-altitude fighter to F.4/40	1940
Single Centaurus Delanne wing light bomber to B.7/40	1940
Single Hercules all-wood fighter to F.19/40	1940
Single Centaurus close support bomber to B.20/40	1940
Twin Merlin high-altitude bomber to B.5/41	1942
Four Griffon Delanne wing heavy bomber to B.8/41	1942
Four Merlin high-altitude bomber to B.3/42	1942
Single H1 turbojet twin-boom fighter to E.5/42	1942
Single Griffon lightweight fighter to F.6/42	1942
Single Sabre torpedo/bomber/reconnaissance aircraft to S.6/43	1943

Model of one of W.E.W. Petter's early jet fighter-bomber projects of March 1944.

Single H1 turbojet naval fighter to N.7/43	1943
Single Griffon naval fighter to N.7/43	1943
One P & W radial and one H1 turbojet torpedo/reconnaissance aircraft to S.11/43	1943
Twin tandem mid-fuselage-mounted pusher Merlin fighter-bomber to F.12/43	1944
Twin turbojet 10/12-seat transport (Brabazon VA) to 26/43	1944
W.34 Single mid-fuselage-mounted Rolls-Royce 24H46 naval strike fighter to N.11/44	1945
Above project for RAF to F.13/44	1945
Twin-engined 12-seat transport (Brabazon VA) to 18/44	1945
Single AJ-65 turbojet naval interceptor to F.11/45	1945
W.35 Single Clyde RAF/naval strike fighter to N.12/45	1945
W.35 Single Bristol or Clyde propeller-turbine naval interceptor to N.12/45	1945
Single Nomad naval strike fighter to N.12/45	1946

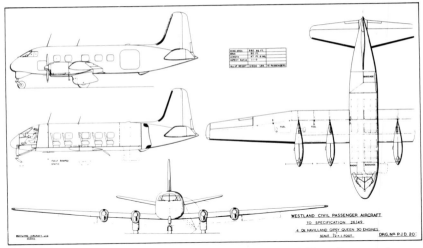

A feeder-liner with 15 rearward-facing seats and de Havilland Gipsy Queen engines, to meet Specification 26/49. (*Westland drawing*)

Single Napier E141 propeller-turbine Wyvern T.F.4 naval strike fighter to N.12/45	1946
Single Double Eland Wyvern S.5E strike aircraft to N.12/45	1946
W.36 Single Avon naval strike fighter to N.12/45	1946

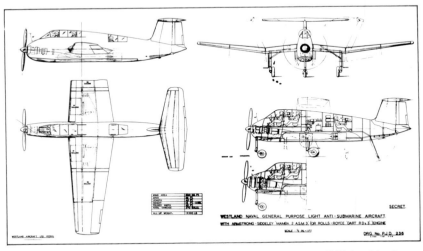

Naval General Purpose light ASW aircraft with one Armstrong Siddeley Mamba or Rolls-Royce Dart propeller-turbine. (*Westland drawing*)

W.36 Single MV F9 or Avon naval strike aircraft to N.12/45   1947

Twin-engined anti-submarine patrol aircraft to GR 17/45.   1945
Design study.

Four propeller-turbine 24-seat transport (Brabazon IIB) to C15/46   1946

Twin Beryl naval all-weather fighter to N.40/46   1946

Rolls-Royce AJ 65 30-seat transport (Brabazon IIB) to 22/46   1946

Single Cheetah or Gipsy Queen basic trainer to T.16/48   1948

Four Gipsy Major 15-seat (aft-facing) civil transport   1949
(Brabazon VA) to 26/49

Single Mamba or Dart naval GP light ASW aircraft.   1950

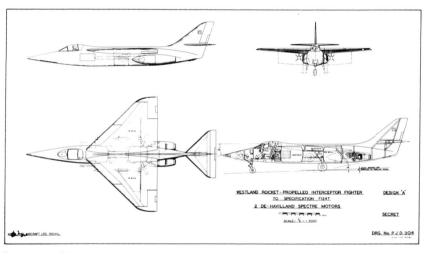

Interceptor fighter Type A to Specification F124T. Span 29 ft. Two de Havilland Spectre
rocket motors. Westland drawing dated 24 April, 1952.

Twin Spectre rocket engined interceptor Type A F124T.   1952

Above project Type B with Delanne type tailplane and   1952
one-over-one engine installation to F124T

Twin Gyron Junior or Rolls-Royce BE.33 naval strike   1952
aircraft to M148T

W.37-1 Single Sapphire two-seat trainer.   1951

495

Two-seat naval carrier strike aircraft to Specification M148T. Span 42 ft 8 in. Two de Havilland Gyron Juniors.

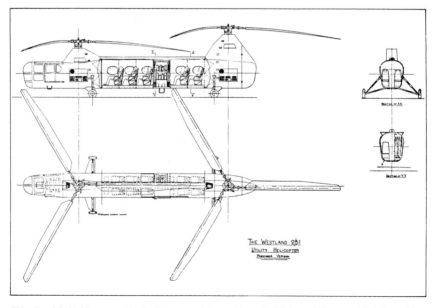

Westland 2/51 10-seat utility helicopter with two Pratt & Whitney Wasp or Alvis Leonides engines.(*Westland drawing*)

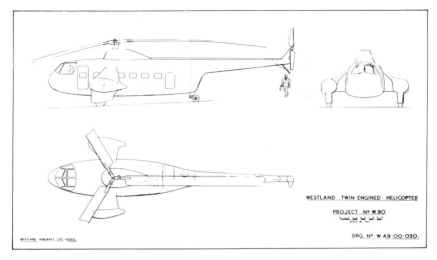

W.80 14-seat civil helicopter with 75 ft diameter main rotor and two turboshaft engines. Loaded weight 11,100 lb. (*1951 Westland drawing*)

W.37-2 Single Sapphire single-seat trainer.   1951

Rotary-wing Projects

W.80 Twin Hercules 14-seat helicopter   1951

W.81 Single Double Mamba 30-seat helicopter   1951

W.90 450-seat troop transport. 195 ft diameter main-rotor. Three Armstrong Siddeley Sapphire turbojets. Loaded weight 93,420 lb. (1951).

Two-seat ultra-light helicopter with two tip jets.

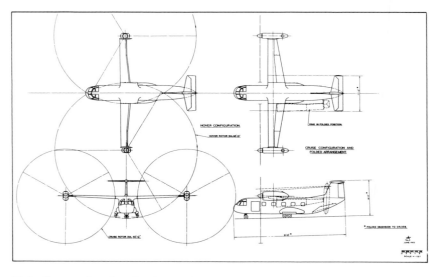

Twin tilt rotor aircraft to OR 358, with a 65 ft diameter main rotor. June 1962. (*Westland drawing*)

W.85 Six (three pairs) Adder rotor blade tip-mounted 102-seat helicopter	1951
W.90 Three Sapphire rotor blade tip-mounted 450-troop helicopter	1951
WS-61 Twin Gazelle Wiltshire civil Sea King.	1951
Three turboshaft ASW helicopter	1962

WG.1 Four Gnome ASW troop/cargo helicopter   1962

Twin tilt rotor aircraft to OR 358   1962

WG.3 Twin Gnome tactical transport helicopter   1963

WG.4 Twin turboshaft ASW/troop/cargo helicopter   1963

WG.5 Single turboshaft light utility helicopter   1964

WG.7 Twin turboshaft ASW medium lift helicopter   1964

WG.11 Four turboshaft 60-troop compound helicopter   1965

WG.12 Single turboshaft light helicopter   1965

WG.13 Twin P & W PT6A 12-seat troop helicopter   1963

WG.13D–P Variants as above with different engine,   1963–64
transmission and rotor systems

WG.13Q–S Utility, escort, utility/escort helicopters   1964

WG.13T–W Armed reconnaissance, utility, naval, civil   1966
helicopters

Twin-engined tilt-rotor five-seat VTOL light executive   1967
aircraft.

Four turboshaft tilt-rotor 85-seat VTOL troop transport   1967

Twin tilt rotor 85-seat troop transport. February 1967.

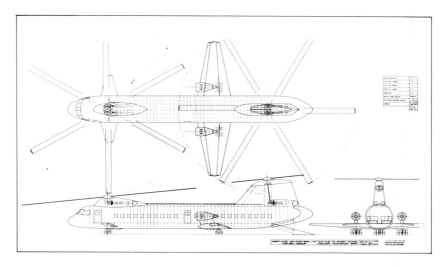

WG.17D. Short-range 138-seat military compound helicopter with 76 ft diameter main-rotor. Four General Electric T64-GE-16 turboshaft and two Bristol Siddeley M.45H turbofan engines. Dated 21 April, 1967. (*Westland drawing*)

WG.22. Tilt wing transport aircraft with four turboshaft engines.

Twin tilt rotor 6/8-seat VTOL aircraft.

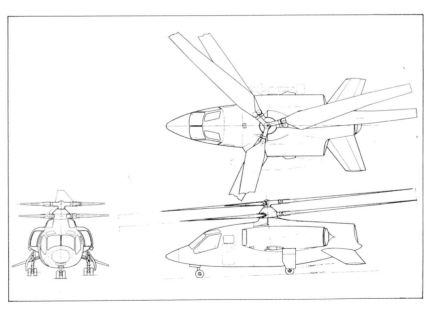

Preliminary study of a naval helicopter with supersonic 49 ft 3 in diameter rotors and three Avco Lycoming LTC.4V1 turboshaft engines. Loaded weight 33,500 lb. Dated 22 June, 1973. (*Westland drawing*)

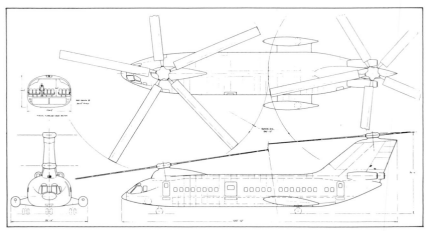

General arrangement of 200-seat mass-transit helicopter with 90 ft diameter main-rotor and three turboshaft engines. (*Westland drawing*)

W.17 Six (four turboshaft, two turbofan) 138-seat compound helicopter.	1967
WG.18 Six (two turboshaft, four propeller-turbine) short-range military transport compound helicopter	1967
WG.22 Four turboshaft tilt-rotor transport helicopter	1968
WE.01 Four T.63 turboshaft tilt-rotor six-seat executive aircraft	1969
Twin turbofan high-speed 40-seat compound helicopter	1971
WG.25 Single turboshaft unmanned surveillance helicopter	1971
Three LTC4.VI turboshaft naval supersonic rotor helicopter	1973
Three turboshaft 200-seat transport compound helicopter	1973
Three (one turboshaft, two turbofan) Advancing Blade Concept high-speed, high-altitude ASW compound helicopter	1976
Single-engined two-seat light helicopter	1978
Two turboshaft supersonic-rotor armed compound helicopter	1978

Remotely-Piloted Helicopters

The Remotely Piloted Vehicle field had been dominated by fixed-wing aircraft until 1966 when Westland began feasibility studies of remotely-piloted helicopters. These RPHs were intended for battlefield surveillance and target acquisition. This work led, in 1971, to Westland's proposal to meet MoD GST 3494 for a medium-range unmanned aerial surveillance system. Named Wideye it was a symmetric shape with co-axial rotors.

Wideye's configuration, described as 'plan-symmetric co-axial rotor' was chosen because it removed the need to steer it in yaw, it was less affected by gusts than other configurations and its heading could be precisely controlled. In addition its sensors had a 360 deg scanning capability by rotating the aircraft and Wideye was very much more compact than fixed-wing RPVs.

Mote

In order to gain early flying experience of small co-axial rotor helicopters, Westland funded the construction of the Mote, which was built initially from available aeromodelling components. It consisted of the co-axial vertical drive-shafts and rotors plus the engines and control system mounted on a platform with four fixed landing legs. Weighing only 18 lb its 5 ft diameter two-bladed teetering rotors were powered by two 1.50 hp model aircraft engines. Mote first flew on 13 June, 1975, and the design was steadily developed to improve its integrity and reliability by substituting Westland-designed components for most of the original model kit parts. Mote went on to become a flying test bed for an electronic gyro-based control system for use on the Wisp, a later Westland RPH, during which time its weight was increased to 35 lb. A total of 37 flights was made before it was retired in June 1976 and given to Southampton University for use as a co-axial rotor research rig.

Wisp

The Mote configuration of twin engines driving the co-axial rotors by means of toothed belts and a dry gearbox was used in the Wisp. This was a short-range surveillance RPH, weighing 70 lb and powered by two 5 hp engines, which was able to carry a television camera. The 'fuselage' was a flattened spheroid shape with the vertical co-axial rotor drive-shafts protruding from the top and with four fixed landing legs. The electronic gyro-based flight control system developed and flight-tested on the Mote was used in the Wisp to establish its performance characteristics.

Three flying examples, a control console and ground handling equipment were produced, the first flight being made in December 1976. The second and third aircraft flew in May and August 1977 respectively and carried small television cameras movable in elevation and stabilised in pitch and roll. Two of these RPHs went on to support the Wideye programme, one going to the RAE Farnborough for flight trials.

Wideye

Wideye was produced as the airborne element of the Supervisor unmanned aerial surveillance system for the MoD. This was developed jointly by Westland Helicopters and Marconi Avionics, the feasibility programme beginning in 1977. In its operational form the Supervisor system consisted of an RPV, a ground station and remote tracker plus a launch and recovery system. Five aircraft and their associated payloads, one ground control station, two sets of ground support equipment to permit test flying within visual range and a flight simulation facility were completed as part of an extended feasibility programme.

Wideye weighed 275 lb, was powered by two 20 hp two-stroke engines and carried a stabilised daylight television sensor. It was of vertical egg shape with the rotor shafts protruding from the top and having four landing legs designed to fold up into recesses in the 'fuselage'. The first aircraft, Wideye 01, flew in August 1978 carrying an instrumentation telemetry payload; the second and third, 02 and 03, flew in April and August 1979 respectively, the second aircraft going to the RAE Farnborough in 1980. Stabilised flight from the ground station, including tramsmission of sensor imagery, was demonstrated with Wideye.

When the MoD cancelled the Supervisor programme Westland concentrated on further studies and definition of developments of RPH systems and explored possible applications of these vehicles. This work was finally abandoned about 1983.

APPENDIX E

Factory Expansions

In addition to new buildings and facilities on the main Westland site at Yeovil, a number of other premises in the town and surrounding area were taken over during World War II and converted for use as machine shops, manufacturing and assembly shops and stores. This was part of a Government policy of dispersing production facilities, to minimise damage in the event of an air attack. The principal ones are listed below.

Sparrows Agricultural Engineers	Martock	Machine shop.
Yeo Brothers Paul	Martock	Machine shop.
No.3 Site	Martock	Machine shop.
Castleton Caravans plus another site	Sherborne	Detail manufacture and sub-assembly.
Odeon Cinema	Yeovil	Detail manufacture.
	Preston	Stores for perishable
	Plucknett	materials.

Southern National Bus Co	Yeovil	Detail manufacture.
Nautilus Works	Yeovil	Sheetmetal stores.
Moffat Garage	Yeovil	Sub-assembly manufacture.

These premises were vacated within a few months after the end of the war.

During the early part of 1940 two existing hangars and a purpose-built hangar on the north side of Doncaster Airport were taken over as part of the Westland Repair Organisation. The No.1 Hangar which belonged to Doncaster Aero Club was used for the receipt of crashed Lysanders, which arrived on RAF 'Queen Mary' type low-loader vehicles, and which were stripped to recover serviceable equipment. When this had been salvaged it was put into stores in No.2 Hangar. The large No.3 Hangar was used for complete aircraft repair and rebuilding using the salvaged equipment plus new components supplied from Yeovil. Some of the salvaged items were also sent back to Yeovil for embodiment in new production aircraft.

About 50 employees worked for Westland at this site including several sent up from Yeovil including C Trigger, P Shott, E Fogg and T Poole. Westland's tenure of this site was short lived; about nine months after this work had started in mid-1940, the company moved it to Yeovil. The hangars were taken over by Brooklands Aviation who moved from Lindholme to do the same job on Wellingtons.

Another purpose-built factory was erected at Ilchester at the western end of Yeovilton aerodrome, beginning in October 1939. Like Doncaster, it was part of the Westland Repair Organisation dealing with Lysanders, Spitfires and Seafires. Unlike Doncaster, it continued to be used until 1984 for repair and rebuild work on RAF Sabres and Meteors and RN Gannets, as a paint shop and for work with composite materials and electrical equipment.

APPENDIX F

Westland Group Companies

While Westland is best known for its creation of a great range of fixed- and rotary-winged aircraft, since the end of the 1939–45 War the company has diversified its interests and activities. This has been achieved organically and by acquisition of other companies.

Westland Engineers Ltd was established in 1944 to provide non-aviation work for its employees when the war-time need for military aircraft ceased. This company produced overhead and sliding doors for the building industry and remained a part of Westland until 1985 when it was sold as its products and markets 'had no strategic relevance to Westland's future'.

Normalair Ltd was formed as a subsidiary of Westland Aircraft in 1946 to exploit the market potential of the 'Westland Valve'. This device was born of the need to provide pressurised cockpits in high-altitude fighter aircraft, beginning with the Welkin. The valve was a compact unit which automatically controlled the air pressure in the sealed cabin by controlling the rate at which air, pumped into it, was allowed to escape away to atmosphere. Postwar development of civil aircraft provided a challenge as the size of the pressure cabin and the aircraft's operating altitudes greatly increased. It was a challenge which was met by Normalair which has continued to produce developments of this valve for a great range of civil and military aircraft. In 1954 licence agreements with the Garrett Corporation in the United States added other environment-control equipment to the Normalair product range; this led to the formation of a joint company, Normalair-Garrett Ltd, in 1967, in which Westland has a 52 per cent holding.

Westland has continued its growth through acquisition of companies with products which complement those of its own, and by the establishment of new companies both in the United Kingdom and overseas.

Westland Group's trading subsidiaries and their activities as at 30 June 1991.

Company and activity	Location
Westland Helicopters Ltd. Holding company. Manufactures helicopters and aerospace products and provides customer support services.	UK
Westland Design Services Ltd. Design and technical service to industry.	UK
Westland Industrial Products Ltd. Design and production of components for the aerospace industry.	UK
Westland System Assessment Ltd. Defence operational analysis, training systems and mission support systems.	UK
Aerosystems International. Airborne systems.	UK
Westland Aerospace Ltd. Holding company.	UK
Westland Aerostructures Ltd. Aerospace industry components in metal and composites, and Hovercraft.	UK
EH Industries Ltd. Design and development of EH 101 helicopter.	UK
EH Industries (Canada) Incorporated. Implementation of EH 101 contracts in Canada.	Canada
FPT Industries Ltd. Rubber components and fabrications and flexible fuel tanks.	UK
Marex Technology Ltd. Advanced systems engineering and process automation.	UK

Westland Technologies Ltd. Holding company.	UK
Normalair-Garrett (Holdings) Ltd	UK
Normalair-Garrett Ltd. Control systems and components for aerospace, defence and engineering industries.	UK
Westland Engineering Ltd. Manufacture of transmission systems, aircraft structures, composite components and rotor blades.	UK
Normalair-Garrett Pty Ltd.	Australia
Normalair-Garrett Manufacturing Pty Ltd	Australia
Westland-Sitec GmbH. Fuel and hydraulic valves.	Germany
Hermetic Aircraft International Corporation. Customer support services.	USA

Four other companies, Westland Dynamics Ltd and Westland Support Services Ltd (UK), Westland Inc (USA), and Westland do Brasil Ltda are concerned with selling and support of Westland Group products.

APPENDIX G

Oldest Extant Westland Aircraft

A Widgeon III, VH-UHU, is the oldest Westland aeroplane in existence, having been built in 1928. Its first C of A was dated 19 March, 1928, and it was registered G-EBUB. Five months later it was exported to Australia as G-AUHU and was owned by Milton C Kent of Sydney, a professional photographer, who was acting as Westland's agent. He used it for his work, pleasure flying and air racing, winning or being placed in many events. In 1940 it was put into store until 1952 when it was sold to a new owner who had it overhauled for C of A renewal and moved it to Wagga Wagga, New South Wales. It was little used until Arthur L Whittaker bought it in 1953. He obtained his pilot's licence the following year and flew it to Boort, Victoria, where it has been based ever since, apart from being loaned to Drage Airworld at Wangaratta in Victoria on several occasions.

Total flying hours in 1990 were about 2,500 and 'UHU passes its mandatory annual inspection for maintenance release with very few problems. Apart from the low-pressure tyres and a modified exhaust system, this Widgeon and its ADC Cirrus II engine are virtually 'as built'.

The use of modern leaded fuels caused the screwed bronze exhaust valve seats to be replaced by steel seats shrunk in. Arthur Whittaker also reported that 'The oil in the crankcase always seemed to have a manic desire to escape smartly . . . going up through the valve tappet guide and escaping to attach itself to anything it could find'. The answer was a small oil trap for the top of each guide connected to a gallery on the engine's side. From there a flexible tube led to a device on the cross-axle where some airflow suction assisted the oil to escape to atmosphere. This modification was embodied more than 25 years ago and the Cirrus has been trouble free ever since.

During 1989 'UHU was used in an Australian TV mini-series *A Thousand Skies* about the life of Sir Charles Kingsford Smith, the renowned Australian pioneer aviator. It was given the registration G-AUKA and the name *Kookaburra* which was another Widgeon III under which Keith Anderson and Bobby Hitchock died of thirst after a forced landing in the outback between Wyndham and Alice Springs, Western Austalia, on 10 April, 1929. They were taking part in a search for 'Smithy's' Fokker monoplane *Southern Cross* in which he had got lost. Kingsford Smith was found.

'UHU still carries the silhouette of a Widgeon on its fuselage side and Arthur Whittaker still gets the comment that 'whoever painted that bird could not have known much about kookaburras'.

APPENDIX H

Westland and the Gulf War

Following Iraq's invasion of Kuwait on 2 August, 1990, there was a steady build-up of British military forces and equipment in Saudi Arabia and the Gulf theatre of operations as part of Operation Granby. Three Royal Navy Lynx helicopters were already there on the 10 years old Armilla Patrol and two Sea King HAS.5s were deployed in the Fleet Tanker RFA *Olna* in the mine spotting and surface search roles.

On 31 October, 1990, four Sea King HC.4s left Plymouth in the RFA *Argus*, a helicopter training ship, which went to the Gulf as a casualty reception vessel. Drawn from No.826 Squadron they were ZA293, ZA296, ZD476 and ZD478. Two more, ZF118 and ZF119 were later deployed on RFA *Fort Grange* for use in supply and communications duties between ships and shore bases.

As the crisis deepened 12 more, from No.845 and the hastily reformed No.848 Squadrons sailed from Southampton on 23 December in the ss *Atlantic Conveyor*, this vessel having replaced one of the same name which was lost in the Falklands War in 1982. They were ZA298, ZA312–314, ZD477, ZD480, ZE427–428, ZF117 and ZG820–822. These aircraft immediately went into the desert alongside the Royal Air Force Helicopter Support Force in support of the British Army's 1st Armoured Division before the land battle began.

Sea King HC.4, ZG821, of No.848 Squadron, Royal Navy, in the Saudia Arabian desert during Operation Granby in January 1991. Note the canvas cover over the engine air intake and a two-letter code on the nose and fuselage side. (*Royal Navy*)

During a period of several days 15 RAF Puma HC.1s were flown to the Gulf in USAF Lockheed C-5A Galaxy transports. They were XW200–201, XW204, XW206–207, XW216–217, XW220, XW222, XW225, ZA934–937 and ZA939 drawn from Nos.33 and 203 Squadrons based at RAF Odiham and Gütersloh respectively. A further four RAF Pumas, among which were XW214, XW226 and XW231, were in ss *Atlantic Conveyor* which sailed on 23 December.

Supporting the Allied ground forces were 23 Lynx AH.7s and 23 Gazelle AH.1s of 4 Regiment, Army Air Corps. The Lynx serials were XZ176, XZ199, XZ208, XZ214–215, XZ217, XZ219, XZ221–222, XZ606, XZ608, XZ610, XZ616–617, XZ642, XZ646, XZ650–651, XZ653, XZ664, XZ670 and XZ679–680. The Gazelles were XW909, XX372, XX389, XX395, XX416, XX437, XX439, XX449, XX453–455, XZ292, XZ298, XZ308, XZ318, XZ337–338, ZX343, ZX347, ZA766, ZA771 and ZB691–692.

On 29 January, 1991, Lynx helicopters from HMS *Gloucester* and *Brazen* fired Sea Skua missiles in actions against seventeen Iraqi patrol boats in the northern Persian Gulf. Very many boats, whose own missiles threatened the Allied fleet, were destroyed. Other vessels in action with Lynx were HMS *Cardiff* and *Manchester*. Then, on 21 February two Sea King HC.4s, ZA291 and ZE425, were flown from RNAS Yeovilton in a C-5A Galaxy to the Gulf theatre to reinforce Nos.845 and 848 Squadrons. At the cease-fire on 28 February there were 32 Royal Navy helicopters operating in the Gulf. When Kuwait City was liberated two Sea Kings landed troops on the roof of the British Embassy.

RAF and AAC aircraft involved in Operation Granby received a 'desert pink' paint scheme; the RN aircraft retained their grey finish. Some helicopters carried white bands on their tail booms and a black inverted V on the forward fuselage sides. The national markings were toned down and reduced in size and single letter codes were carried.

At Yeovil Westland dealt with some 130 different requirements arising directly from Operation Granby. These included modification and design work, including the manufacture and supply of large numbers of sand filters. Because of the urgency a normal year's work was compressed into five months.

(This Appendix was completed before full details of operations by Great Britain's rotary-wing aircraft in the Gulf War had been made public.)

Bibliography

The following is a list of some of the books, reference sources and periodicals consulted by the author. It is provided in the belief that it will be of interest and value to researchers and those wishing to obtain a broader picture of British and world aviation events during the last 75 years and a background to the endeavours and achievements of the Petter and Westland companies since 1870. In addition, there were the countless reports and records which were made available for examination over the years by Westland Helicopters Ltd, the RAE Farnborough, Royal Aeronautical Society, Ministry of Defence (Air Historical Branch), Public Record Office and the Society of British Aerospace Companies.

Aeroplane Structures, A J S Pippard and J L Pritchard (Pitman 1919)
Handbook of Aeronautics, edited by J L Pritchard (Pitman 1931)
The Story of Petters Limited, Percival Petter (Private circulation 1933. Published David W Edington 1989)
Handbook of Aeronautics (Aero Engines), Andrew Swan, (Pitman 1934)
Aeronautics Vols. I–IV, (Newnes 1941)
The Book of Westland Aircraft, A H Lukins (Harborough Press 1944)
Benefits of War, Prof A M Low (Scientific Book Club 1945)
Fellowship of the Air 1901–1951, B J Hurren (Iliffe & Sons 1951)
Wings from the West, (*Flight* 15 April 1955)
Aircraft Engines of the World, Paul Wilkinson (1961–70)
Avro Aircraft since 1908, A J Jackson (Putnam 1990)
The Centenary Journal of the Royal Aeronautical Society (1966)
British Fighter since 1912, The, Peter Lewis (Putnam 1966)
British Bomber since 1914, The, Peter Lewis (Putnam 1967)
British Aviation—The Pioneer Years, Harald Penrose (Putnam 1967)
Blackburn Aircraft since 1909, A J Jackson (Putnam 1968)
Farnborough, Charles Sims (Adam and Charles Black 1970)
Armament of British Aircraft 1909–1939, H F King (Putnam 1971)
Gloster Aircraft since 1917, Derek N James (Putnam 1971)
British Aviation—The Adventuring Years, Harald Penrose (Putnam 1973)
Project Cancelled, Derek Wood (McDonald & Janes 1975)
Rolls-Royce from the Wings, R Harker (Oxford Illustrated Press 1976)
British Aviation—Widening Horizons, Harald Penrose (RAF Museum 1979)
Squadrons of the RAF, J Halley (Air Britain 1980)
British Aviation—Ominous Skies, Harald Penrose (RAF Museum 1980)
Family Engineers, Sir Eric Mensforth (Ward Lock 1981)

Canadian Aircraft since 1909, K M Molson and H A Taylor (Putnam 1982)
British Naval Aircraft since 1912, O G Thetford (Putnam 1982)
Roof of the World, Lord James Douglas-Hamilton (Mainstream Publishing 1983)
Fairey Aircraft since 1915, H A Taylor (Putnam 1984)
The Helicopter, Keith Carey (Patrick Stephens 1986)
British Military Helicopters, J Everett-Heath (Arms and Armour Press 1986)
Royal Aeronautical Society—Yeovil Branch Diamond Jubilee Handbook (1986)
History of Aircraft Piston Engines, Herschel Smith (Sunflower University Press 1986)
The Helicopter, John Fay (David and Charles 1987)
De Havilland Aircraft since 1909, A J Jackson (Putnam 1987)
World Encyclopaedia of Aero Engines, W Gunston (Patrick Stephens 1988)
Setting the Record Straight, David Gibbings (Picton Publishing (Chippenham) 1988)
Bristol Aircraft since 1910, C H Barnes (Putnam 1988)
Saunders and Saro Aircraft since 1917, P London (Putnam 1988)
Vickers Aircraft since 1908, C F Andrews and E B Morgan (Putnam 1988)
Encyclopaedia of the World's Air Forces, Michael J H Taylor (Patrick Stephens 1988)
Rolls-Royce Aero Engines, W Gunston (Patrick Stephens 1988)
Encyclopaedia of Modern Aircraft Armament, C Chant (Patrick Stephens 1988)
British Carrier Aviation, N Friedman (Conway Maritime Press 1988)
Forty Years at Farnborough, John Blake and Mike Hooks (Haynes 1990)
Jane's All the World's Aircraft, (Sampson Low 1914–1990)
Westland Annual Report and Accounts 1950–1990

Periodicals

Aeronautics
Aeroplane, The
Aeroplane Monthly
Aerospace
Aircraft Engineering
Aircraft Illustrated
Flight/Flight International
Helicopter International
Jane's Defence Weekly
Petters Monthly News 1936–37
Royal Aeronautical Society Journal
Royal Aircraft Establishment News
Wingspan

Index